VENTURE CAPITAL AND PRIVATE EQUITY
A Casebook

VENTURE CAPITAL AND PRIVATE EQUITY
A Casebook

Josh Lerner

Harvard Business School
and
National Bureau of Economic Research

John Wiley & Sons, Inc.
New York • Chichester • Weinheim • Brisbane • Singapore • Toronto

Acquisitions Editor	Marissa Ryan
Marketing Manager	Rebecca Hope
Senior Production Editor	Robin Factor
Cover Designer	David Levy
Illustration Editor	Anna Melhorn
Production Management	Hermitage Publishing Services

Cover photo by Greg Pease/Tony Stone Images.

This book was set in 10/12 New Caledonia by Hermitage Publishing Services, and printed and bound by Hamilton Printing. The cover was printed by Lehigh Press.

This book is printed on acid-free paper. ∞

Library of Congress Cataloging in Publication Data:

Lerner, Joshua.
    Venture capital and private equity : a casebook / Josh Lerner.
        p.   cm.
    Includes index.
    ISBN 0-471-32286-5
    1. Venture capital—United States—Case studies.   2. Capital investments—United States—Case studies.   I. Title.
    HG4963.L47   1999
    332'.0415'0973—dc21   99-33115
                                                                                            CIP

Printed in the United States of America

10   9   8   7   6   5   4   3   2   1

Acknowledgments

The writing of a case study is an activity that involves many people. From its initial conception to its publication and revision, a case involves practitioners, students, and colleagues at one's own and other schools. Thus, the problem with the acknowledgments section of a casebook is not deciding which individuals to include, but rather worrying about those one has left out!

First it is important to note that a number of case studies in this volume were written jointly with colleagues, students, and practitioners. Beyond these co-authors, many others provided assistance. The partners and managers of the many private equity groups, institutional investors, and companies featured in these cases not only agreed to be the subject of the analyses, but generously set aside time to answer many questions, review drafts, and make numerous helpful suggestions. Chris Allen responded to frequent requests for data, often under severe time constraints. Colleagues at Harvard Business School and many other business schools offered numerous suggestions after reading or teaching these cases. My assistant, Marianne D'Amico, managed the many logistical details regarding the casewriting process. The Harvard Business School's Division of Research generously funded the considerable cost of developing these case studies. Finally, the encouragement and assistance of Marissa Ryan at John Wiley & Sons was critical in developing this volume.

Three contributions deserve special mention. First, Paul Gompers and I have had an ongoing collaborative research effort examining the economics of the venture capital industry over the past several years. Many of the cases and notes draw on ideas developed in the course of our conversations and research. Second, Bill Sahlman has been exceedingly supportive of my course development efforts, providing many helpful suggestions and a continual stream of new ideas about potential case studies and issues. Many of the cases would not have been developed without his involvement and encouragement. Finally, the late Scott Mason was chairman of the Finance Area during the time when my course was conceived and developed. His unstinting encouragement of this effort was very important.

Finally, the development of these cases required a considerable amount of travel. Thus, I would like to dedicate this book to Scruffy, who was always glad to see me after my casewriting trips!

About the Author

Josh Lerner is an Associate Professor at Harvard Business School, with a joint appointment in the Finance and Entrepreneurial Management Units. He graduated from Yale College with a Special Divisional Major that combined physics with the history of technology. He worked for several years on issues concerning technological innovation and public policy at the Brookings Institution, for a public-private task force in Chicago, and on Capitol Hill. He then undertook his graduate study at Harvard's Economics Department.

His research focuses on the structure of venture capital organizations and their role in transforming scientific discoveries into commercial products. (Much of his research is collected in *The Private Equity Cycle,* published by MIT Press, 1999) He also examines the effects of intellectual property protection, particularly patents, on the competitive strategies of firms in high-technology industries. He is a Faculty Research Fellow in the National Bureau of Economic Research's Productivity and Corporate Finance Program. His work has been published in a variety of academic journals including the *Journal of Finance,* the *Journal of Financial Economics,* the *Journal of Law and Economics,* and the *Rand Journal of Economics,* as well as in over forty case studies.

In addition to his teaching responsibilities, he serves as Faculty Chair of the Focused Financial Management Series, a set of four targeted executive education courses on current issues in finance. As part of this series, he designs and teaches an annual executive course on private equity, and teaches a Ph. D. course on corporate finance.

Private Equity Today and Tomorrow

Over the past 15 years, there has been a tremendous boom in the private equity industry. The pool of U.S. private equity funds—partnerships specializing in venture capital, leveraged buyouts, mezzanine investments, build-ups, distressed debt, and related investments—grew from $5 billion in 1980 to over $175 billion in 1999. Private equity's recent growth has outstripped that of almost every class of financial product.

Despite this growth, many questions about private equity remain unanswered, and many of its features continue to be mysterious. How do venture capital and buyout funds create value? What explains this tremendous growth in these funds? To what extent is the model developed and refined over the past several decades likely to be translated into other countries and types of investments? This volume explores these exciting and important questions.

WHAT IS PRIVATE EQUITY?

A natural first question is what constitutes a private equity fund. Many start-up firms require substantial capital. A firm's founder may not have sufficient funds to finance these projects alone, and therefore must seek outside financing. Entrepreneurial firms that are characterized by significant intangible assets, expect years of negative earnings, and have uncertain prospects are unlikely to receive bank loans or other debt financing. Similarly, troubled firms that need to undergo restructurings may find external financing difficult to raise. Private equity organizations finance these high-risk, potentially high-reward projects. They protect the value of their equity stakes by undertaking careful due diligence before making the investments and retaining powerful oversight rights afterwards.

Typically, these investors do not primarily invest their own capital, but rather raise the bulk of their funds from institutions and individuals. Large institutional investors, such as pension funds and university endowments, are likely to want illiquid long-run investments such as private equity in their portfolio. Often, these groups have neither the staff nor the expertise to make such investments themselves.

The first private equity capital firm, American Research and Development (ARD), was formed in 1946 by MIT President Karl Compton, Harvard Business School Professor Georges F. Doriot, and local business leaders. A small group of venture capitalists made high-risk investments into emerging companies that were based on technology developed for World War II. The success of the investments ranged widely:

almost half of ARD's profits during its 26-year existence as an independent entity came from its $70,000 investment in Digital Equipment Company in 1957, which grew in value to $355 million. Because institutional investors were reluctant to invest, ARD was structured as a publicly traded closed-end fund and marketed mostly to individuals. The few other venture organizations begun in the decade after ARD's formation were also structured as closed-end funds.

The first venture capital limited partnership, Draper, Gaither, and Anderson, was formed in 1958. Imitators soon followed, but limited partnerships accounted for a minority of the venture pool during the 1960s and 1970s. Most venture organizations raised money either through closed-end funds or Small Business Investment Companies (SBICs), federally guaranteed risk-capital pools that proliferated during the 1960s. While the market for SBICs in the late 1960s and early 1970s was strong, incentive problems ultimately led to the collapse of the sector. The annual flow of money into private equity during its first three decades never exceeded a few hundred million dollars and usually was substantially less. During these years, while a few funds made a considerable number of investments in buyouts and other transactions involving mature firms, private equity organization were universally referred to as venture capital funds.

The activity in the private equity industry increased dramatically in late 1970s and early 1980s. Industry observers attributed much of the shift to the U.S. Department of Labor's clarification of the Employee Retirement Income Security Act's "prudent man" rule in 1979. Prior to this year, the legislation limited pension funds from investing substantial amounts of money into venture capital or other high-risk asset classes. The Department of Labor's clarification of the rule explicitly allowed pension managers to invest in high-risk assets, including private equity. Numerous specialized funds—concentrating in areas such as leveraged buyouts, mezzanine transactions, and such hybrids as venture leasing—sprung up during these years. Another important change in the private equity industry during this period was the rise of the limited partnership as the dominant organizational form.

Subsequent years saw both very good and trying times for private equity investors. On the one hand, venture capitalists backed during the 1980s many of the most successful high-technology companies, including Apple Computer, Cisco Systems, Genentech, Microsoft, and Sun Microsystems. Numerous successful buyouts—such as Avis, Beatrice, Dr. Pepper, Gibson Greetings, and McCall Pattern—garnered considerable public attention in the 1980s. At the same time, commitments to the private equity industry during this decade were very uneven. The annual flow of money into venture capital funds increased by a factor of ten during the first half of the 1980s, but steadily declined from 1987 through 1991. Buyouts underwent an even more dramatic rise through the 1980s, followed by a precipitous fall at the end of the decade.

Much of this pattern was driven by the changing fortunes of private equity investments. Returns on venture capital funds had declined sharply in the mid-1980s after being exceedingly attractive in the 1970s. This fall was apparently triggered by overinvestment in a few industries, such as computer hardware, and the entry into the arena of many inexperienced venture capitalists. Buyout returns underwent a similar decline in the late 1980s due in large part to the increased competition between groups for transactions. As investors became disappointed with returns, they committed less capital to the industry.

By way of contrast, the 1990s have seen dramatic growth and excellent returns in almost every part of the private equity industry. This recovery was triggered by several factors. The exit of many inexperienced investors at the beginning of the decade insured that the remaining groups faced less competition for transactions. The healthy market for the initial public offerings during much of the decade meant that it was easier for all investors to exit private equity transactions. Meanwhile, the extent of technological innovation—particularly in information technology-related industries such as electronic commerce—created extraordinary opportunities for venture capitalists. New capital commitments to both venture and buyout funds rose in response to these changing circumstances, increasing to record levels by the late 1990s.

WHY IS PRIVATE EQUITY IMPORTANT?

In order to understand the dramatic growth of the private equity industry, it is important to appreciate the role that these investors play in screening, financing, and overseeing companies. Whether young start-ups hungry for capital or ailing giants that need to restructure, the types of firms that private equity organizations finance pose numerous risks and uncertainties.

In this section, we will first review the risks that these firms pose. We will then consider briefly how private equity organizations address these problems. Finally, we will discuss why other financiers, such as banks, often cannot address these problems as effectively as private equity groups.

The financing of young and restructuring firms is a risky business. Uncertainty and informational gaps often characterize these firms, particularly in high-technology industries. These information problems make it difficult to assess these firms, and permit opportunistic behavior by entrepreneurs after the financing is received.

Let's briefly review the types of conflicts that can emerge in these settings. Conflicts between managers and investors ("agency problems") can affect the willingness of both debt and equity holders to provide capital. If the firm raises equity from outside investors, the manager has an incentive to engage in wasteful expenditures (e.g., lavish offices) because he may benefit disproportionately from these but does not bear their entire cost. Similarly, if the firm raises debt, the manager may increase risk to undesirable levels. Because providers of capital recognize these problems, outside investors demand a higher rate of return than would be the case if the funds were internally generated.[1]

Additional agency problems may appear in the types of entrepreneurial firms in which private equity groups invest. Both result from the large information gaps that characterize these firms. First, entrepreneurs might invest in strategies, research, or projects that have high personal returns but low expected monetary payoffs to shareholders. For example, a biotechnology company founder may choose to invest in a certain type of research that brings him great recognition in the scientific community but provides little return for the venture capitalist. Similarly, entrepreneurs may receive initial results from market trials indicating little demand for a new product, but may want to keep the company going because they receive significant private benefits from managing their own firm.

A second problem relates to the level of risk chosen by the entrepreneurs. Entrepreneurs' equity stakes are essentially options: the firm's management receives much of the upside if the company does well (i.e., their equity will be very valuable), but the investors bear the losses if the firm does poorly. As a result, entrepreneurs may be

---

[1] The classic treatment of these problems is in Michael C. Jensen and William H. Meckling, "Theory of the firm: Managerial behavior, agency costs, and ownership structure," *Journal of Financial Economics,* 3 (1976): 305–360.

tempted to pursue highly, indeed excessively, risky strategies. For instance, an entrepreneur may be tempted to "bet it all" on a risky new product line, even if his investors would prefer him to offer several products.

Even if the manager is motivated to maximize shareholder value, information gaps may make raising external capital more expensive or even preclude it entirely. Equity offerings of firms may be associated with a "lemons" problem: if the manager is better informed about the investment opportunities of the firm and acts in the interest of current shareholders, then he will only issue new shares when the company's stock is overvalued. Indeed, numerous studies have documented that stock prices decline upon the announcement of equity issues, largely because of the negative signal sent to the market. This "lemons" problem leads investors to be less willing to invest in young or restructuring firms, or to be unwilling to invest at all. Similar information problems have also been shown to exist in debt markets.[2]

More generally, the inability to verify outcomes makes it difficult to write contracts that are contingent upon particular events. This inability makes external financing costly. Many economic models[3] argue that when investors find it difficult to verify that certain actions have been taken or certain outcomes have occurred—even if they strongly suspect the entrepreneur has followed a certain action which was counter to their original agreement, they cannot prove it in a court of law—external financing may become costly or difficult to obtain.

If the information problems could be eliminated, financing constraints would disappear. Financial economists argue that specialized intermediaries, such as private equity organizations, can address these problems. By intensively scrutinizing firms before providing capital and then monitoring them afterwards, they can alleviate some of the information gaps and reduce capital constraints. Thus, it is important to understand the tools employed by private equity investors as responses to this difficult environment, which enable firms to ultimately receive the financing that they cannot raise from other sources. It is the nonmonetary aspects of private equity that are critical to its success. It is these tools—the screening of investments, the use of convertible securities, the syndication and staging of investments, and the provision of oversight and informal coaching—that we shall highlight in the second module of the course.

Why cannot other financial intermediaries (e.g., banks) undertake the same sort of monitoring? While it is easy to see why individual investors may not have the expertise to address these types of agency problems, it might be thought that bank credit officers could undertake this type of oversight. Yet even in countries with exceedingly well-developed banking systems, such as Germany and Japan, policymakers today are seeking to encourage the development of a private equity industry to insure more adequate financing for risky entrepreneurial firms.

---

[2] The "lemons" problem was introduced in George A. Akerlof, "The market for 'lemons': Qualitative uncertainty and the market mechanism," *Quarterly Journal of Economics,* 84 (1970): 488–500. Discussions of the implications of this problem for financing decisions are in Bruce C. Greenwald, Joseph E. Stiglitz, and Andrew Weiss, "Information imperfections in the capital market and macroeconomics fluctuations," *American Economic Review Papers and Proceedings* 74 (1984): 194–199 and in Stewart C. Myers and Nicholas S. Majluf, "Corporate financing and investment decisions when firms have information that investors do not have," *Journal of Financial Economics,* 13 (1984): 187–221.

[3] Important examples include Sanford Grossman and Oliver D. Hart, "The costs and benefits of ownership: A theory of vertical and lateral integration," *Journal of Political Economy,* 94 (1986): 691–719 and Oliver D. Hart and John Moore, "Property rights and the nature of the firm," *Journal of Political Economy,* 98 (1990): 1119–1158.

The limitations of banks stem from several of their key institutional features. First, because regulations in the United States limit banks' ability to hold shares, they cannot freely use equity to fund projects. Taking an equity position in the firm allows the private equity group to proportionately share in the upside, guaranteeing that the investor benefits if the firm does well. Second, banks may not have the necessary skills to evaluate projects with few tangible assets and significant uncertainty. In addition, banks in competitive markets may not be able to finance high-risk projects because they are unable to charge borrowers rates high enough to compensate for the firm's riskiness. Finally, private equity funds' high-powered compensation schemes give these investors incentives to monitor firms more closely, because their individual compensation is closely linked to the funds' returns. Banks, corporations, and other institutions that have sponsored venture funds without such high-powered incentives have found it difficult to retain personnel once the investors have developed a performance record that enables them to raise a fund of their own.[4]

WHAT DOES THIS VOLUME COVER?

This volume is based on a course introduced at Harvard Business School in the 1993–94 academic year. "Venture Capital and Private Equity" has attracted students interested in careers as private equity investors, as managers of entrepreneurial firms, or as investment bankers or other intermediaries who work with private equity groups and the companies that they fund. These cases have also been used in a variety of other settings, such as executive education courses at Harvard and graduate and undergraduate entrepreneurship courses at many other business schools.

A natural question for a reader to ask is what he or she will learn from this volume. This casebook has three goals:

First, the private equity industry is complex. Participants in the private equity industry make it even more complicated by using a highly specialized terminology. These factors lead to the world of venture capital and buyout investing often appearing impenetrable to the uninitiated. Understanding the ways in which private equity groups work—as well as the key distinctions between these organizations—is an important goal.

Second, private equity investors face the same problems that other financial investors do, but in extreme form. An understanding of the problems faced in private equity—and the ways that these investors solve them—should provide more general insights into the financing process. Thus, a second goal is to review and apply the key ideas of corporate finance in this exciting setting.

Finally, the process of valuation is critical in private equity. Disputes over valuation—whether between an entrepreneur and a venture capitalist or between a private equity group raising a new fund and a potential investor—are commonplace in this industry. These disputes stem from the fact that valuing early-stage and restructuring firms can be very challenging and highly subjective. This casebook explores a wide variety of valuation approaches, from techniques widely used in practice to methods less frequently seen in practice today but likely to be increasingly important in future years.

---

[4] The limitations of bank financing are explored in such theoretical and empirical academic studies as Joseph E. Stiglitz and Andrew Weiss, "Credit rationing in markets with incomplete information," *American Economic Review,* 71 (1981): 393–409 and Mitchell A. Petersen and Raghuram G. Rajan, "The effect of credit market competition on lending relationships," *Quarterly Journal of Economics,* 110 (1995): 407–444.

The volume is divided into four modules. Its organization mirrors that of the private equity process, which can be viewed as a cycle. The cycle starts with the raising of a private equity fund; proceeds through the investment in, monitoring of, and adding value to firms; continues as the private equity group exits successful deals and returns capital to their investors; and finishes with how the organization renews itself with the seeking of additional funds. Each module will begin with an overview that depicts the themes and approaches of the section. Different courses, however, may choose to use this volume in different ways.[5] Thus, it may be helpful to at briefly summarize the organization of the volume at the outset.

The first module of *Venture Capital and Private Equity* examines how private equity funds are raised and structured. Frequently, these funds have complex features, and the legal issues involved are arcane. But the structure of private equity funds has a profound effect on the behavior of venture and buyout investors. Consequently, it is as important for the entrepreneur raising private equity to understand these issues as it is for a partner in a fund. The module will seek not only to understand the features of private equity funds and the actors in the fundraising process, but also to analyze them. We will map out which institutions serve to increase the profits from private equity investments as a whole and which seem designed mostly to shift profits *between* the parties.

The second module of the course considers the interactions between private equity investors and the entrepreneurs they finance. These interactions are at the core of what private equity investors do. We will approach these interactions through a two-part framework. First, we identify the four critical factors that make it difficult for the types of firms backed by private equity investors to meet their financing needs through traditional mechanisms, such as bank loans. Then we consider six classes of financial and organizational responses by private equity investors to these challenges. This module will illustrate these frameworks with examples from a wide variety of industries and private equity transactions, including venture capital, buyouts, consolidations, and venture leasing.

The third module of *Venture Capital and Private Equity* examines the process through which private equity investors exit their investments. Successful exits are critical to ensuring attractive returns for investors and, in turn, to raising additional capital. But the concerns that private equity investors have about exiting investments—and their behavior during the exiting process itself—can sometimes lead to severe problems for entrepreneurs. We will employ an analytic framework very similar to that used in the first module of the course. We will seek to understand which institutional features associated with exiting private equity investments increase the overall amount of profits from private equity investments, and which actions seem to be intended to shift more of the profits to particular parties.

The final module reviews many of the key ideas developed in the volume. Rather than considering traditional private equity organizations, however, the two cases in this module examine different organization goals. Large corporations, government agencies, and non-profit organizations are increasingly emulating private equity funds. Their goals, however, are quite different: for example, to more effectively commercialize inter-

---

[5] While some courses may closely follow the order of cases in the volume, others may deviate substantially. For instance, a course concentrating on entrepreneurial finance may focus on cases in the second and third modules in this volume.

nal research projects or to revitalize distressed areas. Corporate venture funds are also interesting because they represent an alternative way to break into the competitive private equity industry. These cases will allow us not only to understand these exciting and challenging initiatives, but also to review the elements that are crucial to the success of traditional venture organizations.

At the same time, it is important to emphasize that there are many opportunities for learning about venture capital and private equity outside of this volume. The four module notes—and many of the topical notes interspersed in the body of the text—suggest further readings. These range from trade journals such as the *Private Equity Analyst* and the *Venture Capital Journal* to handbooks on the legal nuances of the private equity process to academic studies. In addition, a note at the end of this volume provides a systematic overview of many information sources for readers who wish to explore a particular aspect of the private equity industry in more detail.

WHAT IS THE FUTURE OF PRIVATE EQUITY?

The cases and notes in this volume are designed to provide an understanding of the history of the private equity industry's development and the workings of the industry today. Because the case studies must of necessity look at events in the past, they may provide less guidance about the future of the private equity industry. The question of how the venture and buyout industries will evolve over the next decade is a particularly critical one because the recent growth has been so spectacular. It is natural to ask whether the growth of private equity can be sustained. Has too much capital been raised? Is the industry destined to experience disappointing returns and shrink dramatically?

These are fair questions. As will be highlighted throughout this volume, short-run shifts in the supply of or demand for private equity investments can have dramatic effects. For instance, periods with a rapid increase in capital commitments have historically led to fewer restrictions on private equity investors, larger investments in portfolio firms, higher valuations for those investments, and lower returns for investors.

These patterns have led many practitioners to conclude that the industry is inherently cyclical. In short, this view implies that periods of rapid growth generate sufficient problems that periods of retrenchment are sure to follow. These cycles may lead us to be pessimistic about the prospects for the industry in the years to come.

It is important, however, to consider the *long-run* determinants of the level of private equity, not just the short-run effects. In the short run, intense competition between private equity groups may lead to a willingness to pay a premium for certain types of firms (e.g., firms specializing in tools and content for the Internet). This is unlikely to be a sustainable strategy in the long run: firms that persist in such a strategy will earn low returns and eventually be unable to raise follow-on funds.

The types of factors that determine the long-run steady-state supply of private equity in the economy are more fundamental. These are likely to include the pace of technological innovation in the economy, the degree of dynamism in the economy, the presence of liquid and competitive markets for investors to sell their investments (whether markets for stock offerings or acquisitions), and the willingness of highly skilled managers and engineers to work in entrepreneurial environments. However painful the short-run adjustments, these more fundamental factors are likely to be critical in establishing the long-run level.

When one examines these more fundamental factors, there appears to have been quite substantial changes for the better over the past several decades.[6] I will highlight two of the determinants of the long-run supply of private equity in the United States, where these changes have been particularly dramatic: the acceleration of the rate of technological innovation and the decreasing "transaction costs" associated with private equity investments.

Although the increase in innovation can be seen though several measures, probably the clearest indication is in the extent of patenting. Patent applications by U.S. inventors, after hovering between 40,000 and 80,000 annually over the first 85 years of this century, have surged over the past decade to over 120,000 per year. This does not appear to reflect the impact of changes in domestic patent policy, shifts in the success rate of applications, or a variety of alternative explanations. Rather, it appears to reflect a fundamental shift in the rate of innovation.[7] The breadth of technology appears wider today than ever before. The greater rate of intellectual innovation provides fertile ground for future investments, especially by venture capitalists.

A second change has been the decreasing cost of making new private equity investments. The efficiency of the private equity process has been greatly augmented by the emergence of other intermediaries familiar with its workings. The presence of such expertise among lawyers, accountants, and others—even real estate brokers—has substantially lowered the transaction costs associated with forming and financing new firms or restructuring existing ones. The increasing number of professionals and managers familiar with and accustomed to the employment arrangements offered by private equity-backed firms (such as heavy reliance on stock options) has also been a major shift. In short, the increasing familiarity with the private equity process has made the long-term prospects for investment more attractive than they have ever been before.

Many of these changes appear to have been driven by the activities of private equity-backed firms: for instance, venture capitalists have funded many innovative firms, which have in turn, created opportunities for new venture investments. A "virtuous circle" may be at work. That is, the growth in the activity of private equity industry has enhanced the conditions for new investments, which has in turn led to more capital formation.

As the various cases in this volume highlight, much remains unknown about the private equity industry. The extent to which the U.S. model will spread overseas and the degree to which the American model will—or can—be successfully adapted during this process are particularly interesting questions. It seems clear, however, that this financial intermediary will be an enduring feature on the global economic landscape in the years to come.

---

[6] Despite its growth, the private equity pool today remains relatively small. For every one dollar of private equity in the portfolio of U.S. institutional investors, there are about $40 of publicly traded equities. The ratios are even more uneven for overseas institutions. At the same time, the size of foreign private equity pool remains far below that of the United States. This suggests considerable possibilities for future growth. The disparity can be illustrated by comparing the ratio of the private equity pool to the size of the economy. In 1995, this ratio was 8.7 times higher in the United States than in Asia and 8.0 times higher in the United States than in continental Europe. (These statistics are taken from the European Venture Capital Association, *1998 EVCA Yearbook*, Zaventum, Belgium, European Venture Capital Association, 1998; and Asian Venture Capital Journal, *Venture Capital in Asia: 1997/98 Edition*, Hong Kong, Asian Venture Capital Journal, 1997). At least to the casual observer, these ratios seem modest when compared to the economic role of new firms, products, and processes in the developed economies.

[7] These changes are discussed in Samuel Kortum and Josh Lerner, "Stronger Protection or Technological Revolution: What is Behind the Recent Surge in Patenting?," *Carnegie-Rochester Conference Series on Public Policy*, 48 (1998): 247–304.

Table of Contents

Martin Smith: February 1998

Martin Smith faced an enviable dilemma, but a dilemma nonetheless. A second-year student in the MBA program at Harvard Business School, Martin had been successful in his private equity job hunt: so much so that he had generated three job offers. What was arguably the most attractive offer, from the prestigious Greenlane Group, had just arrived, but with the proviso that he accept or reject the offer by the next morning. As he walked in the fading winter twilight to the campus gymnasium, Shad Hall, he wondered what he should do.

During the course of his job search, Martin had come to appreciate the very substantial differences between these funds. The Greenlane Group had an excellent track record, and he knew that this was a strong brand name (a "franchise fund" in private equity parlance) in the private equity community. But the organization was in the midst of a transition from the senior to junior partners, which could potentially disrupt the fund's operations. Martin also worried about the fund's approach to compensation. But he also had concerns about Clifton Investment Partners. Until recently, Clifton had made their money by participating as a syndicate member in other funds' deals, not from transactions that they had actually originated themselves. The funds' partners seemed to be much longer on financial than operating experience. Was it good management or merely good luck that had brought the fund success? Finally, the Terra Nova Venture Fund was an unknown quantity. Several general partners, who individually had strong reputations, had established a venture capital fund with a technological emphasis. Their small first fund was off to a good start, and their fund might represent a ground floor opportunity for Martin. But the partners of Terra Nova had not been together as a group for very long and did not even work in the same city. Martin wondered whether they would stay together as a team long enough for him to establish his own track record and reputation.

Another important consideration for Martin was the compensation packages that the different groups offered. Greenlane offered the lowest base pay and made no provision for a share of the carried interest. On the other hand, if he joined Terra Nova, he would receive a higher base level of compensation and immediately begin receiving a share of the fund's profits. The Clifton offer was between these two extremes. While Martin realized that joining a private equity group as an associate was a long-run investment, he was also keenly aware of the impending need to pay off the substantial debt he had accumulated while attending Harvard Business School.

This case was prepared by Josh Lerner. Copyright © 1997 by the President and Fellows of Harvard College. Harvard Business School case 298-076.

OPPORTUNITIES IN THE PRIVATE EQUITY INDUSTRY IN 1998

The U.S. private equity industry had been little more than a cottage industry until the late 1970s. Although the first funds were established in the 1940s, the industry had relied primarily on individual investors during its first three decades. Little of the substantial pools of capital associated with pension funds had gone into private equity, owing both to their unfamiliarity with the asset class and their fears that such investments violated federal government standards.

The U.S. Department of Labor addressed the concerns in 1979 by clarifying the so-called prudent man rule, unleashing a wave of capital into private equity funds that had continued for two decades. Virtually without exception, each year had seen more money invested in private equity, typically in limited partnerships with a contractually specified 10-year life. (The investors served as limited partners—so named because their liability was typically limited to the amount they invested—while the private equity group served as the general partners.) Exhibit 1 illustrates the growth of commitments to private equity funds over this period. The exhibit also illustrates the growing prominence of funds devoted to making leveraged buyout investments among private equity funds.[1]

Private equity groups were traditionally very "lean" organizations, operating without substantial staffs of analysts or associates. This reluctance to add staff was seen as imparting at least two advantages. First, the organizations' small size led to a great deal of flexibility. Private equity, particularly in recent years, was a highly competitive business, where investment opportunities often needed to be acted upon quickly. Small groups could react rapidly with first-hand knowledge. Second, the performance of each partner and associate could be carefully observed and attributed, and compensation and promotion decisions made accordingly. The ability to carefully measure performance limited the internal political activities so common in corporate life.

Despite these concerns, in recent years the number of employees in private equity organizations had climbed. This partially reflected the success of partnerships in raising additional capital and their need to rapidly invest these funds. Exhibit 2 illustrates the recent growth of the private equity industry. Although many private equity funds shunned recent graduates of MBA programs, preferring to hire people with additional experience in operating firms, recruitment of MBA graduates had also increased. Exhibit 2 also indicates the increased recruitment of Harvard Business School graduates into private equity investing.

The use of compensation in private equity organizations had also undergone a substantial evolution with the recent growth of the private equity industry. Initially, there had been quite distinct schemes employed within traditional independent partnerships and groups affiliated with investment or commercial banks. (These affiliated groups have made up about 25% of the private equity groups active over the past 25 years, though accounting for a smaller share of the dollars invested.[2]) Private equity funds would typically pay an annual salary as well as a share of the capital gains (or "carried interest") harvested in that year (the latter would be received only by the partners). Affiliated groups, which typically did not employ a partnership structure (they usually simply invested the parent institution's capital rather than that of outside investors), gen-

---

[1] For an overview of the private equity industry, see George Fenn, Nellie Liang, and Steven Prowse, "The Private Equity Industry: An Overview." *Financial Market, Institutions and Instruments* 6, no. 4 (1997): 70–100.

[2] The prevalence and performance of institutionally affiliated private equity groups are summarized in Paul A. Gompers and Josh Lerner, "Conflict of Interest and Reputation in the Issuance of Public Securities: Evidence from Venture Capital," 42 (1999): 53–80.

erally provided employees with a salary and bonus. Even with the bonus, however, the compensation level in the affiliated funds was rarely equal to that of independent funds, and many of the leading private equity groups had been established by individuals who had left captive private equity groups such as those of the Bank of Boston, Citibank, the First National Bank of Chicago, and Security Pacific.

During the late 1980s, and especially in the 1990s, the patterns of compensation began subtly changing. In particular, the sharp demarcation between affiliated and independent groups blurred. A number of affiliated groups, anxious to limit the defection of personnel, took two new approaches. Many such organizations adopted "shadow" compensation schemes that more directly tied their employees' rewards to their performance. Other institutions allowed their private equity groups to raise part of their funds from outside investors rather than just from the sponsoring institution. For the funds raised from outsiders, there would be a provision for carried interest, at least some of which would be payable to the group's partners.

Meanwhile, intense competition for talented partners and associates had led independent groups to begin awarding bonuses in addition to salaries and carried interest. Although precise data was difficult to obtain, just-published survey estimates of compensation levels by the accounting firm KPMG/Peat Marwick are summarized in Exhibits 3 and 4.

One factor that these surveys did not fully capture was the presence of co-investment rights. Many private equity groups allowed both partners and associates to invest in their transactions. In some cases, there were few restrictions; in other groups, the investors were required to invest an equal amount in each transaction to address the limited partners' concerns about potential incentive problems. In particular, institutional investors were often concerned that large investments by the general partners would reduce their stakes in the most attractive opportunities and that general partners would spend a disproportionate amount of time with the companies in which they had personally invested. In many organizations, associates were extended loans with which to make investments. In many cases, these loans were at a reduced interest level or were only required to be repaid to the extent that the investments yielded any proceeds.

MARTIN SMITH

Martin Smith's background made him attractive to many venture capital organizations. After completing an undergraduate degree in computer science at Stanford University, he had joined Sun Microsystems as a software engineer in the firm's software development area. After a little more than two years, he had left to join several friends from college who had begun a start-up geared to developing Internet tools. This company, which had been a "bootstrap" operation funded largely through contract work developing Web sites for major corporations, had been acquired for $9 million two and a half years later. The acquirer, a venture-backed publicly traded firm whose flagship product was an Internet search engine, was seeking to expand its product line. Martin had left soon after to attend Harvard Business School. While in business school, he had spent a summer internship with a long-established Boston venture capital group. This experience had only reinforced Martin's desire to join the private equity industry after graduation, hopefully in California.

At the same time, he had pursued an effective strategy in identifying private equity opportunities. First, he had focused on the private equity groups that were most likely to be interested in him. Martin had realized that without significant experience in an investment bank or as a financial analyst, it was unlikely that the many groups specializing in buyout or buildup investments would find him an attractive candidate. Consequently, he had targeted groups undertaking venture capital or early-stage investments.

Martin had also avoided more marginal private equity organizations. He had been contacted by a number of groups that were in the process of raising a first fund and had seen his resume in the Venture Capital and Principal Investment Club's resume book. Rather than seriously pursuing these positions, he had focused on more established groups. Martin believed that if he was unable to obtain an offer from a reputable group, he would probably be better served spending several years in an operating position in the software industry and then looking once again.

Finally, Martin had extensively researched the private equity industry in order to target organizations that fit his skill set and to understand their situations. He had identified which groups had just raised funds or were likely to be raising funds in the upcoming year (and hence likely to be thinking about adding personnel), researching the key deals that the partnerships had invested in, and seeking to ascertain the different groups' investment philosophies. As he had narrowed his job search, he had sought first-hand information about the groups from portfolio companies and an institutional investor. While this was time-consuming, and occasionally raised eyebrows at the private equity groups with whom he was interviewing, he believed it was only prudent. After all, accepting a position with a private equity group could be seen as a decision that required the same degree of due diligence as any other investment. The only difference was that here the investment was not of money—just a substantial amount of Martin's "human capital"!

THE DILEMMA

Martin had received offers from three attractive private equity groups. Two of these groups had established track records, whereas the other was newer. Exhibit 5 summarizes the track records of the two established organizations.

The *Greenlane Group* was a top-tier venture firm. Within the private equity community, it had a strong "brand name" and had historically sponsored very successful partnerships. The group built up a franchise in health care and technology beginning in 1986. In mid-1997, the two senior partners had begun "phasing out" and passing work onto good, proven junior partners.

The group had just raised a new fund (Fund IV) that was the same size as the prior fund (Fund III). The share of profits going to the private equity investors had been raised in the new fund to 25% from the 20% that it had been in the previous funds and was still the industry standard. The justification offered was that this increase was due to performance on Fund III. Nonetheless, the second fund (Fund II) had about the same performance as the median fund formed in the same year (often referred to in private equity industry as funds in the same "vintage year"). Furthermore, there was a potentially disturbing variance within the private equity organization. According to Martin's research, in the technology sector, the group had mixed results. In the health-care area, however, the group was consistently good. Observers attributed this to its extraordinary deal-flow due to the "franchise factor" developed by one of the senior and two of the junior partners.

The initial Greenlane fund (Fund I) was established by two senior partners and generated very good returns. It was the three junior partners, many observers felt, who generated the majority of returns of Fund III in 1994. From conversations with a college roommate who now helped manage the private equity portfolio of a major pension fund (who had also provided the performance data reproduced in Exhibit 5), Martin had learned that the distribution of the profit participation in the third fund was very uneven: fully 70% of the gains went to the two senior partners. They had received seven points each (a point is defined as one percentage point of the fund's total profits), whereas the three junior partners received two points each. Although Martin's former roommate had not been involved in his organization's decision to invest in the fourth fund, he had heard that the new fund had improved the distribution of the profits, with about 40% of the profits going to the junior partners. Furthermore, the increase in the carried interest to 25% implied that there would be more profits to divide.

Greenlane's offer did not include any provision for a share of the carried interest for Martin. Nonetheless, the question of how much a "founder" should continue to get and the motives for the increase in the carried interest bothered him. Martin was aware that a number of leading private equity groups had broken up because of disputes between generations of partners. Another issue was the uneven returns by sub-segment. As a specialist in the computer industry, he wondered what the impact of joining such a group would be. Was there any risk in doing so?

The partners of the *Clifton Investment Partners* had strong financial backgrounds but no operating experience. The returns for its two funds were in the upper half, but not the upper quartile, of venture capital funds in general. Exhibit 5 shows the historical performance of the partnership. In conversations with industry observers, Martin learned that Clifton had a history of participating in other people's deals. In the mid-1990s, the fund had changed its strategy by hiring "venture partners" with operating experience. Clifton also developed a database along with a cold calling strategy to generate a proprietary deal-flow for the funds. The partnership seemed to be going after market segments being abandoned by other top-tier venture funds, which had grown much bigger.

The general partners of the group had reasonable reputations, and the carry was equally distributed. The general partners were regarded as equally good performers, but no one was "great." Clifton was currently in the process of raising its third fund, on terms similar to those of its previous two, although it was proposed to be 50% larger. Martin's former roommate seemed to have little doubt that the target would be met, pointing out that the terms were being perceived as "friendly" to the limited partners. Nonetheless, Martin was concerned about the general partners' relative lack of operating experience and modest reputation in the industry. Would this experience be as valuable—either with respect to personal learning or the "stamp of approval" it would provide to the rest of the venture community—as the Greenlane experience? The fund's rapid growth also seemed somewhat problematic.

The *Terra Nova Venture* Fund had just raised a first fund the year before. Only two of the three general partners had worked together before the formation of the fund. The fund was located in offices in San Francisco and Austin, Texas. Since it was a team with an unproven track record, Martin was apprehensive about joining them. On the other hand, the team was developing an interesting deal-flow in a very focused technology niche (Internet infrastructure) that played to Martin's technological training and business experience.

The general partners' backgrounds included a senior analyst from a major investment banking firm, a junior partner at another venture capital fund, and a third from industry. Individually, they had good track records. The banker was successful with his "buy" recommendations, and the industry partner had been chief operating officer at a quality firm. The investment banking and industry partner had worked together, having bought and sold a company that had been very successful.

In early 1996, a $26 million fund had been raised from individual investors. The fund had already invested in 10 companies with what the partners claimed were attractive valuations considering their stage of development. The team had shown an ability to hire key management into portfolio companies, and 3 of the 10 companies had received follow-on financing at higher valuations. The team had one big failure in a syndicated deal. The remaining companies were being carried at cost, but in conversations with several of them, Martin saw indications that several of them appeared to be ahead of plan. Overall, the portfolio had a great deal of potential, but being new, the group had a much higher risk profile. Martin also wondered about the location of the fund's offices. The management style and decision making could be fragmented owing to the geographic spread of the partners. Smith worried that a "lone ranger" general partner could emerge and jeopardize the stability of the organization.

Not only did the situations of the three private equity groups differ considerably, but so did the compensation schemes they offered. Greenlane's offer had called for a salary of about $90,000, with a projected bonus of about 10% of his base salary in the first year. If his investments proved successful, the partners indicated, Martin might receive a share of the carried interest in his third or fourth year at the firm. When Martin tried to push for more specifics, the partners proved unwilling to discuss the matter further. Terra Nova's offer, despite the fund's smaller size and much shorter track record, was considerably more attractive: Martin would receive a base salary of almost $120,000, could expect a bonus of up to 10% of his base pay if he worked out successfully, and would receive one point in the 1996 fund. (This stake would "vest" over four years: that is, if Martin left or was fired before then, he would receive a smaller stake in the profits, according to a set schedule.) Finally, Clifton's offer was midway between the other two offers in terms of salary and bonus. Although Martin would not initially receive a share of the fund's capital gains, the partners indicated that this issue would be revisited after the initial set of investors had agreed to participate in their third fund. The partners projected that this agreement, also known as a "first closing," would occur near the end of 1998.

Martin wondered how to interpret these offers and how much importance to place on compensation in his choice between the three funds.

Exhibit 1 Pattern of Private Equity Fundraising, 1980–1997

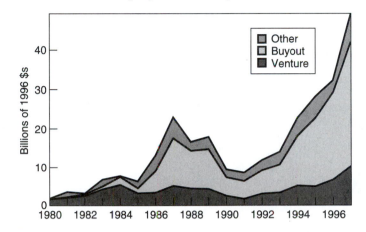

Source: Compiled from the *Private Equity Analyst* and unpublished records of Asset Alternatives.

Exhibit 2 Growth of Private Equity Industry, 1982–1997

	National Venture Capital Association Member Organizations (includes many buyout investors)	Harvard Business School Students Accepting Venture Capital or Buyout Positions	Total Venture Capital Professionals (includes some buyout investors)
1982	114	NA	1,031
1983	130	NA	1,494
1984	144	NA	1,760
1985	180	9	1,899
1986	191	18	2,187
1987	207	20	2,378
1988	225	11	2,479
1989	229	20	2,544
1990	223	12	2,602
1991	220	11	NA
1992	201	8	NA
1993	193	19	NA
1994	187	16	NA
1995	179	22	NA
1996	194	44	NA
1997	240	70	NA

Source: Compiled from unpublished National Venture Capital Association, Harvard Business School, and Venture Economics records.

Note: NA = Not available.

Exhibit 3 Compensation of Private Equity Investors ($000s)

Title	Salary and Bonus		Total Compensation[a]		Carried Interest (%)[b]
	Median	Mean	Median	Mean	Mean
Managing general partner	510	843	1,959	5,249	4.9
Managing partner	450	506	855	2,377	2.9
Partner (mid-level)	250	340	332	1,165	1.5
Junior partner	166	191	215	243	0.7
Senior associate	113	126	124	132	0.4
Associate	78	77	78	78	0.0

Source: Compiled from KPMG/Peat Marwick, *Compensation Survey Performed for Selected Venture Capital Firms*, Boston: KPMG/Peat Marwick, 1998.

[a]Total compensation includes carried interest and co-investment distributions, as well as salary and bonus. Survey data is based on the 1997 calendar year.
[b]Carried interest percentage is for most recent fund.

Exhibit 4 Compensation of Managing Partners and Associates in Private Equity Funds of Different Types ($000s)

	Managing Partners		Senior Associates	
	Mean Salary and Bonus	Mean Total Compensation	Mean Salary and Bonus	Mean Total Compensation
All Funds:				
<$100MM in capital	203	273	107	122
$100-$150MM	335	1,252	125	129
>$500MM	701	3,641	133	135
Private Firms:				
Lower half in size	240	459	149	150
Upper half	523	4,618	133	138
Institutional Funds:				
Lower half in size	300	358	119	129
Upper half	702	1,967	114	116

Source: Compiled from KPMG/Peat Marwick, *Compensation Survey Performed for Selected Venture Capital Firms*, Boston: KPMG/Peat Marwick, 1998. See footnotes above for definitions.

Exhibit 5   Historical Performance of Prior Funds

Table 1:   *GreenLane Group*

Fund	Date	Size (millions)	Fund Return (%)	Venture Economics Median (%) — as of 12/31/96 —	Venture Economics Top ¼ (%)	General Partner (GP) Performance
Fund I	1986	$60	16% (4 times $)	7.2%	12.6%	Senior GPs
Fund II	1990	$100	22% (3 times $)	21.2%	46.7%	Mixed, with GP turnover
Fund III	1994	$150	59% (2 times $)	19.5%	31.3%	Hot public stocks by juniors
Fund IV	1996	$150	(with 25% carry)			

Table 2:   *Clifton Investment Partners*

Fund	Date	Size (millions)	Fund Return (%)	Venture Economics Median (%) — as of 12/31/96 —	Venture Economics Top ¼ (%)	General Partner (GP) Performance
Fund I	1986	$50	10% (3 times $)	7.2%	12.6%	Equal weighted GP performance
Fund II	1990	$60	25% (3 times $)	21.2%	46.7%	Equal weighted GP performance
Fund III	1997	$90	(proposed, with attractive terms)			Proposed new deal sourcing strategy

Fund return shows the internal rate of return to investors to date, as well as (in parentheses) the valuation of distributions plus undistributed assets as a multiple of commited capital.

Source: Compiled from Venture Economics, *Venture Capital Performance*, Boston, Venture Economics, 1997 and casewriters' estimates.

Note: Since the first Terra Nova Venture Fund was less than two years old, no historical data on its performance was yet available.

RAISING AND STRUCTURING PRIVATE EQUITY FUNDS

The first module of *Venture Capital and Private Equity* examines how private equity funds are raised and structured. These funds often have complex features, and the legal issues involved are frequently arcane. But the structure of private equity funds has a profound effect on the behavior of venture and buyout investors. Consequently, it is important to understand these issues, whether one intends to work for, receive money from, or invest in or alongside private equity funds.

In this module we seek not only to understand the features of private equity funds and the actors in the fundraising process, but also to analyze them. We will map out which institutions serve primarily to increase the profits from private equity investments as a whole and which seem designed mostly to shift profits *between* the parties. We will attempt to explain the functions of and reasons for each aspect of private equity fundraising.

WHY THIS MODULE?

The structuring of venture and buyout funds may initially appear to be a complex and technical topic, one better left to legal specialists than to general managers. Private equity partnership agreements are complex documents, often extending for hundreds of pages. Practitioner discussions of the structure of these firms are rife with obscure terms such as "reverse claw-backs."

But the subject is an important one. For the features of private equity funds—whether management fees, profit sharing rules, or contractual terms—have a profound effect on the behavior of these investors. It is important to understand these influences if one is seeking to work for a private equity fund. But an understanding of these dynamics will also be valuable for the entrepreneur financing his company through these investors, the investment banker underwriting a firm backed by private equity funds, the corporate development officer investing alongside venture capitalists in a young company, and the pension fund manager placing her institution's capital into a fund.

An example may help to illustrate this point. Almost all venture and buyout funds are designed to be "self-liquidating": that is, to dissolve after 10 or 12 years. The need to terminate each fund imposes a healthy discipline, forcing private equity investors to take the necessary but painful step of terminating underperforming firms in their portfolios. (These firms are sometimes referred to as the "living dead" or "zombies.") But the pressure to raise an additional fund can sometimes have less pleasant consequences. Young private equity organizations frequently rush young firms to the public marketplace in order to demonstrate a successful track record, even if the companies are not ready to go public. This behavior, known as "grandstanding," can have a harmful effect on the long-run prospects of the firms dragged prematurely into the public markets.

Another rationale for examining the concerns and perspectives of institutional investors and intermediaries is that they provide an often-neglected avenue into the private equity industry. Many students diligently pursue positions at the traditional private equity organizations but neglect other routes to careers as private equity investors. A position evaluating private equity funds and putting capital to work in these organizations is likely to lead to a network of relationships with private equity investors that may eventually pay handsome dividends.

THE FRAMEWORK

The private equity fundraising drama features a wide array of actors. Investors—whether pension funds, individuals, or endowments—each have their own motivations and concerns. These investors frequently hire intermediaries. Sometimes these "gatekeepers" play a consultative role, recommending attractive funds to their clients. In other cases, they organize "funds-of-funds" of their own. Specialized intermediaries concentrate on particular niches of the private equity industry, such as buying and selling interests in limited partnerships from institutional investors. In addition, venture and buyout organizations are increasingly hiring placement agents who facilitate the fundraising process.

This module will examine each of these players. Rather than just describing their roles, however, we will highlight the rationales for and impacts of their behavior. Some institutions and features have evolved to improve the efficiency of the private equity investment process, while others appear to be designed primarily to shift more of the economic benefits to particular parties.

Investing in a private equity fund is in some respects a "leap of faith" for institutional investors. Most pension funds and endowments typically have very small staffs. At the largest organizations, a dozen professionals may be responsible for investing several billion dollars each year. Meanwhile, private equity funds undertake investments that are either in risky new firms pursuing complex new technologies or in troubled mature companies with numerous organizational pathologies and potential legal liabilities.

Many features of private equity funds can be understood as responses to this uncertain environment, rife with many information gaps. For instance, the "carried interest"—the substantial share of profits allocated to the private equity investors—helps address these information asymmetries by ensuring that all parties gain if the investment does well. Similarly, pension funds hire "gatekeepers" to ensure that only sophisticated private equity funds with well-defined objectives get funded with their capital.

At the same time, other features of private equity funds can be seen as attempts to *transfer* wealth between parties, rather than efforts to increase the size of the overall amount of profits generated by private equity investments. An example was the drive by many venture capital funds in the mid-1980s—a period when the demand for their services was very strong—to change the timing of their compensation. Prior to this point, venture capital funds had typically disbursed all the proceeds from their first few successful investments to their investors, until the investors had received their original invested capital back. The venture capitalists would then begin receiving a share of the subsequent investments that they exited. Consider a fund that had raised capital of $50 million, whose first three successful investments yielded $25 million each. Under the traditional arrangement, the proceeds from the first two offerings would have gone entirely to the institutional investors in their fund. The venture capitalists would have only begun receiving a share of the proceeds at the time they exited the third investment.

In the mid-1980s, venture capitalists began demanding—and receiving—the right to start sharing in even the first successfully exited investments. The primary effect of this change was that the venture capitalists began receiving more compensation early in their funds' lives. Put another way, the net present value of their compensation package increased considerably. It is not surprising, then, that as the inflow into venture capital weakened in the late 1980s, institutional investors began demanding that venture capitalists return to the previous approach of deferring compensation.

This twin tension—between behavior that increases the size of the "pie" and actions that simply change the relative sizes of the slices—runs through this module. Using this framework, we will attempt to understand both the workings of and the reasons for the key features of these funds.

THE STRUCTURE OF THE MODULE

The first half of the module introduces the key elements of the private equity fundraising process. Among the actors whose structure and concerns we will examine are institutions, private equity investors, "funds-of-funds," and "gatekeepers." We will put particular emphasis on the agreements that bring these parties together into limited partnerships. Because they play such an important role in shaping behavior, compensation terms will be a special focus.

The second half of the module examines the raising of three funds by private equity organizations. We look at private equity organizations that have very different maturities and varied investment targets: two men seeking to raise a first fund to pursue opportunistic late-stage investments, a venture organization trying to raise its second seed capital fund, and an established British private equity organization considering a new template for a fund to undertake buyouts across Europe. The funds that emerged from these circumstances reflected not only the differences between the investments that each fund promised to make, but also each group's ability to persuade—or demand—a better deal from its investors. We will consider a variety of issues, from the role of the key institutions in the fundraising process to the assessment of the performance of these funds.

FURTHER READING ON PRIVATE EQUITY FUNDRAISING AND PARTNERSHIPS

Legal and Descriptive Works

JOSEPH W. BARTLETT, *Equity Finance: Venture Capital, Buyouts, Restructurings, and Reorganization,* New York, Wiley, 1995, chapters 24 and 29.

CRAIG E. DAUCHY AND MARK T. HARMON, "Structuring Venture Capital Limited Partnerships," *The Computer Lawyer* 3 (November 1986): 1–7.

MICHAEL J. HALLORAN, LEE F. BENTON, ROBERT V. GUNDERSON, JR., KEITH L. KEARNEY, AND JORGE DEL CALVO, *Venture Capital and Public Offering Negotiation,* Englewood Cliffs, NJ, Aspen Law and Business, 1995, volume 1, chapters 1 and 2.

Practitioner and Journalistic Accounts

E. S. ELY, "Dr. Silver's Tarnished Prescription," *Venture* 9 (July 1987): 54–58.

STEVEN P. GALANTE, *Directory of Alternative Investment Programs,* Wellesley, Asset Alternatives, 1997, section II.

WILLIAM M. MERCER, INC., *Key Terms and Conditions for Private Equity Investing* (available on-line at http://www.assetalt.com/ped/mercer.html).

Venture Economics, *1992 Terms and Conditions of Venture Capital Partnerships,* Boston, Venture Economics, 1992.

Numerous articles in *Buyouts, Private Equity Analyst,* and *Venture Capital Journal.*

Academic Studies

GEORGE W. FENN, NELLIE LIANG, AND STEPHEN PROWSE, "The Private Equity Market: An Overview," *Financial Markets, Institutions and Instruments* 6, no. 4 (1997): 70–100.

PAUL A. GOMPERS AND JOSH LERNER, "Risk and Reward in Private Equity Investments: The Challenge of Performance Assessment," *Journal of Private Equity* 1 (Winter 1997): 5–12.

PAUL A. GOMPERS AND JOSH LERNER, *The Venture Capital Cycle,* Cambridge, MIT Press, 1999, chapters 2–5.

PAUL A. GOMPERS AND JOSH LERNER, "What Drives Venture Fundraising?," *Brookings Papers on Economic Activity: Microeconomics.*

BLAINE HUNTSMAN AND JAMES P. HOBAN, JR., "Investment in New Enterprise: Some Empirical Observations on Risk, Return and Market Structure," *Financial Management* 9 (Summer 1980): 44–51.

LESLIE A. JENG AND PHILIPPE C. WELLS, "The Determinants of Venture Capital Funding: An Empirical Analysis," Unpublished working paper, Harvard University, 1997.

PATRICK R. LILES, *Sustaining the Venture Capital Firm,* Cambridge, Management Analysis Center, 1977.

1

Yale University Investments Office: November 1997

David Swensen leaned back from the antique roll-top desk in his otherwise modest office. Outside, the last remaining elm leaves fluttered to the ground, as Swensen and his colleague, Dean Takahashi, reviewed their investment strategies.

As Yale's chief investment officer, Swensen was responsible for managing the university's endowment, which totaled approximately $6 billion in November 1997. Under Swensen's leadership, and with the guidance and approval of the Investment Committee, Yale had developed a rather different approach to endowment management, including substantial investments in "less efficient" equity markets such as private equity (venture capital, buyouts, natural resources, etc.), real estate, and "absolute return" investing. This approach had generated successful, indeed enviable, returns. Swensen and his staff were proud of the record they had compiled, and they believed that Yale should probably focus even more of their efforts and assets in these less efficient markets. At the same time, how far did they think Yale should or could go in this direction? What were the Investment Committee's key concerns likely to be?

BACKGROUND[1]

Yale was established in 1701 by 10 Connecticut clergymen. Over its first century, the college relied on the generosity of the Connecticut General Assembly, which provided more than half of its funding. The creation of a formal endowment for Yale was triggered by the 1818 disestablishment of Congregationalism as Connecticut's state religion. Students and alumni alike demanded that the school respond by establishing a divinity school to offer theological instruction. To fund this effort, numerous alumni made large gifts, the first of a series of successful fund drives. Although Yale used many of these donations to buy land and construct buildings, it invested other funds in corporate and railroad bonds as well as equities. By the century's end, the endowment had reached $5 million.

The growth of the endowment rapidly accelerated during the first three decades of the twentieth century. This was due both to several enormous bequests and to aggressive investments in equities, which comprised well over half the endowment's portfolio

This case was prepared by Josh Lerner. An earlier version of this case was prepared by Josh Lerner and Jay Light. Copyright © 1997 by the President and Fellows of Harvard College. Harvard Business School case 298-077.

[1] This section is based on Brooks Mather Kelley, *Yale: A History*, New Haven, Yale University Press, 1974 and Yale University Investments Office, *The Yale Endowment*, New Haven, Yale University, 1995.

during the "roaring" 1920s. In 1930, equities represented 42% of the Yale endowment; the average university had only 11%.[2] Yale avoided severe erosion of its endowment during the Great Depression, however, because many quite recent bequests were kept in cash or Treasuries rather than being invested in equities.

In the late 1930s, Treasurer Laurence Tighe decided that the share of equities in Yale's portfolio should be dramatically reduced. Tighe argued that higher taxes were likely to expropriate any corporate profits that equity holders would otherwise receive even if a recovery were to occur. He argued that bonds would consequently perform better than stocks. His decision, which stipulated that at least two dollars would be held in fixed income instruments for every dollar of equity, set the template for Yale's asset allocation over the next three decades. The Treasurer and Trustees continued to manage the endowment themselves during this period, selecting individual bonds and high-yield or income-oriented stocks for the portfolio. These policies seemed very prudent in the late 1930s and 1940s, but unfortunately, they were less well suited for the bull market of the 1950s and 1960s. In response, in the mid- and late 1960s, the endowment's trustees decided on two substantial policy shifts.

First, the trustees decided to substantially increase the University's exposure to equity investments. In this decision, they were influenced by a task force sponsored by McGeorge Bundy, president of the Ford Foundation. This committee—which included Kingman Brewster, president of Yale—argued that most university endowments had taken too conservative an approach:

> It is our conclusion that past thinking by many endowment managers has been overly influenced by fear of another major crash. Although nobody can ever be certain what the future may bring, we do not think that a long-term policy founded on such fear can survive dispassionate analysis.[3]

Second, Yale decided to contract out much of the portfolio management function to an external adviser. The school helped to found a new Boston-based money manager, Endowment Management and Research Corporation (EM&R), whose principals were well-known successful growth stock investors recruited from other Boston money management firms. The plan was that EM&R would function as a quasi-independent external firm and would be free to recruit additional clients. At the same time, Yale would be its largest client and would have priority over other clients.

The high expectations for EM&R were never realized. Like almost all other universities, Yale saw its endowment's value plummet in the ensuing years because of a "bear" market, accelerating inflation, and operating deficits. Between 1969 and 1979, the inflation-adjusted value of Yale's endowment declined by 46%. While the investment performance was not that unusual relative to that of other endowments, it nonetheless severely strained the financial fabric of the University. Yale terminated its relationship with EM&R in 1979 and embarked on a program to use a variety of external advisers in its evolving asset management functions.

DAVID SWENSEN AND THE INVESTMENTS OFFICE IN 1997

In 1985, David Swensen was hired to head the Investments Office. William Brainard, Yale's provost at the time, and James Tobin persuaded their former student—Swensen

---

[2] General university information is from Institutional Department, Scudder, Stevens & Clark, *Survey of University and College Endowment Funds,* New York, Scudder, Stevens & Clark, 1947.

[3] Advisory Committee on Endowment Management, *Managing Educational Endowments: Report to the Ford Foundation,* New York, Ford Foundation, 1969.

had earned his Ph.D. in Economics at Yale in 1980—to leave his post at Lehman Brothers. The position offered not only the opportunity to help Yale, but the possibility of some teaching in Yale College as well.

In the succeeding 12 years, Swensen built the capabilities of the Yale Investments Office. Most importantly, he recruited and developed a quite small but high-quality internal staff. Dean Takahashi, whom Swensen had known as a Yale student, was recruited into the Investments Office. He and Ellen Shuman, another graduate of Yale's School of Organization and Management (SOM), became Swensen's primary lieutenants. A number of other staff had also been recruited over the years, often recent graduates of Yale College. There were a total of 15 employees in the office in November 1997. The Investments Office itself filled all three floors of a modest reconstructed Victorian house on the northern edge of Yale's campus. Swensen encouraged his staff to be active members of the larger Yale community. Indeed, he had chosen this location to signal that the Investments Office was an integral part of the University and its financial management function.

Swensen defined the role of the Investments Office broadly. Reporting to the Treasurer and to an Investment Committee (described below), the Investments Office had overall responsibility for endowment matters. Although most of their day-to-day activities involved evaluating, selecting, monitoring, and overseeing external investment advisers, they also played a critical role in the entire policy-making process. For example, they were responsible for recommendations on both the investment policy and the spending policy for the endowment—that is, in broad terms, how the money should be invested and how much of it could be spent in any given year.

The Investment Committee, to whom they reported, was composed of influential and knowledgeable Yale alumni, a number of whom were quite active in different segments of the asset management business. The Committee as a whole functioned as an active, involved board, meeting quarterly and providing advice, counsel, and ultimately approval of the various investment managers. In addition, Swensen often consulted with individual members of the Investment Committee on issues within their areas of specific expertise. This helped guide the thinking and recommendations of the Investments Office on various key issues. It also fostered an atmosphere of advice and support within which the Investments Office could take quite different and sometimes more unconventional stances if it believed in them and could convince the Investment Committee of their merit.

INVESTMENT PHILOSOPHY

Perhaps the most fundamental difference between Yale and other universities was its investment philosophy. Swensen was fond of quoting John Maynard Keynes' maxim that "worldly wisdom teaches us that it is better for reputation to fail conventionally than to succeed unconventionally." Nonetheless, Swensen was willing to take "the risk of being different" when it seemed appropriate and potentially rewarding. By not following the crowd, Yale could develop its investment philosophy from first principles, which are summarized below.

First, Swensen believed strongly in equities, whether publicly traded or private. He pointed out that equities are a claim on a real stream of income, as opposed to a contractual sequence of nominal cash flows (such as bonds). Since the bulk of a university's outlays are devoted to salaries, inflation can place tremendous pressure on its finances. Not only do bonds have low expected returns relative to more equity-like assets, but they often perform poorly during periods of rising or highly uncertain inflation. To demonstrate convincingly why he believed in the long-run advantages of equity investing, Swensen would often refer to the actual cumulative long-run returns over past decades. An original one dollar investment in December 1925 in large-company U.S. stocks (e.g., the S&P 500) would be worth $1371 by the end of 1996; a comparable investment in U.S. Treasury bonds would be worth $34; and Treasury bills, $14.[4]

A second principle was to hold a diversified portfolio. In general, Yale believed that risk could be more effectively reduced by limiting aggregate exposure to any single asset class, rather than by attempting to time markets. Although Swensen and his staff usually had their own informed views of the economy and markets, they believed that most of the time those views were already reflected in market prices. They thus tended to avoid trying to time short-run market fluctuations and would over-weight or under-weight an asset class only if a persuasive case could be made that market prices were substantially out of equilibrium for important and credible reasons.[5]

A third principle was to increasingly seek opportunities in less efficient markets. Swensen noted that over the past decade the difference in performance between U.S. fixed income managers in the 25th and 75th percentiles (of their performance universe) was minimal and that the difference in performance between U.S. common stock portfolio managers in the 25th and 75th percentiles was less than 3% percent per annum. In contrast, in private equity this same performance difference exceeded 15% per annum. This suggested that there could be far greater incremental returns to selecting superior managers in nonpublic markets characterized by incomplete information and illiquidity, and that is exactly what Swensen and his staff endeavored to do.

Fourth, Swensen believed strongly in utilizing outside managers for all but the most routine or indexed of investments. He thought these external investment advisers should be given considerable autonomy to implement their strategies as they saw fit, with relatively little interference or obstructive monitoring by Yale. These managers were chosen very carefully, however, after a lengthy and probing analysis of their abilities, their comparative advantages, their performance records, and their reputations. The Investments Office staff was responsible for developing close and mutually beneficial relationships with each of these external managers. They prided themselves on knowing their managers very well, on listening carefully to their ongoing advice, and on helping to guide them, if and when appropriate, on various policy matters. From time to time, the Investments Office effectively "put a team in business" as a new manager by becoming their first client. It was not uncommon for managers to consider Yale as one of the most important of their clients.

Finally, the Yale philosophy focused critically on the explicit and implicit incentives facing outside managers. In Swensen's view, most of the asset management business had poorly aligned incentives built into typical client–manager relationships. For instance, managers typically prospered if their assets under management grew very large, not necessarily if they just performed well for their clients. The Investments Office tried to structure innovative relationships and fee structures with various external managers so as to better align the manager's interests with Yale's, insofar as that was possible.

RECENT ASSET ALLOCATION AND PERFORMANCE RESULTS

Yale's Investment Committee reviewed its endowment portfolio annually in order to decide on target allocations to the various asset classes. The actual allocations in recent

---

[4] R. G. Ibbotson Associates, *Stocks, Bonds, Bills and Inflation*, Chicago, R. G. Ibbotson Associates, 1997.

[5] Yale actively rebalanced its portfolio to maintain its target asset allocations, however, and this led to some short-term adjustments in its holdings. For instance, as equity values rose in the summer of 1987, Yale sold stocks in order to return to its target allocation level. After the stock market crash later that year, the endowment repurchased many of the same securities as it sought to raise its asset allocation back to the target level.

years are shown in Exhibit 1, which exhibits the recent upward trend in the allocation to the private equity and absolute return classes, as well as the current (1997) target allocations. The comparable asset allocations for several groups of university endowments are shown in Exhibits 2 and 3, and for large institutions (including both pension funds and endowments) in Exhibit 4.

Yale's allocation philosophy and distinctive approach to investing had paid off handsomely over the past decade. In fiscal year 1997, the fund had returned 21.8%, exceeding Yale's benchmark by 7%. This performance was above the institutional funds measured by SEI (which indicated a median performance of 21.4%) and endowments measured by Cambridge Associates (a mean of 20.1%). Perhaps even more impressive had been the fund's long-run performance. Over the 10 years ending in June 1997, Yale's annualized return was 13.5%. This was almost 1% better than the average of its "peers" (other large endowments) and over 2% percent better than the average of all endowments.[6] Yale's record placed it in the top one percent in SEI's rankings of large institutional investors. The endowment's performance during recent years is compared to that of other universities in Exhibit 5; a more detailed breakdown of Yale's returns by asset class is reported in Exhibit 6.

The primary reason for Yale's superior long-term performance record had been the excess returns generated by the portfolio's active managers. Manager selection accounted for more than half the superior performance by Yale relative to the average endowment over the last five years. As expected, the endowment's excess returns had been greatest in the least efficient markets. Over the 10 years ending in June 1997, the difference between Yale's asset class returns and related benchmarks ranged from a low of 0.9% in the most efficiently priced asset class, bonds, to 11.3% in what is probably the least efficient market, private equity.

The Investments Office and the Investment Committee had been pleased with these results. As their experience with the distinctive approach had grown and they had become more confident of their ability to produce sustained above-average results, they had adjusted their spending policy upward. In 1992, in response to an Investments Office recommendation, the Investment Committee adjusted Yale's long-term spending target upward from 4-1/2% to 4-3/4% of endowment assets; in 1995, they adjusted it upward again to 5%.[7] The University was thus benefiting from excellent investment results in two ways: both from a larger endowment and from the justified increase in the target spending rate. The substantial endowment also played a role in Yale receiving the highest rating to finance capital projects (AAA/Aaa) from the two leading bond rating agencies and in enabling the University to borrow money at extremely favorable interest rates.

THE MANAGEMENT OF MARKETABLE SECURITIES

The investment philosophy outlined above guided Yale's management decisions in all of its asset classes. For example, Swensen and his staff approached bonds with skepticism.

---

[6] Had the Yale endowment grown at 12.8% over the past 10 years (the mean of its peers), the endowment in June 1997 would have been $400 million smaller. Had it grown at 11.4% (the equal-weighted average of all university endowments), the endowment would have been $1140 million smaller.

[7] The amount of the endowment spent each year was based on a simple formula, namely, the spending rate (currently 5%) times an exponentially weighted average of the value of the endowment in recent years, with a 30% weight being put on its current value, and exponentially smaller weights on the (inflation-adjusted) values of the endowment in previous years.

They viewed the endowment's current target allocation of 10% in bonds primarily as a disaster reserve, guarding against a severe drop in asset values and/or deflation (such as in the Great Depression). Yale held long-term U.S. government issues (almost exclusively): Swensen was skeptical whether returns from U.S. corporate bonds adequately compensated investors for the added default risk and/or the callability of corporate issues. He was quite skeptical of foreign fixed income securities as well. Unlike most of the rest of its portfolio, the Investments Office managed its bond portfolio internally. Swensen believed that the government bond market was so efficient, and the spread between the performance of government bond fund managers so small, that it did not make sense to hire an outside manager. The portfolio was managed with no attempt to add value through trading on interest rate movements. The endowment staff attempted to generate incremental returns only through modest security selection bets, for example, by using mortgage-backed securities issued by the Government National Mortgage Association (GNMA), which were backed by the full faith and credit of the United States.

Yale also owned a substantial amount of U.S. common stocks, though the current target allocation, 20% of assets, was surprisingly small relative to that of almost all other large institutional investors. Although Yale had been an early adopter of indexing, as the Investments Office staff had become increasingly confident in their ability to find superior managers they eliminated the passive portfolio in favor of a small number of active equity managers. These managers shared several characteristics. First, the majority of Yale's active equity managers tended to emphasize disciplined approaches to investing that could be clearly articulated and differentiated from others. Swensen was convinced that disciplined, fundamentally based approaches, when intelligently applied, could generate reliable and superior long-run performance. Roughly half of Yale's portfolio was allocated to managers who used research-intensive approaches to invest in concentrated portfolios with 10 to 25 stocks. In addition, among Yale's managers were several small stock picking firms that specialized in a particular industry or type of investing. Not surprisingly, none of Yale's managers tended to emphasize market timing, nor did they emphasize fuzzy or intuitive investment approaches that were difficult to articulate. These managers tended to be smaller independent organizations that were owned by their investment professionals. Other things being equal, Yale preferred managers willing to "co-invest" or to be compensated commensurate with their investment performance. Swensen worried that money managers working at many organizations tended to emphasize growth in assets at the expense of performance and/or that ownership by a large institution reduced organizational stability and dampened incentive to perform.

Foreign equities, another 12-1/2% of endowment assets, were a valuable source of diversification, since their returns tended to be only partially correlated with those of the U.S. equity market. But Yale had encountered some real frustrations in transferring its model for successful domestic equity investing to foreign markets. First, the selection of appropriate active money managers had proven particularly challenging. The relatively slower development of institutional investing in many foreign countries meant there were fewer sophisticated "U.S.-style" money managers abroad, managers with credible audited investment performance records and specialized, disciplined investment processes. Perhaps more critically, the best foreign fund managers appeared to work for larger organizations that were in turn owned by large financial institutions, which raised concerns among Swensen and his staff about misaligned incentives. Unlike the United States, few, if any, independent investment advisers were owned solely by their professionals. As a consequence of these problems, Yale had initially chosen two independent

U.S.-based firms to be its foreign equity managers. The University had recently been increasingly successful, however, in identifying and hiring investment managers based in London, Bermuda, and Hong Kong.

Swensen and Senior Director Takahashi found the emerging equity markets of Asia, Latin America, and Eastern Europe particularly intriguing because of the widespread opportunities to find undervalued securities in these less efficient markets. At the end of 1996, roughly 22,000 companies were listed on emerging stock markets exchanges, amounting to 52.5% of all listed companies in the world. Although the market capitalization of these stocks represented 19% of the non-U.S. market capitalization, the economies of emerging markets amounted to more than 25% of the non-U.S. gross domestic product (GDP) in dollar terms and roughly twice that amount when adjusted for purchasing power. In addition to attractive investment opportunities, emerging markets also provided portfolio diversification since their returns generally had a low correlation with those of the United States. Furthermore, emerging markets were growing rapidly, nearly twice the rate of developed countries. There were concerns, of course, including whether these growth prospects would translate into strong investment returns. Although the linkage between growth and profitability for the corporations of these countries was widely assumed, Swensen and his staff were concerned that the link was by no means guaranteed. Nonetheless, they believed that the rapid rate of change in emerging markets provided opportunities for active management to earn superior returns.

Takahashi believed that Yale's foreign equity portfolio should be heavily weighted toward emerging markets, but he was concerned about the limited universe of acceptable managers conducting research-intensive, fundamentally based analysis. Many of the top, successful global emerging markets funds had grown to have many billions of dollars of assets under management, making it difficult to deploy assets in smaller, less well-followed corporations. On the other hand, small funds often lacked the resources to effectively research and cover the tremendous breadth of global emerging markets. Yale had five emerging markets managers in its portfolio. Two were large U.S.-based value managers who used a blend of judgmental and quantitative analysis to allocate between countries and choose stocks. One was a large, London-based global emerging markets manager who used bottom-up fundamental research to invest in a concentrated portfolio. Two were small regionally focused managers concentrating on intensively researched value plays, one in Africa and the other in Southeast Asia.

Yale's emerging market portfolio had generated an annualized 21.7% return since the program's inception in December 1990, 9.3% annually in excess of the International Finance Corporation (IFC) Global Emerging Index. Although Takahashi believed that such excess returns were not sustainable in the long run, he thought that emerging markets generally would continue to be less efficient and provide more opportunities for excess returns than developed markets. Although the Investment Committee did not set a distinct target for emerging market equity holdings, it did so indirectly through definition of a foreign equity benchmark. Currently, foreign equity returns were compared to a benchmark index that comprised 60% of the Morgan Stanley GDP-weighted Europe, Australia, and Far East (EAFE) Index and 40% of the IFC Index. One issue for Yale was that managers other than those in the publicly traded foreign equity portfolio held positions in emerging market securities. For instance, some of Yale's absolute return managers and private equity funds held substantial positions in companies based in developing nations.

A final, more diffuse category of publicly traded investments was called "absolute return" strategies in which Yale currently allocated 25% of its assets. These included a variety of funds specializing in eclectic mixtures of strategies designed to exploit market inefficiencies. Yale divided these into three broad categories: event-driven, value-driven, and opportunistic value investments. Event-driven strategies generally involved creating hedged positions in mispriced securities and were dependent on a specific corporate event, such as a merger or bankruptcy settlement, to achieve targeted returns. Value-driven strategies also entailed hedged investments in mispriced securities but relied on changing company fundamentals or increasing market awareness to drive prices toward fair value. Opportunistic value investments were deep value plays with generally unhedgable market exposure. The common denominator of these strategies was that their returns were expected to be equity-like, and not highly correlated with any particular financial market. Consequently, it made sense to evaluate their investment perfor-mance in terms of the absolute returns achieved rather than relative to any indices of market performance. Most investments by these "absolute return" funds were quite liquid: typically, even the most illiquid of their positions could be sold relatively quickly.

THE MANAGEMENT OF PRIVATE EQUITY

Domestic Venture Capital and Buyout Funds

While Yale had been among the first universities to invest in private equity, entering into its first buyout partnership in 1973 and its first venture capital partnership in 1976, the pace of investing had dramatically increased in recent years. Exhibit 7 summarizes the size of and returns from Yale's private equity portfolio.[8]

Yale's private equity investment strategy was consistent with its overall investment philosophy. First, the Investments Office placed a premium on building long-term relationships with a limited number of premier organizations. Almost 80% of its portfolio was invested in multiple funds sponsored by this limited set of organizations. Yale's prestige, name, and long experience in private equity investing made it a very "desirable" client and allowed it to invest in some well-regarded funds that might otherwise have been closed.

Second, Yale emphasized private equity organizations that took a "value-added" approach to investing (the hallmark of the venture capital industry). It shied away from any funds that sought to generate the bulk of their returns from simply buying assets at attractive prices, refinancing them, and "flipping" them. Its philosophy was explicated in a discussion of buyout organizations:

> While financial skill is a vital component of LBO investing, we seek firms that build fundamentally better businesses. Financial engineering skill is a commodity, readily available and cheaply priced. Value-added operational experience, however, is rare.[9]

Yale believed that value-added investors could generate incremental returns independent of how the broader markets were performing. In addition, it might also find better deals at cheaper prices, deals away from the auction process, that others did not see. For instance, Clayton & Dubilier (in three of whose funds Yale served as limited partner) had purchased Lexmark International from IBM and Allison Engine from

---

[8] Since 1996, Yale had classified real estate funds with more "venture-like" characteristics—for example, golf course development projects—as private equity rather than real estate.

[9] David J. Swensen, Dean J. Takahashi, and Timothy R. Sullivan, "Private Equity—Portfolio Review," memorandum to Investment Committee, September 29, 1994, p. 5.

General Motors after establishing close relationships with those corporations. As a general rule, however, Yale was willing to give considerable latitude to its firms to sensibly define the types of private equity deals that they wanted to do.

Another key principle was to select organizations where the incentives were properly aligned. For instance, Yale was reluctant to invest in private equity organizations affiliated with larger financial institutions. Such situations, the Investments Office believed, were fertile breeding grounds for conflicts of interest, or lack of incentives for the people actually doing the deals, or both. In addition, Yale preferred an overall structure for each of its funds such that the private equity firm could just cover its ongoing costs from the annual fees, earning essentially all of their economic returns from the "carry" tied directly to investment performance. This policy could at times be problematic. For instance, several of the most successful venture funds had dramatically increased their annual management fee income during the late 1980s and early 1990s. Although Yale would have liked to insist that the bulk of the compensation be linked to investment performance, in some cases it had been unable to persuade the venture partners to change the proposed compensation scheme. Some of these venture organizations were sufficiently attractive that the Investments Office decided to participate in their funds anyway. In other cases, because of structural changes, Yale declined to participate.

When Yale's private equity portfolio was compared to those of other universities, three patterns stood out. First, it had a considerably greater exposure to this area: while Yale's current target allocation to private equity was 22.5%, the average university had only 1.5% of its endowment in this asset class. Large endowments (those with over $400 million in assets) had a somewhat greater exposure of 7.2%.[10] Second, Yale had a larger fraction of its holdings concentrated in the funds of top-flight firms. A third difference related to the composition of the private equity investments. In general, many funds could be categorized as either buyout or venture capital funds, though the distinction between the two had become increasingly blurred. The mixture of most major universities' endowments was heavily weighted toward venture capital funds, with the average large endowment (dollar-weighted) holding nearly three-fifths of its investments in this asset class. In contrast, Yale had been gradually increasing investment in other private equity investments, such that the proportion of the portfolio in traditional venture capital had declined from 46% in June 1990 to 28% in June 1997. Yale's private equity portfolio was significantly more diversified than that of the average endowment. (See, for example, Exhibit 4.)

Swensen and his staff believed that Yale should stay committed to private equity for two reasons. First, from its inception in 1973 to June 1997, Yale's private equity portfolio had delivered an annual rate of return of 30%, with modest volatility. (Over the past 15 years, the standard deviation of returns had been only 23%.) Second, over its nearly 25 years of investing, Yale had developed a deep understanding of the process and strong relationships with key managers, which served as an important competitive advantage. An important aspect of this advantage was the continuity of the team managing the private equity program. Swensen, Takahashi, and Director Timothy Sullivan had worked together on the portfolio for more than a decade.

But Yale faced some significant concerns if it were to further increase its allocation to private equity. First, fundraising by venture and buyout organizations had been soar-

---

[10] These figures are from Cambridge Associates, *1997 NACUBO Endowment Study*, Washington, D. C., National Association of College and University Business Officers, 1998. The figure for all universities is an average, with each school weighted equally; the large endowment average is dollar-weighted.

ing in recent years. (Exhibit 8 summarizes the inflow into private equity over an 18-year period). This growth had been fueled by a renewed interest by pension funds and other institutional investors, following a period of few commitments in the early 1990s. Exhibit 9 indicates the changing mixture of the organizations investing in private equity since 1980.

These dynamics were all part of the continuing saga of U.S. private equity flows. Venture capital returns had been extremely attractive in the 1970s, often exceeding 25% per annum. This had attracted great interest from institutional investors in the 1980s. Institutional flows into venture funds peaked in the early 1980s, and those into both buyouts and venture capital funds peaked again in the 1987–88 period. Not surprisingly, the returns generated by the many private equity pools raised in these "peak periods" were poor. For instance, Venture Economics estimated that the average fund begun in 1982 had realized a return of 3% through December 1996, and the average buyout fund begun in 1989 had realized a return of 9%.[11] Many institutions, frustrated with these poor returns, had cut back their commitments to private equity in the early 1990s. Most recently, however, this had all begun to change again. With a soaring stock market and an active initial public offering (IPO) window, the very recent returns from private equity funds had again become very attractive. Institutions had again begun to invest substantial sums in new funds. Sensing a window of real opportunity, many private equity firms had been bringing new funds to the market, perhaps somewhat sooner and perhaps somewhat larger than they might otherwise have done.

This renewed growth in private equity investing raised several concerns. First, it could lead to a considerable increase in competition for deals, just as it had in the venture and buyout markets during the 1980s. As the Investments Office noted:

> Competitive deals … have returned in numbers not seen since the early 1980s. Observers attribute the increased competition primarily to increased institutional capital flowing into the venture business and a lack of discipline on the part of some venture capitalists, particularly those relatively new to the business.[12]

Some quantitative support of this claim was provided by an academic study which showed that with every doubling of inflows into the venture capital funds, the average valuation of a typical investment increased by close to 25%, controlling for company maturity, industry, and public market values.[13]

A second concern was that growth might subtly alter the incentive structures of some firms. In particular, Yale was concerned that the attractive fundraising environment was leading firms to increase the size of the funds they were raising. A particular concern was the plethora of buyout organizations raising funds of $1 billion or more. Asset Alternatives estimated that 13 buyout or merchant banking groups were likely to be raising funds in excess of $1 billion in 1998, in addition to the 6 groups that had done so in 1997.[14] The Investments Office was concerned that these groups would pursue low-risk, low-return transactions in order to ensure their ability to raise a follow-on fund

---

[11] Venture Economics, *1997 Investment Benchmarks Report,* Boston, Venture Economics, 1997.

[12] Swensen, Takahashi, and Sullivan, *op. cit.,* p. 12.

[13] Paul A. Gompers and Josh Lerner, "Money Chasing Deals? The Impact of Fund Inflows on Private Equity Valuations," *Journal of Financial Economics,* Forthcoming.

[14] "Worried about Glut of $1 Billion Funds? Just Wait Till '98," *Private Equity Analyst* 7 (November 1997): 1, 24–26.

(with the substantial associated fees), rather than following innovative strategies that had the potential of generating higher returns. As it noted, "it is hard to see how the capital being raised by LBO sponsors will be invested at rates of return investors associate with LBO equity investments. In fact, it is clear that many buyout firms have lowered their return expectations."[15]

Nonetheless, Yale hoped that it could continue to realize attractive returns from this asset class, just as it had during the 1980s. First, the Investments Office noted, the deterioration of performance in the 1980s had been far from uniform across firms. Although some new "spin-off" organizations had generated very poor returns, as had some established organizations that had grown in an undisciplined manner, many of the funds managed by top-tier private equity organizations had continued to generate superior returns. Because Yale had concentrated its portfolio in several of these funds, such as those organized by Bain Capital, Clayton, Dubilier, and Rice, Greylock, and Kleiner, Perkins, Caufield and Byers, its record had remained intact throughout the earlier period.

Second, Yale had a considerable understanding of the private equity process, which allowed it to manage investments in sophisticated ways. One example of Yale's innovative management was the hedging of its positions. Yale carefully tracked the holdings of the private equity firms in which it invested.[16] When it believed that it had too large an exposure to any particular publicly traded firm, it sought to hedge that exposure through short sales and derivatives. Short sales and put options would generate offsetting profits if the share price declined. This effectively helped to reduce the danger of a severe drop in the public market, wiping out the gains of a private equity investment. This hedging strategy had allowed Yale to receive a higher return from its investment in Snapple, which declined substantially between its peak 14 months after it was taken public and the liquidation of Thomas H. Lee Equity Partners' position.

Finally, being in the private equity market at all times had important benefits. If Yale were to decide not to invest with a top-tier firm merely because the market was "overheated," it might not be able to persuade the organization to accept its money when later market conditions were more favorable. As the Investment Office concluded, if Yale were to alter its steady commitment to private equity and seek to "time" the market, top-tier firms "would not want Yale's unreliable money."[17]

At the same time, Yale realized that the current market conditions might have detrimental effects on private equity. As a consequence, it had altered its behavior in three ways. First, Swensen, Takahashi, and Sullivan examined new funds more skeptically than they might have at other times. Second, they sometimes opted not to push as hard for large allotments in established funds as they might have at other times. Finally, Yale was increasingly making substantial investments as a lead investor in new buyout funds and was actively exploring private equity opportunities other than traditional domestic venture capital and leveraged buyout funds.

[15] David J. Swensen, Dean J. Takahashi, Timothy R. Sullivan, and Alan S. Forman, "Private Equity—Portfolio Review," memorandum to Investment Committee, September 30, 1997, p. 14.

[16] Private equity organizations typically do not sell the shares of firms in their portfolios at the time they go public. They typically promise the underwriter to continue to hold them for a period of months (often termed the "lock-up" period). Many will continue to hold shares after the lock-up period expires, if they believe the shares will appreciate further.

[17] David J. Swensen, Dean J. Takahashi, and Timothy R. Sullivan, "Private Equity—Venture Capital Strategy," memorandum to the Investment Committee, March 4, 1992, p. 7.

International Private Equity Funds

In view of the dynamics in the domestic market, international private equity seemed to be an attractive opportunity. During the past two years, Yale had increased the share of its private equity portfolio devoted to international investments from 6% to 22%. Although its initial strategy had been concentrated on the United Kingdom and France (at the end of 1995 nearly half its foreign investments had been based there), it had increasingly invested in the former Soviet Union and Latin America. The largest overseas concentration of investments in June 1997 was in Russia, which represented 16% of Yale's overall private equity portfolio. One noteworthy characteristic was Yale's lack of emphasis on the developing countries of Asia, which represented the largest single share[18] of many large institutions' international private equity portfolios: less than 0.5% of Yale's private equity investments were in Asian companies.

The Investments Office's move into international private equity had been the result of a careful planning process. As the U.S. market became increasingly competitive, they paid more attention to overseas markets where far fewer funds were competing for deals, suggesting the possibility of more attractive valuations. While many other institutional investors saw international private equity as particularly promising (see Exhibit 10), Yale eschewed the typical strategy of investing in large funds devoted to buyouts in Europe and Asia.[19] This reflected several considerations. First, many of the leading foreign private equity investors were subsidiaries or affiliates of large financial institutions. As discussed above, Swensen and his staff were concerned that such situations were rife with compensation and conflict-of-interest problems. Second, the Investments Office often found it quite difficult to assess foreign private equity organizations. In most countries, Yale lacked the strong network of relationships that it could rely on in the United States to assess the quality of potential new partners. A possible alternative was to invest in a number of the new very large "global private equity" funds that were being sponsored by established and well-regarded U.S. firms. Swensen and his staff liked some of these firms and approved of their incentive structures, but they were a little troubled by the U.S. firms' obvious lack of experience and track records in these very different foreign markets. The managers of these global funds suggested that they could and should become the analog of how Yale had managed similar problems in publicly traded equity, namely, by using U.S. firms, but Swensen and his staff were cautious.

One increasing emphasis was on "quasi-private equity" in emerging markets. For example, several funds were currently being raised to invest in Russian companies, both large "publicly traded" corporations and smaller private firms. There were several similar funds in other Eastern European countries and in China. Notwithstanding their "publicly traded" securities, these funds were best considered as private equity. The upside potential of these funds was enormous if everything worked out well; but the downside risks were equally impressive, particularly the risks of an unstable political environment.

---

[18] Asia represented 24% of all non-U.S. private equity commitments by major institutional investors in 1997, while the former Soviet Union represented only 0.3%. (Comparable figures for 1995 were 35% and 1.1%.) Goldman, Sachs & Co. and Frank Russell Capital, Inc., *1997 Survey of Alternative Investments by Pension Funds Endowments and Foundations,* November 1997.

[19] The venture capital business, in the U.S. sense, did not really exist overseas, except in the United Kingdom and a little in France. In continental Europe, private equity generally meant the buyout business. Asian venture investments, on the other hand, covered a broad array of expansion, joint venture, and infrastructure projects.

Private equity funds were also being raised to invest in Latin America and in Southeast and Southern Asia. Yale had been able to identify a number of these emerging market funds that were managed by general partners which seemed attractive by their normal standards: small entrepreneurial firms, with operational experience on the ground in these emerging markets, some co-investment and/or incentive fees, and an apparently keen sense of where upside opportunities might lie. It was tempting to participate in some of these funds, as a very long-term contrarian bet if nothing else. But the problems of evaluating and selecting managers were challenging here and were perhaps more severe than in almost any other asset class.

Natural Resource Private Equity Funds

A final opportunity was the oil-and-gas and timberland partnerships in the Yale private equity portfolio. In some ways, this market remained attractive. A substantial supply of energy properties was on the market, as major oil companies downsized and smaller firms consolidated. Although some independent firms had been able to raise capital from the public marketplace, the supply of institutional money for such properties remained relatively limited. Timberland was in an even earlier stage of development, having been added to the portfolios of relatively few institutional investors.

It was difficult, however, to find well-designed oil-and-gas partnerships led by attractive managers. Much of the partnership-raising business appeared to be in the hands of agents, who were compensated primarily on the basis of arranging deals. In addition, quite a few operators seemed to get rich, even if their clients didn't. Furthermore, assessing the skills of the general partners in these funds was often difficult. In many cases, individuals raised funds on the basis of their participation in earlier successful partnerships. But it was generally very difficult for the Investments Office to determine which partner had been responsible for a key discovery or production success.[20] Yale's general impression was that investment opportunities and partnerships with sterling track records, unblemished reputations, and proper deal structures were quite uncommon in the oil-and-gas industry.

As a result, Yale's investments in oil and gas tended to focus on partnerships in the business of acquiring existing oil fields and enhancing their operations. In contrast to the high-risk world of exploration, it was somewhat easier to assess performance and responsibility here. More generally, the endowment was considering investing more heavily in publicly traded oil-and-gas firms, where the types of information problems and conflicts seen in the private partnerships were less severe.

Forestland also appeared to be an attractive area for future exploration. Yale had recently invested in one partnership with other institutions and had just committed more than $50 million as the sole limited partner of another. Swensen believed that, unlike commodity indexes, the valuation of natural resource funds did not fully capture the fact that they offered a steady steam of payments in addition to an upside exposure. This appeared to be a ripe area for further expansion in the years to come.

THE MANAGEMENT OF REAL ESTATE

Another important asset class was real estate. Ellen Shuman, the director of investments responsible for real estate, thought that properly managed real estate provided an inter-

---

[20] This was in contrast to venture or buyout investing, where individual partners' successes and failures could be more or less assessed by examining who represented the partnership as a director on various firms' boards.

esting set of investment opportunities. The returns from real property tended to be uncorrelated with those from marketable common stock, and in the long run, real property might produce returns protected from inflation. Most importantly, however, real estate was a quite inefficient, cyclical market where Yale might well be able to generate very attractive returns if it could find the right managers with the right strategies and the right incentive structures. As in other asset classes, Yale concentrated on pure equity investments, avoiding mortgages and other debt. In general, Shuman avoided managers who were just financial advisers who might buy existing buildings with stable rent rolls and apply a little financial engineering. Instead, she sought to establish relationships with real estate operators who had a competitive advantage, either by property type or market, and preferably a focus on an out-of-favor sector.

Historically, Yale's real estate portfolio had consisted primarily of a single very large Manhattan office building at 717 Fifth Avenue, a direct investment that had been singled out and recommended by a group of alumni in the 1970s. The property, which was located at the corner of 56th Street and featured the Steuben Glass showroom, had performed very well. In addition, during the early 1980s the endowment had invested a small amount of money in a number of pools managed by well-known real estate advisers, many of which had performed rather poorly.

During the late 1980s, Yale had been substantially under-weighted in real estate because it could not identify enough attractive investment opportunities in the market of that period. But beginning around 1990, Shuman and Swensen came to believe that the decline in asset values and the savings and loan crisis had created a compelling opportunity. Accordingly, the Investments Office began increasing its real estate investments.

Many institutional investors, having been severely burned, were still wary of this asset class. Yale's strategy was to focus on deliberately contrarian segments of the real estate market where most other investors feared to tread. Shuman was interested in finding partners who targeted distressed sellers and who possessed the operating expertise to implement value-added strategies that could realize substantial returns over the medium term. For example, Yale engaged managers to buy downtown and suburban office buildings from insurance companies facing financial pressures or banks that had foreclosed; close-in developable land, a highly illiquid property type, especially in a capital-constrained environment; or strip shopping centers that needed a reconfiguration or a redirected marketing effort.

Perhaps predictably, however, Swensen and Shuman had encountered some interesting challenges in implementing this real estate strategy. First, they felt that the institutional real estate industry was dominated by firms that were compensated through transaction fees or fees based on assets under management, rather than by sharing in the profits generated for their investors. These firms thus had every incentive to keep their investors' capital tied up over long periods of time, leading to asset accumulation and retention, rather than generation of superior investment returns. As a result, Yale had decided not to deal with the established group of institutional real estate advisers. Luckily, the collapse of the real estate market had provided the Investments Office with an opportunity to find some new firms that might be hungry for funds, and might consequently be willing to accept new kinds of incentive structures. From Yale's perspective, the Investments Office wanted to borrow ideas from, and improve upon, the incentive structures typical in private equity funds. In particular, it wanted all the real estate principals' activities to be focused on one pool at a time, it wanted the principals to make a significant cash investment in the pool (sometimes called co-investment), it preferred an intermediate-term strategy for the pool (after which it might or might not invest in a later pool), and it wanted most of the principals' compensation to come at the end of the fund and to be linked to investors' returns.

Over time, working their networks, Shuman and Director Alan Forman had been able to find a number of independent firms with excellent real estate operating skills that were eager to forge this kind of relationship. But most of these firms were not well known, even by knowledgeable real estate investors. Unlike the case in private equity, where Yale participated in funds considered to be the premier institutional funds, few people knew or even recognized the names of most of their real estate funds. Yale was often the lead investor in these funds, with a sizable percentage of the limited partnership interest. Although it had proven difficult to expand the size of the total real estate portfolio very quickly this way, by mid-1995 Yale had reached its 10% target allocation for the first time, having invested nearly $300 million in pooled funds over the previous five years. Although it would have been much easier to use some of the larger, better-known institutional real estate advisers to expand the real estate portfolio quickly, this would surely have meant compromising on Yale's desired strategy and incentive structures—compromises with which neither Swensen nor Shuman was comfortable.

By the fall of 1997, the endowment had reached an allocation of almost 12% in real estate, resulting in an unusual strategic over-weighting of the asset class. Prices had been rising dramatically in recent years, and institutional equity and debt capital was flooding into real estate through both public and private vehicles. Consequently, many of Yale's managers were considering substantial property sales, especially in the office sector, where assets appeared to be fully valued.

As Shuman and Forman evaluated the impact of these sales on the portfolio, they realized that the real estate allocation would decline substantially over the next two years. On the one hand, they were pleased because performance had been strong, substantially outpacing the NCREIF Property Index (NPI). Moreover, they were delighted that the incentive structures put in place with their real estate managers a few years earlier were providing them with powerful motivation to maximize returns through property sales.

They worried, however, that the decrease in real estate exposure might not serve the needs of the endowment as a whole. Swensen had gained comfort from Yale's substantial real estate allocation, which might provide protection in the event of a significant downturn in the U.S. stock market. Moreover, inception-to-date performance of 14.6% from 1978 to 1997 indicated that despite the tough times experienced in the early 1990s, Yale's allocation to real estate had served the endowment well over a long period of time. Swensen and his staff wondered if they should allow the real estate allocation to drop or whether they should continue to seek out new opportunities, despite the frothy real estate market.

FUTURE DIRECTIONS

In November 1997, Swensen and Takahashi believed that they should probably continue evolving with a heavy weighting in what they viewed as less efficient markets. In particular, they wanted to increase the asset allocations for private equity, real estate, and emerging markets.

As part of the planning process, the Investments Office had completed a "mean-variance analysis" of the expected returns and risks from its current allocation, and had compared them to those of past Yale allocations and the current mean allocation of other universities. These relied on specific assumptions about the expected returns, volatilities, and correlations among asset classes. The results of this comparative mean-variance analysis are shown in Exhibit 11. In addition, it had examined the long-run implications of its allocation for the "downside risk" to the endowment. In keeping with a quantitative format for analyzing long-run downside risk that had been used on prior occasions, it examined the probability that the available endowment spending would fall by more than 25% (adjusted for inflation) over the next five years. It also examined the probability that the inflation-adjusted value of the endowment would fall by more than one-half over the next 50 years. To undertake this analysis, the Investments Office employed a probabilistic Monte Carlo analysis, which simulated and compiled thousands of possible random outcomes drawn from an assumed distribution of returns and correlations used in the simpler "mean-variance analysis." This "downside risk analysis" suggested that the probability of a 25% five-year spending fall was 4.6% and that of the 50% 50-year purchasing power fall was 7.6%.

Stepping back from these selected quantitative analyses, Swensen and Takahashi focused on their long-run strategy. Was private equity, which had been so important in contributing to Yale's superior returns over the years, still an attractive investment in a market awash in liquidity? If so, how should Yale allocate its new commitments? For example, how should the new investments be allocated across venture, buyout, international, and natural resource funds? What should be the mix between new groups and established organizations? Should Yale expand its international program to include a greater emphasis on Asia and continental Europe?

Looking beyond the short run, Swensen wondered about the risks and challenges that the coming years would pose to the Yale endowment and his staff. Over the past few years, the fraction of traditional publicly traded securities in Yale's endowment fell below 50% for the first time. This seemed like an important transition. Just how far could such securities—and fixed income in particular—be reduced? At some point, should they begin to worry seriously about issues of decreasing portfolio liquidity and the increasing difficulty in determining precise valuations for the endowment?[21] Similarly, should they worry about the implications of this evolution for staffing? Should they worry about the fact that an increasing fraction of the portfolio did not really have meaningful benchmarks against which they could reliably measure their managers, themselves, and the success of their strategies? The feedback in these asset classes came only in the very long term, perhaps too long for most individuals' decision horizons. In the long run, how should they think about the issues of risk? Would it really be true that private markets offered greater returns? In the long run, would it be viable for Yale to adopt an asset allocation that was considerably different from that of its closest peers, such as Harvard, Princeton, and Stanford? More generally, could these few endowments as a group persist with asset allocations that were very different from those of almost every other institutional investor?

---

[21] For example, in terms of the valuation estimates used in the spending rule, which had originally assumed that market prices would be available to value the assets.

Exhibit 1 Asset Allocations of Yale Endowment, 1985-1997

	1985	1986	1987	1988	1989	1990	1991	1992	1993	1994	1995	1996	1997	Current (1997) Target Allocation
Domestic equity	61.6%	63.5%	61.7%	56.8%	53.2%	48.0%	30.7%	27.5%	23.9%	21.2%	21.8%	22.6%	21.5%	20.0
Bonds	10.3	12.7	14.6	15.0	16.3	22.1	22.4	23.2	22.6	17.1	12.2	12.3	12.5	10.0
Foreign equity	6.3	8.6	10.8	14.0	15.4	15.2	14.8	15.3	16.5	14.6	12.5	12.4	12.8	12.5
Real estate	8.5	7.5	7.2	7.7	8.7	8.0	7.9	7.1	6.0	8.6	13.5	11.2	11.5	10.0
Private equity	3.2	2.7	3.6	4.4	6.1	6.7	8.3	10.4	14.4	18.1	17.2	20.2	18.6	22.5
Absolute return	0.0	0.0	0.0	0.0	0.0	0.0	15.9	16.5	16.6	20.1	21.0	20.7	23.3	25.0
Cash	10.1	5.0	2.1	2.1	0.3	0.0	0.0	0.0	0.0	0.0	1.8	0.9	-0.2	0.0

Source: University documents

Asset allocations are on June 30th of each year.

Private equity includes venture capital, buyouts, and oil and gas.

Absolute return includes hedge funds, high-yield bonds, distressed securities, and event arbitrage.

Exhibit 2 Asset Allocations of Large University Endowments, 1985-1997

	1985	1986	1987	1988	1989	1990	1991	1992	1993	1994	1995	1996	1997
Domestic equity	51.5%	52.1%	53.8%	50.2%	46.1%	45.3%	43.5%	44.4%	43.0%	41.6%	42.8%	41.1%	42.3%
Foreign equity	2.0	2.6	3.0	5.2	6.6	6.6	7.8	8.1	10.2	14.3	15.2	14.0	15.9
Bonds	26.4	28.3	26.0	26.2	27.5	29.2	30.2	30.7	26.9	22.4	17.5	20.1	18.0
Cash	10.8	8.8	8.9	7.7	6.9	6.9	6.1	5.2	4.6	3.2	4.1	3.2	3.1
Real estate	4.8	4.9	5.2	4.3	5.1	4.4	4.2	3.7	3.7	4.2	5.1	5.2	5.2
Private equity	2.7	1.9	2.0	5.8	6.6	6.2	6.2	5.9	6.6	7.7	8.0	8.1	7.2
Absolute return	0.0	0.0	0.0	0.0	0.0	0.1	0.6	0.8	3.3	5.2	6.2	6.7	6.9
Other	1.8	1.4	1.1	0.6	1.2	1.3	1.4	1.2	1.7	1.5	1.1	1.6	1.5

Source: Compiled from Cambridge Associates, *1997 NACUBO Endowment Study*, Washington, National Association of College and University Business Officers, 1998.

Asset allocations are on June 30th of each year.

Large funds are defined as those with more than $400 million in assets in 1988 through 1997, and as those with more than $200 million in assets in 1985 through 1987.

Private equity includes venture capital, buyouts, and oil and gas.

Funds are weighted equally in calculating average allocations in 1985 through 1987.

Absolute return includes hedge funds, high-yield bonds, distressed securities, and event arbitrage.

Funds are weighted by size in calculating average allocations in 1988 through 1994.

1985-87 classifications may not be completely analogous to those in other years.

Exhibit 3   Asset Allocations of All University Endowments, 1985-1997

	1985	1986	1987	1988	1989	1990	1991	1992	1993	1994	1995	1996	1997
Domestic equity	46.1%	48.7%	51.4%	46.4%	48.5%	48.1%	47.1%	47.1%	48.5%	47.2%	49.2%	51.6%	52.6
Foreign equity	0.8	1.1	1.6	1.5	1.8	2.4	2.4	3.2	4.2	7.5	9.5	9.5	11.2
Bonds	30.6	30.6	30.8	33.8	32.2	33.9	35.3	35.3	34.4	32.2	28.3	27.3	25.2
Cash	14.5	13.1	12.6	14.2	13.0	10.9	10.1	9.9	7.6	7.1	6.5	5.4	4.8
Real estate	4.2	3.9	2.2	2.5	2.7	2.9	2.9	2.3	2.1	2.1	2.3	2.0	2.0
Private equity	0.7	0.6	0.7	0.9	1.1	1.0	1.1	0.9	1.1	1.2	1.3	1.4	1.4
Absolute return	0.0	0.0	0.0	0.0	0.0	0.0	0.2	0.3	1.1	1.8	2.0	2.2	2.4
Other	3.1	2.0	0.7	0.6	0.7	0.7	0.9	1.0	0.9	0.9	0.9	0.5	0.4

Source: Compiled from Cambridge Associates, *1997 NACUBO Endowment Study*, Washington, National Association of College and University Business Officers, 1998.

Asset allocations are on June 30th of each year.

Private equity includes venture capital, buyouts, and oil and gas.

Absolute return includes hedge funds, high-yield bonds, distressed securities, and event arbitrage.

All funds are weighted equally in calculating average allocations.

1985 and 1986 classifications may not be completely analogous to those in other years.

33

Exhibit 4   Asset Allocations of Major Pension Funds and Endowments, 1995 and 1997

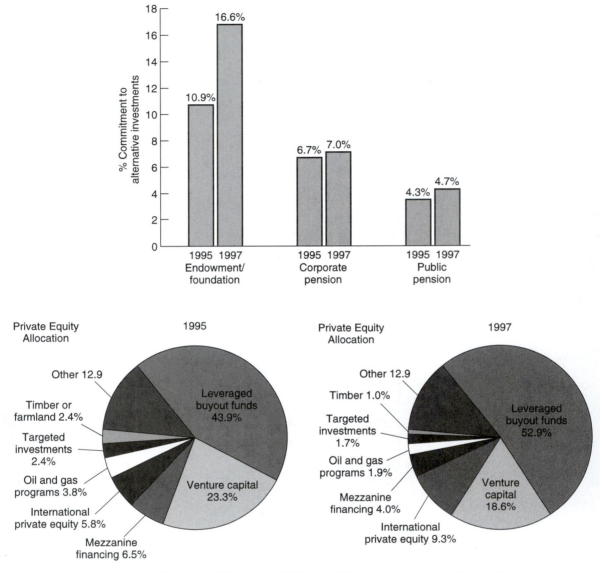

Source: Goldman, Sachs & Co. and Frank Russell Capital Inc., *1997 Survey of Alternative Investments by Pension Funds, Endowments and Foundations,* November 1997

Exhibit 5 Returns of All University Endowments, Yale Endowment, and Benchmark Indexes, Fiscal years 1980-1997

	1980	1981	1982	1983	1984	1985	1986	1987	1988	1989	1990	1991	1992	1993	1994	1995	1996	1997	Annualized 1980-97 Return
Equal-weighted mean	12.6%	14.7%	-0.2%	40.9%	-2.5%	25.4%	26.3%	13.9%	1.4%	13.9%	10.0%	7.3%	13.3%	13.4%	2.9%	15.7%	17.3%	20.5%	13.3%
Dollar-weighted mean	NA	NA	NA	46.0	-2.9	26.1	30.3	16.6	1.1	154.9	10.9	6.2	14.1	14.5	4.4	16.9	20.6	21.7	
Equal-weighted mean, net of fee	NA	NA	NA	40.1	-2.9	25.1	26.3	13.7	1.4	13.9	9.7	7.2	13.3	13.2	2.7	15.6	17.2	20.6	
Yale	18.7	22.7	-4.3	50.1	-0.2	25.8	36.0	22.8	-0.2	17.3	13.1	2.0	13.2	17.3	12.0	15.7	25.7	21.8	16.5
S&P 500	17.0	20.4	-11.5	60.9	-4.8	30.7	35.6	25.1	-7.0	20.5	16.5	7.4	13.4	13.6	1.4	22.3	22.7	31.6	16.3
Wilshire 5000	19.2	25.2	-15.0	66.5	-8.7	31.2	35.3	20.1	-5.9	19.5	12.7	7.0	13.9	16.1	1.2	21.7	26.8	7.5	15.0
Long-term bond index	3.8	-4.1	13.4	29.1	1.8	29.9	20.0	5.5	.1	12.2	7.9	10.7	14.0	11.8	-1.3	20.2	3.1	6.5	10.4
Consumer price index	14.3	9.5	6.9	2.5	3.0	4.1	1.3	3.7	3.8	5.3	4.4	4.6	3.0	2.8	2.4	3.0	2.3	2.9	4.4

Source: Compiled from Cambridge Associates, *1997 NACUBO Endowment Study*, Washington, National Association of College and University Business Officers, 1998, and university documents.

Fiscal years end on June 30th of each year.

The first two averages include endowments that report returns net and gross of fees.

The third average includes only the subset of endowments that report returns net of fees.

No data on dollar-weighted means or net-of-fee equal-weighted mean are available for 1980 through 1982.

Yale's returns are reported net of fees.

Exhibit 6 Returns of Yale Endowment, by Asset Class

Asset Class	Yale 1997 Return	Target Benchmark	Benchmark 1997 Return	Yale vs. Benchmark	Yale 3-Year Annualized	vs. Benchmark	Yale 10-Year Annualized	vs. Benchmark
Domestic equity	25.6	Wilshire 5000	29.3	-3.7	25.9	-0.8	15.0	1.0
Foreign equity	21.0	GDP-weighted EAFE & IFC EMI	13.2	7.8	12.8	3.9	10.8	3.3
Bonds	8.0	LB government	7.4	0.6	8.9	1.0	9.2	0.9
Real estate	19.6	NCREIF	10.7	8.9	17.0	8.1	10.2	5.8
Private equity	36.4	Univ. inflat. plus 10%	13.6	22.8	41.1	27.4	25.7	11.3
Absolute return	15.8	Univ. inflat. plus 8%	11.6	4.2	14.1	2.5	13.1	1.5
Total endowment	21.8	Total benchmark	14.8	7.0	21.0	6.9	13.5	2.9

Source: University documents.

All returns are net of management fees.

Returns are for year ending June 30, 1997.

The total benchmark return is calculated using Yale's target allocations.

Due to the recentness of such investments, returns for absolute return investments could not be calculated over the past decade. The 10-year tabulation is for seven years only.

Exhibit 7   Returns and Size of Private Equity Investments of Yale Endowment 1978-1997

Fiscal Year	Venture	LBO	Natural Resource	Int'l	Real Estate	Total	Portfolio Value	Endowment Value
1978	27.2%	35.3%	NA	NA	NA	33.9%	3.2	545
1979	-2.2	-3.0	NA	NA	NA	-2.8	3.4	578
1980	208.1	231.9	NA	NA	NA	225.5	8.4	669
1981	33.3	-16.6	NA	NA	NA	-0.5	15.6	793
1982	25.6	-47.5	NA	NA	NA	-2.2	19.3	741
1983	123.4	-10.1	NA	NA	NA	91.4	38.6	1,089
1984	3.7	41.6	NA	NA	NA	9.2	37.3	1,061
1985	-10.1	5.6	NA	NA	NA	-5.0	42.0	1,083
1986	2.6	34.0	NA	NA	NA	15.8	46.9	1,739
1987	25.4	23.9	0.0	NA	NA	24.3	75.7	2,098
1988	-0.7	7.8	11.5	-1.9	NA	3.3	91.0	2,044
1989	-0.3	38.7	118.5	13.4	NA	23.4	120.7	2,336
1990	15.6	7.8	20.2	-4.4	NA	11.8	173.7	2,571
1991	11.6	14.7	-19.8	-10.0	NA	6.1	226.8	2,567
1992	28.3	7.2	-2.6	4.1	NA	14.6	294.2	2,833
1993	13.6	57.3	38.8	-0.2	NA	32.3	464.9	3,219
1994	20.2	18.7	65.7	24.0	NA	24.6	640.6	3,529
1995	37.8	26.3	-14.6	13.1	NA	27.0	684.1	3,390
1996	124.8	30.9	2.6	33.7	33.0	60.2	846.6	4,860
1997	35.1	22.3	19.5	90.2	21.8	36.2	1,125.6	5,790
Three-year	64.8	27.4	3.1	51.6	25.8	27.0		
Five-year	41.0	30.8	33.2	30.8		60.2		
Ten-year	27.3	23.9				36.2		
Since Inception	29.0	35.8	21.3	27.6	40.0	29.6		
Venture Economics Benchmark Return	22.0	10.2						
1997 Share in Yale Portfolio	27.9	28.3	4.7	22.2	16.9			

Source: Compiled from Venture Economics, *1997 Investment Benchmark Reports: Venture Capital*, Newark, Venture Economics, 1997, and university documents.

Returns are for year ending June 30th of each year.

Value of private equity portfolio and endowment are as of June 30th, and are expressed in millions of dollars.

NA indicates that Yale had no investments in the asset class during that year.

All real estate investments were classified under the real estate asset class (and not included in private equity) until 1996. At that point, certain real estate funds with more "venture like" characteristics were included in the private equity asset class (and not in the real estate asset class). (At the end of the 1997 fiscal year, Yale also had 11.5% of its portfolio, consisting of more traditional real estate investments, classified under the real estate asset class.) Inception to date and three-year numbers for "Real Estate Private Equity" include data before reclassification from Real Estate to Private Equity.

"Venture Economics Benchmark Return" is the capital-weighted internal rate of return from inception until September 30, 1997 for 601 venture capital funds and 192 buyout funds.

"1997 Share in Yale Portfolio" refers to the share of Yale private equity portfolio devoted to this subclass on June 30, 1997.

Exhibit 8   Private Equity Fundraising, by Fund Type, 1980-1997

	1980	1981	1982	1983	1984	1985	1986	1987	1988	1989	1990	1991	1992	1993	1994	1995	1996	1997
Venture capital	0.6	0.9	1.3	2.6	3.4	2.1	2.1	3.7	3.1	3.3	1.9	1.4	2.6	2.9	4.2	4.7	6.6	6.1
Buyouts	0.1	0.1	0.4	0.6	1.5	1.1	4.3	9.6	7.9	8.8	4.6	4.3	5.7	7.1	13.2	18.0	21.4	19.1
Distressed debt	NA	NA	NA	NA	NA	NA	NA	NA	NA	NA	NA	NA	1.0	1.1	0.0	1.0	1.4	NA
Mezzanine	0.0	0.1	0.0	0.8	0.2	0.8	2.4	4.1	1.7	2.6	1.2	1.7	0.8	0.5	1.2	2.4	1.4	2.7
Other	0.0	0.0	0.1	0.2	0.0	0.3	0.2	0.1	0.4	0.2	0.2	0.3	0.6	1.2	0.8	2.2	1.3	3.3
Total	0.7	1.1	1.8	2.4	5.1	4.3	9.0	17.5	13.1	14.9	6.9	7.7	10.7	12.8	19.4	28.4	32.1	31.3

Source: Compiled from *The Private Equity Analyst* and the records of Asset Alternatives. I thank Steven Galante for his help.

All figures are in billions of dollars.

Other investments include funds-of-funds, secondary purchase funds, and venture leasing funds.

Distressed debt included with other investments prior to 1992 and in 1997.

1997 through October only.

Exhibit 9 Private Equity Fundraising, by Investor Type, 1980-1996

	1980	1981	1982	1983	1984	1985	1986	1987	1988	1989	1990	1991	1992	1993	1994	1995	1996
Pension funds	29.8%	23.1%	33.3%	31.4%	34.1%	33.0%	50.1%	39.0%	45.9%	36.4%	52.5%	42.2%	47.8%	46.8%	49.1%	49.7%	45.4%
Banking/insurance	13.3	15.2	14.0	12.0	13.2	10.9	10.4	15.0	9.4	12.6	9.2	5.4	16.4	15.9	17.0	17.8	19.5
Endowments/foundations	13.9	11.8	6.8	7.8	5.7	7.7	6.3	10.0	11.6	12.3	12.6	24.1	11.4	13.0	11.7	12.4	12.6
Individuals/families	15.4	23.1	20.3	20.9	14.7	13.0	11.8	12.0	8.4	6.1	11.4	12.3	10.4	7.1	10.3	8.4	7.5
Others	27.6	26.8	25.6	27.9	33.4	35.4	21.4	24.0	24.7	32.6	14.3	16.0	14.0	17.3	11.8	11.7	15.1

Source: Compiled from *The Private Equity Analyst* and the records of Venture Economics. I thank Jesse Reyes for his help.

Prior to 1992, the tabulations include only investments in venture capital funds; thereafter, all private equity funds.

Others include corporations, foreign investors, and government bodies (excluding pension funds).

Commitments by funds-of-funds are not included in the tabulations.

Exhibit 10 Institutional Investor Views of Various Private Equity Asset Classes, 1997

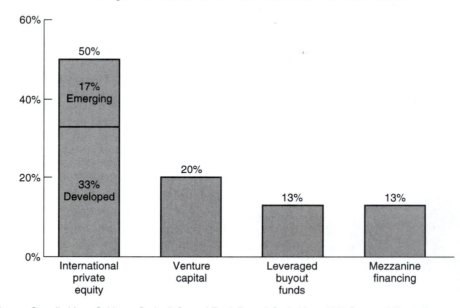

Percentage Who Indicated a Particular Asset Class Was Most Attractive

Source: Compiled from Goldman, Sachs & Co. and Frank Russell Capital Inc., *1997 Survey of Alternative Investments by Pension Funds, Endowments, and Foundations,* November 1997.

Exhibit 11 Risk and Return Chart for Yale University Endowment

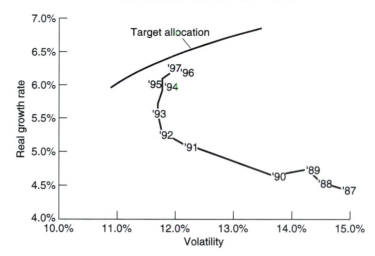

Yale Historical Risk and Return Profile

Source: University documents

2

FOX Venture Partners: Enriching the Private Equity Investor Pool

Peter Lawrence, president of FOX Venture Partners (FVP), sat lost in thought at his desk. Six months earlier, he and Diana Frazier—FVP's chair—had developed the idea of a "fund-of-funds" that would allow sophisticated families to invest in the highest quality private equity funds. Lawrence, confident that the idea would prove to be a success, had left his position as executive vice president of the Marshall Field family office to work without pay as FVP's first full-time employee in July 1994.

The ensuing months had been devoted to developing the concept, test-marketing it, and preparing the private placement memorandum for a $100 million fund. The concept had been enthusiastically received by leading venture capitalists, who saw the fund as an opportunity to broaden their capital base and to involve a particularly influential group of investors. Initial conversations with wealthy families had also been very positive.

Yet a mailing of the placement memorandum to nearly 200 carefully selected families in early November had generated a response rate of only 1%. Followup calls had revealed that while the families were enthusiastic about the concept of the fund in general, they had a variety of reasons for not considering it an appropriate investment for them personally. Keenly aware that time was running out, Lawrence wondered how they should pursue the fundraising effort.

FAMILIES AS PRIVATE EQUITY INVESTORS

Wealthy families historically have played a crucial role in the U.S. private equity industry. Families were a primary source of capital for entrepreneurs in the first half of the twentieth century: for example, the Rockefeller family provided much of the initial financing for Eastern Airlines and Douglas Aircraft; the Phipps family, International Paper and Ingersoll-Rand. In most cases, family members themselves reviewed potential investments and served as active counselors to the entrepreneurs. After World War II, leading families began formalizing their venture activities in corporations or partnerships and hiring outside managers. Although the first venture fund, American Research

This case was prepared by Josh Lerner. Copyright © 1995 by the President and Fellows of Harvard College. Harvard Business School case 296-041.

and Development, was funded by universities, institutions, and the public, many of its contemporaries were established to invest family money. For instance, the Whitney family established J. H. Whitney in 1946, and Joan Payson founded Payson & Trask in 1947.[1] As venture partnerships proliferated in the late 1960s, families remained an important source of capital. The first funds of Greylock, Mayfield, Patricof & Co., and TA Associates (all raised between 1965 and 1969) were capitalized entirely by individuals. As late as 1978, individuals accounted for 32% of the funds flowing into private equity.

The exit of families from venture investing was triggered primarily by the "institutionalization" of private equity in the 1980s. Pension funds had been largely barred from investing in venture funds by the Employment Retirement Income Security Act (ERISA) guidelines. When these guidelines were relaxed in 1979, pension money flooded into the industry. In 1978, pensions invested $64 million in private equity; eight years later, they invested $4.4 billion. One consequence was that the average size of private equity funds increased: venture capital funds raised in 1978 had an average size of $17 million; in 1986, $50 million. Among established private equity organizations, the increase was considerably more pronounced as they raised subsequent funds.

These size increases were important—and problematic—because of U.S. securities regulations. Private equity funds did not need to make filings with the Securities and Exchange Commission as long as they had under 100 investors.[2] In order not to be troubled by the restrictions of the "99 Rule," funds typically required that each investment represent a minimum of between 3% and 5% of the intended capitalization. Frazier and Lawrence felt that it was important for private equity investors to diversify across funds with different geographic, industry, and stage focuses, as well as across funds begun in different years. (Returns for venture capital as a whole have varied dramatically by year.) Such diversification should lower the risk of this inherently risky asset class. However, the growth in the size of private equity funds meant that the construction of a diversified private equity portfolio moved beyond the reach of all but the wealthiest families, that is, those with over $100 million in assets.

Meanwhile, many of the families that did begin venture investment programs during the 1980s encountered difficulties diversifying. First, many of the best funds—seeking to prevent the too rapid growth and organizational disruption that frequently ensued—did not accept funds from new investors. As a result, families investing in private equity for the first time had to invest in less established funds. Second, private equity returns *on average* were poor during the 1980s. Less established funds contributed disproportionately to these poor returns. Consequently, families often withdrew from this asset class. For instance, the absolute amount of investments by families in venture capital fell from $639 million in 1987 to $215 million in 1992. Families' share of investments in this asset class during the late 1980s and early 1990s was only about 8%.[3]

---

[1] For a detailed history, see Charles River Associates, *An Analysis of Capital Market Imperfections: A Report Prepared for the Experimental Technology Incentives Program, National Bureau of Standards, U.S. Department of Commerce* (CRA Report #221), Boston, Charles River Associates, 1976.

[2] These investors also had to meet various tests for "sophistication," based on either net worth or income. This requirement was relaxed in 1996.

[3] These figures are from various publications by Venture Economics and Asset Alternatives. Even these figures understate the decline of investing by wealthy established families. The numerous initial public offerings by venture-backed firms during the 1980s led to the emergence of many newly liquid entrepreneurs. Many of these executives invested much of their new wealth in venture funds, often through companion funds or as special limited partners. The tabulation of investments by individuals was swelled by these entrepreneurs, which represent a somewhat different source of capital than wealthy "old money" families.

Despite this decline, this asset class was particularly appropriate for families for at least two reasons. First, individuals stood to benefit from the preferred tax treatment of long-term investments in private firms. This was in contrast to many institutional investors, such as pension funds, endowments, and foundations, whose investment gains were not taxed. More specifically, after the 1993 tax reform, a substantial gap was created between the tax rate on capital gains and ordinary income. Although the marginal tax rate for the highest income brackets was 39%, long-term capital gains were taxed at 28%. In addition, a special provision in the 1993 tax reform set a 14% rate on capital gains from certain small business equities held for five years and longer.[4]

Second, private equity could have important benefits for estate planning purposes. A major concern of wealthy U.S. families was the avoidance of federal inheritance taxes, which were 50% for individuals with over $18 million in assets. (Bequests to grandchildren of over $1 million were subject to an additional "generation-skipping" tax.) Furthermore, taxpayers' annual gifts to each child or grandchild could not exceed $10,000 without being subject to a gift tax, which was calculated according to the same schedule as estate taxes. Because interests in private equity partnerships were frequently valued very conservatively in the funds' initial years, they made a particularly attractive way to transfer wealth across the generations. In all likelihood, the value of the expected cash flows would be greater than the valuation assigned to the fund. In addition, U.S. tax law allowed the value assigned to such a gift to be reduced (often by as much as 30%) since the security being transferred was both illiquid and a minority interest.

THE FOX VENTURE PARTNERS CONCEPT

FVP's principals, Diana Frazier and Peter Lawrence, were particularly qualified to organize this fund. (Their biographies are reproduced in Exhibit 1.) First, together they had 24 years' experience with venture investing, including both direct investments and funds. Frazier had spent nine years at BancBoston Ventures, starting as an intern in 1981 and working her way up to president. A board member of the National Association of Small Business Investment Companies, she had extensive contacts throughout the private equity industry. Lawrence had expanded Marshall Field's venture investment program, selecting all investments in private equity partnerships by the family's trusts, as well as various direct investments. Second, Frazier and Lawrence had extensive experience in general family office management. During his dozen years with the Field family, Lawrence had spent considerable time on their overall asset allocation strategy. Frazier had started and managed for three years the family office of Mitch Kapor, the founder of Lotus Development Corporation. While in this role, she had achieved high visibility through participation in conferences and forums addressing asset allocation strategies for wealthy families.

In planning their strategy for FVP, Frazier and Lawrence had emphasized two key design goals. First, they would target a specific audience: wealthy families with an ability to commit at least a minimum of $2 million to the fund. Since few families would be willing to devote more than 5% or 10% of their assets to a perceived risky asset class like

---

[4] Eligible businesses were required to have under $50 million in assets at the time the securities were issued. Investments in certain service providers, such as law and consulting firms, were not eligible. An additional complication was introduced by the Alternative Minimum Tax, which attempted to prevent taxpayers from taking advantage of excessive deductions. (Many wealthy families are subject to these provisions.) Investors subject to the Alternative Minimum Tax could only employ half of this special credit and consequently had to pay a 21% [28%–(14%/2)] tax on these capital gains.

private equity, the minimum limited the number of possible investors dramatically. Although the number of families in FVP's target range of above $50 million in investible assets was relatively modest, the wealth that they controlled was substantial. For instance, a 1992 Federal Reserve Board study had shown that the 3% of American families with a net worth of over $1 million controlled 44% of all U.S. household financial assets.[5]

Frazier and Lawrence realized that this group differed substantially from institutions. In order to be comfortable with the asset class, these investors would require education. This role was not without its challenges. Among institutional investors, managers for alternative assets almost universally had M.B.A. degrees and approached the allocation of assets and the evaluation and tracking of funds similarly. Wealthy families, however, varied widely in their degree of sophistication and risk tolerance. Although some were familiar with the rationales for allocating funds to different asset classes and the reasons for including private equity funds in a diversified portfolio, many were not. Furthermore, they had varying desires to be involved with their investments. Frazier noted that an important caveat to F. Scott Fitzgerald's maxim that "the rich are different from you and I" is that "the rich are different from each other."

The second crucial element of FVP's strategy was to invest in a carefully targeted set of funds whose past and expected future performance was in the top quartile. FVP's prospectus pointed out that even in the worst years for private equity investing, top-quartile funds had performed well: for example, the average internal rate of return for limited partners of venture capital funds in the top quartile of those begun in 1982 was 10.6%. (The average return for all funds begun in this year was 2.8%.) Frazier and Lawrence planned to ensure that the funds they selected would be in the top quartile by selecting organizations with

- a successful track record based on a reproducible strategy,
- a strong proprietary deal-flow and industry contacts,
- a tradition of successfully leading investments and adding value,
- a sensitivity to human resource issues, especially planning for succession within their own organization.

Unlike most intermediaries selecting venture investments, FVP's general partners did not intend to pay a great deal of attention to the terms and conditions of the agreements. (Most venture partnership agreements did not have the extreme heterogeneity of leveraged buyout (LBO) funds, particularly concerning complex fee structures.) They planned to leave the negotiation of the details to the institutional investors.

They did care greatly, however, about how the general partners of the venture funds approached their remuneration. They preferred organizations that collectively held a strong philosophy that general partners should share equally, or at least fairly. This compensation, they believed, should take the form primarily of performance-linked pay as opposed to high management fees. These issues were particularly critical in venture organizations sponsoring multiple funds with aging partners.

Frazier and Lawrence intended to invest about $5 million each in approximately 20 funds meeting these criteria. Funds would be selected over the next three years or so. Because the funds would not need all their capital immediately, they anticipated that they would still be disbursing funds as late as the seventh year of FOX Venture Partners' life.

---

[5] Federal Reserve Board, *Survey of Consumer Finances*, Washington, D.C., Federal Reserve Board, 1992.

The founders intended to take a portfolio approach: they did not want to overweight the fund with a particular type of investment. In particular, FVP intended to allocate about 35% of its capital to large funds sponsored by well-known private equity organizations, which invest in a diverse array of situations. Approximately two-fifths of the funds would be devoted to funds specializing in particular regions or industries. These funds tended to be smaller than the diversified ones (with an average size in 1994 of $100 million, about one-half the size of the others). Another 20% would be devoted to new funds (called "first-time funds") raised by experienced venture investors, especially those formed as a result of the breakup of established organizations. Finally, a small share of the portfolio (about 5%) was designated for international funds.[6]

FVP intended to avoid the largest buyout funds. For one thing, minimum commitments of $20 million or more were commonplace in these funds. (FVP's offering memorandum stated that it would not invest more than 10% of its capital in any fund.) More importantly, the FVP partners felt that these funds too often emphasized financial engineering over improving operating performance and growth. The funds that FVP targeted represented about one-third of the total private equity pool by dollar volume but over one-half of the total number of funds. In late 1994, the total invested and uninvested capital of private equity funds was $100.4 billion[7] Of these funds, $32 billion was designated primarily for venture investments. Almost all of the remainder was intended for buyout investments. (About 5% of the pool was raised for mezzanine investments and about 2% for distressed debt purchases.) The number of funds raised, however, presented a different pattern. For instance, of the 362 funds raised between 1992 and 1994, fully 194 specialized in venture capital investments.

The founders hoped that these two design strategies—families and top-tier venture funds—were highly interrelated and unique. The strong local connections, resources, and prestige of FVP's investors would lead private equity funds to welcome FVP as a new limited partner. The funds' general partners would see FVP's investors as potential sources of new deals, as providers of information about potential investments and managers, and even as direct investors in compatible transactions. Meanwhile, FVP's stated intention not to directly invest itself in deals would assure private equity funds that they were not dealing with a potential competitor. Many of the larger institutions and gatekeepers were demanding co-investment rights.

THE HISTORY OF "FUNDS-OF-FUNDS"

"Funds-of-funds" were originally created to allow smaller institutions to pool their resources and build more diversified portfolios than they could alone. The earliest funds-of-funds were organized by investment advisers, who became known as gatekeepers.[8] Gatekeepers have advised pension funds as to how to allocate and structure private investments since 1972, when the First National Bank of Chicago established an

---

[6] Frazier and Lawrence hoped that this could be followed by a subsequent fund, FOX Venture Partners II, with a similar investment mix. In addition, they hoped to raise other funds that targeted smaller segments of the venture industry, such as first-time or international funds.

[7] The figures in this paragraph are drawn from George Fenn, Nellie Liang, and Stephen Prowse, *The Economics of the Private Equity Market,* Washington, D.C., Board of Governors of the Federal Reserve System, 1995, and various publications of Asset Alternatives.

[8] For an overview of private equity investment advisers, see Bruce M. Cohen, "The Increasing Role of Specialized Investment Advisors," in Steven Galante, editor, *Directory of Alternative Investment Programs,* Wellesley, Asset Alternatives, 1995, pp. 33–55.

advisory unit as part of its trust department. (This operation ultimately was purchased in a management buyout in 1989 and took the name Brinson Partners.) In 1994, gate-keepers controlled about $18 billion of private equity assets under management, up from $4 billion in 1989.

These organizations typically provided advisory services to some clients (who still made the ultimate decision as to where to invest), while exercising discretionary control over other clients' assets. In the cases where the gatekeeper had the right to allocate the client's assets, the relationship was structured in one of two ways. Typically, the gate-keepers set up separate accounts for clients allocating $30 million or more to private equity, but commingled the funds of smaller investors into one or more funds-of-funds. Among the pioneers of "funds-of-funds" during the 1980s were Bigler Investment Management, Brinson Partners, and Horsley Bridge Partners (formerly Horsley Keogh).

Recent years had seen an increasing specialization of private equity funds-of-funds. One of the earliest of these was the Common Fund, a nonprofit organization that in 1994 managed a total of $20 billion (in all asset classes) for 1400 college, university, and school endowments. This organization raised an $89 million private equity fund, Endowment Venture Partners, in 1990. Endowment Venture Partners II, a $175 million follow-on fund, was raised in 1993. This fund distinguished itself from its competitors in several ways. First, it was able to get access to several prestigious funds, which normally did not accept new money from investment advisers. Second, these managers were almost unique among funds-of-funds managers in having their compensation linked to the performance of the funds they selected.[9]

Another development had been the introduction of funds-of-funds targeted at spe-cific types of private equity investments. Hancock Venture Partners raised the first such fund in 1991, which exclusively targeted international private equity partnerships. Recent funds targeted other niches, such as venture funds managed by minorities (e.g., funds organized by Fairview Capital Partners and Progress Investment Management) and those based in particular states (for instance, the Cypress Equity Fund, organized by the Enterprise Florida Capital Development Partnership).[10]

DESIGN ISSUES

FOX Venture Partners was to be structured as a limited partnership. Exhibits 2 and 3 summarize the private placement memorandum and the terms of the proposed part-nership agreement; Exhibit 4 provides a schematic illustration of the partnership struc-ture. Frazier and Lawrence would have a controlling interest in FOX Capital Management, a limited liability company that would serve as manager of the fund. This management company would be hired by FOX Venture Company, which served as the general part-ner of the fund. This was also a limited liability company controlled by Frazier and Lawrence. To help limit any potential liabilities, a separate company would serve as the

---

[9] "The Common Fund Announces the Closing of $175 Million Venture Capital Fund," *PR Newswire*, December 1, 1993. One reason that the Common Fund could propose such a performance-linked compen-sation scheme was that it managed much larger funds of publicly traded securities, which generated signifi-cant management fees and covered the overhead. Another reason was that it exclusively managed endowment funds and did not accept money from pension funds. ERISA guidelines limited the ability of investment advisers to collect performance-based fees from "funds-of-funds."

[10] For additional information, see Steven Galante, "Fund of Funds' Find Use by Niche Managers," *Private Equity Analyst*, 5 (September 1995), 5; "Cypress Closes, Plans Quick Return," *Venture Capital Journal*, 35 (September 1995).

general partner of each funds-of-funds. The same management company would be hired to run each fund.

A major advantage of the partnership structure was its tax treatment. First, like any other partnership, it avoided the double-taxation that affected corporations. Corporations were taxed on their profits, and then their dividend payments to individuals were also taxed. In a partnership, all tax obligations "flowed down" and were collected from the partners. Second, investors in the FVP fund could in some cases choose when to realize capital gains. If a private equity fund took a company public and disbursed the shares to the FVP fund and other investors, FVP could distribute the shares in turn to its limited partners. The limited partners would not have to pay capital gains taxes on these securities until they chose to sell them. Meanwhile, each partner's share of FVP's operating expenses could be deducted at the time they were incurred.[11]

Frazier and Lawrence—in addition to investing and disbursing capital—would also strengthen their investors' understanding of and access to private equity funds. Limited partners were to receive quarterly reports, not only on the performance of specific investments but on industry trends more generally. FVP's partners also intended to answer any questions that emerged as their investors learned more about private equity.[12] Assuming permission was granted, FVP would provide a profile of each of their investors to the fund managers. Finally, an annual meeting would bring together FVP's limited partners with the general partners of the underlying venture funds. This provided a forum for FVP's investors to learn more about the companies in which the venture funds intended to invest. Frazier and Lawrence wanted to become the definitive "smart interface" between family investors and venture funds.

At the same time, Frazier and Lawrence sought to avoid evaluating the co-investment opportunities that the fund managers offered FVP's limited partners. They had neither the resources nor the inclination to assess hundreds of potential deals over the five-year investment period. The evaluation of a substantial number of direct deals might rapidly consume all of Frazier and Lawrence's time. Since only some of FVP's investors would be participating in these transactions, this activity would represent a potential conflict with their primary responsibilities. Rather, Frazier and Lawrence believed that they could reasonably devote some time facilitating their limited partners' due diligence, for example, by coordinating their activities and suggesting third-party sources of information. Furthermore, because the venture organizations that FVP selected were highly reputable, there was less risk that the fund managers would opportunistically offer over-

---

[11] The tax code imposed two complications. First, these management fees were considered "miscellaneous expenses," which were deductible only if they exceeded 2% of the taxpayer's adjusted gross income. (Other items included in this category were unreimbursed employee expenses, tax preparation fees, and subscriptions to professional journals.) Second, if the investor was eligible for the Alternative Minimum Tax, the management fee payments would not be deductible at all. Legislation to address the treatment of management fees in investment partnerships under the Alternative Minimum Tax had been introduced in the 104th Congress as House Resolution 747.

[12] An example of the types of issues that might emerge was potential investors' questions about internal rates of return (IRR). Having recently learned about IRRs as a measure of investment performance, some potential investors wondered why Frazier and Lawrence did not simply invest in the organizations whose funds had the highest returns. In response, they emphasized two issues. First, FOX wished to select the funds with the best *future* performance. In some cases, the high returns of an earlier fund was the result of a single fortuitous investment, which might be unlikely to recur. Second, Frazier and Lawrence emphasized that IRRs were not an entirely appropriate measure of performance. A fund might generate a high IRR by returning the initial investment plus a small premium very quickly. Since there were substantial transaction costs associated with investing in a fund, investors might be better off with a somewhat lower return from a fund which held onto the capital for several years.

priced shares for their limited partners to purchase. The funds were financing the firms for the first time as well, at the same price. FVP's limited partners would not need to pay a management fee or carried interest on the investments they made directly, nor a "promote." (This is the term for some venture funds' requirement that their limited partners co-invest at a higher price. For instance, a limited partner might pay $1.25/share while the venture fund is simultaneously purchasing shares for $1.00 each.)

The partnership intended to enter into a consulting agreement with FOX Capital Management, which would assume all routine expenses (such as salaries, rent, and travel) in exchange for an annual management fee of 1% of the partnership's committed capital. This fee would fall to 1% of the lesser of committed capital and the value of the partnership's assets upon FVP's sixth anniversary, or earlier if FVP raised a subsequent fund. In no event would the fee drop below $400,000 while the fund was still active. Although Frazier and Lawrence briefly considered modeling their fee structure on the performance-based compensation employed in the private equity industry, they decided to employ the capital-based compensation structure widely used in the investment management business. One strong reason was that simply persuading families to invest in private equity might be a significant educational challenge. Trying to persuade them to accept an unfamiliar fee structure at the same time might be impossible. Lawrence's model of the fees and returns is presented in Exhibit 5.

Finally, Frazier and Lawrence had established strong relationships with several outside service providers, which would complement and leverage their strengths. These included retaining Arthur Andersen as the fund's auditor and tax adviser. They had also established a strategic alliance with the Family Office Exchange and its founder, Sara Hamilton. This Chicago-based consulting firm provided independent advice to families who had their own investment offices. Their members included many families within FVP's target asset range. Frazier and Lawrence also intended to establish an advisory board of limited partners and other knowledgeable observers from the venture capital world.

COMPETITION

Wealthy families had a few alternative ways in which to make indirect venture investments. The first was venture capital advisory services provided by some bank trust departments. The most similar effort was a private equity fund launched by U.S. Trust at about the same time as FVP. Under the leadership of David Fann, formerly of Citicorp Venture Capital, the bank was seeking investments from its 2500 wealthiest clients (with an investment portfolio of $250,000 or larger). The managers of the UST Private Equity Investors Fund hoped to raise $50 million, with a minimum investment size of $15,000. The focus of the activities, however, would be quite different from that of FVP: 70% would be allocated to direct investments in later-stage companies, and only 30% to investments in venture funds. A few other bank trust departments, such as Mellon, offered their clients opportunities to invest in venture funds, but aside from UST, these were almost universally organized on a case-by-case basis.

Second, some gatekeepers extended services to extremely wealthy families. Their services were still primarily geared to pension funds, and they generally had few insights into the tax and estate planning issues that individuals faced when investing in private equity. Perhaps more significantly, most investment managers did not have the resources or the inclination to cultivate individual relationships with wealthy families that required a considerable degree of education about the asset class. FVP hoped to avoid competitive strains with these advisers by sticking closely to its niche of family investors, and not accepting capital from college endowments or pension funds.

A third option that did not frequently figure in the portfolios of FVP's potential investors was publicly traded venture funds. A variety of funds—for example, Allied Capital, Capital Southwest, and Greater Washington—traded publicly on the NASDAQ exchange. GKN Securities had raised a series of industry-specific "blind pools" that traded on the New York Stock Exchange. These funds would each make one or more investments in entrepreneurial firms. These could be purchased in as small lot sizes as desired and could be sold at any time. But while some of the most prestigious venture firms of the 1950s had been publicly traded, they had been either acquired (e.g., American Research and Development, bought by Textron in 1972) or restructured as private partnerships (Naragansett Capital). With the exception of Pennsylvania-based Safeguard Scientific, today's public funds tended not to be in the top tier. As a result, these funds' access to quality deals was somewhat more limited than that of top-tier private firms.[13]

THE FUNDRAISING CHALLENGE

Lawrence had begun developing the "funds-of-funds" concept in the spring of 1994. Working with an established gatekeeper, he had asked a consultant to examine the potential market. The consultant reported a definite need for such a product and estimated the potential demand as $180 million. Even after extended conversations, however, the gatekeeper had continued to drag its feet, unable to decide whether wealthy families represented a too distinct market from the institutional investors that were its typical clients.

During the course of his initial conversations, Lawrence had been repeatedly urged to contact Diana Frazier. In early July 1994, the two finally met. Their introductory conversation soon turned to sketching the specifics of how such a fund should work. They agreed that the fund would make sense only if they could access the best venture funds. Inspired by this conversation, Frazier had returned to her office to call six prestigious West Coast venture capitalists, whose offices (due to the time zone differential) were still open for business.

Five of these venture capitalists called back within 12 hours, and all expressed enthusiasm for the idea. In addition to the particular advantages that family investors could bring to the table, the venture capitalists believed that these investors would be more patient. Venture capitalists often complained that institutional investors, particularly pension funds, were too prone to herd-like behavior, collectively seeking either to increase or decrease their commitments to private equity and simultaneously clamoring to invest in the "hottest" private equity funds.

Within three weeks, Frazier and Lawrence had drafted an executive summary. Heeding the counsel of their law firm, Testa, Hurwitz & Thibeault, they opted not to initially recruit a lead investor: a family that would contribute $20 million or more to the fund and help defer start-up costs. Often, lead investors in private equity funds demanded either a share of the profits or management fees in the current and subse-

---

[13] Another important—though somewhat different—alternative open to families was direct investments in entrepreneurial firms. These are discussed below.

quent funds. Instead, Frazier and Lawrence decided that the start-up costs should be funded internally.

During the summer of 1994, Frazier and Lawrence held informal conversations with a number of potential investors. Having been assured of considerable enthusiasm for the concept, Lawrence moved out of the Field family office and became FVP's first full-time (if unpaid) employee. In the ensuing months, they drafted a private placement memorandum. Although Frazier and Lawrence intended to raise a total of $100 million, they realized that the fundraising process might present challenges. In particular, they might need to raise capital in several stages and have multiple closings. If less than $50 million of commitments were obtained, they would abandon their fundraising efforts and void any commitments received to that date. The fund was anticipated as having at least a 12-year life, but it could be extended if the venture funds in which they had invested had not concluded by then.

In early November 1994, they mailed 172 copies of the private placement memorandum to a list of particularly promising families. By Thanksgiving, however, about 1% of the recipients had responded. As Frazier and Lawrence began contacting potential investors to determine why they were not more enthusiastic, they learned there were several substantial sources of resistance. Although the respondents seemed to universally agree that the fund was a great idea, they had various reasons as to why it was not appropriate *for them.*

First, several managers of family offices expressed concerns about the proposal. One source of their reluctance was easy to understand. Many of these managers were hired to handle *all* investments of the family, both public and private. They viewed FVP as competition, which supplanted their direct investment role.

Even if these concerns about job description could be overcome, family office managers were also worried about two compensation issues. The first related to the valuation practices of private equity funds. In many cases, venture organizations were very conservative in valuing firms before they were taken public or sold. As discussed above, this feature was attractive for estate-planning purposes. But another consequence was that the reported interim returns of the funds often substantially understated the actual value created—and the office managers' performance-based compensation would also be depressed. Although the investments would ultimately be valued accurately, the office manager might have moved onto another job by then. The most established venture funds, which FVP was targeting, were the most conservative in regard to valuations. Second, some managers received a share of the profits from direct investments in private companies but did not participate in the profits from investments in private equity funds to the same degree, if at all.

The families themselves also had mixed attitudes toward investing in private equity. Direct investments in private companies were undertaken by almost every family that FVP contacted. Wealthy families typically encountered investment opportunities through business associates and personal friends on an *ad hoc* basis. While in some cases these investments had proven to be attractive, many other investors had failed to fully appreciate the risks that were entailed. Most family offices did not have access to the flow of potential investments that venture capitalists did, nor did they have the resources to thoroughly evaluate proposed transactions. Often they learned the hard way that the pricing of deals, the recruitment of management, and the arranging of follow-on financings and sales of firms required highly specialized skills and considerable time. Therefore, some argued that venture investing was too risky because of their poor personal returns from investments in the 1980s. Surprisingly, some of the greatest resistance came from entrepreneurs who had made their own fortunes in growth companies. Many of these individuals failed to appreciate the need to diversify into growth asset classes: for example, their portfolios were weighted heavily toward Treasury bonds and blue-chip stocks.

In addition, there were other stumbling blocks such as the illiquidity of the FVP investments. Although Frazier and Lawrence emphasized that not *all* of a wealthy family's assets needed to be liquid, some potential investors were troubled by the possibility that even *some* of their assets would be inaccessible for a decade or longer. Other families considered FVP to be too risky because it was a "first-time fund" without an established track record.

Finally, a number of wealthy families had consolidated all their accounts at a single trust department. Often they were not yet comfortable with allocating their funds outside the bank to multiple managers. Many banks, which often served as trustees for families' assets, were also reluctant. In many cases, the bank, as trustee, was responsible for approving any outside investments. Yet the banks were frequently compensated based on the assets under their active management. The investment in FVP would reduce their assets under in-house management, and hence their fees. This led to some built-in resistance to approving such investments. Partially limiting this problem, however, was the new prudency requirements imposed on fiduciaries. In 1992, the American Law Institute altered its treatment of private investments in its restatement of the law of trusts. As the law firm Testa, Hurwitz & Thibeault noted:

> The Restatement suggests that in appropriate situations 5% to 10% of trust assets may be invested in private equity funds. ... Historically, trust fiduciaries have been conservative in embracing new trends and developments. [Because of these new standards], fiduciaries may soon be as concerned about being too conservative with trust investments as they are about being too speculative.[14]

The Institute's standards did not have the force of law, but by late 1994 these principles had been adopted into law by at least one dozen states, including New York.[15]

It was becoming increasingly clear, Lawrence noted, that this fund would not raise itself. He wondered how Diana Frazier and he should adjust their fundraising strategy. How could the investors' objections be overcome? Could they take any steps to highlight their strengths prior to the completion of fundraising? Should the terms and conditions of the partnership be modified?

---

[14] Douglas R. Ederle, "Private Trusts May Provide New Source of Capital," *Venture Update* (Fall 1993): 3.

[15] Kenneth R. Page, *A Primer on the New Prudent Investor Rule Governing Investment of Fiduciary Funds Subject to New York Law*, New York, Coudert Brothers, 1994.

Exhibit 1   Resumes of FOX Venture Partners Management

Diana H. Frazier

Professional Experience

1994-: Family Office Exchange, Inc.   Greenwich, CT

Managing Director of independent consulting firm providing strategic advisory services to families investing $50 million or more in assets. Primary consulting focus on diverse investment needs of families and strategic issues of business owners initiating a family office.

1994-: FOX Venture Partners, L.P./FOX Capital Management, LLC   Greenwich, CT

Co-Founder and Chairman of venture capital fund investment consortium made up primarily of Family Office Exchange member families. Focus primarily upon selection of venture capital funds for inclusion in portfolio.

1993-1994: Paloma Partners   Greenwich, CT

Vice President - Director of Development of a broad-based $1 billion hedge fund manager responsible for building and maintaining limited partner marketing and servicing capability.

1990-1993: Kapor Enterprises, Inc.   Cambridge, MA

Managing Director of start-up Family Office, responsible for all personal and business relations as well as public and venture investments for this high net worth entrepreneur.

1981-1990: BancBoston Ventures, Inc.   Boston, MA

Completed Loan Officer Development program and joined the Venture Capital subsidiary in Spring 1982. Progress to Vice President in Fall 1984 and President in 1988 with full responsibility for marketing, investment recommendations, and value-added monitoring (board-level) of equity investments. Director of BBV and BBC, the leveraged buyout subsidiary of Bank of Boston.

1978-1980: Temple, Barker and Sloane, Inc.   Lexington, MA

Research Associate, Energy and Environment Group. Responsible for financial and production simulation model of various industries; designed and implemented recruiting, training, and manager allocation for research staff.

1973-1977: University of Oxford   Oxford, England

Senior Research and Computer Programmer in Psychology Department; Co-director of national computerized Childhood Cancer Database; Senior researcher for a French/English economic history text.

1971-1973: L'Eglise Protestante   Porto Novo, Benin French West Africa

Designed and taught English as a Foreign Language (TEFL), French, personal accounting, and home economics. Reorganized 10,000 volume library. Director of 100-bed women's residence.

1970-1971: **Self-Employed TEFL Instructor**   Grenoble, France

Started business in Americanized Teaching English as a Foreign Language. Clients included IBM, University of Grenoble, private schools, and individuals.

1969-1970: **Institute for Defense Analyses, Inc.**   Arlington, VA

Research Assistant, Program Analysis Division; Responsible for computer simulation models. Author of several publications. Top Security clearance.

Education

1980-1981: **Sloan School of Management, M.I.T.**   Cambridge, MA

Accelerated Masters' degree in Management, June 1981. Concentrations in Applied Economics and Corporate Strategy. Thesis on Management by Exception.

1965-1969: **Wellesley College**   Wellesley, MA

B.A. in Economics and Urban Sociology as Wellesley College Scholar. Volunteer analyst, Boston Redevelopment Authority. Independent honors study at M.I.T. in computerized macroforecasting.

1974-1977 (part-time):

Center for Management Studies, Oxford University   Oxford, England

L'Institute Mathematique Applique, Universite De Grenoble   France

Additional course work in computer science, applied math, and management.

Affiliations

Former Director of National Association of Small Business Investment Companies (NASBIC).

Business Leadership Council of Wellesley College—elected member.

Institute of Private Investors—Founding Director.

L. Peter Lawrence

Professional Experience:

1994-: FOX Venture Partners, LP/FOX Capital Management, LLC Greenwich, CT

Co-Founder and President. Developed concept and structure of this investment consortium of wealthy families designed to pool their resources in order to invest in a diversified group of top-performing venture capital and management buyout funds. Responsible for day-to-day management of the fund including due-diligence, portfolio monitoring, communications, and administration. Along with the Chairman, select venture capital firms for inclusion in portfolio and commit assets of the fund.

1982-1994: Marshall Field Family Office New York, NY

Executive Vice President. Active in all areas of this financial and investment management office of the Marshall Field family including venture capital, real estate, and direct investing; financing and banking relationships; marketable securities manager oversight; financial, tax, estate planning, and trust administration. The family's holdings range from large, wholly-owned companies (e.g., Cabot, Cabot & Forbes) in the real estate and communications industries to non-controlling interests in private companies operating in diverse industries. Primary responsibilities for all direct and indirect venture capital investing, banking and financial institution relationships, and corporate financing activities. Specific commercial real estate and hotel project oversight responsibility. President of related aviation company; director of two venture-backed companies.

1978-1982: The Continental Group, Inc. Stamford, CT

Assistant to the Chairman and CEO. Handled various assignments including special business studies, project/problem follow-up; liaison with operating managers.

Corporate Treasurers Department - Director. Managed staff responsible for providing analytical support and financial planning services to the Treasurer's Office. Specifically responsible for internal and external cash management, capital structure planning, oversight of general and project financings (including IRB, pollution control, company, and timberland financings), rating agency presentations, liaison with company and other financial institutions, acquisition analysis, and funds flow forecasting.

1976-1978: W.R. Grace and Company New York, NY

Treasurer's Division - Financial Analyst. Participated in all areas of international corporate financial management, including corporate debt issues, project financing, analysis of preferred and common stock issues, foreign exchange exposure management, recruiting and training.

1972-1974: Cabot, Cabot & Forbes Land Trust Boston, MA

Portfolio Manager - Northern Region. Responsible for managing the real estate investment trust's preferred equity investments in income producing real estate projects. Tasks include the timely recognition of financial problems and the negotiation of work-out and refinancing programs.

Education

1974-1976: Harvard Graduate School of Business Administration Boston, MA

Master's degree in Business Administration—June 1976.

1967-1971: Trinity College Hartford, CT

BA degree in Psychology—June 1971
Medusa Honor Society, Cerberus Honor Society
Fraternity President, Hockey Team
Class Agent, Decade Chair

Source: Corporate documents.

Exhibit 2 FOX Venture Partners, L.P.: Summary of Terms

The following is a summary of the purpose, structure, and principal terms of FOX Venture Partners, L.P. ("FVP"):

Entity	FOX Venture Partners, L.P., a Delaware limited partnership.
Purpose	FVP's primary purpose is to provide a vehicle for qualified individuals, families, and family trusts (the "Investors") to aggregate their investment dollars in a diversified group of high quality venture capital funds.
Investments	FVP will make investments in a select number of venture capital funds. FVP will also consider secondary purchases of existing partnership interests.
General Partners	FOX Venture Company, LLC, a Connecticut limited liability company, will serve as the general partner of FVP (the "General Partner"). Peter Lawrence, Diana H. Frazier, and Family Office Exchange, Inc. will be the principals of the General Partner.
Offering	The General Partner will initially offer $100 million of interests in FVP (the "Interests"). The General Partner, in its discretion, may increase the size of the offering. FVP will not commence operations without minimum subscriptions for at least $50 million in Interests. Each Investor will be required to subscribe for a minimum of $2 million of Interests, although the General Partner may waive this requirement. Commitments to FVP may be called over a five- to eight-year period, depending on the timing of the calls made by the underlying venture capital funds.
Term	Twelve years, with one-year extensions at the discretion of the General Partner. After the 15th year, Investors will be able to terminate FVP upon a vote of at least a majority of the Interests.
Redemption, Withdrawal, and Transfer of Limited Partnership Interests	Each investor will have the opportunity to redeem all (but not less than all) of its Interest once each year on at least 120 days prior written notice to FVP at a discount to reported value. Payments to Investors pursuant to this redemption may be in cash, notes, or other securities, as determined by the General Partner. FVP shall not be required to pay out more than 5% of its net asset value in any year in connection with redemption of Interests. FVP may assign the right to purchase the Interest of an Investor exercising its right of redemption. Otherwise, Investors may not withdraw from FVP. Investors may not sell, transfer, or assign their Interests except with the consent of the General Partner.
Limited Partner Meetings	FVP will hold meetings at least once a year to provide Investors with the opportunity to review and discuss FVP's investment activity and portfolio and meet selected managers of the underlying funds and representatives of such funds' portfolio companies.
Organizational Expenses	Organizational expenses up to a maximum of $250,000 will be paid by FVP and allocated to all Investors in proportion to capital

contributions.

Reports

All Investors will receive annual reports containing audited financial statements of FVP, and quarterly reports containing unaudited financial statements of FVP.

Legal Counsel

Testa, Hurwitz & Thibeault Boston, Massachusetts

Accountants

Arthur Andersen, LLP Chicago, ILL

Allocations

Allocations of FVP's profits and losses will be made to all Partners pro rata in accordance with their respective capital contributions.

Distributions

FVP will distribute at least quarterly all cash received by FVP, other than amounts retained for expenses and liabilities of FVP. Marketable securities received by FVP will be distributed or sold as appropriate. Distributions will be made to the Partners *pro rata* to their respective capital contributions.

Management Fee

FVP will enter into a Service Agreement with FOX Capital Management, LLC, a Connecticut limited liability company ("FCM"), under which FVP will agree to pay FCM a fee for investment consulting, management, and administrative services. The annual management fee will be calculated and paid quarterly in advance and will be equal to 1% of committed capital through the earlier of (i) the formation by the principals of the General Partner of a fund in scope and purpose similar to FVP; and (ii) the 6th anniversary of FVP. Thereafter, the annual management fee will be equal to the lesser of (i) 1% of committed capital; and (ii) 1% of the fair market value of the assets of FVP. In no event shall the annual management fee be less than $400,000.

General Partner's Contribution

The General Partner will contribute $250,000 in cash or in full recourse promissory notes on the same schedule as the Investors.

Advisory Board

FVP will have an Advisory Board consisting of at least five persons chosen by the General Partner. It is anticipated that the advisory board will be comprised of three persons associated with the Limited Partners and two persons with extensive knowledge and experience in the venture capital industry. The Advisory Board will confer with the General Partner as to the conduct of FVP's investment operations, approved valuation of portfolio securities, and resolve potential conflicts of interest.

Source: Corporate documents.

Exhibit 3   Summary of Limited Partnership Agreement

Distributions

In general, the amount and timing of distributions by FOX Venture Partners ("FVP") to the partners will be at the discretion of the General Partner. Cash proceeds from the investment by FVP in venture capital funds will be distributed at least quarterly by FVP, except to the extent that the General Partner determines that certain amounts should be reserved to pay FVP's reasonably anticipated expenses. Marketable securities received by FVP will be distributed or sold. For administrative convenience, however, FVP will not make any distributions (other than Tax Distributions) until such time as the aggregate amount, otherwise distributable, exceeds $1,000,000. Interest and dividends paid to FVP generally will be distributed annually. Distributions may be in cash or marketable securities. Generally, in any year in which net income is allocated to the Partners, cash distributions ("Tax Distributions") will be made to all Partners in an amount intended to fund federal, state, and local tax liabilities. All other distributions will be made *pro rata* to all Partners in proportion to their capital contributions. "Capital contributions" means, with respect to any Partner, the amount of such Partner's paid-in capital contributions to FVP, including, with respect to the General Partner, contributions made in the form of promissory notes.

Allocations

Allocations of FVP's income, gain, loss and deduction for tax and financial reporting purposes will be made to all Partners pro rata in accordance with their respective capital contributions.

Capital Contributions

Capital contributions will be made upon not less than 15 days' prior written notice from the General Partner.

Failure to Pay Capital Contributions

Upon any failure of a Limited Partner to contribute any portion of its capital commitments when called for by the General Partner in accordance with the Limited Partnership Agreement (unless such payment would be unlawful because of laws or regulations applicable to that Limited Partner) that Partner will be in default. A defaulting Limited Partner's Interest will be reduced by 50% of its capital contributions and will be subject to the General Partner's assignable right to purchase the Interest at the restated value.

Transferability of Interests and Withdrawal

A Limited Partner may not sell, assign, or transfer any Interest in FVP except under certain limited circumstances and with the prior written consent of the General Partner. Withdrawals of Interests are not permitted, except pursuant to each investor's opportunity to redeem its interest once each year (See "Summary of Terms—Redemption, Withdrawal and Transfer of Limited Partnership Interests") or in limited instances when necessary to comply with laws or regulations applicable to a Limited Partner, including applicable ERISA regulations. The Limited Partnership Agreement will prohibit Limited Partners from mailing Section 754 elections under the Internal Revenue Code of 1986 as amended.

Liability of Limited Partners

Limited Partners will not be liable for any debts or be bound by any obligations of FVP, except that they are obligated to make their agreed upon capital contributions and, under Delaware law, may be liable to return to FVP under certain circumstances distributions they have received from FVP.

Liability of General Partner

Under Delaware law, the General Partner is liable for all debts and obligations of FVP. To the extent permitted by law, the General Partner and the principals of the General Partner will not be liable to any Limited Partner for actions or omissions which do not constitute gross negligence or willful misconduct and are undertaken in the best interest of FVP, or for any losses arising therefrom.

Indemnification

Subject to applicable law, if the General Partner, or a principal of the General Partner, or any member of the Advisory Board has acted in good faith, he is entitled to be indemnified by FVP against any cost or expenses incurred by him in connection with any actual or threatened action, suit or proceeding as a result of his being the General Partner or a partner, director, officer or employee of the General Partner or of any organization in which FVP may have an investment interest, or a member of the Advisory Board. In addition, FVP may pay his expenses incurred in defending an actual or threatened civil or criminal action in advance of the final disposition of such action, provided that he undertakes to repay such expenses if it is determined by a court he is not entitled to indemnification.

Management and Control

The General Partner will be responsible for managing the affairs of FVP and will make all investment and policy decisions on behalf of FVP. No changes in the Limited Partnership Agreement may be effected by the General Partner without the approval of Limited Partners holding at least a majority of the Interests.

Term

FVP's term will be twelve years, subject to the General Partner's right to extend the term for additional one-year periods, to permit an orderly liquidation of FVP. After the fifteenth year of FVP, the Limited Partners will be able to terminate FVP upon a vote of Limited Partners holding at least a majority of the Interests.

Unrelated Business Taxable Income

The General Partner will use its best efforts to operate FVP so as not to give rise to unrelated business taxable income to Limited Partners that are exempt from federal income tax.

Portfolio Fund Valuations

All investments will be valued by the General Partner, subject to review by the Advisory Board. Formal valuation of FVP's portfolio will be made quarterly and will be reported to each Limited Partner.

Investment Guidelines

FVP will not make new investments (other than follow-on funding in existing portfolio funds) after four years. FVP will not commit in excess of 10% of its committed capital in any single portfolio fund. The Advisory Board may waive the limitations set forth in this paragraph.

Source: Corporate documents.

Exhibit 4   Illustration of FOX Venture Partners Structure

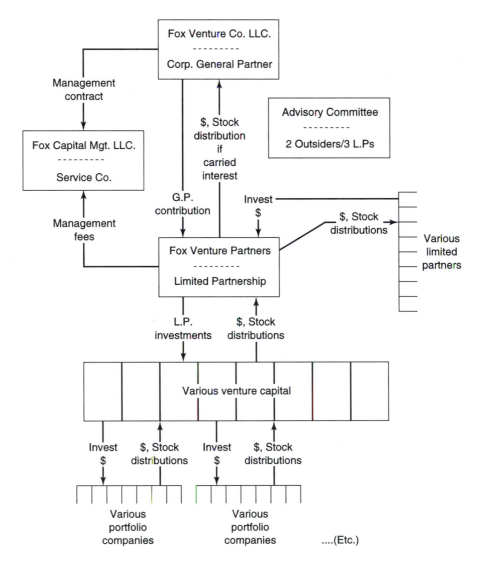

Source: Corporate documents

Exhibit 5   Financial Model ($000s)

	Capital Invested by Year In ...				Capital Each Year For Investments and Fees	% of Total	Total Capital Invested	Payout To Investors	Investors' Cash Flow	Investors' IRR
Year	1st Year Funds	2nd Year Funds	3rd Year Funds	Fees						
1	127			20	147	7.33%	127		-147	
2	127	127		20	273	13.67	253		-273	
3	127	127	127	20	400	20.00	380		-400	
4	127	127	127	20	400	20.00	380	63	-337	
5	76	127	127	15	344	17.22	329	190	-154	
6	51	76	127	5	258	12.92	253	370	112	
7		51	76		127	6.33	127	593	466	
8			51		51	2.53	51	788	737	
9								920	920	
10								887	887	
11								760	760	
12								570	570	
13								312	312	
14								117	117	
Total	633	633	633	100	2,000	100.00%	1,900	5,570	4,390	22.27%

The analysis looks at what would happen to a $2 million investment in the FOX fund.

It is assumed the management fee will be 1% of committed capital for four years; then .75% of committed capital for the remaining ten years.

The first $100,000 of fees is paid out of the committed capital; the remainder, it is assumed, will be paid from the fund's capital gains.

It is assumed the $2 million will be committed to private equity funds established in Years 1 through 3. An equal amount will be committed each year.

It is assumed the funds will draw down 20% of the committed capital in each of the first four years, and the remainder in the fifth and sixth years.

It is assumed the funds will pay out to the investors approximately two times the invested capital, following the pattern laid out in the spreadsheet.

60

3

Acme Investment Trust

In May 1994, officials at Acme Investment Trust were considering an investment in the sixth partnership organized by E.M. Warburg, Pincus & Co. The Trust, the employee pension fund of Acme Corporation, a major manufacturer, had recently raised the private equity allocation of its $10 billion pension fund from 3% to 6%. Warburg intended to raise a $2 billion "mega-fund." This fund, about 15% larger than the organization's 1989 fund (in which Acme had also invested), would be one of the largest funds ever raised by a private equity organization. Yet what concerned Acme's managers was not the size of the fund, but the way in which its profits would be split.

Warburg, Pincus proposed that the investors would receive 85% of the profits from the fund, with the remaining 15% going to the firm's partners. This differed from the 80%–20% split standard within the industry: a division that the *Private Equity Analyst* termed "sacrosanct."[1] The organization also proposed to raise its annual management fee from 1% of capital, as in its previous fund, to 1.5%. Interpretations of these proposed terms differed. While the *New York Times* termed it a "fat discount to investors,"[2] other observers argued that it was an appropriate response to the changing mixture of Warburg, Pincus's investments. Others wondered how this move would affect the compensation terms in less established venture and buyout partnerships.

E.M. WARBURG, PINCUS & CO.[3]

E.M. Warburg & Co. was established in New York in 1938 by Eric Warburg. Warburg was a member of one of the most illustrious German Jewish families, which had played an integral role in Germany's financial life for several centuries. Eric's father, Max, had been an adviser to Kaiser Wilhelm, a participant in the Versailles Peace Conference at the end of World War I, and the head of the powerful Hamburg bank, M.M. Warburg & Co. Nonetheless, the Warburg family was forced to flee Germany in 1938 in the face of Nazi persecution.

This case was prepared by Josh Lerner. Copyright © 1995 by the President and Fellows of Harvard College. Harvard Business School case 296-042.

[1] Steven Galante, "Warburg Points the Way to a Lower Carry," *Private Equity Analyst* 4 (July 1994): 7.

[2] Barry Rehfeld, "Even in Hard Times, He's Still the Top Player in Town," *New York Times,* October 23, 1994, 3:9.

[3] This section is based on Ron Chernow, *The Warburgs,* New York, Vintage Books, 1993; "The Mantle of Warburg," *Forbes,* August 12, 1985, 61; Udayan Gupta, "Megafund Chief Pincus Speaks Softly, Carries a $1.17 Billion Venture Stake," *Wall Street Journal,* March 9, 1987, 1:15; and Rehfeld, *op. cit.*

E.M. Warburg & Co. had initially focused on providing investment services to its German-American clientele. After Eric Warburg returned from service as an intelligence officer in the Army Air Force during World War II, the firm expanded into investment banking activities, participating in underwriting syndicates. Its prominence in the postwar years, however, was eclipsed by that achieved by S.G. Warburg & Co., the London bank founded by Eric's cousin Siegmund.

In 1956, Eric Warburg returned to Germany to reclaim the management of M.M. Warburg & Co. from his father's partners. In the ensuing years, as Eric devoted most of his attention to German affairs, E.M. Warburg & Co. found it difficult to broaden its base of clients and its investment banking activities. In 1966, these concerns led Eric Warburg to sell a half-interest in the New York firm to 34-year-old Lionel Pincus.

Pincus, the grandson of Polish and Russian immigrants, had received an M.B.A. from Columbia University. Instead of entering his family's Philadelphia apparel retailing and real estate business, he had joined the small investment bank Ladenburg, Thalmann & Co. Much of his activity there involved investing wealthy families' money—typically about $1 million in each deal—in small private firms. At age 29, Pincus was made partner and head of the bank's corporate finance activities. In 1964, he had left Ladenburg to found Lionel I. Pincus & Co.

Pincus's experiences persuaded him of the opportunities presented by investing in private firms. At the same time, he realized that far greater returns could be realized if the activity was pursued in a more systematic and professional manner. Shortly after joining E.M. Warburg, he recruited John Vogelstein from Lazard Freres, who shared this vision.

These two men—in conjunction with a team of long-standing managing directors—developed a distinctive approach to private equity investing, which they termed "venture banking." The firm made a diverse array of investments, including traditional start-ups, leveraged buyouts, and purchases of major blocks in publicly traded firms. Although the firm initially invested only its own money, in 1971 it raised its first formal fund. Like other private equity firms, Warburg organized this and subsequent funds as limited partnerships with a life span of approximately 10 years. (Warburg's funds are summarized in Exhibit 1.) The firm served as the general partner of each fund, and the various investors served as limited partners. At about the same time, the firm assumed its current name.

Investors in the five Warburg funds had enjoyed substantial success over the years, earning an average annual return between 1971 and 1990 of over 25%. This was substantially better than the returns of private equity as a whole, summarized in Exhibit 2. The funds had enjoyed very attractive returns from quite different classes of investments. These included buyouts, including Mattel, investments to finance industry consolidations (e.g., Waste Management), and start-ups such as U.S. Health Care Systems. (Major investments that had led to initial public offerings by the end of 1992 are summarized in Exhibit 3.)

Several distinct themes characterized Warburg, Pincus's approach over these years. The first was a willingness to go against industry trends. During the mid-1980s, for instance, the firm had shunned the computer hardware and software investments then in favor at many venture organizations, focusing instead on buyouts and health care. During the 1990s, when many private equity organizations marketed themselves as having a distinctive specialty, Warburg, Pincus retained its eclectic approach. Second, the firm had been willing to build a core group of managers. Although many venture and buyout funds were run with very lean staffs, Warburg, Pincus had 28 managing directors by 1994, many of whom had been with the firm for a decade or longer. Third, the firm had been aggressive in raising capital. The 1980 and 1989 funds had been the largest ever raised to that date by any private equity organization. The firm had successfully attracted investments from some of the most sophisticated investors, including pension funds of AT&T, General Electric, IBM, and New York State, as well as the Harvard University Endowment.

By early 1994, the firm had nearly entirely invested its 1989 fund. Its decision to raise a sixth fund had been widely anticipated. It was the proposed terms of the contract that would govern the fund (contained in the private placement memorandum) that generated widespread discussion within the Acme pension and elsewhere.

COMPENSATION IN PRIVATE EQUITY PARTNERSHIPS[4]

Private equity investors are typically compensated in two ways: a share of the profits and an annual fee. These two elements, however, display many variations. For instance, the way in which the fee is calculated and the timing of the profit-sharing often vary tremendously.

The percentage of profits retained by the private equity investors is known as the carried interest. This share, as noted above, is typically about 20%. Exhibit 4 presents the percentage of capital gains retained after any provision for the return of invested capital, or invested capital plus a premium, for 441 funds established between 1978 and 1993 to make venture or both venture and buyout investments. The carried interest varied from 1.01% to 45%, but the value in 81% of the funds was between 20% and 21%.

Exhibit 5 shows how the average carried interest varied over this period. Funds are divided by their date of formation, as well as by two measures of the experience of the private equity organization. The first measures the relative size of the organization's previous funds (their "market share").[5] The second is the time from the establishment of the organization's first partnership to this fund. Older and larger private equity organizations command a slightly larger carried interest, with about a 1% higher share than the less experienced funds.

The second element of compensation is management fees. These fees are typically paid quarterly and finance day-to-day operations. In many funds, the fees change over time. For instance, the fees will often be reduced in later years, reflecting the expectation that the partnership's costs will be lower during the "harvesting period." The fees may also contain provisions for inflation adjustments. As Exhibit 6 indicates, the base used to calculate the fee varies. While most agreements compute the annual fee as a percentage of invested capital, in some cases the value of the partnership's assets is used. Funds that use asset value as the base often will also limit the maximum and/or minimum fee. A number of firms charge fees not only on the funds raised by the partnership, but also on the indebtedness of the companies in which they invest. This fee structure was commonplace during the 1960s, when Small Business Investment Companies (many of which were affiliates of commercial banks) made equity investments in firms and arranged for their credit lines.

Exhibit 6 also summarizes the level of the fees in the partnerships' fourth year. (As noted above, in some cases the fee will be based on different measures.) The typical fee is 2.5% of capital under management. The table also shows the level of fees for the 15 largest partnerships. Here the percentages are lower, with an average and median fee of about 2.0%.

---

[4] This section and Exhibits 4 through 7 are based on Paul Gompers and Josh Lerner, "An Analysis of Compensation in the U.S. Venture Capital Partnership," *Journal of Financial Economics* 51 (1999) 3–44.

[5] The invested capital in all of the organization's funds established in the 10 years previous to the year this fund closed is totaled. This sum is divided by the total amount raised by independent venture organizations in this period.

Fees based on net asset value have virtually disappeared in recent years. Although 21% of funds formed between 1978 and 1983 had fees based on asset value, this fell to 2% in the period between 1990 and 1993. Some practitioners attribute this decline to opportunistic behavior on the part of private equity partnerships. As investment manager Harold Bigler relates:

> In the 1970s specific partnerships were referred to as a "West Coast Deal" or an "East Coast Deal." The East Coast Deal had its fee generally based on committed capital. ... The West Coast partnerships had a tradition of management fees related to assets. The general [partner] participated in appreciation both through the management fee and the carried interest, thus having the element of "double-dipping."[6]

More specifically, accounts by Venture Economics[7] suggest that asset value-based fees led private equity partnerships to be very aggressive in valuing firms and to delay exiting investments.

There are also many differences in the timing of compensation. Exhibit 7 provides an overview of the restrictions on the receipt of capital gains by general partners. Over 90% of the funds contain some provision which ensures that the private equity investors do not unconditionally receive distributions. This table does not include the exceptions that allow small payments to cover tax obligations.

Most restrictions are of two types. The standard partnership agreement of the 1960s and 1970s called for the private equity investors only to receive distributions after their limited partners had received their invested capital back. Any subsequent distributions were then split according to the carried interest. This arrangement, however, was perceived to have a negative effect on the choice of securities distributed.[8] This is because private equity investors frequently distribute securities of firms that they have taken public rather than selling the shares and distributing cash.[9] Before the committed capital had been returned, some private equity investors were perceived to distribute overvalued securities. Undervalued securities were retained until after committed capital was returned and the investor was eligible to receive distributions.

During the 1980s, a new contractual form appeared, which allowed private equity investors to receive capital gains as long as the value of the portfolio exceeded 100%, 125%, or some other multiple of the invested capital. (The multiple is referred to as the hurdle rate.) Under these arrangements, the cost basis of each investment was first returned to the limited partners. The remainder—the capital gain on this particular investment—was then divided between the limited and general partners according to the agreed-upon formula. Consider the distribution of 1000 shares of a company which the private equity investors had purchased for $2/share and were currently trading at

---

[6] Harold E. Bigler, "Am I Really So Bad?: A 'Gatekeeper's Replies to a Recent Challenge," *Venture Capital Journal* 31 (February 1991): 22–39.

[7] See, for example, Venture Economics, "Venture Partnership–Conventions and Customs," *Venture Capital Journal* 20 (July 1980): 9–11.

[8] Venture Economics, *Venture Capital Performance—1989,* Needham, Venture Economics, 1989.

[9] Private equity investors have at least two reasons for distributing securities rather than cash. First, the limited partners usually include both taxpaying and tax-exempt investors, who may have different preferences concerning the timing of security sales. Second, distributions of securities are valued (both in the partnerships' internal accounting and in the records of gatekeepers and other monitors) using the share price prior to the distribution. The actual price that a private equity investor might realize if he sold a large block of a thinly traded security might be considerably lower. See Venture Economics, "A Perspective on Venture Capital Management Fees," *Venture Capital Journal* 27 (December 1987): 10–14.

$12/share, under a contract where the proceeds were divided 80%–20%. The limited partners would receive shares with a value of $10,000 [1000 ∗ ($2 + .8 ∗ ($12 − $2))] and the general partners shares worth $2000 [1000 ∗ (.2 ∗ ($12 − $2))].[10]

Private equity organizations that have persuaded their investors to allow them to receive accelerated profit-sharing are significantly older and larger. Industry observers argue that the ability of larger partnerships to accelerate their compensation through a hurdle rate reflects their market power. For instance, a Venture Economics report noted: "although there are some limited partners which believe they should receive their original capital back before the general [partners] begin to share in the profits, most of the limited [partners] … were aware that it was difficult to demand, particularly with more experienced groups."[11]

WARBURG, PINCUS VENTURES, L.P.[12]

The fundraising document that Warburg, Pincus circulated in the spring of 1994 proposed to raise $2 billion for a fund that would last 12 years. Warburg, Pincus would receive an annual management fee of 1.5% on the capital that it had actually drawn down from investors. The fund anticipated drawing down these funds fairly evenly over the fund's first six years. Warburg, Pincus would not begin receiving any profits until it had returned the invested capital to investors.

The offering document attracted considerable attention in the private equity community. The Acme pension managers discounted the suggestion that the fee structure was a manifestation of anxiety about reaching the $2 billion fundraising target. The flow of funds into private equity had been accelerating in the past several years, and 1994 was anticipated to be a record year for fundraising. Instead, the reduced carry might reflect the changing mixture of Warburg, Pincus's investments. In particular, a substantial share of its portfolio was publicly traded firms. Public equity managers typically received an annual fee of about 0.5% of assets under management, without any performance-linked compensation. Alternatively, Warburg, Pincus might be anticipating that the recent flow of institutional money into private equity would lead to lower returns, and that the lower carried interest represented a way of "in effect sharing the downside of the market."[13]

Another area of discussion within Acme was the implications of this shift for other private equity organizations. One observer noted that "with their action, Warburg, Pincus has given us all an opportunity to reconsider pricing." Others speculated that the move was especially likely to lead to pressure on less established private equity organizations to reduce their share of the profits.[14]

---

[10] Some recent funds have gone to the other extreme: they do not allow the private equity investors to receive capital gains until *more* than 100% of invested capital has been returned to investors. These tend to have been raised by smaller and younger organizations.

[11] Venture Economics, "Stock Distributions—Fact, Opinion and Comment," *Venture Capital Journal* 27 (August 1987): 8–14.

[12] This section is drawn from "Warburg Pincus Preps Huge Fund Launch," *Buyouts,* 7, April 4, 1994; Jennifer L. Reed, "Warburg, Pincus Seeks Only 15% Carry," *Venture Capital Journal* 34 (May 1994): 6; and Galante, *op. cit.*

[13] Reed, *op. cit.*

[14] Galante, *op. cit.*

Exhibit 1   Funds raised by Warburg, Pincus & Co.

	Year	Fund Size ($ millions)
EMW Ventures	1971	28
Warburg, Pincus Associates	1980	100
Warburg, Pincus Capital Partners	1983	341
Warburg, Pincus Capital Company	1986	1,175
Warburg, Pincus Investors	1989	1,780

Source: Compiled from public reports.

Exhibit 2   Returns of private equity organizations, as compiled by Venture Economics. The table indicates the average and median return for private equity funds begun in various years through the end of 1993.

Year Fund Began	Return Through 12/31/93	
	Mean	Median
1969-1975	23.4	20.6
1976-1979	30.6	24.2
1980	17.4	13.6
1981	6.8	5.0
1982	2.9	2.2
1983	5.5	5.5
1984	4.7	5.1
1985	7.7	9.9
1986	6.6	6.6
1987	5.2	6.2
1988	10.7	8.4
1989	7.4	5.1
1990	3.4	2.1

Source: Compiled from Venture Economics, *1995 Investment Benchmark Report*, Boston, Venture Economics, 1995.

Exhibit 3   Major investments by Warburg, Pincus & Co. in private firms which went public between 1976 and 1992.

Company	Market Value at Time of IPO ($ millions)	IPO Underwriter	Offering Date	Size of Offering ($ millions)
ADVO-SYSTEMS	N/A	None	9/15/86	N/A
AGRIDYNE TECHNOLOGIES	64.9	Piper, Jaffray & Hopwood	2/14/92	17.5
AI CORP	73.0	Alex. Brown & Sons	6/25/90	21.4
ALLIED CLINICAL LABORATORIES	87.1	Alex. Brown & Sons	7/31/90	22.1
ALLSTAR INNS	145.4	Drexel Burnham Lambert	3/27/87	72.9
ALTA HEALTH STRATEGIES	78.6	Alex. Brown & Sons	1/22/91	14.3
BABBAGE'S	65.3	Alex. Brown & Sons	7/14/88	19.5
BRIDGE COMMUNICATIONS	96.7	Morgan Stanley	4/18/85	24.0
CAMBRIDGE NEUROSCIENCE	82.8	Montgomery Securities	6/06/91	18.0
CENTRA FARM GROUP NV	30.5	L.F. Rothschild Unterberg	1/14/85	6.8
CERTIFIED COLLATERAL	18.3	Blunt	12/08/83	4.0
CHIPSOFT	177.4	Robertson, Stephens & Co.	4/03/92	41.2
FOUR-PHASE SYSTEMS	24.6	Lehman Brothers	6/08/76	14.4
GARTNER GROUP	33.7	Shearson Lehman Brothers	7/17/86	11.6
KOLFF MEDICAL	84.9	L.F. Rothschild Unterberg	7/15/83	18.8
MARINE DRILLING CO.	77.8	Dillon, Read	7/28/89	29.8
STARTEL	19.5	Rooney	11/22/83	4.5
SYNERGEN	86.2	Alex. Brown & Sons	3/07/86	17.6
UNITED STATES HEALTHCARE SYSTEMS	71.3	Merrill Lynch	02/09/83	20.0
VALUE HEALTH	146.3	Alex. Brown & Sons	4/04/91	36.0
VESTAR	42.6	Alex. Brown & Sons	11/05/86	10.6
ZILOG	98.3	Alex. Brown & Sons	2/27/91	22.0

*If there were multiple underwriters co-managing the offer, the table reports the one responsible for managing the order book.

Source: Compiled from initial public offering prospectuses.

Exhibit 4 The share of profits retained by private equity organizations. The figure indicates the carried interest (the share of capital gains retained by the organization after any initial return of investment to the limited partners).

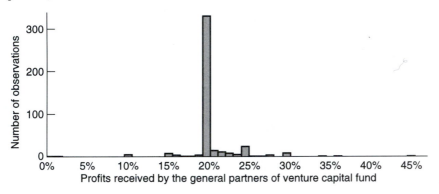

Exhibit 5 The share of profits retained by private equity organizations. The average share of capital gains retained by the organization after any initial return of the original investment to the limited partners is indicated. The second panel indicates the correlation coefficient between the percentage and the other variables.

Panel A: Percentage of Profits		
	Average	*# of Observations*
Date Fund Established:		
January 1978 - December 1984	20.5	100
January 1985 - June 1986	20.9	111
June 1986 - December 1988	20.7	120
January 1989 - December 1992	20.9	85
Size of Private Equity Organization		
No Earlier Funds or Cannot Determine	20.4	170
Between 0.0% and 0.2%	20.9	83
Between 0.2% and 0.7%	20.5	87
Greater than 0.7%	21.6	76
Age of Private Equity Organization:		
No Earlier Funds	20.5	146
Four Years or Less	20.7	87
Between Four and Eight Years	20.6	93
More than Eight Years	21.4	90
Objective of Fund		
Focus on high-technology firms	21.2	198
Other industry focus (or no focus)	20.3	218
Focus on early-stage investments	21.1	172
Other stage focus (or no focus)	20.5	244

Panel B: Correlation Coefficients	
Variables	*correlation*
Date of Closing and Percentage of Profits	0.027
Size of Organization and Percentage of Profits	0.109
Age of Organization and Percentage of Profits	0.104

68

Exhibit 6   The table first summarizes how the annual management fee is determined. The table then summarizes the distribution of fee percentages, for all funds and the 15 largest funds.

Panel A: How Management Fee is Determined	
Percent of capital under management	69.7%
Percent of capital under management, less cost basis of distributions and write-offs	1.3
Percent of net asset value	11.6
Percent of net asset value, but subject to a minimum and/or maximum	7.6
Percent of sometimes capital under management; sometimes capital less distributions	1.9
Percent of sometimes capital under management; sometimes, net asset value	4.6
Percent of debt of portfolio companies, as well as capital or asset value	2.2
Negotiated annually	1.0

Panel B: Fee Percentage	All Funds	15 Largest
3.5% or higher	4.3%	0.0%
3% to 3.49%	10.1	6.7
2.5% to 2.99%	63.0	13.3
2% to 2.49%	16.2	46.7
1.5% to 1.99%	4.3	20.0
1.49% or lower	2.1	13.3

Exhibit 7 Timing of compensation for private equity organizations. The table summarizes the restrictions on the receipt of capital gains.

Restrictions based on return of committed capital	
No distributions until return of 100% of committed capital	43.8%
No distributions until return of 101-25% of committed capital	1.4
No distributions until return of 126-50% of committed capital	0.5
No distributions until return of more than 150% of committed capital	0.2
No distributions until return of 100% of committed capital plus an annual return of 1-10%	0.7
No distributions until return of 100% of committed capital plus an annual return of 11-20%	0.2
No distributions until return of 100% of committed capital plus four times salaries	0.2
No distributions until return of 100% of committed capital plus four times tax distributions	0.5
Restrictions based on return of net asset value	
No distributions until adjusted net asset value exceeds 100% of committed capital	6.2
No distributions until adjusted net asset value exceeds 101-25% of committed capital	15.8
No distributions until adjusted net asset value exceeds 126-50% of committed capital	1.0
No distributions until adjusted net asset value exceeds 150% or more of committed capital	0.5
No distributions until increase in adjusted net asset value exceeds 125% of the S&P 500	0.2
Hybrid restrictions	
No distributions until 100% capital return and adjusted NAV exceeds 100% of capital	0.2
No distributions until 100% capital return and adjusted NAV exceeds 101-25% of capital	1.4
No distributions until 100% capital return and adjusted NAV exceeds 126-50% of capital	1.4
No distributions until 100% capital return and adjusted NAV exceeds 150% or more of capital	0.2
No distributions until 100% capital return or adjusted NAV exceeds 100% of capital	0.5
No distributions until 100% capital return or adjusted NAV exceeds 101-25% of capital	1.2
No distributions until 100% capital return or adjusted NAV exceeds 126-50% of capital	0.2
Requirements to hold distributions in an escrow account	
Distributions held until return of 100% of committed capital	3.4
Distributions held until return of 101-25% of committed capital	1.2
Distributions held until adjusted asset value exceeds 100% of committed capital	0.2
Distributions held until adjusted asset value exceeds 101-26% of committed capital	0.7
Distributions held until 100% capital return and adjusted NAV exceeds 100% of capital	0.2
Distributions held until 100% capital return and adjusted NAV exceeds 126-50% of capital	0.2
Distributions held until 100% capital return or adjusted NAV exceeds 126-50% of capital	0.2
Distributions held set dollar amount reached	0.5
No restriction specified or other restriction	13.9

4

A Note on Private Equity Partnership Agreements

Venture capital and leveraged buyouts are by necessity long-run investments. Consequently, the vast majority of U.S. private equity today is raised through private partnerships with a 10-year or longer life span. To govern these investments, complex contracts have sprung up. These contracts provide an insight into the complex challenge of raising and managing a private equity fund.

There are two critical aspects to these contracts: the incentives offered to the private equity investors and the restrictions placed on their activities. This note discusses the most frequent covenants encountered in these funds.[1,2]

HOW THE FUND IS STRUCTURED

Private equity funds typically have limited and general partners. The limited partners are institutional and individual investors who provide capital. These are limited in the sense that their liability only extends to the capital they contribute. If, for instance, the fund invests in a company that produces a drug which kills some patients, the victims' relatives cannot sue the partnership's investors for damages. The general partners—usually the private equity investors who manage the fund—may, however, be directly liable.[3]

A private equity fund is raised in several stages. Initial investors in a private equity fund are often anxious to avoid opportunistic behavior by the general partners as they raise additional funds. As a result, a series of contractual provisions govern the fundraising process.

This note was prepared by Josh Lerner. Copyright © 1994 by the President and Fellows of Harvard College. Harvard Business School case 294-084.

[1] For an overview of the compensation structure in private equity partnerships, see Chapter 3, "Acme Investment Trust."

[2] This section is based on Joseph W. Bartlett, *Equity Finance: Venture Capital, Buyouts, Restructurings, and Reorganization,* New York: Wiley, 1995; Paul A. Gompers and Josh Lerner, "The Use of Covenants: An Empirical Analysis of Venture Partnership Agreements," *Journal of Law and Economics* 39 (October 1996): 566–599; Jack S. Levin, *Structuring Venture Capital, Private Equity and Entrepreneurial Transactions,* Chicago: Commerce Clearing House, 1994; Venture Economics, *Terms and Conditions of Venture Capital Partnerships,* Needham: Venture Economics, 1989; and Venture Economics, *Terms and Conditions of Venture Capital Partnerships—1992,* Needham: Venture Economics, 1992.

[3] Private equity investors protect themselves, at least partially, by not serving directly as the general partners. Rather, they create a corporation that serves as the general partner, which they in turn are shareholders of.

The first of these provisions is a minimum size of investment. General partners will typically set a minimum size for institutional investors and a smaller minimum for individual investors. Limited partners have at least two reasons for being concerned about the number of partners. Under the Investment Company Act of 1940, funds with more than a few hundred partners (originally 100) must register as investment advisers. This imposes complex regulatory and disclosure requirements. More generally, the costs of administering a private equity fund increase with the number of limited partners.

Most contracts stipulate an explicit minimum and maximum size for the fund. In many cases, limited partners have distinct preferences about fund sizes. If the general partners are unable to attract additional capital from other investors, the initial investors may prefer that the fund be disbanded. The general partners' inability to raise additional funds may imply that other potential limited investors have adverse information that the initial investors do not have.[4] They will in many cases also be concerned that the fund not become too large, lest the management skills of the general partners be strained. In many cases, the private equity investors are allowed to exceed the maximum size stated in the contract by 10% or 20%, as long as they explicitly obtain permission from the existing limited partners. The limited partners who enter late almost always are required to pay the same up-front and organization fees as the original limited partners, and may be restricted from a share of the interest earned on the original limited partner's initial capital commitments.

Prior to the 1986 Tax Reform Act, the contribution of the general partners to the funds was invariably 1%. This was because 1% was the minimum contribution by a general partner required by law. Since this Act, general partners are free to contribute as much or as little as they desire. In most cases, however, 1% is still the general partners' contribution. Deviations are confined to small funds, particularly first funds raised by private equity partnerships. In these cases, a substantial minority of firms contribute either a smaller or larger percentage. A few funds allow general partners not to make the contributions in cash but rather in non–interest-bearing notes.

Contracts uniformly have a "takedown" schedule, which specifies how the funds committed by the limited partners will be paid into the fund. Neither the limited nor general partners are usually eager for the funds to be paid in immediately. Since the private equity partnership will only invest the funds gradually, if the funds are simply sitting in the fund's bank account, they will depress the partnership's rate of return. Typically, partnership agreements will call for a set amount to be disbursed at closing (most often between 10% and 33%). The dates of subsequent payments may be set in the agreement or else left to the general partner's discretion. Larger funds are more likely to leave the schedule to the discretion of the general partners. Even if they are left to the private equity investors' discretion, usually a minimum and maximum period is set. All the funds are usually drawn down by between the second and fourth anniversaries of the fund's formation.

HOW LONG THE FUND WILL LAST

Private equity partnerships almost always have a life of about 10 years. They usually can be extended for at least two more years. In some cases, permission of the limited partners is required; in other cases, only extensions beyond this point need permission. In general, the decision to extend the life of the partnership is not controversial.

---

[4] This is similar to provisions in the riskiest of initial public offerings, the "best efforts" offering. If the underwriter cannot sell a minimum number of shares in a best efforts offering, the offering will be canceled, and the initial investors will be refunded.

Almost all partnerships allow the limited partners to terminate their investments in the partnership under certain extreme conditions. These include the death or withdrawal of the general partners or the bankruptcy of the fund. Most agreements also allow the limited partners to dissolve the partnership or replace the general partners if between 51% and 100% of the limited partners believe that the general partner is damaging the fund. Often, however, the parties in these cases end up in court.[5]

Most contracts will also have provisions for defaulting limited partners who fail to meet their capital commitments. In many cases, the general partners reserve the right to charge interest for late payments, to seize the limited partner's stake in whole or in part, or even to sue the limited partner. In other cases, the terms are less onerous. The general partners may agree to help market the limited partner's interest or pay the limited partner an amount that reflects the current fair market value of the partnership interest (or a fraction of this value). In many cases, if a pension fund must withdraw from a private equity fund due to the complex regulations promulgated by the U.S. Department of Labor, these penalties are waived. In addition, limited partners can frequently transfer their shares to other parties, conditional on the approval of the general partners.

WHAT THE PRIVATE EQUITY INVESTORS CAN AND CANNOT DO

An area of protracted negotiation is the discretion with which the general partner can run the private equity fund. In the 1960s and 1970s, partnership agreements contained few such restrictions. These early venture capital organizations were free to invest as they saw fit. As the 1980s progressed, however, institutional investors began viewing themselves as holding a portfolio of private equity funds, each with a distinct focus. They demanded contractual provisions that would limit the ability of general partners to deviate from their area of expertise. A few of the very oldest organizations, however, have managed to maintain simple contracts with few restrictions.[6] These covenants can be divided into three broad classes: those relating to the overall management of the fund, the activities of the general partners, and the permissible types of investments.

Management of the Fund The first of these restrictions relates to the size of investment in any one firm. These provisions are intended to ensure that the general partners do not attempt to salvage an investment in a poorly performing firm by investing significant resources in follow-on funding. The private equity investors typically do not receive a share of profits until the limited partners have received their original investment back. Consequently, the general partners' share of profits can be thought of as a call option. The general partner may gain disproportionately from increasing risk of the portfolio at the expense of diversification. This limitation is frequently expressed as a percentage of capital invested in the fund (typically called committed capital). Alternatively, it may be expressed as a percent of the current value of the fund's assets. In a few cases, a limit may be placed on the aggregate size of the partnership's two or three largest investments.

---

[5] Articles about such disputes include E.S. Ely, "Dr. Silver's Tarnished Prescription," *Venture* 9 (July 1987): 54–58; "Iowa Suits Test LPs' Authority to Abolish Fund," *Private Equity Analyst* 4 (May 1994): 1 and 9; and "Madison L.P.s Oust G.P., Legal Skirmish Ensues," *Buyouts* (October 23, 1995): 4.

[6] Why do these issues need to be specified within the original partnership agreement? Could not, for instance, the limited partners serve as directors, overseeing the investment decisions of the private equity investors? In actuality, limited partners can retain their limited liability only if they are not involved in the day-to-day operations of the fund. Thus, once the fund is formed, they are limited to a purely consultative role, such as service on the firm's advisory board. This makes the careful delineation of rights in the original partnership agreement critical.

The second class of restriction limits the use of debt. As option holders, the general partners may be tempted to increase the variance of their portfolio's returns by leveraging the fund. Partnership agreements often limit the ability of private equity investors to borrow funds themselves or to guarantee the debt of their portfolio companies (which might be seen as equivalent to direct borrowing). Partnership agreements may restrict debt to a set percentage of committed capital or assets, and in some instances also restrict the maturity of the debt, to ensure that all borrowing is short term.[7]

The third restriction relates to co-investments with the private equity organization's earlier or later funds. Many private equity organizations manage multiple funds, formed several years apart, which can lead to opportunistic behavior. Consider, for instance, a venture organization whose first fund has made an investment in a troubled firm. The general partners may find it optimal for their second fund to invest in this firm, in the hopes of salvaging the investment.[8] Consequently, partnership agreements for second or later funds frequently contain provisions that the fund's advisory board must review such investments or that a majority (or super-majority) of the limited partners approve these transactions. Another way in which these problems are limited is by the requirement that the earlier fund invest simultaneously at the same valuation. Alternatively, the investment may be allowed only if one or more unaffiliated private equity organizations simultaneously invest at the same price.

A fourth class of covenant relates to reinvestment of profits. Private equity investors may have several reasons to reinvest funds rather than distribute profits to the limited partners. First, many partnerships receive fees on the basis of either the value of assets under management or adjusted committed capital (capital less any distributions). Distributing profits will reduce these fees. Second, reinvested capital gains may yield further profits for the general (as well as the limited) partners.[9] The reinvestment of profits may require approval of the advisory board or the limited partners. Alternatively, such reinvestment may be prohibited after a certain date or after a certain percent of the committed capital is invested.

Activities of the Private Equity Investors   Five frequently encountered classes of restrictions limit the activities of the general partners. The first of these restricts the ability of the general partners to invest personal funds in firms. If general partners invest in selected firms, they may devote excessive time to these firms and may not terminate funding if the firms encounter difficulties. To address this problem, general partners are often limited in the size of investment they can make in any of their fund's portfolio firms. This limit may be expressed as a percentage of the total investment by the fund or (less frequently) of the net worth of the private equity investor. In addition, the pri-

---

[7] A related provision—found in virtually all partnership agreements—is that the limited partners will avoid unrelated business taxable income (UBTI). Tax-exempt institutions must pay taxes on UBTI, which is defined as the gross income from any unrelated business that the institution regularly carries out. If the venture partnership is generating significant income from debt-financed property, the limited partners may have tax liabilities.

[8] Distortions may also be introduced by the need for the private equity investors to report an attractive return for their first fund as they seek capital for a third fund. Many venture funds will write up the valuation of firms in their portfolios to the price paid in the last venture round. By having the second fund invest in one of the first fund's firms at an inflated valuation, they can (temporarily) inflate the reported performance of their first fund.

[9] Another reason why private equity investors may wish to reinvest profits is that such investments are unlikely to be mature at the end of the fund's stated life. The presence of investments that are too immature to liquidate is a frequently invoked reason for extending the partnership's life beyond the typical contractual limit of 10 years. In these cases, the private equity investors will continue to generate fees from the limited partners (though often on a reduced basis).

vate equity investors may be required to seek permission from the advisory board or limited partners. An alternative approach employed in some partnership agreements is to require the private equity investors to invest a set dollar amount or percentage in every investment made by the fund.[10]

A second restriction addresses the reverse problem: the sale of partnership interests by general partners. Rather than seeking to increase their personal exposure to selected investments, general partners may sell their share of the fund's profits to other investors. While the general partnership interests are not totally comparable with the limited partners' stakes (for instance, the general partners will typically only receive a share of the capital gains after the return of the limited partners' capital), these may still be attractive investments. The limited partners are likely to be concerned that such a sale would reduce the general partners' incentives to monitor their investments. Partnership agreements may prohibit the sale of general partnership interests outright or else require that these sales be approved by a majority (or super-majority) of the limited partners.

A third area for restrictions on the general partners is future fundraising. The raising of an additional fund will raise the management fees that the general partners receive and may reduce the attention that the private equity investors pay to existing funds. Partnership agreements may prohibit fundraising by the general partners until a set percentage of the portfolio has been invested or until a given date. Alternatively, fundraising may be restricted to a fund of certain size or focus (e.g., a venture organization may be allowed to raise a buyout fund, whose management would presumably be by other general partners).

In a similar vein, some partnership agreements restrict other actions by general partners. Because outside activities are likely to reduce the attention paid to investments, private equity investors may be restricted to spending "substantially all" (or some other fraction) of their time managing the investments of the partnership. Alternatively, the general partners' ability to be involved in businesses other than the companies in which the private equity fund has invested may be restricted. These limitations are often confined to the first years of the partnership or until a set percent of the fund's capital is invested, when the need for attention by the general partners is presumed to be the largest.

A fifth class of covenant relates to the addition of new general partners. By hiring less experienced general partners, private equity investors may reduce the burden on themselves. The quality of the oversight provided, however, is likely to be lower. As a result, many funds require that the addition of new general partners be approved by either the advisory board or a set percentage of the limited partners.

Although many issues involving the behavior of the general partners are addressed through partnership agreements, several others typically are not. One area that is almost never discussed is the vesting schedule of general partnership interests. If a general partner leaves a private equity organization early in the life of the fund, he may forfeit all or some of his share of the profits. If the private equity investors do not receive their entire partnership interest immediately, they are less likely to leave the fund soon after it is formed. A second issue is the division of the profits between the general partners. In the case of some funds, the bulk of the profits accrue to the older general partners, even if the bulk of the day-to-day management is being provided by the younger private

---

[10] Another issue relating to co-investment is the timing of the investments by the general partners. In some cases, venture capitalists involved in establishing a firm will purchase shares at the same time as the other founders at a very low valuation and then immediately invest their partnership's funds at a much higher valuation. Some partnership agreements address this problem by requiring venture capitalists to invest at the same time and price as their funds.

equity investors. These issues are addressed in agreements between the general partners, but are rarely discussed in the contracts between the general and limited partners.

Types of Investments   The third family of covenants limits the types of assets in which the fund will invest. These restrictions are typically structured in similar ways: the private equity fund is allowed to invest no more than a set percentage of capital or asset value in a given investment class. An exception may be made if the advisory board or a set percentage of the limited partners approve. Occasionally, more complex restrictions will be encountered, such as the requirement that the sum of two asset classes not exceed a certain percent of capital.

Two fears appear to motivate these restrictions on investments. First, the general partners may be receiving inappropriately large compensation. For instance, the average money manager who specializes in investing in public securities receives an annual fee of about 0.5% of assets, while private equity investors receive 20% of profits in addition to an annual fee of about 2.5% of capital. Consequently, limited partners seek to limit the ability of private equity investors to invest in public securities. Similarly, the typical investment manager receives a one-time fee of 1% of capital for investing an institution's money in a private equity fund. Partnership agreements often also include covenants that restrict the ability of the general partners to invest capital in other private equity funds.

A second concern is that the general partners will invest in classes of investments in which they have little expertise, in the hopes of gaining experience. For instance, during the 1980s, many venture capital funds began investing in leveraged buyouts. Those that developed a successful track record proceeded to raise funds specializing in buyouts; many more, however, lost considerable sums on these investments.[11] Similarly, many firms explored investing in foreign countries during the 1980s. Only a relative handful proved sufficiently successful to raise funds specializing in these investments.

Exhibit 1 indicates the percent of funds that undertook venture capital or both venture and buyout investments that contained each of these provisions relating to what the private equity investors can and cannot do. Results are presented for three five-year periods (1978–82, 1983–87, and 1988–92). This highlights the growing restrictiveness of contracts during the later years. In general, more restrictive contracts are associated with years in which the private pool was shrinking or the rate of growth of the private equity pool was slowing.

---

[11] The poor performance of venture-backed LBOs such as Prime Computer has been much discussed in the popular press; quantitative support of these claims is found in analyses of the returns of funds with different investment objectives by Venture Economics.

Exhibit 1

The number of covenants in partnership agreements for funds established to undertake venture or venture and buyout investments, by year. For the fourteen most common classes of covenants, the table indicates the percent of partnership agreements with such a restriction in each five-year period.

	% of Contracts with Covenant in ...		
	1978-82	*1983-87*	*1988-92*
Covenants relating to the management of the fund			
Restrictions on size of investment in any one firm	33.3	47.1	77.8
Restrictions on use of debt by partnership	66.7	72.1	95.6
Restrictions on co-investment with organization's other funds	40.7	29.4	62.2
Restrictions on reinvestment of partnership's capital gains	3.7	17.6	35.6
Covenants relating to the activities of the general partners			
Restrictions on co-investment by general partners	81.5	66.2	77.8
Restrictions on sale of partnership interests by general partners	74.1	54.4	51.1
Restrictions on fund-raising by general partners	51.9	42.6	84.4
Restrictions on other actions by general partners	22.2	16.2	13.3
Restrictions on addition of general partners	29.6	35.3	26.7
Covenants relating to the types of investment			
Restrictions on investments in other venture funds	3.7	22.1	62.2
Restrictions on investments in public securities	22.2	17.6	66.7
Restrictions on investments in LBOs	0.0	8.8	60.0
Restrictions on investments in foreign securities	0.0	7.4	44.4
Restrictions on investments in other asset classes	11.1	16.2	31.1
Average number of covenant classes/partnership agreement	4.4	4.5	7.9

Source: Paul A. Gompers and Josh Lerner, "The Use of Covenants: An Empirical Analysis of Venture Partnership Agreements," *Journal of Law and Economics*, 39 (October 1996) 566-599.

5

Weston Presidio Offshore Capital: Confronting the Fundraising Challenge

Michael Cronin glanced once again at the burly bodyguards and shifted uneasily on his stool. It was 9 P.M., and he and his partner, Michael Lazarus, had been waiting for nearly an hour. Cronin mused about the circumstances that had brought them to the unfinished kitchen of an unfurnished apartment in central London, surrounded by suspicious and probably armed men.

Cronin and Lazarus had been raising their first venture fund for the past eight months. The fund, which they had named Weston Presidio Offshore Capital, would focus on a broad array of later-stage private equity investments. Although the two general partners had between them more than two decades of experience in private equity investing, fundraising was proving to be more difficult than they had foreseen when they set out in February 1991.

Potential investors and their advisers had cited a variety of concerns while reviewing the Weston Presidio offering memorandum. Many investors were wary about committing additional capital to venture capital and buyouts, citing the poor returns they had obtained from their investments during the 1980s. Others seemed willing to consider investing in the asset class but were reluctant to consider a first fund or had doubts about the two men's proposed strategy. In some cases, pension fund managers appeared interested in investing, but their advisers had raised objections. While Cronin and Lazarus had been able to structure a deal with Mercury Asset Management to provide an initial $25 million for the fund, some investors had even expressed concerns about this arrangement. In particular, they had demanded the same favorable terms that the lead investor had received.

Finally, a side door opened. Cronin caught a glimpse of a brilliantly lit and carpeted room. "The prince will see you now," a bodyguard announced.

THE PRIVATE EQUITY INDUSTRY IN 1991

Activity in the venture capital and buyout industry had grown during the past 10 years and then declined even more swiftly. After a decade where the annual funds raised did not exceed $100 million, activity soared during the 1980s. During the final three years

This case was prepared by Josh Lerner. Copyright © 1996 by the President and Fellows of Harvard College. Harvard Business School case 296-055.

of the decade, an average of $3.4 billion was raised annually by venture funds. As institutional investors realized how this growth had led to an abrupt decline in returns, however, they rapidly scaled back their commitments. Only $1.9 billion was raised in 1990, and 1991 was shaping up to be an even worse year. The buyout market, another important financing source for small- and midsized firms, had followed a similar pattern. Fundraising by buyout firms had fallen from an average annual rate of nearly $9 billion in the years 1987–89 to $4.6 billion in 1990. The year 1991 was also shaping up as a poor one for raising buyout funds. Exhibit 1 summarizes these trends, especially those affecting later-stage venture funds.

At the same time, other sources of later-stage financing for private firms were also drying up. The most important was bank loans. In 1990, the initial federal regulations implementing the "Basle Accord" went into effect. This international agreement called for banks operating in the major industrialized countries to hold capital in proportion to the riskiness of their activities. In particular, banks were required to hold more capital if their resources were being used for commercial loans (as opposed to being devoted to residential mortgages or Treasury securities). Since few U.S. banks had previously been in compliance with these requirements, many scaled back their commercial lending activities in 1990 and 1991. In addition to policy changes, the well-publicized bank and savings-and-loan failures of the late 1980s had led to increased enforcement of existing rules by regulators. Consequently, there had been an abrupt decline in lending to small- and midsized growth companies in the early 1990s.[1]

In Cronin and Lazarus's eyes, the retrenchment in private equity and the banking "credit crunch" created a substantial opportunity. In particular, the reduced financing alternatives for private firms suggested that a private equity organization specializing in later-stage transactions could find attractive deals at relatively low prices. The attractive conditions today should generate superior returns when the investments were harvested several years hence.

THE PARTNERS

Cronin and Lazarus had between them two-and-a-half decades of experience in private equity investing. During their years at Security Pacific Capital and Montgomery Securities, they had become seasoned investors. They had also built up extensive contacts with entrepreneurial managers, private equity investors, and institutions that would be important sources of new transactions and capital.

Michael Cronin, 37, had nearly 15 years of experience with venture investing. His interest in venture capital had been sparked as a Harvard undergraduate. While managing the student laundry and later as president of Harvard Student Agencies, he had met a director of the student enterprise association, Pat Liles. Liles was a faculty member at Harvard Business School who would later go on to join Charles River Ventures. Cronin had gone into private equity investing immediately after graduating Harvard Business School in 1977. Since 1979, Cronin had been with Security Pacific Capital Corporation, the venture capital subsidiary of a major California bank (now part of the

---

[1] For an academic overview, see Allen N. Berger and Gregory F. Udell, "Did Risk-Based Capital Allocate Bank Credit and Cause a 'Credit Crunch' in the United States?," *Journal of Money, Credit and Banking* 26 (1994): 585–628; for several perspectives from practitioners, see U.S. House, Committee on Government Operations, Commerce, Consumer and Monetary Affairs Subcommittee, *The Credit Crunch and Regulatory Burdens in Bank Lending,* Hearings Held in the 103rd Congress, First Session, March 17–May 10, 1993, Washington, D.C., Government Printing Office, 1993.

Bank of America). During his 12 years with the organization, its capital under management had grown from $25 million to over $600 million. The subsidiary invested in both direct deals and other private equity funds.

Cronin had personally been responsible for investing $95 million in 44 deals. Most of these firms were in the Boston area: Cronin had founded Security Pacific Capital's office in that city in 1984. These firms had been in a wide variety of sectors, including specialty retailing, consumer products, and medical services. The one constant had been the remarkably good returns from these investments: they had realized a 36% rate of return through mid-1991. Exhibit 2 presents Cronin's resume, and Exhibit 3, his investment track record.[2]

Michael Lazarus, 36, was the director of the private placement department at Montgomery Securities, a California investment bank specializing in technology and growth firms. After originally being trained as an accountant at Grove City College, Lazarus had worked for Price Waterhouse for six years. Beginning in his native Pittsburgh and then working in London, he built an expertise in international tax accounting. During his London years, he had forged many relationships with wealthy Europeans who invested in U.S. equities.

In 1983, Lazarus entered the world of private equity investing as part of the founding team of Berkeley International. This firm invested funds of British individuals and institutions in private U.S. growth firms. In 1986, he moved to San Francisco to join Montgomery Securities. While at Montgomery, Lazarus had been responsible for arranging $99 million in private placements in 23 firms. By mid-1991, these securities were worth $375 million. Exhibit 4 presents Lazarus's resume; Exhibit 5, the performance of the private placements that he arranged.

The two men had first met in 1986, soon after Lazarus had joined Montgomery Securities. Lazarus was at the time raising capital for Oral Research Labs. This firm manufactured PLAX, a mouthwash that enhanced the effectiveness of tooth-brushing. The company attracted little interest from venture capitalists. Not only was it a small player in a market dominated by giant firms such as Colgate and Procter & Gamble, but firms targeting the consumer market had in general little appeal to these investors. Despite these considerations, Cronin decided to serve as the lead investor. The firm was acquired 18 months later by Pfizer in a transaction that valued the firm at about $250 million, more than nine times the valuation in the private placement.

After this success, Lazarus made a point of bringing transactions to Cronin's attention. The two men soon came to understand that their investment philosophies had many elements in common. Central among these beliefs was a willingness to go against the herd-like behavior that all-too-frequently characterized venture investors. For instance, Lazarus had arranged the private placement of disk drive start-up Conner Peripherals in 1987. At the time, most venture capitalists—having been hurt by disk drive investments in the early 1980s—still considered the sector to be unattractive. Furthermore, while Lazarus considered the firm's founder, Finis Conner, to be a visionary, many venture capitalists dismissed him as too mercurial. The company went public a year later and in mid-1991 had a market capitalization of over $800 million. This contrarian approach was also central to the criteria Security Pacific used to evaluate investments.

FIRST STEPS

The formation of Weston Presidio was triggered by a series of events in 1990. In July, Mercury Asset Management approached Lazarus regarding potential venture invest-

---

[2]These returns were not based simply on difficult-to-verify interim valuations. By mid-1991, fully 33 of the investments had been harvested, yielding $181 million in cash or marketable securities.

ments. Mercury was a British money manager with approximately $65 billion under management. It was 75% owned by the London-based investment bank S.G. Warburg Group, with the remaining shares traded on the London Stock Exchange. Mercury—which had reviewed, but not invested in, a number of private placements orchestrated by Lazarus over the past several years—had become aware of the precipitous decline in venture fundraising in the United States. They wondered whether this might be an opportune time to enter the private equity market.

Although Lazarus was aware of a number of established venture and buyout organizations currently attempting to raise funds, he recommended that Mercury consider asking Cronin to organize a fund. Lazarus thought that Cronin might be susceptible to such an offer because he, like many bank-affiliated venture capitalists, did not share in the profits generated by his investments. From his experiences at Montgomery Securities, Lazarus was also sensitive to the challenges that Cronin faced in undertaking venture investments within a larger organization.[3]

Mercury indicated that they found the suggestion intriguing and that they would consider it carefully. Much of the appeal lay in the fact that Security Pacific Capital's investment approach was quite similar to that of European private equity funds. In particular, most European funds were affiliated with a financial institution and concentrated on relatively mature companies that needed expansion capital as opposed to start-ups.

Meanwhile, Cronin had begun to consider leaving Security Pacific after one dozen years. The same regulatory scrutiny that was leading many banks to curtail small business lending appeared to be triggering a retrenchment in bank-sponsored venture funds. These pressures had two manifestations. First, venture investments were weighted heavily when bank's capital requirements were tabulated. This led bank managers to question whether their venture units were necessary. Second, regulators had questioned a number of banks about whether their venture subsidiaries were complying with the Glass-Steagall Act. This 1933 Act limited banks to holding no more than 5% of other companies' voting stock. As Timothy Hay, who had founded Security Pacific Capital in 1964 and served as chairman and chief executive officer, noted in 1989, "we have to be increasingly careful not to push over the line of regulatory compliance."[4] As a result of these pressures, banks' total commitments to venture capital fell dramatically.

Because of its illustrious track record, Security Pacific Capital was initially isolated from these pressures. In mid-1990, however, Hay retired from active management of the unit for medical reasons. Hay had begun in the venture industry in 1959, had been among the founding team of Heizer Corporation,[5] and was one of the most well-known and respected venture capitalists. Cronin feared that Hay's retirement would lead to a substantial increase in oversight of and restrictions on the venture unit by Security Pacific's senior management.

Stirred by these concerns, Cronin had taken a number of tentative steps. First, he had held conversations with a number of established venture organizations. These groups had approached him and suggested that he might want to join them as a general partner. After being affiliated for so long with an established venture organization, however, Cronin was more attracted by the prospect of raising his own fund. Thus Cronin—in conjunction with several of his partners at Security Pacific—had held several conversations with a New York-based consultant who specialized in helping venture capitalists raise

[3] Montgomery had organized two funds focusing on medical ventures. These had made a series of troubled investments, including the Scottish hospital HCI Limited, ICU Medical, and Verax Corporation.

[4] Lisabeth Weiner, "Lucrative Leveraged Buyout Deals Are Getting Harder to Find," *American Banker* (June 13, 1989): 2.

[5] In 1969, Heizer became the first venture partnership to raise the bulk of its funds from institutional investors. It went on to be the lead investor in Amdahl, Paradyne, and many other firms.

funds. The adviser, while trying not to drive away their business, was not terribly encouraging. Furthermore, the Security Pacific partners thought that the compensation he demanded was rather substantial. In addition to a fee equal to the greater of $3 million or 2% of assets raised, he also sought one-third of the general partners' share of the profits (carried interest) from the first fund. In addition, he asked for a deposit of $250,000, which would not be refundable, even if the fundraising effort was unsuccessful.

In February 1991, after more than six months of consideration, Mercury got back in touch with Lazarus. They indicated that they were willing to go ahead and provide the lead investment for a new venture fund organized by Cronin. There was, however, one important proviso: this offer was contingent on Lazarus agreeing to join the fund as Cronin's partner. This offer posed a real dilemma for Lazarus. On the one hand, Lazarus was tiring of the transaction-driven environment of investment banking. He felt that it did not fully exploit his special ability in developing and nurturing long-term relationships. Furthermore, undertaking private equity investing in an investment banking setting seemed to pose certain inherent conflicts of interest. On the other hand, leaving Montgomery for a yet-to-be-raised fund would entail a substantial cut in income, the relinquishment of a substantial equity stake in the bank, and a considerable career risk.

INVESTMENT PHILOSOPHY

Cronin and Lazarus held a series of intensive discussions about this offer in the early spring of 1991. To help evaluate whether to accept the offer, they sketched out the key parameters for any fund they might organize. In particular, they agreed that the fund must follow the same approach to private equity investing that had proven successful for them in the past.

More particularly, they agreed on four key principles. First, they would focus primarily on private firms that might be classified as later-stage investments. More specifically, they hoped to exit their investments—whether through an acquisition of the firm or the sale of shares to the public—within three years of their initial investment. Cronin and Lazarus believed that these types of investments had several important advantages. One advantage related to the ability to obtain more realistic valuations. As they noted:

> The Partnership will attempt to value companies based on their current worth rather than discounting future events and projections that have yet to be achieved nor could be achieved without the capital available from the Partnership.[6]

Another advantage was the relatively limited competition in this area. Later-stage investing in the late 1980s had been dominated by a number of "mega-funds": venture organizations that had raised $250 million of capital or more.[7] The flexibility of these large funds was limited. The funds often required that the transactions they undertook were quite large, in order to ensure that their general partners were not distracted by the

---

[6] Weston Presidio Capital, *Private Placement Memorandum,* September 1991, p. 9.

[7] One way to examine this is to compare the venture organizations that raised later-stage funds between 1985 and 1990 with all other venture organizations. The organizations raising later-stage funds were nearly twice as large as the other organizations. More specifically, the typical organizations raising a later-stage fund between 1984 and 1990 controlled .51% of the venture capital under management. The typical organization that raised a fund not focusing on later-stage deals accounted for .29% of the venture pool. (This is based on an unpublished Venture Economics database provided by Jesse Reyes.)

management of too many deals. This meant that Weston Presidio would face less competition for small later-stage deals. Furthermore, despite these controls, many partners in large venture organizations often had become responsible for a considerable number of portfolio firms. This left them less time to originate new investments of any size.

Many of the investment criteria that Weston Presidio intended to employ were designed to identify such later-stage firms. Cronin and Lazarus anticipated that the manufacturing firms in which they invested would have significant revenues and operating profits, as well as (hopefully) positive cash flows. Service firms, they anticipated, would be successfully operating initial facilities. Another important criterion was the management team. They believed that the managers should have a proven ability to grow new enterprises similar to the one in which they were investing.

A second key element of their philosophy was to invest widely across industries and regions. Cronin and Lazarus felt that such an approach would reduce the overall risk of the fund: it would be less adversely affected by regional recessions or downturns in particular industries. This principle went against the approach of many private equity organizations, which had increasingly been raising narrowly targeted funds. For instance, the number of funds stating in their private placement memorandum that they had a focus on a particular industry or industries had increased from 3% in 1980 to 36% in 1990.[8]

One important aspect of the geographic strategy was to place offices in Boston and San Francisco. Cronin would be based out of the former office and Lazarus the latter. This approach would not only limit the danger of parochialism, but would also ensure that each partner was based in the geographic area where he had the most experience and contacts.[9]

A third element was intensive involvement with the firms in their portfolio. In particular, Weston Presidio's general partners anticipated playing an active role in almost all the firms in which they invested, whether through service on the board or informal ties with management. They did not intend, however, to become actively involved in managing these firms, unless required to intervene in a troubled situation.

The final design principle was quite different from that used by most private equity firms. Most organizations, whether focusing on early- or later-stage investments, anticipated a bimodal distribution of returns. The bulk of the returns would be generated from a relatively modest number of investments that went public. This emphasis had been part of the private equity culture since American Research and Development's returns soared with Digital Equipment's success in the late 1950s. Cronin and Lazarus, however, sought to structure transactions that avoided this "all-or-nothing" payout structure. In particular, they sought to include features that would generate an almost immediate payback (such as interest or dividend payments) or else provided at least some payments in case of product–market disappointments (e.g., provisions that allowed the fund to redeem their shares for cash).

THE FUNDRAISING CHALLENGE

Structuring the Relationship with the Lead Investor

Cronin and Lazarus repeatedly traveled together to London in the spring of 1991, seeking to define a relationship with Mercury Asset Management. After several conversa-

---

[8] This is based on an unpublished Venture Economics database provided by Jesse Reyes.

[9] This bi-coastal basing would also facilitate the due diligence process. Cronin and Lazarus foresaw that each proposed transaction would be formally reviewed in a similar manner. One partner would act as the advocate for the transaction, while the other would seek to dispassionately identify risks. Through such a procedure, they hoped to avoid making marginal investments.

tions, the proposed fund structure became clearer. Mercury would invest $25 million in the fund, and Cronin and Lazarus would seek to raise another $50 million. While the bulk of Mercury's funds would be provided alongside the other investors, the British money manager would also make a "seed capital" investment of $500,000 in Weston Presidio. This would provide Cronin and Lazarus with the resources to undertake an initial fundraising effort.

Reflecting this special relationship, Mercury would serve as the sole "special limited partner" of the fund. This would entitle Mercury to a share of the capital gains that the general partners received (the "carried interest"). Cronin and Lazarus proposed that the fund employ the 80%–20% split of the capital gains between the limited partners and the general partners that was standard in the private equity industry. The 20% share would, however, then be divided between Cronin and Lazarus on the one hand and Mercury on the other. The division would be proportionate to the sources of the funds. For instance, if Cronin and Lazarus were able to raise an additional $25 million (so the fund totaled $50 million), then they would receive one-half of the carried interest and Mercury one-half. If they raised an additional $50 million, then they would receive two-thirds of the carried interest, and Mercury one-third.

In addition, Mercury would play a role on the advisory board that the two general partners intended to establish. The board would play three roles: to review the valuation of firms in their portfolio (particularly private concerns where no market price was available), to resolve any potential conflicts of interest that might emerge, and to serve as an adviser on general matters. They had offered a seat on this board to Ian Armitage, a director of Mercury. In addition, they had recruited Timothy Hay, Cronin's mentor and former boss.

Cronin and Lazarus sought to propose terms to Mercury that were as fair as those found in typical venture partnership agreements, or even fairer to the limited partners than normal. They wished to avoid an outcome where Mercury felt that Cronin and Lazarus had exploited their relative inexperience in U.S. private equity investing by offering unusual terms.

Two examples of where Cronin and Lazarus deviated from the standard "vanilla" partnership agreement were the provisions for preferred distributions and the location of the partnership. In each case, they sought to make the terms particularly favorable to the limited partners. In the typical venture partnership, early distributions of cash or securities were first paid to the limited partners. Only after the limited partners had received their capital back did the general partners begin receiving 20% of the capital. Cronin and Lazarus, on the other hand, agreed to defer receiving any share of the profits until their limited partners had not only received their invested capital, but also a 9% return on this capital. Only after this point would the general partners receive any distributions.[10]

A second unusual feature was the design of the fund as an offshore partnership based in the Netherlands Antilles. Venture funds were typically structured as domestic partnerships, but Mercury had requested that they consider alternative structures. As in a domestic partnership, capital gains by foreign limited partners in a foreign fund were not likely to be subject to U.S. tax.[11] The overseas structure had, however, several advan-

[10] In particular, after the limited partners had received their invested capital and their preferred return, then all distributions would be paid to the general partners and Mercury Asset Management. Only after these two parties had received 25% of the amount received by the limited partners would the distributions be split 80%–20%. These restrictions did not apply to certain small distributions to cover any tax obligations that might be incurred.

[11] This was the case as long as the general partners avoided investing in real estate or firms whose primary assets were real estate. Interest and dividend payments, however, were likely to be taxable at a 30% rate.

tages for the foreign limited partners. Among the most important was that foreign limited partners of foreign partnerships had considerably greater flexibility to choose their tax treatment than foreign limited partners of domestic partnerships. This flexibility might enable them to choose the status that minimized the tax obligations in their particular situation. At the same time, the foreign status imposed some costs on the general partners. In particular, some states had more extensive registration requirement for foreign limited partnerships undertaking transactions within their borders.[12]

Other terms were more standard. For instance, like most funds, the two partners would contribute 1% of the capital. (Half of this sum, however, could be in the form of notes.) Similarly, the proposed fee structure was traditional. The memorandum called for the general partners to receive an annual fee of 2% of the capital committed to the partnership. This would be payable in advance each quarter. Thus, assuming that the $75 million target was reached, Cronin and Lazarus would receive $375,000 each quarter. The fee would be the same even if the fund's entire capital had not been fully drawn down. These funds would be indexed to the Consumer Price Index. Thus a 10% increase in consumer prices would trigger an increase in the management fee to 2.2%. The offering memorandum foresaw the possibility that the general partners would collect a variety of directors' or consulting fees from companies in their portfolio. The document proposed that the distributions due to the general partners be reduced by one-half the amount of any such fees that they collected.

The term sheet from the private placement memorandum is reproduced in Exhibit 6; the proposed limited partnership agreement is summarized in Exhibit 7.

The Identification of Other Investors

In June 1991, Cronin stepped down from his position at Security Pacific and begun marketing the fund to other potential investors. The initial understanding with Mercury was that Cronin and Lazarus would raise $25 million, while S.G. Warburg would raise an additional $25 million from their clients. Along with the contribution from Mercury, this would rapidly lead to the formation of a $75 million fund. To this end, Cronin and Lazarus assembled a list of potential investors.

An initial round of meetings had been held in the summer of 1991 with a number of large private and public pension funds. Cronin and Lazarus parlayed their many years of contacts into appointments with some of the most substantial private equity investors. In some cases these institutions had invested in Lazarus's private placements; in others, they had been limited partners in venture funds alongside Security Pacific Capital. Several of these initial meetings had gone very well.

It was only after these initial sessions, however, that Cronin and Lazarus had fully appreciated the role of investment advisers (also known as "gatekeepers"). Many of these institutions would not invest in a private equity fund until their investment advisers had signed off on the transaction. Even in cases where the investment officer at the pension fund made the final investment decision, the gatekeeper's approval seemed to be a necessity. In addition, many investment advisers also managed "funds-of-funds." These funds invested capital from many institutions in a number of venture and buyout partnerships.

---

[12] For an introduction to this complex area of the U.S. tax law, see Fred Feingold and Mark E. Berg, "Whither the Branches?," *New York University Tax Law Review* 44 (1989): 205–257; Susan P. Hamill, "F. Hodge O'Neal Corporate and Securities Law Symposium: The Taxation of Domestic Limited Liability Corporations and Limited Partnerships," *Washington University Law Quarterly* 73 (1995): 565–608; and Jack S. Levin, *Structuring Venture Capital, Private Equity, and Entrepreneurial Transactions*, Boston, Little, Brown, 1995.

Many investment advisers demanded repeated meetings with the Weston Presidio general partners: in one case, eight different meetings had been held with a single gatekeeper. In these sessions, the venture capitalists' backgrounds, their investment track records, and their intended strategy were exhaustively reviewed. For many of these sessions, the advisers demanded that the entire team be present. This entailed flying Lazarus and their first hire, an associate, from California.

The investment advisers raised three substantive concerns about the proposed fund. First, some indicated that they had an absolute rule against funding "first-time funds." Since some of the poorest performances during the 1980s had been by first-time private equity organizations, the advisers indicated that they would rather wait until they had completed their first fund. Similar policies have been widely adopted by investment advisers and pension funds, despite vehement complaints by some private equity investors. For instance, Edwin Goodman, president of Hambro America, argued that

> the "no-first-funds" criterion that has developed is offensive and intellectually bankrupt. …
> If the investing institutions abandon altogether their support for new venture funds, they will leave the field open to the caprice of the wealthy individual dilettante investor. This is not a happy harbinger for the venture capital community of the year 2000.[13]

When Cronin and Lazarus sought to address these concerns by pointing to their past successes, their claims were discounted. For instance, Cronin was extensively queried about the extent to which he was responsible for the deals he had undertaken at Security Pacific Capital. Several gatekeepers seemed to imply that he might have been given the deals by Tim Hay rather than originating them himself.

A second magnet for criticism was Weston Presidio's opportunistic approach. Cronin and Lazarus's arguments about the virtues of flexibility seemed to fall on deaf ears. Many gatekeepers insisted that it made more sense for private equity funds to be targeted. The two men mused that this conviction might partially stem from the fact that narrowly targeted funds added to the power of the gatekeepers: it allowed them to select not only private equity managers for pension funds, but also investment areas.

A final area of criticism was the arrangement with their lead investor, Mercury Asset Management. Several gatekeepers asked that their clients also receive a share of the carried interest. When Cronin and Lazarus explained that this consideration was being provided in recognition of Mercury's status as the lead investor, the gatekeepers asked why their client had not been asked to lead the investment. The structure of the fund as an offshore partnership also raised eyebrows, since it was not a standard arrangement.

The sessions with investment advisers had to date proven to be largely fruitless. Making this especially frustrating to Cronin and Lazarus was the impression that many rejections had little to do with the questions that the gatekeepers had raised about the fund. In some cases, Cronin and Lazarus strongly suspected that the investment adviser was not even authorized to invest in private equity: its clients had pulled back from making new commitments to this asset class. In these instances, it seemed that the gatekeepers were meeting with them only to maintain the impression of being active in this market, as well as to access data about venture investments that they could add to their proprietary databases.

In other cases, it appeared that the gatekeepers' major concern was the impact of Weston Presidio's proposed activities on the funds in which they had already invested. For instance, many gatekeepers had invested in a Boston-based private equity organiza-

---

[13] Edwin A. Goodman, "Gatekeepers' 'Reforms' Reap Negative Consequences," *Venture Capital Journal* 29 (December 1990): 25–28.

tion that specialized in generating later-stage investments through "cold-calling" managers. Many of the questions directed to Cronin and Lazarus seemed to be designed to determine whether they would be competing with this venture organization for deals.

Finally, in some instances Cronin and Lazarus's direct marketing to pension fund officials had generated unforeseen resentments. Often the general partners paid their first visit to a gatekeeper only *after* they had already met with officials at the pension fund who was its client. This was a reverse of the usual process. Typically, the investment adviser would screen the private equity offering memorandums and only allow the managers of the most promising funds to meet with their clients. Several investment advisers seemed to worry that Weston Presidio's direct marketing would lead to an erosion of their own status with their pension fund clients.

Meanwhile, S.G. Warburg's efforts to raise funds had been largely unsuccessful. The bank's brokers did not clearly understand the nature of venture capital and consequently could not address potential investors' concerns about the fund's illiquidity and riskiness. Over the summer of 1991, it became increasingly clear that Cronin and Lazarus would need to raise the entire $50 million.

As they were ushered into the prince's study, a variety of doubts flashed through Cronin's mind. Would they really be able to identify enough individual investors to adequately capitalize the fund? Even if there were enough potential investors, would their seed capital from Mercury Asset Management run out before these individuals could be located? Could the objections of the U.S. investment advisers be overcome? Should they alter the focus of the fund or the conditions of the partnership agreement?

Exhibit 1   Fundraising by Later-Stage Venture Partnerships, 1980-1990

| | Total Amount Raised ($B) | | Later-Stage Venture Funds Only | | |
	Venture Capital	Buyouts	Total Amount ($M)	Number of Funds[a]	Average Fund Size ($M)
1980	0.6	0.1	$ 73	3	$36
1981	0.9	0.1	77	4	19
1982	1.3	0.4	149	7	25
1983	2.6	0.6	741	21	35
1984	3.4	1.5	342	13	26
1985	2.1	1.1	569	17	35
1986	2.1	4.3	453	13	41
1987	3.7	4.3	731	14	56
1988	3.1	9.6	369	10	37
1989	3.3	7.9	450	12	50
1990	1.9	8.8	437	7	62

Source: Compiled from the records of Asset Alternatives and Venture Economics. I thank Steve Galante and Jesse Reyes for their help.

[a]Includes some funds where the fund size is not available (and hence are not used in computation of average fund size).

Exhibit 2   Michael F. Cronin--Curriculum Vitae

EXPERIENCE

8/79 to 6/91   **Security Pacific Capital Corporation, Boston, Massachusetts**

Served as Senior Vice President in Security Pacific Corporation's venture capital subsidiaries, which currently have $200 million in direct investments. Company's activities include equity-type investments in leveraged and/or management "buyouts," growth capital investments, early-stage financing and other capital gain oriented investment opportunities. Responsibilities included origination, structuring, analysis and presentation of investment opportunities, legal documentation of fundings and sales of investment positions and ongoing monitoring of portfolio companies to ensure continued performance based on original investment objectives. Efforts have resulted in closing forty-four transactions, representing approximately $95 million in invested capital which has been a significant portion of the company's direct investment activities. Beginning in 1985, I moved from California to open company's Boston office, served as its managing officer. Served as company's representative to the NASBIC Board of Governors.

6/77 to 7/79   **California Investment Counsel, Inc., San Diego, California**

Served as Assistant to the President of this private investment company, which operated a custom photofinishing lab and developed commercial real estate. Responsibilities included general management of photofinishing business employing over fifty people, supervising tenant improvements of real estate facilities and ongoing analysis of new ventures. Efforts resulted in achieving and maintaining the scheduled delivery goals of the business and initiating a direct mail effort to complement existing magazine advertising. In addition, completed construction of commercial real estate facility.

EDUCATION

1975 to 1977   **Harvard Graduate School of Business Administration, Boston, Massachusetts**

Received Master of Business Administration degree. Managed Harvard Business School's fast-food operation and Student Pub. During summer vacation, served as Facilities Planner for Digital Equipment Corporation and developed a long-term plan for future manufacturing capacity while assessing impact of technological changes on circuit requirements.

1971 to 1975   **Harvard College, Cambridge, Massachusetts**

Received Bachelor of Arts degree, cum laude. Majored in Economics. Worked full time during college to finance education and to gain management experience. Member of the Board of Directors and elected President of Harvard Student Agencies, Inc., the undergraduate business organization. Served as Manager of the Agencies' Laundry Division, a commercial laundry operation. In addition, served as Director of test project, which determined feasibility of utilizing student housing as hotel facilities, and worked as an accountant for chain of retail department stores.

School Affiliations

Harvard Alumni Association: Appointed Member of Human Resource Committee (1985 to present), Chairman of several subcommittees.

Harvard University: Business School and Undergraduate Reunion Committees, College Development Fund Volunteer and College Interviewer for inner-city applicants. Director of Harvard Student Agencies, Inc.

Don Bosco Tech H.S.: Member of Technical Counsel. Development and Scholarship Fund Committee Member.

Source: Corporate documents.

Exhibit 3   Michael F. Cronin--Portfolio Analysis as of June 30, 1991

Year of Initial Investment	Company	Total Investment	Cash Proceeds	Fair Value of Investment 6/30/91	Total Valuation
	Measured Investments				
1979	Crismar	$1,073	$1,313	$0	$ 1,313
1980	OPC/MASTER	1,300	3,204	0	3,204
1980	Harub	800	5,672	0	5,672
1981	ASC Investors	1,300	3,886	0	3,886
1981	Charter Foods	212	463	0	463
1981	Rapada	2,000	457	0	457
1981	Norris Industries	7,000	29,835	0	29,835
1981	Ohio Crane	2,066	2,601	0	2,601
1981	WGM Safety	4,800	13,967	0	13,967
1982	Purex	4,200	9,164	0	9,164
1982	Thermo-Serv	2,127	2,757	0	2,757
1983	Fairfield Pacific	404	981	0	981
1983	Cimflex Tech.	833	0	98	98
1983	FileNet	1,500	3,374	0	3,374
1983	Gem Products	4,000	9,676	0	9,676
1983	Harris Graphics	4,200	19,100	0	19,100
1983	Albany International	3,000	17,980	0	17,980
1983	Ramsay Health	5,274	4,202	4,413	8,615
1984	Quincy Shirt	72	682	0	682
1984	Design Pak	404	1,327	0	1,327
1985	N.E. Critical Care	1,000	6,400	0	6,400
1985	ATP	2,100	115	0	115
1985	Denny's	1,640	7,832	0	7,832
1985	Uniroyal	3,800	10,121	0	10,121
1986	American Medical Plans	2,000	1,433	0	1,433
1986	Oral Research	1,000	5,548	0	5,548
1986	Media Mat.	2,397	281	405	686
1987	Staples	1,573	3,856	0	3,856
1987	Stardent	850	0	100	100
1987	Garfinckels	2,500	137	0	137
1987	Arlington Corp.	1,800	2,201	0	2,201
1988	Wellfleet	1,707	0	7,375	7,375
1989	Ingear of California	1,019	25	0	25
33	Total matured investments	$69,951	$168,590	$12,391	$180,981
	Remaining Investments				
1987	Electro-Films	1,309	22	1,309	1,331
1988	Renal Treatment	3,573	812	3,323	4,135
1988	Mystic Health	2,178	239	2,178	2,417
1989	Micro Source CAD/CAM	313	270	53	323
1989	New Haven Mfg.	5,000	725	5,000	5,725
1989	Electronic Designs	2,000	0	2,000	2,000
1989	PETsMART	2,416	0	3,323	3,323
1989	Pacific Linen	2,000	0	2,000	2,000
1990	Cirrus Technologies	2,165	383	1,865	2,248
1990	Sfuzzi, Inc.	3,500	0	3,500	3,500
1991	Business Depot	286	0	286	286
11	Total remaining investments	$24,740	$ 2,451	$24,837	$ 27,288
44	*Grand total*	$94,691	$171,041	$37,228	$208,269

Exhibit 3 (continued)

I.

Mr. Cronin's portfolio valuation is based on actual cash flows and valuations as of June 1991 and shows an Internal Rate of Return of 36% compounded for the period 1979 through December 1991 for 44 direct investments.

II.

The portfolio valuation estimates realized Internal Rate of Return on the 33 deals that have been sold, written off, or have significant liquidity if it is a public stock. The Internal Rate of Return (1979-1991) equals 36% and consists of $70 million in investments with a value of $180 million.

III.

The portfolio segmented by industry is as follows:

Industries	Investment Cost ($ millions)		Valuation ($ millions)		Deals	
Industrial	$36.9	(39%)	$112.5	(54%)	12	(27%)
Service	7.4	(8)	16.1	(8)	4	(9)
Medical	14.0	(15)	23.0	(11)	5	(11)
Retail	14.9	(16)	21.0	(10)	8	(18)
Technology	10.3	(11)	14.3	(7)	7	(16)
NR/RE/Media	3.5	(4)	2.8	(1)	3	(7)
Consumer	7.6	(7)	18.6	(9)	5	(11)
Total	$94.7	(100%)	$208.3	(100%)	44	(100%)

IV.

The portfolio segmented by investment role is as follows:

Role[a]	Investment Cost ($ millions)		Valuation ($ millions)		Deals	
Lead	$43.4	(46%)	$ 65.8	(32%)	18	(41%)
Co-lead	19.4	(20)	54.7	(26)	9	(20)
Participant	31.9	(33)	87.8	(42)	17	(39)
Total	$94.7	(100%)	$208.3	(100%)	44	(100%)

Source: Corporate documents.

[a]Served on 13 boards of directors.

Exhibit 4   Michael P. Lazarus--Curriculum Vitae

EXPERIENCE

1986 to Present	**Montgomery Securities, San Francisco, California**

Montgomery Securities, founded in 1969, is a fully integrated and highly focused investment banking partnership.

1989 to Present

- *Managing Director*—Corporate Finance
- *Director* of the Private Placement Department
- *Member* of the Firm's Commitment Committee

1988·

- Admitted to the Partnership

1986

- Promoted to *Special Limited Partner*

- Montgomery is recognized as the market leader for arranging private equity for privately-held emerging growth companies in the United States.

- Responsibilities include: Origination, marketing, structuring and worldwide syndication of private equity placements
  — Responsible for the U.S. venture capital relationships
  — Responsible for the institutional investor relationships that service the private capital markets

During my eight-year career in the private capital markets, I have completed over 50 transactions for privately-held U.S. emerging growth companies serving the retailing/consumer, healthcare and technology industries. During my Montgomery tenure (5 years) my group has completed 23 transactions, raising approximately $330 million in equity capital. Six transactions to date have achieved liquidity (sale or public offering) resulting in capital gains to the institutional investors of over $275 million.

1983 to 1986   **Berkeley International, San Francisco, California**

Berkeley is an international financial institution which specializes in arranging development capital finance between non-U.S. institutional and corporate investors and U.S. later-stage, privately-held high technology companies. I was a member of the original senior management team which developed the firm from 1983 to 1986.

- *Principal*
  - **Statistics:**

	1983	1986
a. Revenues	$ 2,000,000	$ 10,000,000
b. Private Placement Financing	$50,000,000	$300,000,000
c. Employees	8	30
d. Offshore Funds	0	3
e. Structure	Privately held	Public-Quoted on the London Stock Exchange

- Structure/execution of partial sale of the firm to a leading English financial institution, Touche Remnant & Co.

- TR Berkeley Development Capital Limited—a Jersey, Channel Islands based offshore fund which raised $55,000,000 from approximately 30 U.K. financial institutions.

- Syndicated approximately $40,000,000 of private placement transactions for privately held U.S. high technology companies from non-U.S. institutional investors.

- Discretionary investment program—developed and raised $20,000,000 for U.S. investment opportunities from an Australian financial institution.

- Berkeley Technology Limited—floated the firm on the London Stock Exchange (Kleinwort Benson—Underwriters; De Zoete and Bevan—Brokers), $44,000,000 raised for the firm's own account.

- Berkeley Australia Development Capital Limited—a Jersey, Channel Islands based offshore fund which raised A$15,000,000 from approximately 10 Australian institutional and corporate investors.

- Management of financial operations/research staff (8), business plan preparation, due diligence reviews, negotiation of share purchase agreements, closings, research and monitoring of funded companies, representation at the board of directors level.

- Investor relations—extensive international travel with primary focus on servicing financial institutions in the United Kingdom and Australia, as well as development of relationships with financial institutions/corporations in Hong Kong, Singapore, Korea, New Zealand, Amsterdam and Switzerland.

1977 to 1983	**Price Waterhouse, San Francisco, California; London, England; Pittsburgh, Pennsylvania**
1982 to 1983·	• *International Tax Manager*, San Francisco, California; London, England
1980 to 1982	• *Assistant Manager*, London, England
	• Participated in the firm's U.S Tax International Program
1979 to 1989	• *Senior Tax Accountant*, Pittsburgh, Pennsylvania
1977 to 1979	• *Staff Accountant*, Pittsburgh, Pennsylvania

EDUCATION

1977 B.A., Grove City College, Grove City, Pennsylvania
1980 Certified Public Accountant

AFFILIATIONS

1984 NASD—Registered Representative
1984 NASD—Principal

Source: Corporate documents.

Exhibit 5   Michael P. Lazarus—Performance of Montgomery's Private Placement Portfolio as Agent ($ million)

Company	Type of Business	Amount Raised	Closing Date	Post-Money Valuation	Current or Exit Valuation
Micro Linear Corp. (private)[a]	Semiconductors	$ 15.0	1986	$ 42.0	$ 114.0
Teradata Corp. (NASDAQ)[b]	Computers	15.0	1986	85.6	511.5
AVIA, Inc. (acquired)	Consumer goods	15.0	1986	86.4	180.0
Scientific Computer (private)	Computers	15.0	1986	81.4	0.0
Oral Research Labs (acquired)	Consumer goods	9.0	1986	28.0	260.0
Tolerant Systems (private)[c]	Software	16.0	1987	32.4	32.4
Loredan Biomedicals (private)[c]	Healthcare products	6.7	1987	17.5	17.5
Conner Peripherals (NASDAQ)[b]	Disk drives	27.5	1987	130.7	820.8
GRiD Systems (acquired)	Computers	7.5	1987	58.1	60.0
SportsTown, Inc. (private)	Retailing	20.0	1988	37.1	37.1
Verax Corporation (private)[c,d]	Healthcare	13.0	1988	38.2	10.0
StrataCon (private)[c,e]	Telecommunications	7.3	1988	54.7	100.0
Toddler U. Inc. (private)[c]	Consumer products	8.0	1989	59.0	59.0
Pacific Linen (private)[c]	Retailing	13.0	1989	37.0	37.0
Total Pharmaceutical Care (NASDAQ)	Healthcare services	10.0	1989	34.0	69.5
MasPar Computer (private)[c,e]	Computers	15.5	1990	66.0	120.0
NetFRAME Systems (private)[c]	Telecommunications	12.0	1990	105.0	105.0
Sfuzzi, Inc. (private)[c]	Retailing	7.0	1990	28.0	28.0
Damark (private)[c]	Mail order retailing	12.0	1991	32.0	32.0
Chevys, Inc.	Retailing	17.1	1991	42.5	42.5
Paul Capital Partners, L.P. (private)[c]	Financial services	63.1	1991	63.0	63.0
Resna Industries (private)[c]	Environmental services	6.5	1991	41.6	41.6
Total		$331.2		$1,200.2	$2,740.9

[a]In registration for an initial public offering.
[b]Institutional investors liquidated the bulk of their holdings through a secondary offering.
[c]Valuation at original cost.
[d]Company currently undergoing a restructuring.
[e]Subsequent private financing completed.

Exhibit 5 (continued)

Capital Gains Analysis: Transactions Realized to Date (includes sales, IPOs and write-offs; $ million)

Valuation	Exit	Initial Cost Basis	Capital Gains	Company Valuation
Teradata Corporation	$511.5	$85.6	$15.0	$ 89.6
AVIA, Inc.	180.0	86.4	15.0	31.3
Oral Research Labs[a]	260.0	28.0	9.0	49.9
Conner Peripherals	820.8	130.8	27.5	172.7
GRiD Systems[b]	60.0	58.1	7.5	11.5
Total Pharmaceutical Care	69.5	34.0	10.0	20.4
Scientific Computer Systems	0.0	81.4	15.0	0.0
Total				$375.4
Cost basis				99.0
Capital gain to date				$276.4

Source: Corporate documents.

As of July 1, 1991.

[a]Factors in interim round of financing.
[b]The GRiD acquisition included a $0.50 earn out over two years.

Exhibit 6   Terms of the Offering

The following is a summary of certain information relating to the Partnership and a parallel domestic partnership which may be organized in the United States (the "Domestic Fund"). As used in this Memorandum, except where the context requires otherwise, the term "Partnership" shall collectively refer to the Partnership and the Domestic Fund. The information contained herein is qualified in all respects by the terms of the Limited Partnership Agreement and Subscription Agreement of the Partnership, copies of which will be made available to all investors meeting the suitability requirements set forth herein.

Securities	An aggregate of US$75 million of Interests in the Partnership are being offered. Subscriptions for the Interests will be accepted only from accredited, sophisticated investors who satisfy certain suitability standards. Mercury Asset Management plc ("MAM") has, to date, purchased US$500,000 of Interests and has committed to purchase US$24.5 million of Interests.
Takedowns	Committed Limited Partner capital will be taken down in installments at such times, and in such amounts, as the Offshore General Partner determines. The Offshore General Partner shall give at least 15 days prior notice of any requested takedown. All takedowns will be in U.S. dollars.
Commitment Period	All capital commitments not taken down within five years of the final closing date will be released from any further obligation to the Partnership.
Term	The term of the Partnership will be 11 years from the final closing date, with an option on the part of the Offshore General Partner to extend for up to three successive one-year periods.
General Partners	The General Partners of the Partnership are Weston Presidio Capital Management, L.P., a Delaware limited partnership (the "Domestic General Partner"), and WPC Offshore Management N.V., a corporation organized under the laws of the Netherlands Antilles (the "Offshore General Partner"). The general partners of the Domestic General Partner and the sole shareholders of the Offshore General Partner are Michael P. Lazarus and Michael F. Cronin (collectively, the "Principals"). As used herein, the term "General Partners" refers generally to both the Offshore General Partner and the Domestic General Partner. The investment management of the Partnership is exclusively vested in the Domestic General Partner, with all other management functions of the Partnership being vested in the Offshore General Partner.
Investment by General Partners/Special Limited Partner	The General Partners will contribute cash to the Partnership in an amount equal to 1% of the capital contributions of all Partners. The timing of these contributions will coincide with takedowns of Limited Partner contributions.

MAM is the sole "Special Limited Partner" of the Partnership. MAM, a public company listed on the London Stock Exchange, has approximately $65 billion under management and is 75% owned by THE S.G. WARBURG GROUP, plc.

MAM, in its capacity as a Special Limited Partner, will contribute cash to the Partnership in an amount equal to .5% of the capital contributions of all Partners. The timing of its contributions will coincide with takedowns of Limited Partner contributions.

Management Fee

The Partnership has entered into a Service Contract with Weston Presidio Management Company, Inc. (the "Service Company"), a Delaware corporation equally and wholly-owned by the Principals, pursuant to which the Partnership will pay the Service Company an annual fee equal to 2% of committed Partnership capital, with such fee being payable quarterly in advance. Such fee shall be payable for, among other things, services provided to the Partnership in identifying, investing in, monitoring and providing assistance to emerging growth companies in the United States. In addition, such fee shall be periodically adjusted on the basis of the Consumer Price Index. Fees payable pursuant to the Service Contract shall be treated as expenses of the Partnership.

Organizational Expenses

All organizational expenses will be paid by the Partnership and will be allocated to all Partners in proportion to their capital contributions.

Distributions

Distributions will be made at the discretion of the Offshore General Partner. Distributions, to the extent made, will be as follows:

(a) First, 100% to all Partners (including the General Partners) in proportion to capital contributions, until such time that the Partners receive an amount equal to their capital contributions;

(b) Next, 100% to the Limited Partners until such time that they receive a simple 9% per annum return on their invested and unreturned capital;

(c) Next, 100% to the General Partners and MAM until such time that they receive 25% of the aggregate preferential return distributed to Limited Partners pursuant to subpart (b) above (the effect of which is to achieve an 80/20 allocation of cumulative distributions); and

(d) Thereafter, all remaining distributions shall be made (i) 80% to the Limited Partners and (ii) 20% to the General Partners and MAM. Final distributions upon Partnership liquidation will be adjusted in accordance with capital accounts.

Allocations of Income, Gain and Loss

Allocations of Partnership income, gain and loss for tax and financial purposes will be made in a manner which will be consistent with, and will give effect to, the distribution procedures outlined above.

Reduction of Distributions to General Partners

Fifty percent of all directors' fees, consulting fees or similar compensation paid to the General Partners (or their affiliates) will generally reduce the amount of distributions otherwise payable to the General Partners as outlined in the above distribution procedures.

Advisory Committee

Representatives of the Limited Partners will be nominated by the Domestic General Partner and approved by a majority in interest of the Limited Partners to serve on an Advisory Committee. MAM will be represented on this Committee. This Committee will meet at least semi-annually to review investment valuations, provide advice and counsel as requested, and resolve any potential conflicts of interest.

ERISA Matters

The General Partners intend to comply with the "venture capital operating company" exception under the U.S. Department of Labor plan asset regulation (the "DOL Regulation") so that assets of the Partnership will not be treated as "plan assets" of Limited Partners subject to ERISA ("ERISA Partners"). The General Partners will use their best efforts to ensure that they and the Partnership will comply with ERISA provisions that are, or may become, applicable to any of them. An ERISA Partner will have a limited right to withdraw from the Partnership if its continued participation would violate ERISA or any assets of the Partnership would constitute "plan assets" of the ERISA Partner under the DOL Regulation.

Default

Upon any failure of a Limited Partner to contribute any portion of its capital commitment when called by the General Partners in accordance with the Limited Partnership Agreement, that Limited Partner will be in default. A defaulting Limited Partners will be subject to various economic penalties, all to the extent specified in the Limited Partnership Agreement.

Parallel Partnership

The Domestic Fund, if established, will be organized on terms and conditions substantially identical to those of the Partnership for U.S. investors who choose not to participate directly in the Partnership. If established, the Domestic Fund and the Partnership will pursue identical investment policies, co-invest in portfolio companies pro rata based on the amount of capital each has available for investment, and share proportionately all fees and expenses payable by each.

Transferability

Transfer of Interests is permitted only with the consent of the General Partners. A right of first refusal in favor of the Limited Partners will exist with respect to any such transfer.

Financial Advisor

S.G. Warburg Securities is the financial advisor to the Partnership and will be paid an advisory fee at closing by the Partnership. S.G. Warburg Securities is a wholly-owned subsidiary of THE S.G. WARBURG GROUP, plc

Source: Corporate documents.

Exhibit 7   Summary of the Limited Partnership Agreement

Liability of Limited Partners

Limited Partners will not be liable for any debts or bound by any obligations to the Partnership, except that they will be obligated to make their agreed-upon capital contributions and to return any part of their capital contributions returned to them in violation of the Partnership Agreement or the laws of the Netherlands Antilles and will be responsible for their pro rata share of offering expenses paid or incurred during any fiscal year of the Partnership.

Management and Control

The management and control of the Partnership shall be vested exclusively in the Offshore General Partner, except that the Domestic General Partner shall be responsible solely for carrying on the investment activities of the Partnership.

Term

The Partnership's term will be 11 years (through July 11, 2002), with provisions for extensions for up to three one-year periods by the Offshore General Partner (up to a maximum term ending July 11, 2005). The Partnership shall terminate earlier than set forth above upon the withdrawal of the Domestic General Partner or, unless the then General partners and at least 75% of interest of the Limited Partners otherwise agree, upon the withdrawal of the Offshore General Partners. In addition, Limited Partners constituting at least 75% in interest of the Limited Partners may dissolve the Partnership if the then-existing general partners of the Domestic General Partner cease to be general partners of the General Partner or die, become bankrupt, insane or permanently incapacitated.

Transferability of Limited Partnership Interests

The Interests are not assignable without the prior written consent of the Offshore General Partner and shall only be made upon receipt of an opinion of counsel for the Partnership that such assignment will not result in the Partnership, any General Partner or the Service Company being subjected to any additional regulatory requirements, a violation of applicable law or the Partnership Agreement, the Partnership being classified as an association taxable as a corporation, or the Partnership being deemed terminated pursuant to Section 708 of the Code, or pursuant to Netherlands Antilles law.

Right of First Refusal

Any Limited Partner which desires to effect a sale for value of its Interest shall afford the other Limited Partners a right of first refusal to purchase the Interest proposed to be sold in accordance with such procedures as the Offshore General Partner shall specify.

ERISA Withdrawal Right

An ERISA Partner will have a limited right to withdraw from the Partnership if it shall obtain and deliver to the General Partners an opinion of counsel to the effect that the ERISA Partner's continued participation would materially violate ERISA or any assets of the Partnership would constitute "plan assets" of the ERISA Partner under the DOL Regulation.

Valuation

Generally, all securities and assets of the Partnership will be valued by the Domestic General Partner, subject to the annual review by the Advisory Committee. In general, freely-tradeable securities for which market quotations are readily available will be valued at the last trade on the exchange where they are primarily traded or, if not traded on an exchange, generally at the last reported sale prices (if reported on the NASDAQ National Market System) or the average of the bid prices or sale prices last quoted by an established over-the-counter quotation service (if not reported on the NASDAQ National Market System). All other securities and assets will be valued by the Domestic General Partner after considering pertinent factors and appropriate information and data.

Indemnification

In general, a General Partner, each general and limited partner of a General Partner, each member of a Partnership Committee (including members of the Advisory Committee) and each director, officer, employee or agent of the Service Company is entitled to indemnification by the Partnership against any costs and expenses incurred by him in connection with any proceeding as a result of his serving in any of the foregoing capacities or having served as a director, officer, employee or agent of any other organization in which the Partnership may have an interest, so long as a court shall not have determined that such costs or expenses resulted primarily from the gross negligence or willful misconduct of such person. In addition, the partnership may pay the expenses incurred by an indemnified party in a proceeding in advance of its final disposition, provided such party undertakes to repay such expenses if he is adjudicated to be not entitled to indemnification.

Potential Conflicts of Interest

Without the consent of at least 75% in interest of the Limited Partners, neither the Domestic General Partner nor the general partners of the Domestic General Partner may organize or act as general partner to any entity (other than the Domestic Fund) similar in purposes and operation to the Partnership until at least 75% of Partners' capital contributions have been invested or contractually committed to be invested by the Partnership. No such consent will be required, however, after at least 75% of the Partners' capital contributions have been so invested or committed for investment.

Source: Corporate documents.

6

ARCH Venture Partners: November 1993

Steve Lazarus opened the final version of the initial public offering prospectus for Illinois Superconductor Corporation with a feeling of satisfaction. This company, which had just gone public with a market capitalization of $38 million, was the first company in ARCH Venture Partners' portfolio to be successfully harvested. Over the past seven years, Lazarus had built up a technology transfer organization and venture capital fund focusing on the commercialization of technologies from the University of Chicago and Argonne National Laboratory. After developing a relationship of trust with researchers and administrators and systemizing licensing procedures, Lazarus had raised a $9 million venture fund in 1989. This fund had invested in one dozen firms and was proving increasingly successful in transforming academic research into new businesses.

Lazarus glanced down to his desk, where the offering memorandum for ARCH Venture Partners II, L.P., lay. This new partnership, whose intended size was $30 million, would allow ARCH to expand both the scale and scope of its activities. Not only could the development of existing portfolio firms be nurtured and more technologies at the University of Chicago and Argonne commercialized, but the new fund would also enable ARCH to extend its reach to other research organizations. The proposed new agreement, however, would alter the nature of his relationship with the institutions with which he had worked most closely in recent years. Furthermore, the risks and rewards that he and his partners—Keith Crandell and Robert Nelsen—faced would be dramatically shifted. As he glanced over the Chicago skyline, Lazarus wondered how these changes would affect the future of the organization that he had built.

THE COMMERCIALIZATION OF FEDERALLY FUNDED RESEARCH[1]

Since World War II, the federal government has financed a significant fraction of the R&D performed in the United States. For instance, in 1993, the federal government paid for $68 billion out the total of $161 billion of R&D performed in the United States. Among the largest recipients of these funds were the more than 700 federal laboratories,

This case was prepared by Josh Lerner. Copyright © 1995 by the President and Fellows of Harvard College. Harvard Business School case 295-105.

[1] For a more detailed discussion of Federal technology transfer policy, see "The Scripps Research Institution: November 1993 (Abridged)," Harvard Business School Case No. 9-295-068.

which spent $25 billion of federal funds on R&D. By contrast, approximately $21 billion was spent on R&D at universities, of which 55% was funded by the federal government.

Universities were responsible for the operations of several of the largest national laboratories. For instance, the University of California operated the Los Alamos, Lawrence Livermore, and Lawrence Berkeley Laboratories; the Massachusetts Institute of Technology, Lincoln Laboratories; and the University of Chicago, Argonne National Laboratory. The operation of these laboratories was assigned to contractors in the hopes of escaping civil service and other burdensome government regulations. But most agencies, such as the U.S. Department of Energy, had created extensive regulatory guidelines that severely limited the flexibility of contractors in managing these laboratories. As a result, decision making at these contractor-operated facilities was often painfully slow, as contractors' recommendations were reviewed by several layers of federal officials.

In the aftermath of World War II, when many of the national laboratories were established and the federal government sharply increased its funding of academic science, the relationship between research and commercial applications was extensively discussed. A consensus emerged that economic benefits from federally funded research would naturally occur through spin-offs, as technologies found applications without governmental interference. As a result, the federal government devoted little effort to encouraging the diffusion of these technologies. In fact, the major concern of federal officials was ensuring that these economic benefits were divided in a fair manner, which they attempted to guarantee by having the government retain in most cases the ownership of the technologies it funded.

As concerns about America's competitive position deepened during the 1970s, the procedures for the transfer of federally funded technologies were repeatedly criticized. It was increasingly realized that the conversion of academic science into commercial products was a difficult and costly process and that private firms would not invest in developing these technologies unless they were confident that they would be able to achieve a satisfactory return. As a result, Congress passed two seminal bills in 1980, the Stevenson–Wydler Innovation Act and the Bayh–Dole Act. These acts, as amended in 1982, 1984, and 1986, fundamentally changed the landscape of technology transfer. Universities and other research institutions were given the right to patent technologies from federally funded research and to commercialize them as they saw fit (subject to a variety of restrictions on licensing to foreign organizations and regarding conflict of interest). National laboratories were encouraged to establish Cooperative Research and Development Agreements (CRADAs) with industry to commercialize their research.

These changes addressed some of the most substantial barriers to technology transfer, particularly at universities. For instance, universities had become more aggressive in patenting discoveries since passage of this Act.[2] At the same time, it was clear that the technology transfer system in 1993 was far from perfect. Although academic laboratories located near centers of venture capital activity were frequently scrutinized by potential investors, in many other regions the commercialization process was haphazard. This was particularly true in technologies other than the life sciences. Furthermore, universities were only receiving a small fraction of the wealth that their research was creating. Even the most successful university technology transfer programs, such as Stanford and M.I.T., generated revenues that were only a small fraction of their annual research bud-

---

[2] For instance, in 1965, U.S. universities were awarded a total of 96 patents; in 1992, they were awarded almost 1500. These trends are discussed in Rebecca Henderson, Adam Jaffe, and Manuel Trajtenberg, "Universities as a source of commercial technology: A detailed analysis of university patenting, 1965–1988" *Review of Economics and Statistics* 80 (1998): 119–127

gets.[3] In many instances where technologies had been licensed, it was clear that universities licensing officials had not succeeded in driving very hard bargains.

The universities' efforts to capture a greater share of these profits, however, had been met with considerable ambivalence. For instance, in 1993 the University of California abandoned an effort to create a $100 million technology transfer fund. The effort disintegrated in the face of criticism by scientists, who charged that it would compromise academic pursuits by emphasizing profit-making, and local venture capitalists, who expressed reservations about the impact of an intermediary organization on the commercialization process.[4]

The situation associated with commercialization of research in the national laboratories was much grimmer. Although the number of CRADAs in the national laboratories was increasing, in many cases firms found them to be of little use because they were extremely difficult to negotiate and implement. The economic impact of those CRADAs that had been signed had also been disappointing. Corporations frequently discovered that Laboratory scientists—accustomed to working on large defense-related projects—had little understanding of the process of commercial innovation. In some instances, it appeared that federal contractors had entered into CRADA agreements simply to generate good-will with federal officials, which they hoped would benefit them in subsequent program funding decisions.[5]

In a number of cases, the CRADA program had led to unexpected costs for both the corporate sponsors and the laboratories.[6] For instance, congressional committees had criticized firms for receiving exclusive rights to federally funded technologies through CRADAs. In other cases, firms had discovered that the intellectual property which they brought to the partnership was carelessly diffused by federal officials, despite assurances of confidentiality. This program had also stirred concerns within the laboratories. Collaborative relationships between researchers with different CRADA sponsors had sometimes been dampened by their sponsors' rivalry. Laboratory researchers had been frustrated by their failure to receive promised cash payments as a reward for successfully developing commercial technologies.[7]

THE CONCEPTION OF ARCH

The Argonne National Laboratory/University of Chicago (ARCH) Development Corporation was established in 1986. Argonne National Laboratory was a national laboratory operated for the Department of Energy (and its predecessor organization, the

[3] Total royalty receipts by academic institutions from technology licenses in 1992 were about $270 million. While this was a vast increase over a decade earlier, it represented only 1.3% of the academic research spending in this year. (See Lou Berneman and Ashley Stevens, "Technology Transfer and Economic Development," Presentation at the Association of University Technology Managers Annual Meeting, 1994.)

[4] This case is discussed in Udayan Gupta, "Marketing Ideas: Hungry for Funds, Universities Embrace Technology Transfer," *Wall Street Journal,* June 30, 1994, pp. A1, A5.

[5] For a discussion of many of these barriers, see Lewis M. Branscomb, "National Laboratories: The Search for New Missions and Structures," in Lewis M. Branscomb, *Empowering Technology: Implementing a U.S. Strategy* (Cambridge, MA: MIT Press, 1993), pp. 103–34.

[6] Several firms' experiences with the CRADA program are documented in U.S. Congress, Office of Technology Assessment, *Defense Conversion: Redirecting R&D* (OTA-ITE-552) (Washington, D.C., Government Printing Office, 1993).

[7] These problems are discussed in U.S. General Accounting Office, *Technology Transfer: Barriers Limit Royalty Sharing's Effectiveness* (GAO/RCED-93-6) (Washington, D.C., U.S. General Accounting Office, 1992).

U.S. Atomic Energy Commission) by the University of Chicago since 1946. In 1993, it employed about 4500 people and had a $500 million budget. Among its areas of expertise were advanced energy systems, hazardous waste detection and cleanup, advanced materials (especially superconducting materials), and high-performance instrumentation. At the end of 1993, Argonne's Advanced Computer Research Facility was the largest center developing software for parallel and massively parallel computers; its Advanced Photon Source, under construction at the time, was to be the world's brightest source of X-rays.

The University of Chicago was a private institution whose researchers had been awarded over 50 Nobel Prizes. In 1993, the University's research budget was over $110 million, and its faculty numbered about 1,200. The University had pioneered a variety of commercially important discoveries, including the first sustained nuclear reaction, the isolation of proinsulin, and the invention of the scanning-transmission electron microscope. The University's record in profiting from these inventions, however, had been much poorer. Among the most conspicuous failures was erythropoietin, which was first isolated at the University of Chicago but not patented. Amgen generated revenue of $575 million in 1993 from this drug, which it marketed as Epogen. (Erythropoietin was also sold by Johnson & Johnson.) The University received no royalties from these sales; nor did it receive equity in Amgen or Johnson & Johnson.

A key role in the conception of ARCH was played by two men: Dr. Walter Massey, who at the time was the University's Vice President for Research and responsible for the operations of Argonne National Laboratory (and who subsequently became Director of the National Science Foundation), and Alan Schriesheim, the Director of Argonne and former General Manager of the Exxon Engineering Technology Department. These men fleshed out the concept for ARCH in conjunction with a number of University trustees, among whom were Kingman Douglass, an investment banker and civic leader; Robert Halperin, President of the Raychem Corporation; Arthur Kelly, a private investor and former President of LaSalle Steel Corporation; and Richard Morrow, the chairman and CEO of Amoco Corporation. Hanna Gray, then President of the University of Chicago, was also a strong supporter of the ARCH concept.

The leaders had several motivations in creating this organization. First, of course, the University stood to generate revenue from licensing revenues and equity in spin-off firms. Second, the effort would contribute to the regional economy by creating new enterprises and jobs. This was especially true because at the time, the bulk of the early-stage venture capital investments—even by venture funds based in Chicago—were devoted to firms based on the East and West Coasts. Finally, Massey believed that ARCH could have a broader impact on the way that scientists looked at business. As Massey noted:

> We really had in mind changing the culture of both institutions. The biggest problem was, how do you capture research without having the scientist feel he or she is being directed?[8]

It was hoped that ARCH could address these multiple goals. Consequently, in late 1986, ARCH Development Corporation was created as a separate, private, not-for-profit corporation affiliated with Argonne and the University of Chicago.

A critical task for the committee was to recruit an appropriate head for ARCH. It was crucial to find an individual who combined familiarity with private-sector practices with an ability to operate in an environment governed by federal regulations and the for-

---

[8] Ann T. Palmer, "Collaboration Turns Research into Jobs," *Chicago Tribune,* June 6, 1993, pp. C1, C3.

mal and informal constraints that characterize academic institutions. The man selected as ARCH's head in late 1986, Steven Lazarus, had a background that spanned both the public and private sectors. A graduate of Dartmouth College and Harvard Business School, Lazarus had served in the U.S. Navy for 21 years. Between 1972 and 1974, he had been Deputy Assistant Secretary of Commerce for East-West Trade. In 1974, Lazarus joined Baxter International. He spent 13 years in this organization, rising to Senior Vice President for Technology and Group Vice President of the Health Care Services Group. (Lazarus's background is summarized in Exhibit 1.) The leaders also recruited a blue-ribbon board of directors, drawn from the University's trustees and other Chicago business leaders. The members of the board are listed in Exhibit 2.

THE IMPLEMENTATION OF ARCH

First Steps

Lazarus had begun with a small office in Walker Museum, the home of the University's Graduate School of Business, and a secretary. He had a broad mandate to develop both the licensing of the University's technology and the promulgation of spin-off companies, but he had few resources. Lazarus consequently sought to implement in stages his charge to develop ARCH.

Among his first steps was to develop an understanding of ARCH's mission on the part of researchers and administrators. Technology transfer organizations such as ARCH initially often encounter some resistance from researchers, for scientists fear that the outsiders will seek to influence the direction of their research. In addition, they may be concerned that they will not be given a chance to be involved in—and to profit from—the commercialization of their discoveries. At the opposite extreme, scientists may push to have favorite projects funded without an understanding of the demands of the commercial marketplace.

The support of the top University and Laboratory administrators was critical in overcoming initial concerns from the organizations' legal staffs. The potential for profits from these enterprises created, in some eyes, the "appearance of a conflict of interest." Their concerns centered on two areas. The first related to the licensing process. Particularly with respect to the Laboratory, the lawyers argued for extensively publicizing technological discoveries and then soliciting formal proposals for nonexclusive licenses. Their concerns were based in part on the extensive scrutiny of earlier efforts to transfer technology from the federal laboratories. For instance, Martin Marietta, which operated Oak Ridge National Laboratory, had been criticized by the U.S. General Accounting Office and Representative John Dingell of Michigan. Marietta had established a venture capital subsidiary, the Tennessee Innovation Center, which sought to establish new businesses around Oak Ridge. This unit had invested in a business that subsequently received an exclusive license to develop an Oak Ridge technology. After congressional criticism, the contractor had been forced to restructure the relationship with its affiliate in a financially unattractive way.[9] While acknowledging these concerns, Lazarus argued that without rapid diffusion and exclusive licenses,

---

[9] For discussions of these issues, see U.S. General Accounting Office, *Energy Management: Problems with Martin Marietta Energy Systems' Affiliate Relationships* (GAO/RCED-87-70) (Washington, D.C., U.S. General Accounting Office, 1987), and U.S. General Accounting Office, *Energy Management: DOE/Martin Marietta Earnings Limitation Agreement* (GAO/RCED-87-147) (Washington, D.C., U.S. General Accounting Office, 1987).

many technologies developed at the University and Laboratory would be unlikely to be commercialized.

A second area of legal concern was the nature of the relationships between Laboratory researchers and spin-off companies. Although researchers were allowed to serve as directors of and consultants to spin-off companies, they were not allowed to hold equity in these enterprises. Lazarus argued forcefully that the researchers needed to benefit directly from these investments. He worked out an arrangement where ARCH, which would invest in spin-off firms, would distribute to the involved researchers 25% of any capital gains. In addition, he pushed for researchers to receive as large a share of royalties as possible, not diminished by any deductions for overhead (as had been the case at other institutions).

A second step was to create a relationship with the University of Chicago's Graduate School of Business (GSB). Under the leadership of Lazarus and GSB Dean John Gould, a program was set up to allow first- and second-year MBA candidates to work with new enterprises as "ARCH Associates." Two dozen students were selected annually. These students typically had previously received technical undergraduate and graduate degrees, and had several years of work experience. The students had to commit to a minimum of 10 hours of work per week. The bulk of the students' work involved evaluating newly disclosed ideas, in an effort to determine whether the innovations were commercially feasible. Others worked directly with portfolio companies. Reflecting the magnitude of this effort and its contribution to the education process, Lazarus was appointed an Associate Dean at the GSB.

Out of this effort, Lazarus recruited two partners to assist him in this project, Keith Crandell and Robert T. Nelsen. Both men were working on their MBA degrees at the GSB. The backgrounds of the partners are described in Exhibit 1. (In addition, they were joined by Thomas L. Churchwell, who left ARCH in 1991 to become the CEO of Calgene Fresh, a wholly owned subsidiary of a publicly traded biotechnology company.)

A third step was the raising of a venture fund. Lazarus realized that to maximize the return to the University, he should be developing new businesses in addition to simply licensing technologies to existing firms. When technology transfer officials at schools such as M.I.T. identify an innovation that appears to be the foundation for a new enterprise, they contact local venture capitalists with whom they have a long-standing relationship. (M.I.T. has invested in venture capital funds since the 1940s, and many alumni work for venture organizations or venture-backed firms.) ARCH did not have that luxury. The venture capital community in Chicago was a relatively modest one and did virtually no early-stage investing in local companies during the 1980s. Consequently, Lazarus realized that ARCH would need to raise a fund of its own. The ARCH partners succeeded in raising a total of $9 million. The limited partners included the University of Chicago, State Farm Insurance, and two venture firms. The sole general partner was ARCH Development Corporation. The structure of the ARCH organizations after the establishment of this partnership is depicted in Exhibit 3.

The Technology Transfer Process

With these elements in place, ARCH refined its technology transfer process.[10] Scientists who make discoveries at the University or Argonne must follow a set procedure. If the invention is "useful," and not identical to something that already exists, they must inform

---

[10] This section is based on ARCH Development Corporation, *ARCH Manual of Procedure* (Chicago: ARCH Development Corporation, 1993).

the University of the discovery. Such an invention might be a particle detector, a medical device, a chemical compound, or a computer program. The University is able to require such disclosures because, like other research institutions, all patentable discoveries and copyrightable software are property of the University.

The principal investigator of the project making the discovery must fill out an invention disclosure form. This describes the nature of the discovery, when the discovery was made, and whether the researcher plans to publish an article about the discovery.[11] The disclosure forms are reviewed by ARCH. If the discovery appears to have commercial promise, ARCH takes title to the invention. In this case, it assigns a professional staff member and a graduate student to the project. If ARCH refuses to develop the technology, the ownership is returned to the University, which will often formally release the technology to the federal agency that provided the funds for the discovery or to the inventor.

If the technology appears to be promising, ARCH officials must then decide how it will be commercialized. Typically, an ARCH associate will interview the principal investigator, in an attempt to assess the value of the invention. The examination will include reviews of the trade press, consultations with academic and industry experts, and limited surveys of potential customers. Among the questions that the associate seeks to answer are:

- the extent to which the discovery can be protected through patents or other means.
- the difficulties that will be encountered in scaling up the manufacture of the product or process.
- the potential for market acceptance and the extent of likely competition.
- the likelihood of rapid obsolescence.

If the product appears to be promising after these tests, ARCH at this point initiates the process of seeking intellectual property protection. Because seeking patent protection can be very costly, particularly if foreign protection is sought as well, ARCH's partners typically ask their outside patent counsel to provide written estimates of the cost of filing patent applications in advance. In this way, they can better balance the costs and benefits of seeking protection.

At this point, ARCH must select between licensing the technology to an existing firm or using it as the basis for a new company. In very few cases, the choice is limited, because a company has retained the right to license all technology in a given area in exchange for funding academic research. ARCH relies on a variety of contacts to identify potential licensees. Most important are informal ties, whether those of Lazarus, his partners, the ARCH associates (typically with former employers), former associates, or ARCH's board. ARCH staff will also pursue targeted contacts with firms where no previous relationship exists, but these have generally proven to be less successful. Once a potential licensee has been identified, ARCH will provide the licensee with an option for up to six months, during which the workability and patent legitimacy of the new technology can be evaluated. The potential licensee will sign an agreement that restricts it from using the technology internally or disclosing it to others during this interval. The potential licensee will pay an up-front fee for this option, as well as monthly "milestone"

---

[11] The latter two pieces of information are important to ARCH because of the nature of the patenting process. Patents must typically be applied for within one year of a discovery. Patents must be applied for prior to the publication of a discovery in virtually all countries aside from the United States. Because ARCH frequently sought European and Japanese patent protection for discoveries, it needed to initiate filings prior to the scientists' publications.

payments while the technology is inspected. These payments will be higher if the firm insists that no other potential licensees be allowed to examine the technology while the option is in force.

If the potential licensee decides to license the technology, an agreement must then be negotiated. A crucial issue is the extent of exclusivity in the arrangement: that is, whether the University will be able to license the technology to others. The more innovative the discovery, the more the licensee is likely to want exclusive rights to the technology. ARCH naturally is reluctant to provide exclusive licenses but will do so if the nature of the invention and the goodness of fit between the licensee and licensor warrant it (and if the compensation is sufficiently attractive). In some cases, the licensee will be granted exclusive rights only for a specific product market or geographic region.

A second critical issue is the structure of the compensation to the University. These payments take three forms. *Up-front license fees* are nonrefundable payments at the time of the signing of the agreement. *Milestone payments* are payments made at specified times in the future, or else conditionally upon the achievement of certain technological thresholds. *Royalties* have ranged from 0.2% to 15% of the sales realized by the product. In many cases, the agreements specify a minimum level of royalties, to provide an incentive for the licensee to develop a product. Often, smaller capital-constrained firms will agree to higher royalties in exchange for reduced up-front payments. Proceeds from the licensing revenues are split in three ways: 40% goes directly to the University, 35% to cover ARCH's operations, and 25% directly to the inventors.

Licenses signed by ARCH have several clauses that protect the University. First, the University seeks explicitly to protect itself against any claims resulting from these licenses. The licensor must indemnify the University against any product liability actions and must acknowledge that the University has made no guarantees that the product will be commercially successful. Typically, the University will only license the patents and not agree to transfer the informal "know-how" associated with the patents. If the licensee wishes to obtain access to informal know-how, it must undertake a consulting agreement directly with the researcher. The University does review the consulting agreements but not the licensing arrangements. ARCH usually will also insist on a confidentiality clause. By agreeing to this clause, the company acknowledges that the University researchers are free to publish all results from their research, though ARCH and the researchers agree to keep all documents and reports from the licensee confidential.

In many cases, however, ARCH staff believes that the technology can be more effectively commercialized through a new enterprise. As ARCH's policy manual states, "ARCH begins with the hypothesis that creating a new enterprise can be a more effective approach to commercialization than traditional licensing."[12] A licensed technology can often end up "on the shelf" at a major corporation, particularly if it encounters resistance from research staff championing an internally developed alternative. Furthermore, the rewards to ARCH, the researchers, and the region as a whole are likely to be more substantial when a new firm commercializes the technology. These benefits often outweigh the greater time and energy required to commercialize a discovery in this manner.

When the ARCH staff identifies a technology that potentially forms the basis of a new business, it is typically in a very early stage of development. ARCH will provide early seed financing to develop the technology and a business plan. The funds provided will be kept to a minimum. The plan will then be presented to the ARCH executive committee (which includes both ARCH officials and members of its board) for a review.

---

[12] ARCH Development Corporation, *ARCH Manual of Procedure* (Chicago: ARCH Development Corporation, 1993), p. 30.

If the decision is made to proceed, outside venture funds will also be contacted regarding a possible co-investment. ARCH managers will also push the company to seek non-equity sources of funds, including funds allocated under the U.S. government's Small Business Innovation Research Program, the U.S. Department of Commerce's Advanced Technology Program, and the State of Illinois' Technology Advancement and Development Act. ARCH staff members will typically serve as temporary general managers, but they will attempt to rapidly replace themselves with recruited entrepreneurs.

From this point forward, ARCH's role resembles that of a typical venture capital fund: consulting informally with management, attending board meetings, and making decisions about whether the firm should receive second- and later-round financings. If the company's venture backers decide to terminate the firm, the technology will revert back to ARCH, who will then seek to license it. ARCH relies more heavily on external legal counsel than most other venture organizations, in order to address the danger of conflicts of interest. For instance, a company funded by ARCH may wish to license a technology developed at the University that ARCH is assigned to license. The early involvement of outside counsel helps ensure that portfolio firms follow the same procedures as others.

The Record to Date

As of November 1993, the companies begun by ARCH had encompassed a broad range of technologies. Many of the companies were traditional outgrowths of the University's research programs. An example was NiOptics Corporation. Researchers in the University's Physics Department developed a method of managing light with several times the efficiency and brightness of traditional lens-based optics. An immediate application was the development of back-lights for the screens of color laptop computers. Other sources of business ideas were less traditional. For instance, Everyday Learning Corporation, a publisher of elementary school mathematics textbooks, grew out of the University's School Mathematics Project, which attempted to design new methods to teach math to grade-school students.

Of the one dozen firms funded by ARCH, the fundamental technology had originated in eight cases at the University of Chicago. Four had been originated at Argonne National Laboratories. The smaller number of companies to have been spun out of Argonne reflected the difficulty of the technology transfer process there. ARCH officials estimated that the spin-off of a new business, which typically took six to twelve months at a private university, consumed two years at a national laboratory. Brief descriptions of ARCH portfolio companies are reported in Exhibit 4.

ARCH's greatest success to date has been an Argonne spin-off, Illinois Superconductor Corp. This Evanston, Illinois firm went public in late October 1993 in an offering underwritten by Gruntal and Co. At the time of the offering, the company had licensed 13 superconducting patents (or patent applications) from Argonne and Northwestern University. In addition, it had been awarded one patent and had four applications pending. This firm had used these discoveries to develop several promising technologies. These included a process that allowed high-temperature superconductors to be applied to surfaces through a process similar to painting. Previously, superconducting film had been applied through chemical vapor deposition, a far more costly process. A second innovation was a superconducting sensor that provides continuous readings of the temperature of ultra-cold refrigerators that store human tissue. Technicians monitoring these refrigerators had previously been required to periodically open the units to check whether levels of refrigerant were adequate. Ultimately, the firm hoped to develop a variety of signal processing and filtering components for the cellular telephone and wireless communication industry that would employ superconducting materials.

The financing history of this firm was typical of ARCH's firms. In October 1989, in conjunction with the formation of the firm, the company issued 136,000 shares of common stock to ARCH. In its Series A financing (undertaken during 1990 and 1991), the company raised $500,000 each from ARCH Venture Partners, Batterson, Johnson & Wang (a Chicago-based venture capital organization), and the Illinois Department of Commerce and Community Affairs. The firm raised several more million dollars from these same sources and others in two additional financing rounds in 1992 and 1993.

One crucial goal of the ARCH partners was to add value through the provision of oversight. Consequently, almost all these firms were based in the city of Chicago or its suburbs. An exception was GenVec, a firm that sought to treat diseases using gene therapies. This firm—which had just signed a $17 million corporate research contract with Genentech—was based on technology developed by Dr. Ron Crystal of the National Institutes of Health and from the Dana-Farber Cancer Institute and the University of Chicago. ARCH co-founded the firm by merging a Chicago-based start-up that it had funded with another company. Reflecting the merged company's East Coast location, ARCH accepted a role as a board observer.

Lazarus sought to involve other venture capitalists as investors as well. Initially, as an outsider to the close circle of venture organizations, Lazarus had found it difficult to interest venture capitalists. This reluctance was exacerbated by the reluctance of many in the industry to consider seed investing. Many felt that the time and effort needed to monitor a seed investment was as large as an investment in a much larger firm and that early-stage investing represented a luxury that could not be afforded in a venture fund with several hundred million dollars of committed capital.

Other venture capitalists insisted that they be located near their early-stage investments and consequently were reluctant to invest in firms based in the Midwest. Finally, ARCH was limited by its charter to investing in deals where the technology had originated at the University of Chicago or Argonne National Laboratory. Consequently, ARCH could not invest in almost all transactions initiated by other venture organizations. Since this deal-sharing was an important component of the venture investment process, the prohibition had limited ARCH's ability to build strong ties with the venture community.

Lazarus was therefore forced to aggressively seek out relationships with the venture community. He sought to exploit old connections from Baxter (a disproportionate number of executives of venture-backed biotechnology firms were from the ranks of Baxter executives), as well as more recent contacts from the University of Chicago. Among the syndication partners of ARCH Venture Partners, L.P., in its first four years were Batterson, Johnson & Wang, Columbine Ventures, Hillman Medical Ventures, Institutional Venture Partners, and Sierra Ventures.

Looking back over the past years, Lazarus noted the record of his fund with pride. (The financial performance of the firms in ARCH's portfolio are reported in Exhibit 5.) Along with his partners, he had founded one dozen firms. These had created 720 jobs directly and promised to create many more. The technology licensing effort had been exciting as well: the number of annual patents filed annually by the University and the Laboratory had increased from about one dozen to between 120 and 150. Over 60 licensing agreements encompassing over 125 products had been signed. These had generated nearly $2 million in royalties for the University and Argonne. Although these revenues were still below the $10 to $20 million in revenues that Stanford and M.I.T. received annually, ARCH had been in existence for a much shorter period.

THE CREATION OF ARCH VENTURE FUND II

By October 1993, ARCH had invested or reserved nearly all of its initial venture fund. Many of the firms were still in the development stage and would require additional infusions of capital. Furthermore, ARCH officials were regularly being contacted by other academic institutions, which sought their involvement in technology transfer at their organizations. Such extensions were not within the scope of the partnership agreement establishing ARCH Venture Partners, L.P.

Prompted by these developments, Lazarus had spent much of 1993 in discussions with University of Chicago officials. They sought to identify ways through which the special relationship between the University and ARCH could be preserved, while allowing the partnership to expand the scale and scope of its operations. From these discussions emerged the outline of a proposed restructuring of the relationship between the fund and the University.

Under the proposed arrangement, Lazarus and his partners would raise a second, more substantial venture fund. Because this fund would entail a substantial scaling-up of venture activities, and reflect the increasing pace of licensing activity, the nature of the relationship between the University and Lazarus and his partners would change. The venture capitalists would retain responsibility for ARCH Venture Partners but would relinquish their direct role in licensing University technology. ARCH Development Corporation, which would now be run by a successor to be hired, would undertake the initial examination of new technologies and decide whether they should be licensed or spun off in a new venture. ARCH Venture Partners would continue to finance new enterprises that sought to commercialize these technologies. The ARCH officials would cease to be employees of ARCH Development Corporation but would continue to provide consulting services to this organization about licensing deals during the transition period. ARCH Venture Partners would also retain responsibility for the investment portfolio of its first fund. As the private placement memorandum described the transition:

> This [transition] will be effected either through (1) subcontracting of ADC's [ARCH Development Corporation] management responsibilities as general partner of ARCH Fund I to AVP [ARCH Venture Partners] or (2) assignment of the general partners' interest in ARCH Fund I from ADC to AVP. In either case, AVP will receive the benefit of the management fee payable to the general partner of Fund I.[13]

It was anticipated that this transition would occur in the months after the first closing of ARCH Venture Partners II, L.P.

The University endowment would invest in the second fund as well and be a limited partner alongside the various institutional and individual investors. The role of ARCH Development Corporation in this fund, however, would be substantially different. In the earlier fund, ARCH Development had been the sole general partner. In this fund, ARCH Development Corporation would serve as a special limited partner, which would allow it to receive a share of the profits without investing any capital. The general partners' carried interest would be divided between the three ARCH venture capitalists. It was anticipated that ARCH Development Corporation's Board of Directors would serve as a Board of Advisors for the venture partnership.[14]

---

[13] ARCH Venture Partners, ARCH Venture Fund, II, L.P. Private Placement Memorandum, mimeo, 1993, p. 19.

[14] The board was given an advisory role because if they had direct oversight of the partnership, the directors would be exposed to litigation involving the firms in ARCH's portfolio.

In addition to the financial relationship, ARCH Venture Partners' special relationship with the University would be preserved through several measures. First, it would retain offices on the Chicago campus and at the Argonne Laboratory. Second, it anticipated including in its agreement with the University a clause formalizing a "right of first look." The private placement memorandum described this right in the following manner:

> The specifics of the Fund's right of "first look" are currently being discussed between Fund Management and the executives of ADC who will be responsible for ADC's technology licensing activities after the Fund's first closing. The General Partner anticipates that the right of "first look" will provide the Fund with a period (which is likely to approximate 60 to 180 days) during which Fund Management can evaluate the suitability of a technology for company formation while ADC is prevented from negotiating with other parties for exploitation of the technology. The Fund will be required to negotiate with ADC during that period to determine the amount of equity in the new company, licensing fees and other consideration (if any) ADC will receive in return for licensing the technology to the Fund for exploitation. Other issues must also be resolved in connection with the relationship between ADC and the Fund with respect to the right of "first look," including the funding of patenting costs during the period when the technology is being developed.[15]

(The offering memorandum and proposed partnership agreement for ARCH Venture Partners II, L.P., are summarized in Exhibits 6 and 7. Exhibit 8 depicts the proposed modified structure of the ARCH organizations.) Finally, and perhaps most important, ARCH officials had developed a broad set of informal relationships with University and Laboratory researchers. These ties would enable them to identify and nurture potential business development ideas from very early on.

At the same time, Lazarus realized that he might be facing considerable challenges in this new fund. First, venture capitalists, who had largely ignored the Midwest in the 1980s, were finding this area increasingly interesting. Second, ARCH Venture Fund II would have a broader geographic focus, which would impose a substantial management challenge. Technologies would be commercialized that had been developed at Argonne and the University of Chicago, but so would discoveries made at other national laboratories and universities. Among the initial institutions with which ARCH planned to build relationships were Northwestern University, the University of Illinois, and the Illinois Institute of Technology. In addition, ARCH officials had been contacted by individuals at Columbia University and Sandia National Laboratory, which sought their involvement in developing their technology transfer programs. Lazarus was sensitive, however, to the danger of spreading ARCH's partners too thinly. Thus he anticipated that the bulk of firms begun by ARCH would be from facilities in the north-central Midwest. In particular, the partners believed that the fund would make 16 investments in its first four years, and then 8 investments in the next four years. Fifty percent of the funds would be devoted to new companies in the Chicago region founded by ARCH, 25% to investments in early-stage companies outside the Chicago area that were also being financed by other venture funds, and 25% to follow-on investments in companies that had already been funded by ARCH Venture Partners, L.P.

---

[15] ARCH Venture Partners, ARCH Venture Fund, II, L.P. Private Placement Memorandum, mimeo, 1993, p. 25.

Exhibit 1   ARCH Venture Partners Management

STEVEN LAZARUS

Steven Lazarus, Managing Director, served as President and CEO of ARCH Development Corporation (ADC) and Associate Dean of University of Chicago's Graduate School of Business. Lazarus has overseen the growth of ADC since its inception in 1986, and has acted as the Managing General Partner for Arch Venture Fund I (AVFI). Lazarus raised $9 million for AVFI, and serves as a director of many AVFI portfolio companies.

Prior to joining ADC, Lazarus was the Senior Vice President for Research and Development, Engineering, Manufacturing and Materials Management for the corporation now known as Baxter International, Inc. During his 13 years at Baxter, he served as Senior Vice President for Strategic Planning, President of the Artificial Organs Division, and Executive Vice President of Baxter's International Division.

From 1972 to 1974, Lazarus served in Washington, DC, as Deputy Assistant Secretary of Commerce for East-West Trade, where he founded and was the first director of the Bureau of East-West Trade. In 1973, he retired as a Captain after 21 years in the U.S. Navy.

Lazarus is a director of Amgen Corporation, Thousand Oaks, California, and Primark Corporation, McLean, Virginia. He is also Chairman of the Board of Highland Park Hospital and a director of the Northwestern Healthcare Network, both of Illinois.

He received a bachelor's degree with honors from Dartmouth College and received his MBA with high distinction from Harvard Business School, where he was also a Baker Scholar.

KEITH L. CRANDELL

Keith L. Crandell, Managing Director, has served as senior manager at ADC with responsibilities for AVFI's activities at Argonne National Laboratory. He joined ARCH Development Corporation in 1987.

Mr. Crandell was instrumental in the creation of Eichrom Industries, Inc., and served as its president from the beginning of 1992 through the first quarter of 1993. In addition, Mr. Crandell has played a leading role in the formation of Nanophase Technologies Corporation, Illinois Superconductor Corporation, Qmax Corporation, and most recently, Clean Surface Technologies. All four companies were formed around technological innovations Mr. Crandell identified at Argonne National Laboratory.

Mr. Crandell has over 10 years of business development experience and has largely focused his venture formation efforts in specialty materials, chemicals, advanced mechanical devices and software. Prior to joining ADC, he spent four years with Hercules Inc., marketing specialty chemical and polymer products to the pharmaceutical, food, and agriculture industries.

Mr. Crandell is a director of Eichrom Industries, Inc., Qmax Corporation, Clean Surface Technologies, and Engineering Animation, Inc., an animation software company located in Ames, Iowa. He holds a BS in chemistry and mathematics from St. Lawrence University, an MS in chemistry from the University of Texas at Arlington, and an MBA from the University of Chicago.

ROBERT T. NELSEN

Robert T. Nelsen is a Managing Director of ARCH Venture Partners. Previously, Mr. Nelsen was responsible for new company formation and ARCH Venture Fund I's activities at the University of Chicago. He joined ARCH Development Corporation in 1987. Mr. Nelsen established and has managed the new venture formation function of ARCH at the University of Chicago since 1987. He focuses his efforts on new company creation primarily in the fields of biotechnology and medical devices.

He led the formation of NiOptics Corporation, Everyday Learning Corporation, AndroBio Corporation, and ARCH's founding role in GenVec, Inc., and R2 Technologies. Mr. Nelsen also managed ARCH Fund I's founding investment in Aviron, Inc., and Idun Pharmaceuticals, Inc.

Mr. Nelsen is a director of Adolor Corporation, Everyday Learning Corporation, AndroBio Corporation, and Aptein, Inc., a biotechnology company based in Seattle, Washington. He holds a B.S. in biology and economics from the University of Puget Sound and an M.B.A. from the University of Chicago.

Source: Compiled from corporate documents.

Exhibit 2   ARCH Development Corporation Board of Directors

James S. Crown
General Partner
Henry Crown and Company

Katharine P. Darrow
Vice President of Broadcasting Service and
Corporate Development Information
New York Times Company

Herbert D. Doan
Retired Chairman and CEO
Dow Chemical Company

Kingman Douglass
Chairman, Kingman Douglass, Inc.

John P. Gould
Dean of the Graduate School of Business
The University of Chicago

Robert M. Halperin
Vice Chairman of the Board
Raychem Corporation

Edgar D. Jannotta
Managing Partner
William Blair and Company

Arthur L. Kelly
Managing Partner
KEL Enterprises Limited

Steven Lazarus
President and Chief Executive Officer
ARCH Development Corporation

Frank W. Luerssen
Chairman and Chief Executive Officer
Inland Steel Industries

Walter E. Massey
Vice President for Research and for Argonne National
Laboratory
The University of Chicago

Richard M. Morrow
Chairman and CEO
Amoco Corporation

Alan Schriesheim
Director
Argonne National Laboratory

Thomas M. Fitzpatrick
Fitzpatrick Law Offices
Secretary Pro Tem

Arthur M. Sussman
General Counsel
The University of Chicago

Source: Compiled from corporate documents.

Exhibit 3   Structure of the ARCH Organization in November 1993

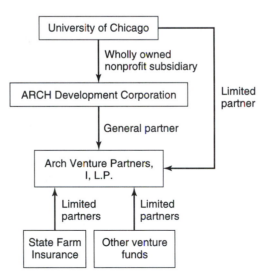

Source: Compiled from corporate documents.

Exhibit 4   ARCH Venture Fund Company Descriptions in November 1993

AndroBio Corporation, Chicago, IL

AndroBio Corporation was formed in August 1989 to license and develop male hormone (androgen) related technology developed at U of C. The company's initial development efforts are targeted for dermatological applications. AndroBio licensed compound screening technology to Ligand Pharmaceutical Corporation in exchange for an equity interest. Ligand Pharmaceuticals Corporation went public in the fourth quarter of 1992. Arch Venture Fund I was a founding seed investor in AndroBio Corporation. Steven Lazarus and Robert Nelsen are directors of the company.

Aviron

Aviron, Inc. develops vaccine and pharmaceuticals based on recombinant viral vectors and other vaccine drug delivery technologies. Recombinant viral vector technology will help create lower cost therapy in the form of more effective vaccines for influenza, herpes and other diseases.

Eichrom

Eichrom Industries, Inc. was formed in February 1990 to manufacture and sell chemical resins that are used to monitor and minimize hazardous wastes. Formed around advanced ion-exchange technology developed at ANL, Eichrom's products address a large international market which is growing rapidly. The company, to date, has raised over $4.0 million in venture capital.

Everyday Learning Corporation, Evanston, IL

Everyday Learning Corporation was formed in November 1988 to reform the mathematics curriculum for grades kindergarten through sixth. The curriculum was designed by a U of C team of mathematicians and educators to revolutionize the way mathematics is taught in the United States. The company is profitable and has experienced over 100% sales growth annually for four years. Everyday Learning Corporation estimates that 125,000 students in grades K-3 are currently using its primary curriculum. Fiscal 1993 revenues were over $7.2 million. AVFI led the formation of the company and recruited an experienced CEO and board of directors to operate it. Steven Lazarus is chairman of the board and Robert Nelsen is a director of the company.

GenVec

GenVec, Inc., is a clinically oriented gene therapy company founded by Hillman Medical Ventures, Genentech, Inc., Prince Ventures, Sierra Ventures, and Dr. Ronald Crystal. GenVec's focus on bringing pharmaceuticals based on gene therapy to the clinic in the next two years, without the use of cell-based delivery systems, is unique among gene therapy companies. GenVec's technology includes adenovirus delivery technology and cystic fibrosis treatment from Dr. Crystal, and radiation inducible promoter cancer treatment technology from University of Chicago and Dana Farber Cancer Institute scientists. ADC, AVFI, the Dana Farber Cancer Institute and four scientists from the University of Chicago and Harvard anticipated in founding the company and invested in GenVec's initial financing round. The company has raised $9 million of venture capital and negotiated a $17 million contract with Genentech to develop products for the treatment of cystic fibrosis. AVFI management is a board observer for GenVec, Inc.

IDUN Pharmaceuticals, Inc.

IDUN Pharmaceuticals was formed in June 1993 to discover and develop new breakthrough pharmaceuticals to treat diseases by modulating the biochemical pathways that control cell death, or "apoptosis." The field of mediated cell death is the focus of intense scientific attention because this process plays an important role throughout the life cycle of organisms. Apoptosis is important in an organism's embryological development, as well as in the development of immune and nervous systems. It is now clear that cell death is a critical element in the etiology of certain diseases, and it is this realization that has led to the formation of IDUN. The company's initial programs aim to identify drugs that inhibit cell death in myocardial infarction, neurodegenerative disease, and chronic inflammation.

Illinois Superconductor Corporation, Evanston, IL

Illinois Superconductor Corporation was formed in October 1989 to address the emerging high-temperature superconductor components market. High-temperature superconductors, when cryogenically cooled, enable resistance-free transmission of electrical current. This unique property of the materials has large commercial potential in the telecommunications, electrical utility, and defense communications industries. Illinois Superconductor is currently developing ultra-low loss components for the next generation of cellular phone base station equipment, with its partners AT&T and Ameritech. In January 1993, Illinois Superconductor was awarded a $2.0 million U.S. Department of Commerce Advanced Technology Program Contract. AVFI was the lead seed investor in Illinois Superconductor and led two additional venture investment rounds totaling $3.2 million. The company completed its IPO of 1.35 million shares at a price of $11.25/share. Steven Lazarus is chairman of the board and a member of its executive committee.

Nanophase Technologies Corporation, Darien, IL

Nanophase Technologies Corporation was formed in November 1989 to develop an entirely new class of ultra-fine ceramic materials which offer the potential to dramatically reduce the brittle nature of ceramics. These materials lead to ceramic components that have enhanced formability and toughness, compared to conventional ceramics. The company was formed around technology developed at ANL and Northwestern University. In 1990 the company won an Advanced Technology Program Contract grant for $1 million from the U.S. Department of Commerce for the development of ceramic engine components. Along with its corporate partner, Caterpillar, the company is scaling-up its powder production and fabricating prototype component parts. The company is also actively developing other ceramic powder market opportunities.

NiOptics Corporation, Evanston, IL

NiOptics Corporation was formed in June 1988 to develop and manufacture highly advanced optical components which can dramatically improve the brightness and efficiency of light sources. The company was formed around proprietary nonimaging optics technology developed at The University of Chicago. The company has research and development partnerships with Apple Computer, and Compaq to develop a high efficiency backlight for LCD screens in portable computers. The company also works with the 3M Corporation and is developing with applications in other industries including color copiers, scanners, control panels, and light pipes.

Opian Pharmaceuticals

Opian Pharmaceuticals is focused on the treatment of pain using recent advances in the molecular biology and chemistry of opioids. The company, founded by AVP, has made substantial progress in recruiting a CEO candidate and a potential co-founder, and is in active discussions which will likely lead to the hiring of a CEO and a vice president-R&D. Both candidates have significant experience in the pharmaceutical and biotechnology industries. Provided that the CEO accepts a position with Opian, the company expects to complete a seed venture round of $1.5-2.0 million with at least one major west coast venture capital investor and possibly others. The company will be located in Philadelphia.

Qmax Inc., Willowbrook, IL

Qmax Corporation was founded in January 1992 to address the need for high-performance heat transfer mechanism in the electronics and x-ray industries. The company's technology, developed by scientists at ANL for use in its Advanced Photon Source, enables the design of liquid metal pumping systems that are highly efficient for heat removal, inexpensive, and physically compact. The company is developing a prototype system for cooling integrated circuits in conjunction with a computer workstation manufacturer. In January 1993, Qmax received a $65,000 contract to build a system for use in the Advanced Photon Source. AVF I was the founding seed investor and led a recent investment round raising $700,000.

R2 Technologies, Inc.

R2 Technologies was co-founded by ARCH Venture Partners, L.P. and several experienced medical imaging executives in Palo Alto, California, to develop and market computer-aided diagnosis products to physicians. The early focus of the effort is to provide advisory products to help radiologists evaluate mammograms more effectively and efficiently. The computer software technology for computer-aided diagnosis has been developed by Dr. Kunio Doi of The University of Chicago, a leading expert in the field. Currently, the technology can identify up to 50% of the cancers (as indicated by microcalcifications) initially missed by radiologists.

Source: Compiled from corporate documents.

Exhibit 5   Summary of ARCH Venture Fund I Investments

	Estimated Market Value[a]	AVF I's % Ownership	AVF I's Share of Estimated Market Value	AVF I's Investment at Cost	Adj. Realized/ Unrealized Gain (Loss)
AndroBio	$ 192,000	25.0%	$ 48,000	$ 37,000	$ 11,000
Assesstek[b]	0	0.0	0	110,000	(110,000)
Aviron	25,260,000	2.5	631,500	350,000	281,500
Eichrom	7,576,565	20.1	1,522,890	519,249	1,003,641
Everyday Learning	13,894,100	17.3	2,403,679	280,000	1,592,759[d]
GenVec	13,284,000	1.9	250,000	250,000	0
HealthQual[b]	0	0.0	0	565,929	(565,929)
Illinois Superconductor	45,175,795	14.3	5,768,511[c]	1,196,572	3,947,675[d]
Information Arts[b]	0	0.0	0	550,000	(550,000)
Nanophase	5,572,190	19.0	1,061,259	1,011,000	50,259
NiOptics	15,965,378	19.5	3,107,200	1,500,000	1,607,200
Qmax	1,200,000	16.7	199,920	137,268	62,652
Subtotal[e]	$128,120,029		$14,992,959	$6,507,018	$7,330,757
Management fee	0		0	1,615,012	(1,615,012)
Net operating expenses[f]	0		0	98,989	(98,989)
Total	$128,120,029		$14,992,959	$8,221,019	$5,616,756

[a]All valuations reflect most recent third-party investment rounds or debt investment as of 9/30/94 except:

AndroBio—based on holdings of 20,000 shares of Ligand Corp. Stock at $9.60/share.

Everyday Learning—18.7 P/E° ratio of similar public company times fiscal 1994 net income after taxes.

Illinois Superconductor—Price: $10.27/per share, weighted average closing price of last 10 trading days of quarter ending 9/30/94.

[b]Companies are in various stages of liquidation, assumed zero value.

[c]Share of estimated market value minus costs of exercising warrants.

[d]Gain discounted 25% to reflect liquidity for Everyday Learning and lock-up status of Illinois Superconductor holdings, which ends 10/94.

[e]Tabulation does not include three firms that had very recently received their initial venture financing from ARCH: IDUN Pharmaceuticals, Opian Pharmaceuticals, and R2 Technologies.

[f]AVF I operating expenses, reduced by interest income on cash on hand. Includes audit and legal fees.

Source: Compiled from corporate documents.

Exhibit 6   Term Sheet for the ARCH Venture Partners II, L.P. Offering

The following is a summary of the principal terms of the Fund:

The Fund

The Fund is a Delaware limited partnership.

Purpose

The purpose of the Fund is to generate substantial long-term capital appreciation by making seed venture capital investments in new and early-stage technology companies. The Fund intends to focus on companies located in the north-central mid-west region of the United States and, in particular, on companies, originating in technology emanating from the University of Chicago and Argonne National Laboratories. ARCH Development Corporation, a University affiliate, is a limited partner of the Management Partnership and will provide a right of "first look" to the Fund with respect to technology under its management.

General Partner

The General Partner of the Fund is ARCH Management Partnership, L.P., a Delaware limited partnership. ARCH Venture Partners, L.P. ("AVP"), a limited partnership controlled by a corporation controlled by Steven Lazarus, is general partner of the General Partner. The address of the Fund is 20 North Wacker Drive, Suite 1849, Chicago, Illinois 60606. Telephone: (312) 704-5830.

Fund Management

The Management of the Fund comprises Steven Lazarus, Keith L. Crandell, and Robert T. Nelsen.

Scientific Advisor

Dr. Shutsung Liao, Professor of The Ben May Institute and the Department of Biochemistry and Molecular Biology at the University of Chicago, will serve as a scientific advisor to the Fund. Dr. Liao is a special limited partner of the Management Partnership.

Amount of Offering

A maximum of $30,000,000. A first closing may occur at any time after a minimum of $5,000,000 has been subscribed.

Minimum Investment

$1,000,000 (subject to acceptance of lesser amounts in the General Partner's discretion), payable 20% upon subscription and the balance within 30 days after notice from the General Partner. The General Partner anticipates that additional capital calls of 20% of Committed Capital will be made annually.

Term

The Fund will have a 10-year maximum term, subject to extension for up to three additional one-year periods with the approval of a majority in interest of the Limited Partners.

International Investors

Subscriptions will be accepted from persons who are neither (i) United States citizens nor (ii) entities formed under the laws of the United States.

Profit Allocation

Fund profits generally will be allocated 80% to the Limited Partners, pro rata in accordance with their capital contributions, and 20% to the General Partner. See "Summary of the Agreement of Limited Partnership—Allocation of Profits and Losses."

Distributions

Except for distributions for the payment of income taxes, all Fund distributions will be paid to the Limited Partners until they have received cumulative distributions in an amount equal to their capital contributions. Thereafter, Fund distributions will be paid 80% to the Limited Partners and 20% to the General Partner. See "Summary of the Agreement of Limited Partnership—Distributions."

Management Fee

Annual fee equal to 2.5% of committed capital with provision for inflation adjustment. The fee will decrease by 0.25% in years 7, 8, and 9 of the Fund's term.

Source: Compiled from corporate documents.

Exhibit 7   Summary of the Proposed Agreement of Limited Partnership for ARCH Venture Partners II, L.P.

The following summarizes the Fund's Agreement of Limited Partnership (the "Partnership Agreement"). These statements are qualified by reference to the text of the Partnership Agreement:

1. *Nature of the Fund; Liability of Partners.* The Fund has been organized as a Delaware limited partnership to pursue its stated investment purposes. Fund investors will become Limited Partners and will receive Interests in the Fund. A Limited Partner will be liable for Partnership losses and obligations only to the extent of the amount of capital it has committed to contribute to the Fund (its "Capital Commitment") and its share of Partnership profits absent representations or other conduct to the contrary by the Limited Partner to a creditor of the Fund. Limited Partners will not be obligated to contribute capital to the Fund in excess of their Capital Commitment.

2. *Management of Partnership Affairs.* The Limited Partners will not take part in the management of the Partnership. The General Partner will make all management, administrative and investment decisions for the Partnership. The role of the Board of Advisors (if such a board is established) will be advisory and its decisions or suggestions will not bind the General Partner in any way.

3. *Distributions.* Each Limited Partner will have a Participating Percentage determined by dividing the capital it actually contributes to the Fund ("Capital Contributions") by the Capital Contributions of all Limited Partners. All distributions made in cash or in kind will be paid to the Limited Partners pro rata in accordance with their Participating Percentages until the Limited Partners have received a full return of their Capital Contributions, except that the General Partner will receive a portion of such distributions designed to enable its partners to pay income taxes on net Partnership income allocated to them. Once the full amount of the Limited Partners' capital contributions has been distributed to them, all subsequent distributions will be paid 80% to the Limited Partners in accordance with their Partnership Percentages and 20% to the General Partner. The Partnership will use its best efforts to make adequate distributions to enable the Limited Partners to pay Federal and state income taxes arising from the purchase of interests in a taxable year. Securities distributed in kind will be valued by the General Partner in its sole discretion.

4. *Allocations of Taxable Income and Loss.* Generally, Fund profits and losses will be allocated 80% to the Limited Partners in accordance with their Participating Percentages and 20% to the General Partner. Fund profits and investment losses will be allocated 100% to the Limited Partners if the General Partner's Fund capital account is at zero at the time of the allocation. If Limited Partners have been allocated 100% of any losses, the Limited Partners will be allocated 100% of future profits to the extent of such losses. Partnership expenses will be allocated to the Limited Partners in accordance with their Participating Percentages.

5. *Organizational Expenses.* The Partnership will bear all costs of its organization and the offer and sale of Interests (including reimbursement of attorneys' fees and other organizational expenses incurred by the General Partner). In addition, the Partnership will reimburse ADC and/or Fund Management for out-of-pocket expenses incurred in connection with efforts to make investments on behalf of the Fund prior to the First Closing.

The General Partner will receive an annual Management Fee equal to 2.5% of Committed Capital, adjusted for inflation annually after the first anniversary of the First Closing and decreasing by .25 percentage points on each of the seventh, eighth, and ninth anniversaries of the First Closing. In return for the Management Fee, the General Partner will pay all expenses of administering and operating the Partnership, except for third-party professional fees such as legal, accounting or brokerage. Each Fund portfolio company will bear its own expenses of formation and operation.

6. *Capitalization*. The Fund is offering a minimum of $5,000,000 and a maximum of $30,000,000 in Interests. Affiliates of the General Partner may purchase Interests. Any such Interests will count towards the minimum offering amount and will have all voting rights accorded to other Limited Partners.

7. *Partnership Term*. The Fund will dissolve so as to precipitate its winding-up and termination on the tenth anniversary of the First Closing, subject to extension for up to three one-year terms at the discretion of the General Partner with the approval of Limited Partners holding a majority of the Interests. The General Partner may dissolve the Fund prior to the tenth anniversary of the First Closing in its discretion.

8. *Transfer of Partnership Interests*. A Limited Partner may assign, sell or otherwise dispose of all or any portion of its Interests only with the written consent of the General Partner, which consent may be withheld in the General Partner's sole discretion. Without limitation of the foregoing, the General Partner may withhold its consent to any transfer of Interests unless counsel satisfactory to the General Partner concludes that the transaction does not violate the registration requirements of applicable federal or state securities laws, will not subject the Fund, the General Partner or Fund Management to additional regulatory requirements (including requirements under the Investment Company Act or the Investment Advisers Act) and will not adversely affect the Fund from an income tax perspective.

Any assignee, purchaser or other transferee of Interests will be admitted as a Limited Partner only upon (a) the consent of the General Partner, (b) execution of such instruments as are necessary or appropriate to effect such admission and, (c) payment of the Fund's reasonable expenses incurred in connection with the transfer and admission.

9. *Reports to Limited Partners*. The General Partner will provide a report to all Limited Partners shortly after the making of each material investment by the Fund and will provide quarterly investment status reports to the Limited Partners. In addition, audited financial statements and tax return information will be provided to all Limited Partners after the end of each fiscal year.

10. *Indemnification and Exculpation*. None of the General Partner, Fund Management or their respective affiliates will be liable to the Fund or any Limited Partner for any act or omission that is made in good faith and does not constitute willful, wanton or intentional misconduct. The Partnership shall indemnify and hold harmless the General Partner, Fund Management and their respective affiliates against any losses, liabilities, expenses and amounts paid in settlement of claims arising in connection with the Partnership, provided that the party to be indemnified acted in good faith and did not engage in willful, wanton or intentional misconduct. Amounts may be paid to a party in advance of the final disposition of an action, suit or proceeding upon receipt by the Fund

of an undertaking provided by or on behalf of the party seeking the advancement to the effect that the advancement will be repaid if the party in question is ultimately determined not to be eligible for indemnification.

11. *Amendment of Partnership Agreement*. Subject to certain limited exceptions, the Partnership Agreement may be amended with the consent of the General Partner and Limited Partners holding not less than two-thirds of the Interests.

12. *Withdrawal*. No Limited Partner may withdraw voluntarily from the Fund. The General Partner is not permitted to withdraw voluntarily from the Fund without the consent of Limited Partners holding a majority of the Interests and the appointment of a replacement general partners(s) acceptable to such Limited Partners. In addition, should Mr. Lazarus' services no longer be available to the Fund, an additional general partner may be admitted with the consent described above. See "Risk and Other Important Factors—Reliance on Management."

13. *Removal*. The General Partner may not be removed unless it commits willful, wanton or intentional misconduct that has a material, adverse effect on the Fund, and then only with the consent of Limited Partners holding a not less than two-thirds of the Interests. If the General Partner is removed, its economic interest in the Fund will be converted to a Limited Partner's interest and it will receive distributions with respect to that interest if, as and when such distributions would have been paid had it remained general partner of the Fund.

14. *Default*. All or any part of a Limited Partner's Capital Commitment will be payable upon 30 days notice from the General Partner. A Limited Partner will have 10 days after receiving notice from the General Partner of a default in such payment to cure the default. Failure to cure the default will result in (a) acquisition by the other Limited Partners of the defaulting Limited Partner's interest for an amount equal to 50% of his then-existing Fund capital account, (b) expulsion of the Limited Partner from the Fund for payment of the amount described in (a) above or (c) suit against the defaulting partner by the Fund for payment of the defaulted amount.

Source: Compiled from corporate documents.

Exhibit 8   New Structure of ARCH Organizations

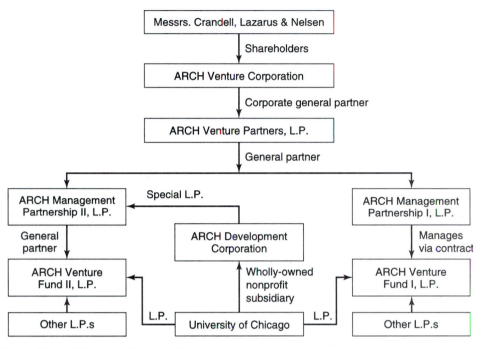

Source: Compiled from corporate documents.

7

Schroder Ventures: Launch of the Euro Fund

Peter Smitham stared out of the Eurostar's gleaming window and thought of wine lakes and butter mountains. Unlike so many initiatives undertaken in the name of European unity, this new train service under the Channel Tunnel linking Britain with continental Europe—or the other way around, as some of his British colleagues saw it—seemed an epitome of efficiency.

As the managing partner of Schroder Ventures' London office, the private equity organization's largest, Smitham was on his way to Paris in March 1995 to chair a meeting with other office heads. The meeting had been scheduled to discuss the strategy and organization of a proposed $750 million buyout fund that would cover all the major countries in Europe. Smitham's aim was to report back in three months' time to Nick Ferguson, the chairman of Schroder Ventures, with a firm plan and timetable that all the European offices supported.

At this early stage in the planning process, Smitham had various important issues to resolve in order to ensure commitment and full cooperation from all the European Schroder Ventures offices. A key goal was to ensure a fund structure in which the interests of the partners were aligned with those of the investors. A fair reward structure that gave incentives to invest in the best deals and avoided pressure on offices to invest locally was also needed, one that linked long-term rewards to individual and fund performance. Other objectives were to create a truly European organization that preserved local autonomy and entrepreneurship, permitted investment in multinational and local companies across Europe, and made possible a flexible allocation of human resources across the different markets.

Smitham nibbled his *pain au chocolat* as he read two memos describing the frustrations of two partners working together on an aborted French buyout, Encrouge SA, and wondered how the Euro Fund should be managed and structured.

HISTORY OF SCHRODER VENTURES

Background

Schroder Ventures was one of the world's largest international venture capital organizations. The name covered a network of advisory entities to venture capital and buyout

This case was prepared by Kate Bingham, Nick Ferguson, and Josh Lerner. Copyright © 1996 by the President and Fellows of Harvard College. Harvard Business School case 297-026.

funds which were managed autonomously and associated with Schroders plc, the United Kingdom (U.K.) investment bank.

Schroders, founded in London during the Napoleonic wars, was one of the oldest and most successful international merchant and investment banking firms. In the nineteenth century, it played a central role in financing world trade and in raising long-term capital for governments and railway companies. Schroders entered the venture capital business in 1936 with the formation in the United States of Schroder Rockefeller, which subsequently became a wholly owned subsidiary of Schroders. In March 1995, Schroders plc was a major public company conducting merchant and investment banking business worldwide. It had a market capitalization of £2.4 billion ($3.6 billion) and funds under management of £64 billion ($96 billion).

Ferguson, the chairman of Schroder Ventures, joined the bank as an investment analyst in 1971 and returned there in 1975 after graduating from Harvard Business School. After managing the bank's Singapore office for several years, in 1984 he assumed responsibility for a small venture capital fund that had been raised in the United States the previous year. Seeing the opportunity to build a worldwide business, he persuaded Schroders to move aggressively into private equity. Schroder Ventures was accordingly founded in 1985, with the launch of the £25 million U.K. Venture Fund and the £75 million U.K. Buy-Out Fund. The U.K. arm still constituted a major part of Schroder Ventures' activities. Since the formation of the U.K. operation, however, Schroder Ventures' entities had been established in eight other countries at the rate of approximately one every 15 months, starting in Japan in late 1985.

By 1995, Schroder Ventures had become one of the largest international buyout and development capital groups in the world. Over 80 investment professionals in 10 countries advised 23 Schroder Ventures funds with committed capital of over $2.4 billion. Twenty-two of these funds were for investment primarily within a single country or region, and one was an international fund focusing on investment in the life sciences sector. To date, $1.5 billion had been invested in over 300 companies and $1.2 billion had been returned to investors, for an average net return of 20% against a comparable stock market return of 11%. The geographic spread of Schroder Ventures funds and the advisory entities of Schroder Ventures is summarized in Table 1.

Organization of the Schroder Ventures Group

For regulatory, control, and tax reasons, Schroder Ventures drew a distinction between the advisers to each fund, whose role was to locate and evaluate attractive investments, and the general partner (which was also the fund manager) who was ultimately responsible to investors for the decision whether or not to invest. Subsidiaries of Schroders

TABLE 1 Summary of Schroder Venture Funds

Region	Number of Schroder Venture funds	Total committed capital ($m)	Location of advisory partnerships
Europe	15	1,661	France, Germany, Italy, Spain, United Kingdom
Asia	4	432	Hong Kong, India, Japan
North America	3	131	Canada, United States
United States & Europe (Life Sciences)	1	100	United Kingdom, United States

acted as general partner and provided central support services to local Schroder Ventures entities, which acted as the fund advisers.

Schroder Ventures' approach was to hire local nationals in each country, many of whom were also industry specialists or former CEOs of operating companies, as its advisory staff. The local advisory businesses operating under the Schroder Ventures name were generally majority owned by its individual principals. These were structured as partnerships and affiliated with Schroders plc. In turn, these advisory entities benefited from the international network of Schroder Ventures and from the expertise and skills available within it.

As general partner, Schroders was responsible for maintaining high professional standards (both in terms of investment procedure and relationship with investors) and integrity throughout the group. Schroders provided central services, including legal, accounting, and fundraising support to the various country-based advisers. For these services and use of its name, it received a proportion of the advisory fees and carried interest. Exhibit 1 shows the structure of the Schroder Ventures group.

Fund Structure

Schroder Ventures funds were generally fixed-life funds of 10 years' duration, which could only be extended with the consent of investors. Some Schroder Ventures funds consisted of a single investment vehicle; others were structured as a number of investment vehicles, usually limited partnerships.

The size, terms, and conditions of the individual Schroder Ventures funds differed, reflecting the investment focus of the fund, the state of development of the market concerned at the launch date, and the investment requirements of the investors. These differences created wide disparities in the overall funds under management in each country, the fees generated, and therefore the partners' compensation. Exhibit 2 shows an example of a typical fund structure.

Sources of Funds

Each local advisory entity was responsible for raising new funds for local investment, supplemented by support from Ferguson and his team. Funds were raised from pension funds, insurance companies, companies, and wealthy families and individuals worldwide (see Figure 1). The majority of cash raised came from U.S. and U.K. investors, with the remainder from Continental Europe, the Middle East, Canada, and the Far East. Thirty-six investors had invested in five or more funds.

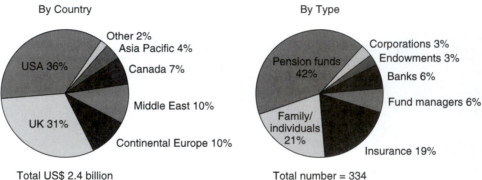

Figure 1 Sources of Capital (% committed capital)

SCHRODER VENTURES' EUROPEAN OPERATIONS

In the latter part of the 1980s, the major focus of Schroder Ventures was on building its business in Europe. Ferguson's responsibilities included planning the expansion into different European countries, recruiting the managing partner for each local adviser, helping these groups build up the team of investment professionals, and raising their funds. One of the key early decisions was to determine which countries to enter and which kind of private equity fund was most appropriate for the particular country. Determining factors included the number and types of investment opportunities available, the breadth of the equity markets, the availability of entrepreneurs willing to take risk, and the supply of bank finance. For example, the U.K. market was sufficiently broad to support both venture capital and buyout funds. Germany, on the other hand, had limited scope for early-stage investments, so Schroder Ventures' German funds focused on buyout opportunities. By 1995, 15 country-focused venture capital and buyout funds had been raised for investment in Germany, France, Italy, Spain, and the United Kingdom. Table 2 gives details of the various Schroder Ventures funds in Europe.

Overall responsibility for the operations and strategic direction of each local adviser lay with a single individual, the managing partner. Given the flat organizational structure of the advisory partnerships, however, this responsibility was exerted through persuasion rather than vested power. Each partnership was locally focused, relatively autonomous, and—although all were affiliated with Schroders plc—had relatively little interaction with the other European partnerships.

It was commonly recognized that autonomy was important in order to hire the most talented and effective individuals, whose creativity would be stifled by a large central bureaucracy. This autonomy meant that the Schroder Ventures group developed as an archipelago of locally focused firms concentrating on deals generated through their local network. Ferguson felt that, apart from Schroders plc and the central team of nine, no person or entity had a financial interest in the overall gains and development of the group as a whole.

In order to develop a sense of teamwork and common purpose within the Schroder Ventures group, Ferguson organized yearly international meetings of all investment professionals. This was also intended to encourage cross fertilization of ideas and increase the day-to-day cooperation of the different people and activities involved. In addition, "CEO Meetings" were held every six months with the managing partners of all the different local advisers, as a forum for discussing matters affecting the strategy and operation of the whole group.

Management fees were typically 2.2% to 2.5% per annum of the gross amount of committed capital and were normally subject to annual increases in line with an agreed inflation index. As incentive payments, carried interests of 20% were payable to the advisers and general partner. For all funds raised after 1989, carried interests of 15% were paid directly to the partners within the local adviser and the remaining 5% to Schroders plc. (Prior to this year, the carried interest had typically been divided equally.) Carried interests in some funds were subject to a hurdle rate.

Investment Decision Making

Each local adviser was responsible for identifying and recommending potential investments, through its Investment Committee, to the general partner. The general partner could choose whether or not to make the investment, although in practice the advisers' investment recommendations were seldom rejected.

The Investment Committee of each adviser was normally made up of four to six people, including the managing partner of the local adviser, a managing partner of

TABLE 2   Details of Schroder Ventures European Funds

Country and fund name	Size: Local currency	Size: US $	Date raised	Number of professionals	Managing partner of adviser
UK					
UKVF	£25m	$27m	1985	14 partners	Peter Smitham
UKVF Extension	£8m	$16m	1991	2 principals	Schroder Venture
UKVF II	£80m	$130m	1987	2 executives	Advisers, UK
UKVF III	£77m	$143m	1990	1 consultant	
UKVF IV	£86m	$131m	1995		
UKBOF	£75m	$104m	1985		
UKBOF II	£168m	$310m	1988		
UKBOF III	£149m	$221m	1993		
Germany					
GBOF	DM139m	$68m	1986	5 partners	Friedrich von der
GBOF 1992	DM235m	$143m	1992	2 executives	Groeben
				1 consultant	Schroder & Partners Beteiligungsberatung GmbH, Germany
France°					
FBOF	FF640m	$102m	1989	4 partners	G rard Tardy
FVF	FF309m	$60m	1992	2 principals	Schroder Partenaires,
				2 executives	France
Italy					
IBOF I	IL95,000m	$66m	1988	4 partners	Paolo Colonna & Mario
IBOF II	IL106,000m	$70m	1993	3 executives	Ferrario
					Schroder Associati, Italy
Spain					
SVF	SP6.1bn	$64m	1991	3 partners	Jaime Grego
				1 executive	Schroder y Asociados, Spain

VF = venture fund

BOF = buy-out fund

° French Buyout Club: In addition, in 1996 FF200m has been committed by three large investors for investment in French buyouts.

another Schroder Ventures adviser, Ferguson, and one or more local partners. Ferguson was responsible for maintaining standards throughout the group: through his involvement on Investment Committees, he sought to ensure that a high quality series of products was consistently presented to investors.

The Investment Committee had a threefold role: it made recommendations to the general partner (including new and follow-on investments and disposals); the committee guided the due diligence and monitoring activities of the investment team; and, it authorized expenditures by the local partnership.

Investment recommendations to the general partner proceeded in two stages. First, the deal team prepared a preliminary investment recommendation (PIR), which outlined the investment opportunity and contained only preliminary due diligence. The PIR enabled the Investment Committee to judge whether the deal fit within the fund's investment guidelines and to give direction to the deal team on which areas of due diligence to concentrate. Then, detailed due diligence was performed and summarized in a final investment recommendation (FIR), which set out the risks, terms, and potential returns of the investment. All members of the deal team presented the investment opportunity to the Investment Committee and were answerable for its quality and practicability. In general, PIRs and FIRs were rarely rejected outright, although the Investment Committee sometimes set conditions that made the eventual completion of the deal unlikely.

Legal, accounting, and other external costs associated with a single deal ranged from $50,000 to $1 million. The Investment Committee decided how much cost the partnership would be willing to bear should the deal fail to complete. Its value was demonstrated by the fact that nearly two out of three deals failed after the PIR. This rate of failure had increased with the general increase in competition in the private equity markets.

Although the Investment Committees generally did not include all partners within the local partnership, all partners, principals, and executives received investment recommendations and were encouraged to give their views on the deal opportunity to any member of the Investment Committee or deal team before the meeting. The Investment Committee's decisions were normally unanimous. Table 3 describes the outcome of this process: the investment records of the mature Schroder Ventures funds in Europe.

SCHRODER VENTURES' INTERNATIONAL FUNDS

In 1994 Schroder Ventures had already launched two international funds. The first non-country-based fund was the industry-focused International Life Sciences Fund. It had also raised a regional fund, Schroder Ventures Asia Pacific Trust. (Schroder Ventures took over the management of an existing pan-Asian fund in 1993.) Both the Life Sciences and Asia Pacific funds were denominated in U.S. dollars.

TABLE 3 Investment Record of the Mature European Funds

	Cash invested in ECU	Number of companies invested in°	Current valuation in ECU	Proceeds and income in ECU	Net IRR to investors (%)	Comparable stock market return (%)
UK						
UKVF	73m	54	17m	136m	19	16
UKVF II	85m	33	37m	38m	1	12
UKVF III	86m	36	117m	77m	32	16
UKBOF	97m	12	25m	251m	27	13
UKBOF II	242m	18	176m	384m	25	15
Germany						
GBOF	64m	13	134m	169m	41	7
France						
FBOF	80m	19	72m	24m	5	3
Italy						
IBOF I	32m	21	58m	22m	14	4
Summary						
UK	583m	153	372m	886m	19	14
Continental Europe	181m	59	283m	217m	22	5

ECU = $1.30 (average over period).
° Includes some double-counting

A key competitive advantage of both these international groups was the spread of investment professionals across several countries. Their international scope attracted entrepreneurs who sought both financial and commercial access to international markets. In addition, the personal networks of the partners helped generate a high-quality deal flow for these funds. Due diligence and portfolio company monitoring also benefited from having both a local and an international presence. At the same time, this dispersion posed organizational and managerial challenges for both groups.

International Life Sciences Fund Before the merger, the life sciences teams in the United Kingdom (London) and United States (Boston and Stamford, Connecticut) came to two important conclusions. First, the existing structure provided little financial incentive to cooperate despite the global nature of their deal opportunities. Second, investee companies were confused by the different faces of Schroder Ventures and the separate Investment Committees of each adviser. By merging the teams and raising a dedicated fund, the team had created important competitive advantages: skills within the advisory team were used more effectively, and decision making was simplified. The process of integrating two previously distinct teams operating in different time zones without demotivating the individuals involved, however, had proven to be a challenging process.

Henry Simon, the chairman of the Life Sciences Fund, succeeded in creating a functional, unified team largely through rigorous management of the investment process, regular team meetings by phone or in person, and daily internal communication (e-mail and voice mail). Trust was built up through a practice of staffing deal teams out of more than one office. Compensation structures were created to give partners incentives to work together as well as to reward individual performance. (Office performance per se was not rewarded.) The Life Sciences Investment Committee, which included all five of the life science partners, two consultants, and Ferguson, created and maintained consistent standards across the group. Operating costs of the different offices were covered by management fees, but the remaining fees were not preallocated in order to remove pressure on the offices to invest and to preserve flexibility.

Asia Pacific Fund Anil Thadani, the managing partner of the Asia Pacific Fund, faced similar challenges. A particular challenge was the need to balance his resources and the investment portfolio across several Asian countries. Different countries in the region had very different economies, inflation, interest, and tax rates, exchange rates, economic cycles, and so on. Cultural assumptions, management practices, customs, and investor expectations also differed. A key financial goal of Thadani's team was to diversify the investments in the Asia Pacific portfolio to take advantage of the different macro- and microeconomic environments. A challenge was posed by the fact that the headquarters and the bulk of the team were based in Hong Kong. Increasing competitive pressure meant that the team needed a greater local presence in the different countries in the region to allow a quick response to new deal opportunities.

A satellite office was established in Bombay, India, in 1995. Other offices elsewhere in Southeast Asia were planned in 1996 and 1997. The Asia Pacific Fund challenge was to balance local presence with central control, to develop access to investment opportunities while controlling costs, and to retain management control over the new corporate structure.

LAUNCH OF THE EUROPEAN FUND

Several events had led Ferguson and the European managing partners in Schroder Ventures to think about launching a pan-European buyout fund. Investors had started to demand a simpler international product, with fewer fundraisings and clearer reporting. The European private equity market was expanding to include large cross-border deals, and other private equity competitors were launching international funds. Each domestic European market in which Schroder Ventures operated, and especially in the United Kingdom, was becoming increasingly competitive. Schroder Ventures' European offices felt they were starting to lose multinational deals to competitors, although the competitors often had less and lower quality international resources. All the European partners saw a huge market opportunity for larger investments in Europe, including privatizations, restructurings, and purchases of family-owned businesses (although the deal-flow in different countries was very different). Finally, the changing economic environment in Europe was creating enormous scope for growth in the private equity markets.

As the only committee with a cross-border focus, the "CEO Meetings"—such as the one Smitham was now heading to in Paris—had been the forum for exploring the concept of the Euro fund. (After this group achieved consensus, it would then be up to the various managing partners to return home and sell the concept to his or her colleagues.) Exhibit 4 shows extracts from the summary draft presentation prepared for marketing the European fund to investors.

This concept inspired optimism because Schroder Ventures had already made several successful multinational investments. Some of these investments were across countries with a shared language and similar legal systems, such as Mitel, a joint Canada/United Kingdom transaction. Other transactions involved more diverse groups. An example of an extremely successful transaction in which teams from Germany, Italy, and the United Kingdom had worked efficiently together was Pisten Bully.

In July 1994, partners from the London office were invited to bid for the large family-owned international bus company, Karl Kassbohrer Fahrzeugwerke GmbH, as part of an auction handled by Goldman Sachs. After Schroder Ventures partners from London and Germany paid a visit to the bus factory, the combined team decided not to pursue the acquisition of the bus company. The partners decided instead to attempt to acquire one of the small operating divisions, Pisten Bully. The Pisten Bully division was responsible for the manufacture and sale of grooming machines for ski pistes (colloquially known as "snow cats"). These vehicles were manufactured in Germany and Austria, and were sold to ski resorts worldwide. Pisten Bully had a worldwide market share of more than 50%, selling approximately 400 new vehicles each year.

As the managing partner of the German office, Friedrich von der Groeben took the role of project leader within Schroder Ventures and persuaded Kassbohrer to sell the Pisten Bully division separately from the bus business. (The bus company was subsequently sold to Daimler Benz.) Von der Groeben then sought help from the British and Italian offices to complete the transaction within a six-week time frame. He developed a detailed timetable for due diligence visits and interviews, banking and legal negotiations, and internal approvals, in order to manage the widespread Schroder Ventures team.

International auditors were appointed to report on the quality and accuracy of the management accounts and systems. Von der Groeben assigned the due diligence activity on U.S. customers and markets to the British team, Italian due diligence to the Italian team, and the primary diligence on the German, Austrian, and other European markets to his German team. All due diligence notes were immediately circulated to the other teams. The whole group talked several times a week through teleconferencing and also had communications by phone, fax, and e-mail. Each member of the transaction team spoke German and English fluently. Eric Walters, who headed the London team, had previously been chairman and a member of the advisory board of several German companies, including a publicly traded brewery. Investment Committee meetings for the different funds were held jointly, and all recommendations had unanimous support.

The effectiveness of the cooperation between the offices was demonstrated by the speed with which the bank finance was assembled. By the second week, it became clear that German banks regarded the management buyout as risky and were unwilling to act as lead lenders in this transaction. Von der Groeben immediately enlisted help from the London office. The London partner specializing in banking successfully raised the necessary senior and subordinate debt from British banks. The $100 million transaction closed on time in mid-August. Walters and a German partner were appointed to the supervisory board of Pisten Bully. Within six months, Pisten Bully successfully refinanced much of Schroder Ventures' equity with mezzanine and senior debt, giving the Schroder Ventures funds an attractive early partial realization.

At the same time, Smitham was aware of some of the challenges inherent in these cross-border private equity transactions. The potential difficulties of such deals had been illustrated by the case of Encrouge SA in France, a recently aborted French buyout, in which the French, U.K., and Life Sciences teams had been involved. As the Eurostar approached the black mouth of the Tunnel itself, Peter Smitham looked out at the low gray clouds shrouding the Dover cliffs. He re-read memos (Exhibit 3) summarizing the frustrations and problems experienced by two of the partners, one French and one English, who had been involved on the Encrouge deal.

Encrouge SA Investment

Encrouge was the subsidiary of a French business called O.R. Cantona SA, owned by the wealthy Monopolet family. Cantona was established at the beginning of the twentieth century and grew successfully until World War I. Its principal business in textiles suffered badly during the war years. Following the end of World War II, Cantona received a heavy subsidy from the government in order to prevent liquidation and the job losses that would inevitably follow. Given its location in an economically depressed part of France, job availability and security was an important political issue to the local and federal governments. The subsidy had continued to the present day.

Through Cantona, the Monopolet family had made some unsuccessful speculative investments and found itself unable to cover its bank borrowings. Its banks forced it to sell Encrouge, a profitable subsidiary, in order to repay the money that had been lent.

Encrouge was a manufacturer and supplier of sterile medical hospital products. It had shown spectacular growth over the last five years since it had been started. Encrouge's sales in 1994 were $40m and operating profits $15m. Eighty percent of its sales were to hospitals in France; the remaining sales were to hospitals in Belgium, Romania, and various developing countries. Management planned to increase market penetration in other major European economies, such as Germany, the Netherlands, and the United Kingdom. Its medical products were approved by the French and Belgian regulatory authorities and were awaiting approval elsewhere in Western Europe. Its principal source of competition was from a large U.S. multinational, which held more than 60% of the world market in this hospital products sector. This competitor was regarded as both the quality and cost leader in most industrialized countries.

Vincent Clouseau, an experienced partner in Schroder Ventures' French office, originally identified the deal through his high-level contacts with banks and the French government. He had introduced Encrouge to the United Kingdom and Life Sciences advisory partnerships in order to access both equity and health-care sector expertise. The French banks, acting as the agent for Encrouge, maintained parallel talks with a potential corporate acquirer during the discussions with Schroder Ventures. The bank appeared to be relatively unfamiliar with the concept of a financial buyer, and also sought the additional insurance and price competitiveness that a strategic acquirer would provide. Due principally to disagreements among the different Schroder Ventures teams about an appropriate price for Encrouge, the deal fell through. The corporate acquirer ultimately paid a higher price for the business once the short lockup period with Schroder Ventures expired.

There was a juddering noise, and the Eurostar ground to a halt some 100 yards short of the tunnel. "There has been a slight technical fault, Ladies and Gentlemen," said a voice on the loudspeaker. "This train has been taken out of service and a new one will be sent through from Paris; there will be a delay of 120 minutes." "Two hours!," thought Smitham. He would be late for his meeting. He thought of the billions of pounds of investment that had gone into the Channel Tunnel and the heavy burden of debt it carried. If this was the fruits of European integration, he would have his work cut out.

As the Eurostar remained resolutely still, Smitham pondered the memos on the Encrouge deal, as well as the more fundamental strategic and managerial questions facing the Euro Fund.

Exhibit 1 Simplified Structure of the Schroder Ventures Group

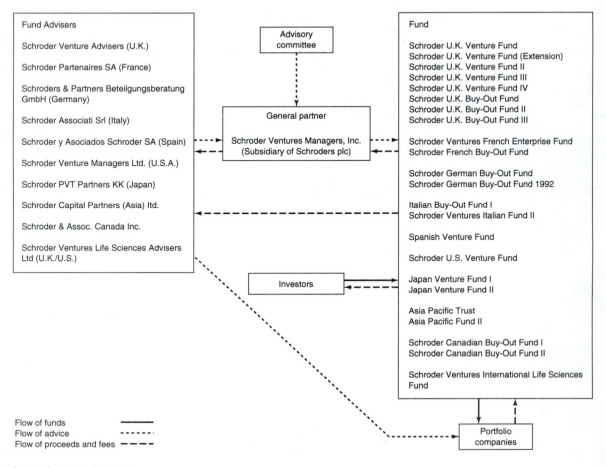

Source: Corporate documents.

Exhibit 2 Structure of a Typical Fund

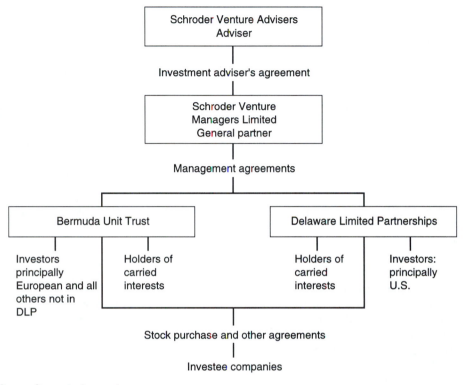

Source: Corporate documents.

Exhibit 3   Memoranda Associated with Proposed Encrouge Transaction

MEMORANDUM

DATE: 25 February 1995

TO: Peter Smitham

FROM: Billy Britten
             Schroder Ventures Life Sciences, London

RE: Encrouge investment process

You asked me to summarise my views on the shortcomings of the Encrouge investment process.

1. Interaction with Encrouge

♦ Overall, there seemed to be little involvement and commitment by the management team to doing an MBO with Schroder Ventures, despite our exclusive agreement with them. It seems surprising that management did not inform us earlier of the trade buyer interest, since they must have been aware of this. Given the structure of the deal, an MBO should have been a more attractive option than a trade sale from management's point of view.

♦ The management seemed oblivious of what was required from them in order to complete the deal; they had little concept of the level of commitment and work required, or the investment process:

- multiple meetings with management were set up to get answers to the due diligence questions which I had outlined in writing at the start of the investment process. Throughout the entire 3 ½ month period, I was never given a detailed business plan outlining the assumptions behind the financial projections. No meeting provided me with detailed forecast projections & assumptions by export country and product, details on competitors' products in the different markets, penetration strategy for Germany, customers outside France etc.

- eventually, a meeting with the full Schroder team was scheduled in which the company's senior management would make presentations on the different areas of the company's operations. However, management had not prepared any presentation or supporting schedules etc. to address the topics I had asked them to discuss and the meeting turned into a free-for-all unstructured discussion. The COO seemed unable to provide answers to fundamental cash management areas, e.g. cash balance, cash flow, working capital etc. The FD was brought in to answer all commercial trading questions; however, management accounts are only generated quarterly and so I could not get hard data on the last two months' trading.

♦ Management believed that they could repeat the excellent growth they had experienced in France in other major European countries. It is obvious from the limited references I took, as well as discussions with their competitors, that the principal reason they won so much business in France was because they were a French company. The French are not alone in protecting their own turf and there is a major US competitor in every developed market which is likely to prevent them from repeating this growth elsewhere. I was given no evidence, such as customer orders etc. to support this assumption of export growth.

2. Investment process

♦ The style of doing investments was very different. Commercial due diligence seems to take place in French deals only once all the financial and legal terms, including the list of the agreed due diligence activities, have been completely agreed. How can the deal be priced in the absence of a clear understanding of the company's current and future value?

If material discrepancies arise between management's view and our due diligence, then it is legally justified to withdraw from the deal. However, if the due diligence (which tends to focus on historical events) approximately reflects the company's history as given by management, then it seems we are legally *bound* to complete the deal. This process allows no scope for analyzing the future forecast performance of the company, since the legal definition of due diligence does not include anything that is not fact. From my point of view, this is not a commercial basis to proceed. If the value of the company arises from its future growth in exports and due diligence suggests that they are unable to meet their export projections, we have no way of getting out of doing the deal—or renegotiating the price. In fact, the Schroder Partenaires told me of several occasions when vendors successfully sued venture capital providers for not completing the agreed deal. Obviously, we have to be very cautious in bidding for deals, or we will be saddled with a bad business!

♦ All documentation (except internal SP documents) were written in French. My French is not good enough to get a proper understanding, so the process was drawn out in order for each document to be verbally summarized in English.

♦ Communication between the French and British teams was poor on this deal. This was partly because of language barriers, and partly because the training of the French and British teams is very different. It took us a long time to agree an acceptable process, timetable, responsibilities etc. because of the need to discuss each part of the process.

♦ I was surprised by the control that the banks exerted over the company. Encrouge had assumed an unusually high amount of debt and the banks seemed to act almost as equity holders. However, on the other hand, I did not understand why the banks allowed Encrouge's CEO, Monsieur Monopolet, to conduct much of the negotiation for the sale of the business, since he was both a buyer and a seller.

♦ Management accounts seem not to be relied on by management for running the business. They are not produced regularly nor in a useful format.

I have shown this memo to colleagues in the UK Schroder Ventures Team, and they share the same frustrations and views.

MEMORANDUM

DATE: 29 February 1995

TO: Peter Smitham

FROM: Vincent Clouseau

           Schroder Partenaires, Paris

RE: Encrouge investment process

You asked me to summarize my thoughts on the problems with the Encrouge deal.

1. Due diligence: I was frustrated by the U.K. and Life Sciences teams' demand for numerous references on management and the business. This is not a company off the street. My family has known Monsieur Monopolet and his family personally for at least 10 years and I trust what he tells me. We sent a very poor message to him by asking for all these external references, especially when he wanted to hide the fact that Encrouge was being sold. This does not look good for him or his family. The external referees were bemused to be approached for references on a man and family whom they have known for years. We at SP have never worked on this basis, nor do other private equity firms, and we have produced perfectly acceptable returns. Indeed our competitiveness would fall significantly if we frightened off companies with an intrusive and aggressive approach to deals.

2. Management accounts: The U.K./Life Science teams wanted detailed weekly management accounts for Encrouge which is just not possible. No private, especially family-owned, business produces accounts so regularly and it is better to spend time with the Finance Director to learn about the operations of the business.

3. The U.K. and Life Science teams were very sceptical about Encrouge's future growth outside France. They suspected that the French government and hospitals were favouring Encrouge over alternative suppliers because it is a French company, which was why it had performed so well. There was limited objective evidence for this view. Encrouge penetrated the mature French market, displacing a major U.S. competitor and now has 40% market share in this high margin medical products sector. There is no reason why they cannot repeat at least part of this spectacular growth elsewhere.

4. The deal process was very unsatisfactory. The vendors and I agreed a price for the business and were ready to sign the preliminary sale and purchase agreement, subject to the due diligence listed in the document. The U. K. and Life Sciences team kept wanting to do due diligence before this agreement was signed. This is not the normal process for French deals. In France, due diligence is required to confirm the factual basis of the sale. Anything else is merely conjecture and is not legally regarded as good grounds to revoke a transaction. Thus, it is customary to sign the documentation first and do the due diligence later. If we do full due diligence before signing the sale and purchase agreement, then we reduce our argument for changing the terms of the deal if the due diligence turns up something of concern, since the vendor can tell us that we were aware of that concern when we signed up at the start.

5. Communication was poor: the U.K. team did not speak good French which slowed up all meetings. Nor could they understand the company's accounts. I spent lots of time just explaining how things work in France and why they are different from the United Kingdom and United States: the U.K./ILSF teams did not adapt to local conditions and insisted on imposing their own cultural presuppositions. I would have found it easier to have worked with another French group.

    Source: Corporate documents.

Exhibit 4 Excerpts from Draft Investor Marketing Materials for European Fund

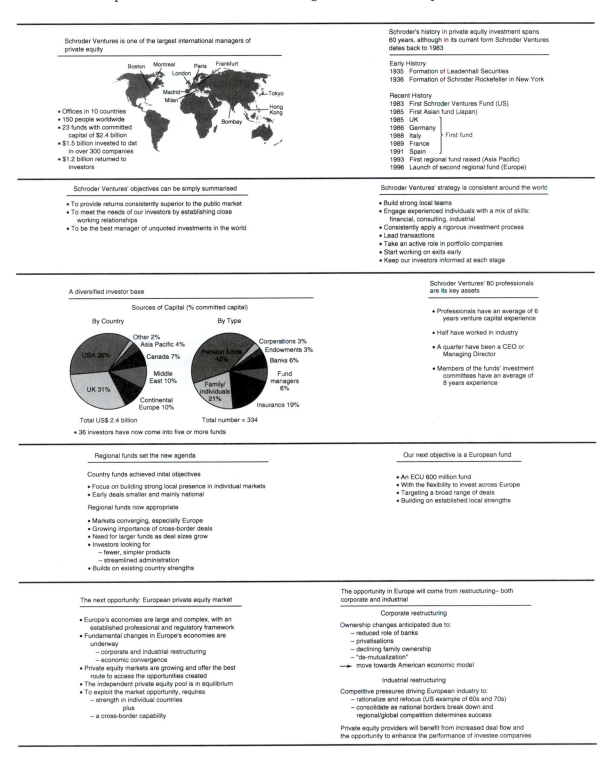

Schroder Ventures is one of the largest international managers of private equity

Boston · Montreal · London · Paris · Frankfurt · Madrid · Milan · Tokyo · Hong Kong · Bombay

- Offices in 10 countries
- 150 people worldwide
- 23 funds with committed capital of $2.4 billion
- $1.5 billion invested to dat in over 300 companies
- $1.2 billion returned to investors

Schroder's history in private equity investment spans 60 years, although in its current form Schroder Ventures dates back to 1983

Early History
1935 Formation of Leadenhall Securities
1936 Formation of Schroder Rockefeller in New York

Recent History
1983 First Schroder Ventures Fund (US)
1985 First Asian fund (Japan)
1985 UK
1986 Germany
1988 Italy   First fund
1989 France
1991 Spain
1993 First regional fund raised (Asia Pacific)
1996 Launch of second regional fund (Europe)

Schroder Ventures' objectives can be simply summarised

- To provide returns consistently superior to the public market
- To meet the needs of our investors by establishing close working relationships
- To be the best manager of unquoted investments in the world

Schroder Ventures' strategy is consistent around the world

- Build strong local teams
- Engage experienced individuals with a mix of skills: financial, consulting, industrial
- Consistently apply a rigorous investment process
- Lead transactions
- Take an active role in portfolio companies
- Start working on exits early
- Keep our investors informed at each stage

A diversified investor base

Sources of Capital (% committed capital)

By Country
USA 36%
UK 31%
Other 2%
Asia Pacific 4%
Canada 7%
Middle East 10%
Continental Europe 10%

Total US$ 2.4 billion

By Type
Pension funds 42%
Family/individuals 21%
Corperations 3%
Endowments 3%
Banks 6%
Fund managers 6%
Insurance 19%

Total number = 334

- 36 investors have now come into five or more funds

Schroder Ventures' 80 professionals are its key assets

- Professionals have an average of 6 years venture capital experience
- Half have worked in industry
- A quarter have been a CEO or Managing Director
- Members of the funds' investment committees have an average of 8 years experience

Regional funds set the new agenda

Country funds achieved inital objectives

- Focus on building strong local presence in individual markets
- Early deals smaller and mainly national

Regional funds now appropriate

- Markets converging, especially Europe
- Growing importance of cross-border deals
- Need for larger funds as deal sizes grow
- Investors looking for
  – fewer, simpler products
  – streamlined administration
- Builds on existing country strengths

Our next objective is a European fund

- An ECU 600 million fund
- With the flexibility to invest across Europe
- Targeting a broad range of deals
- Building on established local strengths

The next opportunity: European private equity market

- Europe's economies are large and complex, with an established professional and regulatory framework
- Fundamental changes in Europe's economies are underway
  – corporate and industrial restructuring
  – economic convergence
- Private equity markets are growing and offer the best route to access the opportunities created
- The independent private equity pool is in equilibrium
- To exploit the market opportunity, requires
  – strength in individual countries
        plus
  – a cross-border capability

The opportunity in Europe will come from restructuring– both corporate and industrial

Corporate restructuring

Ownership changes anticipated due to:
  – reduced role of banks
  – privatisations
  – declining family ownership
  – "de-mutualization"
  → move towards American economic model

Industrial restructuring

Competitive pressures driving European industry to:
  – rationalize and refocus (US example of 60s and 70s)
  – consolidate as national borders break down and regional/global competition determines success

Private equity providers will benefit from increased deal flow and the opportunity to enhance the performance of investee companies

Private equity gives the best access to Continental Europe because the public stock markets are still under-development

Stock Market Capitalization indexed against GDP (1994)

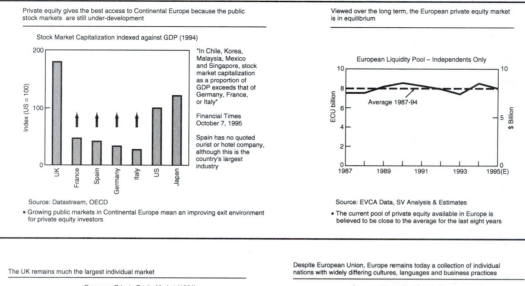

"In Chile, Korea, Malaysia, Mexico and Singapore, stock market capitalization as a proportion of GDP exceeds that of Germany, France, or Italy"

Financial Times October 7, 1995

Spain has no quoted ourist or hotel company, although this is the country's largest industry

Source: Datastream, OECD

• Growing public markets in Continental Europe mean an improving exit environment for private equity investors

Viewed over the long term, the European private equity market is in equilibrium

European Liquidity Pool – Independents Only

Average 1987-94

Source: EVCA Data, SV Analysis & Estimates

• The current pool of private equity available in Europe is believed to be close to the average for the last eight years

---

The UK remains much the largest individual market

European Private Equity Market (1994)

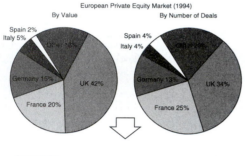

By Value / By Number of Deals

Spain 2%
Italy 5%
Germany 15%
France 20%
UK 42%
Other

Spain 4%
Italy 4%
Germany 13%
France 25%
UK 34%

Source: EVCA

• A strong position in the UK market is essential to any private equity group seeking a balanced presence in Europe
• Schroder Ventures' London office was established over 10 years ago and has a professional team of 24

Despite European Union, Europe remains today a collection of individual nations with widely differing cultures, languages and business practices

Sources of Large Buy-Outs by Number (1994)

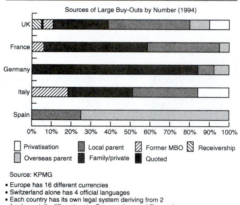

Legend: Privatisation | Local parent | Former MBO | Receivership | Overseas parent | Family/private | Quoted

Source: KPMG

• Europe has 16 different currencies
• Switzerland alone has 4 official languages
• Each country has its own legal system deriving from 2 fundamentally different roots: Common Law and Roman Law

---

Schroder Ventures holds a strong position in the European private equity market

Deals led over ECU 12m 1990–1994

10 Leading Groups	UK #	Continental Europe #					Total #
		France	Germany	Italy	Spain	Other	Total	

10 Leading Groups	UK #	France	Germany	Italy	Spain	Other	Total	Total #
3i	53	2	8	-	-	-	10	63
Schroder Ventures	15	5	3	4	1	-	13	28
CVC	7	2	1	2	1	12	18	25
NatWest Ventures (NWV)	19	1	-	-	-	-	1	20
CINVen	17	-	2	-	-	-	2	19
Charterhouse	9	2	1	-	-	4	7	16
Baring Capital Investors (BCI)	2	7	1	4	-	-	12	14
Montagu Private Equity (MPE)	13	-	-	-	-	1	1	14
Phildrew	13	-	-	-	-	-	0	13
Electra	9	1	-	-	-	1	2	11

Source: KPMG Database

• Although there are local competitors in individual Continental European countries (eg LBO France), they do not have a significant presence across Europe as a whole

Schroder Ventures is unusual in having a strong position both in the UK and on the Continent

Competitive Positioning of 10 Leading Groups (Deals >$15m)

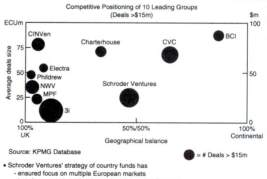

Source: KPMG Database

● = # Deals > $15m

• Schroder Ventures' strategy of country funds has
  - ensured focus on multiple European markets
  - but also constrained the size of deal that can be financed

Schroder Ventures has stable and experienced team

Schroder Ventures' Professional Staff

Country	Year of first fund	Average years with Schroder Ventures		
		Head of office	Partners	All professional staff
UK	1985	11	8	7
Germany	1986	5	5	4
Italy	1988	8	8	5
France	1989	7	6	5
Spain	1991	5	4	3
Average	8 (years open)	7	7	5

Note: Includes whole or part years through to 31.12.95

- In total our European professional staff have 270 years experience with Schroder Ventures
- The emphasis is on local nationals with professional international experience

Schroder Ventures' record in Europe All Buy-Out Funds

ECUm	UK	Continental Europe	Total
Amount invested	415.4	225.7	641.1
Total value of realizations, income, unrealized stakes	887.5	534.7	1,422.2
% realized	68%	39%	57%
% increase in value	214%	237%	222%
Net IRR	25.0%	22.6%	24.1%
Comparable stock market	14.7%	4.4%	10.6%
Premium over stock market	10.3%	18.2%	13.5%

Notes:
1. Schroder Ventures' returns assume liquidation of all investments at 31st October 1995 based on BVCA valuation guidelines and are net return to investors
2. Stock market returns assume reinvestment of dividends

Schroder Ventures' record in Europe Mature Buy-Out Funds*

ECUm	UK	Continental Europe	Total
Amount invested	340.6	170.6	511.2
Total value of realizations, income, unrealized stakes	812.4	473.6	1,285.9
% of total value realized	74%	43%	63%
% increase in value	239%	278%	252%
Net IRR	25.7%	26.3%	25.9%
Comparable stock market	14.7%	3.9%	10.8%
Premium over stock market	11.0%	22.4%	15.1%

* All funds fully drawn down at 31st December 1995
  Schroder UK Buy-Out Funds I & II
  Schroder French Buy-Out Fund
  Schroder German Buy-Outs
  The Italian Venture Fund

Schroder Ventures has invested around ECU 120m per annum in Europe in recent years...

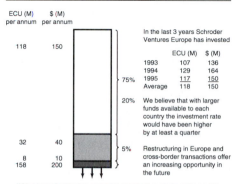

ECU (M) per annum	$ (M) per annum
118	150
32	40
8	10
158	200

In the last 3 years Schroder Ventures Europe has invested

	ECU (M)	$ (M)
1993	107	136
1994	129	164
1995	117	150
Average	118	150

We believe that with larger funds available to each country the investment rate would have been higher by at least a quarter

Restructuring in Europe and cross-border transactions offer an increasing opportunity in the future

... With a larger fund and an expanded opportunity we believe this could be increased to ECU 160m per annum

The European Fund Fund strategy will build on existing strengths

- Investment focus
  - Buy-outs/buy-ins and development capital
  - in the UK, deals requiring >£5m equity
- Sources of deals
  - corporate restructuring
  - family businesses with succession problems
  - privatization
- Nature of deals
  - majority: single country domestic transactions with size appropriate to local market
  - but with cross-border transactions of growing importance
- Active marketing of unequalled European-wide capability
  - 5 offices
  - a professional team of over 50
  - one of the largest funds dedicated to private equity investment in Europe

Source: Corporate documents

8

A Note on European Private Equity

The tremendous growth of European private equity funds have made Europe into the second most developed private equity market after the United States (see Exhibit 1). But Europe is not one market. It is still a collection of individual countries, which vary in some important ways. The largest and most developed private equity market in Europe is the United Kingdom, followed by fast-growing Germany and then France (see Exhibits 1 and 2).

Over 90% of European private equity funds are devoted to buyouts or other later-stage investments. Although the term *venture capital* in Europe is synonymous with private equity, true venture capital (i.e., early-stage investments) has historically been underdeveloped. Some observers have argued that the buyout market may in fact be *too* developed in some European countries and that a dramatic fall in fundraising and investments is likely.

This note will discuss the trends in European private equity through mid-1998, comparing private equity in Europe with the U.S. industry wherever possible. It will also highlight differences among the European countries. The focus will be primarily on buyouts rather than the much-smaller venture capital sector.[1]

BUYOUT FUNDS IN EUROPE

European private equity has gone through a boom-and-bust cycle similar to that in the United States (Exhibit 3). A boom in the late 1980s was followed by a bust in the 1990s. The years 1996 and 1997 witnessed an extraordinary recovery. Fundraising—fueled by the increasing interest in Europe by U.S. institutional investors—far surpassed earlier levels (Exhibit 4). This increase in fundraising was due largely to the strong returns that the European funds have delivered to investors—the returns from European funds have averaged 17% over the past decade—as well as concerns about the degree of competition in the U.S. market.[2] The years 1996 and 1997 were years of strong growth in the volume of deals as well, with the activity in many markets exceeding the levels of the late 1980s.

This note was prepared by Reynir Indahl and Eric Zinterhofer (under the direction of Josh Lerner). Copyright © 1998 by the President and Fellows of Harvard College. Harvard Business School case 299-017.

[1] Unless otherwise noted, this analysis is based on numerous interviews with European and American private equity professionals, as well as on the database of the Centre for Management Buyout Research (CMBOR) at the University of Nottingham and the publications of the European Venture Capital Association and Initiative Europe.

[2] These numbers are based on a preliminary study by Bannock Consulting. For an overview, see "European Performance Surveyed—A Tentative First Step," *European Venture Capital Journal* (December 1996) 3–6.

Although the aggregate trends may be similar to those in the United States, many striking differences exist between the individual European countries and the United States. The United Kingdom had twice the level of invested capital in 1996 than the United States, compared on either a per capita basis or relative to GDP, while several Continental European markets had far less (Exhibits 5 and 6). (Similar patterns appear in the size of the public market relative to GDP.) These differences, however, may be declining with time. In particular, Germany is experiencing rapid growth. Furthermore, the level of private equity in the United Kingdom may be above a sustainable level and may fall in coming years: the dramatic increase of capital under management and the emergence of high-yield debt issues have led to a setting where there is highly competitive bidding for deals.

Historically, European buyout funds grew out of financial institutions, although many of these have lately gone through management buyouts themselves and become independent. Some of the largest and most prestigious independent European funds are offshoots from financial institutions, including Doughty Hanson (Charterhouse and Westdeutsche Landesbank), BC Partners (Barings), Industri Kapital (Skandinaviska Enskilda Banken), and Cinven (the Government Coal Board Pension Fund). Other top-tier funds are still operated as subsidiaries, including Schroder Ventures, Charterhouse, and DMG Capital. The United Kingdom was the cradle of European private equity, and most of the top-tier players are of British origin (Exhibit 7). The industry's capital is increasingly concentrated among a few organizations: the top 15 firms increased their share of the funds raised from 43% in 1995 to 83% in 1996–97.

Germany surpassed France as the largest Continental private equity market in 1996. The driver behind this growth has been the new focus on shareholder value that has forced companies to spin-off companies as part of their restructuring and refocusing efforts. Another reason for the German growth has been the increasing frequency of succession issues among the Mittelstand companies. (The Mittelstand companies are small- to medium-sized family businesses, many of which were started after World War II.) These perceived opportunities have led to widespread optimism among German buyout organizations and the entry of numerous new groups.

France and Italy have been more erratic markets, although France saw a surge of large deals in 1997. The uneven nature of the markets has been attributed to the lackluster performance of some high-profile deals in the 1990s, as well as the difficult regulatory environment, especially in France. Probably the most developed buyout industries outside the United Kingdom are the Dutch and Swiss markets. In both cases, the presence of a strong private pension system has facilitated the raising of funds from local sources. Among the Nordic countries, Sweden has been the only country with a steady transaction flow, although lately Finland has experienced a surge in activity. Denmark and Norway have been more erratic with a limited stream of deals, which is attributed to the many small- to medium-sized family companies and difficult ownership rules.

A majority of the new entrants on the Continent are U.K.-based private equity organizations, along with some American firms. It remains unclear how successful these new entrants will be. It is more challenging to do deals on the Continent than in the United Kingdom or the United States. Accounting standards, government regulations, and union contracts inhibit due diligence and limit the ability to turn around underperforming businesses. Management culture has been another obstacle. Although financial incentives commonly work well in the United Kingdom and the United States, these are less emphasized on the Continent, especially in Germany: numerous observers suggest that German managers put a higher priority on community standing and cooperation at the workplace. Hence, some buyout firms have found it challenging to identify managerial talent who can lead their new acquisitions and make the difficult operational improvements needed.

THE EUROPEAN PRIVATE EQUITY CYCLE

Fundraising

The key sources for European private equity funds have traditionally been segmented by national boundaries. Private equity groups would raise funds from banks, insurance companies, and government bodies in their own country, with little involvement of other investors. The one exception was the United Kingdom, where fundraising has had a strong international flavor—with a heavy involvement of U.S. institutional investors—since the earliest days of the industry.

These barriers are now breaking down. The changes are being driven by two factors. First, institutional investors—particularly in the United States—are becoming increasingly interested in European funds. Second, many international private equity firms are becoming much more active in Europe. American firms such as Carlyle, Texas Pacific Group, KKR, and Chase Capital Partners have entered Europe in one way or another in recent years.

A consequence of these changes is the increasing presence of investment advisers, sometimes called gatekeepers. (These are firms that advise investors, primarily large institutions, about their private equity investments or directly manage their holdings.) In the United States, this is a well-developed market: firms such as Abbott Capital, Brinson Partners, and Cambridge Associates have built strong franchises assisting pension funds and endowments with private equity investments. Gatekeepers and advisers in Europe have been few, reflecting both the immature nature of the private equity market and the lack of large institutional investors with an appetite for private equity. Several of the large U.S. private equity advisers and gatekeepers are currently entering Europe, attracted by pension reforms in Europe as well as an increasing allocation to European private equity by European and American institutional investors. Local advisers are also gaining an increasing following.

One challenge to institutional investors in selecting investments is that there appears to be less strategic differentiation between European private equity firms than between those in the United States. In the United States, private equity players have increasingly focused on developing a niche or a specialty, whereas in Europe the niches are just emerging. For instance, Doughty Hanson, dubbed the KKR of Europe, has achieved considerable success by undertaking large transactions with a heavy reliance on financial engineering and little operating involvement. Exhibit 8 provides a list of the largest European private equity funds in terms of fund size.

Investing

Competition for transactions is intense in Europe, especially in the United Kingdom. According to the Centre for Management Buyout Research at the University of Nottingham, private equity firms are involved in nearly 60% of all mergers and acquisition activity in the United Kingdom, far above the 15% to 20% range seen in the United States. Most of the deals in the United Kingdom are initiated through auctions. Investment banks have made the U.K. auction process very efficient: there is little opportunity to buy firms for below their market value. On the Continent, the process is less efficient. For instance, in Germany and France, personal relationships with lawyers and accountants are important sources of deals for private equity investors. But increasingly, large Continental firms are sold to private equity groups through auctions as well.

The companies purchased by European private equity funds are primarily subsidiaries of conglomerates or family businesses. Unlike the United States, buyouts of public companies are rare in part because of the stringent corporate control rules in some countries. For instance, in France, interest expense of debt can only be deducted if 95% or more of the equity is acquired, which is difficult to accomplish in the case of a public firm with widely scattered holdings.

In the early years of the European private equity industry, a management buyout (MBO) transaction was typical. A typical buyout was initiated by the existing management team. The managers would negotiate with the parent, hire an intermediary to represent them, and find a buyout firm that would provide the equity. Until recently, accounting firms were the intermediary of choice to either auction or "shop around" a firm. During the 1990s, the leading investment banks entered the auction market, and the role of the accountants has been reduced to due diligence work. (They continue to play a role in the auctioning of smaller deals.) On the Continent, lawyers and accounting firms appear to continue to manage more deals than investment banks.

Although many American private equity groups seek to initiate and control transactions themselves, U.K. buyout firms have often been described as "process integrators." For example, buyout firms involve investment banks, accounting firms, and lawyers to support them in preparing the bid, assembling the capital structure, and undertaking the due diligence. A management consulting firm is then involved to improve firm operations post-acquisition. A strong tie to intermediaries may be an important competitive advantage in Europe: Doughty Hanson is reported to have gotten a significant part of its deal-flow through Price Waterhouse in Germany.

As a result of this environment, buyout firms often find it difficult to identify proprietary deal-flow—that is, transactions that are reviewed by only one private equity group. Until recently, this was not too troubling for the major private equity groups, for most investments were syndicated by a number of these groups. (The lead investor would collect a fee from the other participants and could be confident that the other investors would reciprocate in subsequent transactions.) As the size of private equity funds has increased, relationships have become less collegial, and syndication less frequent.[3]

These changes have had two consequences. First, private equity organizations have become much more aggressive in initiating transactions. There has been an increase in management buyins (MBI) and investor buyouts (IBOs); in these transactions, a private equity firm or an outside management team initiates the deal and the existing management team may or may not play a role. Second, the reliance on intermediaries for the identification and management of transactions appears to be declining. Alchemy, Industri Kapital, Schroeder Ventures, CVC, and BC Partners, among others, are reported to rely more on internal resources than on outsourcing.

The financing of deals has also undergone major changes. In particular, the number of high-yield debt transactions more than tripled from 1995 to 1997 and then fell dramatically in 1998.[4] For instance, 1997 saw the first floating-rate French franc, high-yield issue, when Morgan Stanley underwrote a FF 500 million bond offering in conjunction with BC Partners' acquisition of Neopost. The access to high-yield debt allowed BC Partners to decrease the level of equity to U.S. standards, with about 16% equity. (The typical European transaction has about 30% equity.) In 1996 and 1997, mezzanine debt also was easier to raise from local banks. (Mezzanine debt has typically comprised about 10% of the capital structure of U.K. buyouts, with the rest as senior debt [60%] and equity [30%].[5])

---

[3] Similar behavior is seen in many other economic settings. For an overview, see Jean Tirole, *The Theory of Industrial Organization,* Cambridge, MIT Press, 1989, chapter 6.

[4] This is based on an analysis of an unpublished database compiled by Morgan Stanley.

[5] The numbers in this and the following paragraph are based on statistics compiled by CMBOR at the University of Nottingham.

As the size of equity funds and the access to high-yield debt have increased, larger buyouts have become more common. Although there were only 20 transactions over $150 million in size in 1995, there were 33 deals in 1997. Of the 10 largest deals ever done in Europe through the end of 1997, 9 were done in 1997 (Exhibit 9). Half of these transactions involved firms based in Continental Europe.

Exiting

A sale to a corporate acquirer—also known as a trade sale—is the most common form of exit, both in the United Kingdom and on the Continent. The United Kingdom has an advantage over the other European countries in terms of exit, since it has a well-developed capital market. Even when a private equity group sells a company to a corporate acquirer, having the option to take the firm public helps ensure an attractive sale price. The lack of a developed capital market on the Continent has been a particular challenge to smaller, venture-backed companies.[6]

ISSUES FACING EUROPEAN PRIVATE EQUITY INDUSTRY

Many challenges face the European private equity industry today. In this final section, two of these concerns will be highlighted. These are likely to continue to be important issues in the years to come.

First, as the market becomes more competitive—particularly in the United Kingdom—the majority of private equity players will have to focus on adding value to their holdings beyond financial engineering. Numerous European private equity firms in Europe today are grappling with the need to build their competence in helping portfolio firms with their operations. Developing such skills is unlikely to be easy for many groups, whose partners have a primarily financial orientation.

Second, many of the British and American private equity organizations are currently expanding into other European countries. This is driven by the maturity of the British and American markets, the seemingly attractive opportunities on the Continent, and the pressure to deploy the increasingly large equity funds that they are raising. But numerous challenges are associated with growing from a one-office small fund to a larger multinational one. Among the issues are how to provide incentives across countries and offices, how to govern each office's decision processes, and how to implement the expansion. For instance, how should the carried interest be split if the French deal team wants the German deal team to help a French portfolio firm enter Germany? If the German team is highly productive, but the French office does not do any deals for a year, who should get compensated and in what way? How can a team used to working in the United Kingdom break into the German buyout market, given both their lack of business relationships and the different business practices?

---

[6] For a detailed discussion, see Chapter 20, "The European Association of Securities Dealers: November 1994."

Exhibit 1 Overview of the European Buyouts: 1996 Value and Cumulative Annual Growth Rates (CAGRs)

US$ billions invested, 1996

	US$ billions	1989–96	1993–96	1995–96
		CAGR percent		
US	28.8	−13	38	40
UK	12.5	1	44	73
Continental Europe*	7.9	11	26	165
Scandinavia	1.9	1	38	137

* Excluding Scandinavia
Source: Initiative Europe, Buyout Magazine.

Exhibit 2 Continental European Buyouts: 1996 Value and Cumulative Annual Growth Rates

US$ millions, 1996

	US$ millions	1989–96	90–96	93–96	95–96
		CAGR			
Germany	1,837	13%	22%	46%	160%
France	1,722	3%	−11%	9%	38%
Switzerland	1,475	37%	24%	38%	177%
Netherlands	1,094	17%	29%	38%	60%
Italy	1,050	9%	8%	20%	358%
Sweden	832	−6%	−9%	14%	46%
Finland	517	24%	23%	68%	174%
Denmark	379	2%	0%	119%	466%
Spain	256	13%	8%	74%	35%
Norway	160	36%	−7%	152%	1043%
Portugal	158	n/a	33%	33%	30%
Austria	126	0%	5%	60%	690%
Belgium	123	0%	−7%	41%	584%

Source: Initiative Europe.

Exhibit 3   Tabulation of European Buyouts (Transactions over Ten Million British Pounds Only)

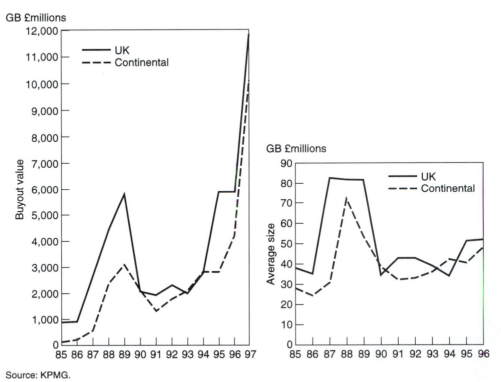

Source: KPMG.

Exhibit 4   Fundraising by European Private Equity Organizations

ECU millions (during this period, 1 ECU equaled on average US$1.22)

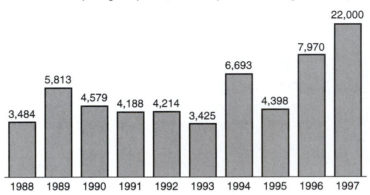

Data sources for 1996 and 1997 are not the same, and differences in methodology could be significant. It is likely that the 1997 estimate is biased downwards.

Source: EVCA; clippings; interviews.

Exhibit 5 Buyout Value as a Fraction of Gross Domestic Product, by Country, 1996

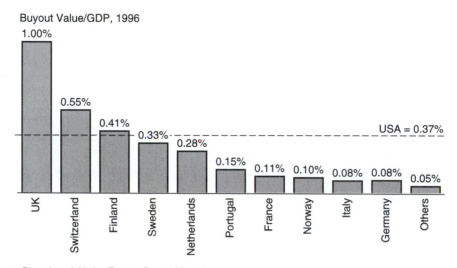

Source: Bloomberg Initiative Europe, Buyout Magazine.

Exhibit 6 Per Capita Buyout Activity, by Country, 1996

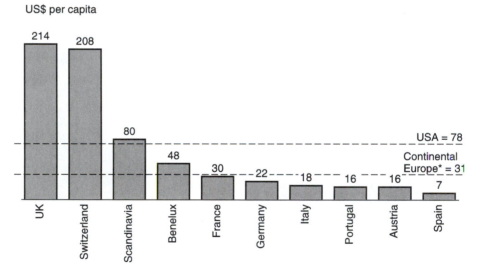

*Including Scandinavia. Excluding Scandinavia the value is 27
Source: Initiative Europe, OECD statistics.

Exhibit 7 Overview of Large Private Equity Organizations at the End of 1997

Company	Size (US$ millions)	Number of Profs	Offices	Past Deals	Comment
BC Partners	1,100	21	UK,FR,IT, GR	Elis, Neopost	Most European of the UK buyout houses
Charterhouse	1,300	23	UK, FR	ITS, Porterbrook	Looking for 2–3 UK deals per year
Candover	1,000	10	UK	Williams Hdgs, BBC	Focuses on large UK transactions
CVC	840	30	UK,FR,IT,SW, GR, SP,DK,UK	Haefely Trench, SEAT	Relies on a strong network of regional offices
CinVen	850	18	UK, GR,SW	Generale de Sante	Targets large/high profile transactions
Doughty Hanson	2,500	16	SW,UK, GR	Geberit, TAG Heuer	In pursuit of large continental buyouts
Industri Kapital	850	15	UK,SW,NO, GR	Ellos, Lindex	Strong in Scandinavia and Germany. Targets mid-cap deals
Schroder Vent.	1,000	55	UK,FR, GR,IT,SP	Siemens Dental, Tetley Tea	Preference for larger deals, but will consider start-ups
Investcorp	n/a	TBD	LN, (NY)	Welcome Break, Helly Hansen, Gucci	Mid-cap to large cap deals. Raise capital for each deal from Arabian investors

Source: Compiled from press accounts.

Exhibit 8   Largest Private Equity Fundraisers in Europe, 1994-1997

	Largest fund each year

Player	Cumulative funds raised 1994–97 GB£ millions	Funds raised in year			
		1997	1996	1995	1994
Doughty Hanson	2,061	1,625	436		
3i	1,593	786	350	200	257
BC Partners	1,168	706			462
Charterhouse	1,138	800			
Candover	920	650	110		270
Schroder Ventures	773	625		38	163
Industri Kapital	693	530			
Apax	643	479		164	26
Advent International	638	612			
HSBC Capital	612	200	497	155	
CVC	497		84		300
DMG Capital	448			64	
Legal & General	355	200		155	
CinVen	300		300		
Total top 15	11,839	7,455	1,777	621	1986
Total # of funds raised	95	31	23	18	23

GB£ millions

* Organizations that have raised over GB£ 200 million in any one year since 1994. Excluded are US organizations and organizations that do not raise external funds.

Source: Acquisitions Monthly.

Exhibit 9   The Ten Largest Private Equity Transactions in Europe through 1997

Acquiree	Value GB£ billions	Year	Country	Acquirer
Gateways	2.2	1989	UK	Isosceles
Spring Inns	2.0	1997	UK	Nomura
SEAT	2.0	1997	Italy	BC Partners/Bain Capital/Investitori Associati
General Healthcare	1.8	1997	France	CinVen
Geberit	1.2	1997	Germany	Doughty Hanson
William Hill	1.2	1997	UK	Nomura
Elis	1.1	1997	France	BC Partners/Goldman Sachs
BTR Polymer	0.9	1997	UK	Legal & General Ventures
Dacne Dry Food	0.9	1997	France/USA	Paribas
Welcome Break	0.8	1997	UK	Investcorp

Source: Acquisitions Monthly; Financial Times.

PRIVATE EQUITY INVESTMENTS

The second module of the course considers the interactions between private equity investors and the entrepreneurs they finance. These interactions are at the core of what private equity investors do. We will approach these interactions through a framework that highlights the particular challenges that portfolio firms pose to private equity investors, as well as the mechanisms that these investors have developed to address these challenges.

WHY THIS MODULE?

It is easy to build a case that the financing and guidance of dynamic private businesses lie at the heart of the private equity process. The frequently complex interactions between investors and the firms in their portfolios could fill several courses! In order to help organize this complex material, we will approach the cases in this module through a two-part framework.

First, we categorize the reasons why the types of firms backed by private equity investors find it difficult to meet their financing needs through traditional mechanisms, such as bank loans. These difficulties can be sorted into four critical factors: uncertainty, asymmetric information, the nature of firm assets, and the conditions in the relevant financial and product markets. At any one point in time, these four factors determine the choices that a firm faces. As a firm evolves over time, however, these factors can change in rapid and unanticipated ways.

We also consider six classes of responses to these challenges by private equity investors. The first three relate to the investment process itself: determining the sources from which the firm should raise capital, how the investment should be structured, and how the profits should be divided. The second set involves the investors' more general interactions with the firm: monitoring management performance, shaping the firm's assets, and evaluating whether to continue or terminate the investment. Thinking about these four classes of problems and six classes of responses will help organize the complex interactions between private equity investors and the firms in their portfolios.

THE FRAMEWORK (1): THE FINANCING CHALLENGE

Entrepreneurs rarely have the capital to see their ideas to fruition and so must rely on outside financiers. Meanwhile, those who control capital—for instance, pension fund trustees and university overseers—are unlikely to have the time or expertise to invest directly in young or restructuring firms. The entrepreneurs would be expected to turn to traditional financing sources, such as bank loans and the issuance of public stock, to meet their needs. But a variety of factors are likely to prohibit some of the most potentially profitable and exciting firms from accessing these financing sources.

Private equity investors are almost invariably attracted to firms that find traditional financing difficult to arrange. Why are these firms difficult to finance? Whether managing a $10 million seed investment pool or a $1 billion leveraged buyout fund, private equity investors are looking for companies that have the potential to evolve in ways that create value. This evolution may take several forms. Early-stage entrepreneurial ventures are likely to grow rapidly and respond swiftly to the changing competitive environment. Alternatively, the managers of buyout and buildup firms may create value by improving operations and acquiring other rivals. In each case, the firm's ability to change dynamically is a key source of competitive advantage, but also a major problem to those who provide the financing.

As mentioned above, these dynamic firms will be analyzed using a four-factor framework. The first of these, *uncertainty,* is a measure of the array of potential outcomes for a company or project. The wider the dispersion of potential outcomes, the greater the uncertainty. By their very nature, young and restructuring companies are associated with significant levels of uncertainty. Uncertainty surrounds whether the research program or new product will succeed. The response of a firm's rivals may also be uncertain. High uncertainty means that investors and entrepreneurs cannot confidently predict what the company will look like in the future.

Uncertainty affects the willingness of investors to contribute capital, the desire of suppliers to extend credit, and the decisions of firms' managers. If managers are averse to taking risks, it may be difficult to induce them to make the right decisions. Conversely, if entrepreneurs are overoptimistic, then investors want to curtail various actions. Uncertainty also affects the timing of investment. Should an investor contribute all the capital at the beginning, or should he stage the investment through time? Investors need to know how information-gathering activities can address these concerns and when they should be undertaken.

The second factor, *asymmetric information,* is distinct from uncertainty. Because of his day-to-day involvement with the firm, an entrepreneur knows more about his company's prospects than investors, suppliers, or strategic partners. Various problems develop in settings where asymmetric information is prevalent. For instance, the entrepreneur may take detrimental actions that investors cannot observe: perhaps undertaking a riskier strategy than initially suggested or not working as hard as the investor expects. The entrepreneur might also invest in projects that build up his reputation at the investors' expense.

Asymmetric information can also lead to selection problems. The entrepreneur may exploit the fact that he knows more about the project or his abilities than investors do. Investors may find it difficult to distinguish between competent entrepreneurs and incompetent ones. Without the ability to screen out unacceptable projects and entrepreneurs, investors are unable to make efficient and appropriate decisions.

The third factor affecting a firm's corporate and financial strategy is *the nature of its assets.* Firms that have tangible assets—for example, machines, buildings, land, or physical inventory—may find financing easier to obtain or may be able to obtain more favorable terms. The ability to abscond with the firm's source of value is more difficult when it relies on physical assets. When the most important assets are intangible, such as trade secrets, raising outside financing from traditional sources may be more challenging.

Market conditions also play a key role in determining the difficulty of financing firms. Both the capital and product markets may be subject to substantial variations. The supply of capital from public investors and the price at which this capital is available may vary dramatically. These changes may be a response to regulatory edicts or shifts in investors' perceptions of future profitability. Similarly, the nature of product markets may vary dramatically, due to shifts either in the intensity of competition with rivals or in the nature of the customers. If there is exceedingly intense competition or a great deal of uncertainty about the size of the potential market, firms may find it very difficult to raise capital from traditional sources.

THE FRAMEWORK (2): THE ACTIVITIES OF PRIVATE EQUITY INVESTORS

Private equity investors may use a variety of mechanisms to address these changing factors. Careful crafting of financial contracts and firm strategies can alleviate many potential roadblocks. We will highlight six of these responses.

The first set of these responses relates to the financing of firms. First, *from whom* a firm acquires capital is not always obvious. Each source—private equity investors, corporations, and the public markets—may be appropriate for a firm at different points in its life. Furthermore, as the firm changes over time, the appropriate source of financing may change. Because the firm may be very different in the future, investors and entrepreneurs need to be able to anticipate change.

Second, the *form* of financing plays a critical role in reducing potential conflicts. Financing provided by private equity investors can be simple debt or equity or may involve hybrid securities such as convertible preferred equity or convertible debt. These financial structures can potentially screen out overconfident or underqualified entrepreneurs. The structure and timing of financing can also reduce the impact of uncertainty on future returns.

A third element is the *division* of the profits between the entrepreneurs and the investors. The most obvious aspect is the pricing of the investment: for a given cash infusion, how much of the company does the private equity investor receive? Compensation contracts can be written that align the incentives of managers and investors. Incentive compensation can be in the form of cash, stock, or options. Performance can be tied to several measures and compared to various benchmarks. Carefully designed incentive schemes can avert destructive behavior.

The second set of activities of private equity investors relate to the strategic control of the firm. *Monitoring* is a critical role. Both parties must ensure that proper actions are taken and that appropriate progress is being made. Critical control mechanisms—for example, active and qualified boards of directors, the right to approve important decisions, and the ability to fire and recruit key managers—need to be effectively allocated in any relationship between an entrepreneur and investors.

Private equity investors can also encourage firms to *alter the nature of their assets* and thus obtain greater financial flexibility. Patents, trademarks, and copyrights are all mechanisms to protect firm assets. Understanding the advantages and limitations of various forms of intellectual property protection, and coordinating financial and intellectual property strategies are essential to ensuring a young firm's growth. Investors can also shape firms' assets by encouraging certain strategic decisions, such as the creation of a set of "locked-in" users who rely on the firm's products.

Evaluation is the final, and perhaps most critical, element of the relationship between entrepreneurs and private equity investors. The ultimate control mechanism exercised by private equity investors is to refuse to provide more financing to a firm. In many cases, through direct or indirect actions—the investor can even block the firm's ability to raise capital from other sources.

THE STRUCTURE OF THE MODULE

This module will illustrate these frameworks with examples from a wide variety of private equity funds and industries. We will carefully identify the types of problems that emerge in different industries and stages of firm development.

This module will also explore the institutional and legal aspects of each type of private equity transaction: venture capital, buyouts, buildups, and venture leasing. We will highlight how private equity organizations employ these mechanisms and react to these regulations to promote success.

Among the specific issues raised in private equity transactions that we will consider are:

- The investment criteria and approaches of venture investors.
- The alternative criteria and approaches employed by later-stage investors, as well as the associated providers of debt financing to these firms.
- The nature of transactions that incorporate elements of both venture capital and buyouts, such as venture leasing and leveraged buildups.
- The extent to which deal structures can be translated into overseas markets, such as developing nations.
- The various ways in which valuation issues are addressed, including many of the methodologies specific to the private equity industry and the opportunities for applying new valuation techniques.
- The relationship between financing choices and firm strategy.
- The structure and implementation of relationships with strategic co-investors.
- The restructuring of entrepreneurial ventures in distress.

FURTHER READING ON PRIVATE EQUITY INVESTING

Legal and Descriptive Works

JOSEPH W. BARTLETT, *Equity Finance: Venture Capital, Buyouts, Restructurings, and Reorganization,* New York, Wiley, 1995, chapters 5–10 and 16–27.

MICHAEL J. HALLORAN, LEE F. BENTON, ROBERT V. GUNDERSON, JR., KEITH L. KEARNEY, AND JORGE DEL CALVO, *Venture Capital and Public Offering Negotiation,* Englewood Cliffs, NJ, Aspen Law and Business, 1995, volume 1, chapters 5 through 9.

JACK S. LEVIN, *Structuring Venture Capital, Private Equity, and Entrepreneurial Transactions,* Boston, Little, Brown, 1995, chapters 2 through 8.

Practicing Law Institute, *Venture Capital* (Commercial Law and Practice Course Handbook Series), New York, Practicing Law Institute, various years, various chapters.

Practitioner and Journalistic Accounts

LEONARD A. BATTERSON, *Raising Venture Capital and the Entrepreneur,* Englewood Cliffs, NJ, Prentice-Hall, 1986.

COOPERS & LYBRAND, *Three Keys to Obtaining Venture Capital,* New York, Coopers & Lybrand, 1993.

HAROLD M. HOFFMAN AND JAMES BLAKEY, "You *Can* Negotiate with Venture Capitalists, *Harvard Business Review* 65 (March–April 1987): 16–24.

ROBERT J. KUNZE, *Nothing Ventured: The Perils and Payoffs of the Great American Venture Capital Game,* New York, HarperBusiness, 1990.

ROBERT C. PEREZ, *Inside Venture Capital: Past, Present and Future,* New York, Praeger, 1986.

JAMES L. PLUMMER, *QED Report on Venture Capital Financial Analysis,* Palo Alto, QED Research, 1987.

Many accounts in *Buyouts, Private Equity Analyst,* and *Venture Capital Journal.*

Academic Studies

GEORGE P. BAKER AND KAREN H. WRUCK, "Organizational Changes and Value Creation in Leveraged Buyouts: The Case of O.M. Scott & Sons Company," *Journal of Financial Economics* 25 (December 1989): 163–190.

GEORGE W. FENN, NELLIE LIANG, AND STEPHEN PROWSE, "The Private Equity Market: An Overview," *Financial Markets, Institutions, and Instruments* 6 (no. 4, 1997): 27–69.

PAUL A. GOMPERS AND JOSH LERNER, *The Venture Capital Cycle,* Cambridge, MIT Press, 1999, chapters 6–9.

PAUL A. GOMPERS AND JOSH LERNER, "Money Chasing Deals? The Impact of Fund Inflows on Private Equity Valuations," *Journal of Financial Economics,* Forthcoming.

THOMAS F. HELLMANN AND MANJU PURI, "The Interaction Between Product Market and Financing Strategy: The Role of Venture Capital," Unpublished Working Paper, Stanford University, 1998.

STEVEN N. KAPLAN AND RICHARD S. RUBACK, "The Valuation of Cash Flow Forecasts: An Empirical Analysis," *Journal of Finance* 50 (September 1995): 1059–1093.

STEVEN N. KAPLAN AND JEREMY STEIN, "The Evolution of Buyout Pricing and Financial Structure in the 1980s," *Quarterly Journal of Economics* 108 (May 1993): 313–358.

SAMUEL KORTUM AND JOSH LERNER, "Does Venture Capital Spur Innovation?," Working paper G846, National Bureau of Economic Research.

KRISHNA G. PALEPU, "Consequences of Leveraged Buyouts," *Journal of Financial Economics* 27 (September 1990): 247–262.

CHRISTINE C. PENCE, *How Venture Capitalists Make Investment Decisions,* Ann Arbor, MI, UMI Research Press, 1982.

WILLIAM A. SAHLMAN, "The Structure and Governance of Venture Capital Organizations," *Journal of Financial Economics* 27 (October 1990): 473–521.

TYZOON T. TYEBJEE AND ALBERT V. BRUNO, "A Model of Venture Capitalist Investment Activity," *Management Science* 30 (September 1984): 1051–1066.

GO Corporation

Jerry Kaplan and Bill Campbell sat in their fourteenth floor office in Foster City in March 1991, watching planes take off and land from nearby San Francisco International Airport. They were contemplating the future of fledgling GO Corporation. Four years earlier, Kaplan founded the company with a dream: to revolutionize the way people used computers by substituting a pen for the keyboard. Kaplan's cohort, Bill Campbell, had joined GO as CEO only weeks ago, having led Apple's Claris software unit for four years.

Just as GO was gaining momentum, Microsoft had announced its commitment to enter the pen-based computing market with a competing system. With a burn rate of $1.5 million a month, only $7 million in the bank, "glitchy" handwriting-recognition software, and corporate crossfire from the likes of IBM, AT&T, and Apple, Kaplan and Campbell dialed the familiar digits to raise John Doerr and Vinod Khosla, their foremost backers at the venture capital firm Kleiner Perkins. Kaplan and Campbell needed to discuss their alternatives in light of Microsoft's announcement. Among the major issues they needed to reconsider were product development schedules, strategic partnerships, and the next round of financing.

THE ORIGIN OF GO CORPORATION

After receiving his Ph.D. degree in computer and information science from the University of Pennsylvania in 1979, Jerry Kaplan joined the research staff of Stanford University. (See Exhibit 1 for a brief biography.) Witnessing the personal computer revolution taking place around him, Kaplan started to develop expert systems that ran on PCs. An expert system is a set of computer instructions that captures human reasoning. With expert systems software, a PC can help users manage information—notes, ideas, to-do lists, phone messages—by "learning" the ways the users manage the information themselves. In 1984, Kaplan met Mitch Kapor, the founder and CEO of Lotus Development Corporation. The two hit it off immediately, and Kapor contracted with Kaplan to develop his ideas into a product. Kaplan continued to work at Stanford and occasionally visited Kapor in his office in Cambridge, Massachusetts.

In February 1987, after one of his visits, Kaplan hitched a ride back to San Francisco on Kapor's new jet. During the entire flight, Kapor was busy sorting his notes, which were written on everything from a napkin to a gum wrapper, and typing them into his new Compaq 286 portable computer. Complaining about the inefficiency of having

This case was prepared by Tarek AbuZayyad and Paul C. Yang (under the direction of Josh Lerner).

to translate information from paper to computer, Kapor asked Kaplan if there were ways to get information directly into the computer. The two began to discuss the limitations of using portable computers in everyday business activities and soon realized that the keyboard was a limiting factor. "How about if a pen is used instead of a keyboard?," Kaplan wondered.

Almost like clockwork, every decade since the computer revolution had seen the emergence of a new class of computer. For instance, in the first years of the 1970s computers evolved from refrigerator-like boxes with spinning tapes and flashing lights into minicomputers that could be hidden in closets and connected to many terminals. In the early 1980s, personal desktop computers became the dominant form of computing. With each generation of device came whole communities of software developers, hardware suppliers, and customers. Each new class of computers did not replace the older computers. Instead, they empowered different people to solve different problems. Whereas mainframe computers automated many back-office functions such as billing and payroll processing, personal computers greatly enhanced the productivity of office workers with spreadsheet and word processing software.

Kaplan and Kapor believed that they had stumbled onto the next wave of computers—a pen-based device that worked like a notebook instead of a typewriter. As an extension of desktop PCs, portable computers were easier to carry but not practical for the true mobile computer users. In many situations where face-to-face activity was necessary, such as meetings and customer visits, using a keyboard could be disruptive and socially unacceptable. In addition, graphical objects such as maps and drawings were difficult to input using a mouse.

Pen-based computers, on the other hand, would fade into the background and would be less obtrusive to both user and audience. They would allow mobile users to focus on activities that demand their concentration. Besides the mobile computer users, both Kaplan and Kapor believed that if they could build a pen-based computer that was intuitive to use, many noncomputer users would join this technological revolution.

INITIAL STRATEGY

After several weeks of further discussion about the technical feasibility of such a new computer, Jerry Kaplan founded GO Corporation with Kapor's encouragement and financial support. The new firm faced many immediate challenges. Whereas the portable computer market was already well developed by the late 1980s (see Exhibit 2), the pen-based computer segment was just starting to emerge. There were no standard hardware platforms, operating systems, or applications.

To address these challenges, Kaplan immediately began building a talented engineering team. Soon after founding the company, he hired Robert Carr, then the chief software scientist at Ashton-Tate, to be the vice president of software development, and Kevin Doren, with whom Kaplan had worked at the University of Pennsylvania, to be the vice president of hardware development. The three founders assembled a talented team of engineers to develop everything from scratch—the hardware, application software, and operating system (the central program, like Microsoft's DOS and Windows, that regulated all operations of the computer).

In order to achieve the vision of a truly intuitive computer the new operating system (OS) had to go beyond the sophistication of available systems. Although the Microsoft Windows and Apple MacIntosh OSs allowed users to work with objects,

Kaplan hoped that the new system would allow users to "create" objects. He considered three options in developing his pen-operating system:

1. To build a "pen compatibility layer" onto an existing QS.

2. To merge selected components of several existing OSs.

3. To create a new operating system from the ground up.

The first two approaches were rejected because layering a pen interface on one or more keyboard-based OSs would significantly compromise the pen's ease of use. With the layered approaches, the pen became an alternative form of keyboard and mouse. By itself, the emulation did nothing to simplify the complexity associated with desktop operating systems such as starting applications, opening and saving files, and working with directories. Such an approach increased the amount of computer memory required, and since more memory required a larger (and heavier) battery, the mobility of the computer would be negatively affected. Lastly, because many mobile, pen-based applications would be fundamentally different from desktop applications—for example, forms completion, electronic calendars, freehand sketching, and note-taking—the benefit of using an existing OS for the sake of application compatibility was minimal. Even traditional applications such as spreadsheets and word processors would require enough rethinking for the pen that the amount of rewriting would be substantial. For these reasons, Kaplan and his team decided to create an entirely new operating system which they named PenPoint™. "The Pen Is the Point" became the company logo.

In addition to an operating system, GO sought to provide well-designed hardware and applications in order to offer users a complete solution. As the pioneer in a market with no other hardware manufacturers and independent software vendors (ISVs) actively involved, GO was forced to design the pen computer and to write the initial personal data management programs.

DEVELOPING THE PEN-BASED COMPUTER INDUSTRY

As GO Corporation commenced operations in late 1987, the engineers soon encountered unforeseen challenges. The hardware development was the center of many difficulties. Although the new computer was designed around an Intel 286 central processing unit (the same family of microprocessor that governed the operations of IBM, Compaq, and many other "clone" personal computers), many of its other components had to be custom-designed. To compound the problem, GO turned to a Japanese supplier to manufacture these components. The physical distance and differences in culture and language made communication very difficult.

Fortunately, pen-based computers quickly stirred up a frenzy in the entire PC industry. Overnight, many large hardware manufacturers like IBM, NEC, Toshiba, and NCR, as well as pen-based computer start-ups like GRiD and Momenta, saw the potential of this new market and announced their own product developments. Industry consultants and trade magazines boldly predicted annual U.S. sales of 1.5 million units by the year 1995. Many Wall Street analysts expected pen-based computers to become "commoditized" even faster than IBM PC clones. Anticipating thin profit margins and development problems, Kaplan ultimately pulled the plug on in-house hardware development, relinquishing it to players like NCR, AT&T, and GRiD, and focused instead on getting these hardware vendors to license PenPoint™ as the operating system.

Similarly, instead of continuing the development of pen-based applications within GO, Kaplan actively pursued ISVs and major PC software companies to adopt PenPoint™. GO typically encouraged ISVs to develop applications by supporting their use of PenPoint™'s application programming interface (API).[1] Beyond this, there were no substantive terms. ISVs were free to sell their programs through any channel. Occasionally, however, applications such as Pensoft's Personal Information Manager (PIM) would be bundled along with PenPoint™, in which case a small royalty per unit would be paid to GO. WordPerfect, Lotus, and Borland came on board and announced that they would develop PenPoint™ versions of their products. In addition, many software start-ups like Slate and Pensoft sprung up to develop applications only tailored to the pen-based computer users.

Pensoft's PIM was intended to make full use of the pen-based capabilities of PenPoint™. With PIM, a user could carry the computer around and use it all the time. Everything the user wrote would be entered into PIM, including notes, contacts, and phone numbers. Slate's product was the Professional Application Development System (PADS), a utility that would allow third-party application developers to create custom pen-based applications for PenPoint™. Expecting that early demand for pen-based computers would be in applications such as collecting and distributing data-using forms, GO first started to develop this utility but later transferred the development to Slate. In exchange, Slate would finish development and market the product under PenPoint™.

Relationships with ISVs often became strained. GO was, first and foremost, promoting its operating system to the market. In order to find customers, it needed applications that its customers valued. In developing applications for these customers, ISVs often had to choose between competing operating system platforms. The decision to support one over another was simply economic: they would expend their limited development budgets on the platforms likely to have the largest installed base in the future.

THREE SCENES FROM THE FINANCING OF GO

Seed Capital (August 1987)

Jerry Kaplan's maroon leather case landed on the table with a loud clap as the partners at Kleiner Perkins looked on. "Gentlemen, here is a model of the next step in the computer revolution," said Kaplan.[2] Without so much as a prototype or a spreadsheet, he was trying to sell the group on the promise of pen-based computing.

By 1987, Kleiner, Perkins, Caulfield & Byers had earned a place among the legendary venture capital firms in the United States. Kleiner Perkins had made investments in such success stories as Apple, Compaq, Genentech, Sun Microsystems, and Tandem. The firm consisted of nine partners and had raised six funds representing hundreds of millions of dollars. The two partners in charge of the GO investment were John Doerr and Vinod Khosla. Doerr was responsible for the partnership's investments in information technology. Khosla, who co-founded Sun Microsystems in 1982, served as one of the firm's technology specialists. (See Exhibit 1 for biographies of Doerr and Khosla.)

---

[1] API referred to the functions that one program makes available for other programs to use. PenPoint™'s API comprised functions that the programmer could access to perform a variety of operations within that system, such as reading or writing data, managing memory, and displaying information inside a window on the screen.

[2] Jerry Kaplan, *Startup: A Silicon Valley Adventure*, Boston, Houghton Mifflin, 1994, p. 25.

A week later, Doerr called Kaplan with the news that Kleiner Perkins had decided to back him. The deal was structured as a $1.5 million Series A Participating Preferred stock issue.[3] If converted into common stock, it would be equal to 33% of the firm's equity. The per-share price was 40 cents. While Kleiner took the lion's share of the issue, Kapor and a few other individual investors also subscribed. Of the remaining equity (issued as common stock), Kaplan took 25%, and the rest went to employees, present and future. GO Corporation was legally incorporated in August 1987.[4]

Three months later, after sharpening the pencil on budgets and schedules, Kaplan raised another $500,000 from the same investors at 60 cents a share. With over 10 million shares outstanding at this time, GO had a valuation of above $6 million.

Second-round Financing (November 1988)

"Let's cut the bull and get to the demo," grinned Mitch Kapor as Kaplan began his address to the board in July 1988.[5] The demonstration was impressive. The team explained how the unit could fit into a shell about an inch thick and how it could be used to improve productivity in many ordinary tasks. Still, many issues remained. How quickly could they make the unit portable? When would they have the handwriting recognition bugs worked out? How much would it cost? GO was burning through $500,000 a month. At their current burn rate, GO had four to six months of cash left. Nevertheless, both Doerr and Khosla felt certain that many investors would want in at the right price. That price, the board believed, was a pre-money valuation[6] of $14 million.

In approaching potential investors, Kaplan had to answer several questions. First, was GO worth the $14 million that the board was asking? One approach might be to value the company according to some market comparables. Second, how much should they raise: $3 million? $5 million? Third, what type of investors should they seek: venture capitalists? pension funds and endowments? independent software vendors? hardware manufacturers? In any case, Doerr and Khosla were reluctant to have Kleiner act as the lead investor (even though they would buy into the new round), because a new investor would allow for the most impartiality in valuation.

While an early-stage firm frequently only had three financing options—one of the handful of seed venture capital funds, the proverbial "family and friends," or reliance on operating cash flows ("bootstraping")—middle-stage firms had many more choices. They could tap further venture capital financing, partner with a corporate behemoth, access public markets, or seek a private placement from an institutional investor. The choice, however, often had profound implications for the company's future development.

GO first approached the ISVs who were flush with cash. Both Jim Manzi of Lotus and Ed Esber of Ashton–Tate passed, while Microsoft agreed to explore applications

---

[3] In the event of liquidation or sale of the company below a certain prescribed price, the Participating Preferred Stock shareholders first receive the face value of their investments. If there is anything left over, the common shareholders will then receive distributions along with the Participating Preferred shareholders, according to the percentage of ownership. Venture investors often use this instrument to protect their investments.

[4] Over the next few years Kleiner Perkins also invested in a variety of other firms developing technologies for pen-based computing, including applications developers Notable Technologies, PenMagic, and Slate, and hardware manufacturer EO (a spin-out from GO).

[5] Kaplan, op. cit., p. 61.

[6] Pre-money is a term generally used to mean a company's valuation exclusive of the funds currently sought: that is, the product of shares outstanding before the offering and the price per share paid in the new financing round.

development but decided not to invest directly. Next, Kaplan hit the road in search of $5 million of venture capital: among the organizations he contacted were Merrill–Pickard, Sequoia, Sevin Rosen, Technology Venture Investments, Accel, Mayfield, Institutional Venture Partners, Oak, Chancellor Capital, and Aeneas (the private equity arm of the Harvard University endowment, which invested not only in private equity partnerships but directly in privately held firms). Some passed; some were studying the market; others were unsure about the $14 million pre-money price.

Late one November afternoon, a frustrated and travel-ragged Kaplan called on Doerr to say that no one was biting and that the company had four weeks of cash left in the bank. On the spot, Doerr called the home number of Scott Sperling, a managing director of Aeneas:

John: *Scott, we need to close up this financing and we don't have a lead. Where do you stand?*

Scott: *We did a lot of work on this and we like the concept. There's a big market if you can make it work, but we feel the deal is overpriced.*

John: *At what price would you be willing to lead?*

Scott: *Eight million pre.*

John: *And how much would you be willing to commit at that level?*

Scott: *Up to two million.*[7]

They had their lead at 75 cents a share, a 25% premium over the last round. Days later, they had commitments for a total of over $6 million.

Corporate Partners (May 1990 and March 1991)

The third financing round began in June 1989, when Kaplan visited State Farm Insurance in Bloomington, Illinois. State Farm represented a huge potential customer. Thousands of adjusters could use a pen-based computer in their daily routine, leading to a substantial improvement in their productivity. IBM, Digital, and Hewlett-Packard were vying for their business as well. Impressed with GO's technology but concerned about the start-up's viability, State Farm awarded GO the business with one caveat— that it work with one of its traditional hardware vendors.

GO approached IBM with a tacit proposal that if IBM were prepared to make an investment of about $10 million in GO, it would be prepared to pursue the State Farm business jointly. IBM agreed in principle. Negotiating with IBM, however, was painstaking, not to mention time-consuming. Everyone in the bureaucratic organization had to be involved. In a series of meetings, each interest group—software, hardware, research, legal—claimed to have decision-making authority, yet none wielded it. The structure of the deal changed with each group with which GO met. First, a combination $5 million loan and $5 million equity investment was pitched. Then IBM proposed to buy GO out. The negotiations seemed to drag on indefinitely.

Meanwhile, by early 1990, GO was burning through $1 million a month. Kaplan could not afford to wait on the IBM deal to close, so he approached State Farm again. He proposed that they be the lead investor at an aggressive valuation—$2.50 per share. (See Exhibit 3 for GO's projections and market comparables during 1990.) After analyzing the investment, State Farm's investment arm agreed to commit $5 million.

---

[7] Kaplan, op. cit., pp. 79–80.

Existing investors came in as well. Then John Doerr arranged a meeting with Intel. Intel initially agreed to a $5 million investment with a public announcement of support if GO agreed to upgrade its architecture to accommodate Intel's more recent 386 microprocessor. At first, Kaplan balked at the expense of upgrading but finally conceded on this issue: the benefit of a public endorsement by Intel would be great. At the last minute, however, Intel reduced its investment to $3 million, shrinking the total financing round to $15 million. To make matters worse, Intel pulled the public endorsement and began serious talks with Microsoft. (Exhibit 4 summarizes the equity financing of GO and the associated valuations.)

GO's intense product development and marketing schedule quickly consumed the $15 million. Kaplan again turned to IBM. This time, he played on IBM's rivalry with Microsoft. "If you back me, I can get you in this market way ahead of Microsoft," bluffed Kaplan, not knowing what the status of their project was. Jim Cannavino, general manager of Personal Systems line of business, took the bait. IBM proposed a combination $2 million loan and $5 million advance—against royalties secured by intellectual property. GO also negotiated a "mutual walkaway" and got IBM to agree to support its application programming interface. GO and IBM announced their new partnership in July 1990. The deal was not signed, however, until March 1991, when GO had just a few weeks of cash to spare.

THE PRODUCT: PENPOINT™ OPERATING SYSTEM

After three turbulent years of writing and rewriting, GO released the first version of PenPoint™ (the "developer's release") in January 1991. The product was designed expressly to meet the needs of the mobile, pen-based computing market. The new release incorporated five key features that made possible a new class of computers that were easier to use than existing systems.

Notebook User Interface (NUI)

PenPoint™ used a notebook metaphor to organize the user's work. (See Exhibit 5 for a picture of the interface.) Users were insulated from the complexities of applications and files, and instead interacted with documents. On the first page was a Table of Contents (TOC) that listed all the documents in the "notebook." Associated with each document was a page number. Documents could be grouped into sections. Tabs could be attached to any document or section. To move from the TOC to a document, the user simply touched the appropriate page number in the TOC, the tab, or the document icon. The user could easily reorganize the contents of the TOC by dragging documents to different locations, and the notebook's pages were then automatically renumbered.

To enable a pen to be significantly easier to use than a mouse and a keyboard, PenPoint™ users issued commands via "gestures," which combined selection and action into a single intuitive motion. Examples of gestures included crossing out words or graphics with an X, turning pages or scrolling with a flick, and moving text or graphics by dragging them with a pen. The 11 basic gestures worked consistently throughout the system and applications. (See Exhibit 6 for a list of gestures.) In addition, users did not have to press a button on the pen or the screen to differentiate between gestures and text. A user could draw a circle on the screen in different applications, or even within the same application, and be assured of different results, depending on the context. Users could also utilize a menu of gesture equivalents if they preferred.

PenPoint™'s NUI provided a handwriting translation system that would accommodate a wide variety of handwriting styles. After text was written into an input pad, it was translated and presented to the user in easy-to-correct editing pads. After any necessary corrections were made, the user inserted the text into the document. A two-way link between applications and the translation system allowed applications to supply context to improve translation results. For example, an application could indicate whether it was expecting alpha or numeric input in a given field or whether a circle would be interpreted as the letter "o" or an edit gesture. The handwriting recognition system also had the ability to "learn" to recognize the unique style of writing. Several users could share a single machine, easily switching between different handwriting profiles without rebooting or complex reconfiguration.

Embedded Document Architecture (EDA)

PenPoint™'s EDA allowed users to embed live documents inside of one another and to create hyperlinks between documents with a single gesture. For example, a user could use a word processor to create a letter and embed a drawing into it. But unlike traditional operating systems, both applications were "live" in the same document—the user could edit the letter or the embedded drawing at the same time. The user could even drag text from the letter into the drawing and vice versa. By creating hyperlink, a user could customize his navigation paths from a file to anywhere in the notebook.

Mobile Connectivity

PenPoint™ provided "instant on." When users turned on their machines, they were returned to the page that was being viewed when the computer was turned off. In addition, the operating system allowed users to issue commands for printing, faxing, filing, or any other form of data storage, even when the computer was not connected to any physical peripherals. PenPoint™ simply moved a copy of the document to the "Out Box." When the user made the appropriate connection, the document was then automatically transferred out of the "Out Box" and processed. Similarly, the PenPoint™ machine could be awakened to request data from a host computer or receive a fax, even if it was left unattended. The machine put the received file in the "In Box" and informed the user when he returned.

PenPoint™ also allowed moving, copying, and manipulating files on PCs and Macintoshes, and any network volume available to them. When a user attempted to copy a foreign data file into PenPoint™, a dialog box appeared which listed the applications that would accept the file.

Compact and Scaleable Implementation

While expressly designed for small, lightweight portable computers, PenPoint™ was highly hardware-independent and scaled to a variety of formats, from pocket-size to wallboard-size computers. Any PenPoint™ application could run unmodified on any PenPoint™ machine.

32-bit Multitasking

PenPoint™'s internal communication protocols and memory configuration took full advantage of the 386 processor. This enabled PenPoint™ to be adapted to other processor families. The multitasking capabilities enabled smooth user interface, background communications, and instant translation of handwriting while the user was writing.

THE FUTURE OF PEN-BASED SYSTEMS

Analysts predicted 40,000 pen-based computers would be shipped in 1991, with prices ranging between $3000 and $6000. At this price range, most of the systems would be purchased by mobile workers such as sales and service professionals. On the other hand, users could buy a desktop computer with equivalent power for about $2000 and a graphical tablet as an add-on for another $1500. By 1993, most analysts expected the price to begin falling by about $1000 a year, thereby broadening the market appeal. Shipments of pen-based systems were predicted to grow to about 1.4 million in 1996. Internationally, sales was projected to grow twice as fast as in the United States. Many non-Western markets (especially Japan, Hong Kong, and Korea) would find a pen to be a more practical input device than a keyboard given the nature of their languages. (Unit shipment and price data are presented in Exhibit 7.)

Pen-based applications such as a personal information manager (PIM), forms completion software, word processors, and spreadsheet programs were expected to carry a price tag between $200 and $500. Operating systems providers typically received as much as a 10% royalty from applications sales. On the hardware side, Microsoft had been charging approximately $30 for every copy of MS-DOS bundled with a computer shipment and another $60 for its Windows program.

COMPETITION

The emergence of this new market—and GO's plans to take advantage of it—had not gone unnoticed. In fact, three formidable competitors had emerged by March 1991, each of whom was apparently intending to produce a competing operating system for pen-based devices.

Microsoft

Microsoft, located in Redmond, Washington, was founded by the now-legendary Bill Gates in 1975. By 1990, the company had surpassed Lotus as the world's largest software developer, with sales of $1.2 billion and net income of $279 million. Microsoft competed in both arenas of the PC software market—operating systems and applications. In the operating systems segment, Microsoft's MS-DOS and Windows had dominant market share (86%) over Apple's Macintosh OS (12%) and IBM's OS/2 (2%).

Microsoft licensed its operating system to hardware manufacturers and received royalty payments on a per-unit basis. Because of its market dominance in this segment, Microsoft negotiated very favorable terms with computer manufacturers. In some instances, the company charged a royalty based on the manufacturer's total Intel-based computer shipments, regardless of the number of operating systems that were actually bundled with these devices. In addition, Microsoft charged ISVs royalties on sales of any applications based on Windows' API. In 1990, the operating systems generated $464 million in sales for Microsoft. The company was also the largest applications developer for the Intel-based computers and the second largest for the Apple Macintosh computers behind Apple's Claris subsidiary. The company's popular applications such as Excel and Word generated $563 million of sales in 1990.

Kaplan first encountered Bill Gates in July 1988, when he was looking for additional investors in GO and ISV support for PenPoint™. GO's board was initially reluctant to approach Gates. Unlike the other major applications companies like Lotus and Ashton–Tate, Microsoft was also in the operating systems business. Moreover, Microsoft had a reputation of detecting promising markets with unseasoned competitors and launching similar products with aggressive pricing. The board believed, however, that working with Microsoft was a necessary evil, given its large market share. It would be impossible, they feared, for PenPoint™ to become an open architecture standard (i.e., one that a large number of ISVs wrote applications for) without Microsoft's support.

Thus, Kaplan invited Gates to visit GO and see a demonstration of PenPoint™ under the condition that Gates sign a nondisclosure agreement. After seeing the PenPoint™ demonstration, Gates said to Kaplan, "this is something different, like a Mac, … and that means we have a choice. We can start to work with you now or play catch-up if it succeeds."[8] Despite sending one of his applications engineers to look at PenPoint™ in more depth, Gates never decided to develop applications for GO or to invest in it. (See Exhibit 8 for Gates' e-mail to senior management regarding GO.)

Instead, Gates decided to compete. The "war" broke out in early 1991. After GO announced the "developer's release" in January and subsequently received wide industry acclaim, Microsoft announced its own version of a pen-based operating system—PenWindows. Unlike GO's develop-from-scratch approach, Microsoft built PenWindows as an extension of its desktop version of Windows. Although PenWindow's 16-bit architecture was less "user friendly" than PenPoint™'s 32-bit, Microsoft promised users perfect file compatibility and ISVs minimal modifications to existing applications. Jeff Raikes, Microsoft's vice president of office systems, openly discredited GO's approach in his interview with the magazine *Infoworld*:

> GO is a little off base to say you need a new operating environment because of a pen. … PC users will not tolerate two operating systems—one for their desktop PCs and another for their portables—and ignore their investment in Windows applications. … And it is not necessarily clear that the world is out there demanding a new 32-bit operating system.[9]

Not knowing which operating system would eventually become standard in the marketplace, many large software vendors and large hardware manufacturers decided to hedge their bets, developing products that allowed end-users to run either PenPoint™ or PenWindows. Smaller ISVs, however, had to choose between the two operating systems because of their limited resources. After Microsoft's announcement, one small ISV said to Kaplan,

> I've been thinking about Windows, and I'm having second thoughts about writing applications for PenPoint™. … Your system is compelling, but Windows is compatible with an installed base of millions of PCs. As a developer with capital constraints, it's hard to ignore that.[10]

Tim Bajarin, vice president at Creative Strategies Research International, summarized: "if the market is going to be driven by technology, GO has the edge, … but if it's going to be driven by business, Microsoft will have the lead."[11]

---

[8] Kaplan, op. cit., p. 66.

[9] Laurie Flynn, "The Power of the Pen," *Infoworld* 13 (March 4, 1991): 44*ff*.

[10] Kaplan, op. cit., p. 170.

[11] Flynn, op. cit.

Apple

Sensing the rapid convergence of telecommunication and mobile computing, John Sculley, CEO of Apple Computer, became interested in developing a "personal digital assistant" which he later named "Newton." Much like GO's vision, Sculley wanted to design Newton as a pen-based device that could manage all the user's personal and business information. Instead of having the complete functionality of a desktop computer, however, Newton focused on mobile communication capability: e-mail, wireless fax, and network linkage. Consequently, it was positioned as a companion system to the desktop computers.

Sculley had initially shown interest in working with Kaplan and GO. Sculley had invited Kaplan to visit him in Cupertino soon after GO's founding and personally tried to recruit Kaplan to join his effort in developing Newton. Later, Sculley considered licensing PenPoint™ as the operating system for Newton, but the idea was dropped because of the strong opposition among the Apple software developers. Kaplan observed, "the idea of buying technology rather than developing it internally was entirely contrary to Apple's culture. This technical xenophobia was known in Silicon Valley by the initials NIH—not invented here."[12]

In the midst of the market's enthusiasm for PenPoint™ and PenWindows, Apple decided to join the battle. Apple chose to design its own operating system with a graphical interface similar to the Apple desktop computers. Its decision to proceed added legitimacy and momentum in this developing market. Nevertheless, in March 1991, Newton's product launch was believed to be at least two years away.

Momenta Corporation

Like GO, Momenta was a young start-up company in the pen-based computer industry. The company adopted the strategy that Apple had employed in the desktop market: it kept both the hardware and the operating system in-house. Its operating system, Momenta Applications Development Environment (MADE), was an object-oriented operating system very similar to PenPoint™, and its Intel 386 pen-centric computers were fully IBM-compatible. In addition, Momenta's hardware could also run PenWindows and DOS. Analysts appeared to be enthusiastic about Momenta's new product. As one noted:

> Momenta's interface seemed like a rough-and-ready combination of superb innovations and throwbacks to earlier desktop models. The menu panel was a welcome change from the busyness of the PenPoint™ interface, and the Command Compass is a real advancement in the interface design. Cascading menus, however, were confusing to use.[13]

DECISIONS

> Look gang, it's time to bet the company. IBM is getting antsy again; Microsoft is breathing down our neck; the investors are anxious; and our reputation is fading. We can't afford to delay any further, period. It's time to stand and deliver.[14]

[12] Kaplan, op. cit., p. 156.

[13] "Pen Systems at a Glance," *Pentop*, vol. 1 (November–December 1991), pages unnumbered.

[14] Kaplan, op. cit., p. 161.

As they waited for the Kleiner Perkins partners to take their call, Kaplan and newly appointed CEO Bill Campbell mulled over several pressing issues. First, product development schedules for the full release of PenPoint™ were slipping behind. What could the team do to ensure a more timely launch? How could they maintain momentum among ISVs, investors, and, perhaps most critically, end users?

Second, how should they face off with the likes of Microsoft? Should they consider a partner such as AT&T which had just developed a RISC microprocessor called the Hobbit?[15] (Unlike Intel's 286 and 386 microprocessors, the Hobbit was designed specifically for mobile computing systems and featured lower consumption and heat dissipation.) What would they sacrifice by such a move? What would the competition's likely counter-move be?

Third, GO was burning through over $1.5 million a month. How should GO finance all these activities? Should it consider further venture capital, additional strategic partners, or an initial public offering?

Finally, was the mass market strategy that GO had been following the wrong approach? There seemed to be strong demand for pen-based computers in specialized markets: for example, insurance adjusters. These customers were less price sensitive and did not require flawless handwriting recognition. On the other hand, Kleiner Perkins and the other venture investors were counting on GO to be the next Microsoft. How would Kaplan and Campbell pacify these investors if they were to switch strategies?

---

[15] RISC is the acronym for *Reduced Instruction Set Computing*. It allowed for greater processing speed by employing fewer and simpler instructions.

Exhibit 1   Selected Management and Board of Directors Profiles

Jerry Kaplan, *Founder and Chairman*

Prior to founding GO Corp., Kaplan served as principal technologist at Lotus Development Corporation, where he co-authored Lotus Agenda, the first personal information management software. In 1981, Kaplan co-founded Teknowledge, now a public artificial intelligence company. Kaplan received a BA in history and philosophy of science from the University of Chicago and a Ph.D. in computer and information science from the University of Pennsylvania.

Bill Campbell, *Chief Executive Officer*

Campbell was founder, president and CEO of Claris Corporation which was purchased by Apple Computer in 1990. Before starting Claris, he was U.S. Group Executive at Apple. In 1983, Campbell joined Apple as vice president of marketing. By 1984, his responsibilities broadened to include sales as well as distribution, service and support. Prior to Apple, Campbell worked at Eastman Kodak and J. Walter Thompson, an advertising agency in New York. Bill Campbell was head football coach at Columbia University for six years before entering commercial industry.

John Doerr, *Director*

Doerr joined Kleiner Perkins in 1980 and sponsored a series of investments including Compaq, Cypress, Intuit, Lotus, and Sun Microsystems. He was the founding CEO of Silicon Compilers. Prior to joining Intel as a line manager, Doerr earned an MBA at Harvard and a masters in electrical engineering at Rice University.

Vinod Khosla, *Director*

Khosla was a co-founder of Daisy Systems and founding Chief Executive Officer of Sun Microsystems. He served on the boards of PictureTel and Spectrum Holobyte. Khosla held a bachelor of technology in electrical engineering from the Indian Institute of Technology in New Delhi, a masters in biomedical engineering from Carnegie Mellon, and an MBA from Stanford.

Source: Corporate documents.

Exhibit 2 Overview of Portable Computer Market

Units Shipped ('000s)

	1986	1987	1988	1989	CAGR
	100	180	320	570	79%

Market Share of Portable Computer Makers, 1989

Toshiba	23%
Zenith	19%
Compaq	14%
Tandy	12%
NEC	10%
Epson	3%
All other	19%

Source: Compiled from International Data Corp., 1990.

Exhibit 3   GO's Pro Forma Financial Projections and Market Comparables

GO Pro Forma Financial Projections (dollar figures in thousands)

	1990	1991	1992	1993	1994	1995	1996
Hardware licensing	$ 0	$1,200	$4,500	$ 8,400	$15,150	$27,150	$42,000
ISV licensing	0	566	2,342	4,707	8,512	14,436	20,278
Application/utilities	0	0	0	1,311	3,549	8,317	15,569
Total revenues	*0*	*1,766*	*6,842*	*14,418*	*27,212*	*49,903*	*77,847*
Cost of goods sold	0	265	1,026	2,163	4,082	7,485	11,677
Development	3,750	4,500	5,250	6,000	6,750	7,500	8,250
Marketing	1,000	1,250	1,600	2,884	5,442	9,981	15,569
Sales	0	141	547	1,153	2,177	3,992	6,228
SG&A	400	500	600	1,442	2,721	4,990	7,785
Total expense	*5,150*	*6,391*	*7,997*	*11,479*	*17,090*	*26,463*	*37,832*
Operating income	(5,150)	(4,890)	(2,181)	777	6,040	15,955	28,338
Tax	0	0	0	0	0	3,587	9,635
Net income	*(5,150)*	*(4,890)*	*(2,181)*	*777*	*6,040*	*12,368*	*18,703*

Source: Casewriter estimates. The typical major software manufacturer had capital expenditures equal to 9% of sales in 1990, and net working capital equal to 40% of sales. NM = not mentioned.

1990 Comparables of PC Software Companies (dollar figures in millions)

	Microsoft	Lotus	Ashton-Tate	Novell	Borland
Revenue	$1,183	$685	$231	$498	$227
Net income	$279	$23	$(18)	$94	$27
Earnings growth:					
1 year	63.7%	-65.8%	NM	94.3%	127.2%
5 year	63.2%	-9.4%	NM	86.7%	NA
Year-end market value	$8,631	$844	$126	$2,324	$437
Year-end debt	$17	$165	$6	$4	$10
P-E ratio:					
High	35	73	NM	25	18
Low	18	23	NM	10	5
Beta	1.40	1.35	1.45	1.30	1.70

Beta is calculated using weekly data from 1990. In 1990, the average yield on a 10-year Treasury bond was 8.55%; the mean prime rate was 10.01%. NM = not meaningful.

Source: Compiled from Standard & Poor's Industry Surveys, 1991.

Exhibit 4   GO's Historical Fund-Raising Activities and Valuations[a]

Fund Raising Summary and Valuations (millions of dollars, except per share figures)

Investors	Year Invested	Amount ($ millions)	Price per Share	Number of Common Stock-Equivalent Shares Sold in Financing Round
Kaplan	August 1987	-	-	1.88
Management/employees	August 1987	-	-	5.62
First round—A	August 1987	$1.5	$0.40	3.75
First round—B	November 1987	0.5	0.60	0.83
Second round	November 1988	6.3	0.75	8.40
State Farm round[a]	May 1990	15.3	2.50	6.12

The totals assume the exercise of all outstanding warrants and the conversion of the preferred shares (*i.e.,* those purchased in the first, second and State Farm rounds) into common stock. Not all shares reserved for management were immediately distributed. Consequently, the valuations discussed in the case (which in some cases were based on shares actually outstanding) may differ somewhat from those implied by these calculations.

[a]State Farm round includes Intel, a few Japanese banks, as well as investors in earlier funds.

Sources: Compiled from the VentureOne database and Jerry Kaplan, *Startup: A Silicon Valley Adventure*, Boston, Houghton Mifflin, 1994.

Exhibit 5   PenPoint™ Notebook User Interface

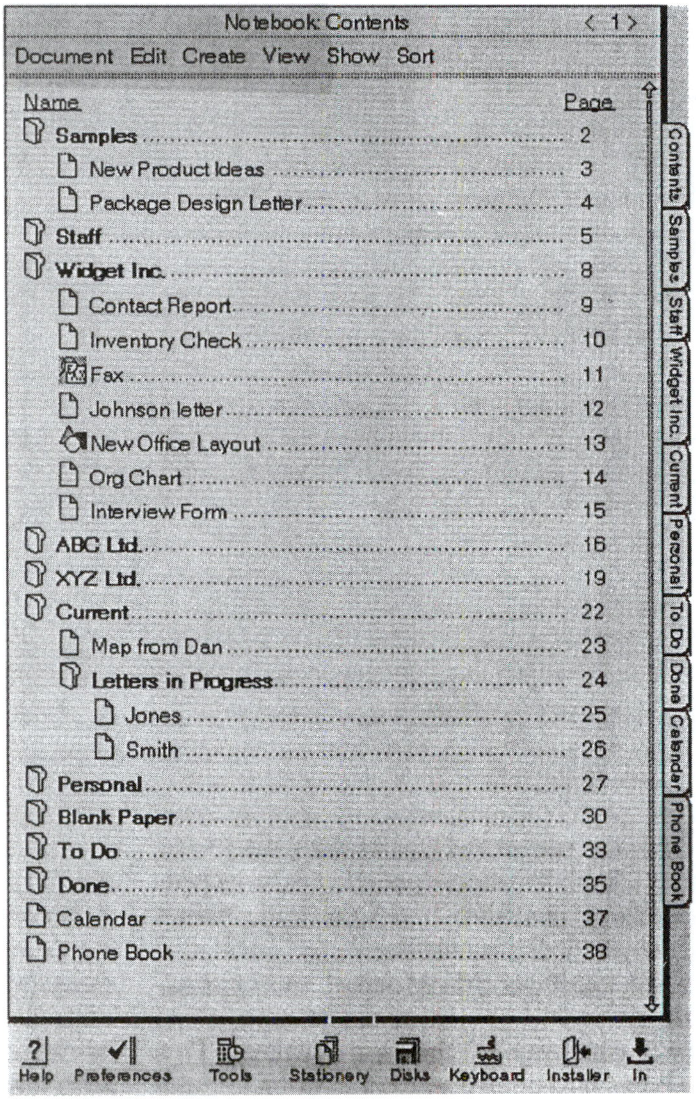

Source: Corporate documents.

Exhibit 6 PenPoint™'s Basic Gestures

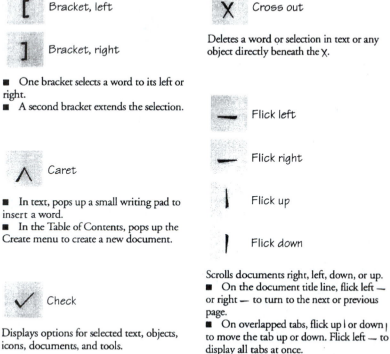

[Bracket, left

] Bracket, right

■ One bracket selects a word to its left or right.
■ A second bracket extends the selection.

∧ Caret

■ In text, pops up a small writing pad to insert a word.
■ In the Table of Contents, pops up the Create menu to create a new document.

✓ Check

Displays options for selected text, objects, icons, documents, and tools.

○ Circle

Opens an edit pad for a word or selection in text, text fields, and labels.

X Cross out

Deletes a word or selection in text or any object directly beneath the X.

— Flick left

— Flick right

| Flick up

| Flick down

Scrolls documents right, left, down, or up.
■ On the document title line, flick left — or right — to turn to the next or previous page.
■ On overlapped tabs, flick up | or down | to move the tab up or down. Flick left — to display all tabs at once.

L Insert space

■ In text, adds a space.
■ In writing and edit pads, adds one or more spaces.

 9 Pigtail

Deletes a character in a writing or edit pad character box, or an individual character in text.

▸ Press

■ Begins a move.
■ Begins a drag-through selection.

▸ Tap

Selects or activates what you touch with the pen.
■ In text, selects one character.

▸ Tap press

Begins a copy.

Source: Corporate documents.

Exhibit 7   Forecast Unit Shipment and Revenue Data for the Pen Computing Industry

Total U.S. Unit Shipments (000s)

	1990	1991	1992	1993	1994	1995	1996	CAGR %
Desktop	6,070	5,486	5,100	4,899	4,561	4,247	3,954	-7%
Notebook/laptop	832	1,258	1,820	2,601	3,803	5,561	8,131	46
Pen-based	0	40	150	280	505	905	1,400	104[a]
Total	6,902	6,784	7,070	7,780	8,869	10,713	13,485	12

[a]CAGR for pen-based computers is based on unit growth between 1991 and 1996.

Source: Compiled from Forrester Research, 1990.

Total U.S. Revenue ($ millions)

	1990	1991	1992	1993	1994	1995	1996	CAGR %
Desktop	$12,140	$10,972	$10,200	$9,308	$8,666	$7,644	$7,117	-9%
Notebook/laptop	2,912	3,774	5,096	6,503	8,937	12,234	17,076	34
Pen-based	0	200	675	1,120	1,768	2,263	3,220	74[b]
Total	$15,052	$14,946	$15,971	$16,931	$19,371	$22,141	$27,413	11

[b]CAGR for pen-based computers is based on sales growth between 1991 and 1996.

Source: Compiled from Forrester Research, 1990.

Pre-packaged PC Software Revenue

	1990	1991	1992	1993	1994	1995	1996	CAGR %
Total U.S. sales	$6.90	$8.00	$9.20	$10.90	$12.46	$14.24	$16.28	14.30%

Source: Compiled from Data Analysis Group, September 1990.

Total PC End-User Spending ($ billions)

	1990	1991	1992	1993	1994	1995	1996	CAGR %
Home	$ 3.50	$ 3.64	$ 3.88	$ 4.08	$ 4.14	$ 4.29	$ 4.50	4%
Business	51.10	58.60	65.20	72.50	79.20	84.80	93.79	11
Total	$54.60	$62.24	$69.08	$76.58	$83.34	$89.09	$98.29	10

Includes computer, peripherals, operating systems and applications.

Source: Compiled from BIS Strategic Decisions, September 1991.

Exhibit 8   Gates's Memo to Microsoft Senior Management Regarding GO

From: billg Thu Jul 14 16:42:49 1988
To: [6 names deleted]
Subject: GO Corporation
Cc: [3 names deleted]
Date: Thu Jul 14 16:42:45 1988

Jeff Harbers and I met with Jerry Kaplan and Bob Carr of GO corporation Monday afternoon. Basically they are building a machine that Kay and I talked about building a long time ago - a machine with no keyboard and no disk using static memory. It's like an 80286 version of the model 200 with 2meg-8meg using a writing stylus with handwriting recognition for input. According to Marquardt there are a few other people building things like this - in fact there was one discussed in the WSJ this week. It's notebook size. The LCD is 640x400 so about 55DPI (which I don't think is enough).

They are doing ALL their own system software - a protect mode OS for 286 using visual objects (like everyone!). It's multitasking. The interface metaphor is a set of named folders with tabs on the right hand side each containing any number of numbered pages and each page has on it just ink (writing) or rectangles that contain application sessions (which can be zoomed/unzoomed). All the old ideas like using gestures for various commands they have "rediscovered". They will announce in 1990 at $3k. Modem is optional. They will bundle some drawing/wp/filing/notetaking/ mail software but they want to get third party ISVs including Microsoft.

We tried out their handwriting stuff and it was terrible. It's very possible to do this stuff correctly and maybe they will but they haven't yet.

ANALYSIS: This machine should be built as an open standard by a bunch of Japanese makers. The software layers should be more compatible with desktop stuff. Kaplan isn't the best CEO. They have some OK ideas but I don't think this thing will be big. We do need to think about note taking and the fact that small machines can be used everywhere especially with this input approach but I don't think we should be an ISV for them.

ACTION ITEMS: Gregw - Carr wants our debug format to do a remote debugger. If it is written up and easy to send then send it to him with a letter saying they will use it for developing on their machine only. If it is hard then have someone call and say sorry.

Joachimk/Steveb - we should be selling system software to people like this. He is fairly far along at this point. What would we sell him? Either stripped down PM or WINDOWS. WINDOWS is the best choice I think. Tell him to use extended memory. He won't like this but it will sure help him with applications developers. Who can take a pass at this with Carr?

Mikemap - Another applications opportunity but unless we want something that fits on this machine for the desktop I doubt it makes sense. They do want to create connections between stuff on their machine and popular desktop stuff so we want to be friends with them even if they are not an ISV. They offered to come up and present their concepts to a larger group up here. I doubt that makes sense. I will talk about this class of machine in our Saturday morning meeting.

10

A Note on Valuation in Private Equity Settings

The valuation of private companies, especially those in the earlier stages of their life cycle, is a difficult and often subjective process. Early-stage companies typically forecast a period of negative cash flows with highly uncertain—but tantalizing—future rewards. This cash-flow profile is very sensitive to the valuation assumptions made.

This note will discuss valuation techniques that can be used in private equity settings. The intention is to provide a practical toolkit to be used when tackling cases in the second and third modules of *Venture Capital and Private Equity.* Much of the background theory will be glossed over: the focus will be on the essential underlying mechanics of each method and a discussion of strengths and weaknesses. The references at the end of this note provide more detailed information on the various valuation techniques discussed.

This note addresses the Comparables, Net Present Value, Adjusted Present Value, Venture Capital, and Options valuation methods. We also discuss the use of Monte Carlo simulation employing the software package Crystal Ball® to enhance these valuations. Each of the following five sections is dedicated to one valuation method and has a corresponding appendix with a detailed example of the method.

COMPARABLES

Comparables often provide a quick and easy way to obtain a "ballpark" valuation for a firm. When searching for comparables, we seek other firms that display similar "value characteristics" to the company we are interested in. These value characteristics include risk, growth rate, capital structure, and the size and timing of cash flows. Often, these value characteristics are driven by other underlying attributes of the company which can be incorporated in a multiple. For example, the anticipated cash flows for a new Health Maintenance Organization (HMO) might be accurately predicted by the number of members it has enrolled (see the example in Appendix 1).

Using comparables for private companies poses many potential problems, however. (The strengths and weaknesses of each method are summarized in Exhibit 1.) First, it is often difficult to ascertain what valuations have been assigned to other privately held firms. Consequently, it may be impossible to compare our firm to the companies that are the most similar. Second, because accounting and other performance information on private firms are often unavailable, key ratios may not be calculable, or other important impacts on valuation may be missed. Finally, the valuations assigned to comparable firms may be misguided. Periodically, whole classes of firms have been valued at prices that seem unjustifiable on a cash-flow basis.

Sound judgment should therefore drive the use of comparables. One must search for potential measures of value that can be sensibly applied from one company to the next. In public markets, common ratios are *(i)* the share price divided by the earnings per share (the P-E ratio), *(ii)* the market value of the firm's equity divided by total revenue, and *(iii)* the market value of the firm's equity divided by the shareholder's equity on the balance sheet (market-to-book ratio). These ratios, however, may be misleading. Consider the price-earnings ratio. The earnings (profit after tax) reflect the company's capital structure, since earnings are computed after interest expenses and taxes. Common sense would therefore tell us that when comparing two companies with similar characteristics except for substantially different capital structures, it would be more appropriate to use a multiple based on earnings before interest and taxes (EBIT). By using this latter comparable, we compensate for the differing capital structures of the two entities. This is because EBIT ignores the different levels of interest expense incurred by the two companies. (Of course, the use of EBIT ignores the interest tax shields associated with these capital structures, which we may wish to factor into the comparisons.)

Accounting-based comparables, such as those mentioned above, are less suitable in a private equity setting where companies are often unprofitable and experiencing rapid growth. One must therefore look for other sensible measures of value. For example, in an Internet business a good indicator of value may be the number of subscribers enrolled by a company. A valid proxy for the value of a biotechnology firm may be the number of patents awarded. In a gold exploration company, a typical measure of value is the number of ounces of gold indicated by initial drilling results. These are just a few examples of nonfinancial, industry-specific measures that can be used to estimate the value of a firm.

A recent study suggests that industry-specific multiples have strong explanatory power for the offering prices of IPOs. In contrast, accounting-based multiples, such as the price-earnings ratio and the ratio of the market-to-book value of equity, were found to have little predictive ability. The reason is that among young, publicly traded firms in the same industry, accounting-based multiples vary substantially.[1]

Another issue related to the use of public market comparables to value private companies is the marketability of the equity. Because shares in private firms are less marketable than those of publicly traded firms, it may be appropriate to apply a discount for liquidity. The size of the proper discount will depend on the particular circumstances. Surveys suggest, however, that discounts for lack of marketability used in practice fall within a very narrow band, often between 25% and 30%.[2]

THE NET PRESENT VALUE METHOD

The Net Present Value (NPV) method is one of the most common methods of cash-flow valuation. (Others include the Equity Cash Flow and Capital Cash Flow methods. The Adjusted Present Value method discussed in the next section is a variation on the Capital Cash Flow method.) This section briefly visits the basics of the NPV method.

---

[1] Mounchul Kim and Jay R. Ritter, "Valuing IPOs," *Journal of Financial Economics*, Forthcoming.

[2] Shannon P. Pratt, *Valuing a Business: The Analysis and Appraisal of Closely Held Companies*, Homewood, Illinois, Dow Jones-Irwin, 1996.

The NPV method incorporates the benefit of tax shields from tax-deductible interest payments in the discount rate (i.e., the Weighted Average Cost of Capital, or WACC). To avoid double-counting these tax shields, interest payments must not be deducted from cash flows. Equation (1) shows how to calculate cash flows (subscripts denote time periods):

$$CF_t = EBIT_t * (1 - \tau) + DEPR_t - CAPEX_t - \Delta NWC_t + other_t \tag{1}$$

where:

CF	= cash flow
$EBIT$	= earnings before interest and tax
τ	= corporate tax rate
$DEPR$	= depreciation
$CAPEX$	= capital expenditures
ΔNWC	= increase in net working capital
other	= increases in taxes payable, wages payable, etc.

Next, the terminal value should be calculated. This estimate is very important as the majority of the value of a company, especially one in an early-stage setting, may be in the terminal value. A common method for estimating the terminal value of an enterprise is the perpetuity method.

Equation (2) gives the formula for calculating a terminal value (TV) at time T using the perpetuity method, assuming a growth rate in perpetuity of g and a discount rate equal to r. The cash flows and discount rates used in the NPV method are typically nominal values (i.e., they are not adjusted for inflation). If forecasts indicate that the cash flow will be constant in inflation-adjusted dollars, a terminal growth rate equal to the rate of inflation should be used:

$$TV_\tau = [CF_\tau * (1 + g)]/(r - g) \tag{2}$$

Other common methods of terminal value calculation used in practice include price-earnings ratios and market-to-book value multiples, but these short-cuts are not encouraged!

The net present value of the firm is then calculated as shown in Equation (3):

$$NPV = [CF_1/(1 + r)] + [CF_2/(1 + r)^2] + [CF_3/(1 + r)^3] + \ldots + [(CF_\tau + TV_\tau)/(1 + r)^\tau] \tag{3}$$

The discount rate is calculated using Equation (4):

$$r = (D/V) * r_d * (1 - \tau) + (E/V) * r_e \tag{4}$$

where:

r_d	= discount rate for debt
r_e	= discount rate for equity
τ	= corporate tax rate
D	= market value of debt
E	= market value of equity
V	= $D + E$

If the firm is not at its target capital structure, however, the target values should be used for D/V and E/V.

The cost of equity r_e is calculated using the familiar Capital Asset Pricing Model shown in Equation (5):

$$r_e = r + \beta + (r_m - r_f) \qquad (5)$$

where:

r_e = discount rate for equity

r_f = risk-free rate

β = beta, or degree of correlation with the market

r_m = market rate of return on common stock

$(r_m - r_f)$ = market risk premium

When determining the appropriate risk-free rate (r_f), one should attempt to match the maturity of the investment project with that of the risk-free rate. Typically, we use the 10-year rate. Estimates of the market risk premium can vary widely: for the sake of the course, 7.5% can be assumed.

For private companies, or spin-offs from public companies, betas can be estimated by looking at comparable public firms. The beta for public companies can be found in a beta book or on the Bloomberg machine. If the firm is not at its target capital structure, it is necessary to "unlever" and "relever" the beta. This is accomplished using Equation (6):

$$\beta_u = \beta_L * (E/V) = \beta_L * [E/(E + D)] \qquad (6)$$

where:

β_u = unlevered beta

β_L = levered beta

E = market value of equity

D = market value of debt

An issue arises where there are no comparable companies, especially in entrepreneurial settings. In this situation, common sense is the best guide. Think about the cyclical nature of the particular firm and whether the risk is systematic or can be diversified away. If accounting data is available, another way is to calculate "earnings betas," which have some correlation with equity betas. An earnings beta is calculated by comparing a private company's net income to a stock market index such as the S&P 500. Using least squares regression techniques, we can calculate the slope of the line of best fit (the beta).

Strengths and Weaknesses of the NPV Method

Estimating firm values by discounting relevant cash flows is widely regarded as technically sound. The values should be less subject than comparables to distortions that can occur in public and, more commonly, private markets.

Given the many assumptions and estimates that have been made during the valuation process, however, it is unrealistic to arrive at a single, or "point," value for the firm. Different cash flows should be estimated under "best," "most likely," and "worst" case assumptions. These should then be discounted using a range of values for WACC and the terminal growth rate *(g)* to give a likely range of values. If you can assign probabilities to each scenario, a weighted average will determine the expected value of the firm.

Even with these steps, the NPV method still has some drawbacks. First, we need betas to calculate the discount rate. A valid comparable company should have financial performance, growth prospects, and operating characteristics similar to those of the company being valued. A public company with these characteristics may not exist. Second, the target capital structure is often estimated using comparables. Using comparable companies to estimate a target capital structure has much the same drawbacks as finding comparable betas. Third, the typical start-up company cash-flow profile of large initial expenditures followed by distant inflows leads to much (or even all) of the value being in the terminal value. Terminal values are very sensitive to assumptions about both discount and terminal growth rates. Finally, recent finance research has raised questions as to whether beta is the proper measure of firm risk. Numerous studies suggest that firm size or the ratio of book-to-market equity values may be more appropriate.[3] Few have tried to implement these suggestions, however, in a practical valuation context.

Another drawback of the NPV method lies in the valuation of companies with changing capital structures or effective tax rates. Changing capital structures are often associated with highly leveraged transactions, such as leveraged buyouts. Changing effective tax rates can be due to the consumption of tax credits, such as net operating losses, or the expiration of tax subsidies sometimes granted to fledgling firms. Under the NPV method, both the capital structure and effective tax rate are incorporated in the discount rate (WACC) and assumed to be constant. For this reason, the Adjusted Present Value method is recommended in these cases.

Monte Carlo Simulation

When calculating values using spreadsheets, we arrive at a single, or "point," estimate of value. Even when undertaking sensitivity analysis, we simply alter variables one at a time and determine the change in the valuations. Monte Carlo simulation is an improvement over simple sensitivity analysis because it considers all possible combinations of input variables. The user defines probability distributions for each input variable, and the program generates a probability distribution describing the possible outcomes.

One such package, which will be described here and used in class, is Crystal Ball®.[4] The first step is to set up the base case spreadsheet. We then define the assumption and forecast variables: we will determine the effect of changes in the assumption cells on the value contained in the forecast cell. Assumption cells contain variables such as the discount rate, terminal growth rate, and cash flows. Assumption cells must contain numerical values, not formulas or text. Probability distributions are used to define the way in which the values in the assumption cells vary. Crystal Ball® has a suite of probability distributions to choose in describing the behavior of each variable. The user needs to select an appropriate distribution and estimate the key parameters (e.g., mean and standard deviation).

---

[3] For an overview, see Eugene F. Fama and Kenneth R. French, "The Cross-Section of Expected Stock Returns," *Journal of Finance.* 47 (1992), 427–465.

[4] Crystal Ball® is a personal computer simulation package produced by Decisioneering, Inc., which is located at 1515 Arapahoe Street, Suite 1311, Denver, CO 80202. Its phone is 800-289-2550 or 303-534-515; its fax, 303-534-4818; and address on the World Wide Web, http://www.decisioneering.com.

Assumptions can be defined by highlighting one variable at a time and using the command *Cell Define Assumption.* Similarly, the forecast is defined by highlighting the cell with the valuation calculation and using the command *Cell Define Forecast.* A simulation is then generated using the command *Run Run.* To create a report, use the command *Run Create Report.* A summary of the report for the NPV valuation performed in Appendix 2 is shown in Exhibit 2. It shows the probability distribution for the value of the subsidiary, Hi-Tech. The report also indicates that the assumptions were defined as normal distributions with means equal to the values initially contained in the cells, and standard deviations set at 10% of the mean.

The availability and simplicity of simulation packages make them a useful tool. Simulation allows a more thorough analysis of the possible outcomes than does regular sensitivity analysis. An additional benefit is that simulation packages allow the user to consider the interrelationships between the different input variables: as the manual describes, it is easy to define correlations between the various explanatory variables. One must remember, however, that in reality the shapes of distributions, and interrelationships between variables, can be very hard to discover. As sophisticated as the output reports look, the old adage about a model being only as good as the assumptions behind it still applies.

THE ADJUSTED PRESENT VALUE METHOD

The Adjusted Present Value (APV) method is a variation of the NPV method. APV is preferred to the NPV method when a firm's capital structure is changing or it has net operating losses (NOLs) that can be used to offset taxable income. (An example demonstrating the APV method can be found in Appendix 3.)

The NPV method assumes that the firm's capital structure remains constant at a prespecified target level. This is inappropriate in situations such as leveraged buyouts, where initially the capital structure is highly leveraged, but the level of debt is reduced as repayments are made. In this case, the "target" capital structure changes over time. A way of illustrating this issue is to consider an LBO firm with an ultimate target capital structure of zero: that is after a certain period it aims to have paid off all its debt. Under the NPV method, the discount rate (WACC) would be calculated using an all-equity capital structure. This ignores the fact that the firm has been levered up. APV overcomes this drawback by considering the cash flows generated by the assets of a company, ignoring its capital structure. The savings from tax-deductible interest payments are then valued separately.

The NPV method also assumes that the firm's effective tax rate, incorporated in the WACC, remains constant. This is inappropriate where a firm's effective tax rate changes over time. For example, typically a start-up company incurs NOLs before it attains profitability. Under certain circumstances, these NOLs can be carried forward for tax purposes and netted against taxable income. APV accounts for the effect of the firm's changing tax status by valuing the NOLs separately.

Under APV, the valuation task is divided into three steps. First, the cash flows are valued, ignoring the capital structure. The firm's cash flows are discounted in the same manner as under the NPV method, except that a different discount rate is used. We essentially assume that the company is financed totally by equity. This implies that the discount rate should be calculated using an unlevered beta, rather than the levered beta used to compute the WACC used in the NPV analysis. The discount rate is calculated using the Capital Asset Pricing Model shown in Equation (5).

The tax benefits associated with the capital structure are then estimated. The net present value of the tax savings from tax-deductible interest payments has value to a company and must be quantified. The interest payments will change over time as debt levels increase or decrease. By convention, the discount rate often used to calculate the net present value of the tax benefits is the pretax rate of return on debt. This will be lower than the cost of equity. Conceptually, this is sensible. The claims of debtholders rank higher than those of ordinary shareholders and therefore are a safer stream of cash flows.

Finally, NOLs available to the company also have value that must be quantified. NOLs can be offset against pretax income and often provide a useful source of cash to a company in its initial profitable years of operation. For instance, if a company has $10 million of NOLs and the prevailing tax rate is 40%, the company will have tax savings of $4 million. (Note, however, that this ignores the time value of money. The net present value of the NOLs will only be $4 million if the firm has taxable income of $10 million in its first year. If the NOLs are utilized over more than one year, then discounting will reduce their value to some amount less than $4 million.)

The discount rate used to value NOLs is often the pretax rate on debt. If you believe that the realization of tax benefits from the NOLs is certain (i.e., the firm will definitely generate sufficient profits to consume them), then you should use the risk-free rate. If, however, there is some risk that the firm will not generate enough profits to use up the NOLs, then discounting them by the pretax rate of corporate debt makes sense.

THE VENTURE CAPITAL METHOD

The Venture Capital method is a valuation tool commonly applied in the private equity industry. As discussed, private equity investments are often characterized by negative cash flows and earnings and highly uncertain but potentially substantial future rewards. The Venture Capital method accounts for this cash-flow profile by valuing the company, typically using a multiple, at a time in the future when it is projected to have achieved positive cash flows and/or earnings. This "terminal value" is then discounted back to the present using a high discount rate, typically between 40% and 75%. (The rationales for these very high target rates are discussed below.)

The venture capitalist uses this discounted terminal value and the size of the proposed investment to calculate her desired ownership interest in the company. For example, if the company's discounted terminal value is $10 million, and the venture capitalist intends to make a $5 million investment, she will want 50% of the company in exchange for her investment. This assumes, however, that there will be no dilution of the venture capitalist's interest through future rounds of financing. This is an unrealistic assumption, given that most successful venture-backed companies sell shares to the public through an IPO.

The underlying mechanics of the Venture Capital method are demonstrated by the following four steps. (An example demonstrating the Venture Capital method can be found in Appendix 4.) The method starts by estimating the company's value in some future year of interest, typically shortly after the venture capitalist foresees taking the firm public. The "terminal value" is usually calculated using a multiple: for example, a price-earnings ratio may be multiplied by the projected net income in the exit year. (See the earlier discussion of comparables.) The Terminal Value can, of course, be calculated using other techniques, including discounted cash-flow methods.

The Discounted Terminal Value of the company is determined, not surprisingly, by discounting the Terminal Value calculated in the first step. Instead of using a traditional cost of capital as the discount rate, however, venture capitalists typically use a Target Rate of Return. The Target Rate of Return is the yield the venture capitalist feels is required to justify the risk and effort of the particular investment. The formula for calculating the Discounted Terminal Value is shown in Equation (7):

$$\text{Discounted Terminal Value} = \text{Terminal Value}/(1 + \text{Target Rate})^{years} \qquad (7)$$

The venture capitalist then calculates the Required Final Percent Ownership. The amount of the proposed investment is divided by the Discounted Terminal Value to determine the ownership necessary for the venture capitalist to earn her desired return (assuming that there is no subsequent dilution of her investment):

$$\text{Required Final Percent Ownership} = \text{Investment}/\text{Discounted Terminal Value} \qquad (8)$$

Finally, she estimates future dilution and calculates the required current percent ownership. Equation (8) is the correct answer if there are no subsequent "rounds" of financing to dilute the venture capitalist's interest in the company. As we have seen in the course, venture-backed companies commonly receive multiple rounds of financing, followed by an IPO. Hence, this assumption is usually unrealistic. To compensate for the effect of dilution from future rounds of financing, she needs to calculate the Retention Ratio. The Retention Ratio quantifies the expected dilutive effect of future rounds of financing on the venture capitalist's ownership. Consider a firm that intends to undertake one more financing round, in which shares representing an additional 25% of the firm's equity will be sold, and then to sell shares representing an additional 30% of the firm at the time of the IPO. If the venture capitalist owns 10% today, after these financings her stake will be 10%/(1+.25)/(1+.3) = 6.15%. Her retention ratio is 6.15%/10% = 61.5%.

The Required Current Percent Ownership necessary for the venture capitalist to realize her Target Rate of Return is then calculated using Equation (9):

$$\text{Required Current Percent Ownership} =$$
$$\text{Required Final Percent Ownership}/\text{Retention Ratio} \qquad (9)$$

Strengths and Weaknesses of the Venture Capital Method

A major criticism of the Venture Capital method is the use of very large discount rates, typically between 40% and 75%. Venture capitalists justify the use of these high target returns on a number of grounds. First, they argue that large discount rates are used to compensate for the illiquidity of private firms. As discussed in Module 1, equity of private companies is usually less marketable than public stock, and investors demand a higher return in exchange for this lack of marketability. Second, venture capitalists view their services as valuable and consider the large discount rate as providing compensation for their efforts. For example, they provide strategic advice, credibility, and access to specialized intermediaries such as lawyers and investment bankers. Finally, venture capitalists believe that projections presented by entrepreneurs tend to be overly optimistic. They submit that the large discount rate compensates for these inflated projections.

Financial economists suggest that although the issues raised by venture capitalists may be valid, they should not be addressed through a high discount rate. They propose that each "justification" should be valued separately using more objective techniques. First, they argue that the discount for lack of marketability makes sense but that the estimated premium is far too large: there are numerous investors with long-run time horizons, including endowments, foundations, and individuals. Second, financial economists contend that the services provided by the venture capitalist should be valued by determining what amount would have to be paid to acquire equivalent professional services on a contract basis. Once the fair market value of the services provided is determined, shares equal to this value can be given to the venture capitalist. Finally, financial economists submit that discount rates should not be inflated to compensate for the entrepreneurs' overly optimistic projections. They argue that judgment should be applied to determine the likely values of various scenarios and the probability that they will occur. This will result in unbiased estimates of the firm's cash flow.

The use of high discount rates suggests an element of arbitrariness in the venture capitalist's approach to valuing a company. A better process is to scrutinize the projections and perform reality checks. This involves asking a number of questions. What has been the performance of comparable companies? What share of the market does the company need to meet its projections? How long will it take? What are the key risks? Are contingency plans in place? What are the key success factors? This type of analysis is far more meaningful than just taking the entrepreneur's pro formas and discounting them at a very large rate.

OPTIONS ANALYSIS

In some cases, it is appropriate and desirable to use option pricing techniques to value investment opportunities. Discounted cash-flow methods such as NPV and APV can be deficient in situations where a manager or investor has "flexibility." Flexibility can take many forms, including the ability to increase or decrease the rate of production, defer development, or abandon a project. These changes all affect the firm's value in ways that are not accurately measured using discounted cash-flow techniques. One form of flexibility that is of particular interest to the venture capitalist is the ability to make "follow-on" investments.

Private equity-backed companies are often characterized by multiple rounds of financing. Venture capitalists use this multistage investment approach to motivate the entrepreneur to "earn" future rounds of financing as well as to limit the fund's exposure to a particular portfolio company. Often, the first right of refusal for a later stage of financing is written into the investment contract.

The right to make a follow-on investment has many of the same characteristics as a call option on a company's stock. Both comprise the right, but not the obligation, to acquire an asset by paying a sum of money on or before a certain date. As we shall see, this flexibility is not readily accounted for by discounted cash-flow techniques. By way of contrast, option pricing theory accounts for the manager's ability to "wait and then decide whether to invest" in the project at a later date.

To illustrate the drawback of using NPV flow methods when pricing options, consider the following simplified example. A project requiring an investment of $150 today is equally likely to generate revenues next year, that—discounted to today's dollars—total $200, $160, or $120. Consequently, the project will have a net present value of $50, $10, or −$30. The expected return is $10 [= (1/3) * (50 + 10 − 30)].

Now consider an investor who has the ability to delay his investment until period 1.[5] By delaying investing until he obtains further information, he can avoid investing when revenues will only be $120. Essentially, by waiting and gathering more information, the

---

[5] We assume the net present value of the investment in today's dollars is still $150, whether the investment is made in Period 0 or Period 1.

investor modifies the expected return profile from [$50, $10, –$30] to [$50, $10, $0]. The option to delay investing is worth $10, the difference between the new expected NPV of $20 [= ($^1/_3$) * (50 + 10 + 0)] and the earlier $10 expected value.

This section introduces a developing area in finance. For the purposes of brevity, a basic knowledge of option pricing theory (at the level, for instance, of Brealey and Myers) is assumed. Readers are referred to the references at the end of this note for further literature on option pricing techniques.

Valuing Firms as Options

The Black-Scholes model values European options using five variables as inputs. For an option on a stock, these comprise the exercise price (X), the stock price (S), the time to expiration (t), the standard deviation (or volatility) of returns on the stock (σ), and the risk free rate (r_f). Using these variables, we can value the right to buy a share of stock at some future point. We can evaluate a firm's decision to invest in a project using a similar framework. The equivalents are shown in Table 1.

Once the input variables have been estimated, the value of the option can be calculated using a Black-Scholes computer model or a call option valuation table.

Reducing Complex Problems to Options Analyses

Real-world decisions can be difficult to reduce to mathematically solvable problems. There is often great value, however, in attempting to simplify these types of problems. For example, the right to abandon the development of a gold mine is similar to a put option. A finance lease gives the leaseholder both the right to cancel the lease by paying a fee (a put option) and the right to purchase the asset for a fixed price at the end of the lease (a call option). This note will consider only the solution of call options using the Black-Scholes formula for European options (which can only be exercised at the end of the period).

Table 1 describes the five inputs necessary to value an investment option by a firm. The approximation of four of the variables (X, S, t, r_f) is fairly intuitive and is illustrated in the example in Appendix 5. The process of estimating the fifth variable, the standard deviation (σ), merits further discussion. One way to estimate the standard deviation is to look at the stock price volatility for businesses with assets comparable to the project or company under consideration. These are, for instance, available on the Bloomberg machine. An important point is that volatilities estimated using this method will require adjustment to take into account the leverage of the comparable company. Remember that leverage amplifies risk, and hence comparable companies with higher leverage than the project under consideration will have higher risk. As a guide, volatilities of 20% to

TABLE 1   Financial and Firm Option Variables.

Variable	Financial option	Firm option
X	Exercise price	Present value of the expenditures required to undertake the project
S	Stock price	Present value of the expected cash flows generated by the project
t	Time to expiration	The length of time that the investment decision can be deferred
σ	Standard deviation of returns on the stock	Riskiness of the underlying assets
r_f	Time value of money	Risk-free rate of return

30% are not unusually high for single companies, and many small technology companies have volatilities of between 40% and 50%.

Strengths and Weaknesses of Using Option Pricing to Value Investment Opportunities

Option pricing theory is useful in situations where there is the "flexibility" to wait, learn more about the prospects of the proposed investment, and then decide whether to invest. As discussed, opportunities that incorporate flexibility will consistently be undervalued using discounted cash-flow techniques.

At least three concerns are associated with the use of option pricing methodology. First, it is not well known to many businesspeople, particularly in the private equity community. As with most "new technologies," it may be difficult to convince associates and counterparties that its use is valid. A second drawback of the option pricing methodology is the difficulty of reducing real-world opportunities to simple problems that can be valued. Although the models can accommodate cases where the firm pays dividends or where the option can be exercised early, the calculations may be more complex. Option pricing used inappropriately can inflate values achieved using other methods, thereby falsely justifying projects that would otherwise be rejected. Finally, some situations may not be appropriate for the Black-Scholes formula. For instance, the exact pricing of a series of call options that are nested (i.e., where one cannot be exercised before the other one is) is a difficult problem. In these cases, it may be best to use simulation techniques.

FOR FURTHER READING

RICHARD A. BREALEY AND STEWART MYERS, *Principles of Corporate Finance*, New York, McGraw-Hill, 1996.

TOM COPELAND, TIM KOLLER, AND JACK MURRIN, *Valuation: Measuring and Managing the Value of Companies*, New York, John Wiley & Sons, 1991.

European Venture Capital Association, "The EVCA Performance Measurement Guidelines," Zaventum, Belgium, EVCA Venture Capital Special Paper, 1994.

EUGENE F. FAMA AND KENNETH R. FRENCH, "The Cross-Section of Expected Stock Returns," *Journal of Finance* 47 (1992): 427–465.

STEVEN FENSTER AND STUART C. GILSON, "The Adjusted Present Value Method for Capital Assets," Note 9-294-047, Harvard Business School, 1994.

ROBERT C. HIGGINS, *Analysis for Financial Management*, New York, Irwin, 1992.

STEVEN N. KAPLAN AND RICHARD S. RUBACK, "The Valuation of Cash Flow Forecasts: An Empirical Analysis," *Journal of Finance* 51 (1995): 1059–1093.

MOUCHUL KIM AND JAY R. RITTER, "Valuing IPOs," *Journal of Financial Economics*, Forthcoming.

TIMOTHY A. LUEHRMAN, "Capital Projects as Real Options: An Introduction," Note 9-295-074, Harvard Business School, 1995.

JAMES L. PADDOCK, DANIEL R. SIEGEL, AND JAMES L. SMITH, "Valuing Offshore Oil Properties with Option Pricing Models," *Quarterly Journal of Economics* 103 (1988): 473–508.

SHANNON P. PRATT, *Valuing a Business: The Analysis and Appraisal of Closely Held Companies*, Homewood, IL, Dow Jones – Irwin, 1996.

RICHARD S. RUBACK, "An Introduction to Capital Cash Flow Methods," Note 9-295-155, Harvard Business School, 1995.

Exhibit 1 Strengths and Weaknesses of Various Valuation Methods in Private Equity Settings

Method	Strengths	Weaknesses
1. Comparables	• Quick to use • Simple to understand • Commonly used in industry • Market based	• Private company comparables may be difficult to find and evaluate • If use public company comparables, need to adjust resulting valuation to take into account private company's illiquidity
2. Net Present Value	• Theoretically sound	• Cash flows may be difficult to estimate • Private company comparables (β and capital structure) can be difficult to find and evaluate • WACC assumes a constant capital structure • WACC assumes a constant effective tax rate • Typical cash flow profile of outflows followed by distant, uncertain inflows is very sensitive to discount and terminal growth rate assumptions
3. Adjusted Present Value	• Theoretically sound • Suitable (and simple to use) in situations where the capital structure is changing (e.g., highly leveraged transactions such as leveraged buyouts) • Suitable in situations where the effective tax rate is changing (e.g., when there are NOLs)	• More complicated to calculate than the NPV method • Same disadvantages as NPV Method except overcomes the shortfalls of the WACC assumption (*i.e.*, constant capital structure and tax rate)
4. Venture Capital	• Simple to understand • Quick to use • Commonly used	• Relies on terminal values derived from other methods • Oversimplified (large discount rate "fudge factor")
5. Asset Options	• Theoretically sound • Overcomes drawbacks of NPV and APV techniques in situations where managers have flexibility	• Methodology is not commonly used in industry and may not be understood • Real world situations may be difficult to reduce to solvable option problems • Limitations of Black-Scholes model

Exhibit 2   Simulation Report Produced by Crystal Ball Using Data from Appendix 2

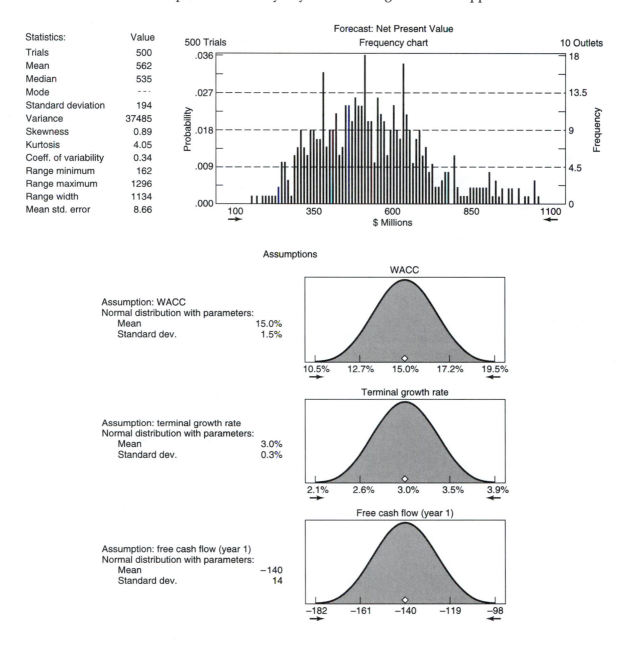

Statistics:	Value
Trials	500
Mean	562
Median	535
Mode	- - -
Standard deviation	194
Variance	37485
Skewness	0.89
Kurtosis	4.05
Coeff. of variability	0.34
Range minimum	162
Range maximum	1296
Range width	1134
Mean std. error	8.66

Forecast: Net Present Value

500 Trials   Frequency chart   10 Outlets

$ Millions

Assumptions

WACC

Assumption: WACC
Normal distribution with parameters:
Mean   15.0%
Standard dev.   1.5%

Terminal growth rate

Assumption: terminal growth rate
Normal distribution with parameters:
Mean   3.0%
Standard dev. 0.3%

Free cash flow (year 1)

Assumption: free cash flow (year 1)
Normal distribution with parameters:
Mean   −140
Standard dev.   14

Appendix 1: Sample Valuation Using Comparables

The fifty-year-old chairman and major shareholder of Private Health, a private regional health maintenance organization (HMO), is considering selling his stake in the company and retiring. He has asked Private Health's chief financial officer (CFO) to calculate the value of the firm by the following morning. The two main options that he is entertaining are the sale of his interest to an Employee Share Ownership Plan (ESOP) and to one of the firm's publicly traded competitors. The CFO regularly receives research reports from investment bankers eager to take the company public. From these reports she is able to compare the following information for Private Health and two public HMOs operating in the same region. Data is for the 1995 financial year (amounts in millions of dollars unless indicated):

	Private Health	Happy Healthcare	Community Health
Balance Sheet			
Assets	160	300	380
Long-Term Debt	5	100	0
Net Worth	80	120	175
Income Statement			
Revenues	350	420	850
EBITDA	45	55	130
Net Income	30	20.0	75.0
Market Data			
Earnings per Share ($/share)	3.00	0.67	2.14
Price-Earnings Ratio (times)	n/a	21.0	14.5
Shares Outstanding (m)	10	30	35
Number of Members	500,000	600,000	1,100,000

From the above information, the CFO was able to calculate the following multiples and implied valuations for Private Health:

	Happy Healthcare	Community Health	Average	Private Health Implied Value ($m)
Price-Earnings Ratio	21.0	14.5	17.7	533
Market Value/EBITDA	7.64	8.37	8.00	360
Market Value/Sales	1.00	1.28	1.14	399
Market Value/Book Value of Equity	3.52	6.21	4.86	389
Market Value/Member	700	989	844	422

The CFO felt that on an overall basis the multiples gave a good indication of the value of Private Health, but that it was overvalued on a P/E multiple basis. She believed this was because Happy Healthcare (long-term debt to total assets of 33%) was substantially more leveraged than Private Health (3%). Valuing Private Health using Community Health's P/E ratio of 14.5 gave an implied valuation of $435 million. Based on her analysis, she was confident that the value of Private Health was in the range of $360-435 million if sold to a public company. If the shares were sold to an ESOP she believed that, because of the company's private status, it would be appropriate to assume a discount of 15-20%, or a valuation of $290-360 million.

Appendix 2: Sample Valuation Using the Net Present Value Method

Lo-Tech's shareholders have voted to cease its diversification strategy and refocus on its core businesses. As a part of this process the company is seeking to divest Hi-Tech, its start-up high-technology subsidiary. George, a venture capitalist, has been approached by the management of Hi-Tech, who want to purchase the company. He decides to value Hi-Tech using the NPV method. George and Hi-Tech management have agreed on the following projections (all data are in millions of dollars):

	Year 1	Year 2	Year 3	Year 4	Year 5	Year 6	Year 7	Year 8	Year 9
Revenues	100	140	210	250	290	380	500	650	900
Costs	230	240	260	275	290	310	350	400	470
EBIT	−130	−100	−50	−25	0	70	150	250	430

The company has $100 million of NOLs that can be carried forward and offset against future income. In addition, Hi-Tech is projected to generate further losses in its early years of operation that it will also be able to carry forward. The tax rate is 40%. The average unlevered beta of five comparable high-technology companies is 1.2. Hi-Tech has no long-term debt. Treasury yields for ten-year bonds are 6.0%. Capital expenditure requirements are assumed to be equal to depreciation. The market risk premium is assumed to be 7.5%. Net working capital requirements are forecast as 10% of sales. EBIT is projected to grow at 3% per year in perpetuity after Year 9.

George first calculated the Weighted Average Cost of Capital (WACC):

$$WACC = (D/V) * r_d * (1 - \tau) + (E/V) * r_e = 0 + 100\% * [6.0 + 1.2 * (7.5)] = 15\%$$

He then valued the cash flows, which showed the company had a net present value of $525 million. As suspected, all the value of the company was accounted for in the terminal value (the present value of the cash flows was $(44) million and the present value of the terminal value $569 million, giving a net present value of $525 million).

The terminal value was calculated as follows:

$$TV_T = [CF_T * (1 + g)]/(r - g) = [233 * (1 + 3\%)]/(15\% - 3\%) = \$2,000$$

George also performed a scenario analysis to determine the sensitivity of the value of Hi-Tech to changes in the discount rate and the terminal growth rate. He developed a scenario table[6] shown in the attached spreadsheet.

George's scenario analysis gave a series of values ranging from $323 million to $876 million. Clearly this large range did not provide precise guidance as to Hi-Tech's actual value. He noted that the cash flow profile of negative early cash flows followed by distant positive cash flows made the valuation very sensitive to both the discount rate and the terminal growth rate. George considered the NPV method a first step in the valuation process and planned to use other methods to narrow the range of possible values for Hi-Tech.

---

[6] Sensitivity analyses can be easily undertaken using the Microsoft Excel command *Data Table*.

Appendix 2 (continued)

WACC Calculation

Tax Rate	40%
Rm – Rf	7.5%
E/V	100%
Bu	1.2
10 Year Treasury Bond	6.0%
WACC	15.0%

Cash Flows

Terminal Growth Rate   3.0%

Year	0	1	2	3	4	5	6	7	8	9
Revenues		100	140	210	250	290	380	500	650	900
Less: Costs		230	240	260	275	290	310	350	400	470
EBIT		−130	−100	−50	−25	0	70	150	250	430
Less: Tax		0	0	0	0	0	0	0	26	172
EBIAT		−130	−100	−50	−25	0	70	150	224	258
Less: Ch. NWC		10	4	7	4	4	9	12	15	25
Free Cash Flow		−140	−104	−57	−29	−4	61	138	209	233
Discount Factor		0.870	0.756	0.658	0.572	0.497	0.432	0.376	0.327	0.284
PV (Cash Flow)		−122	−79	−37	−17	−2	26	52	68	66
PV (Cash Flows)	(44)									
Terminal Value										2000
PV (Terminal Value)										569

Net Present Value and Sensitivity Analysis

				WACC		
				13%	15%	17%
PV (Cash Flows)	(44)					
PV (Terminal Value)	569		Terminal	2%	699	476	323
Net Present Value	525		Growth	3%	778	525	355
			Rate	4%	876	583	391

Tax Calculation

EBIT	−130	−100	−50	−25	0	70	150	250	430
NOLs Used	0	0	0	0	0	70	150	185	0
NOLs Added	130	100	50	25	0	0	0	0	0
Tax	0	0	0	0	0	0	0	26	172
Beginning NOLs	100	230	330	380	405	405	335	185	0
Ending NOLs	230	330	380	405	405	335	185	0	0

Net Working Capital (10% sales)

Beg NWC		10	14	21	25	29	38	50	65
End NWC	10	14	21	25	29	38	50	65	90
Ch. NWC	10	4	7	4	4	9	12	15	25

Appendix 3: Sample Valuation Using the Adjusted Present Value Method

Vulture Partners, a private equity organization specializing in distressed company investing, was interested in purchasing Turnaround. Mr. Fang, a general partner at Vulture, used the following projections to value Turnaround (all data are in millions of dollars):

	Year 1	Year 2	Year 3	Year 4	Year 5
Revenues	200	210	220	230	240
Costs	100	105	110	115	120
EBIT	100	105	110	115	120
ΔNWC	3	3	4	4	5

Turnaround had $220 million of NOLs which were available to be offset against future income. At the beginning of Year 1, the company had $75 million of 8% debt which was expected to be repaid in three $25 million installments, beginning at the end of Year 1. The tax rate was 40%. Mr. Fang believed an appropriate unlevered beta for Turnaround was 0.8. The ten-year Treasury Bond yield was 7.0% and the market risk premium 7.5%. Net cash flows were forecast to grow at 3% per year in perpetuity after Year 5. Mr. Fang performed the following steps.

Mr. Fang employed the APV method to value Turnaround and, as such, used the cost of equity as the discount rate:

Cost of Equity $= r_f + b_u * (r_m - r_f) = 7.0 + 0.8 * (7.5) = 13.0\%$

Cash flows and the terminal value were both calculated in the same manner as under the NPV method. Mr. Fang arrived at a terminal value of $690 million using the perpetuity method (assuming a growth rate of 3% per annum).

Mr. Fang then calculated the interest tax shields by multiplying the interest expense for each period by the tax rate of 40%. The interest expense was calculated using the debt repayment schedule. The present value of the interest tax shields, equal to $4.2 million, was determined by discounting each year's interest tax shield at the pre-tax cost of debt.

To value the tax shields from the NOLs, Mr. Fang first determined the taxable earnings for each period and hence the rate at which the NOLs would be utilized. By subtracting the interest expense on debt from taxable earnings (EBIT), he determined the amount of NOLs that would be used each period. The NOL tax shields were then calculated by multiplying the NOLs consumed each period by the tax rate. Mr. Fang discounted the NOL tax shields at the pre-tax cost of debt. The present value of the NOLs was equal to $77 million.

The sensitivity analysis showed the likely valuation range for Turnaround to be on the order of $650 to $750 million. The range of values indicated the valuation was reasonably sensitive to both the discount and terminal growth rate assumptions.

Appendix 3 (continued)

Discount Rate Calculation					
Tax Rate	40%	Rm – Rf	7.5%		
10 Year Treasury Bond	7.0%	Bu	0.8		
Discount Rate (Unlevered)	13.00%				

Step 1: Value Cash Flows					
Terminal Growth Rate	3.00%				

Year	0	1	2	3	4	5
Revenues		200	210	220	230	240
Less: Costs		100	105	110	115	120
EBIT		100	105	110	115	120
Less: Tax		40	42	44	46	48
EBIAT		60	63	66	69	72
Less: Ch. NWC		3	3	4	4	5
Net Cash Flow		57	60	62	65	67
Discount Factor		0.885	0.783	0.693	0.613	0.543
PV (Cash Flow)		50	47	43	40	36
PV (Cash Flows)	217					
Terminal Value						690
PV (Terminal Value)						375

Step 2: Value Interest Tax Shields						
Beginning Debt		75	50	25	0	0
Repayment (End of Year)		25	25	25	0	0
Ending Debt		50	25	0	0	0
Interest Expense		6.0	4.0	2.0	0.0	0.0
Interest Tax Shield		2.4	1.6	0.8	0.0	0.0
Discount Factor	8.00%	0.926	0.857	0.794	0.735	0.681
Present Value		2.2	1.4	0.6	0.0	0.0
Net Present Value	4.2					

Step 3: Value NOLs						
EBIT		100	105	110	115	120
Interest Expense		6.0	4.0	2.0	0.0	0.0
EBIT less Interest Expense		94	101	108	115	120
NOLs Used		94	101	25	0	0
Beginning NOLs		220	126	25	0	0
Ending NOLs		126	25	0	0	0
NOLs Used		94	101	25	0	0
NOL Tax Shield		38	40	10	0	0
Discount Factor	8.00%	0.926	0.857	0.794	0.735	0.681
Present Value (NOL)		35	35	8	0	0
Net Present Value (NOLs)	77					

Step 4: NPV and Sensitivity Analysis				WACC		
				12.0%	13.0%	14.0%
PV (Cash Flows)	217					
PV (Terminal Value)	375	Terminal	2%	692	635	589
PV (Tax Shields)	4	Growth	3%	739	673	619
PV (NOLs)	77	Rate	4%	798	718	655
Net Present Value	673					

Appendix 4: Sample Valuation Using the Venture Capital Method

James is a partner in a very successful Boston-based venture capital firm. He plans to invest $5 million in a start-up biotechnology venture and must decide what share of the company he should demand for his investment. Projections he developed with company management show net income in year seven of $20 million. The few profitable biotechnology companies are trading at an average price-earnings ratio of 15. The company currently has 500,000 shares outstanding. James believes that a target rate of return of 50% is required for a venture of this risk. He performs the following calculations:

*Discounted Terminal Value = Terminal Value / (1 + Target Rate)^{years} = (20 * 15) / (1+ 50%)^7 = $17.5 million*

Required Percent Ownership = Investment / Discounted Terminal Value = 5 / 17.5 = 28.5%

Number of New Shares = 500,000 / (1 - 28.5%) - 500,000 = 200,000

Price per New Share = $5 million / 200,000 shares = $25 per share

*Implied Pre-money Valuation = 500,000 shares * $25 per share = $12.5 million*

*Implied Post-money Valuation = 700,000 shares * $25 per share = $17.5 million*

James and his partners are of the opinion that three more senior staff will need to be hired. In James's experience this number of top caliber recruits would require options amounting to 10% of the common stock outstanding. Additionally, he believes that, at the time the firm goes public, additional shares equivalent to 30% of the common stock will be sold to the public. He amends his calculations as follows:

Retention Ratio = [1 / (1 + .1)] / (1 + .3) = 70%

Required Current Percent Ownership = Required Final Percent Ownership / Retention Ratio = 28.5% / 70% = 40.7%

Number of New Shares = 500,000 / (1 - 40.7%) - 500,000 = 343,373

Price per New Share = $5 million / 343,373 shares = $14.56 per share

Appendix 5: Sample Valuation Using Option Pricing

Sharon Rock, a famous venture capitalist, was considering whether to invest in ThinkTank, Inc., a company owned and managed by Mr. Brain. ThinkTank had developed a new product that was ready to be manufactured and marketed. An expenditure of $120 million was required for the construction of research and manufacturing facilities. Rock was of the opinion that the following projections developed by Mr. Brain and his associates were justifiable (all data are in millions of dollars):

	Year 0	Year 1	Year 2	Year 3	Year 4	Year 5
Cash Flow except CapEx	0.0	0.0	0.0	10.0	25.0	50.0
Capital Expenditures	−120.0	0.0	0.0	0.0	0.0	0.0
Total Cash Flow	−120.0	0.0	0.0	10.0	25.0	50.0

Rock performed a NPV valuation using a discount rate (WACC) of 25% and a terminal growth rate of 3%. She was unimpressed with the resulting valuation of −$11.55 million.

After thinking more carefully, Rock realized that the investment could be broken into two stages. The initial investment, which would need to be made immediately, would be $20 million for R&D equipment and personnel. The $100 million expenditure on the plant could be undertaken any time in the first two years. (Whenever the project would be undertaken, the present value of the plant construction expenditures would total $100 million in today's dollars.) Rock decided that the option to expand should not be valued using discounted cash flow methods, as she would only pursue the opportunity if the first stage of the project were successful. The expansion opportunity could more validly be considered as an initial $20 investment bundled with a two-year European call option and priced using the Black-Scholes model.

The easiest variables to estimate were the time to expiration (t) and the risk free rate (r_f), being 2 years and 7%, respectively. The "exercise price" (X) was equal to the present value of the investment to build the plant, or $100 million. The "stock price" (S) was estimated by discounting the expected cash flows to be generated by the underlying assets associated with the expansion opportunity. Using a discount rate of 25% and a terminal growth rate of 3% per year, S was calculated as worth as $108.45 million in Year 0. The only Black-Scholes input variable remaining to be calculated was the standard deviation (σ,). Rock found this difficult to estimate but proceeded to look at some comparable companies. She estimated that the value of σ, was likely to lie in the range of 0.5 to 0.6.

Using this data Rock then calculated the Black-Scholes European call option to be worth between $38.8 and $43.7 million. The total net present value of the project, equal to the cost of the first stage investment and the value of the call option (the stage 2 opportunity), was therefore between $18.8 and $23.7 million [= −$20 million + $38.8 to $43.7 million].

Based on this analysis, Sharon Rock decided to invest in ThinkTank on the provision that she would be granted first right of refusal on any subsequent rounds of financing.

11

Apex Investment Partners (A): April 1995

As the three venture capitalists from Apex Investment Partners headed to the Seattle–Tacoma Airport, their mood was pensive. Rick Bolander, George Middlemas, and Oliver Nicklin—along with several analysts from an affiliated firm—had just spent nearly 12 hours with officials from AccessLine Technologies, an emerging telecommunications firm based in Bellevue, Washington. The company appeared to have extraordinary potential for rapid growth. If Apex was to be the lead venture investor, it would need to move quickly. But before the transaction could be completed, two major obstacles needed to be surmounted.

AccessLine had pioneered the development of the first commercial system to deliver a broad array of personal communication services. It was the developer of the "One Person, One Number" concept, which allows individuals to manage all of their telecommunications (personal and business calls, faxes, voice messaging, and paging) through a single phone number. A caller need not know the location or phone number of a subscriber's communication device, but could simply dial the AccessLine number.

Apex was excited not only about AccessLine's technology, but also about its business approach. The intense competition among traditional telephone companies and new entrants had led carriers to offer new services to differentiate themselves. The AccessLine System provided such a differentiating service, with relatively modest capital and operating expenditures. The firm had signed agreements with several key players in the telecommunications industry, which allowed it to generate increasing fees as the use of these services increased. The company also was poised for rapid international growth through its relationships with European and Canadian carriers. Unlike most early-stage deals in which Apex considered investing, AccessLine had relatively limited risk: cash flow was projected to turn positive in the third quarter of 1995. Another source of strength was AccessLine's management team, which combined extensive technical expertise with business experience in many facets of the telecommunications industry and had met or exceeded financial projections during the last seven quarters.

AccessLine had raised $15 million in a private placement with nonventure investors in July 1994, but there were no earlier venture investors. Much of this meeting between AccessLine and Apex, as well as an earlier session, had been spent building mutual understanding and establishing a relationship of trust between the corporate managers and the venture capitalists. At the same time, it was clear that two contentious issues needed to be resolved before any deal could proceed. In each case, the position of the two parties seemed far apart.

First, AccessLine's valuation posed a complex challenge. Although AccessLine was an extremely promising firm, there was a considerable degree of uncertainty about its prospects. Apex would need to invest at a valuation that was low enough to ensure a sufficient return if the firm proved successful, in order to compensate the fund for the risk it was assuming. But AccessLine's management team felt strongly that the investment had to be priced at a premium to the valuation in the previous financing round.

Second, Dan Kranzler, AccessLine's president and CEO, had proposed a set of terms and conditions that were very similar to those in the company's Series A financing. Apex typically invested in deals with much more stringent terms and conditions. Determining what protections were needed for Apex in this case and persuading AccessLine that these terms were needed were proving to be complex challenges.

APEX INVESTMENT PARTNERS

Apex Investment Partners was founded in 1987 by James A. Johnson and the First Analysis Corporation. Prior to forming Apex, Johnson had been chief financial officer of Beatrice Foods. He had also, in conjunction with a Beatrice colleague, been a partner in Knightsbridge Associates, a small buyout fund. While with Knightsbridge, Johnson and his partners did a buyout of the haircut chain, Supercuts, in a transaction valued at $21 million. (When the firm went public in 1991, the company's equity was priced at $48 million.)[1] Another successful buyout was Tasty Frozen Products, which was sold to H. J. Heinz for several times the purchase price in 1991.

First Analysis Corporation, which served as a general partner of Apex, was founded in 1982 by Oliver Nicklin. Nicklin had previously been chief operating partner at the investment banking firm William Blair & Co. Originally a "research boutique" (an organization concentrating on equity research in a particular industry), First Analysis had diversified into corporate finance and mergers and acquisition activity. All of its work focused on environmental and industrial productivity technologies. Beginning in 1985, First Analysis had begun raising a series of targeted venture funds focusing on productivity-enhancing and environmental technologies. The six funds they had raised in the ensuing decade had total committed capital of $210 million.[2]

In December 1991, George Middlemas joined Apex. Middlemas had been in the venture industry since 1979, first at Citicorp Venture Capital and then at Inco Venture Management. Among the companies that Middlemas had been responsible for were America Online (and its predecessor, Control Video Corporation), Plant Genetics (which merged with Calgene), and Security Dynamics Technologies Inc. Middlemas had left Inco after the venture organization returned to its original objective of managing venture investments for its corporate parent, the Toronto-based nickel producer Inco, Ltd. (In the interim, it had raised and invested capital from external investors.[3]) Rick Bolander, a recent graduate of Harvard Business School who had spent seven years as an operating manager at AT&T, had joined Apex in 1994. (Biographies of the principals of Apex are summarized in Exhibit 1.)

---

[1] Supercuts Initial Public Offering Prospectus, October 30, 1991.

[2] "Environmental Venture Fund/Environmental Private Equity Fund," *Venture Capital Journal* 35 (January 1995): 45.

[3] "Inco's Peabody Succeeds Feiner as President," *Venture Capital Journal* 32 (March 1992): 29.

In its eight-year life, Apex had raised three funds.[4] Its first fund, Apex Investment Fund I, closed in 1987, and Apex Investment Fund II, in 1990. Together, the two funds had committed capital of about $70 million. As of April 1995, Apex was in the process of raising its third fund, which had a $75 million target. The Ameritech Pension Trust had committed $10 million for this next fund. Several of the key investments of Apex's first two funds (out of a total of about 40) are summarized in Exhibit 2. These were concentrated in four broad areas:

- Telecommunications, information technology, and software
- Environmental and industrial productivity-related technologies
- Consumer products and specialty retail
- Health care and related technologies

In making its investments, Apex had sought to balance early-stage investments with those that were already generating positive operating cash flows. As of the end of 1994, fully 35% of Apex's portfolio was classified as start-up or first-stage. About one-sixth of its investments were in buyouts or industry consolidations. Whatever the stage of the investment, Apex generally sought a leading role. In nearly two-thirds of its portfolio at the end of 1994, Apex was the lead investor; in three-quarters of the investments, an Apex representative had joined on the board. As of early 1995, Apex Investment Fund II had yielded a cash return of 26% to the limited partners.[5]

ACCESSLINE TECHNOLOGIES

AccessLine Technologies (originally known as AccessPlus Communications) was established in early 1989 in Bellevue, Washington.[6] Robert Fuller had invented its basic technology. Fuller had begun working on the "One Person, One Number" concept in 1983, after he had sold his first company, US Communications (a manufacturer of cellular equipment for telephone companies), to E. F. Johnson Co. In 1984 Fuller had initiated a patent application that ultimately led to two important awards governing telecommunications network technologies: patent number 4,893,335, "Remote Access Telephone Control System," issued in 1990; and number 5,375,161, "Telephone Control System with Branch Routing," awarded in 1994.

Fuller recruited Daniel Kranzler in 1986 to commercialize his technological ideas. (Biographies of AccessLine principals are presented in Exhibit 3.) After a brief stint as a school psychologist after graduating college in the mid-1970s, Kranzler had spent his working life in the mobile communications industry. His first position in the industry

---

[4] This information is drawn from "Portfolio Profiles: Chicago—Apex Investment Partners," *Venture Capital Journal* 33 (November 1993): 43–44, and "Apex Gets Ameritech as Lead Investor," *Venture Capital Journal* 35 (April 1995): 18. This should not be construed as an offering document for the sale of securities or otherwise. Apex Investment Partners, its general partners, and its principals specifically disclaim liability with respect to the contents hereof.

[5] "Apex Gets Ameritech as Lead Investor," op. cit.

[6] This history of AccessLine is based in large part on Tim Healy, "Entrepreneur Knows When to Hold Ideals, When to Fold Them," *Seattle Times*, January 29, 1990, D4; Jerry Michalski, "AccessLine, the Communications Coordinator," *Release 1.0* 93 (January 1993): 13; and "AccessLine Revisited: Friend of the Intelligent Network," *Release 1.0* 94 (October 1994): 10.

was selling paging equipment for the Harris Corporation. After a brief hiatus as a sailboat salesman in California, Kranzler moved to the Seattle area. He worked out an arrangement with an existing paging company, which allowed him to begin his own paging firm using the same frequency. Within a year, his firm, Beepers Northwest, was one of the fastest growing in the U.S. industry. Kranzler's firm caught the eye of Craig McCaw, who acquired Beepers Northwest in 1983. Kranzler became the eighteenth employee at McCaw Cellular Communications and helped grow McCaw's cellular and paging businesses. (McCaw emerged as the nation's largest cellular firm before being acquired by AT&T.)

Kranzler met Fuller while working at McCaw. Fuller had been impressed with Kranzler's entrepreneurial zeal and tenacity. The two men's partnership had evolved over time. An initial focus of their efforts was US Metrolink, a company that enabled Seattle-area customers to pay lower rates for in-state calls than charged by the local telephone provider, US West, by arbitraging discrepancies in the local rates. After a fiercely fought, multiyear battle with US West before State of Washington's Utilities and Transportation Commission, Kranzler and Fuller shifted their emphasis to the "One Person, One Number" technology. As president of AccessLine, Kranzler played several roles. In addition to designing the firm's marketing strategy, he was instrumental in reshaping this technology to enhance market acceptance. Robert Fuller served as chairman of the new firm.

AccessLine's vision was to integrate cellular phone, paging, voice messaging, and traditional telephone service. A subscriber was assigned a single telephone number. (See Exhibit 4 for a detailed product description.) Calls to a subscriber could be routed to him (e.g., to his car or office phone), to his fax machine, or else to his voice mailbox. If a subscriber was in transit at the time of an urgent call, the system was able to page him. The subscriber could then dial into the system and be connected with the caller. Users could program the system in a myriad of ways: for instance, a subscriber could screen or block all but selected business calls to his home after a certain hour.

Thus, AccessLine strategy was distinct from the numerous manufacturers of personal communications systems who were contemporaneously attracting financing. (An analysis of AccessLine's competitors is reproduced in Exhibit 5.) Although a variety of competitors were focusing on developing special units that were usable inside and outside the office, AccessLine sought to achieve similar goals using the customer's existing telephone network. Kranzler argued (as it turned out, correctly) that consumers would be reluctant to invest $700 or more for a Newton or other personal communicator. He believed that they would be much more willing to pay a few dollars a month to get most of these communicators' features from AccessLine.

The firm sought to commercialize its technology through the aggressive use of strategic alliances. Although telephone companies had originally intended to develop the software for single-number systems in-house, they soon discovered it was far more cost-effective to license the technology. In 1989, AccessLine undertook its initial strategic relationship with McCaw Cellular Communications. McCaw not only launched AccessLine's product but also provided a considerable fraction of the firm's initial financing. In the ensuing three years, AccessLine undertook licenses with many carriers, including Ameritech, Bell Atlantic, Southern New England Telephone, and Bell Canada. The telephone companies then marketed the service to its customers under their own brand names. (For instance, Bell Atlantic marketed the service as ContactLine, and Southern New England as Linx AccessLine.) In exchange for a higher fee, a phone company could be granted an exclusive franchise in a particular market. In addition, AccessLine undertook strategic alliances with equipment manufacturers such as Stratus Computer (manufacturer of the fault-tolerant mainframes used in many telephone networks) and Motorola.

AccessLine turned to professional equity investors for the first time in June 1994. Under the leadership of AccessLine's chief financial officer, Bill Stuart, and Bill Brady from Morgan Stanley & Co., it undertook a $15.5 million private placement from five investors. As part of the transaction, Jay Hoag, at the time managing director of Chancellor Capital Management, was elected to the board.[7] Exhibit 6 reproduces the term sheet of the transaction. In the ensuing year, the pace of strategic alliances had continued apace, including a major arrangement with IBM, which agreed to use AccessLine's technology in its forthcoming personal communicator device. AccessLine's historical finances and projected growth are summarized in Exhibit 7.[8]

THE PROPOSED TRANSACTION

Reflecting this rapid growth, AccessLine sought additional financing in early 1995. The firm sought to raise approximately $16 million, which it intended to use for acquisitions and developing strategic partnerships. Bolander had learned about AccessLine during his job search as he was completing his MBA in early 1994. Although he had not accepted the business development position that the firm offered him, he had stayed in touch with the management team. As AccessLine began looking for another financing round, he arranged a meeting between Apex and AccessLine officials.

The two teams had met for an informal dinner in late February. After pursuing a variety of due diligence investigations, Apex had decided to visit Seattle in early April. After an evening at the scenic Salish Lodge in Snoqualmie (the site where the "Twin Peaks" series was filmed) informally conversing over dinner and watching the NCAA basketball finals, the two teams had spent the day reviewing the company, its technology, and its prospects. At the day's end, the Apex team was excited by AccessLine's prospects. The investment also fit in well with their current objectives. Most of Apex's technology investments to date had been early-stage ones. Apex Investment Fund II, however, was approaching middle age, and its third fund was still being raised. Consequently, the prospect of an investment in an imminently positive-cash-flow firm that had the prospect of going public relatively quickly was attractive.

Nonetheless, Apex's management had two sets of concerns with the deal as proposed. The first related to the proposed valuation of the deal. AccessLine's management felt strongly that the Series B investment had to be priced at a premium to the valuation in the prior financing round. As AccessLine's chief financial officer, Bill Stuart, noted:

> We will not enter into a transaction which is unfair to our existing shareholders, especially those who invested last June. That's not the way we operate and, in any event, the Series A

---

[7] "AccessLine Technologies Completes $15.5 Million in Private Placement," *PR Newswire,* July 25, 1994. Hoag left Chancellor shortly after this transaction to begin his own firm but retained his board seat. No other director was added to the board to represent the Series A investors.

[8] AccessLine's sales were projected to continue to grow steadily, reaching about $208 million by 1999. 1994 sales were $14.2 million, and 1995 sales were projected as $32.5 million ("NIT to Deploy 'One Number Service' in Japan: NTT to Form a New Company with an American Corporation by End of September," *Nikkei Sangyo Shimbun,* September 6, 1995, p. 1). While after-tax net income was projected to be very modest in 1995 and 1996, by 1999 it was projected to represent 22% of sales. New capital expenditures (i.e., distinct from expenditures to replace depreciation) were expected to be about $1.5 million in 1995 (a year in which sales growth was $18.3 million). New capital expenditures were likely to be proportional to the dollar growth in sales in subsequent years. Net working capital would remain approximately constant.

Preferred shareholders will need to approve the financing. If we give better terms on this deal, we will need to renegotiate our last financing with those Series A shareholders. From their standpoint, the question would be why provide better terms than those of the last financing—AccessLine has met and, in fact, exceeded their expectations. There is more value in the company—not less.

But Apex needed to ensure that if the company was successful the fund would receive a very attractive return. They believed that AccessLine had received a relatively high valuation in its initial external financing round. Investing at too high a valuation in this round would limit the fund's upside. In considering its potential return, Apex also examined two comparable firms that were publicly traded (summarized in Exhibit 8).

Even if Apex was willing to invest at a high valuation, it would need to persuade one or more syndication partners to do likewise. Apex Investment Fund II's partnership agreement prohibited the venture capitalists from investing more than a few million dollars in any one deal. Apex intended to serve as lead investor[9] for this transaction, contributing a total of $2 million of its own capital and arranging for much of the additional financing. If Apex was to persuade others to invest, the investment could not be priced at too high a level.

At the same time, Apex realized that AccessLine was talking to a number of other venture capitalists, including Accel Partners and at least one other group. Accel, based in San Francisco and Princeton, was a formidable competitor, with $350 million under management and a specialization in telecommunications investments. (Its previous investments had included Network Equipment Technologies and Vitalink Communications.) If Apex sought to drive too hard a bargain, AccessLine might turn to these other investors for capital.

Second, Apex had concerns with the particulars of AccessLine's proposed term sheet (presented in Exhibit 9). Apex felt that the agreement should more directly provide incentives for the management team to pursue a mutually satisfactory outcome (i.e., an initial public offering at an attractive valuation). This might be accomplished through a variety of mechanisms. Among the approaches that might accomplish this goal would be provisions that required punitive interest or dividend payments if the firm did not go public. This gave the venture capitalists the right to fire management if the firm did not go public by a certain date, and it allowed the venture capitalists to force the firm to repurchase their shares (a put option).

In addition, Apex management felt that there was a greater need for measures that would protect the Series B investors from steps that were detrimental to their interests, such as the sale of shares to public or private investors at too low a valuation. The proposed AccessLine term sheet had provided some protections. For instance, the investors did not need to convert their preferred shares into common stock if an IPO was completed at a price under $10.50 per share. Their failure to convert the shares would essentially block the firm from going public. Nonetheless, Apex management believed that stronger measures would be helpful. These might include making the existing protections stronger (e.g., by raising the price at which the investors would be required to automatically convert their shares into common stock), as well as giving rights of first refusal on future financing.

The Apex team realized that these steps would likely meet with resistance from AccessLine. In particular, Kranzler interpreted suggestions along these lines as indica-

---

[9] As lead investor, Apex anticipated that it would represent the Series B shareholders on AccessLine's board.

tions that Apex was viewing the investment in purely financial terms and was seeking to earn a quick profit by "flipping" the shares after an IPO. If Apex was not interested in quick profits, he asked, why should it demand a set of terms that would punish management for not going public?

In two weeks, the two sides planned to meet again. This session, set for the Union League Club in Philadelphia, would involve Stuart from AccessLine, Middlemas and Bolander from Apex, and Brady from Morgan Stanley. The outstanding issues, the Apex team realized, would need to be resolved quickly if the deal was to come to fruition.

Exhibit 1   Profiles of Key Personnel

Apex Management

James A. Johnson   Prior to founding Apex, Jim Johnson was one of three founding partners of Knightsbridge Partners, a private investment firm. Knightsbridge sponsored investments in small- to medium-size companies with excellent growth prospects. After the partnership was disbanded, Mr. Johnson retained ongoing responsibility for two companies from which the investors have now successfully exited. Previously, Mr. Johnson was associated with Beatrice Foods, serving in a number of positions including CFO of the parent corporation and senior vice president of the $6 billion revenue U.S. Foods operating subsidiary. During this period, he was active in numerous acquisitions and divestitures including Esmark, Tropicana, Culligan, Air Stream Trailers, Coca-Cola Bottling of Los Angeles, and Dannon Yogurt. Mr. Johnson holds an MBA from Northwestern University and is a CPA. He is director of Acstar, American Waste Services, Industrial Services Technologies, Pure Fill Corporation, and Select Comfort, and currently serves as the president of the Juvenile Protection Association. Mr. Johnson concentrates on consumer-related opportunities and later stage deals.

George M. Middlemas   George Middlemas joined Apex in 1991 and has been involved in the venture capital industry since 1979. Prior to joining Apex, he was senior vice president and principal with Inco Venture Capital Management and prior to that was vice president and member of the investment commitment committee of Citicorp Venture Capital. Mr. Middlemas was a founding investor in Arnold Palmer Golf, Security Dynamics, America Online, Autotote, Conductron, and ALC (Lexitel). In addition, he was instrumental in the early financings of GRID Systems, Chomerics, Omni Cable TV, and Plant Genetics (Calgene). He is currently a director of PureCycle, American Communication Services, Steinbrecher, Data Critical, Security Dynamics, Tut Systems, and Arnold Palmer Golf. Mr. Middlemas holds bachelors of arts degrees in history and political science from the Pennsylvania State University, a masters of arts degree in political science from the University of Pittsburgh, an MBA from Harvard University, and is a CPA. He also serves on the Library Development Board of the Pennsylvania State University. Mr. Middlemas concentrates on telecommunications, software, and information technology.

Frederick W. W. Bolander   Rick Bolander joined Apex in 1994 after participating in a start-up venture to fund telecommunications projects, including a shared private telecommunications network in Tanzania, Africa in the summer during his MBA enrollment. Mr. Bolander was with AT&T for seven years where he served in various operating management roles including product development, project management, operations, engineering, sales, and marketing. He holds an MBA from Harvard University. After receiving his bachelors and masters of science degrees in electrical engineering from the University of Michigan, Mr. Bolander developed course material and lectured at the University on computer architecture. He is currently a director at Concord Communications. Mr. Bolander concentrates on telecommunications, software, and information technology.

First Analysis Corporation

F. Oliver Nicklin, Jr.   Oliver Nicklin founded First Analysis Corporation and is its president. He is an acknowledged expert in the broad environmental waste services field, having 25 years of experience in this area, as well as over 27 years of private investment experience. Prior to founding FAC, he served 12 years as an analyst, director of research, and chief operating partner at William Blair & Company, an investment banking, brokerage firm located in Chicago. His other experience includes strategic planning and European project evaluations for Amoco Corp. and Exxon Corp. A major emphasis throughout his career has been finding, evaluating, and nurturing emerging growth situations. He is a chartered financial analyst and received a bachelor's degree in chemical engineering from the University of Texas and an MBA from Harvard University. Currently, Mr. Nicklin is on the Board of Acstar, American Waste, and GNI Corp.

Bret R. Maxwell Bret Maxwell is a managing director of First Analysis Corporation responsible for coordinating private equity activities. Mr. Maxwell has more than 12 years of experience in the environmental and telecommunications private equity markets with the solid waste management field among his primary areas of expertise. His prior experience includes consulting for Arthur Andersen & Co. on manufacturing control systems and engineering work for General Electric Co. on automated inspection systems, robots, and sensing devices for jet engines. He is a chartered financial analyst and received a bachelor's degree in industrial engineering and an MBA, both from Northwestern University. Mr. Maxwell participates or has participated on the Boards of American Waste, American Communication Services, Continental Waste, Dialogic Corporation/GammaLink, National Recovery Systems, Salopek Golf Cars, and The Zond Group.

Other Investment Professionals

Nancy L. Corrie—Chief Financial Officer Nancy Corrie joined Apex in 1991 after serving as an accountant with Arthur Andersen & Co. for six years. She is a CPA and graduated with highest honors from DePaul University. Ms. Corrie is responsible for the financial administration of Apex as well as limited partner reporting and communications.

Source: Corporate documents.

Exhibit 2   Selected Apex Investments in April 1995

Telecommunications, Information Technology, and Software

American Communication Services, Inc. (ACSI)—Oakbrook, IL (NASDAQ:ACNS)
ACSI is a competitive access provider (CAP) and a developer and operator of fiber optic networks. CAP networks are used by high volume telecommunication users and long distance providers to bypass the Local Exchange Carriers. The company has five networks in operation, five networks under construction, and 10 more being planned. By the year 2000, it is estimated that CAP industry revenues will exceed $2.5 billion, and ACSI expects to achieve several percentage points of the available market. ACSI was founded by Apex, Global Capital, and The Productivity Fund, along with the management team. Publicly held, ACSI recently completed a private placement of $20 million to finance the completion of networks under construction. *Apex holds a board seat and the current valuation is 1.6x cost.*

Applied Digital Access, Inc. (ADA)—San Diego, CA (NASDAQ:ADAX)
ADA is a leading provider of network test and performance monitoring systems for high speed telecommunications circuits. Its customers are primarily the Regional Bell Operating Companies. The company is also developing a product that could be installed on customer premises, thereby greatly enlarging the market for their products. To our knowledge, ADA is the only company with technology capable of processing test data from DS3 circuits without inducing degradation in the circuit itself. ADA went public in March 1994. Apex participated in a recapitalization financing of ADA in early 1992 and was responsible for introducing Ameritech Development Corporation to the company. *Current valuation is 7.3x cost.*

Data Critical Corporation—Seattle, WA/Oklahoma City, OK
Data Critical has developed a patented technology for using the paging network (or any other wireless bandwidths) for sending large data files to remote locations. Applications for the technology include medical information, law enforcement, broadcast fax, and financial information. The company has already signed agreements with several companies for the development of services and has finished one extensive trial leading to a commercial roll-out in 1995. Apex led a bridge round in 1994 and a $3 million round in early 1995. *Apex holds a board seat and carries the investment at cost.*

Dialogic Corporation/GammaLink—Parsippany, NJ (NASDAQ:DLGC)
Dialogic is a leading developer, manufacturer, and distributor of call-processing system products. The company went public in April 1994. First Analysis Corporation was a founder of GammaLink in 1986 and Apex originally invested in GammaLink in 1990. GammaLink and Dialogic agreed to merge via a pooling of interests in September 1993. GammaLink is a leading manufacturer of PC-fax communication products. Since the IPO and merger, the company has been performing above expectations. *Holdings in Dialogic were liquidated at 5.75x cost.*

Security Dynamics Technologies, Inc. (SDI)—Cambridge, MA (NASDAQ:SDTI)
SDI develops and supplies a family of products used for computer and network security. The company's basic technology ("SecurID") is based on over 14 patents in the United States and overseas, and their products are used by many "Fortune 1000" companies, as well as government agencies. Profitable since the fourth quarter of 1989, SDI has been growing at over 50% per annum and enjoys 70%+ gross margins. SDI was founded in 1986 by a group including George Middlemas and the original management team. Apex invested in SDI in 1992 as part of a recapitalization and the company went public in December 1994. *Apex holds a board seat and the current valuation is 7.5x cost.*

Steinbrecher Corp.—Burlington, MA
Steinbrecher is the leading designer and supplier of wideband digital radio systems, which are primarily used in wireless communication networks. The company's technology enables wireless

networks to process signals digitally with higher fidelity at lower signal strengths. The company's patented technology is less expensive than current analog solutions and more versatile. The company is currently supplying data transceivers to McCaw, Airtouch, and other cellular network operators. They are also developing a new product ("mini-cell") targeted for the worldwide cellular voice industry in late 1995/early 1996. The technology can easily be adapted to PCS or other voice and data uses. Apex and McCaw Corporation led an $8.6 million venture financing in February 1993, a $20 million private placement in December 1993, and a $15 million private placement in October 1994. *Apex holds a board seat and Steinbrecher is currently valued at 2x cost.*

Tut Systems, Inc.—Pleasant Hill, CA
Tut designs and distributes transceiver products that improve the transmission characteristics of copper wire. The core technology employs a patented balun circuit to enhance the signal-to-noise ratio by over 100 times better than other existing balun technologies. Tut's unique solution offers a cost advantage over the competition's solution. Tut will leverage their core technology to develop additional products. Apex led a $5 million venture financing in April 1995 which allowed the company to expand its marketing efforts. *Apex holds a board seat and carries the investment at cost.*

Environmental/Industrial Productivity

PureCycle Corporation—Commerce City, CO (NASDAQ:PCYC)
PureCycle is a water resource and development company that owns the rights to market and develop ground and surface water in the state of Colorado. In addition, the company has a proprietary technology for the treatment of waste water. The company's main asset is a large amount of water (three million acre feet) that is located within seven miles of Denver. This water, when developed, represents an asset worth at least $200 million and annual revenues to the company exceeding $12 million. The company is in the midst of developing the assets for use by several communities in the Denver area. Apex structured and led two financings of PureCycle that have financed operations during development. *Apex holds a board seat and the company is valued at cost.*

Zemex Corporation—Toronto, Ontario, Canada (NYSE:ZMX)
Zemex is involved in the extraction and processing of industrial minerals as well as the production of powdered metals. Assuming only the growth in Zemex's existing business, due to programs already in place or announced, net income would increase from $1.8 million in 1993 to $6.8 million in 1996. Zemex represented an opportunistic and relatively low risk means of participating in an upsurge in cyclical issues and came to our attention through our deal flow via FAC. *Current valuation is 1.6x cost.*

The Zond Group, Inc.—Tehachapi, CA
Zond develops, constructs, operates, and manages wind power generating facilities and sells related technology. The company has developed wind power projects comprising of approximately 260 megawatts of generating capacity and currently operates over 2,400 wind turbines. Zond is completing tests of its new wind turbine, the Z-40. *Apex holds a board seat and the current valuation is at cost, plus Zond pays a current dividend.*

Consumer Products /Specialty Retail/Other Investments

Arnold Palmer Golf Management Co. (Pacific Golf, Inc.)—Orlando, FL
Pacific Golf was founded to acquire Arnold Palmer Golf Management (APGM) and to acquire, lease, upgrade, and manage golf course facilities. Apex led this investment and holds a major position. Since the investment was made in September 1993, the company has added four additional facilities and has more than tripled in size and is cash flow positive. *Apex holds two board seats and APGM is currently valued at 2.5x cost, based on a multiple of cash flow comparable to other companies in this area.*

Continental Waste Industries, Inc.—Clark, NJ (NASDAQ:CONT)

acquisitions. As of fourth quarter 1994, the company reported an increase in revenues of 130% from the previous year and fully diluted earnings per share was $0.17, up from $0.05 in 1993. *Apex was a founder of Continental Waste in 1990, holds a board seat, and currently values the company at 3.2x cost.*

Expressly Portraits, Inc. — Foster City, CA

Expressly Portraits operates more than 150 photographic portrait studios in high traffic shopping malls throughout the United States. The company is based on the concept of providing finished portraits for the consumer in one hour. The customer, frequently a family, has their appointed sitting and returns for their finished portraits one hour later. The concept is popular with the malls since the family, often including both spouses, normally spends the hour in the mall. Expressly Portraits has increased its number of stores by over 130 and sales by over $45 million since Apex's investment in 1990. The company has also attracted two very significant corporate partners, one of whom invested $10 million. *Expressly is currently valued at 1.8x cost.*

Mothers Work, Inc. — Philadelphia, PA (NASDAQ:MWRK)

Mothers Work is a specialty retailer in the upscale maternity market and currently operates over 160 stores nationwide under the names Mothers Work, Mimi's Maternity, and Maternity Works. Apex was among the initial venture investors in this company. Since our investment, Mothers Work has had a successful public offering, increased the number of stores 350%, and increased revenues by more than 400%. In addition, the company designs and manufactures 70% of their goods and utilizes a sophisticated internally developed MIS system. Mothers Work acquired Page Boy, a direct competitor, and recently announced the acquisition of A Pea in the Pod, its next largest competitor in this niche. *Apex held a board seat and the company is currently valued at 2.6x cost.*

Select Comfort Corporation — Minneapolis, MN

Select Comfort manufactures and distributes a line of adjustable air support mattresses for home use through both direct marketing and its own retail stores. The company has undertaken a retail roll-out and has over 30 stores as of December 1994, an increase of 27 stores from the time of our initial investment in March 1993. The company recently began a new sales promotion effort utilizing "road shows" aimed at potential customers. The use of multiple distribution channels has allowed the company to more than quadruple its sales since Apex's investment, with another 100% increase projected for 1995. *Apex held a board seat and the company is currently valued at 2.75x cost.*

Preferred Solutions, Inc. — New York, NY

Preferred Solutions provide prescription benefit management services which lower drug costs for companies and managed care entities. Drug costs are reduced via a combination of enforcing generic substitutions, dispensing optimum prescription size, eliminating duplications, and negotiating and enforcing discounts with pharmacies and manufacturers. Despite its relatively early stage, Preferred Solutions has already achieved a reputation for being far ahead of the competition in its analytical features. *The company was sold for cash in January 1995 for 2x investment.*

Richwood Pharmaceuticals, Inc. — Florence, KY

Richwood has developed a drug distribution network focused on specific drug categories not normally addressed by the large integrated pharmaceutical companies. Richwood's efforts are currently focused on pain management and neurological disorders. The company has found an exciting prospect in one drug in a portfolio it recently acquired from another company. As currently evaluated, the drug has promise as a treatment for attention deficit disorders, currently a $150 million market. The company has several clinical trials underway to assess efficacy and the early results are quite promising. *Apex holds a board seat and Richwood is currently valued at 1.75x cost.*

Source: Corporate documents.

Exhibit 3   AccessLine Management Profiles

Daniel Kranzler
President and Chief Executive Officer
See description in case study.

Robert M. Fuller
Founder and Chairman of the Board of Directors
Bob Fuller has been a member of the mobile electronics and telephone communications industries since 1971. He began his career as principal engineer of Harris Corporation, R.F. Communications in Rochester, New York. In 1976, Fuller co-founded U.S. Communications which produced mobile phone products for the mobile and cellular industries. As president and CEO, Fuller grew the firm to sales of $2.5 million. U.S. Communications merged with E.F. Johnson/Western Union in 1981 and Fuller subsequently became corporate vice president for E.F. Johnson, continuing to head the U.S. Communications division until 1983. Fuller is the owner of patents and patents pending for the technology he invented on which the AccessLine System® is based.

Frederick A. Epler
Senior Vice President, Engineering
Fred Epler is one of the founding members of AccessLine Technologies and in addition to being senior vice president of engineering, he is also a member of the board of directors. Epler has been associated with Robert Fuller and his companies since 1977 and played a major role in the development of the AccessLine System technology. His expertise includes specialties in electrical/mechanical engineering, electronics design, and telecommunications interface. At U.S. Communications, Epler was the director of engineering, supervising the engineering and technical staffs in the design and development of cellular telephones.

William J. Stuart
Senior Vice President and Chief Financial Officer
Bill Stuart has had 15 years of broad financial management experience in both large and small corporate environments. He has a strong record of success with high growth companies, and expertise in the areas of joint ventures, mergers and acquisitions, financing, planning, and international operations. Prior to joining AccessLine Technologies, Stuart was vice president of AT&T Paradyne, where he had responsibilities as an area controller for several business units and as an international controller overseeing financial operations of the company's international subsidiaries and distributors. Prior to its acquisition by AT&T, Stuart was treasurer for Paradyne Corporation. At Prime Computer, Inc., prior to joining AT&T Paradyne, Stuart held various financial management positions during which time the company grew from $60 million to $640 million in annual revenues. Stuart joined AccessLine Technologies in May of 1992.

Mark A. Louison
Senior Vice President and Chief Operating Officer
Mark Louison has a wide variety of experience in sales, marketing, and general management in the wireless telecommunications industry with particular expertise in management of start-up operations and distribution channel development. Prior to joining AccessLine Technologies, Louison was vice president and general manager for the New York metropolitan area of NYNEX Mobile Communications Company. Louison was promoted to the management team as a result of the partnership in New York between Bell Atlantic and NYNEX. Louison joined AccessLine Technologies as senior vice president of operations in December of 1992.

Brian T. McManus
Senior Vice President and General Counsel
Prior to joining AccessLine Technologies in 1994 as senior vice president and general counsel, Brian McManus was a partner in the Seattle law firm of Mundt, MacGregor, Happel, Falconer, Zulauf &

Hall, and was AccessLine's chief legal counsel. He has also been corporate secretary since January 1993. McManus has concentrated his legal practice in the areas of partnership and corporate formation and finance, software licensing and other forms of intellectual property protection.

Edwin A. Hopper
Member of the Board

Ed Hopper was one of the pioneers in developing cable television franchises and distributing cable service to homes around the country. His first involvement was with National Communication Service Corp. Hopper then joined McCaw as the lead executive for cellular telephone when McCaw was beginning to apply for FCC licenses prior to the introduction of cellular service in the United States. Hopper led the cellular team at McCaw in developing and securing cellular licenses. As McCaw spread its operations throughout the United States and went public, Hopper became vice chairman and was responsible for financial structuring, as well as acquisitions and organization of partnerships and operations. In 1988, Hopper retired and now lives in Portland, Oregon.

Jay C. Hoag
Member of the Board

Jay Hoag is a founder and managing director of Technology Crossover Ventures, a fund investing in late-stage private and young public information-technology firms. From 1982 to 1995, Hoag was with Chancellor Capital Management, Inc. (formerly Citicorp Investment Management, Inc.). At Chancellor, he led the management of the technology portfolio. Hoag first was an analyst for the electronics and computer software and services industry, joined the Alternative Asset Group in 1985 and was appointed managing director in 1990.

James R. Carreker
Member of the Board

Jim Carreker has been president and CEO of Aspect Telecommunications since its inception in 1985 where he guides the overall strategy of the company. From 1982 through 1985, Carreker served in various management positions at Dataquest, Inc., a leading provider of high technology market research. From 1976 through 1982, Carreker headed product development at a division of Datapoint Corporation, a computer and communications manufacturer. During the latter part of this period, Carreker was vice president and general manager of Datapoint's Communications Management Products Division. Prior to joining Datapoint, he worked for AT&T Bell Laboratories and EDS.

John C. Bolger
Member of the Board

John Bolger recently retired from Cisco Systems, Inc. where he had been vice president and chief financial officer since 1989. Prior to that, he served as vice president of finance and administration for KLA Instruments, Inc., a semiconductor equipment manufacturer, from March 1988 to February 1989. He was also vice president of finance at Monolithic Memories, Inc. from 1983 until its acquisition by Advanced Micro Devices, Inc. in 1987.

Source: Corporate documents

Exhibit 4   AccessLine Product Description

By linking state-of-the-art computer compatibility with a telephone network, the AccessLine System® combines the full power of today's computer technology with a telephone number and has introduced the AccessLine Smart Number.® Having a Smart Number on your phone is analogous to putting a personal computer on your desktop. Once you have an *intelligent* platform which is easily accessed, you can choose applications to meet your needs as they arise. Some users may use their computers for just word processing, spreadsheets, or graphics, while others may use many of the applications together to give them more power to be effective and productive. In the same way, an AccessLine Smart Number user can make his or her communications more effective and productive by *choosing* one or more of the AccessLine applications. Below is a list of some of the functions:

Personal AccessLine®
This feature is often referred to as the Phone Number Assigned to People, Not Places.® It's a personal phone number—a number associated with a person, not a particular phone. It has the ability to look for a subscriber at his or her current location, and move from location to location based on a subscriber's schedule. Call routing to the cellular phone is now fully automatic—a first in a single number technology.

Screened AccessLine®
While the AccessLine service can increase the accessibility of key people on the move, the ability to be inaccessible during certain times is of equal importance. A busy professional wants important calls to reach him or her on the first attempt but does not want to be disturbed by unimportant calls that could be handled at another time or by others. Screened AccessLine allows a subscriber to have this kind of call management. Based on criteria such as time of day, location, and availability status, each subscriber may screen and control her calls in her own way. Therefore, the AccessLine System lets the subscriber choose the amount of and kind of screening desired. Following is a list of the kinds of screening available to an AccessLine subscriber:

> **Informed Forwarding**—"You've reached the AccessLine for Bob Jones who is currently on his cellular phone. If you wish to speak to him now, touch 1 and we will connect you. Otherwise, please hold the line and speak with his office."

> **Urgent Screened Forwarding**—"You've reached the AccessLine for Bob Jones who is currently on his cellular phone. If it is important that you speak to him now, touch 1 and we will connect you. Otherwise, hold the line and speak with his office."

> **Emergency Screen**—"You've reached the AccessLine for Dr. Jones who is currently away from his office. If this is an emergency, requiring that you speak to him now, touch 1 and we will page him. If you'd like to speak to his office, touch 2. Otherwise, hold the line and leave a detailed message."

> **VIP Access Only**—"You've reached the AccessLine for Benjamin Morgan, who is currently with a client. If it is important that you speak with him now, touch in his privacy code and we will connect you. Otherwise, hold the line and leave a detailed message."

> **Voice Screen**—"You've reached the AccessLine for Marianne Quinlan. Please state your name and the purpose of your call and we will attempt to connect the call to your party."

A subscriber can choose from many screening options and levels of control.

AccessLine Connection®
AccessLine Connection lets a subscriber pick up a call on **any** phone. Her pager becomes the "ringer" for her phone. When a caller dials a subscriber's number and hears the ringing, the subscriber *feels* the ring on her silent vibrating pager. The subscriber then goes to **any** phone and dials her AccessLine number to connect with the caller who is holding on the line. This virtually puts

an end to telephone tag, pager tag, and (the newest game) voice mail tag. In addition, this product solves the problems of portable users: limited battery life, poor reception areas, and poor cellular telephone etiquette (i.e., taking calls in inappropriate public places such as a theater or restaurant).

AccessLine Messaging®

Incorporated into the AccessLine service is a messaging service. The difference between AccessLine Messaging and other voice messaging systems is that AccessLine always takes care of callers. The system always gives callers the option of speaking to a live person thereby eliminating "voice mail jail." In addition, voice mail messages are accessible directly through a subscriber's AccessLine which gives subscribers additional functions such as the ability to instantly call back a caller who left a message without having to dial the number. This has tremendous value in terms of convenience and safety for subscribers in their cars who can't take their eyes from the road to look up a number.

Rebound[SM]

This feature lets a subscriber return or rebound back into his AccessLine System after completing an outbound call (automatically or by using touchtones). This enables the subscriber to answer a series of voice mail messages within a single call or to use AccessLine as a call card.

Fax Reflection[SM]

The AccessLine Smart Number also integrates fax. The intelligence in the system automatically detects when a fax machine is calling and routes the call to the fax machine of the subscriber's choice.

AccessLine Traveler[SM]

More and more, telephone users are finding the need to be mobile, not only in town, but anywhere in the United States and the world. AccessLine Traveler allows subscribers the ability to travel to any city throughout the world and still receive important calls. AccessLine Traveler informs callers that the subscriber is out of town and screens the calls (as designated by the subscriber) and then forwards the call to the subscriber at any location. A subscriber can pick up calls at her remote field office, hotel, or on any cellular network and the caller does not need to know any roaming codes or procedures. The AccessLine knows how to find you and does it all transparently to the caller. In order to utilize the Personal AccessLine, a subscriber need only to provide a basic schedule of where he or she is most likely to be located during a given week. As an example, a subscriber may usually be at his office between 8:00 a.m. and 6:00 p.m., commuting between 7:30 and 8:00 a.m. and 6:00 and 6:30 p.m., at home between 6:30 and 10:00 p.m. and available only for family calls after 10:00 p.m.

In summary, AccessLine gives telephone subscribers the ability to coordinate and simplify their accessibility for important calls while also controlling communications so that they receive only the calls they want. Using the AccessLine is as simple to use as it is sophisticated.

Source: Corporate documents.

Exhibit 5   AccessLine Competitive Analysis

There will be significant competition in the industry. This area may account for over one billion dollars of revenue per year in the next few years. With that potential revenue base, competition will be in two forms. First, there will be "point-solutions" which deliver one or several pieces of the AccessLine suite of services. Second, there will be companies who will introduce a similar suite of services to AccessLine's. In general, it is important to note that while there are a number of systems announced, AccessLine is the *only* commercially deployed system in the market.

Constant Touch—Glenayre

Glenayre's one number solution is a software package on Glenayre's Modular Voice Processing Family (MVP) platform. The MVP was an enhancement to the existing paging services offered by Glenayre. Glenayre has been marketing the service since 1994 although there are no announced customers to date. The company has an excellent reputation in the industry and a very strong sales force. The system has a complex and cumbersome user interface compared to AccessLine's. (The interface is one of the more important criteria for market acceptance.) AllTel in the United States has looked at the Glenayre system but is now in discussion with AccessLine. In Europe, there is a test system in BelgiCom. AccessLine is in discussion with BelgiCom, apparently indicating some dissatisfaction on their part with the Glenayre system.

Ericsson

Ericsson is apparently planning to put some functionality in their switch and has deployed a trial system with the Norwegian telecommunications firm. AccessLine has licensed the Swedish firm Telia, which had attempted unsuccessfully to obtain personal number functionality from Ericsson. In mid-1994, Telia determined that, despite their close relationship, Ericsson could not be relied upon to deliver the solution anytime soon. Also, AccessLine is in discussions with the Norwegian firm, indicating disappointment with the product being delivered by Ericsson.

McCaw

Recently introduced Universal Number in the U.S. as a direct competitor to earlier AccessLine customers. The interface is cumbersome and inflexible. No take rate statistics are available. However, McCaw's marketing of the service will probably benefit AccessLine. McCaw is an aggressive marketer and will help drive demand by licensees for a competitive solution from AccessLine and force AccessLine licensees to market the AccessLine solution more aggressively. Recent information indicates that the company is trying to purchase another product, "Magic Number," to replace its current one. It is unclear as to why.

Northern Telecom

In early 1995, Northern Telecom announced a marketing agreement with BellSouth to use their ProLink software as the foundation for Personal Number Service. No timeframe for commercial availability was announced. Northern Telecom plans to develop its own wireless mobility services for availability beginning in late 1995. AccessLine is currently discussing with Northern Telecom the steps necessary to port its application. Also, AccessLine has licensed the technology to two of Northern's sister companies— Bell Canada and Bell Mobility.

OneVoice PCS—InterVoice

InterVoice, a Dallas-based call automation company announced OneVoice PCS in February 1994, an enhanced product on the InterVoice OneVoice Network Solutions Platform. According to their literature, subscribers are able to consolidate their office, home, cellular, fax and pager numbers into a single personal number. The company has also indicated that their products can provide voice recognition and verification capabilities on their integrated services platform. AccessLine is aware of no installation of the OneVoice PCS platform in the U.S., other than one trial in Los Angeles.

Precision Systems Inc. (PSI)

PSI is a developer and manufacturer of voice and call processing systems for use with local and long distance companies and has been in business since 1981. The company is based in Clearwater, Florida. In 1994, Single Number Service (SNS) was acquired by PSI. The SNS is said to allow callers to locate a subscriber at any of several locations by dialing a single phone number. According to the company, when a caller dials the SNS number, the SNS application will dial different numbers to "find" the subscriber based upon the time of day and a predetermined schedule or pattern. The company indicates that features such as voice dialing, simultaneous phone ringing, and scheduling are offered. The company president has contacted AccessLine's president and proposed the use by PSI of the AccessLine software on their platform. AccessLine has not responded at this time. There are no known sites where SNS is installed.

Prairie Systems

Prairie Systems is a five-year old, privately-held company headquartered in Omaha, Nebraska. It has been successful to date in selling the wireless fax and 800-number paging components in the ARDIS Personal Messaging Service (ARDIS is the largest wireless Motorola packet radio network in the United States). The company announced "The Next Generation One-Number Solution" in January 1995. The Information Services Platform (ISP) is advertised to support messaging, broadcasting, network switching and interactive application solutions and services such as personal number, messaging, credit card access and enhanced fax services. Prairie Systems has announced its intention to license its system and have test installations in the United Kingdom and Hong Kong.

Priority Call Management

The PCM platform is understood to be basically an automatic call director (ACD) that provides the caller with several options, touch 1 for ---, touch 2 for ---, etc. The system offers only one of the dozens of applications available on the AccessLine system.

ProLink

ProLink is a proprietary development out of Bell South Corporation who thought it could sell this call-processing functionality to other carriers. The ProLink service is less feature-rich and less user-friendly compared to the AccessLine service offerings (i.e., the system "hunts" from place to place until it finds the subscriber, or the caller hangs up). Bell South has attempted to sell its software system to a number of carriers in the past few years (AccessLine has been up against it on several occasions and has won in every instance). No other carrier in the United States or internationally has endorsed this platform to date.

TPS

TPS is a U.S.- and U.K.-based firm with 45 employees. It offers in both countries a wide array of enhanced communications services, including voice-activated dialing, voice and fax mail, and one-number features. It also provides intelligent agent services, allowing callers to sort through large amounts of e-mail, news stories, and other information.

Wildfire

The Wildfire Assistant, developed by start-up Wildfire Communications Inc., can place phone calls on your behalf, announce incoming calls and, knowing your routine, automatically forward calls to your phone or pager. Wildfire offers a voice recognition "personal assistant" system that can help in making calls and checking messages. This system uses standard "off-the-shelf" industry voice recognition algorithms to execute its functions, and is very progressive and effective in the use of "conversational" voice recognition. (You can receive a demonstration of the system by dialing 1-800-945-3347.) While the system has immediate high-tech appeal, there are few, if any, "live" systems out in the field. The applicability of the service from mobile phones or phones with any background noise is unknown. According to the company, the Wildfire server includes an internal switch for routing calls and processes spoken commands to initiate or redirect calls by accessing a directory of names and telephone numbers users have established. The product is scheduled to begin shipment in mid-1995. It is extremely expensive—$1,200 to $2,000 per user subject to system size. This expense is largely due to the reliance on voice recognition throughout all conversations through the platform.

Source: Corporate documents.

Exhibit 6   Access Series A Term Sheet: June 4, 1994

Securities:	2,500,000 shares of Series A Preferred Stock and, for each share so purchased, warrants to purchase an additional 0.15 shares of Series A Preferred Stock at an exercise price of $7.00 per share ("Units").[a]
Investors:	The Units will be offered only to "accredited investors" as defined in Regulation D under the Securities Act.
Aggregate Proceeds:	$17,500,000
Price:	$7.00 per Unit (the "Sale Price").
Placement Agent:	Morgan Stanley & Co. Incorporated (the "Placement Agent") to act on a "best efforts" basis. The Company will pay in cash a placement fee equal to 5% of the aggregate offering proceeds.

The capitalization of the Company giving effect to the Financing will be as follows:

Name or Entity	Class of Stock	Number of Shares	Total Percentage Ownership
Existing Investors[b]	Common (Class A and B)	7,931,060	61%
New Investors	Series A Preferred	2,500,000	19%
	Warrants to Purchase		
	Series A Preferred	375,000	3%
Reserved for Management and Employees[c]	Common (Class A and B)	2,143,846	17%
Total		12,949,906	100%

Rights and Preferences of Series A Preferred

The Series A Preferred shall be entitled to:

(1) An 8% non-cumulative *dividend preference*; any such dividend to be paid when and if declared by the Board of Directors out of funds legally available for such purpose.

(2) A *liquidation preference* equal to the Sale Price per share plus declared and unpaid dividends. Thereafter, all remaining assets shall be distributed among the holders of Common Stock ("Common"). A change in control of the Company by way of merger, sale of assets or other reorganization shall constitute a liquidation event.

(3) The right of *conversion* of the Series A Preferred into Class A Common Stock at the option of the holder, at the initial ratio of one-for-one ("Conversion Ratio") at any time; *provided* however, the Series A Preferred shall automatically convert upon (i) an initial public offering ("IPO") with gross proceeds of at least $10,000,000 and a per share price of at least $10.50 until June 30, 1996, or (ii) the written consent of holders of at least two-thirds of the Series A Preferred.

(4) *Antidilution* adjustment, on a weighted-average basis using a

broad-based formula, for any new issues at a purchase price less than the Series A conversion price, except for issues of employee shares or on recapitalizations, but including shares reserved for issuance to employees but not yet subject to any option or other acquisition right. Proportional adjustment of the Series A conversion price in the event of a stock split, combination, reclassification and the like.

(5) The right to *vote* on an as-converted basis with Class A Common Stock as a single class on all matters (except to the extent that voting as a separate class or series is required by law): *provided,* however, that a vote of the holders of at least two-thirds of the Series A Preferred, voting as a separate class, shall be required for (a) any material adverse change in the rights, preferences or privileges of the Series A Preferred; (b) any creation of a new class of shares having rights or preferences senior to or on a parity with the Series A Preferred; (c) declaration or payment of any cash dividends on the Common Stock; (d) any redemption, purchase or other acquisition of the Company's capital stock or any payments with respect to stock appreciation rights or similar rights; (e) a recapitalization or reorganization into a limited liability company or other noncorporate form; (f) entering into any business other than the telecommunications business; (g) any increase in compensation of any officer, director or any other employee holding 5% or more of the Company's capital stock unless approved by a disinterested majority of the Board; or (h) entering into certain specified related-party transactions.

(6) The right to *elect* one director to the Board.

Term of Warrants

The warrant shall expire on June 3, 1999 or earlier upon the occurrence of a change in control of the Company.

Information and Inspection Rights

The holders of Series A Preferred or Class A Common Stock issued upon conversion of Series A Preferred ("Conversion Stock") shall be entitled to receive quarterly and annual financial statements prepared in accordance with GAAP. The annual statements shall be certified by a nationally known accounting firm.

Each holder of 100,000 shares or more of Series A Preferred Stock and/or Conversion Stock shall be entitled to monthly financial statements prepared in accordance with GAAP, to inspect the Company's books and records and to discuss the Company's affairs with its officers.

The foregoing information and inspection rights shall terminate upon an IPO.

Registration Rights

At any time following the earlier of (i) June 3, 1997 or (ii) one year after an IPO, the holders of a majority of the Series A Preferred and the Conversion Stock shall be entitled to demand registration of at least 50% (or such lesser amount if the anticipated aggregate offering price would exceed $10 million) of the Class A Common Stock issued or issuable upon conversion of the Series A Preferred under the Securities Act of 1933 (the "1933 Act") for a public offering on a firm commitment underwritten basis (the "Demand Rights"). The Demand Rights may only be exercised once during any 12-month period, and the Company shall not be obligated to effect more than two registrations under the Demand Rights. The Demand Rights may not be exercised during the 180 days following the effective date (or subsequent to the filing date at any time prior to the effective date) of a registration statement filed by the Company under the 1933 Act.

The holders of Series A Preferred and Conversion Stock shall be entitled to "piggyback" registration rights (the "Piggyback Rights") on registrations by the Company (or any other holders), subject to pro rata "cutback" (including to zero on an IPO) to accommodate shares to be sold for the account of the Company.

If available for use by the Company, at any time following the second anniversary of the IPO the holders of Series A Preferred and Conversion Stock shall be entitled to unlimited S-3 registrations (the "S-3 Rights"); provided the aggregate offering price of each such offering is at least $1,000,000.

The Company shall pay for the expense (exclusive of underwriting discounts or commissions or special counsel of a selling stockholder) of all registrations under the Demand Rights and Piggyback Rights. The selling stockholders shall pay for the expenses of all registrations under the S-3 Rights.

Registration rights may be transferred to related entities, constituent partners and a transferee who acquires at least 100,000 registrable securities (or such lesser number as constitutes all such securities held by the transferor) upon written notice to the Company.

Registration rights shall terminate with regard to any holders who can sell all of their shares under Rule 144 (exclusive of Rule 144 (k)) in a three month period.

All holders of registration rights will agree to a 120-day lock-up period after an IPO, conditional upon all officers and directors similarly agreeing.

Other standard provisions with respect to registration rights shall apply, including limits on subsequent registration rights, cross indemnification, the Company's ability to delay the filing of demand registration for a period of at least 120 days, the period of time in which the registration statements shall be kept effective, underwriting arrangements and the like.

| Redemption Rights | Each holder of Series A Preferred Stock shall have the right to require the Company to repurchase their share of Series A Preferred Stock (but *not* any Conversion Stock) at $7.00 per share plus any declared and unpaid dividends on each anniversary of the first closing date (June 3), beginning June 3, 2,000, provided that no holder may require the Company to repurchase more than one-third of its share of Series A Preferred Stock on any anniversary date. If a holder exercises such right, the Company may elect to repurchase all of such holder's shares. |

| Rights to Maintain | Each holder of at least 100,000 shares of Series A Preferred Stock and/or Conversion Stock shall have a right to maintain its percentage ownership interest in the Company in the event the Company issues stock at a price less than $7.00 per share, subject to exceptions for stock issued pursuant to mergers and acquisitions, |

technology licensing arrangements, strategic alliances, employee stock options, stock issued on an IPO and other standard exceptions.

Right of Co-Sale

Each purchaser of Units shall have a right of co-sale in the event that either Daniel Kranzler or Robert Fuller shall propose to sell his stock to third parties, subject to certain exceptions for transfers to family members and other shareholders, transfers to the Company pursuant to its right of first refusal, and sales of up to 26-2/3% of Mr. Kranzler's shares and up to 33-1/3% of Mr. Fuller's shares.

Option to Buy Common Stock

Each purchaser of Units shall have an option to purchase 0.583 shares (rounded to the nearest share) of Class A Common Stock from the current shareholders for each Unit purchased. The option shall be exercised and the shares of Common Stock purchased, if at all, on or before July 31, 1994. The purchase price shall be $5.00 per share, payable in cash at closing.

Voting Agreement

Each holder of Series A Preferred Stock shall agree to vote all of its shares in favor of a designee of Chancellor Venture Capital Fund II as the director which such holders are entitled to elect.

Board of Directors

It shall be a condition to closing that Jay Hoag of Chancellor Capital Management shall be appointed to the Board. In addition, the stockholders subject to the existing Shareholders' Agreement shall amend that agreement to provide that they will vote for two directors independent of the company.

Closing

The first closing for the Financing shall occur on or about June 3, 1994 at the offices of Wilson, Sonsini, Goodrich & Rosati; a second closing may occur by July 1, 1994.

Purchase Agreement

The Financing shall be evidenced by a Unit Purchase Agreement and other related agreements satisfactory to counsel to the Investors.

---

[a]While the term sheet was prepared assuming the sale of 2.5 million shares, 2.22 million shares were actually sold.

[b]Includes 157,677 shares issued as part of the Fuller Research & Development Company merger, 389,820 shares issued pursuant to restricted stock grants and 1,087,962 shares subject to options granted to Daniel R. Kranzler.

[c]Excludes 643,600 shares reserved for future grant.

Source: Corporate documents.

Exhibit 7   Historical Financial Performance and Projected Growth of AccessLine Technologies, Inc.

Consolidated Statements of Operations, Year Ended December 31, 1993

	1993
Revenue	
Systems revenue	$7,551,090
Licensing and maintenance	808,699
Total revenue	$8,359,789
Cost of systems	2,815,292
Gross margin	$5,544,497
Operating expenses	
Sales, general and administrative	4,985,320
Engineering, research and development	1,421,099
Total operating expenses	$6,406,419
Operating loss	(861,922)
Other income, net	12,348
Net loss	$(849,574)
Net loss per share	$(0.10)
Weighted average common share outstanding	8,751,598

Consolidated Balance Sheet, December 31, 1993

Assets	1993
Current assets	
Cash and cash equivalent	$ 50,337
Accounts receivable	685,962
Inventory	823,181
Prepaid expenses and deposits	240,482
Total current assets	1,799,962
Property and equipment, net	638,503
Other assets, net	396,793
Total	$2,835,258

Liabilities and Stockholders' Equity	1993
Current liabilities	
Accounts payable	$1,946,739
Accrued wages, benefits, taxes	413,597
Other accrued liabilities	256,854
Deferred revenue	1,628,506
Total current liabilities	$4,245,696
Note payable	1,888,139
Other liabilities	73,226
Total stockholders' equity (deficiency in assets)	(3,371,803)
Total	$2,835,258

	1995	1996	1997	1998	1999
U.S. Personal number market:					
Cellular	244,350	839,700	2,208,150	3,861,000	5,798,250
PCS	0	59,200	296,000	621,600	1,184,000
Paging	182,650	576,933	1,667,000	2,648,333	4,232,667
Personal number market	427,000	1,475,833	4,171,150	7,130,933	11,214,917
Combined penetration (%)	0.75%	2.13%	5.13%	7.63%	10.61%
AccessLine U.S. subscribers:					
Subscribers	29,890	118,067	417,115	1,069,640	2,242,983
Penetration of cellular, paging & PCS	0.05%	0.17%	0.51%	1.14%	2.12%
Penetration of personal number market	7.00%	8.00%	10.00%	15.00%	20.00%
Non U.S. subscribers:					
Canada	12,000	18,000	40,000	75,000	150,000
Europe	20,000	30,000	100,000	600,000	1,300,000
Japan	0	40,000	150,000	350,000	800,000
Asia	0	25,000	100,000	275,000	600,000
Total non U.S. subscribers	32,000	113,000	390,000	1,300,000	2,850,000
Total AccessLine subscribers	61,890	231,067	807,115	2,369,640	5,092,983

Source: Corporate documents.

Exhibit 8   Comparable Public Companies

3Com

One of the data networking industry's largest and fastest-growing firms, 3Com provides a scalable architecture to allow business and homes to gain access to critical information through high-speed networks.

Recent Performance ($m)	1994	1993	1992
FY Revenues	827.0	617.2	408.4
FY Net Income	19.5	68.2	5.2
Market Capitalization at Calendar Year End	3,320	1,419	662
Beta	1.39		

Boston Technologies

A global leader in the delivery of network based enhanced services for telephone companies, cellular service providers, and other telecommunications firms.

Recent Performance ($m)	1994	1993	1992
FY Revenues	70.3	49.5	36.4
FY Net Income	6.7	3.1	-2.4
Market Capitalization at Calendar Year End	364	199	180
Beta	2.03		

Both firms had virtually all-equity capital structures in April 1995. The 10-year Treasury bond in April 1995 had a yield of 7.1%.

Source: Compiled from corporate securities filings and public databases.

Exhibit 9   Series B Term Sheet Proposed by AccessLine Management

Securities:	2,000,000 shares of Series B Preferred Stock ("Shares").
Investors:	The Shares will be offered only to "accredited investors" as defined in Regulation D under the Securities Act.
Aggregate Proceeds:	$16,000,000
Price:	$8.00 per Share (the "Sale Price").
Placement Agent:	Morgan Stanley & Co. Incorporated (the "Placement Agent") on a "best efforts" basis. The Company will pay in cash a placement fee equal to 5% of the aggregate offering proceeds.

The capitalization of the Company giving effect to the Financing will be as follows:

Name or Entity	Class of Stock	Number of Shares	Total Percentage Ownership
Existing Investors[a]	Common (Class A and B)	8,086,099	53%
	Series A Preferred	2,220,726	15%
	Warrants to Purchase		
	Series A Preferred	333,110	2%
New Investors	Series B Preferred	2,000,000	13%
Reserved for Directors, Management & Employees	Common (Class A and B)	2,582,047	17%
Total		15,221,982	100%

Rights and Preferences of Series B Preferred

The Series B Preferred shall be entitled to:

(1) An 8% non-cumulative *dividend preference* in pari passu with the Series A Preferred Stock (the Series A and Series B Preferred Stock are collectively referred to herein as the "Preferred"); any such dividend to be paid when and if declared by the Board of Directors out of funds legally available for such purpose.

(2) A *liquidation preference* equal to the Sale Price per share plus declared and unpaid dividends payable in pari passu with the Series A Preferred. Thereafter, all remaining assets shall be distributed among the holders of Common Stock ("Common"). A change in control of the Company by way of merger, sale of assets or other reorganization shall constitute a liquidation event.

(3) The right of *conversion* of the Series B Preferred into Class A Common Stock, at the option of the holder, at the initial ratio of one-for-one ("Conversion Ratio") at any time; *provided*, however, the Series B Preferred shall automatically convert upon (i) an initial public offering ("IPO") with gross proceeds of at least $10,000,000 and a per share price of at least $10.50 until June 30, 1996 or at least $12.00 after June 30, 1996, or (ii) the written consent of holders of at least two-least least two-thirds of the Preferred.

(4) *Antidilution* adjustment, on a weighted-average basis using a broad-based formula, for any new issues at a purchase price less than the Series B conversion price, except for issues of employee shares or on recapitalizations. Proportional adjustment of the Series B conversion price in the event of a stock split, combination, reclassification and the like.

(5) The right to *vote* on an as-converted basis with Class A Common Stock and Series A Preferred Stock as a single class on all matters (except to the extent that voting as a separate class or series is required by law); *provided*, however, that a vote of the holders of at least two-thirds of the Preferred, voting as a separate class, shall be required for (a) any material adverse change in the rights, preferences or privileges of the Series B Preferred; (b) any creation of a new class of shares having rights or preferences senior to or on a parity with the Series B Preferred; (c) declaration or payment of any cash dividends on the Common Stock; (d) any redemption, purchase or other acquisition of the Company's capital stock or any payments with respect to stock appreciation rights or similar rights; (e) a recapitalization or reorganization into a limited liability company or other noncorporate form; (f) entering into any business other than the telecommunications business; (g) any increase in compensation of any officer, director or any other employee holding 5% or more of the Company's capital stock unless approved by a disinterested majority of the Board; or (h) entering into certain specified related-party transactions.

Information and Inspection Rights	The holder of Series B Preferred or Class A Common Stock issued upon conversion of Series B Preferred ("Conversion Stock") shall be entitled to receive quarterly and annual financial statements prepared in accordance with GAAP. The annual statements shall be certified by a nationally known accounting firm.

Each holder of 100,000 shares or more of Series B Preferred Stock and/or Conversion Stock shall be entitled to monthly financial statements prepared in accordance with GAAP, to inspect the Company's books and records and to discuss the Company's affairs with its officers.

The foregoing information and inspection rights shall terminate upon an IPO.

Registration Rights

At any time following the earlier of (i) June 3, 1997 or (ii) one year after an IPO, the holders of a majority of the Preferred and the Conversion Stock shall be entitled to demand registration of at least 50% (or such lesser amount if the anticipated aggregate offering price would exceed $10 million) of the Class A Common Stock issued or issuable upon conversion of the Preferred under the Securities Act of 1933 (the "1933" Act") for a public offering on a firm commitment underwritten basis (the "Demand Rights"). The Demand Rights may only be exercised once during any 12-month period, and the Company shall not be obligated to effect more than two registrations under the Demand Rights. The Demand Rights may not be exercised during the 180 days following the effective date (or subsequent to the filing date at any time prior to the effective date) of a registration statement filed by the Company under the 1933 Act.

The holders of Series B Preferred and Conversion Stock shall be entitled to "piggyback" registration rights (the "Piggyback Rights") on registrations by the Company (or any other holders), subject to pro rata "cutback" (including to zero on an IPO) to accommodate shares to be sold for the account of the Company.

If available for use by the Company, at any time following the second anniversary of the IPO the holders of Series B Preferred and Conversion Stock shall be entitled to unlimited S-3 registration (the "S-3 Rights"); provided the aggregate offering price of each such offering is at least $1,000,000.

The Company shall pay for the expenses (exclusive of underwriting discounts or commissions or special counsel of a selling stockholder) of all registrations under the Demand Rights and Piggyback Rights. The selling stockholders shall pay for the expenses of all registrations under the S-3 Rights.

Registration rights may be transferred to related entities, constituent partners and a transferee who acquires at least 100,000 registrable securities (or such lesser number as constitutes all such securities held by the transferor) upon written notice to the Company.

Registration rights shall terminate with regard to any holders who can sell all of their shares under Rule 144 (exclusive of Rule 144(k)) in a three- month period.

All holders of registration rights will agree to a 120-day lock-up period after an IPO, conditional upon all officers and directors similarly agreeing.

Other standard provisions with respect to registration rights shall apply, including limits on subsequent registration rights, cross indemnification, the Company's ability to delay the filing of demand registration for a period of at least 120 days, the period of time in which the registration statement shall be kept effective, underwriting arrangements and the like.

Redemption Rights	Each holder of Series B Preferred Stock shall have the right to require the Company to repurchase their shares of Series B Preferred Stock (but *not* any Conversion Stock) at $8.00 per share plus any declared and unpaid dividends on each anniversary of the closing date, beginning with the fifth anniversary, provided that no holder may require the Company to repurchase more than one-third of its share of Series B Preferred Stock on any anniversary date. If a holder exercises such right, the Company may elect to repurchase all of such holder's shares.
Right to Maintain	Each holder of at least 100,000 shares of Series B Preferred Stock and/or Conversion Stock shall have a right to maintain its percentage ownership interest in the Company in the event the Company issues stock at a price less than $8.00 per share, subject to exceptions for stock issued pursuant to mergers and acquisitions, technology licensing arrangements, strategic alliances, employee stock options, stock issued in an IPO and other standard exceptions.
Closing	The closing for the Financing shall occur on or about _____ at the offices of Wilson, Sonsini, Goodrich & Rosati.
Purchase Agreement	The Financing shall be evidence by a Purchase Agreement and other related agreements reasonably satisfactory to counsel to the Investors.

[a]Includes 1,087,962 shares subject to options granted to Daniel R. Kranzler

.Source: Corporate documents.

12

The Exxel Group: September 1995

Juan Navarro put out his cigar as he glanced at the Buenos Aires harbor from the Exxel Group's office high over the River Plate. It was the close of a beautiful spring day, but neither he nor his partners had had the time to enjoy it. For Exxel was in the midst of structuring the purchase of a 56% stake in Argencard, the credit card transaction processor and exclusive Mastercard licensee for Argentina and Uruguay. Argencard would represent a new departure for the private equity organization. Although Exxel was the largest Argentine private equity fund and one of the two most important Latin-based private equity organizations, this transaction would be five times larger than any other they had undertaken.

Navarro thought over the troubled history of the Argencard transaction. One year earlier, Argencard had been within weeks of being sold in an auction arranged by CS First Boston. The auction had collapsed after the crash of the Mexican peso—and its resounding effects throughout Latin America—scared away investors. After being offered a brief window of exclusivity, the Exxel team had undertaken a detailed analysis of the company and its market. The analysis had proved to be a challenging one: the dynamic character of the credit card industry made assigning an appropriate valuation challenging. For instance, while the firm was projected to have very attractive earnings growth, the assumptions could be significantly flawed. After an intensive analysis over a two-week period, Exxel had made a $136.5 million bid for a controlling interest in the company.

Now Navarro had a mere 45 days in which to close the transaction before Exxel's exclusive right to undertake the transaction expired. The transaction posed some special problems. In order to finance this transaction, Exxel would need to raise additional funds from its limited partners and other investors. Could a large transaction of this complexity be arranged in this market in so short a time? Was Exxel's proposed structure the ideal one?

Navarro also wondered about the evolution of the Exxel Group. The private equity organization currently controlled a portfolio of companies acquired with its $47 million first fund, raised in 1992. It had successfully raised a second fund of $150 million in February. Over the next few years, Exxel would face the challenge of harvesting the first fund's investments, as well as investing the considerably larger amount of capital now under management. More generally, the recent interest by institutional investors in Argentina was likely to lead to the development of the nation's public and private equity markets. This growth would pose both opportunities and challenges for Exxel.

This case was prepared by Alex Hoye and Josh Lerner. Copyright © 1997 by the President and Fellows of Harvard College. Harvard Business School case 297-068.

THE ARGENTINE OPPORTUNITY[1]

Sharing the southern cone of South America with Chile, Argentina is the second-largest country in South America. Nearly half of the nation's 34 million inhabitants live in the greater Buenos Aires area. The nation has a 95% literacy rate, and its 1994 per capita gross domestic product (GDP) of about $7500 was the highest in Latin America by nearly a factor of two.

In 1910, Argentina ranked ninth among the world's nations in wealth, with a per capita GDP only $30 below that of France.[2] But its highly remunerative trade with western Europe—especially exports of grain, wool, and beef—dwindled after World War I. Particularly after 1945, the country turned to a protectionist economic policy and was beset by both economic and political chaos. After many years of military dictatorship, the nation returned to democracy in 1983 when the ruling junta yielded power after a costly war with Great Britain. But the political transformation did not produce economic stability. By 1989, when the current president, Carlos Menem, was elected into office, the nation was gripped by hyperinflation with rates nearing 5000%. (Exhibit 1 summarizes the recent performance of the Argentine economy.) The hyperinflation created an environment in which businesses succeeded through financial management rather than productivity advances.

In 1991 Economics Minister Domingo Cavallo, a Harvard-trained economist, implemented a monetary plan. He established a currency board, which was responsible for ensuring that the money supply was fully backed with foreign currency. The Convertibility Law fixed the Argentine peso as worth exactly one U.S. dollar. Inflation rates slowed rapidly, mirroring that of the United States in recent years.

Concurrently, Menem and Cavallo implemented a series of policies, sanctioned by the International Monetary Fund, to privatize businesses, reduce trade barriers, and deregulate industries. By September 1995, the privatization process was almost complete. Operations in industries as diverse as telecommunications, airlines, oil exploration, and power generation had been transferred to the private sector. In April 1994 Argentine tariff barriers had been lowered from 22.3% in October 1989 to 9.1%, and that same year Argentina, Brazil, Paraguay, and Uruguay had formed a trading bloc called the Mercosur. Many of the economic reforms had focused on the capital-raising process. Regulatory changes included the elimination of taxes on capital gains and dividends, the reduction of fees on stock market transactions, and the institution of futures and options transactions, as well as eased procedures for initial public offerings (IPOs).

These bold steps had a substantial effect.[3] The country's per capita GDP grew at an annual rate of 7.7% between 1991 and 1994; total imports and exports, at 23%. The capitalization of the stock market rose from $5 billion in 1991 to $49.7 billion in January 1994. This reflected not only increases in security prices, but also IPOs of privatized companies.

---

[1] Unless noted otherwise, this section is drawn from Daniel Artana and Fernando Navajas, *Stabilization, Growth and Institutional Build-Up: An Overview of the Macroeconomics of Argentina, 1991–1995,* Buenos Aires, Fundacion de Investigaciones de Economicas Latinoamericanas, 1995; Economist Intelligence Unit, *Country Report: Argentina,* London, Economist Intelligence Unit, 1996; Republic of Argentina, Ministry of Economy, Public Works and Services, *Economic Report,* Buenos Aires, Republic of Argentina, various years.

[2] In 1994, France's per capita GDP was $21,800. Detailed economic histories of Argentina include Carlos F. Diaz Alejandro, *Essays on the Economic History of the Argentine Republic,* New Haven, Yale University Press, 1970; Paul H. Lewis, *The Crisis of Argentine Capitalism,* Chapel Hill, University of North Carolina Press, 1992; and Laura Randall, *An Economic History of Argentina in the Twentieth Century,* New York, Columbia University Press, 1978.

[3] This paragraph is drawn in large part from "Argentina: A Supplement," *Euromoney,* June 1994.

(To cite one example, the oil enterprise YPF was the world's fifth largest IPO, with a market capitalization of $3.04 billion). These offerings were frequently purchased by overseas investors: a June 1994 estimate suggested that foreigners held between 50% and 60% of the outstanding float on the Argentine market and 20% to 25% of total capitalization.

The rapid progress of the Argentine economy came to an abrupt halt on December 20, 1994. Almost as soon as the Mexican peso was devalued, growth and foreign direct investment in Argentina ceased. Many international institutions began rapidly liquidating their Latin holdings, while wealthy Argentines transferred their liquid assets to banks in major financial centers. The Mercado de Valores (Merval) index, which tracked blue-chip stocks, lost 23% of its value from December 1994 to June 1995 (depicted in Exhibit 2). Deposits in domestic banks and domestic branches of international banks dropped by 19%, a "bank run" of greater magnitude than the United States suffered during the entire Great Depression. Furthermore, the banks' loan portfolios deteriorated sharply: within a few months 30% of loans were nonperforming.[4]

Within a few months, the broader impacts of the peso crisis (dubbed by Argentines the "Tequila Effect") were readily apparent. The economy was facing a GDP contraction for the first time in six years. Unemployment rates reached 18.4% in May 1995. The growth in unemployment reflected massive layoffs of newly privatized companies, the slowing investment associated with high interest rates, and an expensive currency that hampered exports. Speculators eyed Argentina closely to see if the banking system would collapse and whether popular dissent would push government to abandon its strict convertibility policy.

As it became clear that the government was sticking to its policies in the wake of the Mexican crisis, the peso began trading even closer to the dollar than before the crisis (depicted in Exhibit 2). The financial sector was restructured, with troubled institutions consolidated into stronger ones: by September 1995, 40 financial institutions had been closed. Deposits were expected to recover to pre-crisis levels by the end of 1995. New issues of bonds to service debts to the International Monetary Fund and other international development agencies had met enthusiastic responses in Europe, Japan, and the United States. Analysts increasingly believed that the growth of the Argentine economy was likely to resume in 1996.[5]

The equity markets appeared to be particularly ripe for recovery and renewed growth. The exchange was capitalized at $38 billion in December 1994. This represented approximately 15% of GDP versus 74% in the United States at the same time. Market capitalization and trading volume were heavily concentrated among a few firms, while most concerns traded with great infrequency. Furthermore, recent new exchange listings had been largely reserved for large corporations and privatizations (see Exhibit 3 for a list of recent Argentine IPOs). The four largest companies accounted for 58% of market capitalization and 85% of trading volume in June of 1994. Expanding that roster to include the top nine companies increased the proportion of trading volume to 89%.[6]

[4] These estimates are drawn from "Argentina Bounces Back from a Short, Sharp Shock," *Financial Times*, December 13, 1996, p. 6; and "Argentina After Cavallo," *The Economist*, 340, (August 3, 1996): 17. For a more academic analysis, see Mauricio Carrizosa, Danny M. Leipzinger, and Hemant Shah, "The Tequila Effect and Argentina's Banking Reform," *Finance and Development*, 33 (March 1996): 22–29.

[5] See, for instance, the summaries of growth forecasts in Economist Intelligence Unit, *Country Report: Argentina*, London, Economist Intelligence Unit, 1995.

[6] For detailed accounts and market data, see Maria Suarez, "Latin Equities 1995," *LatinFinance*, April 1995, 36–40; "Argentina: A Supplement," *Euromoney*, June 1994; "Survey of Latin American Finance and Investment," *Financial Times*, March 25, 1996, I–VIII; and "Argentina—The Silver Giant: A Supplement," *LatinFinance*, March 1996.

In addition to overseas institutional investors, a future source of liquidity was likely to be the Argentine pension system. In July 1994, Argentina instituted a program emulating the highly successful pension system in Chile. Since that time, $3 billion of domestic savings had been raised, with $200 million of inflows each month. These funds were permitted to invest up to 35% of their assets in equities. The development of pension funds, long an important investor in U.S. stock markets, was expected to generate a broader domestic equity base in Argentina.[7]

Private equity investing in Argentina grew out of the debt crises of the previous decade. Many global banks, having lent aggressively to Latin businesses and governments in the 1970s and early 1980s, found themselves with substantial portfolios of nonperforming loans by the late 1980s. Meanwhile, many of these institutions faced increasing regulatory scrutiny in the United States and elsewhere. Eager to "clean up" their balance sheets, many of these banks agreed to convert loans into equity stakes. One of the first outsiders to make equity investments in private Latin firms was George Soros in the late 1980s. A few others followed. Many of the early private equity investments in Latin America, however, encountered severe difficulties. An example was a $34 million fund organized by a U.S. investment bank in 1990 to invest in Chile. More than $9 million was invested in a private cemetery, a project that collapsed (with a total loss to the investors) six months later when it was discovered that its regulatory permits had been obtained illegally.

THE EXXEL GROUP

Juan Navarro was born in Uruguay in 1952. Both his father and his father's father had been leaders of Uruguay's medical and scientific establishments. His mother's family had influential positions in the Argentine scientific and banking communities. After briefly attending university in Uruguay, where he found the curriculum to be steeped in leftist ideology and of little interest, Navarro moved to Argentina. While completing his education, he joined an Argentine bank in which his mother's family had a major role.

In 1980, seeking greater challenges, Navarro joined Citibank's Argentine subsidiary. Citibank Argentina was the largest international bank in Argentina and was the U.S. parent's first international affiliate, having been established in 1914. Navarro spent the next six years as a banker in Buenos Aires and New York City.

Navarro's involvement in the private equity industry began in 1986, when he was offered the number two position at Citibank Argentina. After carefully considering the offer, Navarro realized that he was not particularly interested in a career as a senior corporate manager, and so he declined the position. Simultaneously, Citibank's headquarters asked its Latin American subsidiaries to consider an "asset redeployment": the replacement of its troubled loans with equity. Meanwhile, Citicorp Global Investment Banking, which was directly responsible for the bank's New York–based private equity group, Citicorp Venture Capital, was expressing increasing interest in investing in Latin firms. In lieu of the offered position, Navarro agreed to head up Citibank Argentina's new private equity mandate.

Before assuming the chairmanship of the new Citibank Capital Investors (CCI), Navarro spent several months with Citibank Venture Capital. The group's chairman, William Comfort, gave him many valuable insights into the private equity process,

---

[7] "Survey of Latin American Finance and Investment," *Financial Times,* March 25, 1996, I–VIII; "Argentina—The Silver Giant: A Supplement," *LatinFinance,* March 1996.

including the instruction "to discard everything that he had learned as a banker"! Between 1987 and 1991, Navarro directed CCI's involvement in over a dozen substantial investments in Argentine entities. Many of these deals were highly complex ones. For instance, in order to ensure the stability of several financially troubled provincial banks, the Argentine central bank had transferred foreign obligations to them. Although these provided the banks with immediate liquidity, they ultimately needed to be repaid. In return for assuming the responsibility of making the repayments, CCI would receive commercial property that the provincial bank had seized from defaulting creditors. The returns from these complex transactions were attractive. Navarro increasingly realized, however, that a considerable opportunity lay in making *new* private equity investments. The bulk of the demand for such financing was from local firms rather than from the multinational corporations with whom Citicorp did the bulk of its business.

In 1991, Navarro decided the time was right to undertake an effort of his own. He was motivated by four beliefs. The first two related to the overall economic environment. First, the recent reforms, he believed, had led to a turning point for the Argentine economy. They would create numerous attractive investment opportunities, as many established conglomerates restructured and family businesses struggled to adjust to the newly competitive environment. Second, the public and private equity of Argentine firms were attracting increasing attention from overseas financial investors, who previously had little interest in these securities. Local firms had previously financed themselves largely through other means, among which were direct investments from multinational partners and bank loans.

Navarro's second set of motivations for beginning his own fund were derived from his observations of the private equity industry. He noted that most successful private equity organizations in the United States were not affiliated with a major financial institution. He believed that free-standing organizations avoided many of the conflicts of interest and interorganizational battles that plagued groups affiliated with major investment and commercial banks. Finally, he was convinced there was an opportunity to build a franchise as a buyout fund geared to Argentine firms. Because of the early stage of the market, it would be possible to pioneer this effort as a free-standing organization rather than as a subsidiary of a major financial institution.

In planning his effort, Navarro was guided by several principles:

- The new fund would invest in buyouts, recapitalizations, privatizations, and mergers of Argentine firms. Given that returns were uncertain enough in these later-stage investments in the region, Navarro believed that venture-oriented or early-stage operations were impractical. Rather, Navarro would seek to build on his unique strength: his ability to originate deals, based on his strong ties with local business community, and then to add value to these enterprises.

- The group would be an independent organization with strong U.S. ties. The strong connections to U.S. financial institutions and institutional investors would bring credibility to the private equity group. The ties with U.S. institutions would also allow Navarro and his partners to help the firms in their portfolio in ways that they could not otherwise. In order to create a fund that was attractive to U.S. investors, Navarro sought to "clone" a U.S. buyout fund: for example, using the same partnership structure and law firms.

- He would develop a network of service providers to complement the work of his partnership. In 1990, Argentine lawyers, accountants, bankers, and notaries[8] were not familiar with the workings of and philosophy behind the U.S. buyout industry. Thus, Navarro resolved to focus his energies not only on the development of his own organization, but on the cultivation and education of a network of intermediaries and service providers.

To implement this vision, Navarro sought to leverage his resources. First, he recruited an advisory board that included some of the leading lawyers, bankers, and businessmen in Buenos Aires. This group gave an immediate credibility to the new fund. Second, he attracted a management team of experienced professionals including Jorge Demaria, the former Argentine undersecretary of privatizations who would play a key role as the fund's second-in-command, Marcelo Aubone and several other former colleagues from CCI, and Jose Ortiz from the Techint Group (a major Argentine industrial conglomerate), as well as various management consultants from McKinsey & Company and Booz, Allen & Hamilton, and the former CEO of Xerox Argentina.

One of Exxel's first decisions was to select a U.S. bank to solicit investments from institutional and individual investors. Navarro selected Oppenheimer & Company to play this role. Oppenheimer's Private Equity Group had raised capital for funds in areas as diverse as Chile, India, and Israel. In presentations to investors, Jeffrey Stern, who managed Oppenheimer's Private Equity Group, highlighted his view that "foreign controlled assets that have been protected from competition for generations must transform to meet foreign competition, improved local competition, and achieve greater flexibility."[9] This need for capital, combined with increasing competition among private equity funds investing in the United States, made emerging market funds increasingly attractive.

Exxel and Oppenheimer had organized two funds as of September 1995. The first, the Argentine Private Equity Fund I, L.P., closed in April 1992 with $46.8 million. The initial fund had been raised largely from sophisticated individual investors in the United States, as well as the Brown University Endowment, Batterymarch Financial Advisors, Oppenheimer & Company, and Rockefeller & Company (the Rockefeller family office). Their follow-on fund, the Argentine Private Equity Fund II, L.P., raised $150 million between September 1994 and February 1995. The second fund attracted a variety of institutional investors: for example, the insurers Aetna, Allstate, Liberty Mutual, and SunAmerica; the endowments of Brown University, the Ford Foundation, the Riverside Church, and the Wellcome Trust; the financial advisers Batterymarch, the Common Fund, and Hancock Venture Partners; and Oppenheimer.

In these two funds, Exxel and Oppenheimer shared responsibilities. In the first fund, Oppenheimer served as the general partner and the Exxel Group as the investment adviser. In the second, these relationships changed somewhat: Oppenheimer acted as the administrative general partner, and the Exxel Group was the managing general partner. Oppenheimer's responsibilities included assisting fundraising, advising on tax issues, managing communications with the limited partners, and selecting three of the seven members on the Investment Committee that approved all investments. It contributed an initial investment as a limited partner, but it also received a portion of the profits (the "carried interest") and management fees. Exxel was responsible for the identification, acquisition, management, monitoring, and disposition of fund investments. Exxel appointed four of the seven members on the Investment Committee. The Exxel

[8] Most key documents in Argentina needed to be notarized. To become a notary there, one required several years of special practice after obtaining a law degree.

[9] Jeffrey Stern, "Analyzing the Surge in International Leveraged Buyouts," Presentation at the Institute for International Research's Symposium on Leveraged Buyouts, April 26, 1996.

Group itself was 70% owned by Navarro, with the balance held by Banco Mariva, run by Steven Darch, the former CEO of J.P. Morgan Argentina. Navarro's key partners in the fund, however, shared in the carried interest.

The investment covenants of the two funds were relatively broad, reflecting the uncertainty implicit in emerging markets. For example, in contrast to stipulations in U.S. fund agreements preventing investments in publicly traded securities, Exxel was permitted to invest in public equity, equity-related, and even debt securities. Investments, however, had to be made in Argentina or Uruguay or to directly impact operations in these countries. Up to 35% of the fund could be devoted to any one investment. Larger "facilitating investments" could be made in order to execute a transaction, as long as Exxel had the objective of refinancing these contributions relatively promptly. This clause was especially important given the region's limited mezzanine debt market.

In return, Exxel and Oppenheimer received 20% of all capital gains, as well as a management fee of 2% of committed funds. There was, however, a "hurdle rate" of 10%: all distributions would go to the limited partners until they have received their capital back plus a return of 10%.[10] The fund would bear the investment banking, financial advisory, and transaction fees associated with the buyouts. The management fee paid by each fund, however, would be reduced on a dollar-for-dollar basis for any transaction fees that flowed to Exxel from the fund. (For instance, if the fund was responsible for 75% of a firm's investment, the fund's future management fees would be reduced by 75% of the transaction fees paid to Exxel.) Finally, key employees had the obligation to invest an amount totaling 5% of the fund's investment in each transaction and could invest more (up to 10% of the total).

Over the past 5 years, Exxel had undertaken a total of 13 acquisitions, which had been folded into 6 portfolio companies (summarized in Exhibit 4).[11] As three representative transactions depict, Exxel in each case paid considerable attention to building value:

- Ciabasa S.A. was one of Argentina's leading providers of consumer detergents: Poett S.A., one of the leading manufacturers of air fresheners and liquid cleaners. Exxel purchased these two firms in January and May 1993, respectively, merged them, and added several smaller family-owned concerns that were acquired subsequently. Wherever possible, the Exxel team sought to exploit synergies between the firms and with the new acquisitions.[12]

- Edesal S.A., a power company serving midwestern Argentina, was acquired by a team led by Exxel in March 1993. (A minority stake was acquired by Roggio & Co., one of the largest corporations in Argentina, and the Spanish utility Union

---

[10] Once the limited partners had received their capital back and a 10% annual return, all distributions would flow to the general partners until they had "caught up": that is, received 20% of all capital gains paid out. Subsequent distributions would be divided on an 80%–20% basis. Between 20% and 30% of the carried interest and management fee were allocated to the administrative general partner. The precise share was determined through a sliding scale based on the amount of capital raised from various sources. Of the funds invested by the administrative general partner into the fund, only a 10% carried interest was charged rather than the 20% levied on the limited partners. The same 2% fee was, however, paid into the fund.

[11] All the acquired firms were held privately, with the exception of La Papelera del Plata S.A., where the fund had bought a 23% block. This was the leading tissue paper company in Argentina. Since the time the block had been acquired, the share price had initially doubled, but then it declined after the December 1994 "tequila effect."

[12] In September 1995, the fund was in the midst of intense negotiations to sell the merged household products company to a strategic acquirer at more than four times the combined purchase price.

Fenosa served as technical adviser.) Exxel was able to purchase the company for less than half the price (in dollars per megawatt hour sold) than three privatizations of similar firms in the Buenos Aires region. The firm's workforce, management systems, and equipment underwent substantial restructuring after the purchase.

- Beginning in November 1994, Exxel began merging and consolidating a number of health maintenance organizations (HMOs) and clinics. In addition to benefiting from the numerous operational efficiencies introduced by the Exxel team, the organization (now known as Galeno y Life) expected to profit from the reforms in the Argentine health-care sector announced by the Menem administration soon after the purchase.

A crucial aspect of these transactions was Exxel's demand that it control the acquired firms. Exxel had received control of the firms in all but one transaction it had undertaken, where it had shared control with another investor. A second important element was persuading the management of the acquired firm of the necessity and importance of restructuring operations. Although this could be partially achieved by financial incentives, in many cases old-line managers did not understand the value of stock options or did not believe that they would have any worth. As a result, an important role was to identify managers who were attracted by the prospect of working with Exxel. This task had become easier in recent years, as the private equity organization's successes had become publicized in the Argentine press.

As a result of the success of Exxel and the Brazilian fund, G.P. Capital Partners (an affiliate of Banco de Investimentos Garantia), as well as the general improvement in macroeconomic conditions, Latin American private equity markets were attracting considerable attention in September 1995. A series of Latin funds had recently been formed, several of which targeted Argentina. Among the most visible were (also see Exhibit 5):[13]

- The AIG-GE Capital Latin American Infrastructure Fund, a joint venture between the insurance giant American Insurance Group and the project financing arm of General Electric, was currently raising $1 billion to make investments in transportation, power generation, telecommunications, and natural resources projects throughout Latin America.

- BEA Associates, a New York based investment adviser controlled by CS First Boston, had raised a $36 million fund, made a wide range of equity and debt investments in private Latin firms, and was raising a follow-on fund.

- BISA, a corporation, raised a fund with $60 million in cash assets in January 1994. This was designed to make private equity investments in Argentina. The lead investor was the Bemberg Group, which represented the French–Argentine family that owned Quilmes Industrial S.A., one of the largest brewers in South America.

- Darby Overseas Investments Ltd., whose managing team included Nicholas Brady, the former U.S. Treasury secretary and author of the 1989 "Brady Plan" for restructuring Latin debt, and Daniel Marx, the former undersecretary of

---

[13] Exhibit 5 and this discussion are based on "Crisis? What Crisis? Mexican Woes Fail to Dent Interest in Latin Funds," *Private Equity Analyst* 5 (February 1995): 1, 4, 9; Victoria Griffith, "The Advent of Venture Capital," *Latin Finance,* March 1996, 46–49; Lorenzo Weissman, "The Advent of Private Equity in Latin America," *Columbia Journal of World Business* 31 (Spring 1996): 60–68; and assorted other press accounts.

finance for Argentina and a player in the YPF privatization (the oil company, privatized in 1993, was formerly known as Yacimientos Petroliferos Fiscules), was raising a pan-Latin fund.

- The investment bank ING Barings sponsored a pan-Latin private equity fund organized by Pedro-Pablo Kuczynski, a former investment banker at CS First Boston and Peruvian government official. While fundraising was still ongoing, the fund had already closed on $175 million.

- The South American Private Equity Fund, organized by Westsphere Capital Management, was currently seeking capital. This New York based buyout fund, spun out of Chase Manhattan in 1989, sought to expand its focus to a variety of Latin American countries. They had succeeded in obtaining a guarantee from the quasi-governmental U.S. Overseas Private Investment Corporation, which limited the losses that the fund's investors would have to bear.

Although these groups might in some cases be competing for deals, Navarro thought it was likely that they would also invest in transactions that Exxel originated.

ARGENCARD S.A.

Argencard S.A. was an integrated credit card processor. The company held the exclusive license for Mastercard in both Argentina and Uruguay and owned two other proprietary credit card brands (Argencard and Lider). In 1994, Argencard and Mastercard accounted for 36% of cards outstanding in Argentina and 38% of the charge volume. Visa, the next largest card, had a 29% and 30% share, respectively. Argencard S.A. did not issue cards, nor did it finance outstanding balances; rather it derived revenues from processing and administrative services for credit card issuing banks, merchants, and the merchants' banks, as well as from brand management and promotion. In addition, the firm operated the leading point-of-sale network and held a stake in one of two ATM networks in Argentina.

Argencard S.A. introduced the first third-party credit card network in Argentina in 1971. (American Express and Diners' Club, by way of contrast, are "closed" systems where the same organization is the licensee and card issuer.) In 1977, Argencard obtained the exclusive Mastercard license for Argentina. In 1978 Argencard expanded its credit card network into Uruguay and in 1992 secured the exclusive Mastercard license in this neighboring country. Most recently, Argencard rolled out Mastercard's debit card (Maestro) and launched a proprietary brand, Lider, that focused on lower-income markets.

In 1994, the firm had revenues of $130 million and net income of $24.7 million. Argencard derived revenues from four primary activities. Merchant discount fees generated the lion's share of income, with 47% of revenues in 1994.[14] In the same year, 21% of revenues emanated from data processing services, which consisted of issuing account statements to merchant banks and cardholders (for the 80% of issuing banks that out-

---

[14] Credit card transaction processing is illustrated in Exhibit 6. When a consumer makes a $100 purchase from an issuing bank [1A], authorization is requested and received from the bank that issues the credit card [steps 1B through 2C]. The issuing bank will then transfer a somewhat smaller sum (e.g., $96) to the merchant's bank, which the merchant will ultimately withdraw [steps 4A through 4C]. The difference between the amount the consumer pays the issuing bank [5B] and the merchant's bank credits to his account [4C] (in this case 4%) is the discount rate. This payment is made in three installments: when the issuing bank transfers funds to the card administrator [4A], when the card administrator transfers funds to the merchant bank [4B], and when the merchant bank transfers the funds into the merchant's account [4C].

sourced this function). Twelve percent of income originated from a development fund dedicated to advertising and promoting the credit card brands. This was financed through a portion of annual fees paid by cardholders. A warning bulletin, printed four times per month, advised merchants of delinquent or stolen cards. This generated 10% of Argencard's income. The remaining revenues were derived primarily from bounties received from adding new merchants to the system, transaction authorizations, and operations in Uruguay. Argencard had recently added two new lines of business. A 12.75% share of Red Link,[15] one of two ATM networks in Argentina, as well as the full ownership of Posnet, a point-of-sale network with 8,000 terminals, were both acquired. They were projected to generate $8 million, or 6% of revenues, in 1995.

Argencard stood to benefit from three very favorable industry dynamics. First, there was an ongoing migration to noncash payment systems worldwide. Credit card charge volume worldwide reached $1.03 trillion in 1994, with 661 million credit cards and 10 billion transactions. This represented, however, only 6.8% of total personal consumption. Income derived from electronic transaction processing stood at $30.3 billion in 1993 and was projected to grow 7% annually worldwide over the next decade. Within electronic transaction processing, credit card processing in particular was projected to grow at 17% over the same period. Many promising applications, such as electronic funds transfer and health-care processing, had room for substantial growth. Reflecting these growth opportunities, many transaction processing firms in the United States were trading at high price/earnings ratios, and leading institutions were still giving many of these firms strong buy recommendations.[16]

Second, significant advantage in the credit card processing industry accrued to first movers, large players, and early investors in technology and marketing. Card processing companies obtained competitive advantage by offering lower discount rates to merchants, providing superior service, and having a strong brand image. In the past, three different processors may have been involved in one transaction authorization, each taking a fee. Companies like First Financial Management in the United States sought to be involved in all aspects of credit card processing and had driven out competitors through economies of scale and lower transaction fees.

This trend was very favorable to Argencard. Argencard was fully integrated, offering processing services to merchant and issuing banks, as well as network and card administration. It offered not just one card, but three well-differentiated products: the high-end (and most expensive) Mastercard, the middle-range Argencard, and the Lider. The firm had begun introducing innovations that had been successful elsewhere, such as co-branding with companies from airlines to cable companies, traveler's insurance, calling card capability, and frequent-flyer programs. Finally, Argencard had invested significantly in technology. In a country with very expensive telephones, Argencard maintained a satellite network to make authorizations outside of Buenos Aires. The firm had also invested in hardware and software that enabled issuing banks to statistically analyze their customers' usage and payment history. These systems allowed banks to improve profitability by imposing or extending limits on cardholders, varying interest rates, and changing membership charges.

Finally, many observers believed that the growth in credit card usage would be particularly rapid outside the major economies. Net income from electronic transaction

---

[15] 33.75% was purchased, but 21% was expected to be transferred to local banks.

[16] Much of the information in this paragraph is drawn from J.P. Morgan, *The Transaction Processing Services Industry,* December 14, 1994; and Alex. Brown & Sons, *The Transaction Processing Services Industry,* May 25, 1995.

processing was projected to grow at 13% in Latin America over the next decade, nearly twice the rate elsewhere. This largely reflected the rapid economic growth in these countries. Cross-sectional regression analyses suggested that spending per card—and hence demand for processing services—was strongly linked to economic growth.[17] Exxel believed that the opportunity was particularly strong in Argentina for three reasons:

- Mastercards (including Argencard) and Visas per capita were almost as prevalent in Argentina as in Mexico and Chile, where average incomes were less than half those of Argentina. Argentina's ratio of 0.11 Visas or Mastercards was just above the Latin American average of 0.08, compared to the United States' 1.16 cards per person. Exxel's projected 6.4% growth rate put penetration at only 0.15 per person in 1999. Argentina employed cash for 80% of transactions in 1995 versus 46% in the United States.

- The number of people with bank accounts in Argentina was growing rapidly. Years of severe inflation had driven the number of bank depositors down to around 19% of households in 1991. That rate stood at near 23% in September 1995 and was growing rapidly, but it was still far behind the U.S. level. Banks found credit cards a useful way to attract new customers, to whom they could then offer various other services.

- Mastercard (including Argencard) and Visa in Argentina accounted for 64.2% of all credit cards, whereas the Latin American average was 92% and Europe's 80%. In other countries, growth in credit card usage had been associated with rapid consolidation. In Chile, the two leading cards' combined share rose from 68% in 1990 to 89.5% in 1995.

At the same time, two industry dynamics worldwide raised real concerns. The first of these was the decline in merchant discount rates. Exxel estimated that the discount rate had been declining in the United States at an annual rate of 3.5% over the past five years: the discount rate for Mastercard had gone from 3.34% to 2.83%. Discount rates in less developed markets were falling as well, but from a higher level. Three trends drove this evolution to lower discount rates. First, the increase in scale had permitted card processors to reduce the discount that they offered merchants as a competitive move against other cards or processors. Second, a broadening retailer base had increased card-charging volume at lower-margin operations, such as grocery stores and gas stations. These operations typically had rates as low as 1% in both developed and developing economies, in contrast to establishments such as clothing shops and travel agencies. Third, retailers were consolidating, which increased their bargaining position when negotiating discount rates. The leverage held by massive retailing enterprises like Wal-Mart had impacted discount rates worldwide.

These trends were likely to be important in Argentina as well. Between 1990 and 1994, Argencard's average discount rate had fallen from 6.76% to 5.97%. This was still above the discount rates in other Latin countries (e.g., Mexico's rate was 3.2% and Chile's 3.8%), not to mention the United States. In particular, Argencard might be vulnerable to pressure to bring down the discount rate for clothing purchases, which had an average discount rate of 8.8% and accounted for 32% of Argencard's revenue.

---

[17] A regression prepared by Exxel's consultants related charge volume growth to gains in per capita GDP from 1991 to 1994. It yielded a coefficient of greater than two and an overall goodness-of-fit of 99%. That is, in an economy projected to grow at an annual rate of 7%, charge volume growth should exceed 14%.

The second dynamic was a redistribution worldwide in how the discount rate was divided between issuing banks and credit card processors [transaction 4A in Exhibit 6]. This would probably be a special problem for Argencard because of the recent trend toward bank consolidation in Argentina. As a result of the financial crisis, between January and August 1995, 47 of Argencard's 147 member banks had changed ownership. Furthermore, nearly 20% of Argencard's cards were issued by banks that might yet change ownership due to privatization or financial difficulties. As banks became larger, they could take a tougher negotiating position with credit card processors, demanding a larger percentage of the merchant discount fees. The share of the merchant discount received by credit card processors—as well as their other fees—might attract more scrutiny in upcoming years. Argencard was shielded from this effect to some degree by the number of issuing banks. Only three banks issued more than 9% of Argencard's outstanding cards.

A compounding factor was Visa's aggressive pricing moves. Argencard was one of the very few Mastercard licensees to be the market leader. In 1980, Visa—a late entrant into the Argentine market—had 1% of the outstanding cards; by 1995, this figure was 29%. This came largely at the expense of Diners' Club and American Express, whose share of outstanding cards had fallen from 51% in 1980 to 12% in 1995. But Visa in Argentina was increasingly eyeing Mastercard. Visa had priced its services aggressively, charging a lower merchant discount (5.4%) and leaving a greater share of that fee for the issuing bank (72.5% vs. Argencard's 63.3%). (These patterns are summarized in Exhibit 6.) Visa was rumored to be considering increasing the issuing bank's share even further, perhaps to 80%. Through these aggressive moves, Visa was trying to encourage issuing banks to offer and merchants to accept their card before Mastercard.

THE PROPOSED TRANSACTION

The proposed transaction entailed the purchase of the 56.04% stake of Argencard owned by the Italian state-owned bank Banca Nazionale del Lavoro (BNL) through its subsidiary Fondiaria Inversions Argentinas S.A. (The remainder of Argencard was held by other Argentine shareholders who had founded the company 20 years before and their relatives.) The Italian bank—in the process of preparing itself for privatization— had been plagued by a host of problems and scandals. The new management was focusing on core markets in Italy and was shedding assets worldwide. In particular, it was eager to sell Argencard to generate earnings that would offset write-downs associated with over 4 billion lira worth of improper loans to Iraq and underperforming Argentine investments.

Although Navarro had had some initial conversations in mid-1994 with Argencard's management team about the possibility of arranging a management buyout, there had been no great interest in this option. By July 1994, BNL and the other shareholders decided to sell the entirety of Argencard. The investment bank CS First Boston was hired to conduct an auction. While Exxel registered and received the offering memorandum, it concluded that this was unlikely to be an attractive investment opportunity for its fund. Preliminary indications of interest were received in September 1994 from suitors as diverse as Mexico's Banamex, GE Capital, and merchant transaction processor National BanCard Corporation (Nabanco). The auction was proceeding well, with the various teams pursuing routine due diligence, until markets throughout Latin America were rocked by Mexico's peso devaluation and the associated capital flight.

After the December 1994 crisis, only one party remained in pursuit of Argencard, a consortium of eight Argentine banks affiliated with Visa. They offered about $240 million for the 100% stake. Realizing that they were the only party still interested in Argencard, the banks began demanding various concessions, such as the retention of 30% of the purchase price in a noninterest bearing escrow account for three years.

In August 1995, Navarro learned that BNL, eager to liquidate its stake quickly, would consider an offer from Exxel if it was received in the next 15 days. At the time, the Exxel Group was extraordinarily busy, with a number of transactions nearing completion. Navarro asked Scott Mason, a senior finance professor at Harvard Business School whom Navarro had met while at Citibank, to lead an intensive examination of Argencard. Over a two-week period, the team had undertaken a detailed analysis of the firm. It had enjoyed considerable cooperation from Argencard's management, which was concerned about the potential impact of the sale to the bank group.

In analyzing the proposed transaction, the team rapidly identified several sources of value that Exxel could bring to Argencard in a way that the bank consortium might not. Unlike the competing group, Exxel had no banking interests. Consequently, it could credibly promise to treat each bank in the network equally and to maximize profits from the transaction network. The private equity organization's experience in streamlining over a dozen Argentine companies suggested that it would be able to identify and execute a wide variety of efficiency-enhancing measures. Finally, as owner of one of the largest HMOs in Argentina and several other firms, Exxel believed that it could encourage noncash payment processing in new sectors such as health care.

Exxel's ability to implement these changes would be enhanced by strong control rights in the proposed transaction. The new shareholders would control the majority of the voting rights and would have the ability to appoint key officers and directors. In particular, they would have the right to appoint 8 of the 12 directors, the president, and the two key vice presidents.

Much of Exxel's assessment of the transaction had focused on assigning a valuation to Argencard. Unlike a stable manufacturing business, it was difficult to assess the firm's future financial health. Exxel had undertaken two approaches to valuing Argencard: the multiples and the "venture capital" methods. Both approaches suggested that Argencard was attractively valued in the current transaction.

First, the group had examined the ratio of May 1995 share prices to projected 1995 earnings per share for 12 publicly traded U.S. credit card processing companies. These fell between 11 and 41, with an average of 24. The multiples of the four most comparable firms ranged from 16 to 35, averaging 25. Unlike the U.S. firms, Argencard would be privately held: consequently, it might be appropriate to discount these multiples in order to compensate investors for their illiquidity. This problem could be avoided by examining the valuations in several acquisitions and buyouts of credit card processors. The June 1995 acquisition of First Financial by First Data was at a multiple of 29.8 times earnings. In August 1995, Ceridian acquired Comdata Holdings, which processed funds transfer and cash advance transactions, for a multiple of 30 times earnings. In a slightly older transaction, First Data acquired Card Establishment Services in November 1994 for 29 times the earnings before interest and taxes.[18] The Exxel team generally used the multiples of comparable firms in the United States as a starting point, which they adjusted downward according to a formula, which factored in such measures as the relative long-term interest rates and GDP growth rates in the two countries.

A second valuation approach employed was the "venture capital" method. Exxel calculated what it believed the firm would be worth in three years, when it hoped to take

---

[18] Because of substantial interest payments, CES's net income was negative at the time. The EBIT was calculated by doubling the results of the first two quarters of the fiscal year in which the acquisition took place.

the concern public. To project this value, it first constructed a pro forma income statement, reproduced in Exhibit 7. It then multiplied projected 1998 earnings by a price–earnings ratio of 15, which roughly characterized the Argentine market in September 1995. Exxel was confident that Argencard would command a higher multiple than the average Argentine firm.[19] It then computed the internal rate of return of the transaction, including the initial investment, the annual dividends to shareholders, and the final payment from liquidating the shares. These projections incorporated a round of layoffs at Argencard that had recently been announced by the firm's existing management, as well as considerable reductions in printing and other operating costs. The projections did not consider, however, long-run efforts to expand into other areas of processing that had developed in the United States. Exxel, its limited partners, and its consultants were confident that the Argentine processing industry was about 15 years behind the United States and would be likely to follow a similar growth trajectory. Nor did it reflect the development of corporate and health-care procurement services or any future efforts to extend credit card services to other Latin American nations. Exxel also undertook detailed scenario analyses exploring the sensitivity of the returns to the projections, a few of which are summarized in Exhibit 8.

After intensive analysis and due diligence, Exxel had made a preliminary offer of $136.5 million for BNL's stake in a mere 14 days (one day before the deadline). Now the fund had 45 days in which to close the transaction. If the transaction was not completed in this period, Exxel's exclusivity ("lock-up") agreement would expire and the bank consortium could return into the bidding.

Closing this transaction in so short a time period would pose an enormous challenge. Although Exxel had developed a proposed transaction structure (summarized in Exhibits 9 and 10), it raised several concerns. Neither the first nor the second fund could cover the entire purchase price and remain within the terms of the partnership agreements. Rather, Exxel proposed to raise additional financing from a variety of sources. Exxel would establish a new company known as Credit Card Holding Company. The company would raise $142.5 million, $136.5 million of which would go to the purchase of BNL's stake and $6 million to fees and expenses. The sources of these funds would be diverse. $50 million would come from BNL; $30 million from the second fund; and $62.5 million from individual limited partners and other private equity investors. BNL would provide mezzanine seller financing of $50 million for four years, at an interest rate of 3% above the Libor rate. Unless Argencard paid substantial dividends, only very modest principal payments (totaling $10.5 million) would be required by BNL before the loan came due. If a mismatch developed between the entry of the limited partners and the closing of the deal, Exxel was allowed to invest up to an additional $22.5 million from the second fund as a "facilitating investment." Such an investment would be refinanced within one year.[20]

---

[19] This confidence reflected not only their belief in the attractiveness of Argencard as a company, but the nature of the firms traded on the Argentine market. Utilities, energy, telecommunications, and banking concerns represented nearly 90% of the Argentine market capitalization, and there was an absence of publicly traded financial transaction processing concerns. An Argencard offering would enable money managers to expand their portfolios to include this important aspect of the economy.

[20] While several private equity investors had expressed enthusiasm about co-investing in Argencard, they had raised some concerns about the proposed structure of Credit Card Holding Co-Investment, L.P., the vehicle through which the $62.5 million from outside investors would be raised. In particular, they pointed out that private equity organizations in the United States typically did not collect carried interest on investments made by other funds in deals that they led. Navarro believed, however, that such a payment was an appropriate compensation for Exxel's unique ability to originate Argentine transactions and that this issue should be resolved during the fundraising process.

A related issue was whether Exxel could interest Mastercard International ("MCI"), the New York–based "parent" of the Mastercard family, in being one of the investors in Argencard. MCI had never before considered an equity investment into one of its franchisees. If MCI invested, it would be a great benefit to Exxel and increase the value of Argencard.

Navarro had to convince William I. Jacobs, MCI's new executive vice president, that the investment would offer both excellent financial returns and strategic benefits to MCI. In particular, there were several powerful reasons, Navarro believed, why MCI should prefer the sale of Argencard to Exxel rather than to the other bidder, the consortium of Argentine banks. In particular, the banks would likely consolidate many of Argencard's operations with those of Visa, which the banks already managed. While undertaking joint marketing of the two cards might result in short-run cost savings, this was likely to lead to the long-run devaluation of Mastercard's franchise in Argentina: the different credit card brands would be increasingly viewed as interchangeable commodities. In addition, the banks already owned the only other credit card processor in Argentina. If the processors were merged, the processing costs were likely to increase and the quality of service would deteriorate. This could also affect the viability of the Mastercard franchise in Argentina. Both Navarro and Mason (who served with Jacobs on the board of the New York based trading firm, ITG) had discussed these issues with Jacobs.

DECISIONS

As the dusk began to settle on Buenos Aires, Navarro considered his options. Although the significant returns Exxel projected in the Argencard transaction were attractive, they were not without risk. Was the price that Exxel was offering, he wondered, a reasonable one? Was the proposed transaction structure appropriate and practical? How important was it to involve Mastercard International as an investor?

More generally, Navarro contemplated the future of the Argentine private equity market. The key to future growth was likely to be successful exits from its existing portfolio. Navarro did not like to imagine himself selling Exxel's investments at fire-sale prices in a market thin on buyers. How rapidly would Exxel be able to harvest its first fund's portfolio and on what terms? What would be the impact of the increasing interest in Latin American private equity markets by institutional investors? Would Exxel's leadership position be enhanced, as these institutions co-invested in deals it led? Or would ruinous competition result, as characterized the U.S. private equity market in the 1980s following a rapid increase in capital under management and the entry of numerous inexperienced investors? As his secretary announced that Bill Jacobs of MCI was on the line, Navarro turned back to the present and picked up the telephone.

Exhibit 1   Argentine Macroeconomic Data

	Inflation-Adjusted GDP Change (%)	Per Capita GDP ($)	Consumer Price Index Inflation (%)	Average Exchange Rate (Peso per $1)	Money Market Rate (%)	Deposit Rate (%)	Exports ($ billions)	Imports ($ billions)	Average Unemployment (%)	Population (millions)
1985	-6.6	6,227	600.0	0.00006	1,161	630	10.4	5.6		30.32
1986	7.3	6,584	81.9	0.00009	135	95	9.1	7.0		30.77
1987	2.6	6,659	174.8	0.00021	253	176	8.7	8.4		31.22
1988	-1.9	6,438	387.7	0.00087	524	372	12.2	7.9	3.1	31.67
1989	-6.2	5,958	4,923.9	0.04233	1,387,179	17,236	10.0	5.0	7.1	32.11
1990	0.1	5,883	1,341.9	0.48759	9,695,422	1,518	14.6	6.5	6.3	32.55
1991	8.9	6,324	84.0	0.95355	71	62	14.6	11.2	6.0	32.97
1992	8.7	7,198	17.5	0.99064	15	17	15.4	18.8	7.0	33.37
1993	6.0	6,706	7.4	0.99895	6	11	16.3	20.9	9.3	33.67
1994	7.1	7,484	3.9	0.99901	8	8	19.2	25.7	10.7	34.18
1995[a]	-1.5	7,430	2.0	0.99975	9	12	22.0	19.8	19.0	34.60

[a]As projected in mid-September.

Source: Compiled from various International Monetary Fund and Argentine government reports.

244

Exhibit 2 Merval Index and Argentine Peso-U.S. Dollar Exchange Rate

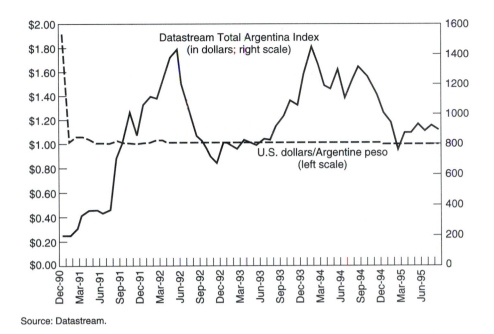

Source: Datastream.

Exhibit 3 Recent Initial Public Offerings of Argentine Firms as of September 1995

Date	Issuer	Proceeds ($ million)	
7/21/95	Transportadora de Gas Norte	$ 141.5	
	1995 (through mid-September)		$ 141.5
11/10/94	Latin American Fund	70.0	
10/20/94	Mirgor SACIFIA	18.8	
10/14/94	Dragados y Construcciones	32.6	
6/13/94	Capex Argentina	47.4	
5/09/94	CADIPSA	9.7	
	1994 Total		$ 178.5
7/14/93	YPF	3,040.0	
	1993 Total		$3,040.0
12/29/92	Minetti	6.1	
6/23/92	Massuh SAIC	0.0	
6/17/92	Sevel Argentina	126.4	
5/28/92	BAESA	135.0	
5/28/92	Guillermo Decker	5.5	
3/24/92	Telecom Argentina STET	310.6	
	1992 Total		$ 583.6

Source: Compiled from Securities Data Company's Corporate New Issues Database.

245

Exhibit 4   Exxel Investments as of September 1995

Date	Company	Sector	Purchase Price ($ million)	%	Funding Source	Current Status
Jan. 1993	CIABASA	Household cleaning	$9.6	100%	Fund I	Merged with Poett
Jan. 1993	Papelera Mar del Plata	Tissue paper products	4.0	98	Fund I	
Mar. 1993	EDESAL	Electric power distribution	13.8	75	Fund I	
May 1993	Poett San Juan	Household cleaning	11.8	100	Fund I	
June 1993	La Papelera del Plata	Tissue paper products	15.0	23	Fund I	
July 1993	Papelera Daniel Chozas (division)	Paper products	a	100	Fund I	Acquired by Papelera Mar del Plata
Jan. 1994	Pizza Hut (Bestov Foods)	Pizza chain	12.0	60	Funds I and II	Also includes 2nd purchase in 1995
May 1994	Linea Hogar de YPF	Insecticides	1.0	100	Fund I	Merged with Poett
Nov. 1994	Galeno-Vesalio	Health maintenance organization	27.0	92	Fund II	Merged to form Galeno y Life
Nov. 1994	La Trinidad	Clinic	b	75	Fund II	Part of Galeno purchase
Nov. 1994	The Jockey Club, San Isidro	Clinic	b	90	Fund II	Part of Galeno purchase
Mar. 1995	Life	Health maintenance organization	11.0	100	Fund II	Merged to form Galeno y Life
May 1995	EDELAR	Electric power distribution	12.2	90	Fund II	

aPurchase price included in Papelera Mar del Plata total.
bPurchase price included in Galeno total.

Source: Corporate documents.

Exhibit 5 Latin American Private Equity Funds as of September 1995

Sponsor	Fund Name	Last Closing Date[a]	Amount Raised ($ million)[b]	Target Area	Note
Advent International Corporation	Latin America Private Equity Fund			Argentina, Brazil, Chile and Mexico	$200 million target; first closing expected in late 1995
Baring Latin America Capital Ltd.	Latin American Enterprise Fund	June 1995	$175	Latin America	Fundraising still active; final closing expected in late 1995
Baring Venture Partners de Mexico	Baring Mexico Private Equity Partners			Mexico	$60 million target; first closing expected in early 1996
Banco de Investimentos Garantia	G.P. Capital Partners	Jan. 1994	500	Brazil	
Banco Garantia/BEA	Brazilian Equity Partnership	Sep. 1995	84	Brazil	
BEA Associates	Latin America Capital Partners	Mar. 1993	36	Latin America	
BEA Capital	Latin America Capital Partners II			Latin America	$400 million target
Bemberg Investments S.A.	Bemberg Investments S.A. (BISA)	Jan. 1994	60[c]	Argentina	
Darby Overseas Limited	Latin America Capital Partners	Dec. 1994	54	Latin America	Fundraising still active; final closing expected in late 1995
Del Sol Capital Management	Andean Emerging Growth Fund			Peru and Chile	$50 million target; first closing expected in mid-1996
Emerging Markets Partnership	AIG-GE Latin American Infrastructure Fund			Latin America	$1 billion target; first closing expected in mid-1996
Exxel Group/Oppenheimer	Argentine Private Equity Fund I	Apr. 1992	46.8	Argentina	
Exxel Group/Oppenheimer	Argentine Private Equity Fund II	Feb. 1995	150	Argentina	
FondElec Capital Management	Latin American Energy and Electricity Fund I			Latin America	$50 million target; first closing expected in late 1995
J.G. Fogg & Co.	Westburg Peru Partners	Mar. 1995	40	Peru	Fundraising still active; final closing expected in late 1995
Wasserstein Perella	Latin America Equity Partners			Latin America	$300 million target; first closing expected in early 1996
Weston Group	Mexico Private Capital Fund			Mexico	$250 million target; first closing expected in 1996
WestSphere Equity Investors	South America Private Equity Growth Fund			Latin America	$180 million target; first closing expected in late 1995

a If the fund had multiple closing dates, this denotes the date of the final closing. If fundraising was still active in September 1995, this denotes the last closing before September 1995.

b If the fund had multiple closing dates, this denotes the total raised. If fundraising was still active in September 1995, this denotes the amount raised before September 1995.

c BISA was structured as a corporation, and thus is not strictly comparable to the others. This total only includes the cash assets of BISA.

Source: See footnote 13.

Exhibit 6 Payment System Dynamics and Average Argentine Merchant Discount Rates

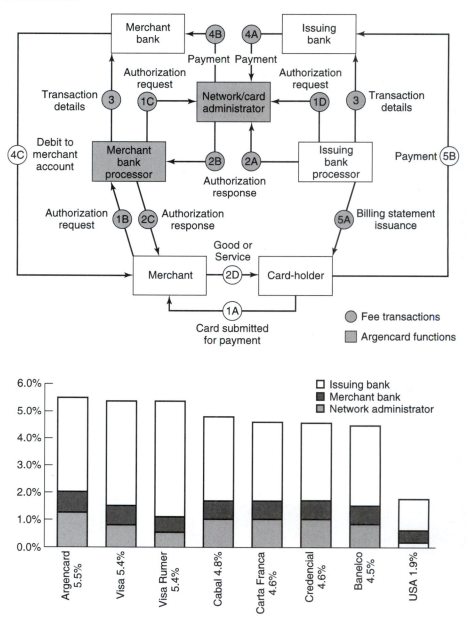

Source: Corporate documents.

Exhibit 7 Argencard Historical Performance and Projections (US$ million, unless otherwise noted)

	1992	1993	1994	1995[a]	1996[b]	1997[b]	1998[b]	1999[b]
					Year Ended December 31			
Assumptions								
Gross volume[c]	2,469	3,327	4,112	3,998	4,499	5,374	6,319	7,348
Cards outstanding (millions)	2.18	2.45	2.39	2.55	2.86	3.14	3.39	3.65
Transactions (millions)	69.6	81.2	93.8	95.6	109.5	130.4	151.8	173.1
Merchant discount (%)	6.50	6.12	5.97	5.50	5.21	4.91	4.61	4.31
Merchant discount share (%)	23.40	23.40	23.40	23.40	23.25	23.10	22.95	22.80
% growth gross volume		34.8%	23.6%	-2.8%	12.5%	19.4%	17.6%	16.3%
% growth cards outstanding		12.4	-2.4	6.7	12.3	9.8	8.0	7.7
% growth transactions	36.8	16.7	15.5	1.9	14.5	19.1	16.4	14.0
% growth merchant discount	-2.5	-5.8	-2.5	-7.9	-5.3	-5.8	-6.1	-6.5
Revenues								
Merchant discounts[d]	$36.6	$54.2	$60.8	$54.4	$56.7	$63.4	$69.5	$75.1
Data processing[e]	18.3	22.3	27.1	28.2	30.1	31.2	32.0	32.1
Warning bulletin[f]	5.4	10.0	13.0	12.7	11.3	9.5	8.6	7.5
Other[g]	5.8	7.4	13.7	22.6	24.6	27.2	29.5	31.3
Development fund	8.4	11.7	15.0	16.1	17.8	17.9	18.2	17.8
Total revenue	$74.5	$105.6	$129.6	$134.0	$140.5	$149.2	$157.8	$163.8
% change	69.9%	41.7%	22.7%	0.4%[h]	4.9%	6.2%	5.8%	3.8%
Operating costs[i]	3.4	19.7	27.9	37.7	34.3	33.0	32.9	32.5
% revenues	4.6%	18.7%	21.5%	28.1%	24.4%	22.1%	20.8%	19.8%
Depreciation and amortization[j]	2.1	3.0	8.0	8.0	6.5	5.5	4.4	3.3
Marketing and selling expenses[k]	29.7	31.7	40.4	36.2	38.8	41.3	44.3	47.1
% revenues	39.9%	30.0%	31.3%	27.0%	27.6%	27.7%	28.1%	28.8%
Administrative expenses[l]	21.8	27.0	33.1	19.8	19.0	17.7	18.4	19.2
% revenues	29.3%	25.6%	25.5%	14.8%	13.5%	11.9%	11.7%	11.7%
E.B.I.T.	19.5	27.1	28.3	40.3	48.6	57.3	62.3	65.1
% revenues	26.3%	25.8%	21.8%	30.1%	34.4%	38.3%	39.4%	39.7%
Income from affiliated companies	0.1	0.2	0.6	1.0	1.7	2.6	3.7	3.9
Severances	0.0	0.0	0.0	(0.8)	(1.6)	0.0	0.0	0.0
Interest income (expense)[m]	2.7	4.5	3.9	(1.0)	(0.6)	(0.6)	(0.6)	(0.7)
Other income (expense)	0.4	1.0	1.7	(0.4)	(1.4)	0.0	0.0	0.0
Income tax[n]	(6.3)	(9.7)	(9.8)	(12.2)	(14.5)	(17.9)	(19.6)	(20.5)
Net income	16.5	23.2	24.6	26.9	32.0	41.3	45.7	47.7
% revenues	22.1%	22.0%	19.0%	20.1%	22.8%	27.7%	29.0%	29.1%
Selected Balance Sheet Items								
Net working capital	(4.2)	(2.9)	(2.0)	1.7	2.0	2.3	2.5	2.7
% revenues	-5.6%	-2.7%	-1.5%	1.3%	1.4%	1.5%	1.6%	1.6%
Change in NWC ($ million)		1.3	0.9	3.7	0.3	0.3	0.2	0.2
Capital expenditures (US$ million)	1.3	16.9	17.7	3.2	8.4	3.7	2.7	1.5
% revenues[o]	1.7%	16.0%	13.7%	2.4%	6.0%	2.5%	1.7%	0.9%
Cash[p]	1.1	1.6	3.0					
Total assets[p]	35.5	63.1	62.4					
Long-term debt[p]	0.0	2.3	0.0					
Shareholders' equity[p]	15.5	26.5	28.1					

Exhibit 7 (continued)   Footnotes to Exhibit 7

[a]1995 data is preliminary.

[b]1996 through 1999 data are projections by Exxel and its consultants.

[c]Includes both charge volume and cash advances.

[d]Merchant discounts = Gross volume * Merchant discount * Merchant discount share. This calculation, however, is not exact, because Argencard receives different shares of purchases made by Argencard holders abroad and those by foreign Mastercard holders in Argentina.

[e]In detailed projections, fees were seen as declining at annual rates of between 8.0% and 12.6% in 1997-99, but the number of accounts and transactions were seen as increasing.

[f]In detailed projections, delinquency and theft rates were seen as declining, leading to a fall in these revenues (which are based on the number of cards listed).

[g]Includes card issuance, ATM, merchant acquisition, and marketing fees, as well as Uruguay operations. Includes interest income in the period 1995 through 1999, but not in earlier years.

[h]Had interest income been included, 1994 income would have been $3.8 million higher. The percentage revenue growth between 1994 and 1995 is calculated using revenue with interest income in both years.

[i]Includes salaries and benefits in operations, printing costs, depreciation, and amortization. Incorporates already-announced layoffs scheduled for 1995 and 1996, as well as some additional cost savings anticipated by Exxel.

[j]Already included in operating costs.

[k]Includes salaries and benefits in sales and marketing, sales tax, Mastercard fees, travel, and legal expenses.

[l]Includes salaries and benefits in administration, buildings, Uruguay operations, and other expenses.

[m]After 1994, interest income is included with other revenues. Interest expenses do not include additional interest payments for debt associated with the proposed buyout.

[n]Argencard pays a federal income tax rate of 30%.

[o]Capital expenditures for 1993 and 1994 would have been 3.9% and 6.8% without one-time expenses associated with the construction of a new headquarters building.

[p]These balance sheet items will vary with the timing of Argencard's initial public offering, as well as with the pace at which the debt assumed in the buyout is repaid. Immediately after the proposed transaction, Argencard would have assumed $50 million of debt.

Source: Corporate documents.

Exhibit 8   Analysis of Internal Rate of Return to Argencard Equityholders (US$ million)

	Day 0	1996	1997	1998
Purchase price[a]	$142.5			
Equity	92.5			
Outstanding debt	50.0	$50.0[b]	$47.3[b]	$42.6[b]
Interest payments[c]		(4.5)	(4.3)	(3.8)
Required debt repayments		(1.5)	(3.0)	(6.0)
Fees and expenses		(1.2)	(1.2)	(1.2)
Additional debt repayments		(1.2)	(1.7)	(36.6)
56% of Argencard cash flow[d]		17.7	24.9	27.3
56% of Argencard sale price[e]				385.0
Total cash flow to equityholders	$ (92.5)	$ 9.3	$14.8	$364.7
IRR to equityholders	64.8%			

IRR to Equityholders Under Different Assumptions

Merchant discount rate falls to 4.33% in 1998	57.7%
Merchant discount rate falls to 4.05% in 1998	53.6
Merchant discount rate falls to 3.76% in 1998	48.6
Argencard's share of merchant discount falls to 22.5% in 1998	60.4
Argencard's share of merchant discount falls to 22.05% in 1998	59.2
Average consumption per account grows at one-half projected rate	58.1
Costs each year are $3 million greater	60.6

[a]Includes $6 million of transaction costs.

[b]Debt outstanding at beginning of year.

[c]Assumes interest rate of 9%.

[d]Argencard cash flows are calculated from pro-forma income statements in **Exhibit 7**. The net income figure must be adjusted for (i) expenses that should not be removed from the cash flow statement (depreciation, amortization, and interest expense), (ii) changes in net working capital and capital expenditures, and (iii) the reduction of tax obligations associated with the debt assumed in the buyout (note that **Exhibit 7** does not incorporate the additional interest expenses associated with a buyout).

[e]Purchase price projected using a price-earnings multiple of 15.

Note: Two credit card processors publicly traded in the United States were First Data Corporation and Total System Services. Over the previous year, the two firms had betas (using weekly data) of 1.01 and 0.99 respectively. Both had virtually all-equity capital structures. In September 1995, 10-year U.S. Treasury bonds had a yield of 6.16%; Argentine government dollar-denominated bonds of approximately the same maturity had a yield of 11.02%. The 30-day rate for loans in pesos to top-tier corporations was 1.05%; the monthly rate for government-guaranteed peso-denominated securities was 0.69%.

Source: Corporate documents.

Exhibit 9 Proposed Acquisition Transaction Structure

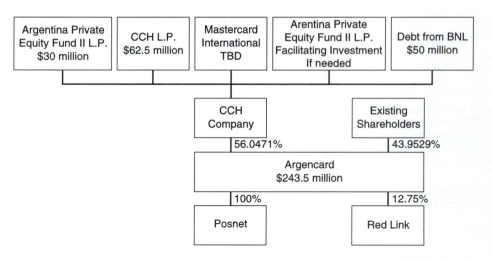

Note: CCH L.P. = "Credit Card Holding Co-Investment, L.P."; CCH Company = "Credit Card Holding Company"; TBD = "To be determined."

Source: Corporate documents.

Exhibit 10   Excerpts From Term Sheet for Credit Card Holding Co-Investment, L.P.

The Fund	Credit Card Holding Co-Investment, L.P., a Cayman Islands exempted limited partnership.
The General Partner	The Exxel Group II (Cayman Islands) Inc., a Cayman Islands limited liability company, will be the sole general partner of the Fund.
Promoted and Non-Promoted Limited Partners	Promoted Limited Partners are all the Limited Partners except for the Argentine Private Equity II, L.P. ("Fund II"), The Exxel Group S.A. and its Affiliates (collectively, "Exxel") and any Affiliate thereof, which shall be designated as Non-Promoted Limited Partners. Distributions to Non-Promoted Limited Partners are not subject to Carried Interest.
Fund Investment	The Fund will make a single equity investment (the "Fund Investment") in Argencard S.A. ("Argencard," or the "Company"), the exclusive licensee of Mastercard International Incorporated ("MasterCard") in Argentina and Uruguay. The fund Investment will be made through an equity investment in Credit Card Holding Co. ("CCH Co."), a Cayman Islands Corporation, which in turn will acquire a 56.0471% interest in Argencard. CCH Co.'s total [equity] capitalization will be $92,500,000.
Size of Fund	The Fund will have a maximum of $92,500,000 in capital commitments. The General Partner may schedule multiple closings for subscriptions. See "Closings" below.
Limited Partner Commitment	Each Limited Partner in the entire document will be required to make a minimum commitment of $2,500,000. The General Partner may, in its discretion, accept a commitment for a lesser amount.
Exxel Commitment	The General Partner will be required to make a minimum commitment in the Fund in connection with its general partnership interest in an amount equal to 1% of the Fund's total capital commitments at any time.
Closings	The first closing will occur as promptly as practicable after the General Partner determines, in its discretion, that a sufficient amount of subscriptions for limited partnership interests have been obtained. The General Partner expects that the first closing will occur on or before November 22, 1995 ("First Closing Date"). After the First Closing Date, provided the total capital commitments have not reached the maximum amount of capital commitments of the Fund (see "Size of Fund" above), the General Partner will have the right, in its discretion, to accept subscriptions for additional limited partnership interests and to permit existing limited partners to increase their capital commitments (the "Admission Period") for up to such maximum amount. Subsequent closings may occur until the close of business on the day which is one year after the First Closing Date (each a "Closing Date").
Capital Contributions	Upon its admission to the Fund and its execution of the Partnership Agreement of the Fund, each Limited Partner will be required to make a capital contribution equal to its entire capital commitment. All capital contributions will be required to be funded by wire transfer in immediately available funds in U.S. dollars.
Term	Subject to the provisions listed under "Dissolution" below, the Fund shall continue in existence until November 17, 2002, which term may be extended for up to three one-year terms with the approval of the General Partner and Limited Partners representing at least a majority of the total capital commitments.

Distributions, Carried Interest

Upon receipt of any current income or proceeds with respect to the disposition of any portion or all of the Fund Investment, the General Partner will determine the portion of such income or proceeds required to be used to pay Partnership Expenses and shall then determine for each Limited Partner, the amount of such limited partner's share of the proposed distribution and distribute such amount as described in Article VIII of the Partnership Agreement. Promoted Limited Partners are subject to the following Carried Interest Amounts, after such Limited Partner shall have received, taking into account the amount being so distributed and all prior distributions to such Limited Partner, an aggregate amount equal to such Limited Partner's Realized Invested Capital as of such Distribution date:

Promoted Limited Partner Internal Rate of Return	Applicable Carried Interest Percentage
Less than or equal to 20%	0.0%
More than 20% but less than or equal to 30%	5.0
More than 30% but less than or equal to 40%	7.5
More than 40% but less than or equal to 50%	10.0
More than 50%	15.0

The aggregate amount, if any, distributed to the General Partner in respect of any Promoted Limited Partner's Partner Distribution Amount shall be referred to as a "Carried Interest Amount." At dissolution of the Fund, if the General Partner has a deficit balance in its capital account it will be obligated to restore the amount of such deficit balance resulting from distributions of the Carried Interest Amount.

Any securities or other property constituting all or any portion of the Fund Investment to be distributed by the Fund will be valued by the General Partner, subject to review by the Advisory Committee (as defined below). The Fund will not make distributions in kind of nonmarketable securities, except in connection with the dissolution of the Fund.

Expenses

The Fund will be responsible for and will pay all Partnership Expenses. Partnership Expenses will be classified as follows: (i) all out-of-pocket expenses incurred by the Fund or on its behalf that are directly related to the organization of the Fund (including legal fees) will be classified as "Partnership Organizational Expenses"; (ii) all expenses incurred by the Fund or on its behalf that are directly related to the acquisition, monitoring, management, restructuring, reinvestment, or sale or other disposition of the Fund Investment will be classified as "Partnership Investment Expenses," including (a) professional fees (e.g., legal, tax, engineering, accounting and consulting fees) and (b) expenses incurred by Affiliates of the General Partner in connection with their services as advisors to the Fund with respect to the Fund Investment; and (iii) all other expenses incurred by the Fund or on its behalf (including without limitation the reasonable travel and other out-of-pocket expenses of the Advisory Committee (as defined below)) will be classified as "Partnership Administrative Expenses." Partnership Investment Expenses are expected to be borne by the Company or its Affiliates. Such expenses will be borne by the Fund pro rata with the other shareholders of CCH Co. to the extent not covered by the Company and its Affiliates.

Transfer Restrictions

Limited partnership interests in the Fund will not be registered under any securities laws and cannot be sold, pledged, assigned, transferred or otherwise disposed of without the written consent of the General Partner (which consent may be withheld in its sole discretion).

Advisory Committee

The Fund will have an advisory committee consisting of all limited partners (the "Advisory Committee"). The persons comprising the Advisory Committee will be determined as follows: (i) the General Partner will, in its discretion, annually select no less than two limited partners to serve as members of the Advisory Committee for a one-year term; and (ii) in addition to the limited partners selected by the General Partner, each limited partner having a capital commitment of at least $8.5 million will have the right to be a member of the Advisory Committee. The Advisory Committee will meet with the General Partner once a year in order to review Fund matters and to advise the General Partner. The General Partner will consult the Advisory Committee on the following matters: (i) any receipt of Portfolio Fees; (ii) advances of funds by the General Partner or any of its Affiliates, including the interest rate charged with respect to such advance; (iii) any transaction entered into during the prior year by the Fund or the Company as permitted by the Partnership Agreement; (iv) any Investment Banking Fees received by the General Partner and its Affiliates in connection with the performance of investment banking, financial, advisory, consulting, or other related services for the benefit of the Company or any of its Affiliates, which Investment Banking Fees shall be on terms no less favorable to the Company and its Affiliates than the terms that would be obtained on an arms' length basis; (v) any lending fees received by the General Partner or any of its Affiliates from the Company or any of its Affiliates; (vi) the most recent financial statements of the Fund available; (vii) the status of the Fund Investment; and (viii) such other matters relating to the business of the Fund or the Partnership Agreement as the General Partner may determine, or any member of the Advisory Committee may reasonably propose to the General Partner, from time to time. Except with respect to the actions discussed below, any actions taken by the Advisory Committee will be advisory only and the General Partner will not be required or otherwise bound to act in accordance with any such actions. The actions of the Advisory Committee set forth below are binding on the Fund and all the partners.

Board of Directors of Argencard and Its Affiliates

So long as it does not result in the General Partner ceasing to be able to elect a majority of the directors of CCH Co. and Argencard, limited partners investing $20 million or more shall have the right to appoint one member of the Board of Directors of CCH Co. and of Argencard.

Portfolio Fees

In connection with providing active management and consulting advisory services, the General Partner may charge normal and customary fees to the Fund and its Affiliates.

Dissolution

The Fund will be dissolved and its affairs wound up upon the earliest of: (i) the expiration of its term described above; (ii) the written consent of the General Partner and limited partners representing a majority of the aggregate capital commitments of all limited partners' capital commitments at such time; (iii) the bankruptcy, liquidation, dissolution or insolvency of the General Partner; (iv) the withdrawal of the General Partner; and (v) the General Partner engages in willful malfeasance, fraud or gross negligence, unless limited partners representing at least two-thirds of the aggregate capital commitments of all limited partners' vote to continue the Fund. Upon dissolution, the General Partner will, in its discretion, liquidate the Fund in an orderly manner.

Reports

Limited partners will receive: (i) annual audited financial statements for the Fund (including a statement of each partner's closing capital account balance); (ii) quarterly unaudited financial statements for the Fund; (iii) annual tax information necessary for the completion of tax returns; and (iv) a quarterly and annual overview of the Fund Investment, prepared by the General Partner.

ERISA
The General Partner will use its reasonable best efforts to operate the Fund in such a way that so long as the Fund has an ERISA partner the Fund will meet the requirements of a "venture capital operating company" within the meaning of U.S. Department of Labor Regulations.

Auditors
Coopers & Lybrand.

U.S. Counsel
Davis Polk & Wardwell.

Argentine Counsel
Quattrini, Laprida & Asociados.

Cayman Islands Counsel
W.S. Walker & Company.

Source: Corporate document.

13

A Note on Private Equity in Developing Nations

The past several years have seen a boom in private equity activity in the developing world. This has been fueled largely by institutional investors based in the United States. The reasons for this growth are several. Among them has been the recent rapid growth of many developing nations and the relaxation of curbs on foreign investments in many of these nations. Perhaps equally important has been the recent perception by many institutional investors that the returns from private equity investments in the United States are likely to decrease in upcoming years.

Although comprehensive data is hard to come by, a few examples may help illustrate these patterns.[1] In 1994 alone, private equity funds based in Hong Kong and China raised a total of $3.1 billion in capital. Two-thirds of the capital came from outside Asia, with the single largest source being U.S. institutions. This sum was more than the *total* raised by professional private equity organizations there since the first fund was raised in Hong Kong in 1981. In 1994 and 1995, Latin American funds raised $1.4 billion. This represented several times the amount that had been raised previously by funds in the region. India, Eastern Europe, South Africa, and Israel are just a few of the other areas where multiple private equity funds have recently been or currently are being raised. In addition, funds based in the United States are increasingly investing directly in transactions in the developing world, often in conjunction with these funds.

This note seeks to identify some of the key challenges and opportunities that private equity investors in developing nations will face. The first section presents a broad overview of some of the key reasons developing nations are increasingly seen as an attractive investment environment by institutional investors and private equity funds. The note then considers the "private equity cycle." The second through fourth sections examine the process from fundraising through investing to exiting, contrasting developing and developed nations. The opportunities that make private equity in developing countries so attractive are highlighted, as well as the potential risks.

It is worth cautioning that this note only tries to identify broad patterns. This discussion should not blind the reader to the substantial heterogeneity in the private equity

This note was prepared by Gonzalo Pacanins (under the direction of Josh Lerner). Copyright © 1996 by the President and Fellows of Harvard College. Harvard Business School case 297-039.

[1] No single directory captures private equity activity in the developing world. The Asian data is drawn from Asian Venture Capital Journal, *The Guide to Venture Capital in Asia: 1995/1996 Edition,* Hong Kong, Asian Venture Capital Journal, 1995; the Latin American data is compiled from the *Private Equity Analyst* and various stories and studies cited in the "Further Readings" section.

industries of various developing countries. A key reason for these differences, of course, is that developing nations differ along many dimensions among themselves.

WHY INVEST IN DEVELOPING NATIONS?

In this section, we will discuss two sets of rationales for the growth of private equity activity in the developing world.[2] The first relates to the changes in the developing nations themselves. Many have undertaken radical reforms. External changes—for example, technological innovations—have also helped make these nations more attractive arenas for investment. The second set relates to the changing condition in the developed nations. Many institutional investors are skeptical that attractive returns that have recently characterized venture capital and leveraged buyout investments in many developed nations can be sustained, and they are looking for new arenas in which to invest.

The Increasing Attractiveness of Developing Nations

Much of the interest in private equity investing in developing nations must be attributed to their economic progress over the past decade. A critical impetus to much of this progress, in turn, has been the economic reforms many of these nations have adopted. The pace at which capitalism has rolled through developing economies is breathtaking. It is easy to forget that as recently as a decade ago, only 1 billion of the world's citizens were in capitalist economies. Today, three times that number are in economies that are strongly capitalist in orientation.[3]

Although a detailed discussion of these changes is beyond the scope of this note, a few of these reforms will be detailed here. One of the most substantial macroeconomic shifts was the 1989 Brady Plan. This allowed several Latin American countries to restructure their external debt. The enormous reduction in debt service led to a substantial boost in the economic health of these markets. In turn, the successful reform process led to an increase in major investors' confidence in developing nations, as seen, for instance, in the increase in the market prices of these nations' debt.

Other macroeconomic reforms were initiated by the developing nations themselves, though often with the prodding of such international bodies as the International Monetary Fund. One arena for such reforms has been major tax reforms. Many developing countries realized that one way to fuel the economy was by lowering taxes on capital gains, thereby encouraging equity investment and stock market growth. Similarly, in many nations, restrictions on foreign investment—which often prohibited investments in particular industries, stipulated that foreign investors needed to hold a minority stake, or limited the repatriation of profits—have been relaxed. Finally, several developing nations have made great progress in improving their accounting and disclosure standards. These changes have helped lower the costs of investing in these nations, as well as diminish the information asymmetries that foreign investors face.

---

[2] According to the World Bank, developing nations are those countries that have either low- or middle-level per capita incomes; have underdeveloped capital markets; and/or are not industrialized. The application of these criteria is somewhat subjective, however. For instance, Kuwait appears on many lists of developing nations despite its high per capita gross domestic product. The reason for its inclusion lies in the income distribution inequality that exists there, which has not allowed it to reach the general living standards of developed countries.

[3] For a provocative discussion of these changes from a practitioner perspective, see Lucy Conger, "Interview-Garantia Launches Brazil Equity Fund," *Reuters News Service*, September 26, 1995.

Other drivers of the economic progress of developing nations have been external. An example is the lowering by many developed nations of many tariff and nontariff barriers to imports from developing nations. Both exports and imports by developing nations more than tripled between 1987 and 1995.[4] A second example is technological change. Thanks to innovations in information and communication technologies, investors in developed countries—whether corporations or institutions—can better monitor their investments. A substantial decline in inflation-adjusted transportation costs has also made greater trade and investment feasible. These trends have led to spectacular growth in many of the developing nations. Although the developed economies grew at an inflation-adjusted annual rate of 1.9% between 1990 and 1994, emerging market economies grew at 5.2%.[5]

The Decreasing Attractiveness of Developed Nations

A second critical factor in the growth of private equity investing in developing countries has been the perception of diminishing investment opportunities in the developed nations, particularly the United States. The pool of private equity under management in the United States grew from $4 billion in 1980 to about $125 billion in 1995. This growth was largely attributable to the relaxation of the formal and informal curbs that limited private and pension funds from investing in private equity.

This growth, many institutional investors argue, has had three deleterious consequences. First, the increase in the size of many private equity funds has led to an alteration in the incentive structure of these funds. In particular, the management fees charged by private equity investors have remained relatively constant, averaging about 2% (typically calculated as a percentage of capital under management). But since the capital managed per partner has increased dramatically, this has meant that these fees have become a significant source of income. Many investors fear that the incentive provided by the share of the profits reserved for the private equity investors has consequently become less effective. Second, many private equity organizations have encountered strong demand when they seek to raise new funds. This allowed them to negotiate partnership agreements without the many covenants that protect investors in these funds. If an institution insisted on the inclusion of a particular form of protection, the venture capitalists could simply exclude them from the transaction. Finally, many institutional investors argue that the current market is characterized by an imbalance between the supply of capital and attractive investments. Many argue that this has led to unjustifiable increases in valuations, or, more colloquially, the phenomenon of "money chasing deals."

These concerns are also causing institutional investors, particularly in the United States, to consider more favorably private equity funds specializing elsewhere. One focus has been continental Europe, which has lagged both the United States and United Kingdom in the supply of private equity. But the low inflation-adjusted growth rates in many European nations have led many institutions to focus on the developing nations.

Why Private Equity?

In view of the above patterns, it may not be surprising that institutional investors have been investing in a broad array of asset classes in developing nations. Institutional hold-

[4] International Monetary Fund, *International Financial Statistics Yearbook,* Washington, D.C., International Monetary Fund, 1996.
[5] *Ibid.*

ings of both public equities and corporate and government debt have increased sharply in recent years. But a recent focus of interest has been international private equity funds.

This interest is illustrated by a 1997 survey of 204 of the largest U.S. institutional investors conducted by Goldman Sachs and Frank Russell Capital. It found that international private equity had increased from representing 0.0% of all alternative investments in 1992 to 9.3% in 1997. In a few short years, participation in this asset class (by the institutions that had invested in any alternative assets) went from virtually zero to 51%. Of the remaining firms, more than one-half indicated that they were currently considering investments in international private equity funds. Furthermore, international private equity was the asset class that the institutions identified as the most attractive and offering the highest expected future returns.[6]

Institutional investors frequently justify their interest in private equity funds in developing nations by highlighting the similarities to venture capital in the United States. Like venture capital investments, many companies in developing nations are characterized by great uncertainty, difficult-to-value assets, and substantial information asymmetries. In the developing world, a venture capital-like style of investment should consequently yield attractive returns.

THE PRIVATE EQUITY CYCLE: FUNDRAISING

In many respects, private equity in developing and developed countries is similar. In both settings, professional investors provide equity or equity-linked capital to privately held firms. Another key element is the ongoing involvement of the private equity investor in monitoring and assisting the company. Where private equity in developing countries differs is in its implementation. The next three sections will highlight some of these differences.

Fund Structures

The fund structure standard in developed countries is the limited partnership. The general partners are the individual venture capitalists (or an investment management firm controlled by these individuals). The general partners are in charge of raising, making, monitoring, and exiting the investments. In return they are paid a management fee plus a share of the profits. The limited partners are prohibited from playing an active role in managing the investments and usually enjoy tax benefits. For instance, taxes are typically paid not at the fund level, but rather by the individual general and limited partners. This enables tax-exempt investors to avoid almost all tax obligations.

This limited partnership structure has served as a model for many private equity funds in developing countries. For instance, all but one of the funds focusing in Latin America have been structured along the lines of U.S.-style limited partnerships.[7] A major issue for venture capital funds in Asia, however, has been the general lack of legal structures that allow the establishment of limited partnerships.

Without the ability to form a limited partnership, most Asian venture capital funds are structured as corporations. This corporate structure puts several limitations on the

---

[6] Goldman, Sachs & Co. and Frank Russell Capital Inc., *1997 Report on Alternative Investments by Tax-Exempt Originazations,* New York: Goldman, Sachs & Co. and Frank Russell Capital Inc., 1998.

[7] Lorenzo Weissman, "The Advent of Private Equity in Latin America," *The Columbia Journal of World Business* 31 (Spring 1996) 60–68 (this information is on page 68).

limited partners' ability to ensure that the fund will dissolve at the end of a stated period (e.g., ten years). With the corporate structure, it is easier for the general partners to prolong the fund's life. Since the forced liquidation—and the consequent need for general partners to return for additional funds—is one of the most powerful control rights exercised by limited partners, it is not surprising that this has been a major concern.

Capital Sources

The sources of funds for private equity funds in the developing nations have largely been the same ones that invest in private equity funds based in the United States: pension funds, corporations, insurance companies, and high net worth individuals. To date, U.S.-based organizations have made up the bulk of these investors. European investors are gradually increasing in importance.

Several additional sets of parties, however, have played an important role in raising private equity funds in developing nations. These have included U.S. foreign aid organizations like the U.S. Agency for International Development (USAID), quasi-governmental corporations like the Overseas Private Investment Corporation (OPIC), and multilateral financial institutions like the International Finance Corporation (IFC). Their role has been twofold. First, USAID and IFC have invested in funds directly. Rather than serving as traditional limited partners, however, they have typically provided financial support through long-term loans or direct grants. Second, these agencies have provided guarantees to private investors that they will receive some or all of their capital back. OPIC has been particularly aggressive in providing such guarantees.

The track record of these public efforts has been somewhat mixed. A recent internal critique at USAID[8] argued that of all the funds that it had supported over the past two decades, only one—the Latin American Agribusiness Development Corporation (LAAD)—had proven over time to be sustainable. Furthermore, it argued, this fund had become sustainable only by shifting from equity funding to more conventional agribusiness lending.

The critique attributed this poor performance to two factors. First, the government bodies often chose the wrong investors to invest in or guarantee. In many cases, the implementing institution had little or no previous experience as a private equity investor. The funds' ability to attract the right individuals to manage the portfolios was often limited by government restrictions on the compensation of the investors. A second problem was the excessive constraints on the implementers. Many private equity funds were given very narrow mandates, such as very small businesses, the agricultural sector, and women-owned businesses. Since the number of potential investments was somewhat limited at best, the sustainability of the funds was severely impacted by these restrictions. In other cases, the government bodies conducted lengthy reviews of potential investments, and consequently the funds lost the opportunity to participate in attractive deals. It should be noted, however, it would have been very difficult to obtain attractive returns from private equity investments in most developing nations during the 1970s and 1980s, even under the best of circumstances.

One source that is likely to become an increasingly important source of capital for private equity funds is retirement savings in the developing nations themselves. East Asian nations have very high savings rates, often about 30% of gross domestic product. These high rates partially reflect the younger average age in developing countries, as

---

[8] James W. Fox, "The Venture Capital Mirage: An Assessment of USAID Experience with Equity Investment," Working paper, Center for Development Information and Evaluation, U.S. Agency for International Development, Washington, D.C., 1996.

well as cultural differences. While many of these individual savings are invested informally in the privately held businesses of relatives and friends, little has been directed into institutional private equity funds.

These patterns are likely to change in future years. Leading the way has been Chile, which has privatized much of its retirement savings. Assets in private pension plans have risen to $25 billion—50% of current GDP. Pension funds have already helped to finance privatization programs in Chile, taking equity positions of between 10% and 35% in privatized firms. As the funds have grown, regulators have increasingly widened the fields in which they can invest. Several are considering initiating private equity investment programs.[9]

THE PRIVATE EQUITY CYCLE: INVESTING

The investment process in developing and developed nations is often very different. In this section, we will discuss four aspects of these differences: the types of deals that are considered, the process by which companies are identified and evaluated, the structuring of the investments, and valuation.

Types of Investments

Private equity funds in developed nations undertake a diverse array of potential transactions. Venture capitalists in the United States usually target high-technology sectors of the economy, while buyout firms focus on more mature firms in a variety of industries which need to restructure or combine. By way of contrast, funds in developing nations generally target already-established firms in traditional industries. (A notable exception is India, where software firms have been successfully attracting investments.)

Typical investments by developing country private equity funds fall into four broad categories. The first are privatizations. The World Bank estimates that 80 countries in recent years have made privatization a primary public-policy concern. More than 7000 large-scale privatizations have been undertaken, at an annual rate of $25 billion per year.[10] Many of these newly privatized enterprises are undercapitalized and desperately need to modernize. The simple distribution of shares to employees or others will not solve their need for financing. In many cases, the national capital markets are still not well developed, and access to international markets is limited to the largest firms. Consequently, governments and the private sector are turning to private equity to fill the investment gap.

A second market opportunity has been corporate restructurings. Globalization has implied increased competition for many businesses in developing countries: lower trade barriers and new regulatory frameworks have forced companies to refocus their activities. Furthermore, the transfer of technologies and techniques from developed nations has provided new challenges, which existing management has often not been capable of meeting. Consequently, many private equity investments in developing nations have focused on either (*i*) purchasing and improving the operations of established firms or

---

[9] For a general overview, see Jim Freer, "The Private Pension Path," *LatinFinance* (July/August 1995), 34–38; for a specific discussion of future investment plans, see Felipe Sandoval, "CORFO Targets Small and Medium Enterprises," *Chile Economic Report* (Summer 1995) 2–9.

[10] These statistics are from William L. Megginson, Robert C. Nash, and Matthias van Randenborgh, "The Financial and Operating Performance of Newly Privatized Firms," *Journal of Finance* 49 (1994) 403–452 (the information is on page 404).

business units, or *(ii)* consolidating smaller businesses to achieve large, more cost-effective enterprises.

The final two categories of private equity investors are unique largely to the developing world. The first of these is investments in strategic alliances. In many cases, major corporations have made strategic investments (acquisitions, joint ventures, and alliances) in developing countries without detailed knowledge of the business environment or their partners. To address these information gaps, corporations have increasingly welcomed private equity funds as third-party investors. The private equity investor is expected to provide much of the informed monitoring of the local partner that the corporation finds difficult to undertake.

A final class of investment has been infrastructure funds. Most infrastructure projects in the developed world have been financed through the issuance of bonds. In some developing nations, particularly in Asia, private equity funds have financed major projects, such as bridges, docks, and highways.

Private equity investors in developing nations are reluctant to make the kinds of early-stage, technology-intensive investments that U.S. venture capitalists specialize in. First, of course, in many markets trained technical talent and the necessary infrastructure (e.g., state-of-the-art research laboratories) are scarce. Second, in many nations intellectual property protection is weak, or the enforcement of these rights questionable. Thus, even if one was able to develop a successful product, it is unclear how rapid imitation could be avoided. A third factor is the difficulty in exiting these investments (discussed in more detail below). Finally, many investors argue that investing in a developing country is already a very risky act. To take on additional business risk would be imprudent. Consequently, they concentrate on mature enterprises with established track records.

Deal Identification and Due Diligence

The screening of investments is a major focus of private equity funds in developed nations. Typically, a venture capitalist in the United States receives several hundred times more proposals than he could invest in. Funds develop broad criteria to select the deals that will later be subject to in-depth evaluation.

In developing countries, private equity investors have to be more opportunistic, since the number of attractive investments is lower. Although deals are identified from the same sources—for example, other entrepreneurs and business intermediaries like lawyers and accountants—most investors adopt a much more active strategy. They exploit tight relationships among business and social groups in the region. This often gives them a first-mover advantage over outside investors without such ties.

The criteria employed by private equity investors are similar in developed and developing nations. In interviews, both sets of investors cite management as the overriding factor in the success of any venture. Many speak of the need for "chemistry" among venture capitalists and the entrepreneur, and seek to evaluate the management team's commitment, drive, honesty, reputation, and creativity. Other criteria—such as the size of the market, the threat of obsolescence, and the ability to exit the investment—are also similar.

In evaluating potential deals, however, private equity investors in developing nations emphasize two sets of risks often not encountered in developed nations. The first of these is country risk. A revolution, for instance, might lead to the nationalization of foreign investments. A more common threat, however, is the potential cost of rent-seeking behavior. The highly regulated infrastructure sector is usually of great concern to investors because politically motivated regulatory changes can directly affect cash flows. Investors need to carefully analyze the institutions and legal framework as well as industry regulations. One very visible example of the potential costs of this behavior was the Enron Dabhol project in India. In this case, the recently elected government of Maharashtra, a state in India, canceled the power plant contract of Enron for the largest proposed foreign investment in India. Accused of bribery and overcharging, Enron agreed to renegotiate the contract even though it claimed already to have spent $300 million on the unfinished plant.[11] Working to limit these dangers, however, may be government's concerns about the reputational consequences of such actions; that is, the potential of their actions to deter future private investment and to invite criticism from multilateral financial organizations.

A second concern is exchange rate risk. Although this is hardly unique to developing countries, the Mexican peso devaluation dramatically demonstrated the volatility of these markets. A major devaluation of a developing nation's currency could lead to a sharp drop in the returns enjoyed by its U.S. investors. Ways to mitigate this risk include entering into currency swaps, purchasing options based on relative currency prices, or purchasing forward currency. Since the nature and timing of future payments is usually unknown to private equity investors, however, exchange risk management poses some real challenges. While hedging tools have attracted increasing interest, their actual use by private equity investors in developing nations appears to be very limited to date.

Deal Structuring

The choice of financing vehicle also differs between developed and developing markets. Investors in developed nations use a variety of instruments, including common and several classes of preferred stock, debt, and convertible preferred. These financial instruments allow the private equity investors to stage investments, allocate risk, control management, provide incentives to executives, and demarcate ownership.

In many developing countries, private equity investors primarily use plain common stock. This choice reflects several factors. First, in several countries, especially in Asia, different classes of stock with different voting powers are not permitted. Thus, investors must seek other ways in which to control the firm. These alternatives are often of extreme importance, since most of the companies are family owned or controlled. Such control rights allow the venture capitalists to step in during such messy controversies such as a dispute between two sons as to who should succeed the father as president.

Although the structure of the investments may differ, shareholder agreements in developed and developing countries are likely to include the same control rights. Among these control rights are affirmative covenants—such as the investors' right to access the firm's premises and records—as well as negative covenants that limit actions that the entrepreneur might take, such as the sale or purchase of significant assets of the firm. Although the terms may be similar, their enforceability may vary. The enforceability of these shareholders' agreements depends strongly on the country or region of the investment. For instance, they are usually enforceable in Latin courts, but they may not hold in some Asian courts like China's.

Pricing

Significant differences also appear in the pricing of transactions in developed and developing nations. Reflecting the later stage of most investments, the types of spectacular

---

[11] For an overview, see Jonathan Bearman, "Death of Enron's Dabhol LNG Project Sends Shockwaves Through Industry," *Oil Daily* 45 (August 9): 1995, 1*ff.*

returns seen in U.S. ventures such as Digital Equipment, Genentech, and Netscape are not often encountered. As William Hambrecht, chairman of the San Francisco–based investment bank Hambrecht & Quist, points out, "Asian investing success in baseball terms is characterized by double and triples, not the occasional home run characteristic of U.S. venture capital."[12]

Venture capitalists' assessment of the value of a company in a developing nation is often problematic. Challenges abound at many levels. For instance, many developing countries lack timely and accurate macroeconomic and financial information. Sometimes macroeconomic variables published by central banks are manipulated by governments to portray a healthier economy. These uncertainties—combined with political and regulatory risks—may make it extremely difficult to draw up reasonably accurate projections. The uncertainty increases further since most private companies do not even have audited financial statements, especially family-run businesses. Furthermore, accounting principles and practices, though improving, are still very different from Western standards.

THE PRIVATE EQUITY CYCLE: EXITING

Perhaps the most vexing aspect of venture investing in developing nations has been the difficulty of exit. The fortunes of private equity investors in the developed world have been largely linked to those of the market for initial public offerings (IPOs). Studies of the U.S. market suggest that the most profitable private equity investments have, on average, been disproportionately exited by way of IPOs. In both Europe and the United States, there has been a strong link between the health of the IPO market and the ability of private equity funds to raise more capital.

Private equity investors in developing countries cannot rely on these offerings. Even in "hot markets" where large foreign capital inflows are occurring, institutional funds are usually concentrated in a few of the largest corporations. Smaller and new firms typically do not attract significant institutional holdings and have much less liquidity.

An illustration of these claims is India, which saw over 2000 IPOs between January 1991 and April 1995. Despite the volume of IPOs, the public market has not been an attractive avenue for exiting private equity investments. The bulk of these offerings appear to be bought by individual investors, who purchase them at huge discounts. (The typical share trades on the day of its offering at 106% above its offering price.) After the offering, trading appears to be very thin for most offerings. For instance, 18% of the offerings do not trade on the day immediately after the offering (most of these apparently never trade again). It would be very difficult for a private equity investor to liquidate a substantial stake in a young firm through this mechanism.[13] The situation in many other emerging markets, which lack the infrastructure of settlement procedures, payment systems, custodial or safekeeping facilities, and regulations, is even bleaker.

Consequently, private equity investors in developing countries have tended to rely on the sale of portfolio firms to strategic investors. This can be problematic, however, when the number of potential buyers is small. The purchaser can exploit the private equity investor's need to exit the investment and can acquire the company for below its

---

[12] Wendi Tanaka, "Advising the Asia Investor: Experts Say It May Be a Gold Mine, But No Quick Rewards," *The San Francisco Examiner,* September 20, 1994.

[13] Ajay Shah, "The Indian IPO Market: Empirical Facts," Working paper, Centre for Monitoring the Indian Economy, Bombay, 1995.

fair value. This is particularly likely to be the case when the firm invests in a strategic alliance: the only feasible purchasers are likely to be the other partners in the alliance.

Several private organizations have tried to develop creative approaches to the exiting problem. Examples include the listing of the shares on an exchange in a developed country and the acquisition of a similar firm in a developed country (which is subsequently merged with the firm in the developing nation). In the years to come this is likely to be an area for continued innovation.

LOOKING FORWARD

The future of private equity in the developing world remains highly uncertain, but there are reasons to be optimistic. The growth in interest among U.S. institutional investors suggests that—at least for the next few years—capital should be available. The increasing involvement of leading private equity organizations in investments in developing nations should increase the quality of the deal selection and management. The evolution of institutions such as national securities exchanges, regulatory agencies, banking systems, and capital markets suggests that the difficult problem of exiting investments may eventually be addressed. Perhaps most persuasively, the types of environments where private equity funds have thrived in the United States are quite similar to those in developing nations: the investors have specialized in financing illiquid, difficult-to-value firms in environments with substantial uncertainty and information asymmetries. In short, it will not be surprising if the private equity industry in developing nations slowly matures, with the investment cycle becoming increasingly similar to that of developed nations.

FURTHER READINGS

STIJN, CLAESSENS AND MOON-WHOAN RHEE, "The Effect of Equity Barriers on Foreign Investment in Developing Countries," Working Paper No. 4579 (1993), National Bureau of Economic Research, Cambridge.

DEAN FOUST, KAREN L. MILLER, AND BILL JAVETSKI, "Special Report: Financing World Growth," *Business Week* (October 3, 1994): 100–103.

JAMES W. FOX, "The Venture Capital Mirage: An Assessment of USAID Experience with Equity Investment," Working Paper, Center for Development Information and Evaluation (1996), U.S. Agency for International Development, Washington, D.C.

DEIRDRE FRETZ, "Emerging Markets' Push for Private Equity," *Institutional Investor* 29 (October 1995): 319–320.

MARK MOBIUS, *The Investors Guide to Emerging Markets* (1992), Burr Ridge, Illinois, Irwin Professional Publishing.

SILVIA B. SAGARI AND GABRIELA GUIDOTTI, "Venture Capital: Lessons from the Developed World for the Developing Markets," Discussion Paper No. 13 (1992), International Finance Corporation, Washington, D.C.

LARRY W. SCHWARTZ, "Venture Abroad: Developing Countries Need Venture Capital Strategies," *Foreign Affairs* 73 (November–December 1994): 14–19.

LISA SEDELNICK, "Sector Funds Surge," *LatinFinance* (December 1995): 13–16.

LORENZO WEISSMAN, "The Advent of Private Equity in Latin America," *The Columbia Journal of World Business* 31 (Spring 1996): 60–98.

14

The Fojtasek Companies and Heritage Partners: March 1995

Randall Fojtasek (pronounced "Phot-ah-shay"), president and CEO of the Fojtasek Companies, drove through the Dallas suburbs early on a Saturday morning in March 1995. The normally crowded streets were empty, Fojtasek mused, but for once he would have welcomed some delays in order to have time to think further. He was on his way to a meeting with his father, Joe Fojtasek, to discuss the future of the window and door manufacturing and distribution company that Joe had founded five decades earlier.

The two Fojtaseks—along with several trusted managers and family members—would be meeting on Monday morning with representatives from the Dallas office of the investment banking firm Bear, Stearns. The company had retained the investment bankers eight months earlier, after a buyout fund had made an initial offer for their family business. Prompted by this outside interest, as well as by the need to address generational succession issues, the Fojtaseks had made the decision to explore the sale of their firm.

The review of the potential choices available to the family had generated not just one but a variety of options. First, several buyout funds had expressed interest in acquiring the firm outright. Although these offers would ensure a healthy payout to the firm's shareholders, it was unclear whether these buyout funds intended to radically restructure the firm. Furthermore, the involvement of the Fojtasek family and the rest of the management team in the firm after a transaction was completed was uncertain.

Second, several of the investment bankers had urged the firm to explore a leveraged recapitalization. Not only were the Fojtaseks uncertain about running the business after assuming such a large level of indebtedness, but there were questions as to whether the family could even arrange such a transaction.

Finally, a private equity group from Boston, Heritage Partners, had urged the firm to consider undertaking a hybrid transaction. Heritage claimed that the transaction would entail lower debt levels, permit continued operating control for the family, and allow the existing shareholders to retain a majority ownership of the firm. As Randall Fojtasek pulled his car into his father's driveway, he wondered what to make of these options.

This case was prepared by Josh Lerner and Sam Hayes. Copyright © 1997 by the President and Fellows of Harvard College. Harvard Business School case 297–046.

THE BUILDING MATERIALS MARKET IN MARCH 1995

Americans spend a great deal of their wealth on their homes. According to the consulting firm F.W. Dodge, the U.S. market for new home construction was estimated at $190 billion in 1994, and the repair and remodeling market at $110 billion. Window products was estimated to represent $2.0 and $4.5 billion of these two markets, respectively. The overall building materials market is closely tied to the cyclical new housing market but is balanced through the countercyclical repair and remodeling market.

The window and door industry was exceedingly fragmented, both by region and product segment. Only a handful of firms had a dominant position in particular niches, as for instance Andersen and Pella do in wooden windows. Most of the industry was dominated by privately held small and midsized companies. The smaller manufacturers typically targeted the custom home builders and lumberyards; the midsized firms focused on the large-volume home builders, major home retail chains, and major distributors. Lumberyards primarily served professional remodelers and small home builders, while the home retail chains targeted the do-it-yourself market.

The market was fragmented, particularly when compared to other mature manufacturing sectors. For instance, in 1992 the U.S. Department of Commerce estimated that 75% of the over 300 establishments in the United States whose primary products were wood doors and windows had fewer than 20 employees. These units accounted for 14% of the employment in the industry. Among manufacturing firms as a whole in the United States, the 67% of the firms with fewer than 20 employees accounted for only 7% of the employment.[1] The industry had recently seen a number of acquisitions, however, as manufacturers sought to achieve wider distribution and better economies of scale. For instance, Caradon had purchased Better-Bilt and Lebanon Aluminum, and Andersen had bought Dashwood Industries in attempts to build a wider customer base.

One of the key reasons for the continuing lack of concentration in this industry is the substantial heterogeneity in the materials used for window and door construction in the United States. Windows and doors are made primarily of three classes of materials: wood, aluminum, and vinyl. Wood is the most thermally efficient of the three products: that is, it provides the best insulation against cold in the winter and heat in the summer. Wood windows and doors, however, are considerably more expensive than those made out of aluminum or vinyl. Furthermore, to be properly maintained, wood windows need more intensive service and tend to be replaced more often than those made out of other materials. Consequently, the share of windows and doors made out of wood had been declining in recent years. Wood still had a strong position in the new construction market for more expensive homes, particularly in the northern United States.

The use of vinyl windows and doors had been growing in recent years. These were generally less expensive than wood products but more costly than aluminum ones. Although newer models were almost as thermally efficient as wood windows and doors and required virtually no maintenance, many high-end builders avoided them on aesthetic grounds. The penetration of vinyl products in the southwestern United States had been limited by their performance under prolonged exposure to bright sunshine. The ultraviolet rays led the vinyl to become brittle, causing unsightly cracks and the degradation of the window's ability to insulate.

Aluminum windows and doors were the lowest in cost and the most durable. They had, however, poor thermal efficiency and an annoying tendency to "sweat," or build up

---

[1] U.S. Department of Commerce, Bureau of the Census, *1992 Census of Manufacturers—Industry Series*, Washington, D.C., Government Printing Office, 1995. Some firms in the survey had multiple manufacturing establishments.

condensation, in cold temperatures. Aluminum windows were the regional standard in the South and Southwest, with the largest markets in Arizona, Florida, Georgia, Nevada, and Texas, but they had little penetration elsewhere. In recent years, technological innovations in the tinting, glazing, and coating of glass have substantially improved the insulating properties of aluminum windows. Another innovation likely to lead to the greater diffusion of these windows was the development of composite windows, which consist of a vinyl composite coating on an aluminum frame. Although these composites cost less than vinyl windows, they retain many of the desirable features of vinyl.

The overall pattern of the unit sales of doors and windows built out of these three materials—in both the new construction and repair/remodeling markets—is summarized in the first panel of Exhibit 1. Similar patterns emerge from federal estimates of the dollar volume of sales. For instance, between 1992 and 1994, shipment of aluminum doors and windows had risen at a 3.6% annual rate, whereas wooden doors and windows had grown at a slightly slower 3.2% rate. Although precise numbers on vinyl windows were not available, the broader category in which they were aggregated had enjoyed considerably faster growth.[2]

Despite the large number of competitors, manufacturers of windows and doors had a considerable degree of market power. It was costly for a distributor to switch manufacturers, because each had a large number of customers who designed houses or renovation projects around certain popular sizes and types of windows and doors. These customers often were resistant to change. In addition, the distributors had to continue to stock replacement parts and screens for discontinued brands. Finally, the demand from builders was highly seasonable and often difficult to predict in advance. As a result, distributors were willing to pay a small premium for reliable delivery, attentive service, and the assurance of an ongoing relationship.

THE FOJTASEK COMPANIES

Lumberman Door and Sash was founded in 1943 in Dallas, Texas by Joe Fojtasek. The firm initially served as a distributor of building materials. In the 1950s, it began manufacturing aluminum windows. Reflecting the company's new, broader focus, it was renamed the Fojtasek Companies. Through a combination of internal growth and acquisition, the firm gradually expanded into wood windows, interior wooden doors, molding materials, and most recently vinyl windows. The firm also owned a series of wholesale distribution centers throughout the Southwest and a contract manufacturing operation that sold aluminum and vinyl extrusions to other firms for use in a wide variety of products.

By 1995, the Fojtasek Companies were among the 10 largest manufacturers and distributors of a wide range of wood, aluminum, and vinyl building materials. Approximately 70% of the firm's sales were to the new home construction market; the remainder were to major retail home center chains. Its brand names—such as Atrium Door and Windows, H-R Windows, and Skotty Aluminum—enjoyed widespread recognition among builders. Although the firm offered a broad array of products, aluminum-based products accounted for about 85% of its sales.

As with other building materials suppliers, Fojtasek's business was quite localized: more than 50% of the firm's sales were in the five largest markets for aluminum doors and windows. In these markets, Fojtasek had an average market share of 24%. It also had a strong presence in several smaller markets, including Mississippi and New

---

[2] U.S. Department of Commerce, *1994 Annual Survey of Manufacturers,* Washington, D.C., Government Printing Office, 1996.

Mexico. The strong link between the firm's sales and the health of the housing markets in these states is shown in the second panel of Exhibit 1.

In recent years, Fojtasek had experienced rapid growth: sales climbed from $46 million in 1991 to $83 million in 1994. (Recent income statements and balance sheets are presented in Exhibit 2.) This was partially due to growth in new home construction in the South and West, which increased at an annual rate of 11.3% and 16.7% in these years. It was also attributable to Fojtasek's aggressive pursuit of new distribution channels and product innovations. The company's strategy was to maximize market penetration in each geographic market where the firm competed. To do this, the firm used several trade names and sold products through a variety of channels, including company-operated distribution centers, lumberyards, home center chains, and building products distributors. In many cases, the firm succeeded in obtaining exclusive relationships with distributors, based primarily on their attention to timely delivery, product quality, service excellence, and price competitiveness.

Although the company had enjoyed almost universal success over the past 12 years, one division had not shared in that growth. The remainder of the firm had grown at an 11% annual rate between 1986 and 1994, but the sales of the Baloleum® Division had actually declined at a 9% rate. This was largely due to a series of strategic miscues by the firm and the unique competitive dynamic of the market niche in which the division competed. Unlike its core businesses, where competitors were highly fragmented, here a strong market leader had succeeded in driving down Fojtasek's sales and profits. The firm had just hired a new general manager and a new plant manager for the division, both of whom had extensive industry experience. These key individuals, along with Fojtasek's senior management, were currently undertaking a major restructuring of the division.

Finally, the firm has attractive prospects for future growth. In particular, it had just introduced a more thermally efficient aluminum window. This had significant cost advantages over vinyl windows and might lead to market penetration in several states adjoining its current strongholds. Second, it had recently opened its own production facility for the manufacture of vinyl windows. The firm intended to rapidly grow its vinyl window business, first using its established brand names and distribution channels to reach its existing customers, and then targeting the northern half of the United States.

HERITAGE PARTNERS

Heritage Partners had its origins in 1986, when the fund's three managing partners had established Equity Partners, a unit of BancBoston Capital. BancBoston Capital was the subsidiary of the Bank of Boston responsible for mezzanine and later-stage equity investments. Each of the three partners—Michael F. Gilligan, Peter Z. Hermann, and Michel Reichert—had extensive experience at the Bank of Boston. Their biographies are reproduced in Exhibit 3.

The fund's founders sought to develop a business strategy that differentiated the new group from other private equity organizations by targeting the market segment of family companies. They then consulted with family business owners to research what the market needed. Between January and August, the partners contacted 245 family businesses; 121 of these CEOs were willing to meet to discuss their future financing needs in depth.

Their interviews highlighted the extent to which these businesses faced an interrelated set of family and financial problems. In many cases, aging founders were seeking to spend more time away from the business. In addition, many felt the need to at least partially liquidate their positions for a variety of reasons, including a need to diversify their portfolios, to provide cash to minority shareholders and children not actively participating in the business, or to make provisions for estate taxes. Furthermore, the partners heard many accounts of situations where family business founders had done no estate planning prior to their death. These situations frequently had very sad outcomes. In many cases, the firm had been sold to cover the huge estate tax obligations to the federal government; in others, disputes over succession and control had led to the damage or even destruction of company and family relationships.

The entrepreneurs seemed not only to be facing similar challenges in effecting a transition across the generations, but also to be sharing perspectives about how they wanted their businesses to be financed. In particular, they were typically adverse to high levels of debt, preferring that their firms' growth be financed through equity. The high levels of debt associated with leveraged buyouts and recapitalizations were often seen as having two disadvantages. First, they limited the opportunities to pursue future growth options that might require substantial capital investments, and the required interest and principal payments were often so large that even a small economic downturn could throw the company into default. Second, the founders were concerned about retaining control of the firms. In particular, they were concerned that financial buyers might seek to wrest away control, once the transaction was completed.

The partners also examined the available literature on family businesses. One often-cited study projected that more than $6.8 trillion would be changing hands through generational transitions in the next two decades, much of which was currently concentrated in private family businesses.[3] The partners estimated that at any one time, about 10% of 42,000 private companies in the United States with sales of more than $25 million were actively pursuing an outright sale, a recapitalization, or the sale of shares to an employee stock ownership plan (ESOP). The remaining 90% of firms, however, faced a wide array of issues that could ultimately lead to a change in ownership or capitalization.

With these concerns in mind, the partners sought to develop a distinctive form of private equity investing that would be responsive to the needs of family businesses. They realized that many of their activities—for example, careful due diligence of prospective deals, active involvement in their portfolio companies, and exiting through an acquisition or initial public offering—would be similar to those undertaken by other private equity firms. There would be three elements, however, that would distinguish them from their peers.

First, the partners targeted a segment of privately held firms that was simultaneously large but inaccessible: mature, but successful, family businesses. They targeted the 90% of firms not currently "in play." They would consider a broad array of firms, from manufacturing to distribution to services companies. Although they would consider firms with sales between $25 and $300 million, they placed a particular emphasis on firms between $50 and $150 million in revenues. At the same time, the partners attempted to limit the risks of the situations in which they invested: firms were expected to have stable profits, rather than being in the midst of restructurings or in industries where earnings were highly variable. High-technology or research-intensive firms that required highly technical knowledge to assess were also avoided.

The second key differentiating aspect was the marketing of their fund to potential portfolio firms. Private equity investors are often deluged with business plans, whether

---

[3] Robert B. Avery and Michael S. Rendall, "Estimating the size and distribution of baby boomers' prospective inheritances," *Proceedings of the Annual Meeting of the American Statistical Association, Social Statistics Section* (1993): 11–19.

from entrepreneurs seeking venture financing or managers striving to spin off corporate divisions. In targeting "not-for-sale" family businesses, however, a much more aggressive marketing effort was required. Consequently, the partners focused on developing a network of over 2000 CEOs, commercial and investment bankers, and business intermediaries such as lawyers and accountants. In working with these intermediaries, they sought to raise their sensitivity to the problems that succession could pose to small firms, as well as learn how the transaction could create value for them (e.g., a liquid entrepreneur was likely to turn over his resources to a private banking group to manage).

The final, most important aspect was how the deals were to be structured. The partners developed a distinctive cornerstone structure—which they dubbed the "Private IPO"®—that responded to the needs of many mature family businesses. Consider, for instance, a firm that could be sold to a leveraged buyout firm for $50 million (see Exhibit 4). This money would flow to the founder and other shareholders, who in turn would relinquish all their equity. In such a typical transaction, the firm would be capitalized with approximately 10% to 20% equity, which would be held by the buyout firm. (Some performance-based warrants would be issued to the key managers.) The debt would be divided between senior debt (typically at a rate of approximately the prime rate plus 2%) and subordinated debt with warrants.

As mentioned earlier, many founders of family businesses were anxious about the loss of control and the hefty interest payments implied by highly leveraged buyouts and recapitalizations. Nor were the other options appealing. Many modest-sized firms in traditional industries would find an initial public offering (IPO) with a reputable underwriter impossible to arrange. Even those firms that could go public were frequently anxious about the degree of public disclosure and scrutiny that being publicly traded entailed. ESOPs involved complex federal regulatory requirements designed to protect the employee–owners and arcane tax concessions granted to both the buyer and seller. The outright sale of the firms to a competitor frequently led to wholesale restructurings, including the frequent closing of manufacturing facilities, the termination of long-time employees, and the loss of the family business.

In a typical "Private IPO,"® the partners would offer a fair market value. (Competing financial buyers would often offer as much as 10% more in an LBO structure, reflecting both a control premium and the greater leverage employed.) In this example, the purchase price would be $45 million. In a "Private IPO,"® the shareholders would only be paid $38 million in cash, not the whole $45 million. But instead of ceding all their ownership, the founder and management would retain 51% of the equity in exchange for $7 million which they would reinvest on a tax-deferred basis in the firm (the difference between the $45 million purchase price and the $38 million cash payment).[4]

The remaining $38 million of the purchase price would be financed from three sources. First, the firm would issue $24 million in senior debt. Because of the lower leverage of this transaction, it was anticipated that the cost of the senior debt would be the prime rate plus 1.5% (as compared to the 2.0% in the more levered structure). In exchange for 49% of the common stock, the fund would invest $7 million. The new corporate charter would include super-majority provisions on a broad range of issues for the fund. These provisions prohibited the firm from undertaking certain steps unless more than a majority (typically 60%) of the shareholders agreed, including distributions, cap-

---

[4] One important advantage of this alternative structure was its implications for estate taxation. If the founder simply sold his shares outright, he would be faced with the challenge of passing on the full value of the firm. In a "Private IPO," he can gift his 51% of the shares immediately after the transaction. In all probability, the founder can value these at the price paid for them at the time of the transaction, with a discount for illiquidity. The subsequent appreciation will not be subject to estate taxes.

ital expenditures, asset purchases or sales, issuance of additional debt, management hiring or firing, and so forth. Finally, the fund would invest an additional $7 million for a block of preferred shares. These preferred shares not only would have an annual dividend (which would not be paid in cash in the first years of the transaction), but also sufficient warrants for common stock to bring the fund's ownership stake in the firm up to 65%. These warrants could only be exercisable, however, if management did not make its projections.[5]

The enthusiasm evidenced in initial interviews—where fully 92% of the CEOs interviewed expressed an interest in the proposed product—was soon borne out in practice. Between 1988 and 1993, Equity Partners had achieved an admirable record. They acquired eight primary companies and made seven add-on acquisitions. By the end of 1993, the successes of this strategy were evident. By this date, two of these investments (representing a total equity investment of $13.2 million and fees of $1.2 million) had been sold, yielding a total return (including dividends) of $57.8 million. The remaining six investments had not yet been realized but had total sales in 1993 of about $490 million and a 1993 EBIT of $38 million. These not-yet-exited firms represented a total investment of $38.5 million, with an additional $2.2 million going to fees. The partners assigned a total value of $53.4 million. (A small amount—$1.3 million—had also been received from these investments in the form of dividends and other payments.) The partners estimated their annual return at the end of 1993 as 81%. Not only had they built a strong reputation and network of relationships that would serve as a substantial competitive advantage, but they had established relationships with many financial institutions that had provided their senior and subordinated debt. (In only one case had they raised debt from the Bank of Boston.)

The independent Heritage Partners was founded in late 1993, when Gilligan, Hermann, and Reichert left the Bank of Boston. In February 1994, they unveiled their private placement memorandum, which sought $125 million for Heritage Fund I, L.P. After obtaining commitments for nearly $200 million, by September 1994 they held a closing (at which point the partnership agreements were signed and the initial capital commitments paid). Rather than taking the entire amount, however, they chose to scale back investors' commitments to $150 million. Although BancBoston Capital was an early investor in the fund, the Pennsylvania Public School Employees' Retirement System took the lead. Other investors included Ameritech, the Bank of America, the Hillman Company, Kleinwort Benson, Lincoln National Life Insurance, Massachusetts Mutual Life Insurance, RogersCasey Alternative Investments, the University of Richmond, and several individuals and family offices. The term sheet from the fund is reproduced in Exhibit 5.

THE DECISION

The Fojtasek family had been actively thinking about making a change in the financial and organizational structure of their company since the spring of 1994. At that point, they had been approached by a buyout organization regarding a possible purchase of the firm. These negotiations—and subsequent developments—had triggered a period of self-evaluation by the Fojtasek family.

Shortly before the offer was received, the firm had gone through a major transition. Prior to 1992, the firm had been managed by founder Joe Fojtasek, along with four general managers. These managers were well seasoned, having spent on average more than

---

[5] At the same time, the partners did not foresee limiting themselves to a single type of transaction. They would, for instance, undertake traditional transactions, such as low-leverage recapitalizations.

20 years at Fojtasek and 30 years in the industry. (This was also true of the second layer of management, which had on average 11 years of experience at Fojtasek and 25 years in the industry.) At age 73, however, Joe Fojtasek had felt that it was time to step aside for the next generation. Fojtasek relinquished his role as chief executive officer to his son Randall in 1992, though he retained the title of chairman of the board. Randall Fojtasek, who was 29 at the time he became president and CEO, had spent two years at the firm and had seven years of industry experience. At the same time, Lou Simi, a 28-year veteran who was one of the general managers, was named executive vice president.

The business was currently owned by Joe Fojtasek (who had the single largest stake) and his five sons. Three of the sons, however, were not active in the business and were eager to liquidate all or some of their investment. The firm also needed to address the challenges posed by the specter of heavy inheritance taxes when ownership of the family businesses was passed to the next generation. Even though the federal tax code makes several provisions for family businesses—for example, if a family business represents at least 35% of an estate's value, inheritance taxes can be paid over a period of 15 years—these taxes can still pose a heavy burden.

The Fojtaseks' interactions with the initial potential financial acquirer had been disappointing. The company had spent over three months engaged in conversation with the buyout fund and had made extensive disclosures of operating and financial information. After initial indications that the fund would offer about $70 million to acquire the company, it made a significantly lower offer. Perhaps even more frustrating, the lowering of the offer did not appear to have been triggered by any disappointing discoveries about the firm.

After this discouraging experience, the Fojtasek family felt that it needed to conduct a more thorough examination of its options. Consequently, it retained the Dallas office of the investment bank Bear, Stearns, which prepared a private placement memorandum describing the company. This memorandum was distributed to a variety of investors. As part of the process, the management team and investment bankers prepared two sets of projections of the firm's future performance. One set they denoted as the most likely projections. They also prepared a base case that used considerably more conservative assumptions. The managers and bankers also identified a set of comparable firms whose valuations might provide useful guidance. These firms are summarized in Exhibit 6.

By March 1995, three different buyout groups had expressed interest in acquiring Fojtasek outright. Their initial offers ranged from $58 to $62 million for the entity. (These offers were for the enterprise as a whole; that is, they were the sum of the purchase price of the equity and the debt that would be taken on.) The investment bankers from Bear, Stearns, however, were confident that they could exploit the competition in order to extract a better valuation for the firm. Based on past experience, they felt it was reasonable to expect a valuation of about $65 million for the transaction.

At the same time, the Fojtasek family had three main reservations about these offers. First, it was clear that these groups intended to implement a substantial restructuring of the firm. The family understood that the persistent losses at the Baloleum® Division needed to be addressed: the division needed either to be radically streamlined or divested to another buyer. More generally, they acknowledged that there were opportunities for cost savings by integrating manufacturing and executive functions across the divisions. At the same time, it was unclear what impact the buyout groups' plans would have on the continued job security of the firm's many long-time employees.

Second, even though the family would no longer have controlling interest in the firm, the Fojtaseks worried about the impact of a buyout on the company's future growth. In particular, the high debt levels associated with the transaction would severely limit the firm's financial flexibility going forward. Much of the firm's success in the past was attributable to the strategic purchase of small, undercapitalized manufacturers and suppliers. The industry continued to be characterized by numerous small firms, and attractive acquisition candidates were abundant. If the firm was to be in a position to take advantage of these opportunities, it would need to avoid taking on a high debt load that would unduly limit its flexibility.

Finally, the buyout firms had been unclear about the extent to which the existing management of Fojtasek would continue to be involved with the firm. This was a particular concern of Randall Fojtasek, who had recently taken over as CEO. In particular, it appeared that some of these groups had a set of seasoned managers who had already taken part in a number of buyout transactions that they had financed. These managers might replace some or all of the management team. Even if the existing management team was not immediately replaced, they worried that any revenue or earnings shortfall would lead to their swift replacement.

In light of the family's concerns about control, the Bear, Stearns bankers urged the family to consider a leveraged recapitalization. Under this plan, the sons active in the business, as well as the management team, could borrow enough money to buy out the interests of their father and the family members not active in the business. Just as in a leveraged buyout, the debt and interest would then be repaid, according to a strict schedule that would absorb most of the cash flow that the firm generated. The end result would be that the equity in the firm would be owned by the Fojtasek family and management rather than controlled by an outside investor.

This financial strategy, however, raised the same concerns about high debt levels that the buyout strategy had posed. In addition, two important ambiguities surrounded the feasibility of the transaction. First, there was some concern about the tax treatment of the payout, which might not be treated as a capital gain but rather as a dividend. Second, there was concern about whether the financing for a leveraged recapitalization involving Fojtasek could be arranged. In many instances, commercial banks were reluctant to finance a transaction in which the managers of a family business received a large cash payout, unless a significant amount of new equity was committed to the firm.

Heritage Partners, on the other hand, had proposed to undertake a "Private IPO."® Following the template outlined above, the purchase price would be $56 million. At the time of the transaction, the Fojtasek Companies would pay off the $4.3 million of long-term debt that was currently outstanding. Thus, the value to the existing equity holders would be $51.7 million. The cash proceeds (less the reinvestment discussed below) would be considered as a capital gain and would consequently be taxable at a lower rate than ordinary income.

Of the $56 million value, $7 million would be reinvested into the firm by the existing shareholders. In return, the existing shareholders would receive 50.1% of the common stock of the new firm. Because this transaction was considered to be an exchange of securities, no tax obligation would be incurred on the $7 million until the new shares were liquidated. Only a subset of the shareholders would invest, primarily those members of the Fojtasek family actively involved in the firm, as well as key managers.

Heritage would arrange the remainder of the financing. First, the fund would invest $7 million for 49.9% of the common stock in the firm. Heritage would also invest another $7 million for a block of preferred shares. These would earn an 8% dividend, which would be accrued in the first three years after the closing; that is, they would be converted into equity of the firm. These shares would also have warrants for the company's common stock, which could be exercised at a nominal price. Finally, the firm would take on $36.25 million in senior debt.[6] The structure of the transaction—using the management and base case projections—is summarized in Exhibits 7 and 8.

Although the equity assigned to management and old shareholders would control 50.1% of the initial voting rights of the firm, it would constitute between 35% and 50.1% of the economic ownership of the firm. In particular, if the firm met the valuation targets specified in the *management* projections, the family and managers would receive 50.1% of the proceeds from the eventual disposition of the firm (e.g., the funds paid by an acquirer for the equity at the time of an IPO). If performance fell below that level, more of the ownership would be assigned to Heritage (through the exercise of warrants attached to the preferred stock). If the firm's valuation at the time of the ultimate sale fell below or to the level stipulated in the *base* case, the management and new shareholders would receive 35% of the proceeds. As the offer letter explained:

> Warrants only convert on the liquidation of Heritage's common stock investment. Between the management case and the Heritage's "Base Case," the warrants convert on a sliding scale basis at liquidation based on the Company's ultimate Terminal Value.

Perhaps the best way to illustrate the division of the ultimate proceeds is through an example. Consider the case, for instance, where Fojtasek was sold four years after the proposed transaction (at the end of 1998). The eventual value of the liquidity event would be compared against the terminal values implied by the base and management cases. In calculating the terminal value implied by the projections, the partners multiplied projected operating earnings by the projected exit multiple (in this case 5.5), then subtracted the projected value of the outstanding debt and preferred stock, and added the projected cash outstanding at the time of the liquidity event. The base case implied a terminal value at the end of year four of $76.0 million: projected EBIT of $17.3 million multiplied by the exit multiple of 5.5, less $10.3 million of debt and $8.8 million of preferred stock. The management case similarly implied a valuation of $118.6 million. If the actual value of the equity at the time of the sale at the end of year four was $100 million, management would receive 43.5% of the proceeds and Heritage 56.5%. (Management's share would be computed as follows: 35% + (($100 − 76)/(118.6 − 76)) *15%.) Heritage prepared cash-flow and valuation analyses of Fojtasek which suggested that in either the base or management case, the investors and managers would enjoy attractive returns. These analyses are summarized in Exhibits 9 and 10.

Although Fojtasek would at least initially retain voting control of the firm, Heritage proposed that it would have a number of protections. As discussed above, it asked that the firm's bylaws be amended so that minority investors would have super-majority rights to block major changes. Heritage would also be represented on the board of directors. The revised board, they suggested, would consist of Randall Fojtasek, two of his key lieutenants, one of Heritage's general partners, and a mutually agreed-upon outsider. Finally, if the firm's performance fell substantially below the level foreseen in the *base* case for four consecutive quarters, Heritage reserved the right to take control of the firm's board of directors.

As Randall and Joe Fojtasek sat down in the family study to consider their options, Randall continued to wonder about Heritage's offer. What would be the costs and benefits? How much real loss of control would the transaction entail, relative to the more traditional leveraged buyouts being proposed? What would be the potential upside to management if the firm was successful?

---

[6] The difference between the $57.25 million of financing raised and the $56 million purchase price would go for legal, accounting, environmental consulting, senior lenders', and other transaction fees. Heritage typically does not charge transaction fees for "Private IPOs."® It would not take a fee in this transaction.

Exhibit 1 Basic Industry Data

Division of Unit Sales of Window and Door Products in the United States

	Aluminum	Wood	Vinyl	Other
New Construction				
1990	52.4%	44.2%	1.2%	2.2%
1991	49.4	47.4	1.7	1.5
1992	57.6	34.9	7.4	0.1
1993	50.7	38.1	11.2	0.0
1994	52.0	37.0	10.9	0.1
Repair and Remodeling				
1990	25.5	34.7	29.3	10.5
1991	25.5	34.6	29.2	10.7
1992	36.8	21.4	39.9	1.9
1993	33.0	21.4	43.7	1.9
1994	33.1	21.3	43.6	2.0
Total Home Construction				
1990	35.0	38.0	19.6	7.4
1991	33.5	38.9	20.1	7.5
1992	43.7	25.9	28.7	1.7
1993	38.5	26.5	33.7	1.3
1994	39.1	26.3	33.2	1.4

Housing Starts and Fojtasek Sales

	U.S. Housing Starts	Core Market Housing Starts	Fojtasek Sales without Baloleum® Division	Fojtasek Sales with Baloleum® Division
1986	1,812	259	30,321	56,599
1987	1,631	189	29,200	61,902
1988	1,488	171	36,509	68,089
1989	1,382	151	39,358	59,635
1990	1,203	155	42,701	55,370
1991	1,011	149	37,830	46,083
1992	1,208	183	45,240	53,954
1993	1,291	205	56,576	66,457
1994	1,429	242	70,525	82,810

Source: Corporate documents.

Exhibit 2   Historical Income Statements and Balance Sheets ($000s)

	1991	1992	1993	1994
Total revenues[a]	$46,083	$53,954	$66,458	$82,833
Cost of goods sold	34,468	36,904	45,472	56,378
Total gross profit	11,615	17,050	20,986	26,455
General administrative[b]	12,991	11,910	14,761	17,482
Operating income	(1,375)	5,141	6,225	8,973
Restate for Baloleum® [c]	(4,047)	(1,706)	(2,415)	(2,363)
Other restatements[d]	(1,314)	(248)	(1,051)	(1,385)
Adjusted EBIT	$3,986	$7,095	$9,691	$12,721
Total interest expense	443	333	245	231
Interest/other income	2,123	686	680	(1,082)
Income before taxes	305	5,494	6,660	7,661
Income taxes	0	71	106	393[e]
Net income	$305	$5,423	$6,554	$7,268

	1991	1992	1993	1994
Assets				
Cash	$2,234	$3,543	$1,888	$ 785
Accounts receivable	4,831	5,600	8,081	10,610
Inventory (LIFO in 1994)	7,070	6,078	7,899	9,421
Other current assets	524	618	762	950
Total current assets	$14,659	$15,839	$18,628	$21,765
Net fixed assets	10,638	11,179	12,668	12,979
Other assets	4,124	4,234	2,840	3,286
Total assets	$29,421	$31,252	$34,136	$38,030
Liabilities & Shareholders Equity				
Accounts payable	$891	$995	$1,679	$3,804
Accrued expenses	2,543	1,979	2,441	3,031
Current long-term debt	954	941	2,221	671
Total current liabilities	$4,388	$3,915	$6,341	$7,506
Existing long-term debt	6,106	5,138	2,986	4,286
Total liabilities	$10,494	$9,054	$9,327	$11,792
Common stock	315	315	315	315
Retained earnings	18,612	21,883	24,494	25,923
Total equity	$18,927	$22,198	$24,809	$26,237
Total liabilities and equity	$29,421	$31,252	$34,136	$38,030

[a]EBIT is presented on a FIFO basis (the company moved to LIFO in 1994).

[b]Projected G&A is net of corporate services, franchise taxes, and outside interest.

[c]Baloleum® restatement is used to create adjusted EBIT, which represents the EBIT had the Baloleum® Division not been active.

[d]Other restatements for one-time or non-recurring items. 1991 also includes a $1.2 million restatement for pension termination expense.

[e]Because the company was structured as an S-corporation, the firm paid no Federal taxes. (Like a partnership, tax obligations flowed through to the shareholders.)

Source: Corporate documents.

Exhibit 3   Biographies of General Partners

Michel Reichert   43, Managing General Partner, orchestrates the group's overall activities. He works closely with Mr. Hermann in the formulation as well as the execution of the marketing strategy and origination effort. He is also actively involved with Mr. Gilligan in the negotiation of deal terms and conditions, and oversees management of the portfolio. Before establishing Equity Partners, Mr. Reichert was asked in 1984 to manage a team of lenders covering California and the Northwest, territories the bank had repeatedly tried to penetrate unsuccessfully. In two years, the unit grew substantially and more than tripled its asset base. Prior experiences at the bank included four years as a Vice President responsible for U.S.-based multinational companies, a year in the Bank's asset review unit and a six month training program commencing in July 1979. Before joining the Bank, Mr. Reichert worked for over a year for a French engineering company headquartered in Chateauroux, France. During that time he was asked to establish a subsidiary involved in a related field and was made its CEO in 1978. At its height, the subsidiary had 60 employees. From 1973 to 1977, Mr. Reichert worked for the Brazilian subsidiary of the French multinational Saint Gobain, ultimately as Director of Budget and Planning. Mr. Reichert is a graduate of the University of Bourges, France with a specialty in Business Administration. He is married and has two children.

Peter Z. Hermann   40, General Partner, co-founded Equity Partners and is primarily responsible for transaction origination, development of marketing strategy and new product creation. Working with Mr. Reichert, he is actively engaged in all aspects of investment transactions up to the signing of the Letter of Intent. After closing, Mr. Hermann plays a central role in the generation of add-on investments for portfolio companies. Prior to the founding of Equity Partners in 1986, Mr. Hermann spent seven years at the Bank of Boston specializing in acquisition and multinational finance. After joining the bank in 1979 and completing his training program (followed by a year spent in the problem loan work-out area), he was asked to manage a $325 million loan portfolio comprised of project finance, sovereign risk, inter-bank and corporate lending. In 1984, he was recruited by Mr. Reichert to spearhead the lending effort of a new team focused on California and the Northwest, and established a deal origination network based on West Coast intermediaries and principals. This effort generated a substantial flow of highly profitable lending opportunities in LBO transactions. In June 1986, Mr. Reichert and Mr. Hermann founded the unit of the Bank of Boston that later became Equity Partners. Mr. Hermann has a BA and MA from the University of Sussex, England and an M. Phil in business and economics from Oxford University. He is married and has two children.

Michael F. Gilligan   38, General Partner, is principally responsible for orchestrating the acquisition process from immediately after the selection of Heritage as the buyer. In this capacity, he negotiates with the sellers and management deal terms and conditions from Letter of Intent stage and oversees the business due diligence and underwriting processes. Mr. Gilligan also manages the placement of senior and subordinated debt along with the overall relationship with Heritage's key lenders. He has been actively engaged in the management if EP's investment in most portfolio companies, and, in conjunction with Michael Reichert, has coordinated the development and execution of the companies' business plans. Finally, he also orchestrates the perpetual refinement and ultimate execution of the exit strategies, leading the negotiations. Prior to assuming his role with EP, Mr. Gilligan had developed an extensive background with the Bank of Boston. Following an undergraduate liberal arts degree from Boston College in 1977 and completion of the Bank's management training program, Mr. Gilligan commenced his lending career in the Bank's Multinational Lending Division. Following four years, Mr. Gilligan spent twelve months in the Bank's Middle Market Lending Division, where he assumed responsibility for $125 million in credit facilities and the group's prospecting efforts. Mr. Gilligan then joined the Bank's Entertainment Lending Division, where he managed over $300 million in credit facilities. In his final assignment before joining EP, Mr. Gilligan was asked to co-manage the Bank's Loan Officer Development Program. Mr. Gillian is married and has two children.

Source: Corporate documents.

279

Exhibit 4   Typical LBO Structure vs. The Private IPO®

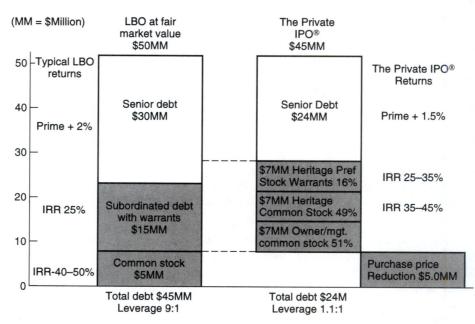

(MM = $Million)

Source: Corporate documents.

Exhibit 5   Excerpts from Heritage Fund I, L.P. Term Sheet

Overview:	Heritage Fund I, L.P. ("Heritage" or the "Fund") has been formed to make equity and equity-related investments primarily in acquisitions of private companies. Heritage expects to invest in mature, highly successful businesses, with strong management teams, solid market shares and stable cash flows.
Fund Size:	Heritage is seeking commitments aggregating $150 million.
Minimum Commitment:	Each limited partner will be expected to contribute a minimum of $5 million to the Fund.
General Partner:	HF Partners I, L.P., a Delaware corporation (the "General Partner"), of which Michel Reichert, Peter Z. Hermann and Michael F. Gilligan are individual members, is the general partner of the Fund.
Management:	Heritage Partners Management Company, Inc., a Delaware corporation (The "Management Company"), of which Michel Reichert, Peter Z. Hermann and Michael F. Gilligan are Directors, will enter into a Management Agreement with the Fund to originate, analyze, close, monitor and divest the Fund's investments.
Closing:	An initial closing may be held when the Fund obtains commitments totaling at least $50 million. The final closing will take place no more than one year after the initial closing.
Drawdowns:	At the initial closing of the Fund, the General Partner and each Limited Partner (collectively the "Fund Partners") will contribute two percent of its committed capital. Additional commitments will be drawn as needed, on a minimum of 10 days prior notice. As used in this Summary of Terms, "Committed Capital" means the aggregate amount committed by a Fund Partner, whether or not it is actually invested.
Allocations:	Income and gain on investment will be allocated as follows: (i) *first*, to all Fund Partners, until they have received a 10% annual rate of return (the "Preferred Return") on all of their invested capital, (ii) *second*, to the General Partner until it has received 20% of all income and gains allocated to that point, and (iii) *third*, 80% to all Fund Partners in proportion to their Committed Capital and 20% to the General Partner.
GP Capital:	The General Partner will invest an amount equal to 1% of all capital invested by the Fund Partners, and will be entitled to allocations which are proportionate to the Limited Partners, with respect to such invested capital.
Distributions:	Subject to the following paragraph, distributions will be made (i) *first,* to the Fund Partners, on a pro rata basis, until all of the Fund Partners' invested capital has been returned, and (ii) *second,* to the Fund Partners in accordance with the allocations described above.
	The Fund may distribute the proceeds of an investment without first returning capital or paying the Preferred Return on other investments held by it if, at the time of distribution, the fair market value of its other investments is at least 120% of the amount necessary to return capital and pay the Preferred Return on those other investments (as determined by the General Partner and the Advisory Board).
Timing of Distributions; Tax Distributions	The Fund will distribute proceeds from investments, less reasonable reserves as soon as practicable, and will use reasonable efforts to distribute a sufficient amount of cash to enable Fund Partners to pay taxes on allocations of income and gain from the Fund.
Investment Period:	The Fund may make investments from the initial closing until the earlier of (i) the date when all Committed Capital of the Fund has been invested, and (ii) the fifth

anniversary of the final closing (the "Investment Period"). Committed Capital not drawn down or committed for investment by the end of the Investment Period will, with certain exemptions, be released from further obligation.

Diversification: The Fund will invest no more than 20% of its Committed Capital in any single investment.

Management Fee: The Fund will pay the Management Company an annual management fee of (i) 2.0% of the Fund's Committed Capital, during the Investment Period, and (ii) 2.0% of the Fund's Committed Capital which is then invested in investments held by the Fund (determined on a cost basis), after the Investment Period. Management fees will be reduced by 100% of all transaction, break-up and monitoring fees received by the Management Company.

Organization Expenses: The Management Company will bear all organization expenses, including legal and accounting fees in connection with the organization of the Fund, in excess of $250,000.

Transaction and Operating Expenses: In addition to all normal operating expenses, the Management Company will bear all expenses relating to investments which do not close unless a letter of intent or purchase agreement has been signed, in which case the Fund will bear such expenses.

Advisory Board: The Fund's advisory board will comprise representatives of at least three limited partners. The Board's role will be one of counsel to the General Partner in connection with new investments, conflicts of interest that may arise from time to time and other operating issues concerning the Fund. In addition, the advisory board will determine valuations of portfolio investments of the Fund based on information provided by the General Partner. The General Partner will ultimately retain responsibility for all operational and investment decisions.

Co-Investment: Investors may be offered co-investment opportunities in equity investments of the Fund and may also be offered the opportunity to provide senior or subordinated debt for such investments.

Term: The Fund will continue in existence for 10 years, but may be extended for up to two additional years to permit the orderly disposition of its investments.

Tax Exempt Partners: The Fund will use its best efforts to qualify as a "venture capital operating company."

Withdrawal and Transfer: Fund Partners may not withdraw from the Fund, and may not transfer their interests, without the consent of the General Partner.

Other Activities: Until the earlier of (i) the date on which at least 75% of the Committed Capital of the Fund has been invested or committed for investment, and (ii) the end of the Investment Period, the principals of the General Partner will not establish another investment fund.

Reports: Fund Partners will receive audited annual financial statements and unaudited quarterly financial statements of the Fund.

Indemnification: The Fund will indemnify the General Partner, the Management Company and their affiliates against all claims, liabilities, damages and expenses, including legal fees, relating to the Fund, in the absence of gross negligence, fraud or willful violation of law.

Legal Opinions: The Fund will receive an opinion from Choate, Hall & Stewart, counsel to the Fund, to the effect that for U.S. Federal income tax purposes, the Fund will be treated as a Partnership and not as an association taxable as a corporation.

Source: Corporate documents.

Exhibit 6   Comparable Publicly Traded Companies ($ millions)

	ABT Building Products Corp.	Elcor Corp.	Falcon Building Products, Inc.	International Aluminum	Ply-Gem Industries	TJ International, Inc.	Simpson Manufacturing, Inc.
Ticker:	ABTC	ELK	FB	IAL	PGI	TJCP	SMCO
Location:	Neenah, WI	Dallas, TX	Chicago, IL	Monterey Park, CA	New York, NY	Boise, ID	Pleasanton, CA
Business Description:	A leading manufacturer of specialty building products made from hard board and plastics that serve as substitutes to natural wood and ceramic tile. The Company's products are sold to wholesalers, home center retailers, manufactured housing builders, and industrial finishers.	Makes and sells asphalt roofing material, including fiberglass asphalt shingles. Produces other industrial products including: hard chrome plating, solid waste and paper balers, and scrap metal recycling equipment.	Leading domestic manufacturer and distributor of air distribution products: ceramic, enameled steel, and acrylic bathroom fixtures; and air compressors, electric generators, pressure washers, and OEM compressors.	An integrated manufacturer and supplier of aluminum, wood, vinyl, and glass products. The Company's products include windows, doors, tub enclosures, aluminum extrusions, and glass furniture.	The Company produces and markets specialty products for home improvement and filtration. Products include: bi-fold doors, skylights, paneling, and filtration devices for air pollution control.	Manufacturer of wood building products for residential, light commercial, and industrial construction.	Manufacturer of connectors and venting systems for gas and wood-burning appliances. The Company markets its products to the residential, light industrial, commercial, remodeling, and do-it-yourself markets.
Market capitalization	155.68	215.26	223.29	102.07	278.29	300.26	121.21
Shareholders equity	80.48	85.23	-24.55	103.43	161.64	240.56	66.52
Beta	0.59	0.88	a	0.63	1.54	1.12	b
Total assets	143.54	108.23	187.46	129.03	345.57	614.48	80.31
Working capital	42.01	39.51	-27.20	63.45	110.50	126.08	44.13
Cash	0.22	5.92	2.22	15.70	14.40	57.63	5.81
Long-term debt	33.12	0.00	103.79	1.10	86.66	102.50	0.00
Sales	203.26	157.03	440.66	174.77	796.42	618.88	151.29
EBIT	37.65	25.13	51.74	11.61	-4.47	48.84	14.12
Depreciation	5.41	4.39	12.43	4.70	13.39	28.34	3.97
Net income	21.75	14.74	25.88	8.80	-8.53	8.85	5.45

Cumulative annual growth rate (CAGR), 1992-1994

(%)							
Net income	78.45	33.14	40.25	216.86	c	10.01	-31.61
Sales	17.07	2.62	18.35	5.07	13.05	24.31	32.80
EBIT	124.70	61.74	14.46	166.77	c	d	-2.96

Note: All data is for year-end 1994 or the 1994 calendar year.
a Only began trading in November 1994; not enough data to calculate beta.
b Only began trading in May 1994; not enough data to calculate beta.
c Negative 1994 net income and EBIT; growth rate calculation is not meaningful.
d Negative 1992 EBIT; growth rate calculation is not meaningful.

Exhibit 6 (continued)   Analysis of Comparable Transactions, 1990-1993 ($ millions)

	SPX Corp. (Truth Division)	Ritz Pillar Ltd.	Abitibi-Price Bldg. Products	Robertson-Ceco Doors, Versacor	American Door, Mohawk Flush Doors, Castlegate	M. Kamenstein Inc.	Philips Industries
Target							
Acquirer	FKI PLC	MB-Caradon	Investor Group	Canadian Pacific, Ltd.	Canadian Premdor, Inc.	CHSMK Corp.	Tomkins PLC
Announcement date	10/01/93	8/25/93	8/22/92	11/22/91	7/09/91	6/11/91	6/05/90
Business Description	Producer of hardware for windows, doors, and skylights	Products include wood, storm windows and doors, door bells and chimes, automotive frames and residential replacement windows	Manufacturer of wall panels	Pennsylvania manufacturer of siding, doors and insulation	Door manufacturer	New York manufacturer of kitchen cabinets	Ohio manufacturer of ventilation equipment, fiberglass bathtubs and plastic plumbing fixtures, aluminum and wooden doors and windows and truck axles and conveyor equipment
Offer for equity	$102.8	$1,217.8	$95.8	$135.0	$35.0	$26.2	$529.0
Offer for equity to:							
Book value	2.6X	NA	1.4X	1.6X	NA	2.0X	2.4X
LTM e net income	16.2X	20.5X	20.8X	NA	NA	9.4X	NM
Offer for assets	$108.2	$1,228.3	$96.2	$135.1	$35.0	$26.6	$587.4
Offer for assets to:							
LTM revenues	1.3X	0.8X	0.6X	0.5X	0.3X	0.6X	0.6X
LTM EBIT	10.4X	9.8X	10.8X	15.1X	7.3X	5.7X	10.0X
3 year average	NA	NA	NA	NA	NA	8.3X	8.3X
LTM EBITDA	NA	NA	6.1X	10.3X	NA	5.2X	6.9X
3 year average EBITDA	NA	NA	NA	NA	NA	7.4x	6.3X
Net assets	2.7X	1.7X	1.4X	1.5X	NA	2.0X	2.1X
Target							
3 year revenue CAGR	NA	-0.8%	NA	NA	NA	16.8%	15.7%
LTM EBIT margin	12.5%	7.9%	6.0%	3.4%	3.8%	11.1%	8.3%
LTM EBITDA margin	NA	NA	10.6%	5.0%	NA	12.1%	9.2%

e LTM = Last twelve months'.

Source: Compiled from Compustat, SEC filings, and corporate documents.

Exhibit 7 Pro Forma Income Statements and Balance Sheets: Management Case ($000s)

	1994	Projected				
		1995	1996	1997	1998	1999
Total revenues	$82,833	$97,329	$111,929	$128,718	148,026	$170,229
CGS-Material (FIFO)[a]		50,299	57,439	66,223	76,280	88,370
CGS-Labor		11,342	12,782	14,318	16,063	18,107
CGS-Overhead		5,393	5,976	6,437	7,151	8,028
Total cost of goods sold	$56,378	$67,033	$76,198	$86,978	$99,494	$114,502
Total gross profit	$26,455	$30,296	$35,730	$41,740	$48,531	$55,727
General & administrative[b]		4,904	5,389	6,173	7,082	8,140
Selling		4,417	5,001	5,736	6,604	7,605
Delivery		6,317	7,308	8,368	9,596	11,029
Bonuses		548	608	640	677	716
Total operating expenses	17,482	16,186	18,305	20,916	23,959	27,491
Operating income	$8,973	$14,110	$17,426	$20,824	$24,573	$28,237
Restate for Baloleum®	(2,363)	0	0	0	0	0
Other restatements	(1,385)	0	0	0	0	0
Adjusted EBIT	$12,721	$14,110	$17,426	$20,824	$24,573	$28,237
Revolver interest		994	983	798	501	165
Term debt interest		2,616	2,108	1,531	848	61
Total interest expense	231	$3,610	$3,091	$2,329	$1,349	$226
Interest/other income	(1,082)	0	0	(0)	0	0
Income before taxes	$7,661	$10,500	$14,334	$18,495	$23,223	$28,011
Income taxes	393	4,200	5,734	7,398	9,289	11,204
Net income	$7,268	$6,300	$8,601	$11,097	$13,934	$16,807
Beginning net worth		(5,840)[c]	460	9,061	20,158	33,386
Plus net income		6,300	8,601	11,097	13,934	16,807
Less dividends		(560)	(605)	(653)	(705)	(705)
Plus increase in equity[d]		560	605	653	0	0
Ending net worth		460	9,061	20,158	33,386	49,487

[a]EBIT is presented on a FIFO basis (the company moved to LIFO in 1994).
[b]Projected G&A is net of corporate services, franchise taxes, and outside interest.
[c]Heritage proposed to structure the transaction in order to accommodate " recapitalization accounting": the firm's net worth would be reduced by the proceeds of the transaction, resulting in a negative net worth. In this way, the firm will not need to amortize goodwill in the future.
[d]The dividend would be accrued in the first three years after the closing: *i.e.*, it would be converted into equity of the firm.

Exhibit 7 (continued)   Management Case

	1994	Day One	1995	1996	1997	1998	1999
Assets							
Cash	$ 785	$ 0	$ 0	$ 0	$ 0	$ 0	$ 5,079
Accounts receivable	10,610	10,610	12,466	14,336	16,487	18,960	21,804
Inventory (LIFO in '94)	9,421	9,421	11,069	12,730	14,639	16,835	19,360
Other current assets	950	950	950	950	950	950	950
Total current assets	$21,765	$20,980	$24,485	$28,016	$32,075	$36,744	$47,193
Net fixed assets	$12,979	$12,979	$13,227	$13,369	$13,396	$13,295	$13,055
Other assets	3,286	3,286	3,286	3,286	3,286	3,286	3,286
Total assets	$38,030	$37,245	$40,998	$44,671	$48,757	$53,325	$63,533
Liabilities and shareholders equity							
Accounts payable	$3,804	$3,804	$4,470	$5,141	$5,912	$6,799	$7,818
Accrued expenses	3,031	3,031	3,561	4,095	4,709	5,416	6,228
Current long-term debt	671	671	0	0	0	0	0
Total current liabilities	$7,506	$7,506	$8,031	$9,236	$10,621	$12,214	$14,046
Revolver	0	9,000	9,928	8,796	6,400	3,146	0
Term loan	0	26,579	22,579	17,579	11,579	4,579	0
Long-term debt	4,286	0	0	0	0	0	0
Total unsubordinated debt	$4,286	$35,579	$32,507	$26,374	$17,978	$7,725	0
Total liabilities	$11,792	$43,085	$40,538	$35,610	$28,599	$19,939	$14,046
Preferred stock	0	7,000	7,560	8,165	8,818	8,818	8,818
Common stock	315	14,000	14,000	14,000	14,000	14,000	14,000
Retained earnings	25,923	(26,840)	(21,100)	(13,104)	(2,660)	10,568	26,669
Total equity	$26,237	($5,840)	$460	$9,061	$20,158	$33,386	$49,487
Total liabilities and equity	$38,030	$37,245	$40,998	$44,671	$48,757	$53,325	$63,533

1994 data are the actual numbers; all others are projections using base case numbers.

Source: Corporate documents.

Exhibit 8   Pro Forma Income Statements and Balance Sheets: Base Case ($000s)

	1994	Projected				
		1995	1996	1997	1998	1999
Total revenues	$82,833	$91,117	$95,673	$100,456	$105,479	$110,753
CGS-Material (FIFO)[a]		47,088	49,097	51,683	54,355	57,494
CGS-Labor		10,618	10,926	11,174	11,446	11,780
CGS-Overhead		5,048	5,108	5,024	5,096	5,222
Total cost of goods sold	$56,378	$62,755	$65,131	$67,881	$70,897	$74,496
Total gross profit	$26,455	$28,362	$30,541	$32,575	$34,582	$36,257
General & administrative[b]		4,591	4,606	4,817	5,047	5,296
Selling		4,135	4,274	4,476	4,705	4,948
Delivery		5,914	6,246	6,530	6,838	7,176
Bonuses		548	608	640	677	716
Total operating expenses	17,482	15,188	15,735	16,464	17,267	18,136
Operating income	$8,973	$13,174	$14,807	$16,111	$17,315	$18,121
Restate for Balunimum	(2,363)	0	0	0	0	0
Other restatements[c]	(1,385)	0	0	0	0	0
Adjusted EBIT	$12,721	$13,174	$14,807	$16,111	$17,315	$18,121
Revolver interest		971	934	793	659	538
Term debt interest		2,616	2,108	1,531	848	61
Total interest expense	231	$3,587	$3,042	$2,324	$1,507	$599
Interest/other income	(1,082)	0	0	0	0	0
Income before taxes	$7,661	$9,588	$11,765	$13,787	$15,809	$17,522
Income taxes	393	3,835	4,706	5,515	6,323	7,009
Net income	$7,268	$5,573	$7,059	$8,272	$9,485	$10,513
Beginning net worth[c]		(5,840)	(88)	6,971	15,244	24,023
Plus net income		5,753	7,059	8,272	9,485	10,513
Less dividends		(560)	(605)	(653)	(705)	(705)
Plus increase in equity[d]		560	605	653	0	0
Ending net worth		(88)	6,971	15,244	24,023	33,831

[a]EBIT is presented on a FIFO basis (the company moved to LIFO in 1994).
[b]Projected G&A is net of corporate services, franchise taxes, and outside interest.
[c]Heritage proposed to structure the transaction in order to accommodate "recapitalization accounting": the firm's net worth would be reduced by the proceeds of the transaction, resulting in a negative net worth. In this way, the firm will not need to amortize goodwill in the future.
[d]The dividend would be accrued in the first three years after the closing: *i.e.*, it would be converted into equity of the firm.

Exhibit 8 (continued)   Base Case

	1994	Day One	1995	1996	1997	1998	1999
Assets (at yr end)							
Cash	$ 785	$ 0	$ 0	$ (0)	$ 0	$ 0	$ 3,421
Accounts receivable	10,610	10,610	11,671	12,254	12,867	13,510	14,186
Inventory (LIFO in '94)	9,421	9,421	10,363	10,881	11,425	11,986	12,596
Other current assets	950	950	950	950	950	950	950
Total current assets	$21,765	$20,980	$22,983	$24,085	$25,241	$26,456	$31,153
Net fixed assets	$12,979	$12,979	$13,227	$13,369	$13,396	$13,295	$13,055
Other assets	3,286	3,286	3,286	3,286	3,286	3,286	3,286
Total assets	$38,030	$37,245	$39,496	$40,740	$41,923	$43,037	$47,493
Liabilities and shareholders equity							
Accounts payable	$3,804	$3,804	$4,185	$4,394	$4,614	$4,845	$5,087
Accrued expenses	3,031	3,031	3,334	3,500	3,675	3,859	4,052
Current long-term debt	671	671	0	0	0	0	0
Total current liabilities	$7,506	$7,506	$7,518	$7,894	$8,289	$8,704	$9,139
Revolver	0	9,000	9,486	8,295	6,812	5,731	4,523
Term loan	0	26,579	22,579	17,579	11,579	4,579	0
Long-term debt	4,286	0	0	0	0	0	0
Total unsubordinated debt	$4,286	$35,579	$32,065	$25,874	$18,390	$10,310	$4,523
Total liabilities	$11,792	$32,085	$39,583	$33,768	$26,679	$19,013	$13,662
Preferred stock	0	7,000	7,560	8,165	8,818	8,818	8,818
Common stock	315	14,000	14,000	14,000	14,000	14,000	14,000
Retained earnings	25,923	(26,840)	(21,648)	(15,193)	(7,574)	1,205	11,013
Total equity	$26,237	($5,840)	($88)	$6,971	$15,244	$24,023	$33,831
Total liabilities and equity	$38,030	$37,245	$39,496	$40,740	$41,923	$43,037	$47,493

1994 data are the actual numbers; all others are projections using base case numbers.

Source: Corporate documents.

Exhibit 9   Heritage Projections of Cash Flows from Heritage Investment ($000s)

	1994	1995	1996	1997	1998	1999
USING BASE CASE PROJECTIONS						
Revenues	$82,833	$91,117	$95,673	$100,456	$105,479	$110,753
EBIT	12,721	13,174	14,807	16,111	17,315	18,121
- Cash taxes	(393)	(3,835)	(4,706)	(5,515)	(6,323)	(7,009)
+ Depreciation	1,268	1,052	1,158	1,273	1,401	1,541
+/- Change in working capital	(1,336)	(1,320)	(726)	(762)	(800)	(840)
- Non-discretionary capital expenditure	(2,203)	(1,300)	(1,300)	(1,300)	(1,300)	(1,300)
Operating cash flow	$10,057	$7,772	$9,233	$9,807	$10,292	$10,513
Debt service requirements						
Revolver interest	0	(971)	(934)	(793)	(659)	(538)
Term loan interest	(231)	(2,616)	(2,108)	(1,531)	(848)	(61)
Current long-term debt	(2,221)	0	0	0	0	0
Total debt service	($2,452)	($3,587)	(3,042)	(2,324)	($1,507)	(599)
USING MANAGEMENT PROJECTIONS						
Revenues	$83,833	$97,329	$111,929	$128,718	$148,026	$170,229
EBIT	17,721	14,110	17,426	20,824	24,573	28,237
- Cash taxes	(393)	(4,200)	(5,734)	(7,398)	(9,289)	(11,204)
+ Depreciation	1,268	1,052	1,158	1,273	1,401	1,541
+/- Change in working capital	(1,336)	(2,309)	(2,326)	(2,675)	(3,076)	(3,537)
- Non-discretionary capital expenditure	(2,203)	(1,300)	(1,300)	(1,300)	(1,300)	(1,300)
Operating cash flow	10,057	7,353	9,224	10,724	12,308	13,736
Debt service requirements						
Revolver interest	0	(994)	(983)	(798)	(501)	(165)
Term loan interest	(231)	(2,616)	(2,108)	(1,531)	(848)	(61)
Current long-term debt	(2,221)	0	0	0	0	0
Total debt service	(2,452)	(3,610)	(3,091)	(2,329)	(1,349)	(226)

1994 data are the actual numbers (adjusted EBIT rather than EBIT is presented); all others are projected. The yield on Treasury bonds maturing in ten years was 7.20% in March 1995; the prime rate was 9.0%.

Source: Corporate documents.

Exhibit 10   Heritage Assessment of Returns from Fojtasek Investment ($000s)

	Day 1	Year 1	Year 2	Year 3	Year 4	Year 5
USING BASE CASE PROJECTIONS						
Heritage Preferred Stock						
Basis	(7,000)	0	0	0	0	7,000
Dividends	0	0	0	0	705	2,523
Cash flow =	(7,000)	0	0	0	705	9,523
IRR = 8.0%						
Heritage Common Stock						
Cash flow =	(7,000)	0	0	0	0	58,334
IRR = 52.8%						
Heritage Blended Cash Flow/Return	(14,000)	0	0	0	705	67,858
IRR = 37.5%						
Management Common Stock						
Cash flow =	(7,000)	0	0	0	0	31,411
IRR = 35.0%						
USING MANAGEMENT PROJECTIONS						
Heritage Preferred Stock						
Basis	(7,000)	0	0	0	0	7,000
Dividends	0	0	0	0	705	2,523
Cash flow =	(7,000)	0	0	0	705	9,523
IRR = 8.0%						
Heritage Common Stock						
Cash flow =	(7,000)	0	0	0	0	75,782
IRR = 61.0%						
Heritage Blended Cash Flow/Return	(14,000)	0	0	0	705	85,306
IRR = 43.9%						
Management Common Stock						
Cash flow =	(7,000)	0	0	0	0	75,782
IRR = 61.0%						

Both scenarios foresee an initial purchase price of $56 million and an exit in year 5 at a multiple of 5.5 times the EBIT in that year.

Source: Corporate documents.

Aberlyn Capital Management: July 1993

In early July 1993, several senior managers of Aberlyn—Lawrence Hoffman, David Sakura, Douglas Brian, and Dana Ono—sat down to consider a novel proposal. Aberlyn was an emerging company in the nascent venture leasing business, which leased tangible assets such as laboratory equipment to high-risk young firms. In exchange for undertaking these financial transactions, Aberlyn was compensated with promised regular cash payments as well as warrants to purchase the common stock of the firms for which it provided financing. The proposed new deal called for Aberlyn to base a lease on an intangible asset: the patent of a biotechnology firm. A firm, RhoMed, would sell its patent to Aberlyn and then lease it back for the life of the three-year deal. As Aberlyn's management met to consider the proposal, they had to ponder several issues. How much was the U.S. patent on which they were basing the lease (U.S. Patent #4,940,670) really worth? Was Aberlyn being fairly compensated? What were the risks in this novel transaction? There were also intriguing long-run questions to consider. If this transaction was successful, how could Aberlyn—as a new and relatively small player in the venture leasing business—capture the most profits from its innovation?

ABERLYN CAPITAL MANAGEMENT

Aberlyn was established in 1989 to provide investment banking services to the biotechnology and biomedical industries. It provided capital to its clients through bridge financings, private placements, and (since 1992) venture leasing, and it also advised them on mergers and other business development activity.

In order to access the capital markets, Aberlyn joined forces with a Dutch investment bank, MeesPierson, N.V. As a result of an early 1993 merger, MeesPierson was one of the largest merchant banks in Europe, with over $40 billion in assets. It was a subsidiary of ABN-AMRO Holding, N.V., which was the world's eighteenth largest bank with assets over $250 billion in 1993. In addition to providing Aberlyn with operating capital, MeesPierson played a key role in raising funds from individual investors in Europe and the Middle East for Aberlyn's first venture leasing fund.[1]

This case was prepared by Josh Lerner and Peter Tufano. Copyright © 1994 by the President and Fellows of Harvard College. Harvard Business School case 294-083.

[1] Because Aberlyn's limited partners were overseas investors, they faced a considerably different tax environment than Aberlyn's U.S.-based general partners.

Aberlyn concluded that the biotechnology sector would be a suitable candidate for venture lease transactions. At least three factors supported this conclusion. First, biotechnology was representing an increasing share of venture transactions. This reflected both the accelerating pace of technological progress in this area and the public market's interest in these securities. Second, the biotechnology firms' ability to access the public markets was quite uneven, with lengthy droughts while the "financing window" was shut. Compounding these cycles, during periods when public financing was scarce, venture capitalists also became less willing to fund new firms. During these droughts, industry executives were willing to explore any financing avenue.[2] Finally, biotechnology was very capital intensive. For instance, as one consultant reported to Aberlyn:

> Biotechnology firms are expected to invest $78.23 billion (1990 dollars) in new plant and equipment over the five-year period ending in 1995. The biotech industry has emerged—even in its initial stages of development—as one of the most capital intensive industries in our economic history. Capital spending ratios for the industry amount to nearly $75,000 per employee—a sharp contrast to that for all manufacturing industries at about $6,000–$10,000 per employee.[3]

The nature of the capital equipment lent itself to venture leasing. Much of the laboratory equipment used by biotechnology firms, such as bioreactors, was expensive but relatively standardized, which made it a natural target for venture leasing arrangements. Exhibit 1 summarizes the terms and conditions of a representative venture lease involving a biotechnology firm.

As venture leasing became increasingly important to Aberlyn, Aberlyn Capital Management Company (ACMC) was set up as a subsidiary of Aberlyn Holding Company. Under this organization lay two other organizations. The first, BioQuest Venture Leasing Company, N.V., was the offshore company that Aberlyn established to finance its venture leasing activities. The second, Aberlyn Capital Management Limited Partnership, served as the general manager (akin to the general partner) of the venture leasing fund. (Aberlyn's organization chart in July 1993 is summarized in Exhibit 2; biographies of the management team and advisers appear in Exhibit 3; and the terms and conditions of BioQuest Venture Leasing Company, N.V., are summarized in Exhibit 4.) Aberlyn Capital Management retained its lean organization by undertaking a collaboration in August 1992 with Phoenix Leasing, another leasing firm. ACMC contracted out the back-office administration of its lease portfolio—billing, data processing, and financial reporting—to Phoenix, allowing its management to focus on generating new business.

Aberlyn attempted to adjust the risk and return of its venture leasing portfolio in a variety of ways. Perhaps most importantly, it kept a number of technical specialists both on its staff and on its advisory boards. With more technically skilled staff than other venture leasing firms, Aberlyn felt it could better evaluate, lend to, and profit from leases to younger firms than most of its competition. Unlike other firms that only felt comfortable

---

[2] Many of these firms had negative net worth, and hence were technically insolvent. This made bank loans implausible, especially in light of the increased federal scrutiny of bank lending in the early 1990s. Only a few banks would make such loans. The bank with the largest presence in biotechnology lending was the Silicon Valley Bank, the 400th largest bank in the nation, which targeted high-technology firms. Silicon Valley was one of the few banks willing to consider making loans to companies that had no earnings but were likely to obtain future equity financings.

[3] The Howell Group, *Overview of the Biotechnology Industry in the United States and Capital Equipment Financing Requirements,* unpublished consulting report, 1992. The projections assume a 65% annual rate of increase in employment over this period and a 10% yearly increase in annual capital spending per employee.

extending lease financing to cover tangible laboratory equipment or computers, the Aberlyn staff was capable of evaluating technologies.

To limit its risks ex ante, Aberlyn intentionally constrained the firms to which it would provide venture leasing. It typically only invested in firms that had received at least two "rounds" of venture financing. For firms with insufficient cash flows or cash reserves to ensure the timely payment of the promised lease payments, Aberlyn met with the firm's venture investors to discuss the probability of refinancing the lease position.

To further control its risk exposure, Aberlyn evaluated potential lessees on a five-part scale that attempted to rank firms on the basis of the likelihood that Aberlyn would be repaid. (See Exhibit 5.) The policy goal was to invest no more than 5% of the lease portfolio to Class 5 (low-risk firms), with 15% to Class 4, 35% to Classes 3 and 2 each, and 10% to Class 1.

Finally, to protect itself from risks that might arise after the lease documents were signed, Aberlyn's management in some cases asked to have a nonvoting representative placed on the board of directors of any firm to which it provided lease financing.[4] In virtually all cases, it attached certain covenants to the lease financing documents that clearly specified the equipment to be leased (sometimes including the model number of tangible equipment) and a maintenance schedule for the equipment.

Aberlyn's return as a venture lessor was received in three forms. First, it received regular lease payments. These lease payments, similar in form to interest payments, were periodic promised payments to be made from the lessee to Aberlyn. These interest rates typically reflected a spread over Treasury rates or prime. For example, in the lease given in Exhibit 1, the lessor demanded a promised rate of 3.1% above the four-year Treasury note. The spread over treasuries charged was a function of the perceived riskiness of the investment as well as the alternatives open to the parties, and ranged from 1% to 10% above reference rates such as prime.

In the summer of 1993, the venture leasing spread over treasuries was at historically high levels, reflecting the scarcity of venture capital financing, as well as the closed "window" for initial public stock offerings. The second component of a venture lessor's returns came in the form of the money paid as a purchase option at the end of the lease. After the lease period concluded, the lessee typically had the right, but not the obligation, to purchase the equipment from the lessor. In the example given in Exhibit 1, the lessee can pay "fair market value," not exceeding 25% of the original cost of the equipment, and then take legal ownership of the equipment at the end of the lease. This would be similar to an auto lease in which the lessee has the right to make a lump-sum payment at the end of the lease and own the car. If the item leased was highly firm-specific, the purchase option price could be quite small.

Unlike an auto lease, a venture lease included a third mechanism by which the venture lessor could earn a return. The lessor was typically granted warrants to purchase the common stock of the lessee, at a certain date, for a prespecified exercise price. In the Embryogen Corporation example, Equitec was given 80,000 warrants. On or before the end of five years, Equitec Leasing has the right, but not the obligation, to buy up to 80,000 shares of Embryogen for $1.00 per share. Generally, warrants given to venture lessors were protected by antidilution rights (which would adjust the conversion ratio if the firm issued any additional shares of stock or paid a cash or stock dividend to shareholders).

Because these firms typically were privately held, a venture lessor's ability to sell or otherwise transfer these warrants (or the shares into which these shares were convert-

---

[4] Were Aberlyn to be represented by a voting director, its legal status as a lender might be compromised in any bankruptcy proceeding.

ible) for three years was sharply restricted by the Securities and Exchange Commission's Rule 144. In July 1993, this forbade the public sale of unregistered securities for two years after the transaction and limited the volume of sales in the following year. Typically however, the warrants have "piggyback" registration rights. These allow the holders of restricted shares to register the shares for public sale at the time of the firm's initial public offering or shortly thereafter.

It is convention in the venture leasing industry to describe the warrant portion of a lessor's compensation in terms of its "warrant coverage," expressed as a percentage of the value of the cash advanced by the venture lessor. A "warrant coverage" of 10% means that the lessor who finances $1 million receives warrants that—if exercised— would cost the lessor 10% of $1 million, or $100,000 to exercise. Venture lessors obtain warrants whose exercise or strike price equals the per share valuation of the firm at its last venture financing round, which might have been months or years prior to the lease. Thus, if the last venture financing round had valued the firm's equity at $5.00 per share, the lessor would receive $100,000/$5 or 20,000 warrants. Warrant coverage is a convention to describe the amount of warrants granted but does not reflect the value of the warrants granted to the venture lessor.

The combination of the lease payments and purchase prices (akin to the payment of interest and repayment of principal in a bond) and warrant coverage define the return available to a venture lessor. By adjusting the lease payments, purchase prices, and warrant coverage, a venture lessor could create a more bondlike or a more stocklike return. Aberlyn established policy guidelines for the terms it charged lessees, as a function of their position in Aberlyn's five-part risk class. The transaction's implicit rate is merely the internal rate of return if all lease payments and purchase payments are made but exclude any return from the warrants. Leases to companies in Class 4 and 5 had an implicit yield of between 9% and 10% with few or no warrants; Class 3 firms, 13% to 15% with 10% to 20% warrant coverage; Class 2 firms, 15% to 17% with 15% to 20% warrant coverage; and Class 1 firms, 17% with between 25% and 40% coverage.

THE PROPOSED INTELLECTUAL PROPERTY LEASES

In 1992, Aberlyn's management team had developed the concept of providing leases based on patents. This would allow growing firms to finance their need for working capital through leasing, rather than just equipment purchases. Aberlyn (the lessor) would purchase one of the firm's patents, and the firm (the lessee) would then lease the patent from Aberlyn and therefore gain the legal right to use the patent. Aberlyn would hold or own the title to the patent until the lease had expired, at which point the lessee could exercise its option to purchase the patent at a nominal price. This transaction was akin to the sale and leaseback of a building. Aberlyn termed the new instrument a *FLIP* (short for a Finance Lease on Intellectual Property).

FLIP financing was attractive for several reasons. First, the lessee would be able to obtain working capital while giving up only a small equity stake. The only viable alternative, obtaining additional venture financing, would require that the firm give up a larger share of the firm than required by the venture lessor. (Because these firms were finding banks unwilling to finance equipment purchases, working capital loans from banks would be quite improbable.)

Second, FLIPs could help reconcile firms' economic value with their accounting statements. Firms that develop discoveries can value them only for the cost of the patent application: typically, between $10,000 and $50,000. In contrast, firms that acquire patents record them on their balance sheet at their purchase price, which presumably reflects their market value. For instance, Hoffmann–La Roche's 1991 annual report lists the three polymer chain reaction patents that it purchased from Cetus as an intangible asset worth $286 million, approximately the purchase price. Roche's partially owned subsidiary Genentech provides a contrasting example. At the end of 1992, the firm owned over 150 patents, including some of the most valuable in biotechnology. Almost all of these had been developed internally. Genentech's 1992 annual report does not list these patents separately but rather with the firm's "other assets." The patents and other assets have a book value of $37 million.

Although analysts understood this convention and closely examined the patent positions of biotechnology firms, many managers felt that accounting affects market valuations in subtle ways. For instance, the chief financial officer of Merck & Co., Judy Lewent, stated that "the fact that intellectual property is not included as an asset on the balance sheet is a deficiency in current accounting rules. The best way to address that deficiency requires further study by the industry, and this is a key area of focus in Merck finance."[5] The leasing of intellectual property would help address this problem temporarily by allowing the firm to include as a balance sheet asset the value of the leased patent. Aberlyn realized, however, that this would be a temporary benefit: the value of the patent on the firm's balance sheet would shrink as the lease was repaid.

The implementation of the proposed FLIPs posed several management problems for Aberlyn. Foremost among these problems would be the valuation of the patent. The procedure that Aberlyn and its advisers proposed to employ was to estimate the ultimate profits from the patent, discount the cash flows back to the present at a rate that reflects the transaction's risk, and then execute a sales and leaseback for up to 75% of the patent's assessed value. Much of this estimation process involved subjective assessments.

A second difficulty would be if a patent was ever seized from a defaulting firm. Predicting the value that the patent would fetch in the resale market would be difficult. The patent would be valuable to a firm with an active research program in the same area. Selling the patent would entail identifying the firms undertaking research in the area and assessing how valuable the patent would be to each in light of their current patent position. Because biotechnology patents can take a long time to issue, this evaluation would also need to include pending patent applications. These can be evaluated only imperfectly.

Furthermore, Aberlyn could find itself forced to defend the patent while marketing it. Maintaining a patent position entails carefully monitoring other firms for potential infringement. If biotechnology firms sensed that Aberlyn was unwilling to enforce the rights to seized patents through costly litigation, they might be tempted to use the technology covered by these awards without permission. Several biotechnology firms, for instance, are reputed to regularly infringe patents held by research universities, secure in the knowledge that the schools do not have extensive budgets for undertaking litigation. This might become a problem if the bulk of the lessee's research proved unpromising (so it was unable to obtain any further financing), but the patent itself seemed promising.

A final difficulty was the selection of the patent on which to base the lease. If the patent was too closely linked with the firm's other awards, it might be very difficult for Aberlyn to market the seized patent to a third party. Potential purchasers of the patent might be deterred because of concerns about litigation. Even if the lessee had given up the rights to the leased patent, if it retained closely related patents, it could make the

---

[5] Michael Schrage, "Intellectual Property Should Be Managed as a Real Asset," *Boston Globe,* April 19, 1992.

use of the leased patent by a third party very difficult. Thus, it was important that Aberlyn select patents covering intellectual property that was distinct and separate from the firm's other claims.

In the course of raising the funds for their subsidiary, BioQuest Venture Leasing Company, Aberlyn had stated certain limitations on their use of intellectual property leases. First, licenses would be restricted to issued U.S. patents. No leases would be made on the basis of pending patent applications, which might not ultimately be approved, or awards in different countries. (Because the United States was the world's largest health-care market, U.S. awards generally had more economic value than those covering smaller markets. In addition, it was difficult to enforce patent rights in several countries, most notably Japan.) Aberlyn would not execute a lease for more than 80% of the computed net present value of the patent. (These valuations would be performed by Aberlyn's outside advisers.) Finally, patent leases would be restricted to 10% of the overall investments by the fund.

RHOMED, INC.

Although Aberlyn's management team had accepted the idea of providing FLIPs in principle, an appropriate opportunity for a substantial transaction of this type had not yet presented itself as of late 1992. (Aberlyn had undertaken three very small transactions of this type.) This changed in early 1993, when Aberlyn's management met Robert Stern, the chief financial officer of RhoMed. While conversations initially focused on a traditional equipment lease, it soon became clear that RhoMed would be an ideal candidate for a FLIP.

RhoMed was a biotechnology firm specializing in developing radio-pharmaceutical (i.e., nuclear medicine) products for diagnosing and ultimately treating diseases. RhoMed's founder was Dr. Buck A. Rhodes, who also served as RhoMed's president and chief scientist. While on the faculty of Johns Hopkins University in the 1970s, Rhodes had begun working on application of the radioactive element Technetium to the diagnosis of disease. At the time, the biochemists were discovering how to clone identical cultures of antibodies. These "monoclonal" antibodies, it was hoped, could serve to identify and ultimately to treat a wide variety of diseases. (The popular description was "magic bullets.")

Rhodes and his fellow researchers had examined how to combine these new bio-engineered products with nuclear medicine (the introduction of radioactivity into the body for imaging and treatment). In particular, with his colleagues, Rhodes developed ways to label antibodies with small amounts of radioactive Technetium. These cells could then be (in theory) injected into the human body and tracked to identify a variety of potentially serious conditions. As one of the pioneers in this area, Rhodes had written six textbooks and over 160 articles in refereed journals.

In 1978, Rhodes accepted a position at the University of New Mexico, which gave him an opportunity to return to his native state. Due to its proximity to Los Alamos National Laboratory, the University had a keen interest in nuclear medicine. The Department of Energy spent over $4 billion on research at contractor-operated facilities (termed national laboratories) in fiscal year 1992. Los Alamos, with a research focus on nuclear weapons and energy, was one of the largest, with an R&D budget of $629 million in fiscal year 1990. Not only was the research community in the area lively, but the nuclear medicine department included a commercial radio-pharmacy laboratory, the largest commercial facility of this type in the United States. University faculty were given a chance to span the academic and commercial worlds. They were not only teaching industry about their discoveries, but they were helping to shape the business environment in which they would be commercialized.

With an increasing interest in business, Rhodes joined a local biotechnology concern, Summa Medical Corporation, as the senior vice president for scientific affairs. This proved to be a trying affair, for the firm experienced severe financing pressures that led to its bankruptcy and the abandonment of its biotechnology research effort. In 1986, Rhodes left to begin a firm of his own, specializing in the application of nuclear medicine. He resolved to avoid the mistakes that he had seen other firms make. One of these was reliance on venture financing. Rhodes felt that venture capitalists frequently erred, particularly by insisting that firms in the development stage meet previously agreed-upon targets even after they were revealed to be scientific dead ends.

Beginning the firm out of his garage, Rhodes sought funds from the Small Business Innovation Research (SBIR) program. This $500 million-per-year federal initiative gives grants to businesses with under 500 employees, primarily in high-technology fields. The program enables federal agencies to fund private-sector research, with Phase I awards of approximately $75,000 and Phase II awards of up to $750,000. Helping Rhodes draft the SBIR proposals was Steven Slusher, who soon joined the firm. A graduate of St. John's College, Slusher had received his law degree in 1977 from the University of New Mexico and then spent nine years as a deputy district attorney general for the state of New Mexico.

Within its first year of operations, RhoMed had won two Phase I awards. One, from the National Institutes of Health, examined whether it would be possible to identify the quality of diagnostic products that employ monoclonal antibodies. In particular, Rhodes sought to determine whether it was possible to measure the proportion of antibodies that are immunoreactive or able to interact with other cells. This information is important because it allows the dose of the medicine to be precisely determined. This initial project led to a Phase II award in 1988.

The second Phase I grant, awarded by the Department of Energy, examined whether it might be possible to use radioactive antibodies to identify intestinal abscesses. Intestinal abscesses, while potentially fatal, often had no visible manifestations other than a persistent fever. RhoMed examined whether these abscesses could be identified by tracing the progress of the radioactive antibodies, using computed tomography or another imaging technology. Previously, doctors had relied on radioactive-labeled white blood cells, which involved the injection of eight times as much radioactivity into the human body. Furthermore, the blood cells needed to be withdrawn from the human body and processed—a time-consuming, costly, and potentially dangerous step. In 1989, RhoMed received a $500,000 grant from the Department of Energy to commercialize this technology.

Rhodes and Slusher also had turned to the state of New Mexico for additional financing.[6] The state, eager to encourage high-technology development, established the New Mexico Research and Development Institute (NMRDI) in 1981. This organization sought to encourage new firms to commercialize technologies in New Mexico. Initially focusing on energy-related technologies, NMRDI awarded contracts to companies seeking to develop innovative technologies. In exchange for the loans, NMRDI received a royalty based on future sales. Their contract with RhoMed called for RhoMed to pay a 2% royalty for New Mexico–manufactured products and a 5% royalty on other products. In return, NMRDI awarded RhoMed a $448,000 contract in 1987.

---

[6] This paragraph is based in part on Damon Benningfield, "High-Tech Success: Rio Grande Research Corridor Initiative Profits from Federal Laboratories," *New Mexico Business Journal,* August 1989.

In addition to developing Rhodes's technology, RhoMed aggressively sought to develop collaborations with national laboratories. The mechanism RhoMed employed was Cooperative Research and Development Agreements (CRADAs).[7] RhoMed had signed two CRADAS with a researcher at Brookhaven National Laboratory with whom Rhodes had worked at Johns Hopkins. In October 1992, RhoMed signed a two-year agreement with Los Alamos to label antibodies with highly radioactive copper isotopes. This work used a lead-lined facility for handling highly radioactive materials at Los Alamos that was likely to have been closed had this agreement not been signed.

As RhoMed technology advanced, it became necessary to tap a third source of financing, strategic alliances with large pharmaceutical firms. These large firms were motivated to work with and fund RhoMed because of its diverse product line under development:

- Its first product, RhoChek, was introduced in 1990. This product grew out of the first SBIR grant from the National Institutes of Health. It sought to measure the effectiveness of antibodies before they were administered to patients. The product was made up of small beads covered with antibody binding molecules. The U.S. Food and Drug Administration (FDA) had required that it be used in the manufacture of the first antibody-based therapeutic reaching the marketplace, Cytogen's Oncoscint. Growth was likely to be considerable as more antibody-based products reach the marketplace.

- RhoMed's radioactive antibody abscess-imaging technology, LeukoScan, was currently in Phase I trials (small sample human studies to determine if a proposed new drug was safe). This had been the subject of RhoMed's first SBIR award from the Department of Energy. DuPont-Merck Pharmaceutical had the product under option and was expected to exercise its right to license the product if the trials went well.

- In December 1992, RhoMed had signed a collaborative agreement with Sterling Winthrop, a major pharmaceutical firm, to use radioactive-labeled antibodies to diagnose and treat cancer. The cancer delivery and treatment product was the subject of both the Los Alamos CRADA and the Sterling Winthrop agreement. Part of the funds paid by Sterling Winthrop to RhoMed would be paid to Los Alamos to cover part of the costs of the facility that RhoMed was using.

- RhoMed had developed an approach to develop antibodies that worked more effectively in the human body than the mouse-based antibodies that most biotechnology firms were developing. While this technology was still in an early stage, it had attracted the interest of Genentech, which had signed an agreement to develop one cell line. RhoMed anticipated other collaborative agreements.

- Related projects to identify blood clots, ulcers, and more general inflammations were currently underway as well.

THE PROPOSED TRANSACTION

Aberlyn saw several reasons why RhoMed was an attractive candidate for the initial FLIP transaction. First, its intellectual property position was very strong. Rhodes had been a pioneer in marrying biotechnology and nuclear medicine, which gave RhoMed

---

[7] In 1986, Congress passed the Federal Technology Transfer Act, which authorized federal agencies to enter into CRADAS with private firms and other entities for the purpose of commercializing federal research (PL 99-502). The 1989 National Competitiveness and Technology Transfer Act (PL 101-189) allowed national laboratories, which are run by contractors for the federal government, to enter into CRADAS.

an initial lead over the competition. Perhaps even more critically, RhoMed's small management team had aggressively pursued patent protection. The firm's research strategy had involved careful consideration of whether the work could lead to a defensible patent position as well as meaningful strategic alliances. RhoMed's first patent (4,940,670) covered the antibody delivery system to treat cancer. Among the patents for labeling antibodies with Technetium were two that had been awarded to the firm (5,078,985 and 5,102,990) and one under license from the University of New Mexico that Rhodes had co-invented. The firm had several dozen applications pending that they felt confident would ultimately be awarded.

Second, the management team, having retained a controlling interest in the firm to this point, was unwilling to give up a large share of the firm to venture capitalists. When Rhodes had been sought to obtain equity financing in the late 1980s, he had approached venture capitalists but found little interest. This was largely due to RhoMed's distance from geographic centers of venture activity. More recent inquiries had suggested that RhoMed would be an attractive venture investment in 1993. Few venture investors, however, would be satisfied with less than a 30% stake in the firm, as well as effective control through strict covenants.[8]

Finally, because RhoMed had so little external financing in the past, it was a prime example of the disparity between accounting and economic value. Not only did it have a considerable number of patent awards and pending applications, but it also had a substantial inventory of refined antibodies that it had extracted over the past seven years. While this material had a market value of several million dollars, it was recorded at the raw material's cost of purchase. (RhoMed's income statements and balance sheets are reported in Exhibit 6, and projected cash flows in Exhibit 7.)

Doug Brian, senior vice president at Aberlyn, had developed the initial terms of the proposed transaction. As initially envisioned, RhoMed would receive $1 million from Aberlyn at the outset of the FLIP. RhoMed would not have to make any interest payments until the beginning of the second year. RhoMed would make three even payments of principal, at the end of years 1, 2, and 3, as well as 15% of the amount outstanding before the repayment.

Because the patent was valued at nearly $5 million (an analysis for Aberlyn performed by an outside consultant, Lulu Pickering, Ph.D., of Infomagen, Inc., is excerpted in Exhibit 8), this provided a very satisfactory safety margin for Aberlyn. RhoMed could purchase its patent back for one dollar at the end of the three-year lease after repaying Aberlyn's loan.

The interest rate on the outstanding amount of the lease would be 15%, reflecting their classification of the firm in Risk Class 2. (Background information on economic conditions in early July 1993 is provided in Exhibit 9; information on the volatility of recent biotechnology IPOs is provided in Exhibit 10.) Brian proposed a "warrant coverage" of 10%. Setting an exercise price for the warrants had been problematic, because the firm had not had a previous venture financing that would provide a benchmark for setting the price. After some negotiation with RhoMed officials, Aberlyn proposed setting the warrants' life at five years and their exercise price at $1.45.[9]

---

[8] Most venture investments in private firms are made through the purchase of convertible preferred stock (equity with priority over common stock in the event of liquidation that converts into common stock at set ratio). These shares typically have many rights, including those that essentially give the venture capitalist the right to force the firm to repurchase its shares. This action frequently is tantamount to forcing the firm into bankruptcy.

[9] This was between the $1/share initially proposed by Aberlyn and the $3/share that RhoMed had asked for. The beta of six small publicly traded biotechnology firms specializing in human diagnostics was between 1.2 and 2.0, with a mean of 1.53, using weekly data from July 1991 through June 1993.

Aberlyn had the impression that RhoMed's management team had been excited about the proposal. First, RhoMed's management saw the venture leasing proposal as consistent with their goal of assuring the firm's progress while maximizing their control over the firm's equity. This financing would entail a minimal reduction in their owner-ship stake. Second, they were intrigued by Aberlyn's ability to raise capital from European and Middle Eastern sources. This transaction could serve as a bridge until a private placement. The private placement would then assure financial stability until it made sense to go public. RhoMed's chief financial officer, Robert Stern, thought that an appropriate time for an IPO might be in October 1994, after its product development effort was further advanced.[10]

Stern, who had handled the preliminary negotiations, appeared to have few con-cerns about the transaction. The relatively limited dilution implied by the 10% warrant coverage had not been problematic. He felt confident that collaborative arrangements and private and public financings would provide the capital to repay the loan over the three-year period. He had not felt that the sale and leaseback of the patent would com-plicate any potential strategic arrangements.

---

[10] Both the subsequent private placement or the initial public offering might potentially consist of a combi-nation of shares and warrants. Unit offerings consisting of shares and warrants are a common structure for many small stock offerings.

Exhibit 1   Representative Venture Lease Agreement Involving Biotechnology Firm

Embryogen Corporation

Venture lease agreement with Equitec Leasing Company, as amended July 29, 1989, for purchasing research equipment

Lease Line:	$800,000
Warrants sold:	80,000 warrants exercisable at $1/share
Warrant life:	Five years after issue
Period when purchases can be made:	12 months from execution of the agreement
Repayment period:	48 months from receipt of equipment
Interest rate:	3.1% in excess of the per annum asked yield for the four-year treasury note closest to par in the *Wall Street Journal*, adjusted quarterly
Purchase option:	Fair market value, but no more than 25% of original cost of equipment

Source: Embryogen corporate document.

Exhibit 2   Aberlyn's Organization Chart

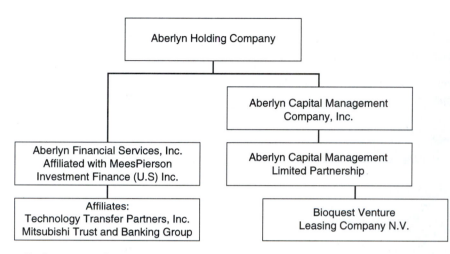

Source: Aberlyn corporate documents.

Exhibit 3 Aberlyn Management Team and Advisors

Lawrence M. Hoffman (Chairman) has over 25 years of experience in trading and investment banking. Mr. Hoffman held senior trading positions with Glore Forgan, William R. Staats, DuPont & Co., Burnham & Co., and Dean Witter. From 1986 to 1988, Mr. Hoffman founded and was Chairman of Nicholas, Lawrence & Co., an investment banking firm that specialized in biotechnology research and institutional trading. Since 1989, Mr. Hoffman has served as President and Chief Executive Officer of the Aberlyn Group, Inc., a firm specializing in providing investment banking services to biotechnology companies. Mr. Hoffman has managed a number of public offerings. He sits on the boards of American BioMed, Nurture, Inc., New Horizons Diagnostics, Inc., and Medclone, Inc. Mr. Hoffman holds a B.S. in Economics from New York University.

J. David Sakura, Ph.D. (President) has over 20 years' experience in the biotechnology and biomedical area. From 1970 to 1980, Dr. Sakura was a member of the research faculty at Harvard Medical School, where he conducted a research program in the neurosciences. In 1980, Dr. Sakura became a senior consultant in biotechnology with Arthur D. Little, Inc., an international high technology and management consulting company. His clients included multinational pharmaceutical and specialty chemical companies, biotechnology companies, and federal and state government agencies. Since 1988, Dr. Sakura has also held senior marketing, business development, and product development positions with several high-technology companies, including early-stage companies. Dr. Sakura has published over 50 scientific papers and reports, and has been an invited speaker at numerous international biotechnology conferences and symposia. Dr. Sakura holds a Ph.D. in protein biochemistry from the University of Arizona and an M.P.H. from the Harvard School of Public Health.

Lulu Pickering, Ph.D. (Biotechnology Analyst) has over 14 years' experience in the fields of molecular biology and genetic engineering, with a concentration in molecular immunology. From 1985 to 1992, Dr. Pickering held positions at T Cell Sciences, Inc., a biotechnology company located in Cambridge, Massachusetts, including positions of Vice President of Technology Licensing, Patent Liaison, and Group Leader of Molecular Immunology. Dr. Pickering passed the United States Patent Bar Exam in 1989 to become a registered patent agent and has five years of experience in evaluating and managing a patent portfolio. Dr. Pickering is a member of the Association of University Technology Managers, the Licensing Executives Society, the American Bar Association, and the American Intellectual Property Law Association. Dr. Pickering received her doctorate from Cornell University in 1980, studying the expression of interferon proteins and RNAs.

R. Dana Ono, Ph.D. (Biotechnology Industry Analyst) has spent the past decade in the biotechnology and health-care industries. Most recently, Dr. Ono served as President and Chief Executive Officer of ARCTURUS Pharmaceutical Corporation, a privately held company which he cofounded. His prior experience includes senior management positions at several biotechnology companies. His expertise ranges from strategic planning, product management, technology acquisition and development, licensing, and commercial development. Dr. Ono has also served as a consultant to both *Fortune* 500 companies and early-stage companies. As a founding director of the Massachusetts Biotechnology Council, Inc., a trade association of member biotechnology companies and affiliates, Dr. Ono is a frequent spokesperson in the field. The author of numerous scientific articles, he recently edited the book, *The Business of Biotechnology from the Bench to the Street*. Mr. Ono has also co-authored a book in the environmental field. He is a founding member of the Marine Science and Technology Committee of the Environmental Business Council, Inc. Dr. Ono received his A.B. in Earth and Planetary Sciences from the Johns Hopkins University, and his A.M. and Ph.D. in Biology from Harvard University, where he also completed an accelerated program in business administration.

Douglas R. Brian (Senior Vice President) has over 20 years' experience, with over 10 years' experience in both domestic and international leasing. During that time, Mr. Brian has arranged over $500 million worth of leases which include leases on state-of-the-art and high-technology medical equipment. Prior to joining Aberlyn Capital Management, Mr. Brian helped establish NordFinance, Inc. as a subsidiary of a large Swedish bank (Nordbanken) and developed it into a major leasing company specializing in medical equipment leases. Mr. Brian also held various senior-level management positions with the John Hancock Insurance Company and with the John Hancock Leasing Corporation.

Richard G. Power (Director of Business Development), founder of R.G. Power Associates in 1980, has designed and implemented business development strategies for emerging health care companies, with a major emphasis on the biotechnology industry. Prior to 1980, Mr. Power held senior management positions with several major pharmaceutical companies, including Vice President of Business Development for Ortho Pharmaceutical, a division of Johnson & Johnson, Director of Corporate Development for G.D. Searle, Marketing Director (International) for Warner Lambert, and Director of New Product Marketing for Smith Kline & French. Mr. Power has been an active member of the venture capital community and has served as a special consultant to Domain Partners (Princeton, NJ). Mr. Power was the founder of two biotechnology companies, Pharmatec and Xenon Vision, where he served as President and CEO.

Andrew Stanhope (Director of Research) has over 20 years of experience in investment banking and business development. Since 1985 Mr. Stanhope was Director of Corporate Finance for a banking and brokerage affiliate of D.H. Blair & Co. where he originated, negotiated, and structured private and public offerings of emerging growth companies. From 1983 to 1985 Mr. Stanhope was associated with Robert A. Stanger & Co., a renowned Wall Street investment advisory firm. During this time he developed qualitative rating and performance measures of public limited partnership investments that were reviewed in the monthly Stanger publications. Prior to 1983, Mr. Stanhope served in various business development capacities, including Manager of Business Development for a subsidiary of a *Fortune* 100 firm. Mr. Stanhope is a graduate of Brown University with a major in political science and a minor in mathematics and also holds an MBA degree from Northeastern University.

Richard J. Bell (Director of Marketing) is a seasoned investment analyst and business advisor with a technical background involved in the financing of young growth companies. He also has substantial management experience in marketing, manufacturing, and research and development. He has been the founder or held senior management positions in Yig-Tek Corporation, Watkins Johnson Co., and Microwave Chemicals Laboratory. Mr. Bell holds a B.A. from the University of Minnesota.

Jerald Belofsky (Managing Director, MeesPierson Investment Finance [U.S.] Inc.) has over 20 years in investment banking and equipment lease financing. Prior to joining MeesPierson Investment Finance (U.S.) Inc., Mr. Belofsky was in charge of equipment leasing and venture leasing activities at Bear Stearns. In total, Mr. Belofsky has financed well in excess of $1 billion of various projects, including approximately 30 equipment leasing and project finance partnerships or trusts.

Financial and Business Advisors included Schering Plough Corporation—a research-based company engaged primarily in the discovery, development, manufacturing, and marketing of pharmaceutical and health care products worldwide, with annual sales of $3 billion, and Stiefel Laboratories—a privately held leading dermatology specialty company with sales in more than 100 countries throughout the world.

Legal Advisors included Bromberg and Sunstein (Patent Advisor) and Graham & James (Legal Advisor).

Scientific and Technical Advisors included six researchers, all affiliated with major academic institutions (Stanford, Harvard, New York University, University of Maryland, and MIT).

Medical and Clinical Advisors included five researchers, all of whom hold M.D./Ph.D. degrees and are affiliated with major research hospitals.

Source: Aberlyn corporate documents.

Exhibit 4   Offering Document for Bioquest Venture Leasing Company, N.V.

BioQuest Venture Leasing Company-A N.V.

U.S.$20,000,000

Common Stock

Overview

BioQuest Venture Leasing Company-A N.V. (the "Fund"), a Netherlands Antilles company to be formed, intends to engage in the business of acquiring, holding, and disposing of full-payout finance leases that will be secured by first liens on equipment and patents of technologies, owned by U.S. biomedical and biotechnology companies. The Fund's primary objectives are to make steady current distributions and to achieve an attractive overall return through equity participation rights, such as common stocks or warrants, in select portfolio companies. The Fund believes that its investment philosophy combines desirable attributes of lease finance and venture capital investment.

Key Investment Considerations

Current distributions   The Fund's objective is to distribute a minimum cash distribution of 8% per annum, payable monthly.

Attractive total return   The Fund's investment objective is to return to shareholders an Internal Rate of Return ("IRR") of approximately 16% over the anticipated five-year life of the investment.

Multinational corporate participants   Schering-Plough Corporation, one of the world's largest pharmaceutical companies, and Stiefel Laboratories, Inc., one of the world's leading dermatological specialty companies, will provide advisory services to the general manager.

No residual risk   Over 100% of the original equipment cost is anticipated to be recovered through cash flow generated from lease payments during the lease term. All leases are anticipated to be written with a fixed equipment sale price or a mandatory lease renewal clause.

No leverage   All portfolio investments in leases will be made on an all-cash basis.

Security   Investment made by the fund will be fully secured by first liens on equipment and patents on technologies.

Investment Rationale

Fast-growing biotechnology market   The Fund believes that the biotechnology industry has emerged as one of the most promising investment opportunities since the early days of the computer industry. Projections put its annual revenue growth rate over the next five years at 25%. Sparking this growth will be the anticipated commercial introduction of numerous products now in development. By the year 2000, cumulative sales of biotechnology products will reach a projected $12 billion in the United States and $50 billion worldwide. To sustain this growth, the extremely capital-intensive biotechnology industry will require major expenditures for plants and equipment totaling an anticipated $78 billion in just the next five years.

Lack of sufficient alternative financing sources   Traditional financing sources—banks, insurance companies, and venture capitalists—can not meet this demand for capital. For biotechnology companies with limited access to capital markets, the Fund represents an attractive financing alternative.

Experienced principals   The principals of the Fund's general manager offer the combination of (a) broad experience in domestic and international leasing, having managed collectively over $2.0 billion of equipment leases in the other organizations; and (b) over 20 years' collective experience consulting for the biotechnology industry and financing biotechnology companies.

Corporate participants   Corporate participants, who will advise the general manager, includes *Schering-Plough Corporation*, a leading multinational pharmaceutical company, and *Phoenix Leasing Inc.*, a subsidiary of Phoenix American, Inc., which has managed an equipment lease portfolio of approximately $1.8 billion. *Stiefel Laboratories, Inc.*, one of the world's leading dermatological specialty companies with sales in more than 100 countries, is a limited partner in the general manager and will also provide advisory services to the general manager.

Industry experts on Scientific and Technical Advisory Board   The Scientific and Technical Advisory Board (the "Advisory Board") will advise the general manager on matters relating to emerging industry trends, general technology, and scientific information.   The Advisory Board is comprised of recognized experts from the *Massachusetts Institute of Technology, Harvard Medical School,* the *Harvard School of Public Health, New York University, Stanford University,* the *University of Maryland,* and the *Maryland Biotechnology Institute.*

Summary of Preliminary Offering Terms

Securities to be offered:	Common stock
Offering size:	$20,000,000
Price per share:	$10.00
Anticipated offering date:	October 1, 1992
Anticipated investment term:	Approximately five years
Leverage:	None
Management fees:	2.5% of the assets under management, 100% subordinated to shareholders receiving the 8% minimum cash distribution per annum. After shareholders receive a full return of their original investment plus the 8% minimum cash distribution, the general manager will receive an incentive management fee of 20% of the Fund's profits and the shareholders the remaining 80%.
Projected return:	
Base case[a]	16% IRR
High case[b]	19% IRR
Low case[c]	8% IRR

Source: Aberlyn corporate documents.

[a]Assumes warrants are obtained from 20% of the companies in portfolio, with a 20% appreciation rate per annum.

[b]Assumes warrants are obtained from 30% of the companies in portfolio, with a 20% appreciation rate per annum.

[c]Represents lease income and residuals only, and on warrants obtained.

Exhibit 5   Aberlyn Firm Evaluation System

Risk Class "5"
- Annual sales in excess of $50 million.
- Company profitable for at least four years.
- Both sales and income growing annually.
- Tangible net worth in excess of $10 million.
- Total liabilities to tangible net worth not greater than 3 to 1.
- Company burn ratio[a] greater than two years.
- Company in business more than 10 years.
- Company may be public.
- Liquidity strong, current ratio greater than 2 to 1.
- Cash flow to debt service[b] greater than 3 to 1.
- Company has many products for sale and in the pipeline.
- Company's management strong in all functions.

Risk Class "4"
- Annual sales in excess of $10 million.
- Company profitable for at least one year.
- Both sales and income growing annually.
- Tangible net worth in excess of $5 million.
- Company already has had second round of venture capital.
- Total liabilities to tangible net worth not greater than 4 to 1—company burn ratio greater than one year.
- Company in business more than five years.
- Company may be considering going public soon.
- Liquidity strong, current ratio greater than 2 to 1.
- Cash flow to debt service greater than 2 to 1.
- Company has few products for sale but many in the pipeline.
- Company's management good in all functions.

Risk Class "3"
- Annual sales in excess of $2 million.
- Company starting to lose less money each year.
- Sales growing annually, losses turning around.
- Tangible net worth in excess of $3 million.
- Company on or about to go for second round venture capital.
- Total liabilities to tangible net worth not greater than 3 to 1.
- Company burn ratio greater than nine months.
- Company in business more than three years.
- Company may be considering going public within three years.
- Liquidity strong, current ratio greater than 3 to 1.
- Little debt, large amount of cash.
- Company has few products for sale but gearing up production.
- Company protected by patents on new products or pending.
- Company's management good in sales and research.
- May have affiliation with hospital or drug company.

Risk Class "2"
- Little or no sales.
- Company sees profits in three years or less.
- Tangible net worth in excess of $1 million.
- Company on first round of venture capital.
- Total liabilities to tangible net worth not greater than 4 to 1.
- Company burn ratio greater than six months.
- Company in business more than one year.
- Company may be considering going public within three years.
- Liquidity strong, current ratio greater than 2 to 1.

- Little debt.
- Company may have only one product for sale.
- Company protected by patents on new products or pending.
- Company products in FDA approval or clinical stage.
- Company management good in research.
- May have an affiliation with hospital or drug company.

Risk Class "1"

- Little or no sales.
- Company sees profits in three years or more.
- Company less than two years away from sales.
- Tangible net worth less than $1 million.
- Company on first round of venture capital or seed only.
- Little or no debt.
- Company burn ratio greater than six months.
- Company in business less than one year.
- Company may be considering going public within five years.
- Liquidity strong, current ratio greater than 2 to 1.
- Company working on products in clinical trials or research labs.
- Company protected by patents on new products or pending.
- Company products in FDA approval or clinical stages.
- Company's management good in research.
- May have an affiliation with hospital or drug company.

Source: Aberlyn corporate documents.

[a] Defined as the amount of time (at the current level of negative cash flow) that the firm could continue to operate until it depleted its current holdings of cash and marketable securities.

[b] Defined as the ratio of earnings before depreciation, interest or taxes over the required interest and principal repayments.

Exhibit 6   RhoMed Historical Financial Statements

Balance Sheet

	August 31, 1992
Assets	
Current assets:	
Cash	$ 21,351
Accounts receivable:	
Grant and contract	67,162
Trade and other	11,006
Prepaid expenses	9,032
Other	2,479
Total current assets	$111,030
Property and Equipment, net of accumulated depreciation of $32,525	24,163
Patents, net of accumulated amortization of $13,391	134,367
	$269,560
Liabilities and Shareholders' Deficit	
Current liabilities:	
Accounts payable	$ 64,051
Accrued expenses, including amounts owed to officers and shareholders of $210,504	269,231
Unearned revenue	17,700
Total current liabilities	$350,982
Convertible notes payable to shareholders, including accrued interest of $13,312	85,312
Other payables	4,000
	$ 89,312
Commitments and contingencies	
Shareholders' deficit: Common stock, no par value, authorized 10,000,000 shares; issued and outstanding 5,670,747 shares	326,647
Deficit accumulated during development stage	(497,381)
	($170,734)
	$269,560

Exhibit 6 (continued)

Statement of Cash Flows

	Years Ended August 31,	
	1992	1991
Cash Flows from Operating Activities:		
Net loss	$(84,667)	$(98,550)
Adjustments to reconcile net loss to net cash provided by (used for) operating activities:		
Depreciation and amortization	14,766	9,913
Interest expense on related party debt	5,312	5,760
Common stock and notes payable issued for consulting and equipment expenses	3,000	9,818
Settlement with consultant	(28,731)	—
Changes in certain operating assets and liabilities:		
Grants and contracts receivable	(57,162)	(10,000)
Trade accounts receivable	(4,498)	17,345
Inventory	1,700	1,538
Prepaid expenses and other	1,935	(8,895)
Patents	(68,041)	(22,356)
Accounts payable	14,168	26,307
Accrued expenses	86,291	73,157
Unearned revenue	17,700	(24,922)
Other payables	4,000	—
Net cash provided by (used for) operating activities	$(94,227)	$(20,885)
Cash Flows from Investing Activities:		
Purchases of property and equipment	$(13,506)	$ (9,866)
Cash Flows from Financing Activities:		
Payments on notes payable	$ (4,700)	$ —
Proceeds from notes payable	60,000	24,700
Proceeds from stock issuances	14,650	12,830
Net Increase (Decrease) in Cash	($37,783)	$ 6,779
Cash, beginning of period	59,134	52,355
Cash, end of period	$21,351	$ 59,134
Noncash Stock Activity:		
Conversion of loans from employees to common stock	$ —	$ 74,187
Common stock issued for services	3,000	—
Employee stock bonus distributed	—	9,818
	$ 3,000	$ 84,005

Exhibit 6 (continued)

Statements of Operations for the Years Ended August 31, 1993 (projected), 1992, and 1991

	For the Years Ended August 31,		
	Projected 1993	1992	1991
Revenues:			
Grant and contract	$ 330,000	$669,105	$ 562,829
Sales	67,000	58,517	42,209
License fees and royalties	187,000	33,000	—
Total revenues	$ 584,000	$760,622	$ 605,038
Expenses:			
Research and development	$ 524,000	$426,826	$ 391,046
General and administrative	579,000	415,161	310,334
Total expenses	$1,103,000	$841,987	$ 701,380
Other Income (Expenses):			
Other income	$ 21,000	$ 2,956	$ 3,900
Interest expense	(27,000)	(6,258)	(6,108)
Total other expenses, net	$ (6,000)	$ (3,302)	$ (2,208)
Net Loss	$ (525,000)	$ (84,667)	$ (98,550)

Source: RhoMed corporate documents

Exhibit 7 RhoMed Projected Revenue and Net Income ($ millions)

	1994	1995	1996	1997	1998	1999	2000	2001	2003	2003	2004
Antibody Derivative Products											
LeukoScan	2.2	4.2	7.2	9.6	7.4	8.6	8.7	9.0	10.2	11.3	12.5
Human antibody program	0.6	3.9	6.2	8.0	10.6	12.2	13.0	11.0	10.5	9.0	6.2
GastRho Scan	0.0	1.2	1.7	2.0	16.0	18.0	20.2	21.2	21.0	18.5	18.0
RhoChek I and II	0.4	0.5	0.7	1.5	2.0	2.0	2.0	2.0	2.0	2.0	2.0
Labeling Patent License	0.5	0.8	1.7	1.9	2.2	2.4	3.4	3.9	4.7	5.2	6.6
Peptide Derivative Products											
Clot Imaging	0.0	0.0	0.0	1.0	2.7	3.5	4.7	2.0	6.2	8.0	8.0
Lung Imaging	0.0	0.0	0.0	0.0	0.0	0.0	0.0	1.0	2.3	4.1	6.0
Inflammation Imaging	0.0	0.0	0.0	0.2	0.4	1.0	2.2	3.5	3.8	4.0	5.2
Infection Imaging	0.0	0.0	0.0	0.2	0.4	2.1	3.0	4.5	6.5	7.5	8.0
Grant Revenue	0.2	0.7	0.7	0.7	0.7	0.7	0.7	0.7	0.7	0.7	0.7
Contract Research	0.5	0.5	0.5	0.5	0.5	0.5	0.5	0.5	0.5	0.5	0.5
Total Revenue	4.5	11.8	18.8	25.6	43.0	51.0	58.4	59.4	68.4	70.8	73.8
Total Expenses	-1.2	-3.7	-4.7	-6.0	-5.7	-6.8	-7.8	-8.8	-10.4	-11.3	-12.3
Net Income	3.3	8.1	14.0	19.6	37.3	44.2	50.6	50.6	58.0	59.5	61.5

Source: RhoMed corporate documents.

Exhibit 8   Patent Valuation of U.S. Patent #4,940,670

Relevant Patent for the Patent Leaseback Arrangement

Although RhoMed is involved in several different areas of technology and research, the only area subject to this patent leaseback agreement is [the] technology involving RhoMed's proprietary Antibody Delivery and Cancer Management System. This technology is the subject of U.S. patent #4,940,670; Canadian patent #1,305,919, European Patent #EP 0234612, and Japanese patent application #62-014967.

Overview of Relevant Market

U.S. patent #4,940,670 concerns the *in vivo* (inside the body) use of specific antibodies in the diagnosis (*immunodetection or imaging*) and treatment (*immunotherapy*) of cancer.

There are a number of different procedures used to diagnose cancers. The single most important diagnostic tool is the analysis of a biopsy of the tumor by direct histology. Other diagnostic procedures include X-rays, mammography, endoscopy, barium studies, magnetic resonance imaging (MRI) scans and computed tomography scans, such as CAT scans (computed axial tomography) and PET (positron emission tomography) scans. In addition to these procedures, detection of tumors can also be done by radioimmunodetection using antibodies that bind to tumor cells that are radioactively labeled with isotopes such as ^{90}Y, ^{123}I, ^{131}I, ^{111}In, and ^{90}Tc.

Detection of known tumor markers, such as CEA, does not confirm diagnosis by itself. Several of the known cancer antigens, such as CEA, arise from different types of cancer. Furthermore, cancer antigens, such as CEA, are NOT especially diagnostic of cancer, since the correlation between the levels of CEA present and tumor stage and/or tumor burden is not precise.

Currently when a patient is diagnosed with cancer, the available therapeutic procedures involve chemotherapy, radiation treatment and/or surgical removal of the tumor. Although it is thought that immunotherapy using cancer-specific antibodies may be a less invasive, less toxic, and more specific alternative, it has not yet been conclusively demonstrated. Thus, there is no current cancer immunotherapy market. The major breakthrough that will open up the cancer markets to immunotherapy procedures will be the identification of more precise cancer antigens and antibodies that bind to them. The strongest patent claims will be product claims that claim the antibodies, antigens, and pharmaceutical antibody compositions themselves; followed by method claims of using the compositions to treat or diagnose cancer; followed by methods of producing or analyzing the antibodies or antigens.

Factors Considered in Evaluating U.S. Patent #4,940,670

Claims of U.S. patent #4,940,670 cover methods of selecting and formulating antibody-based drugs for *in vivo* cancer detection and therapy (claim 1); coupled with specific labeling of the antibody drug, e.g., with a radioisotope (claim 8) and further coupled with quality control testing of the labeled drug to determine whether the antibodies in the drug are still immunoreactive with their specific cancer antigen after labeling (claim 11).

During the prosecution file history for this patent, the claims were restricted to recite:

1. A "variable formula" for the drug as opposed to a "fixed formula."

2. The formula is "patient specific" for "a specific patient," rather than formula that can be used with many patients.

3. The samples are "solid tumors" which eliminates blood cancers.

4. "More than one" antibody is combined to formulate the drug.

The practical consequences of the claims restrictions are:

(1)   From a commercial standpoint, it is generally less commercially feasible to create diagnostic or therapeutic products on an individual patient basis ("variable formula") than to develop one product that can be used for multiple patients ("fixed formula"). Due to all of the clinical trial, efficacy, and safety studies that are required for regulatory approvals, as well as the cost, time, and efficiency of manufacturing processes, products are generally developed that can be used to treat many patients. A tailor-made product that is optimized for an individual patient may be the most efficacious therapy for that patient. However, a tradeoff between cost, time, manufacturing, regulatory issues, and efficacy may be required in order to reach the largest number of patients possible with a product that works satisfactorily for most patients, although the product may not be the best possible product for any particular individual.

(2)   The methods cover a drug that contains no less than two antibodies; e.g., "more than one." The use of only one antibody is not protected by these claims. This language also indicates that the drug that would be injected into a patient for diagnosis or treatment is a *mixture* of at least two antibodies. Of interest, is the possibility that someone could potentially get around the claims by injecting first one drug and then another.

(3)   Due to the multiple steps in the claims, it appears that no one person would be involved in infringing each of the steps. Thus, the person that preselects the antibody panel (scientist?), that obtains the tumor specimen (the doctor?), that chooses the antibodies (technician?); that labels the antibodies (another technician?); that quality controls the antibodies, etc. may be different people. Who is the infringer? Who could be sued? This underscores the problems with this type of method claim. How do you know that someone is infringing your claim? It is more difficult to determine infringement on method (use or process) claims than on product (composition-of-matter) claims.

(4)   Each of the claims involves the use of a panel of antibodies, which may need to be licensed incurring royalty obligations. Some of the claims further contain the use of positive or negative controls that may or may not need to be licensed depending upon their source and third-party patent rights. Some of the steps in the "immunoassay"-type procedures may be the subject of third-party patents (e.g., the detection means or the solid phase immunoassay format). Thus, there is a potential for multiple royalty obligations being necessary to use the patent methods.

(5)   Due to the above considerations, the claim coverage afforded by this patent appears to cover a *subset* of imaging and treatment uses (e.g., individual patients, variable formula drugs, at least two antibodies, etc.). As such, *the patent is more valuable from a defensive position (protect yourself) than from an offensive one (prevent others)*.

Evaluation of Patent Rights

Estimated market size   Cancer is the second leading cause of death in the United States following death by heart diseases. The incidence of different types of cancer in the United States per 100,000 people is 58.0 (lung and bronchus), 34.4 (colon), 114.7 (female breast), 101.2 (prostrate), 8.7 (pancreas), and 9.6 (leukemias) [*The Cancer Statistics Review, 1973-1987*, by the National Cancer Institute]. The

314

incidence of colorectal cancers has risen over the last few years to 50.5 cases per 100,000 Americans in 1986 (*The Healthcare Competitive Intelligence Summary: Colon and Rectal Cancer Rates, Research Studies-Strategic Intelligence Systems*, December 1989, p. 29). Thus, over a one-year period, approximately 131,300 new cases of colorectal cancer will be diagnosed in the United States (50.5 per 100,000 people x 260 million Americans).

Assumptions:

1. Since there is no market, beyond investigational uses, that currently exists for immunotherapy of cancer, base the patent valuation on estimates of the market for detection of cancer.

2. Ignore cancer prevalence rates (e.g., the number of people in the overall population that currently have cancer) and use cancer incidence rates (e.g., the number of people in the overall population who will get cancer, e.g., these people will represent part of the diagnostic market).

3. Double the incidence rates to include annual reanalysis of patients who have already been diagnosed.

Thus, estimate 131,300 new cases of colorectal cancer to be diagnosed and 262,600 detection procedures to be performed each year. At an estimated cost of $200 per test, the yearly U.S. population = $52.52 million.

Patent U.S.#4,940,670 issued on July 10, 1990 and has a 17-year term, or 14 more years from 1993. The detection market for colorectal cancer over these 14 years = $735.3 million [$52.52 million x 14 years].

Market share   The use of radio-labeled antibodies to detect tumors is one of several available procedures that can be used to confirm a diagnosis of cancer and to localize tumors. Other procedures include barium studies, MRI scans, CAT scans, PET scans, etc. Radioimmunodetection may be able to detect occult tumors that were missed by the other procedures. However, due to the expense and limited availability of equipment and trained personnel, any given hospital will probably use only one of these procedures. If a PET machine is available, it will probably be used over any of the other methods. Thus, radioimmunodetection may be able to effectively penetrate this market, but at most, it will achieve a limited market share. It is unlikely that it will replace the other market segments. If the kits are easy to use, require little advanced training or additional equipment, market penetration should occur rapidly. For lack of additional information, market share is estimated at 20% (one out of five available procedures), all else being equal. Radioimmunodetection in the colorectal market = 20% of $735.3 million or $147 million.

Development stage   In 1988 RhoMed entered into agreements with Biomira (Canada) and Syngene (Netherlands) to jointly develop cancer imaging and therapy products using its Antibody Delivery System. Many antibodies are being analyzed for this purpose, but to date, none have been selected for further development. There is a risk that this research may not identify viable candidates (estimated at 50%). This risk would be significantly lower if antibody candidates were already in clinical trials. Estimated market = 50% of $147 or $73.5 million due to the unknowns inherent in research and development.

Claim limitation   A further reduction factor of 50% is applied due to the special considerations discussed above = $36.8 million.

Valuation based upon license-royalties   One way to estimate the value of this particular patent is to determine what royalty income could be obtained if RhoMed decided to completely license the technology to a third party in exchange for royalty fees. A typical royalty rate, based upon product sales, for a diagnostic product is 5%. Over the 14-year time period of the estimate, this equals $1.84 million [5% of $36.8 million].

Total cancer market   The estimate of $1.84 was calculated for just colorectal cancer, but the claim coverage of the patent is not limited to this type of cancer. Assume the total cancer market is 10 times the colorectal cancer market = $18.4 million.

Present value   Assuming a discount factor of 10%, the present value calculated if $18.4 million were obtained at year 14 would be: $18.4 million/$(1+0.1)^{14}$ = $4.85 million. At a 10% discount factor, the present value is calculated to be $4.85 million and at a 25% discount factor, the present value would be $0.81 million.

Executive Summary

Given the assumptions discussed above, the present value valuation of U.S. patent #4,940,670 is about $5 million at a 10% discount factor and less than $1 million at a 25% discount factor, based upon the 14-year lifespan still remaining for the patent. These numbers reflect the "defensive" nature of this particular patent. The actual diagnostic and therapeutic products to be developed are specific monoclonal antibodies, proteins, and peptides that are not claimed in the patent. If such claims exist in other patents or pending applications in the Antibody Delivery System Patent Portfolio, that would strengthen the overall patent package. However, as a stand-alone patent, its value is as discussed.

Scope of Review

Copies of U.S. patent #4,940,670, its file wrapper, and a business plan received from the company were reviewed and analyzed. No external database searches were performed to identify or to evaluate other intellectual property or technology, but about 26 news releases or trade journal abstracts relating to RhoMed were obtained and reviewed. No prior art was reviewed or analyzed relative to the patent rights and no foreign patent file histories, applications, or publications were reviewed.

Source: Aberlyn corporate document.

Exhibit 9   Capital Market Data, July 1, 1993

Yield Implied by the Ask Price of Treasury Bills and Bonds, Maturing in:

Three Months	3.03%
Six Months	3.16%
One Year	3.50%
Two Years	3.95%
Three Years	4.42%
Four Years	4.73%
Five Years	5.05%
Ten Years	6.05%
Thirty Years	6.68%

Average Yield of Corporate Bonds, Maturing in:

1-10 Years, High Quality	5.77%
1-10 Years, Medium Quality	6.24%
10+ Years, High Quality	7.42%
10+ Years, Medium Quality	7.82%
All Years, Low Quality	9.91%

Source: *Wall Street Journal*, July 2, 1993.

Exhibit 10   Annualized Volatility of the Returns of 75 Biotechnology Firms

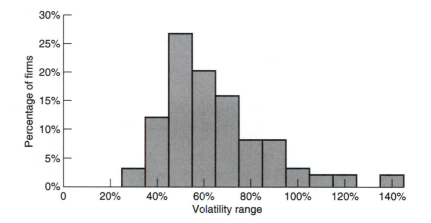

Source: Casewriter's calculations.

This chart plots the annualized volatility of 75 biotechnology firms' common stocks. Daily volatility was calculated for each stock from the 15th trading day subsequent to the stocks' initial public offering until the end of the third year of trading, with returns observable for approximately 745 trading days. The mean annualized volatility for this sample is 68% and the median volatility 67%. In 37% of the 51,771 trading days, these stocks experienced a zero return. The stocks experienced single day returns exceeding 3%, 5%, and 10% on 31%, 16%, and 4% of all trading days, respectively.

16

A Note on the Venture Leasing Industry

INTRODUCTION TO LEASING[1]

Equipment leasing is among the most ancient of financing mechanisms, dating back to the Phoenician shipping industry of 3000 years ago. In the U.S. economy, however, rapid growth in equipment leasing did not occur until the boom of the early 1950s. Fast-growing firms then began leasing a wide variety of capital equipment from construction machinery to aircraft to computers.

The essential characteristic of a lease is that the user of the equipment (the lessee) does not own the equipment. Rather, the title rests with the lessor, who receives periodic payments from the lessee. Although long-term leasing is similar to purchasing equipment with a secured loan (that is, debt that is guaranteed by a pledge of the firm's assets), leasing has several advantages that can make it an attractive financing option for firms.

The first consideration is taxes. If the firm is in a low-tax bracket, it cannot take full advantage of the tax deduction for the depreciation of its capital equipment. In fact, if the firm is losing money, it will have to defer using the deductions for depreciation until it reaches profitability. Leasing can address this problem. Since the title to the equipment remains with the lessor, he can deduct the depreciation for income taxes as long as certain tests specified by the U.S. Internal Revenue Service are met. But taxes have a limited ability to explain which firms employ leasing and how much equipment they lease.[2]

One of the most important nontax motivations for leasing is the possibility of bankruptcy. In these cases, holders of secured debt often find it hard to obtain the property pledged to them, even if their legal rights to the property are well established. Because the lessor retains title to the asset, and the lessee uses the asset only as long as there are no defaults on lease payments, it is often easier for the lessor to

This note was prepared by Josh Lerner. Copyright © 1994 by the President and Fellows of Harvard College. Harvard Business School case 294–069.

[1] This background section is based primarily on Stephen A. Ross, Randolph W. Westerfield, and Jeffrey F. Jaffe, "Leasing," *Corporate Finance* (Homewood, Ill.: Irwin, 1993), pp. 673–702, and U.S. Department of Commerce, International Trade Administration, *A Competitive Assessment of the U.S. Equipment Leasing Industry* (Washington, D.C.: ITC, 1985).

[2] See, for instance, Clifford E. Smith and L. MacDonald Wakefield, "Determinants of Corporate Leasing Policy," *Journal of Finance,* vol. 40 (1985), pp. 895–908; and James Ang and Pamela P. Peterson, "The Leasing Puzzle," *Journal of Finance* 39 (1984), 1055–65.

recover his equipment.[3] A consequence of this improved security is that lessors typically provide 100% financing for equipment purchases. Banks will often require that the firm pay up front in cash 10% or more of the purchase price.

Several other explanations for choosing leasing over secured debt are frequently offered. First, many management compensation schemes are based on return on invested capital. Leasing may lead to a lower computed level of invested capital, and consequently to higher bonuses. Second, lessors may become specialists in assessing the quality of maintenance and the resale value of equipment. Leasing organizations may thus be better at avoiding costly defaults than bankers, who make loans secured by many classes of assets. Finally, managers of risky enterprises often prefer leases to bank loans because of the limited collateral. Although bank loans are often secured by all the firm's assets, leases are secured only by the equipment being leased. Thus, a default on a lease may not entail the same level of disruption to the firm as the failure to meet a bank payment.

THE ORIGIN OF VENTURE LEASING[4]

Venture leasing had its origins in the late 1960s, as the boom in venture capital financing in that decade slowed. Several West Coast venture capital organizations sensed the opportunity to lease equipment to start-up firms as well as provide equity financing. As the new firms found it more difficult to obtain equity financing, they sought to finance major equipment purchases with debt. Bank loan officers, however, had little interest in firms without operating revenues, much less profits. Even when they were willing to extend loans, they typically demanded that the firms purchase the equipment with between 30% and 70% cash up front. This was usually impossible to manage. Similarly, the start-ups encountered difficulties structuring arrangements with traditional leasing agencies, which often used criteria similar to those employed by commercial banks.

The early venture leasing deals typically involved three parties. Not only was the lessee and the venture capitalist–lessor involved, but frequently another venture fund was as well: the lead venture capitalist investing in the firm. This was because a relatively small number of venture funds undertook venture leasing. Consequently, venture lessors were reliant on the referrals of other venture financiers for deals. As in a traditional lease, the lessor maintained title to the equipment over the life of the lease. Unlike traditional leasing, both the lessor and the lead venture capitalist who had provided the referral received warrants in the firm.

These early leases were usually structured as triple-net full-payout leases. This meant the lessee would make payments that covered the entire cost of the leased equipment over the course of the lease. In addition, the lessee would assume responsibility for costs such as maintenance, taxes, and insurance.

Although several successful transactions were completed in the early 1970s, the boom was short-lived. This new financial product faced several difficulties. First, the venture capitalists promoting this product encountered considerable resistance from the start-up firms. The new firms were concerned that the leases would add to an already

[3] For a detailed description, see Linda L. Boss, "Uniform Commercial Code Article 2A—Leases: Structuring Priorities of Competing Claimants to Leased Property," *Minnesota Law Review,* vol. 73 (October 1988), pp. 208–245.

[4] The most comprehensive history of venture leasing—on which this section is largely based—is Venture Economics, *Venture Leasing* (Needham: Venture Economics, 1989).

substantial arsenal of mechanisms through which venture capitalists could exercise control over their firms.

Second, the management of these arrangements proved daunting to the venture capital organizations. The administration of the leases called for considerable paperwork on a monthly basis. Many venture capital firms were run as very "lean" organizations, with little capability to handle routine administrative tasks.

Finally, the reduced capital commitments to the venture capital industry during the 1970s led to a retrenchment. Venture capitalists focused primarily on raising funds to support their core business of investing in new firms rather than on expanding their product offerings.

The rebirth of venture leasing was fueled by the growth of investments in the semiconductor industry in the early 1980s. The chip fabrication equipment that semiconductor manufacturers needed was enormously expensive. In late 1982, a West Coast venture capital fund encouraged Equitec Financial Group, a major real estate syndicator, to extend leases for the purchase of semiconductor manufacturing equipment. Out of these discussions, a new Equitec subsidiary, Equitec Leasing Company, was born. Between 1984 and 1987, Equitec raised 11 limited partnerships of approximately $30 million each, to undertake equipment leases to high-risk firms.

Between the first venture leases and these funds, the treatment of leases had been codified by the Financial Accounting Standards Board (FASB). The new venture leases were structured as capital leases. This was required if at least one of several tests, as stated in FASB's Statement 13, was met. These tests sought to ascertain if the economic ownership in the leased equipment had been transferred to the lessee.[5] In these cases, the firm was required to include the leased asset as an additional asset and the lease obligation as a liability. (In other cases, the lease would just be noted in a footnote to the financial statements.)

This success of the early Equitec funds led to entry by a number of other firms. These included other real estate syndicators, investment banks, equipment leasing firms, and several organizations dedicated to venture leasing. These firms active in venture leasing since 1982 are summarized in Exhibit 1. The volume of venture leasing in several years is reported in Exhibit 2, as well as that of traditional venture investments.

THE VENTURE LEASING PROCESS

The first step in the venture leasing process, it could be argued, is fundraising. A few of these organizations have employed their internal capital, but it has been far more common for venture lessors to access capital through limited partnerships. These specialized pools of money have been raised through private placements with solo investors and syndicated partnerships with a number of limited partners.

The venture leasing partnerships are structured in many respects like venture capital partnerships. The foremost of these similarities is in the compensation of the general partners (the venture lessors). Venture lessors will charge the fund a management fee and receive a percentage of profits. The annual management fees are often 2% to

---

[5] These tests included if (*i*) the present value of the lease payments was at least 90% of the asset value, (*ii*) the lease life was at least 75% of the economic life of the asset, and (*iii*) the lessee is able to purchase the asset at a below-market value price at the end of the period.

3% of the capital committed to the fund or the assets under management. Other funds structure fees up to 5% of the partnership's gross revenues from rental fees and equipment sales. Additional charges may be made per each lease signed.

In addition, the general partners will receive between 15% and 30% of the profits from the fund, but most usually receive 20%. These funds are usually received only after the limited partners receive their initial investment back. In recent years, it has become more common to provide as well for a minimum annual rate of return to the limited partners before the general partners begin receiving distributions.

Venture leasing partnerships differ from venture capital organizations, however, in two respects. First, the timing of the cash flows out of the fund is quite different. Venture capital funds typically must wait years until the first investments are "harvested" through an acquisition or an initial public offering. Venture leasing funds, however, generate funds from lease payments almost immediately. Consequently, the funds will typically pay out distributions quarterly, beginning in the first year of operations.

The second difference is the nature of the investors. Venture lessors have found the primary contemporary sources of venture capital, pension funds and endowments, to be reluctant to invest in their partnerships. The reluctance of the institutions to invest stems from three factors. The first is the information costs associated with educating pension fund managers about venture leasing. Venture investments make up only a small percentage of most pension portfolios. Pension managers are unlikely to spend much time learning about the opportunities inherent in venture leasing, a small subfield of this area. Second, many pension managers are reluctant to invest funds for which they bear a fiduciary responsibility in a relatively unproven asset class.

A final concern is the tax treatment of nonprofit institutional investors' investments in venture leasing funds. In particular, the U.S. Internal Revenue Service regards the interest payments from the lessee to the fund as unrelated business income. Many nonprofit institutions are required to pay taxes on such income, even if the lease payments are retained by the partnership and not distributed to the limited partners. Since the vast majority of endowment earnings are not taxable (e.g., traditional dividends), the tax status of leasing funds imposes a substantial administrative burden and may lead to a less attractive financial return.

Thus, the primary limited partners in leasing partnerships funds have been—just as in the early days of the venture capital—individuals. Increasingly important sources of funds are insurance companies and foreign individuals and institutions. These investors have been attracted to the high returns promised by venture leasing funds, particularly in light of the relatively low yields of Treasury bonds and bills.

Consistent with the origins of the venture leasing industry, these firms have cultivated the venture capital industry. Most firms have close ties with two or three venture capital organizations, who will steer portfolio companies to them. The primary incentive for the venture capitalist is that this provides a chance for their firms to receive additional financing while reducing their stake in the firm by only a few percentage points.

In many respects, the venture lessors play a role for the venture capitalists that is akin to that of marginal or fringe venture partnerships. The venture lessors provide financing after the lead venture capitalist makes the bulk of his investment, in exchange for a much smaller share of the firm's equity. The venture lessors will similarly rely on the lead venture capitalist to monitor management through his role on the board and to provide them with accurate information about the firm's prospects. But because the same venture capitalists and venture lessors frequently interact on deals, their relationships avoid the exploitative behavior that has sometimes characterized established venture capitalists' relationships with less experienced venture funds.

Many of the remaining deals come from the same network of service providers to high-technology firms—law firms, auditors, academic consultants—that venture capitalists employ to generate prospective investments. A small number of firms—most notably, Meier Mitchell and Company and Venlease Associates—have established themselves as brokers of venture leases. These firms locate prospective lessors and perform preliminary background research on the firms. The one-time fee for the broker's services is usually paid by the venture lessor. Having identified a prospective deal, venture leasing organizations differ considerably in the ways in which the potential transactions are evaluated. These differences reflect whether the lessor is a specialist in low-risk, late-stage investments or higher-risk, early-stage ones. All venture leasing organizations examine the extent to which the equipment can be resold if the lessee defaults and the ability of the firm to meet its lease payments. The ability to resell the equipment is largely a function of the extent to which a liquid secondary market exists and the equipment is standard (i.e., it did not require physical retrofitting or application-specific software).

Venture leasing organizations undertaking deals with higher-risk firms (particularly cases where the equipment is specialized) evaluate the firms like a venture capitalist, considering issues such as the strength of the management team and the competitive dynamics of the market. More traditional lessors, however, stress analyses employed by bank lending officers, such as historical and pro forma ratio analysis.

Four key issues frequently emerge in lease negotiations. The first of these is the size and timing of the equipment purchase. Most venture leases will allow the firm to lease a set dollar amount of equipment, which will often be described down to the manufacturer's product number. The average lease has historically been for about $1 million, though this has varied by stage of firm and industry. If the firm does not use all of its lease financing, its interest and principal payments will be reduced, but no adjustment is made to the number of warrants that are provided to the lessor. Exhibits 3 and 4 summarize the average size of lease by the stage of the lessee and its industry. The exhibits also provide comparative information on the size of traditional venture capital investments.[6] Second, the timing of the lease payments presents several issues. First, the lessee will frequently have a set period of time after the lease begins in which it can request that the equipment purchase be made. This "takedown" period is often 6 to 12 months. Once the request is made, the lessor purchases the equipment and the lease payments begin. In many cases, not all the principal is repaid over the life of the lease. Thus, the final payment is a "balloon" payment, containing the unpaid principal. At the opposite extreme, in some cases lessors demand that the firm make a security deposit of up to 20%. In these cases, a percentage of the loan is withheld. This is somewhat similar to a commercial bank's demand that a lending firm retain a minimum level of deposits (a "compensating balance") in their bank account at all times.

A third issue is the length of the lease. Most venture leases are between three and four years in length. But considerable diversity exists across industries. The longer development times of certain industries—such as medical and biotechnology firms—lead them to opt for longer-term leases. Since the return of principal is delayed longer, lessors regard longer-term leases as riskier. Exhibits 5 and 6 summarize the average length of leases by the stage of the lessee's development and its industry. It also provides comparative information on the time between rounds of traditional venture capital investments for each stage and industry.

---

[6] Rather than providing funds in one large sum, U.S. venture capital organizations typically provide financings in several stages (rounds). This allows them to terminate funding if the firm does not live up to its initial promise.

The final area of discussion is the pricing of these transactions. Lessors typically view the pricing of the lease as having two aspects. The first of these, the implicit rate, is the internal rate of return of the promised principal and interest payments associated with the lease, as well as the anticipated cash flows from the final disposition of the property. (The impact of the warrants is not considered.) These rates often range across deals, from just one or two percentage points above the prime interest rate to 10 or more percent above this rate. Typically, lessors will provide lessees with an option to purchase the equipment at the end of the lease. If the equipment is quite firm-specific, the purchase price is likely to be nominal. If the equipment is more generally marketable, the option price may be as high as 25% of the original purchase price. By specifying the price in the transaction, the parties avoid conflicts at the end of the transaction. In the early days of U.S. leasing, the failure to specify the purchase option price led to cases where the lessors would sell equipment—for instance, a telephone system—back to the lessee at *above* the market price, because the disruption entailed by its replacement would be incredibly costly!

The second component of pricing is termed "warrant coverage." Venture lessors are typically granted warrants that are exercisable at the price paid per share of the last venture round. Venture lessors calculate the amount of warrants that they should receive using a unique method. They compute the ratio of the amount they would pay to exercise the warrant to the funds advanced in the lease.

Consider, for instance, a firm that undertakes a $1 million venture lease, whose last venture round was priced at $5/share. If the venture lessor desired 10% "warrant coverage," he would seek to have warrants that could be exercised for a total of $100,000. The exercise price of $5/share (the price of the previous venture round) would imply that he would receive 20,000 warrants.

The unique system of compensation must be understood in the context of the venture financing process. Venture capitalists will typically make several rounds of investment in a firm, at progressively higher valuations. First-round investments are often valued at $1/share, subsequent rounds at a few dollars per share, and initial public offerings at $10/share or higher. Thus, a lessor can be confident that the venture firm will—if it is not terminated—appreciate sharply in value.

The extent of "warrant coverage" that venture lessors will obtain ranges from 5% to 40% of the lease amount, with most lessors receiving between 10% and 15%. In many cases, however, the underwriter of a firm going public will purchase the warrants from the venture lessor at the time of the firm's initial public offering (IPO). This may be because the warrants represent a small and potentially confusing complication of the firm's capital structure.

Exhibit 1 Major Actors in Venture Leasing Business, 1982–1998

Aberlyn Capital Management
Waltham, Massachusetts
An investment banking that entered venture leasing in 1992

Comdisco Ventures (about $500 million in assets under management in the beginning of 1998)
Rosemont, Illinois
Primary line of business: equipment leasing
Entered venture leasing in 1987.

Costella Kirsch
Mountain View, California
Solely devoted to venture leasing.
Established in 1986; apparently exited in the late 1980s.

Dominion Ventures (about $250 million in assets under management in the beginning of 1998)
San Francisco, California
A subsidiary of two venture capital firms and the leasing holding company PLM Co.
Established in 1985 to solely do venture leasing; emphasis on early-stage deals.

Eden Hannon and Co.
Menlo Park, California
Primary line of business: government asset and energy financing.
Entered venture leasing in the mid-1980s, but exited soon thereafter.

Equitec Leasing Company
Oakland, California
A subsidiary of a real-estate syndicator.
Established in 1982 as the first venture leasing organization; acquired by Pacificorp Financial Services
(a utility's financial subsidiary in 1990); declared bankruptcy in 1991.

Fairfax Financial Group
Fairfax, Virginia
Primary line of business is tax-exempt leasing.
Entered venture leasing in the mid-1980s; apparently exited in the late 1980s.

Lease Management Services
Menlo Park, California
One of earliest venture leasing organizations.

Lighthouse Capital Partners (about $120 million in assets under management in the beginning of 1998)
Greenbrae, California
Emphasis on early-stage transactions.
Founded in 1994.

Linc Capital Partners (about $125 million in assets under management in the beginning of 1998)
Chicago, Illinois
A subsidiary of a specialist in health-care equipment lease financing for hospitals.

Phoenix Growth, Inc. (about $250 million in assets under management in the beginning of 1998)
San Rafael, California
A subsidiary of Phoenix America, a leasing firm and limited partnership broker, with a strong leasing emphasis.

R&D Funding Corporation
New York, New York
A subsidiary of Prudential Securities. Served as a general partner, beginning in 1984, in two limited partnerships that provided venture leasing: PruTech I and II. Currently inactive and subject to litigation.

Technology Funding Securities
San Mateo, California
Subsidiary of a venture capital organization, Technology Funding, which had marketed R&D limited partnerships in the early 1980s.

Third Coast Capital (about $66 million in assets under management in the beginning of 1998)
Chicago, Illinois
Founded in 1996; acquired by DVI, Inc. in 1998.

Western Technology Investment
San Jose, California

Source: Complied from numerous media accounts, web pages, and corporate filings with the Securities and Exchange Commission.

Exhibit 2 Venture Leasing and Traditional Venture Capital Investments by Year

Year	Venture Leasing				Traditional Venture Capital		
	Total Firms Funded	Total Amount Invested ($000)	Average Amount Invested ($000)	Range ($000)	Median Investment ($000)	Total Firms Funded	Total Amount invested ($billion)
1986	55	$ 54,511	$991	$ 57-$4,500	$750	1,504	3.23
1987	97	92,672	945	150- 5,000	750	1,729	3.94
1988	177	154,939	875	50- 3,000	500	1,472	3.65
1989	-	200,000[a]	-	-	-	1,355	3.26

Source: Compiled from Venture Economics, *Venture Leasing* (Needham: Venture Economics, 1989); and Venture Economics, "Special Report: Disbursements Fall for Second Year," *Venture Capital Journal*, vol. 30 (July 1990), pp. 14-22.

Some firms may have received several traditional venture rounds in a single year.

[a]Estimate

Exhibit 3 Average Size of Venture Leasing and Traditional Venture Capital Investments, by Stage

Stage	Venture Leasing				Average Venture Round ($000)[a]
	Amount Invested ($000)	% of Total Invested	Number of Companies	Average Amount Invested ($000)	
Seed	4,620	1.5%	11	$ 420	$ 712
Startup	39,102	13.0	44	889	2,387
Other early stage	51,946	17.3	59	880	1,651
Second stage	102,988	34.2%	113	911	2,501
Later stage	102,466	34.0	102	1,005	2,459
Total	$301,122	100.0%	329	$ 915	$ 1,939

Source: Compiled from Venture Economics, *Venture Leasing* (Needham: Venture Economics, 1989); and Paul A. Gompers, "Optimal Investment, Monitoring, and the Staging of Venture Capital," *Journal of Finance*, 50 (December 1995) 1461-1489.

[a]Based on a random sample of 2138 traditional venture capital rounds at 795 venture-backed firms between 1969 and 1992.

Exhibit 4   Average Size of Venture Leasing and Traditional Venture Capital Investments, by Industry

Industry	Venture Leasing				Average Venture Round[a] ($000)
	Amount Invested ($000)	% of Total Invested	Number of Companies	Average Amount Invested ($000)	
Biotechnology	$13,391	4.4%	21	$ 638	$2,412
Commercial communications	1,600	0.5	2	800	[b]
Computer hardware and systems	61,751	20.5	65	950	4,197
Computer software and services	24,125	8.0	31	778	1,916
Consumer related	48,450	16.1	38	1,275	3,120
Other electronics	67,834	22.5	71	955	1,649
Industrial automation	4,700	1.5	9	522	[c]
Industrial products and machinery	13,100	4.4	20	655	1,406
Medical/health	40,838	13.6	42	972	1,900
Telephone and data communications	21,833	7.3	27	809	2,644
Other	3,500	1.2	3	1,167	2,829
Total	$301,122	100.0%	329	$ 915	$ 1,939

Source: Compiled from Venture Economics, *Venture Leasing* (Needham: Venture Economics, 1989); and Paul A. Gompers, "Optimal Investment, Monitoring, and the Staging of Venture Capital," *Journal of Finance*, 50 (December 1995) 1461-1489.

[a]Based on a random sample of 2138 traditional venture capital rounds at 795 venture-backed firms between 1969 and 1992.
[b]Included with "Telephone and data communication."
[c]Included with "Industrial products and machinery."

Exhibit 5   Average Length of Venture Leasing and Traditional Venture Capital Investments, by Stage

Stage	Venture Leasing							Average Length of Venture Round[a]
	Lenght of Lease (Months)						Average	
	1-12	13-24	25-36	37-48	49-60	16+		
	(number of companies)							
Seed	-	-	6	3	-	-	39	25
Startup	-	-	9	22	2	1	44	15
Other early stage	1	-	22	29	2	1	41	13
Second stage	2	4	30	65	6	1	42	12
Later stage	6	-	28	56	7	2	41	13
Total	9	4	95	175	17	5	42	16

Source: Compiled from Venture Economics, *Venture Leasing* (Needham: Venture Economics, 1989); and Paul A. Gompers, "Optimal Investment, Monitoring, and the Staging of Venture Capital," *Journal of Finance*, 50 (December 1995) 1461-1489.

[a]Based on a random sample of 2138 traditional venture capital rounds at 795 venture-backed firms between 1969 and 1992.

Exhibit 6   Average Length of Venture Leasing and Traditional Venture Capital Investments, by Industry

Industry	Venture Leasing							Average Length of Venture Round[a]
	1-12	13-24	25-36	37-48	49-60	16+	Average	
				Months				
Biotechnology	-	-	1	15	1	1	47	15
Commercial communications	-	-	2	-	-	-	36	[b]
Computer hardware and systems	2	-	21	36	5	-	41	15
Computer software and services	1	-	9	16	1	-	40	13
Consumer related	1	1	9	21	-	2	42	17
Other electronics	1	-	24	39	1	-	41	15
Industrial automation	1	2	3	3	-	-	32	[c]
Industrial products and machinery	1	1	8	9	-	-	38	12
Medical/health	-	-	9	18	8	2	47	17
Telephone and data communications	2	-		15	1	-	40	19
Other	-	-	-	3	-	-	45	13
Total	9	4	95	175	17	5	42	16

Source: Compiled from Venture Economics, *Venture Leasing* (Needham: Venture Economics, 1989); and Paul A. Gompers, "Optimal Investment, Monitoring, and the Staging of Venture Capital," *Journal of Finance*, 50 (December 1995) 1461-1489.

[a]Based on a random sample of 2138 traditional venture capital rounds at 795 venture-backed firms between 1969 and 1992.
[b]Included with "Telephone and data communication."
[c]Included with "Industrial products and machinery."

17

An Introduction to Patents and Trade Secrets

INTRODUCTION

One of the key questions in evaluating potential firms is whether their competitive position is sustainable. Firms can protect these positions in many ways, including by developing a favorable reputation ("brand equity") and economies of scale in manufacturing that other firms cannot duplicate. In most high-technology industries, however, two methods of protecting discoveries are most critical: patents and trade secrets.

Volumes can—and have!—been written about each of these ways to protect intellectual property. This note can do little more than provide an introduction to these sources of protection. I refer to several articles and books, however, that provide much more detailed information.

PATENT PROTECTION

A patent application to the U.S. Patent and Trademark Office (USPTO) essentially consists of a series of claims and supporting documentation. (Much of this section is based on Klitzman, 1984; Schwartz, 1988; and U.S. Department of Commerce, 1992.) Some of the claims in a patent application will be cast in very specific terms; others may be sweeping. A supervising primary examiner reviews each incoming patent application, and assigns it to one of the over 120,000 U.S. patent subclasses. This classification determines which examining group reviews the application.

A patent examiner in the assigned group then evaluates the proposed patent. To assess the novelty of the application, he searches previous patents issued in the original and related subclasses and several on-line databases. To be entitled to utility patent protection (the most common form of U.S. grant), an innovation must satisfy three criteria. Under 35 U.S.C. 101–103 and 112, it must be:

- a process, machine, manufacture, or composition of matter.
- new, useful, and nonobvious.
- disclosed in sufficient detail that a skilled person could build and operate it.

This note was prepared by Josh Lerner. Copyright © 1994 by the President and Fellows of Harvard College. Harvard Business School case 295-062.

The scope of patentable subject matter has traditionally not included fundamental scientific discoveries. A frequently invoked rationale for this omission is that many scientists care little for monetary rewards, and would consequently have pursued the discoveries in any case. To grant patent awards for purely scientific discoveries would consequently be socially wasteful.[1]

If the application appears to conform to the other standards for patentability, the patent examiner will then determine whether the claimed innovation conflicts with any in-process applications or recent patent awards. Unlike most nations, the United States grants patents to the party that is "first to invent" a new product or process rather than the one who is "first to file" for an award. If the application appears to supersede another application or a recent award, the examiner will declare the patent application to be in interference. Often applicants will provoke interferences. The standard approach is for the firm to "copy claims"; that is, to include in its application the same wording as in another firm's claim. Even though USPTO holds pending applications confidential, firms often provoke interferences with patents that are still pending. They are able to do so because of the timing of the patent application process. To receive European patent protection, firms must file an application at the European Patent Office (EPO) within one year of the U.S. application. Eighteen months after the original application, the EPO publishes the key information about the pending patent.

Disputes are turned over to the USPTO's Board of Patent Appeals and Interferences. The firm whose patent has been interfered with (the senior party) is notified, and each party reviews the other's application. The Board will hold a hearing to determine which inventor first made the discovery. It will decide whether the junior party's patent should be allowed in its entirety or whether some claims should be disallowed. If the senior party's patent has not yet been issued, its claims may be scaled back or even rejected entirely. If the senior party's patent has been issued, the Board cannot take away the award or retroactively reduce its scope. A finding casting doubt on the senior party's patent, however, can be used by the junior party if and when it challenges the patent in Federal court.

Thus, prior to the award of the junior party's patent, the two parties are often aware of each other's patent position. The lengthy interference process serves to bring firms together early in the dispute process and facilitates the negotiation of a cross-licensing agreement to settle the controversy. In recent years, 80% of the interferences have been settled prior to a final hearing by the Board (Calvert and Sofocleous, 1992).

At the time of award, the patent examiner assigns the patent to one or more U.S. patent subclasses. The examiner has a strong incentive to classify these patents carefully, because he uses these classifications in his searches of the prior state of the art. To ensure the accuracy of the classification and to maintain consistency across examining groups, an official known as a "post classifier" reviews the classification of all issuing patents.

After the patent is issued, the primary forum for formally resolving disputes is the Federal courts. The Federal courts have exclusive jurisdiction over disputes involving the infringement of patents, as well as over appeals of USPTO decisions. Other disputes—for example, a disagreement between a firm and an employee over a royalty—are routinely referred back to the state courts. If a firm believes that a patent is being infringed, it may sue the infringer for damages and/or injunctive relief (a judgment ordering the defendant to cease infringing the patent). Conversely, the alleged infring-

---

[1] See, for instance, *Katz v. Horni Signal Manufacturing Corp.,* 52 F.Supp. 453, 59 U.S.P.Q. (BNA) 196 (D.N.Y. 1943), rev'd, 145 F.2d 961, 63 U.S.P.Q. (BNA) 190 (2d Cir. 1944), cert. denied, 324 U.S. 882, 65 U.S.P.Q. 588 (U.S. 1945).

ing firm may preemptively use the other firm for declaratory relief (a judgment that the plaintiff is not infringing any patent held by the defendant).

In either event, the initial litigation must be undertaken in a district court. Prior to 1982, appeals were heard in the court of appeals of the district in which the case was tried. These circuit courts varied considerably in their interpretation of patent law, and the resolution of these differences through appeals to the U.S. Supreme Court was a lengthy and uncertain process. Consequently, the Court of Appeals for the Federal Circuit (CAFC) was established as the appellate court for all patent-related Federal cases. CAFC decisions may still be appealed to the U.S. Supreme Court, but the latter seldom agrees to hear such appeals.

At any point in the litigation process, the adversarial parties may settle their dispute. This agreement may or may not be accompanied by compensation for retroactive relief and/or a patent license or cross-license agreement. If the settlement is reached before the filing of a suit or a decision within USPTO, the existence of the dispute is unlikely to become public knowledge. The settlement of interferences or post-award disputes are rarely announced, and certainly not in any systematic manner.

Practitioner accounts suggest that the impact of patent litigation has grown with the strengthening of patent rights. This shift towards a more "pro-patent" policy has been effected partially through legislation—for example, the Computer Software Protection Act of 1980 and the Semiconductor Chip Protection Act of 1984—but even more so through the decisions of the CAFC. When the CAFC was created in 1982, its stated purpose was to be a streamlined venue for treating patent cases in a systemized manner. But as Merges (1992) notes,

> While the CAFC was ostensibly formed strictly to unify patent doctrine, it was no doubt hoped by some (and expected by others) that the new court would make subtle alterations in the doctrinal fabric, with an eye to enhancing the patent system. To judge by results, that is exactly what happened.

This claim is supported through a comparison of CAFC's rulings with previous appellate decisions in patent infringement cases. Between 1953 and 1978, circuit courts affirmed 62% of district court decisions holding patents to be valid and infringed, and reversed 12% of the decisions holding patents to be invalid or not infringed (Koenig, 1980). In the years 1982–90, the CAFC affirmed 90% of district court decisions holding patents to be valid and infringed, and reversed 28% of the judgments of invalidity or noninfringement (Harmon, 1991).

As a consequence, corporate patent litigation today appears to be quite frequent. In an analysis of intellectual property litigation involving a sample of 530 firms based in Middlesex County, Massachusetts, Lerner (1994) finds that these firms engaged in 78 distinct patent suits between January 1990 and June 1994 in Federal District for Massachusetts and Middlesex County Superior Court. During the same period, these firms were awarded 2533 patents. Because firms generally attempt to litigate cases in the district encompassing their headquarters,[2] this litigation probably represents about one-half the patent suits involving these firms. The analysis suggests that approximately 6

---

[2] Because there was considerable variation in the interpretation of patent laws across the federal circuits before the creation of the CAFC in 1982, firms frequently attempted to litigate cases in districts that they believed were predisposed to their arguments. The creation of the centralized appellate court has led to a considerable reduction in the differences in intellectual property law across the circuits. As a result, "forum shopping"—the filing of cases in districts perceived to be favorable—declined sharply. Firms today generally attempt to litigate these cases in the same district as their headquarters. This allows them to employ the same outside lawyers that they usually utilize, and to make greater use of internal corporate counsel.

patent suits are filed for each 100 corporate patent awards. Particularly striking, practitioner accounts suggest, has been the growth of litigation—and threats of litigation—between large and small firms. Several well-capitalized firms, including Texas Instruments, Digital Equipment, and Intel, have established groups that approach rivals to demand royalties on old patent awards. In addition to litigation in the courts, in recent years nearly 4,000 quasi-judicial administrative procedures have been conducted annually within the USPTO (U.S. Department of Commerce, 1991).

These suits lead to significant expenditures by firms. Based on historical costs, the patent litigation within USPTO and the Federal courts begun in 1991 will lead to total legal expenditures (in 1991 dollars) of about $1 billion,[3] a substantial amount relative to the $3.7 billion spent by U.S. firms on basic research in 1991.

Litigation also leads to substantial indirect costs. The discovery process is likely to require the alleged infringer to produce extensive documentation, as well as time-consuming depositions from researchers and general managers. The firm may be portrayed unfavorably in the trade press, and be disparaged by rival salesmen. In addition, the CAFC has repeatedly emphasized a patentee's "affirmative duty to exercise due care to determine whether or not he is infringing"[4] other firms' patents. If the infringement is held to be willful, the firm risks being assessed trebled damages, opponent's legal fees, and court costs. Its officers and directors may also be held individually liable.

Event studies can provide one indication of the total costs of litigation. Bhagat, Brickley, and Coles (1994) examine the market reaction to the filing of 20 patent infringement lawsuits between 1981 and 1983 where (i) the filing was reported in the *Wall Street Journal,* (ii) there is only one plaintiff and defendant, and (iii) both the plaintiff's and defendant's stock returns are included in the Center for Research in Security Prices' (CRSP) Daily Returns File. In the two-day window ending on the day the story appears in the *Journal,* the combined market-adjusted value of the firms fell by an average of –3.1% (significant at the one percent confidence level).

These developments have sparked concern that the pattern of costly litigation—or payments to forestall litigation—are leading to reductions or distortions in innovative investments, particularly for small firms. [Several examples are discussed in Rutter, 1993 and Chu, 1992. These concerns also appear to have been an important motivation for the Department of Justice's emphasis on "innovation markets" in their proposed new intellectual property guidelines.] This anecdotal evidence is supported by more formal examinations. Lanjouw (1994) uses European patent renewal data and a model of patenting behavior to estimate how litigation affects the pace of innovation. Her simulations suggest that a doubling of legal costs will lead about a 30% reduction in the value of the average patent. Claims regarding differences with firm size are corroborated by a 1990 survey of 376 firms (Koen, 1992). This survey found that the time and expense of intellectual property litigation was a major factor in the decision to pursue an innovation for 55% of the enterprises with under 500 employees, but was a major concern for only 33% of larger businesses. In general, small firms believed that their patents were infringed more frequently, but were considerably less likely to litigate these infringements.

---

[3] This estimate is based on documents by the USPTO and other sources. USPTO's estimate of the number of patent suits is likely to be low, because (i) many cases that involve patents are classified as contract, miscellaneous tort, or other cases, and (ii) many suits classified as patent cases are nonetheless not reported by the federal clerks to USPTO.

[4] *Underwater Devices v. Morrison-Knudsen,* 717 F.2d 1380, 1389; 219 U.S.P.Q. (BNA) 569 (Fed. Cir. 1983).

TRADE SECRET PROTECTION

The definition of trade secrecy with the widest acceptance is that in the American Law Institute's *Restatement of Torts* (1939).

> A trade secret may consist of any formula, pattern, device or compilation of information which is used in one's business, and which gives him an opportunity to obtain an advantage over competitors who do not know or use it. … A substantial element of secrecy must exist, so that, except by the use of improper means, there would be difficulty in acquiring the information.

Trade secrecy is quite different from other forms of intellectual property protection. This note will highlight three of these differences. (For fuller discussions, see Kitch, 1980 and Cheung, 1982.)

First, in at least three respects trade secrecy provides stronger protection than patents. While other forms of intellectual property protection are contingent on novelty or originality, the standard for trade secret protection is lower. A firm can protect an innovation in this manner, even if several competitors have made the same discovery independently. (The other firms, however, also must not disclose the discovery.) The span of trade secret protection is indefinite, not limited to a set term as other forms of protection. An inventor need not (indeed cannot) disclose a trade secret, while publication by the U.S. Patent and Trademark Office is a requirement for the award of a patent.

In other ways, the nature of trade secret protection is more limited than alternative forms of intellectual property protection. Trade secrets are only protected against misappropriation: "the acquisition of a trade secret by a person who knows or has reason to know that the trade secret was acquired by improper means" (Milgrim, 1993). Thus, a firm whose trade secret is discovered by another firm independently or through "reverse engineering" (the disassembly of a device to discover how it works) would not have grounds to sue. This is unlike patent protection, which allows the awardee to prosecute others who infringe, regardless of the source of the infringers' ideas.

Finally, while the other forms of intellectual property protection are governed by federal law, trade secrets are protected by state laws. As of July 1994, 40 states had adopted the Uniform Trade Secrets Act (Jager, 1994). This Act codifies many of the features of trade secret law that were already incorporated in the common law (Friedman, Landes, and Posner, 1991). The essence of trade secret law was already established in the United States by the end of the nineteenth century, and the law has changed relatively little since the publication of the first edition of the *Restatement of Torts* in 1939 (Milgrim, 1993).

Trade secrecy has also been the subject of ongoing public policy activity. A substantial reform of trade secret policy has recently been implemented in Japan (McKeown, 1993). The U.S. Senate passed the Patent Prior User Rights Act of 1994 [S.2272], which would insulate those who protect discoveries through trade secrecy from subsequent patent infringement suits. (The 103rd Congress adjourned before this issue was considered by the House of Representatives.) More changes are anticipated as nations struggle to harmonize their intellectual property systems. In addition to legislative initiatives, governmental agencies are devoting greater administrative resources to the prevention of trade secret theft. In the United States and other Western nations, intelligence agencies have made a major effort to shift resources from monitoring Communist nations to thwarting trade secret spying by foreign industrial concerns (for an overview, see U.S. House, 1992).

Economists and lawyers have devoted relatively little attention to firms' choice between trade secrecy and other methods of protecting intellectual property. Two rationales, however, are suggested by the limited work on this question.

First, firms may choose to employ trade secrecy because it is more cost effective than patent protection. Friedman, Landes, and Posner (1991) suggest several examples where this rationale might hold. The innovation may be relatively minor, and hence the cost of filing and prosecuting an application may exceed the benefit of patent protection. Second, the expected duration of trade secret protection (i.e., until a rival discovers the secret independently or through reverse engineering) may exceed the fixed length of a patent grant. Finally, the firm may believe that the invention is not patentable.

Two other models of the decision to patent introduce an additional cost of patenting: the disclosure of information to rivals. In Horstmann, MacDonald, and Slivinski (1985), a patent reveals to competitors that a certain technological area is promising, but does not always block rivals from imitating the patent. Firms consequently only patent discoveries with some probability that is positive but less than one. As patents become less effective in blocking infringements, the propensity of firms to patent declines. Scotchmer and Green (1990) develop a model in which a relatively minor finding provides information about an as-yet-undiscovered innovation. A firm may choose not to patent the intermediate discovery, lest the information disclosed allow its rival to catch up in the race to make the ultimate innovation. The probability that a firm will patent an intermediate discovery decreases with the cost of pursuing the innovation and the probability of discovery.[5]

EVIDENCE ON THE CHOICE BETWEEN PATENTS AND TRADE SECRETS

In the paper mentioned above, Lerner examines the importance of trade secrecy relative to other forms of intellectual property protection for a sample of 530 manufacturing firms based in Middlesex County, Massachusetts. He examines this by using civil litigation case files. While the pattern of litigation is certainly not a perfect indicator of economic importance, it can suggest where particular forms of intellectual property protection are most critical.

He identifies all litigation involving these firms in the federal and state judicial districts encompassing their headquarters over a four-and-a-half year period. Patent and trade secret issues are commonplace and occur with about the same frequency. He examines how the involvement of firms in trade secret and other forms of intellectual property litigation varies with firm size, research intensity, and access to capital. Intellectual property cases litigated by smaller firms disproportionately involve trade secrecy. The coefficients in a regression analysis are economically as well as statistically significant. In the average firm, 43% of the intellectual property cases involve trade secrecy. In a firm with employment one standard deviation above the mean, only 33% of the intellectual property cases involve trade secrecy. This result is consistent with the view that less established firms employ trade secrecy because the direct and indirect costs of patenting are too large.

---

[5] While not discussed by the authors, the process of applying for international patent protection may also contribute to the reluctance to patent. Patent applications in the United States are held confidential until the time of award: hence, rejected applications are not made public. But firms that seek patent protection in the United States are almost certain to also seek it in other major markets as well. Patent applications in Europe and Japan are published 18 months after the original application is filed. Because firms often do not know at the time that they pursue a European patent whether the invention is patentable, they run the risk of losing both patent and trade secret protection if the application is subsequently denied after its publication. A case in which these issues figured prominently is *Paterson v. Chemical Engineering*, Docket No. 82-10-1709, State of Michigan Circuit Court, Country of Lewanee, June 10, 1983; *aff'd*, Michigan Supreme Court, March 8, 1985; *cert. denied*, 479 U.S. 828, 107 S.Ct. 109 (1986).

REFERENCES AND FURTHER READING

BHAGAT, SANJAI, JAMES A. BRICKLEY, AND JEFFREY L. COLES, 1994, "The Costs of Inefficient Bargaining and Financial Distress: Evidence from Corporate Lawsuits," *Journal of Financial Economics*. 35, 221–47.

CALVERT, IAN A., AND SOFOCLEOUS, MICHAEL, 1992, "Interference Statistics for Fiscal Years 1989 to 1991," *Journal of the Patent and Trademark Office Society* 74, 822–26.

CHEUNG, STEVEN N.S., 1982, "Property Rights in Trade Secrets," *Economic Inquiry*. 20, 40–53.

CHU, MICHAEL P., 1992, "An Antitrust Solution to the New Wave of Predatory Patent Infringement Litigation," *William and Mary Law Review* 33, 1341–68.

FRIEDMAN, DAVID D., WILLIAM M. LANDES, AND RICHARD A. POSNER, 1991, "Some Economics of Trade Secret Law," *Journal of Economic Perspectives* 5 (Winter): 61–72.

HARMON, ROBERT L., 1991, *Patents and the Federal Circuit*. Washington, D.C.: Bureau of National Affairs.

HORSTMANN, IGNATIUS, GLENN M. MACDONALD, AND ALAN SLIVINSKI, 1985, "Patents as Information Transfer Mechanisms: To Patent or (Maybe) Not to Patent," *Journal of Political Economy* 93, 837–58.

JAGER, MELVIN F., 1994, *Trade Secrets Law*. New York: Clark Boardman Callahan.

KITCH, EDMUND W., 1980, "The Law and Economics of Rights in Valuable Information," *Journal of Legal Studies* 9, 683–723.

KLITZMAN, MAURICE H., 1984, *Patent Interference: Law and Practice*. New York: Practicing Law Institute.

KOEN, MARY S., 1990, *Survey of Small Business Use of Intellectual Property Protection: Report of a Survey Conducted by MO-SCI Corporation for the Small Business Administration*. Rolla, MO: MO-SCI Corp.

KOENIG, GLORIA K., 1990, *Patent Invalidity: A Statistical and Substantive Analysis*. New York: Clark Boardman.

LANJOUW, JEAN O., 1994, "Economic Consequences of a Changing Litigation Environment: The Case of Patents," National Bureau of Economic Research Working Paper No. 4835. Cambridge, MA: National Bureau of Economic Research.

LERNER, JOSH, 1994, "The Importance of Trade Secrecy: Evidence from Civil Litigation." Unpublished manuscript. Boston: Harvard University.

MERGES, ROBERT P., 1992, *Patent Law and Policy*. Charlottesville, VA: Michie Company.

MILGRIM, ROGER M., 1993, *Milgrim on Trade Secrets*. New York: Matthew Bender.

RUTTER, NANCY, 1993, "The Great Patent Plague," *Forbes ASAP*. (March 29): 58–66.

SCHWARTZ, HERBERT F., 1988, *Patent Law and Practice*. Washington, D.C.: Federal Judicial Center.

SCOTCHMER, SUZANNE, AND JERRY GREEN, 1990, "Novelty and Disclosure in Patent Law," *Rand Journal of Economics* 21, 131–46.

U.S. Department of Commerce, Patent and Trademark Office, 1991, *Annual Report: Fiscal Year 1991*. Washington, D.C.: Government Printing Office.

U.S. Department of Commerce, Patent and Trademark Office, 1992, *Manual of Patent Examining Procedure*. 5th ed, Revision 14, Washington, D.C.: Government Printing Office.

U.S. House of Representatives, Committee on the Judiciary, Subcommittee on Economic and Commercial Law, 1992, *The Threat of Foreign Economic Espionage to U.S. Corporations*. (102nd Congress, Second Session, April 29 and May 7, 1992). Washington, D.C.: U.S. Government Printing Office.

18

BCI Growth III: May 1993

Don Remey, a managing director at the mezzanine fund BCI Growth III, sat stuck in traffic on Interstate 95. The sky was a forbidding gray, which matched Remey's pensive mood. What was deeply troubling Remey, however, was neither the New Jersey traffic nor the fact that the management team of a company in his portfolio was already waiting for him in his office. Rather, his thoughts were several hundred miles away, in the green hills of Vermont.

Remey and his partners were considering making a $5 million investment in a company based in Rutland, Vermont—Casella Waste Systems, which specialized in solid waste hauling and disposal. The company was planning to use the proceeds of the BCI investment to acquire its first two lined landfills, which would be a major step in undertaking a consolidation ("roll up") of waste firms in northern New England. Remey was troubled, however, by the fact that the proposed transaction was in many respects an earlier stage deal than BCI's typical mezzanine investments. In particular, Casella Waste Systems appeared to be much closer to the type of high-risk transaction that a venture capital fund might consider.

At the same time, Casella's proposed strategy was sound. Its management team was an attractive one. Furthermore, the financial characteristics of the solid waste business lent themselves to a mezzanine financing structure. Finally, BCI had invested considerable time in researching the opportunity and structuring the proposed transaction. The key issue in Remey's mind was whether he was really taking an equity risk for a mezzanine return. The detailed terms had been aggressively negotiated, and the closing was only a few weeks away. It would be difficult to back away at this late date, but Remey still had some major concerns about the risks to BCI. Should he proceed with the closing or back away?

MEZZANINE PRIVATE EQUITY

Mezzanine investments emerged as a distinct class of private equity in the early 1980s. As Exhibit 1 depicts, the amount of funds raised by mezzanine investors climbed sharply through 1987 and then rapidly declined. Behind this pattern of growth and retrenchment, however, lay a more complex story.

The type of investment made by mezzanine funds—the provision of capital to small firms with a greater return than straight debt and a lower risk than straight equity—has

This case was prepared by Josh Lerner. Copyright © 1998 by the President and Fellows of Harvard College. Harvard Business School case 298–093.

long been a feature of the U.S. economy.[1] At least since the 1950s, insurance companies have allocated a portion of their capital reserves for equity-linked investments in private firms, which typically are already-established companies in low-technology industries. Because of the long-term nature of their liabilities (life insurance policies and annuities), these financial institutions were willing to invest in illiquid securities that did not pay out for a number of years. (Many of these were also among the earliest institutional investors in venture capital funds.) In return for their investments, the insurance companies received not only the repayment of debt and interest, but a modest "equity kicker," typically a small number of warrants to purchase the firm's common stock. The insurance companies found that while these investments did not offer the exceedingly high returns that venture capitalists could enjoy, the protection provided by the firms' stable cash flows and liquid assets limited the potential for substantial losses. Meanwhile, the higher returns allowed them to consider investing in many firms that banks (which typically did not—and often could not—take equity stakes in firms they lent to) had rejected as too risky.[2]

One characteristic of mezzanine lending since its inception was a great deal of flexibility in the structure of the transactions. Based on the projected cash flows of the firm, the interest rate and speed with which the principal would need to be repaid could vary substantially. The equity provided as part of the transaction could vary considerably as well. Whatever the debt-equity mixture, typically these transactions at the time were designed to return a rate of return of between 20% and 30%. Another area of innovation was the development of complex call and put provisions. These enabled the issuer to buy back the outstanding warrants within certain time windows, either at a price set in advance or at fair market value, or allowed the investor to force the issuer to repurchase these financial instruments.

During the 1970s, the insurance companies were joined in this activity by banks and several venture capital organizations. But the early 1980s saw a more substantial change: the emergence of the first independent partnerships geared solely to mezzanine investments. (Dedicated funds devoted solely to leveraged buyouts—LBOs—had emerged just a few years before.) These groups, using the same limited partnership structure that venture capital groups employed, tended to concentrate on riskier transactions than insurance companies. This alternative investment approach reflected three considerations:

- The new groups needed to differentiate themselves, and consequently chose an area that was not the insurance companies' historic strength.

- Many of the insurance companies' private placement groups were structured as very "lean" operations, without the staff to intensively scrutinize potential transactions.

---

[1] The account of the origins of the mezzanine market was largely based on American Life Convention and Life Insurance Association, *Direct Placements,* Chicago, American Life Convention, 1957; and Eli Shapiro, "Developments in the Private Placement Market: The Changing Role of the Life Insurance Industry," in J. David Cummins, editor, *Investment Activities of Life Insurance Companies,* Homewood, Illinois, R. D. Irwin for the S. S. Huebner Foundation for Insurance Education, 1977, chapter 3. The description of the evolution of mezzanine finance in the 1980s and early 1990s was based partially on the narratives in Ronald A. Kahn and Susan W. Wilson, "The Bifurcated Mezzanine Finance Market," *Secured Lender* 51 (July/August 1995), pp. 46–50, William J. Torpley and Jerry A. Viscione, "Mezzanine Money for Smaller Business," *Harvard Business Review* 65 (May/June 1987): pp. 116–118, and "Are Institutions Missing the Boat by Overlooking Mezzanine Funds?," *Private Equity Analyst* 2 (March 1992): pp. 1, 10–12.

[2] A substantial literature documents the types of regulatory and agency problems that can limit the effectiveness of banks as financing sources. Two thoughtful review articles are Sudipto Bhattacharya and Anjan V. Thakor, "Contemporary Banking Theory," *Journal of Financial Intermediation* 3 (1993): pp. 2–50; and Raghuram G. Rajan, "Why Banks Have a Future: Towards a New Theory of Banking," *Journal of Applied Corporate Finance,* 9 (Summer 1996), pp. 114–128. For a more general discussion of the constraints that prevent small firms from obtaining the capital that they need, see R. Glenn Hubbard, "Capital Market Imperfections and Investment," *Journal of Economic Literature* 36 (1998): 193–225.

- The insurance companies—unlike the private equity partnerships—were subject to a considerable degree of regulatory oversight from state authorities. Fearing scrutiny and adverse publicity, they tended to shy away from investments with a substantial probability of default.

The mezzanine market underwent another wrenching transition in the mid-1980s, as the popularity of LBOs soared. A considerable number of mezzanine funds, often affiliated with major financial institutions or private equity investors, were established solely to invest in LBO transactions. The investment focus of these funds was quite different from that of traditional mezzanine investors. Rather than providing growth capital to emerging firms, these groups invested in the intermediate trenches of buyout transactions: that is, claims junior to the bank debt but senior to the equity provided by the LBO partnerships. The peak year of mezzanine fundraising, 1987, was driven by the formation of several very large LBO-related funds, including the $2 billion Forstmann Little Subordinated Debt Fund IV.

These buyout-oriented mezzanine funds experienced very poor returns. This was partially attributable to the poor performance of the LBOs initiated in the mid- and late-1980s. (Many funds begun around this time to make equity investments in buyouts had very poor returns as well.) An additional problem at many of the mezzanine funds sponsored by financial institutions or private equity groups was conflicts of interest, as the general partners at the funds were pressured to invest in their sponsors' transactions on unattractive terms. As a result, the returns of mezzanine funds as a whole were very low. As of the end of 1992, the average mezzanine fund had an annual return of 0.1% since its inception, while the median fund had a return of 6.7%.[3]

These problems did not go unnoticed by institutional investors. Many of these investors, not appreciating the distinctions between mezzanine funds, abandoned this subclass of private equity entirely. As a result, numerous private equity groups dedicated to mezzanine investing disbanded in the early 1990s. Ironically, just as many mezzanine funds were exiting the market, the range of attractive investment opportunities increased dramatically. The recession and real estate crisis of the early 1990s prompted much tighter regulation of banks by state and federal regulators. In the resulting "credit crunch," many firms had their bank lines of credit trimmed and experienced severe financial pressures. The surviving mezzanine funds—who tended to be those who had remained with the traditional formula of providing growth capital—suddenly had an abundance of attractive opportunities.

BCI ADVISORS[4]

BCI Advisors was a private equity group concentrating on providing expansion capital to small businesses. Their target investment was well beyond the start-up phase: a firm with revenues between $5 and $100 million. Typically, the firms in the BCI portfolio had positive cash flows from operations and established products or services, but were seeking to grow rapidly. Although the fund considered potential investments in almost any industry outside of high technology, historically one-third of BCI's investments had been in radio and television companies. The biographies of BCI's four general partners in 1993—Hoyt Goodrich, Bart Goodwin, Ted Horton, and Don Remey—as well as Peter Wilde, the key associate working on the Casella transaction, are reproduced in Exhibit 2.

---

[3] Venture Economics, *1997 Investment Benchmark Reports: Buyouts and Other Private Equity*, New York, Venture Economics, 1997.

[4] Unless otherwise noted, this section is based on various private placement memoranda of and news stories about BCI Advisors.

BCI's first office had a photograph of the Brooklyn Bridge in its conference room, which was an apt metaphor for the private equity organization's mission. In their decades of private equity experience at Aetna, Citibank, Kidder, Peabody, and New Court Securities (the private equity affiliate of Rothschild & Co.), BCI founders Goodrich and Remey had observed that a substantial gap existed between venture capital and traditional financing sources such as banks and public investors. In particular, as Goodrich observed, many "companies have dramatic growth opportunities but have problems getting capital to expand from the usual sources."[5] These challenges were particularly acute at the time of BCI's formation. While venture investors were concentrating on high-technology firms, many insurance companies were experiencing cash-flow problems and were cutting back their investments in private placements. Meanwhile, banks were frequently unwilling to finance aggressive expansion programs that might endanger their principal.

BCI Advisors had raised its first fund, Bridge Capital Investors, in 1983 with $51 million in capital. Its follow-on fund, Bridge Capital Investors II, was raised in 1986 and totaled $100 million. The firm decided to switch to its current name because during the late 1980s, bridge financing increasingly became associated with leveraged buyouts and short-term financings. BCI Growth, its third fund, had closed in 1990 with committed capital of $135.5 million. These funds had been raised from a wide variety of pension funds, such as those of General Electric, Honeywell, Kodak, and the state of Wisconsin, and investment advisers, including Abbott Capital Management and Chancellor Capital Management.

BCI typically made investments of between $3 and $8 million in companies. These were usually structured as debt and subordinated to any bank debt the companies had outstanding. In exchange for the greater risk that BCI was assuming, the private equity group received compensation and demanded protections that banks could not (or typically did not) receive. In each transaction, BCI would receive equity in the firm, either in the form of warrants or convertible debt. It also approached its relationship with the portfolio company like a venture investor: it typically obtained a board seat and a close working relationship with the portfolio firm. As a result of these preferences, BCI tended to invest in deals that it originated itself, rather than deals in which other private equity groups served as the lead investor. This approach to deal origination also allowed BCI to avoid being drawn into auctions, enabling it to invest at more attractive valuations.

BCI's approach to proposed transactions combined the perspective of a venture capitalist and a banker. In its due diligence, the partners sought not only to understand the upside potential—that is, whether the firm would be able to go public or be acquired within a few years—but also the likelihood of the return of principal. In particular, the firm's ability to service its debt, the liquidity of its assets, and the ease of exit were key aspects of the analysis.

In structuring its transactions, BCI also employed a variety of hybrid structures to protect its interests. An illustration of this approach was its 1985 investment of $10 million in Jiffy Lube, the quick-change oil service.[6] BCI had agreed to provide the company with subordinated debt, on which interest payments would begin immediately. The principal would be repaid in eight semiannual installments, beginning in the fourth year after the transaction. Finally, the company agreed to provide BCI with warrants equal

---

[5] "Mezzanine Financing: Backing Companies Once They're Off the Ground," *Business Week,* May 7, 1984, p. 136.

[6] This description is based on Jeffry R. Timmons, "Jiffy Lube International, Inc.," *New Venture Creation,* 4th ed., Burr Ridge, Illinois, Irwin, 1994, pp. 586–595; and *Initial Public Offering Prospectus: Jiffy Lube International, Inc.,* Shearson Lehman Brothers Inc. and Alex. Brown & Sons Inc., July 22, 1986.

to 10% of the firm. These warrants were "puttable"—that is, BCI could force the company to repurchase the warrants—if Jiffy Lube did not go public within five years and trade at a price that ensured BCI an attractive return. (The minimum share price, which increased over time, was stipulated in the stock purchase agreement.) If BCI exercised the put option, it could force the company to repurchase the shares at a price that provided it with an overall return on its investment of at least 30%. If the company could not repurchase the shares, then BCI would have the right to nominate a majority of the board.

This approach had served BCI well. The rate of return from BCI Advisors' first two funds considerably exceeded that of the average buyout or mezzanine fund formed in the same year, as calculated by Venture Economics. Given the considerably lower risk associated with its investments relative to those of a traditional buyout or venture fund, it is likely that BCI's outperformance was even more substantial than these simple comparisons suggest.

THE WASTE HAULING INDUSTRY IN 1993[7]

The revenues of the solid waste industry were estimated to be about $30 billion in 1993. Despite the consolidation activity that had occurred over the previous decade, it remained a highly fragmented industry. Environmental regulations were placing increased pressure on the industry, particularly on the smaller firms. Although obtaining a comprehensive picture of the solid waste industry was challenging, both investment bank analysts and the Census Bureau compiled estimates of activity. (Key Census data is summarized in Exhibit 3.) At the end of 1992, 11 publicly traded firms accounted for revenue of almost $9 billion, or about 30% of the industry total. (These firms are summarized in Exhibit 4.) Several thousand independent firms (typically operating on a local or regional basis) accounted for about 25% of revenues, while the remainder was in the hands of municipal or other governmental bodies. The role of the public sector was even more pronounced when the ownership of landfills was examined: fully 85% of the solid waste landfills were owned by public bodies.[8] The industry had experienced declining profitability over the first years of the 1990s. This partially reflected the impact of the recession of 1991–1992: the downturn in economic activity had led to a 4% fall in solid waste tonnage in 1991 and a similar decline in 1992. Another factor was the decision of two of the largest firms in the industry, Browning–Ferris and Waste Management, to engage in aggressive price competition. The declining profitability also reflected pressures by municipalities on waste companies to initiate recycling programs (or to increase the percentage of waste recycled). These directives frequently were quite expensive to implement. Another factor had been the tightening of bank credit policies in response to the troubled real estate market: many waste firms found themselves with sharply reduced credit lines and higher interest costs.

The most profound change affecting the solid waste industry in the early 1990s, however, was regulatory in nature. The Resource Conservation and Recovery Act of

[7] This section is based in large part on "The Solid Waste Industry: 1992 Review and 1993 Outlook," *Waste Age* 23 (December 1992): pp. 47–57. It also relies on a variety of filings by solid waste firms with the U.S. Securities and Exchange Commission, analyst reports, and U.S. Bureau of the Census publications.

[8] While an increasing share of publicly owned landfills had been privatized, or contracted to private managers, the fraction was quite modest: for instance, of the over 3000 counties in the United States, the number with contractor-operated, government-owned landfills had increased from 323 in 1987 to 415 in 1992. For a detailed analysis, see Florencio Lopez-de-Silanes, Andrei Shleifer, and Robert W. Vishny, "Privatization in the United States," *Rand Journal of Economics* 28 (1997): pp. 447–471.

1976 had been enacted to govern the generation, treatment, storage, transportation, and disposal of both hazardous and nonhazardous solid waste. The regulations issued by the U.S. Environmental Protection Agency (EPA) had initially focused on hazardous wastes. In October 1991, however, the EPA adopted "Subtitle D Regulations," which governed landfills for nonhazardous solid waste. These regulations required the states to implement regulations within the two years that covered the design, operation, monitoring, and financial security of solid waste landfills. Particularly critical was the requirement that all landfills have synthetic linings to prevent the leaching of contaminants into the local water supply by October 1993. The vast majority of landfills, particularly in northern New England, were unlined and would need to be closed.

These new requirements coincided with growing concerns about the solid waste industry's exposure under the Comprehensive Environmental Response, Compensation and Liability Act (CERCLA) of 1980. This act sought to encourage the cleanup of hazardous waste sites. To accomplish this, it made both current and past property owners liable for the cost of any investigation or cleanup involving hazardous substances. The act defined hazardous substances very broadly, including many substances found in household waste. Under this legislation, if any party was found to be partially responsible for the hazardous substances, it could be required to bear the entire cost of the investigation and cleanup. The liable party would then need to file suit against other responsible parties in order to get them to contribute to the remediation effort.

As a result of these pressures, the firms and investors showed increasing interest in undertaking consolidations in the solid waste industry. While for many years, two companies—Browning–Ferris and Waste Management—had pursued active consolidation strategies, in recent years they had been joined by Mid-American Waste, Sanifill, and a variety of smaller competitors. While many of these firms concentrated on major metropolitan areas, others (most notably United Waste, which had gone public in December 1992) focused on acquiring solid waste firms in rural areas and small cities across the nation.

CASELLA WASTE SYSTEMS[9]

Doug Casella had founded Casella Refuse Removal, the predecessor entity to Casella Waste Systems, in 1975 with an $8000 investment. (See Exhibit 5 for the biographies of Casella and other members of the management team.) A year later, his brother John joined the firm upon completing a B.S. in Business Education from nearby Castleton State College. Casella Waste Systems grew gradually over the next two decades, reaching a total of nearly $11 million in annual revenues in calendar year 1992. The company had emerged as a major player in the Vermont solid waste industry: it hauled, recycled, and processed nearly 20% of all nonhazardous waste generated in the state, and it had more than twice the market share of any other firm in the state. (Major national consolidators had generally not been active in Vermont through mid-1993.) This growth had been achieved through a variety of mechanisms:

- *Acquisitions.* Beginning with the purchase of Rutland-based Beaver & Sons in November 1976 for $40,000, Casella Waste Systems had made judicious acquisitions of Vermont competitors. By June 1993, the firm had spent almost $3.5 million on 22

---

[9] The next two sections are largely based on *Private Placement Memorandum: Casella Waste Systems,* Houghton and Co., February 1993; internal due diligence memoranda prepared by BCI Advisors and the Vermont Venture Capital Fund; selected press accounts; and interviews with case protagonists.

acquisitions. The purchase price in these hauling company acquisitions was usually about three to four times adjusted earnings before interest, taxes, depreciation, and amortization (**EBITDA**) and about equal to the revenues of the acquired firm.

- *Service innovations.* The company had aggressively responded to their customers' needs. One important area of innovation had been the introduction of the first recycling program in the state of Vermont in 1977, and its aggressive expansion over the subsequent decades. Many solid waste firms found these programs difficult and costly to implement, but Casella Waste Systems believed that a strong recycling capability was an important marketing asset in environmentally sensitive Vermont.

- *Integration.* The firm established a construction subsidiary, Casella Construction Company, which it used in its projects. In 1988, Doug Casella assumed the management of the construction firm and relinquished day-to-day operations of the solid waste company to his brother. Doug continued to make key contributions to Casella in the design and construction of its landfills. Casella Waste Management had also made a minority investment into a waste-to-energy plant (which had been closed by 1993).

Over 90% of Casella Waste Systems' hauling revenues came from over 13,000 commercial and residential customers, each of whom paid a subscription fee. A small but growing area of activity was contracting with local municipalities to provide hauling and disposal of solid waste and/or recyclable materials. Casella Waste Systems also had designed, owned, and operated nine waste transfer stations, where trash was consolidated before being shipped to landfills. The firm owned three unlined landfills, which were used for waste that it collected, and that brought by other haulers. These haulers would pay Casella Waste Systems "tipping fees" for the right to dump solid waste there. In response to EPA and state regulations, two of these landfills were being closed. (This was also true for the other unlined landfills in the state.) Casella Waste Systems was in the arduous process of obtaining permits to retrofit the third facility into a lined landfill.

John Casella and Senior Vice President Jim Bohlig had been considering the idea of raising long-term capital for some time. Previously, however, the firm had rejected this idea, preferring to rely on cash flow from operations and bank loans. In particular, a local banker had financed much of the firm's expansion during the 1980s through generous loans. The decision to actively pursue external equity financing was largely a result of the changes in the early 1990s. First, the tightened bank regulation led to an abrupt reduction in the firm's ability to finance its expansion through further bank loans. Second, the shift to lined landfills was creating substantial financing pressures, which meant that an industry consolidation was likely. A large number of small hauling companies and landfills in the region were attractive acquisition candidates. In fact, in 1992 Waste Management made an offer for Casella Waste, in which slightly over $5 million (based on performance) would have gone to the equity holders. The firm faced a stark choice between aggressively acquiring competitors and being acquired itself.

The solid waste industry in Vermont had traditionally been dominated by over 70 unlined "town dumps." At each site, there were approximately one half-dozen small carriers, who were able to dump their solid waste for a nominal fee. Entry barriers for haulers were minimal. With the advent of the EPA's Subtitle D directive and Vermont's Act 78 (which mandated even stricter standards than the federal regulations), the landscape was changing dramatically. Several dozen Vermont landfills had been forced to close in 1992. Many other landfills were experiencing serious financial hardships as they sought to comply with regulatory closure directives. Meanwhile, many haulers were facing sharply higher tipping fees and the need to carry waste much longer distances. These changes placed a severe strain on the smaller haulers, who frequently had weak balance sheets and limited management teams. The economics of running a lined landfill was dramatically different from that of an unlined one: the minimum efficient size, capital requirements, and logistical skills required were much greater.

The firm's management team believed that they would be effective in competing not only against small operators but other consolidators in the solid waste industry. Their success in operating under Vermont's strict regulatory environment would enable them to pursue a successful consolidation strategy elsewhere as the EPA standards came into force. Furthermore, the strict regulation of the industry would serve as a substantial barrier to entry to any potential competitor who wished to challenge their dominance of the market in their native state.

As a first step, the firm had identified two ideal acquisition candidates: two lined landfills, fully permitted and already in operation. These two facilities, Consumat Sanco in western New Hampshire and Waste USA in upper Vermont, would give them ownership of two of the four lined landfills in operation in New Hampshire and Vermont and would allow the firm to aggressively expand across northern Vermont and New Hampshire. More generally, they believed that the acquisitions would position them well for future consolidation activity, in the hopes of extending their dominance of waste and environmental services from Vermont throughout the entire region. Eight local hauling companies, with total revenues of approximately $10 million, also appeared to be attractive acquisition candidates.

In November 1992, the firm had undertaken a purchase and sale agreement to acquire the Sanco landfill. Since 1989, the landfill had been owned by a Richmond, Virginia-based Consumat Systems, whose primary line of business was the manufacture of air pollution control systems. After a disastrous foray into the development and operation of medical waste disposal facilities, however, the company had encountered a severe, continuing liquidity crisis in 1991. The proposed transaction called for the landfill to be purchased by National Waste Industries (NWI), a Pittsburgh-based investment company specializing in landfill transactions with whom Bohlig had worked during his years at Westinghouse, and then to be immediately transferred to Casella Waste Systems. In exchange, Casella Waste Systems would issue NWI a total of 600,000 shares of common stock. As part of the transaction, NWI planned to renegotiate the outstanding landfill bonds (special securities secured by future fees commonly employed in the solid waste industry) that Sanco had sold to Allstate Insurance. As envisioned, Sanco would sell an additional $4.3 million of bonds to Allstate. The proceeds from this sale, as well as an additional cash payment, would be paid to Consumat (or its creditors) in exchange for title to the landfill. The strained relationships between the landfill and the community in which it was based posed additional challenges.

The firm was also negotiating (though a purchase and sale agreement had not yet been signed) to acquire the entire outstanding equity of Waste USA—a company that had been established by several aggressive Canadian entrepreneurs—for a cash payment of $500,000, the assumption of the firm's debt, and a royalty of 10% of gross revenues. The cumulative royalty was capped at $6 million. If the cumulative royalty payments at the end of seven years did not reach $6 million, Casella Waste Systems would be required to make a lump-sum payment of the difference. Any such lump-sum payment was conditional, however, on a substantial expansion of the landfill's capacity.

Meanwhile, the Casellas and Bohlig realized that the financing mechanisms they had employed to date would no longer be enough. To undertake such an acquisitions strategy, Casella Waste Systems would need a substantial amount of funds. Not only would the two landfill acquisitions require some cash outlays,[10] but they also hoped to acquire a number of small haulers. The terms of the typical hauling acquisition called for 80% of the purchase price to be paid in cash (with the remainder financed through sellers' notes). Many of the acquired units would also require substantial investments to improve operations.

THE PROPOSED TRANSACTION

For these reasons, the firm decided to seek equity financing in late 1992. An important choice was whether to turn to a local venture investor or to conduct a more general search. The firm had had repeated interactions with Greg Peters, a general partner and co-founder of the North Atlantic Capital Corporation and the Vermont Venture Capital Fund. The Vermont fund, established in 1988, had been "seeded" by a $1.5 million state tax credit. Using this credit, Peters and his partner, David Coit—both Harvard Business School graduates with extensive experience in entrepreneurial firms, independent venture organizations, and a small business investment company—had raised a total of $7.6 million. (Coit and Peters had employed a similar structure when raising a total of $17.2 million for the Portland, Maine-based North Atlantic Capital Partners one year earlier.) After considerable negotiations, the fund had obtained a charter from the state of Vermont which allowed it to invest elsewhere in New England as well. Such flexibility, Peters believed, was essential if the fund was to build a set of relationships with the larger venture community. He argued that these ties would ultimately yield many dividends in the form of outside investments in Vermont firms as the state emerged into the venture capital mainstream.

Although the Casellas had been intrigued by the idea of raising outside capital, they initially resisted Peters' suggestion. Of particular concern was the substantial dilution implied by an early-stage venture financing: the venture group and its syndication partners would probably expect a significant amount of the firm's equity, as well as onerous control rights. While Peters argued that the Casellas would be better off with the proverbial "smaller slice of a larger pie," the brothers rejected this argument.

These concerns had led to a series of conversations with Steve Houghton, chairman of a New York investment banking boutique, Houghton & Company. Prior to founding his firm in 1977, Houghton had been an investment banker at G. H. Walker & Co. and White, Weld & Co. Houghton, who was a friend of the firm's long-standing legal adviser, urged the brothers to look farther afield for equity financing. In particular, he argued that the company should be able to raise $5 million in private equity while selling no more than 25% of its shares.

After a series of conversations, the Casellas had authorized Houghton to prepare a private placement memorandum. This document called for the firm to issue 900,000 convertible preferred shares at $5.55/share. Once converted, these shares would represent 22.5% of the total shares in the firm.[11] Because the founders held a special class of

---

[10] Both prospective landfill acquisitions were already heavily leveraged with landfill bonds and bank loans secured by heavy equipment and real estate. (The outstanding debt of the merged company would carry interest rates varying from 7% to 11%, with an average rate of 9 and 1/2%.) Under pressure from Federal Deposit Insurance Company regulators regarding some troubled real estate loans, Casella Waste Systems' bank had indicated that they could not provide any additional financing unless the firm received an equity infusion of approximately $5 million.

[11] Subsequent to the close of the proposed transactions, the Casella brothers would hold 2.35 million shares of common stock, NWI would hold 600,000 shares, and 150,000 shares would be held by Houghton & Co. as part of its fee for arranging the transaction. All shares would be Class A common stock except for the convertible preferred shares discussed above and one million of Class B common shares held by the Casella brothers. These Class B shares were entitled to ten votes per share, as opposed to all other shares, which were entitled to only one vote per share.

common stock with enhanced voting rights (Class B common stock), the preferred shares would have fewer voting rights. The holders of these shares would, however, have the right to elect one director to the firm's board.

The company prepared a series of detailed financial statements for inclusion in the private placement memorandum. These included historical information about the financial performance of Casella Waste Systems and its proposed acquisitions in calendar year 1992 (Exhibit 6) and projections of the combined firm's performance over the next five years (Exhibit 7).

In February 1993, Houghton sent a copy of the proposal to Don Remey at BCI Growth. Remey—put off by what he considered to be a high valuation and the company's early stage of development—was initially inclined to reject the proposal out of hand. Houghton, however, urged him to meet the management team. In their initial meeting, as well as several subsequent conversations, Remey was favorably impressed by the management team's energy, experience, and vision. He further felt that the industry was poised for a rebound from the recession of 1990–91 and that the regulatory changes were creating attractive opportunities for investors in the industry. Of particular appeal was the company's strategy of being the major consolidator of rural New England markets. To date, these markets were considered too small by the existing industry consolidators. As a local New England company, management had a competitive advantage in acquiring haulers and landfills in Vermont, New Hampshire, and Maine. As a result, he and Peter Wilde began seriously evaluating the transaction. In response to BCI's queries, Houghton & Co. had prepared a discussion of assumptions (reproduced in Exhibit 8).

Remey believed that the proposed valuation of $5.55 per share was about double the fair market value of the equity (see Exhibit 4). Proposing a lower valuation, however, would mean substantially more dilution than the Casellas were willing to consider. Using a mezzanine debt structure, BCI could get part of its return with an interest payment and reduce its risk by having a debt security that was senior to the equity with covenants and default provisions. The equity kicker necessary to achieve the targeted return of 20% to 30% would remain in the million share range, but at a lower exercise price than the $5.55 per share valuation originally proposed. These elements of a current return and senior debt security provided a lower risk/return structure for BCI but represented acceptable dilution for the Casellas.

As the negotiations progressed, BCI drafted a term sheet for its investment in Casella Waste Systems, which is reproduced in Exhibit 9. In exchange for its $5 million investment, BCI would receive interest and principal repayments, as well as warrants exercisable at $2.75 for 25% of the firm's equity. To be sure, the warrant exercise price was considerably below the $5.50 price per share of equity that Houghton & Co. had proposed, but Casella would achieve its primary goal of raising $5 million while giving up no more than one-quarter of the equity in the firm.

Certainly, the firm would be highly leveraged after the transaction. At the end of Year 1, the firm would have assumed net long-term liabilities of approximately $25.6 million and have shareholders' equity of only $4.1 million.[12] The projected EBIT would exceed the interest expenses by only 13%.[13] Moreover, the successful implementation

---

[12] The liabilities was based on the $28.3 million of liabilities shown on the pro forma balance sheet in Exhibit 7, plus the $5 million in debt raised from BCI (the balance sheet had been prepared under the assumption that the firm would raise $5 million in equity), less the $7.7 million of restricted funds recorded as an asset. The equity was based on the projected shareholders equity, less the $5 million that would be now raised as debt and the (tax-adjusted) interest that would be due to BCI in the first year.

[13] This calculation incorporates the additional $375,000 of interest that would be due to BCI in the first year. (The income statement in Exhibit 7 had been prepared under the assumption that the firm would raise $5 million in equity.)

of the consolidation strategy was dependent on the firm's continued ability to borrow: although the firm was projected to generate positive cash flows from operations, the projected rate of business acquisitions and capital expenditures would be even greater in the first few years. Nonetheless, should BCI be able to sell its investment at a multiple of earnings common among publicly traded firms in the industry, it could obtain an attractive return. (Exhibit 4 indicates the enterprise value—the sum of equity market capitalization and long-term debt—of small waste firms and the earnings before interest, taxes, depreciation, and amortization.)

The next weeks were devoted largely to negotiating the terms of the transaction and intensive due diligence. By the end of May 1993, the paperwork was almost completed. As a result of their investigations, however, Remey and his partners were increasingly concerned about the proposed investment. Three issues appeared critical:

- First, the projections seemed too optimistic. They called for very aggressive growth, both in revenues and profitability. Despite efforts to address them, questions remained about management's ability to achieve such an aggressive plan.[14]

- Second, the two proposed landfill acquisitions seemed to be highly risky. The Waste USA acquisition was structured as a purchase of stock. As such, Casella Waste Systems could potentially be assuming all liabilities associated with the activities of the previous management team. Meanwhile, Consumat's precarious financial condition might delay, if not entirely derail, the closing of the Sanco transaction.

- Finally, Remey remained concerned about a number of accounting and financial issues. Historically, the firm's accounts had never been audited and the projections had been prepared by Bohlig, who was not a trained financial expert. Remey and his partners had little confidence in the historical and projected figures. At BCI's request, Casella had hired a local auditor to review the company's books and to prepare actual and pro forma statements. In light of this primitive financial and accounting situation, BCI had conditioned its investment on hiring a CFO with waste industry experience. Management, however, appeared to be not fully committed to adding a CFO at this time.

These concerns were fundamental to the risk/reward tradeoffs between the proposed mezzanine financing and a higher-risk straight equity investment. In most of their mezzanine financings, BCI had a higher degree of confidence. Were these risks too great for a mezzanine deal? Were they assuming what were truly equity risks?

Thus, Remey and his partners faced a considerable dilemma. Should they proceed with the transaction? Could the deal be restructured in some manner to address these concerns? For instance, should the exercise price of the warrant be lowered or the put provision altered? Or should BCI opt out of the transaction entirely? As the radio traffic report announced that the backup had been caused by a multivehicle collision five miles ahead, Remey pondered his options.

---

[14] A related issue was a number of questions about accounting practices in the solid waste industry. One crucial issue was the amortization of landfill space. In the typical landfill, the entire capacity was not initially developed: rather, the space was developed (and regulatory approvals obtained) as existing space was filled. As a result, solid waste firms often had a considerable degree of discretion as to how rapidly to depreciate the acquisition or development cost of the landfill. A second issue was how the costs associated with the landfill after closure were accounted for. The practices of waste management firms differed widely in how they estimated the cost of closure and post-closure environmental liabilities, and their policies for making accruals against these costs.

Exhibit 1 Mezzanine and Buyout Fundraising

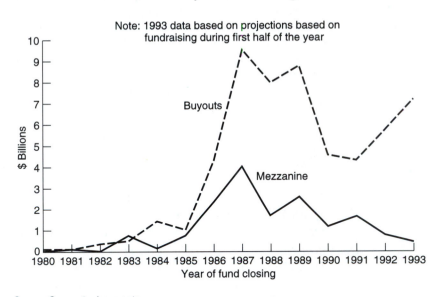

Source: Corporate documents.

Exhibit 2   BCI Biographies

Hoyt J. Goodrich is a Managing Director. In addition to his investing activities since co-founding BCI in 1983, Hoyt spent over 20 years at Aetna Life & Casualty doing mostly private placement investments in smaller and medium-sized companies. He has been a director of 15 BCI companies. Hoyt has become a recognized expert in the financing of radio and television, having been involved in 21 investments made by BCI. Hoyt is a graduate of Dartmouth College.

J. Barton Goodwin is a Managing Director. For 12 years prior to joining BCI, he was with Kidder, Peabody, where he was first a generalist investment banker, then a private placement specialist. Bart has been a director of seven BCI portfolio companies and has developed an expertise in the financial services industry. Bart is a graduate of Washington & Lee University and holds an MBA from Columbia Business School.

Theodore T. Horton, Jr. is a Managing Director. He has been a director of ten BCI portfolio companies and has expertise in the broadcasting and media/entertainment industries. Prior to joining BCI, Ted was a Managing Director of Dillon Read & Co. Inc. and from 1974 to 1982 held increasingly responsible investment positions with Barclays Bank and Home Life. He received his MBA from St. John's University and is a graduate of St. Michael's College.

Donald P. Remey is a Managing Director. He has extensive experience in investing and investment banking. As an investment banker at Kidder, Peabody, Citicorp, and Rothschild Inc., Don specialized in private placements and venture capital for small-growth companies. Since forming BCI in 1983, Don has been a director of 15 BCI portfolio companies and has developed an expertise in the environmental services industry. He is a graduate of Colgate University and Harvard Business School.

Peter O. Wilde, Jr. is a Principal and first joined BCI in 1992 after working at LaSalle Partners. His undergraduate degree was from Colorado College.

Source: Corporate documents

Exhibit 3   Summary of Solid Waste Industry in 1992

Growth of Solid Waste Industry, 1987 to 1992

Kind of Business	Establishments		Revenue		Annual Payroll	
	1992 (Number)	1987 (Number)	1992 ($1,000)	1987 ($1,000)	1992 ($1,000)	1987 ($1,000)
Garbage and trash collection	6,782	6,395	10,984,763	3,763,768	2,473,305	983,496
Refuse systems	2,284	NA	14,101,667	NA	2,577,856	NA

Revenues of Solid Waste Firms, 1992

Kind of Business and Revenue Size of Firms	Firms (Number)	Establish-ments (#)	Revenue ($1,000)	Annual Payroll ($1,000)	Employees (Number)
Garbage and trash collection					
Firms with annual revenue of:					
$25,000,000 or more	24	489	4,717,869	1,014,085	33,921
$10,000,000 to $24,000,000	79	109	1,151,900	233,171	7,096
$5,000,000 to $9,999,999	166	207	1,127,838	260,118	7,808
$2,500,000 to $4,999,999	302	340	1,036,585	249,192	8,636
$1,00,000 to 2,499,999	865	904	1,338,597	335,300	13,481
$500,000 to $999,999	1,020	1,027	719,080	180,476	9,117
$250,000 to $4999,999	1,241	1,241	438,504	104,569	6,345
$100,000 to $249,999	1,476	1,478	247,306	51,679	4,141
Less than $100,000	814	814	49,604	10,889	1,268
Firms not operated entire year	795	796	157,480	33,826	2,240
Refuse systems					
Firms with annual revenue of:					
$25,000,000 or more	65	863	9,772,501	1,617,660	47,706
$10,000,000 to $24,000,000	101	117	1,457,793	281,367	8,116
$5,000,000 to $9,999,999	145	213	1,033,833	249,919	7,751
$2,500,000 to $4,999,999	219	258	785,519	172,170	5,767
$1,00,000 to 2,499,999	354	391	559,663	138,273	5,108
$500,000 to $999,999	289	296	206,345	51,069	2,467
$250,000 to $4999,999	275	276	97,914	24,853	1,333
$100,000 to $249,999	287	287	48,449	12,607	878
Less than $100,000	199	199	11,195	3,045	346
Firms not operated entire year	355	357	128,455	26,893	1,445

Source: Compiled from U.S. Bureau of the Census, *Census of Transportation Communications and Utilities: 1992*, Washington, Bureau of the Census, 1996

Establishments primarily engaged in the collection and disposal of refuse by processing or destruction or in the operation of incinerators, waste treatment plants, landfills, or other sites for disposal of such materials are classified in Refuse Systems. Establishments primarily engaged in collection and transporting refuse without such disposal are classified in Garbage and Collection.

Exhibit 4   Comparable Public Solid Waste Firms as of May 1993

Basic Statistics on Publicly-Traded Firms in Industry

Ticker	Name	Trailing Twelve Month Data									
		Revenues	EBIT	EBITDA	Net Income	Total Assets	Shareholder's Equity	Market Capitalization	Long-Term Debt	Beta	Annualized Volatility
AWIN	Allied Waste Inds Inc.	43.4	8.2	19.0	1.7	131.9	39.9	49.8	58.5	NA	25.9%
A.2	Attwoods Plc	550.9	64.5	141.4	48.3	NA	NA	500.5	NA	0.93	14.7
BFI	Browning-Ferris Inds	3,423.2	407.5	1,309.5	194.5	4,216.1	1,489.7	4,656.7	1,073.2	1.42	11.1
LLE	Laidlaw Environmental Svcs	227.2	32.3	81.4	20.5	277.8	213.7	444.9	4.6	1.34	15.6
3MAWS	Mid-American Waste Sys Inc.	171.0	57.9	90.6	18.3	696.4	301.5	299.5	323.8	1.89	21.3
OG	Ogden Corp	1,898.9	222.6	336.0	57.0	3,271.5	483.0	1,140.5	2,018.9	1.37	10.5
FIL	Sanifill Inc.	98.2	23.0	59.0	10.2	347.2	110.9	252.1	124.7	0.78	18.7
UW	USA Waste Services Inc.	66.3	16.0	33.9	5.7	113.4	41.4	139.7	53.2	0.38	15.8
WMX	Waste Management Inc.	8,891.7	1,824.3	3,467.1	816.6	15,673.4	4,280.4	15,616.1	5,245.7	1.23	11.7
WTI	Wheelabrator technologies	1,327.9	304.8	432.7	153.8	2,919.2	1,184.3	3,356.5	798.1	1.34	13.5
UWST	United Waste Sys Inc.	49.7	10.0	27.1	5.2	156.0	62.9	107.4	51.3	NA	35.4

Comparison of Projections of Casella and Most Directly Comparable Firms

Ticker	Name	1993 Projections			
		Revenues	EBIT	EBITDA	Net Income
	Casella (Years 1 and 2)	24.8	3.8	8.0	0.3
UW	USA Waste Services Inc.	82.3	19.3	26.0	8.6
UWST	United Waste Sys Inc.	74.6	18.9	26.9	11.2

Ticker	Name	1993 Projections			
		L-T Debt	Mkt. Cap.	EV	EV/EBITDA
	Casella (Years 1 and 2)	33.3	NA	NA	NA
UW	USA Waste Services Inc.	55.0	174.1	229.1	8.8
UWST	United Waste Sys Inc.	19.0	102.2	121.2	4.5

Ticker	Name	1994 Projections			
		Revenues	EBIT	EBITDA	Net Income
	Casella (Years 1 and 2)	31.0	5.4	10.3	1.0
UW	USA Waste Services Inc.	102.3	24.3	34.1	14.1
UWST	United Waste Sys Inc.	100.0	24.8	38.1	10.9

Ticker	Name	1994 Projections			
		L-T Debt	Mkt. Cap.	EV	EV/EBITDA
	Casella (Years 1 and 2)	33.5	NA	NA	NA
UW	USA Waste Services Inc.	55.0	177.5	232.5	6.8
UWST	United Waste Sys Inc.	19.0	126.0	145.0	3.8

Source: Compiled from Compustat and corporate records.

Notes: EBIT = Earnings before interest and taxes. EDITDA = Earnings before interest, taxes, depreciation, and amortization. EV = Enterprise Value = Equity market capitalization + long-term debt. NA = not applicable. All dollar figures in millions. The ten-year treasury rate in June 1993 was 5.96%. Casella's projections in Year 1 and 2 are based on the pro forma statements in Exhibit 7, adjusted to reflect the terms of the proposed BCI Growth transaction (i.e., the reliance on debt rather than equity). Because the debt of the comparable firms is not adjusted for restricted funds, neither is Casella's.

Exhibit 5   Management and Employees

The Company employs 130 people, 50 of whom are employed in the recycling centers None of the Company's employees are represented by a collective bargaining organization.

John W. Casella, Chairman and CEO   John W. Casella has actively supervised all aspects of operations since 1976. He also sets overall corporate policies and has served as the chief strategic planner of corporate development. John Casella has been a member of numerous industry-related and community service-related state and local boards and commissions, including the Board of Directors of the Associated Industries of Vermont, The Association of Vermont Recyclers, Vermont State Chamber of Commerce, and the Rutland Industrial Development Corporation. He has also served on the various state task forces serving in an advisory capacity to the Governor on solid waste issues. He holds an A.S. in Business Management from Bryant & Stratton and a B.S. in Business Education from Castleton State College.

Douglas R. Casella, President   Douglas R. Casella founded Casella Waste Management in 1975 with an eight thousand dollar investment. His responsibilities have focused on the operations, landfill development and construction aspects of the business. Douglas graduated from Mount St. Joseph Academy in 1972 and has continued his education since then in the concentrated area of waste management.

James W. Bohlig, Senior Vice President   Jim Bohlig joined Casella Waste Management in 1992 and has worked closely with John Casella in developing the strategy for developing CWS into an integrated waste management company. He has also played an active role in the acquisition negotiations for Waste USA and Sanco. Mr. Bohlig's business, marketing and senior management experience developed from proven practice in the co-generation, energy, hazardous waste and construction industries. He has had extensive turnkey (EFC) project management responsibility and experience in product commercialization and strategic planning. From 1974 to 1989, Mr. Bohlig was associated with Westinghouse Electric Corporation, first in nuclear plant engineering and construction, and later in several manager positions in waste to energy plant design and construction. From 1989 until he joined Casella Waste Management, Mr. Bohlig was executive vice president and chief operating officer of a general contractor and developer. Mr. Bohlig holds a B.S. in Engineering and Chemistry from the U.S. Naval Academy, and an M.B.A. from Columbia University. He is a licensed professional engineer.

Gerald L. Hansen, Manager, Administration   Jerry Hansen joined Casella Waste Management in 1990, bringing with him 22 years of management experience with other northern New England corporations. Mr. Hansen played a major role in structuring Casella's corporate purchasing, human resources and safety programs.

Beth R. Shak, Environmental Affairs   Beth Shak joined Casella Waste Management in 1988 with a background in public administration and small business ownership. She was a legislative representative for the League of Cities and Towns for three years with specific responsibilities for solid waste management issues. Ms. Shak is responsible for the design and sales of all solid waste management and recycling programs throughout the State of Vermont. She serves as the corporate contact with engineering consultants as well as state and local governments on permitting issues. Ms. Shak holds a B.A. in Political Science and Environmental Studies (Phi Beta Kappa, Magna Cum Laude) from the University of Vermont.

Robert G. Jacob, Controller   Robert Jacob served as Casella Waste Management's controller since 1983. Mr. Jacob is responsible for all internal accounting functions including monthly and annual P&L and balance sheet reporting. In addition to his controller's responsibilities, Mr. Jacob has been involved with acquisitions and operations as well as strategic planning. Mr. Jacob holds a B.S. in Accountancy from the Walsh College of Accountancy and Business Administration, Troy, Michigan.

Lance E. Stout, Manager, Information Systems   Lance Stout joined Casella Waste Management in 1987. Mr. Stout designed and implemented new computer programs, reports and data entry screens relative to routing, receivables and operational support services for Casella. He continues to improve systems to increase efficiency and productivity, thereby saving time and money and reducing errors. Mr. Stout is a graduate of the State University of New York and holds a B.S. in Accounting and an A.S. degree in Applied Science.

Susan W. Monaco, Manager, Human Resources   Susan Monaco joined Casella Waste Management in 1987 and is responsible for developing with management, personnel policies, procedures and employee relations programs. Susan is the administrator of employee benefit programs and is responsible for the weekly payroll of Casella and its affiliate companies. She processes and monitors unemployment claims, workers compensation claims and employment verification requests. Ms. Monaco also served as administrative assistant to the chairman and CEO of Casella Waste Management from September 1990 to August 1992.

David M. Fretz, Manager, Recycling Division   David joined Casella in 1992 as manager for the recycling operations for the corporation. David is responsible for marketing all materials at all Casella recycling centers and manages the day-to-day operations of Casella's Center Rutland Recycling Facility. Prior to joining Casella, Mr. Fretz was with the Hawk Mountain Corporation for almost 20 years, responsible for all liaison, submission, negotiation and compliance of development-related projects.

Source: Corporate documents

Exhibit 6   Unaudited Financial Statements for Year End 1992

Income Statements

	Casella Aggregate	Sanco	Waste USA
Revenues			
Landfill	538,524	4,487,482	1,154,780
Collection			
Recycling	1,242,000	0	0
Hauling	8,876,000	0	0
Septage	75,000	0	0
Interest income	0	198,209	0
Other income	218,544	0	0
Total	10,950,068	4,685,691	1,154,780
Expenses			
Landfill	568,637	832,045	608,133
Collection			
Recycling	1,708,000	0	0
Hauling	2,900,335	0	0
Disposal	1,272,380	0	0
Total cost of sales	6,449,352	832,045	608,133
Gross profits	4,500,716	3,853,646	546,647
Percent of sales	41%	82%	47%
General and administrative			
Landfill overhead	172,305	1,021,837	192,347
Landfill closure	452,726	220,998	5,483
Hauling/recycling	1,665,753	0	0
Operating income	2,209,932	2,610,811	348,817
Percent of sales	20%	56%	30%
Depreciation	1,105,281	98,840	57,386
Amortization	226,806	83,435	0
Depletion	87,140	963,386	99,972
Noncompete expense	0	296,777	0
EBIT	790,705	1,168,373	191,459
Interest expense	668,190	843,971	110,605
Pre-tax income	122,515	324,402	80,854

Exhibit 6 (continued)   Balance Sheet

	Casella Aggregate	Sanco	Waste USA
Assets			
Current assets			
Cash & equivalent	95,240	88,404	2,797
Accounts receivable	1,808,243	595,024	234,317
Doubtful accounts	-121,095	0	-1,765
Inventory	93,739	0	0
Prepaid expenses	175,194	21,451	11,924
Other current assets	1,054,638	963,028	0
Property & equipment			
Landfills	1,364,632	8,771,504	5,414,283
Vehicles & equipment	8,634,868	1,199,559	580,242
Buildings	1,606,248	272,720	256,361
Accumulated depreciation	-4,971,725	-3,199,784	0
Accumulated depletion	-370,350	0	0
Other assets			
Land	489,235	215,699	250,974
Goodwill	2,127,605	0	7,000
Accumulated amortization	-665,752	0	-202,754
Notes receivable	468,044	0	0
Restricted funds	219,933	2,744,510	0
Other assets	150,357	352,316	0
Total assets	12,159,054	12,024,431	6,553,379
Liabilities & Shareholders Equity			
Current liabilities			
Accounts payable	840,159	172,529	1,213,814
Accounts payable—related companies	1,135,975	0	0
Current notes	1,223,761	1,009,977	245,060
Accrued expenses	92,899	468,047	0
Taxes payable	13,962	0	0
Long-term liabilities			
Landfill bonds	188,000	7,030,000	0
Other long-term debt	4,892,870	162,035	3,797,141
Long-term sellers' notes	1,032,224	0	955,608
Deferred taxes	295,230	0	82,250
Other liabilities	890,941	1,094,471	5,483
Shareholders equity			
Common stock	5,300	1,000	10,000
Capital in excess of par value	16,000	0	0
Retained earnings	1,531,733	2,086,372	244,023
Total liabilities & shareholders equity	12,159,054	12,024,431	6,553,379

Source: Corporate documents

Note: While information on selected Casella subsidiaries was available for the fiscal year ending in December 1991, no comprehensive information was available.

Exhibit 7   Projections by Casella Management

	Day 0	Year 1	Year 2	Year 3	Year 4	Year 5
			Assumptions			
Equity infusion	5,000,000					
Capital expenditure and acquisitions		6,650,000	4,750,000	1,850,000	1,950,000	3,050,000
			Income Statement Projections			
Income (P&L)						
Landfill revenues		7,660,860	9,487,500	10,632,500	11,962,500	12,562,500
Collection revenues						
Recycling		1,330,430	1,383,648	1,483,994	1,496,553	1,556,415
Hauling		9,507,971	9,888,290	10,238,822	10,695,175	11,122,981
Septage		73,251	76,181	79,229	82,398	85,694
Acquisition hauling		5,785,263	9,571,705	10,545,954	11,679,773	12,821,739
Processing income		125,000	175,000	225,000	275,000	350,000
Interest income		356,393	429,956	508,382	589,710	661,059
Total revenues		24,839,169	31,012,280	33,713,880	36,781,108	39,160,389
Expenses						
Landfill		2,317,400	2,442,750	2,489,750	2,520,750	2,522,750
Collection		10,176,293	13,128,041	13,896,038	14,815,339	15,334,192
General & administrative		3,798,535	4,480,159	4,818,215	5,152,107	5,468,296
Operating income		8,546,941	10,961,330	12,509,877	14,292,911	15,835,151
Depreciation		1,670,090	1,834,518	1,736,518	1,671,518	1,626,518
Amortization		413,282	558,737	595,100	631,464	667,828
Depletion		2,092,623	2,514,209	2,920,893	3,423,712	2,860,327
Noncompete expense		550,200	662,500	744,500	821,000	848,000
EBIT		3,820,746	5,391,367	6,512,865	7,745,218	9,832,479
Interest expense		2,987,249	3,393,900	3,481,380	3,374,086	3,487,335
Pre-tax income		833,498	1,997,467	3,031,486	4,371,131	6,345,143
Less taxes		316,729	759,037	1,151,965	1,661,030	2,411,154
Net income		516,769	1,238,429	1,879,521	2,710,101	3,933,989

Exhibit 7 (continued)

	Day 0	Year 1	Year 2	Year 3	Year 4	Year 5
			Balance Sheet Projections			
Assets						
Current assets						
Cash & cash equivalent	3,152,921	2,057,161	2,387,578	5,512,266	7,377,260	10,570,149
Accounts receivable	2,126,549	3,248,979	3,969,416	4,364,090	4,787,122	5,130,506
Less doubtful accounts	-141,500	-323,170	-357,247	-392,768	-430,841	-461,746
Inventory	93,739	199,565	207,547	215,849	224,483	233,462
Prepaid expenses	175,194	208,524	208,524	208,524	208,524	208,524
Other current assets	-67,850	808,732	808,732	808,732	808,732	808,732
Property & equipment						
Landfill/other investments	1,364,632	19,300,419	19,300,419	19,300,419	19,300,419	19,300,419
Vehicles & equipment	8,835,741	14,864,786	18,014,786	19,464,786	21,014,786	22,664,786
Buildings & improvements	1,606,248	2,158,234	2,158,234	2,158,234	2,158,234	2,158,234
Less accumulated depreciation	-6,038,749	-11,074,636	-12,909,154	-14,645,672	-16,317,190	-17,943,708
Less accumulated depletion	-428,170	-2,979,867	-5,494,076	-8,414,969	-11,838,681	-14,699,007
Other assets						
Land	489,235	955,908	955,908	955,908	955,908	955,908
Construction in progress	0	100,000	100,000	100,000	100,000	100,000
Goodwill, etc.	2,127,605	4,534,605	6,134,605	6,534,605	6,934,605	7,334,605
Less accumulated amortization	-876,333	-1,289,615	-1,848,352	-2,443,453	-3,074,917	-3,742,744
Notes receivable related company	468,044	421,240	379,116	341,204	307,084	276,375
Restricted funds/bond shield	356,933	7,731,797	9,617,553	10,235,574	12,911,627	15,388,116
Other assets & investments	676,903	1,495,765	1,495,765	1,495,765	1,495,765	1,495,765
Total assets	13,921,142	42,418,426	45,129,354	45,799,094	46,922,920	49,778,376
Liabilities and Stockholders Equity						
Current liabilities						
Accounts payable	744,639	1,218,994	1,948,021	2,140,690	2,349,283	2,519,814
Accounts payable related companies	66,804	66,804	66,804	66,804	66,804	66,804
Current notes/obligations	1,163,967	2,972,279	3,463,699	3,985,869	4,540,064	3,853,869
Accrued expenses	147,899	449,191	449,191	449,191	449,191	449,191
Income taxes payable	19,868	103,368	103,368	103,368	103,368	103,368
Long-term liabilities						
Long-term bond (landfill) debt	176,000	16,879,582	16,222,715	15,505,281	14,721,685	13,865,817
Long-term debt (other)	4,604,195	4,757,407	4,385,322	2,822,371	981,973	764,862
Long-term seller/land notes	1,032,244	3,625,117	4,340,370	4,084,887	3,718,816	3,587,927
Deferred taxes	295,230	377,480	377,480	377,480	377,480	377,480
Other liabilities	886,202	2,623,230	3,188,980	3,800,230	4,441,230	5,082,230
Stockholders equity						
Common stock	3,005,300	5,006,300	5,006,300	5,006,300	5,006,300	5,006,300
Capital excess par	16,000	17,000	17,000	17,000	17,000	17,000
Retained earnings	1,762,795	4,321,674	5,560,103	7,439,624	10,149,726	14,083,715
Total liabilities & stockholders equity	13,921,142	42,418,426	45,129,354	45,799,095	46,922,920	49,778,376

Notes to Financial Statements

Unless otherwise indicated, uniform escalation assumptions of 3% have been applied throughout to all revenues and expenses, except for depreciation, amortization, and interest. Eliminations have been based on conservative estimates of duplicate streams.

Landfill annual use is based on actual records or assumption of waste currently within the control of CWS. Landfill prices are based on actual prices currently charged. Landfill and landfill acquisition costs are depleted on the unit production method. The terms of the Waste USA and Sanco acquisitions are based on a signed purchase and sale agreement or a negotiated letter of intent. Depletion has been taken against expected actual permitted capacities. Debt service reserve funds (DSRF) are established by bond purchasers' requirements. Release of DSRF funds will be convented between the bond purchasers and the Company. Cost rejections are based on actual operating history and CWS estimates of future operating costs. Closure cost estimates are established by independent engineers. Closure costs of Sunderland will be accrued during the C&D operation expected to start in 1994. Landfill capacities are based on estimates by independent engineers, but utilization of the capacity is likely to vary, dependent on fill techniques employed.

Hauling revenues are based on actual current experience of CWS and acquired companies, escalated by the uniform escalation factor. No increase in the number of customers or per capita waste production has been assumed and the effect of a recovery from the present recession, especially in the retail and recreation or hospitality sectors, has not been taken into account. Acquisition of hauling companies is based on negotiation with companies currently underway or developed during the past 18 months. In the case of acquisitions within the existing CWS service area, certain fixed costs will be absorbed by the existing CWS infrastructure.

The Company's recycling activities have been developed as part of an integrated waste management service. Recycling contracts typically have provisions for renegotiation of processing fees based on the prices received for recycled materials. The projections assume that only 20% of the contracts will be so renegotiated, although the Company expects to renegotiate a substantially higher number.

Source: Corporate documents

Exhibit 8   Memorandum on Projections

To:	Don Remey
	Bart Goodwin
	Peter Wilde
From:	Richard H. Lindgren
Date	May 10, 1993
Subject:	Casella Waste Systems Cash Flow Projections

In the projections furnished you relating to Casella Waste Systems, EBITDA in Year 1 totals $7,996,000 compared with $4,896,000 actually achieved in the year ending December 31, 1992, an increase of $3,100,000 You have asked that we spell out more fully the assumptions underlying that increase.

Casella Waste Systems consists of three operating entities, the Casella Aggregate, and the SANCO and Waste USA landfills. Casella Aggregate is the combination of the activities conducted by the Casella brothers, including hauling, recycling, unlined landfills and real estate ownership of the underlying properties. The breakdown of EBITD among those three for the periods is as follows:

($000 omitted)	Year Ended December 31, 1992	Year 1
Sanco	2,314	2,755
Waste USA	349	1,231
Casella	2,206	4,010
	4,896	7,996

Sanco   During Year 1, it is assumed that revenues remain constant and the gross margin actually declines modestly from 82% to 78%. The increase in EBITDA is occasioned largely by a decrease in Landfill Overhead from $1,021,837 to $375,000. In 1992, General and Administrative expenses were inflated by $200,000 in legal expenses which will be terminated before closing, $400,000 in excess payroll which has already been reduced under Casella management and $100,000 relating to construction expenses. The ownership of SANCO by CWS will reduce that charge to a realistic level.

Waste USA   EBITDA generated by Waste USA increases by $882,000 in Year 1. Landfill Revenues increase from $1,154,780 to $2,842,000, brought about by an increase in volume to 58,000 tons. The tonnage is derived from the following sources:

Currently under contract	35,000
Diverted from CWS's Newbury landfill	10,000
Diverted from unlined landfills	13,000
	58,000

It is estimated that the waste stream of the Montpelier/Barre area generates approximately 35,000 tons and the counties surrounding Burlington generate 75,000 tons. In addition, it is estimated that the Northeast Kingdom generates perhaps 15,000 tons that is not now delivered to WASTE USA. All of the existing non-lined landfills in Vermont must close by October 1993. Waste USA is the nearest lined landfill to the three areas outlined above. The CWS projections assume, however, that only approximately 10% of that waste stream will find its way to Waste USA in Year 1.

Casella   EBITDA from Casella increases by $1,804,000 in Year 1. In Year 1, Casella revenues increase from $10,950,068 to $17,175,775, brought about by an increase in existing hauling revenues of 4% and revenues from hauling company acquisitions totaling $5,785,263. CWS assumes that its gross margin will drop from 41% in 1992 to 38% in Year 1, reflecting, in part, the costs of assimilation. Assuming a 35% margin on the acquired businesses, that would provide $2,024,00 in additional EBITDA. Casella has targeted nine hauling companies with current revenues of $11.1 million for acquisition. Casella's has traditionally expanded through the acquisition route. The lack of bank lending in Vermont, however, made it impossible for Casella to make acquisitions in the last two years. At the same time, there is a consolidation going on among hauling companies and Casella's dominant position makes it a likely acquirer. Consequently, the five acquisitions contemplated in Year 1, one of which has already been completed, represent a backlog of transactions that were unable to be consummated until growth capital was available to the Company. The closing of the unlined landfills and the requirements for recycling dramatically change the economic environment for small haulers, further increasing the pressure to sell out.

You have also asked how EBITDA increases from $7,996,741 in Year 1 to $14,987,151 in Year 5. The basic assumptions are as follows:

Sanco   Tipping fees increase by 4% per year and volume increases by 5% per year. Because, the landfill business is largely a fixed cost business, gross margins increase from 38% to 41%, during the period.

Waste USA   Tipping fees increase by 4% per year and volume increases to 75,000 tons in Year 2, 85,000 tons in Year 3 and 90,000 tons in Years 4 and 5, reflecting greater assimilation of the waste stream available. Using the waste stream available to Waste USA in Year 1 from the areas outlined above of 170,000 tons and inflating the stream by 4% per year, Waste USA captures 34% of the tonnage in Year 1, increasing to 42% in Year 2, 46% in Year 3 and 47% in Year 4. Given the lack of alternative sites and CWS's increasing control of the waste stream through acquisition, the Company believes that its projections will prove conservative.

Casella   Casella projects revenues from existing hauling activities increasing 4% per year and acquisitions providing volume increases of approximately $6 million in Year 1, $4 million in Year 2 and $ I million in each year thereafter. The gross margin increases from 38% to 41% by Year 5, a level of profitability its existing operations achieved in 1992. In all likelihood, acquisition volume will surpass projections during the period. Projections of acquisitions only encompassed known companies in the Casella operating area. It is extremely likely that acquisition volume in Years 3-5 will be substantially higher. Given the cash available to the Company in Years 3-5, the Company will be able to take advantage of opportunities to further extend its operating area.

Source: Corporate documents.

Note: The slight deviations from the pro forma projections are as in the original document.

Exhibit 9   Proposed BCI Investment in Casella Waste Systems, Inc.

Issuer:	Casella Waste Systems, Inc. (The "Company" or "CWS" (a holding company.
Purchaser:	BCI Growth L.P. ("Growth') Glenpointe Centre West Teaneck, New Jersey 07666
	Donald P. Remey J. Barton Goodwin Peter O. Wilde, Jr.
Issues:	Senior note due July 15, 2000 (the "Note")
	Warrants to purchase Class A stock of CWS ("Warrants")
Amount:	$5,000,000
Closing:	On or before July 15, 1993. Subject to completion of due diligence and legal documentation.
Use of Proceeds:	(1) Acquisition of Consumat Sanco, Inc. for approximately $1.6 million initial cash payment (2) Acquisition of Waste USA, Inc. for approximately $500,000 initial cash payment. (3) Working capital totaling $500,000 for Casella Waste Management, Inc. and CWS. (4) Acquisitions of hauling companies.
Takedowns:	The initial takedown will be approximately 1.5 million for the acquisition of Consumat Sanco, Inc. plus working capital. Subsequent takedowns will be at the option of CWS subject to customary representations and warranties. 50% of the Warrants will be issued upon the initial closing, with 25% upon each of the next takedowns.
Fees and Expenses:	Upon authorization to proceed, the Company will pay: (1) a nonrefundable fee of $25,000 to BCI Advisors, Inc. ("BCA"). BCA will be responsible for its own expenses, including fees for any outside experts hired as part of their due diligence. (2) An advance of $25,000 to Reboul, MacMurray, Hewitt, Maynard & Kristol ("Reboul") for credit against their fees and expenses At closing, the Company shall pay all of the fees and expenses of Reboul.

The Note

Purchase price: 100%

Interest rate: 7.50% per annum, payable monthly on the amount drawn down.

Maturity: Seven years

Sinking fund: Beginning in 42 months, 10% of the principal amount shall be payable semiannually with the balance (30%) due at the end of the seventh year.

Month	Principal	%
42	$500,000	10%
48	500,000	10
54	500,000	10
60	500,000	10
66	500,000	10
72	500,000	10
78	500,000	10
84	1,500,000	30
	$5,000,000	100%

Prepayment: The note may be prepaid in part or in whole at any time with no penalty except, the Note will become due and payable:
(1) Upon an IPO of $15 million or more net proceeds to the Company.
(2) In the event of a change of control.
(3) Upon merger or sale of significant assets.

Ranking and Collateral: The notes will be the sole debt in CWS, a holding company. The common stock of all subsidiaries will be pledged as collateral to the Note.

Financial Covenants: The purchase agreement will contain customary financial covenants to include:
(1) Limitation on consolidated funded indebtedness of CWS. Ratio to be determined based on pro-forma and projected capitalization.
(2) Maintain fixed change coverage on a consolidated basis and for CWS alone.
(3) Consolidated net worth to be maintained at certain dollar amounts, initially the amount as of July 30, 1993, increasing annually by 50% of projected net income.
(4) No sale of equity securities by subsidiaries.

Restricted Payments: No dividends or stock redemptions by CWS as long as the Notes are outstanding.

Management Compensation and Non-Arm's Length Transactions: Subject to approval by the non-management directors.

The Warrants

Warrants: Initially to purchase 1,168,333 shares of Class A common stock representing 25.0% of the fully diluted shares of the Company. Pro forma ownership would be approximately as follows:

	# of Shares	Percent
BCI Growth Class A warrants	1,168,333	25.00%
National Waste Industries	600,000[a]	12.84
Houghton & Company	150,000	3.21
James W. Bohlig	125,000	2.67

360

Harry Ryan	100,000	2.14
John & Doug Casella	1,130,000	24.18
John & Doug Casella (Class B)	1,000,000	21.40
Warrants	100,000	2.14
Management options	300,000	6.42
Total	4,673,333	100.00%

[a]Maximum

Exercise Price:	$2.75 payable in cash or Notes, subject to anti-dilution protection.
Warrant Ratchet:	In the event that EBITDA for the fiscal year ending April 30 (or March 31), 1995, is less than $3.6 million, BCI Growth would receive 120,000 additional warrants (2.5%), and the exercise price would be reduced to $2.00.
Purchase Price:	Nominal.
Expiration:	10 years
Repurchase:	The Company, at its option, may repurchase the Warrants: (1) After 4.5 years at the higher of fair market value or five times EBITDA less long term debt. The Company must, upon notification by BCI Growth, repurchase the Warrants: (1) At a price of 200% of the exercise price if prior to July 15, 1995, there is a sale of assets, merger, or change of control; (2) After 4.5 years at the higher of fair market value or five times EBITDA less long term debt.
IPO Exercise:	Upon an IPO at a price of not less than 250% of the exercise price, BCI Growth must exercise all the Warrants provided BCI Growth has the opportunity to sell not less than 25% of its exercised shares at the IPO price.
Pre-Emptive Rights:	Of all future issuances of equity securities for cash. Excludes securities issued for acquisitions or management options.
Voting:	Vote on an as exercised basis.
Registration:	Two demand and unlimited piggyback rights.
Stockholders Agreement:	The owners of equity securities will enter into a Stockholders Agreement that will provide normal and customary provisions including Board of Directors size and composition; approval of merger, sale and other major corporate transactions; Restrictions and terms for sales/transfers of securities.
Other Conditions to Closing:	To include, but not limited to: (1) Audited statements by Gallagher, Flynn & Company of Casella Waste Management, Inc., Bristol Waste Management, Inc., Newbury Waste Management, Inc., Sunderland Waste Management, Inc., individually and pro-forma consolidated as of April 30, 1993. (2) Confidential disclosure by John and Doug Casella to Donald P. Remey of all non-CWS business activities and personal financial statements. (3) Non-compete agreements with John Casella, Doug Casella and Jim Bohlig. Agreement that all future business dealings will be limited to CWS. (4) Retention of qualified search firm to recruit a chief financial officer. Targeted hire within three months. (5) Agreement on composition of Board of Directors. (6) Agreement of responsibilities and compensation of senior management.

Source: Corporate documents

361

19

Apex Investment Partners (B): May 1995

The three key parties concerned with the proposed financing of AccessLine Technologies by Apex Investment Partners—the company's chief financial officer, two venture capitalists from Apex, and an investment banker from Morgan Stanley—had met in Philadelphia in early May 1995. The meeting's goal was to finalize the transaction. Apex had proposed to be the lead investor in AccessLine's $16 million Series B financing round. The term sheet stipulated that the investors would invest $8.00 for each unit, which would consist of a preferred share of AccessLine and 0.7 of a warrant to purchase an additional share. Apex, as lead investor, would have a seat on AccessLine's board.

Apex's final offer had addressed the bulk of each party's concerns and sought to achieve a proper alignment of interests. The venture capitalists, however, had failed to appreciate how great a discrepancy existed between their proposed valuation and that desired by the firm's management. Apex's Rick Bolander and George Middlemas had been forced to return to Chicago without a deal in hand. AccessLine's investment banker had called a few days later on a Friday afternoon, to reiterate that Apex's proposed valuation was unsatisfactory. The issue, he indicated, had to be resolved by Sunday night, when a conference call to finalize the deal was scheduled.

In the just-completed call, the investment banker had indicated that he believed the price per share of preferred stock in the proposed Series B financing would be below the per share price paid in the previous financing round (which had been priced at $7.00 per share-and-warrant unit). If so, management would almost surely reject the proposed deal. Bolander was unsure, however, whether Apex would be willing to pay more than $8 for the share-and-warrant unit. Even if his fund was willing to invest, its potential syndication partners might decide not to participate in the deal.

The essential problem, Bolander realized, was how much of the $8 price of the unit should be assigned to the Series B preferred share and how much to the warrant. Morgan Stanley had done an analysis using the Black-Scholes model. This suggested that the valuation of the preferred stock in the proposed deal would be substantially lower than in AccessLine's previous financing. Bolander acknowledged that the warrant had some economic value, but felt that he needed to understand both the strengths and limitations of the Morgan Stanley analysis better.

This case was prepared by Sanjiv Das and Josh Lerner. Copyright © 1995 by the President and Fellows of Harvard College. Harvard Business School case 296–029.

THE PROPOSED DEAL

After considerable due diligence, Apex had decided that it wished to invest in AccessLine Technologies. AccessLine, an emerging telecommunications firm based in Bellevue, Washington, was the developer of the "One Person, One Number" concept, which allows an individual to have a single phone number at which he or she can be reached at any time.[1]

In conjunction with its legal adviser, George Thibeault of Testa, Hurwitz and Thibeault, Apex had prepared a term sheet for the proposed deal (reproduced in Exhibit 1). This called for a total investment of $16 million, of which Apex and its affiliated investors would contribute between $4.5 and $6.5 million. As is natural in such situations, the terms and conditions outlined in the term sheet had raised a variety of concerns on the part of management. These difficulties, however, had largely been ironed out in the negotiating process.

Much more serious was the problem of valuation. The Morgan Stanley bankers had valued the AccessLine warrants through the Black-Scholes formula. This commonly used model allows one to derive the price of an option to purchase a publicly traded share of stock. The Black-Scholes model assumes that the payouts of the option can be duplicated by buying and selling shares of the underlying stock and a Treasury bond. Given several simple variables—the price of the share, the exercise price of the option, the volatility of the firm's stock price, the time to expiration of the option, and the risk-free interest rate—the option's price can then be determined.

The bankers had solved for the value of the warrant in an iterative manner. They began with the assumption that the share of stock and two-thirds of the warrant are together worth $8.[2] Through the use of various assumptions[3] and alternative prices for the stock, they were able to reach a price that set the unit equal to $8. Bolander worried whether this calculation was appropriate. An essential assumption of the Black-Scholes formula, however, is that one can buy and sell shares of the security at any time without transaction costs and that the value of the underlying security evolves in a smooth and continuous manner. AccessLine, however, was not publicly traded. The changes in its valuation could only be observed at infrequent intervals, at the time of new financing rounds. Furthermore, many young technology companies that did trade publicly were characterized by large discontinuities, as the market reacted dramatically to earnings announcements or technological breakthroughs.

Bolander wondered as to whether the Morgan bankers had correctly applied the Black-Scholes formula, and even if they had, whether it was the right tool to apply in this situation. Bolander thought about the complexity of the problem, and about the imminent Sunday night conference call.

---

[1] For background information on AccessLine and Apex Investment Partners, see "Apex Investment Partners (A): April 1995," Chapter 11.

[2] The Black-Scholes formula provides the value for an option. One can adjust this formula to obtain the value of a warrant by correcting for the dilution associated with the issue of the shares to fulfill the warrants. In this case, the warrant will be worth about 10% to 15% less than the comparable option.

[3] AccessLine did not trade publicly, so no volatility figure was available. A comparable company, BroadBand Technologies, had a recent volatility of between 40% and 45% (using daily and weekly data).

Exhibit 1   Summary of Terms for Private Placement of Series B Convertible Preferred Stock and Warrants to Purchase Series B Convertible Preferred Stock: Final "Walk-Away" Offer Presented at Philadelphia Union League Club by Apex Investment Partners

Issuer:	AccessLine Technologies, Inc. ("Company")
Investors:	(1) Apex Investment Fund II L.P., various of its affiliated funds and other entities introduced by Apex (the "Apex Purchasers"); (2) existing investors in the Company; and (3) certain other new investors, (collectively, the "Investors").
Currently Outstanding Securities:	8,086,099 Class A & B Common Stock ("Common"); 2,220,726 Series A Preferred ("Series A"); 333,110 Warrants for Series A; and 2,582,047 Common reserved for employees.
Amount of Investment:	$16,000,000, of which the Apex Purchasers will provide approximately $4,500,000-$6,500,000.
Time of Investment:	The Investors will purchase all of the Series B Shares and Series B Warrants on the date of the Closing under the Purchase Agreement hereinafter referred to.
Types of Securities:	Series B Convertible Preferred Stock ("Series B") and Warrants to purchase Series B ("Series B Warrants").
Number of Series B and Series B Warrants:	2,000,000 shares of Series B and 1,400,000 (70%) Series B Warrants.
Purchase Price per Series B And per Series B Warrants:	$8.00 per Series B Share ("Original Purchase Price") and Series B Warrant at no cost
Exercise Price per Warrant:	$8.00 as to warrants exercised on or before June 30, 1996; $9.00 as to warrants exercised on or after July 1, 1996; and $10.00 as to warrants exercised on or after January 1, 1997 ("Warrant Exercise Price").
Terms of Series B Warrants:	Earlier of five (5) years following a Qualified Public Offering (as hereafter defined) and ten (10) years from the date of the Closing. The Warrants will provide for "cashless" exercise provision.
Rights, Preferences, Privileges, and Restrictions of Series B:	(1) *Dividend Provisions*: A cumulative dividend on the Series B will accrue at the rate of eight percent (8%) per annum of the Original Purchase Price or Warrant Exercise Price, as the case may be, commencing on the date such share is issued; provided, however, that if the Company has not consummated a Qualified Public Offering (as hereinafter defined) before January 1, 1997, then effective on and from such date the dividend rate will be increased by an additional two-thirds of a percent per annum at the start of each and every calendar month thereafter ("Accruing Dividends") until a Qualified Public Offering has occurred or until redeemed as described under "Redemption." Accruing Dividends will be payable only: (a) if, as and when determined by the Board of Directors ("Board"); (b) upon the liquidation or winding up of the Company; or (c) upon a redemption as described under "Redemption." No dividend will be paid on the Common, and no shares of Common will be repurchased by the Company except for unvested shares repurchased from former employees at their original purchase price.

(2) *Liquidation Preference:* In the event of the liquidation or winding up of the Company, the holders of Series A and Series B, on a par passu basis, will be entitled to receive in preference to the holders of Common an amount equal to the greater of (a) the Original Purchase Price in the case of the Series A and the Original Purchase Price in the case of the Series B or the Warrant Exercise Price, as the case may be, plus any dividends (including Accruing Dividends) accrued on the Series B but not paid; or (b) the amount they would have received had they converted the Series A and Series B to Common immediately prior to such liquidation or winding up. A consolidation or merger of the Company or sale of all or substantially all of its assets will be deemed to be a liquidation or winding up for purposes of the liquidation preference.

(3) *Redemption:* On _____, _____ [to be a date after the date the Series B Warrants expire], the Company will redeem the Series B by paying in cash the Original Purchase Price or Warrant Exercise Price, as the case may be, plus any dividends (including Accruing Dividends) accrued on the Series B but not paid. If the Company fails to redeem the Series B when due, the conversion price of the Series B thereafter will decrease at the rate of 10% per quarter and the holders of the Series B will be entitled to elect a majority of the directors.

(4) *Conversion:* A holder of Series B will have the right to convert the Series B, at the option of the holder, at any time, into shares of Common. The total number of shares of Common into which the Series B may be converted initially will be determined by dividing the Original Purchase Price or Warrant Exercise Price, as the case may be, by the Conversion Price. The initial conversion price will be the Original Purchase Price or the Warrant Exercise Price, as the case may be. The Conversion Price will be subject to adjustment as provided in paragraph (3) above and paragraph (6) below.

(5) *Automatic Conversion:* The Series B will be automatically converted into Common, at the then applicable conversion price, in the event of an underwritten public offering of share of the Common in an offering with gross proceed to the Company of not less than $10,000,000 and at a public offering price per share that is not less than $12.00 if such offering occurs on or before June 30, 1996, $14.00 if such offering occurs on or after July 1, 1996 and on or before December 31, 1996 and $16.00 if such offering occurs on or after January 1, 1997 (a "Qualified Public Offering"). In such event, the Warrants will automatically convert into warrants to purchase such number of shares of Common as the Series B subject to the Warrants could then be converted into Common. Two-thirds of Series B vote will be required to change Automatic Conversion Price.

(6) *Antidilution Provisions:* If the Company issues additional shares (other than the Reserved Shares described under "Reserved Shares" below) at a purchase price less than the applicable conversion price, the conversion price of the Series B and the Warrant Exercise Price will each be reduced on a weighted average formula basis to diminish the effect of such dilutive issuance. Pay to Play provision shall be in effect for any future financing round.

(7) *Voting Rights:* Except with respect to election of director and certain protective provisions, the holders of Series B will have the right to that number of votes equal to the number of shares of Common issuable upon conversion of the Series B. Election of directors and the protective provisions will be as described under "Board Representation and Meetings" and "Protective Provisions", respectively, below.

(8) *Protective Provisions*: Consent of the holders of at least two-thirds of the Series A and Series B will be required for (1) any sale by the Company of substantially all of its assets; (2) any merger of the Company with another entity; (3) any liquidation or winding up of the Company; (4) any amendment of the Company's charter or by-laws; or (5) certain other actions materially affecting the Series B.

Information Rights:

As long as any of the Series B or Series B Warrants are outstanding, the Company will deliver to each Investor annual, quarterly, and monthly financial statements, annual budgets, and other information reasonably requested by an Investor.

Registration Rights:

(1) *Demand Rights*: If, at any time after the earlier of the Company's initial public offering and the date two (2) years from the purchase of the Series B, Investors holding at least 40% of the Common issued or issuable upon conversion of the Series B and exercise of the Series B warrants request that the Company file a Registration Statement covering at least 20% of the Common issued or issuable upon conversion of the Series B and exercise of the Series B Warrants (or any lesser percentage if the anticipated aggregate offering price would exceed $5,000,000), the Company will use its best efforts to cause such share to be registered.

The Company will not be obligated to effect more than two registrations (other than on Form S-3) under these demand right provisions.

(2) *Registrations on Form S-3*: Holders of Common issued or issuable upon conversion of the Series B and exercise of the Series B Warrants will have the right to require the Company to file an unlimited number of Registration Statements on Form S-3 (or any equivalent successor form), provided the anticipated aggregate offering price in each registration on Form S-3 will exceed $250,000.

(3) *Piggy-Back Registration*: The Investors will be entitled to "piggy-back" registration rights on registrations of the Company, subject to the right of the Company and its underwriters to reduce in view of market conditions the number of shares of the Investors proposed to be registered to not less than one-third of the total number of shares in the offering.

(4) *Registration Expenses*: The registration expenses (exclusive of underwriting discounts and commissions) of all of the registrations under paragraphs (1), (2), and (3) above will be borne by the Company.

(5) *Transfer of Registration Rights*: The registration rights may be transferred to a transferee who acquires any of the Series B or Series B Warrants.

(6) *Other Registration Provisions*: Other provisions will be contained in the Purchase Agreement with respect to registration rights as are reasonable, including cross-indemnification, the Company's ability to delay the filing of a demand registration for a period of not more than 90 days in certain circumstances, the agreement by the Investors (if requested by the underwriters in a public offering) not to sell any unregistered Common they hold for a period of 120 days following the effective date of the Registration Statement of such offering, the period of time in which the Registration Statement will be kept effective, underwriting arrangements and the like.

(7) *No Registration of Series B*: The registration rights set forth herein apply only to the Common and the Company will never be obligated to register any of the Series B or Series B Warrants.

Use of Proceeds:

The Proceeds from the sale of the Series B or Series B Warrants will be used for working capital.

Board Representation and Meeting:	The charter will provide that the authorized number of directors is seven (7). The Series B (voting as a class) will elect one (1) director (F.W.W. Bolander will be the representative of Apex), the Series A (voting as a class) will elect one (1) director and the Common Series A and Series B (voting together as a single class) will elect five (5) directors. The Board will meet at least quarterly. The by laws will provide, in addition to any provisions required by law, that any two directors or holders of at least 25% of the Series B may call a meeting of the Board. Investors holding at least 400,000 shares of Series B will be entitled to have an observer attend Board meetings.
Key Person Insurance:	\$_____ on each of _____, _____, and _____, with the proceeds payable to the Company.
First Refusal Right for Purchase of New Securities:	As long as any of the Series B or Series B Warrants are outstanding, if the Company proposes to offer any shares for the purpose of financing its business (other than Reserved Shares, shares issued in the acquisition of another company, or shares offered to the public pursuant to an underwritten public offering), the Company will first offer all such shares to the Investors.
Stock Restriction Agreements:	_____, _____, and _____ will each execute a Stock Restriction Agreement with the Investors and the Company pursuant to which the Investors will have a right of first refusal with respect to any shares proposed to be sold by such persons. The Stock Restriction Agreement will also contain a right of co-sale providing that before any such person may sell any of his shares, he will first give the Investors an opportunity to participate in such sale on the basis proportionate to the amount of securities held by the seller and those held by the Investors. In addition, the Stock Restriction Agreement will restrict such person from selling more than ____% of his shares for ____ years from the purchase of the Series B. The Stock Restriction Agreement will also give the Company the right to repurchase such person's unvested shares at a price equal to his original purchase price, in the event his employment with the Company terminates. Shares will vest at the rate of ____% per annum. The Stock Restriction Agreement will terminate after ten years or, if earlier, a Qualified Public Offering.
Reserved Shares:	The Company currently has 2,582,047 shares of Common reserved for issuance to directors, officers, employees (the "Reserved Shares").
	The Reserved Shares will be issued from time to time to directors, officers, employees, and consultants of the Company under such agreements, contracts, or plans as are recommended by management and approved by the Board, provided that without the unanimous consent of the directors elected solely by the Series B, the vesting of any such shares (of options therefore) issued to any such person shall not be at a rate in excess of 20% per annum from the date of issuance. Unless subsequently agreed to the contrary by the investors, any issuance of shares in excess of the Reserved Shares will be a dilutive event requiring adjustment of the conversion price as provided above and will be subject to the Investors' first refusal right as described above. Holders of Reserved Shares who are officers or employees of the Company will be required to execute Stock Restriction Agreements generally as described above.
Noncompetition Agreement:	To the extent permitted by applicable law, employees, directors, and _____ will each enter into a noncompetition agreement with the Company in a form reasonably acceptable to the Investors.
Nondisclosure and Developments Agreement:	Each officer and key employee of the Company will enter into a nondisclosure and developments agreement in a form reasonably acceptable to the Investors.

The Purchase Agreement:

The purchase of the Series B and the Series B Warrants will be made pursuant to a Series B Stock and Warrant Purchase Agreement drafted by counsel to the Investors. Such agreement shall contain, among other things, appropriate representations and warranties of the Company, covenants of the Company reflecting the provisions set forth herein and other typical covenants, and appropriate conditions of closing, including, among other things, qualification of the securities under applicable Blue Sky laws, the filing of a certificate of amendments to the Company's charter to authorize the Series B, and an opinion of counsel. Until the Purchase Agreement is signed by both the Company and the Investors, there will not exist any binding obligation on the part of either party to consummate the transaction. This Summary of Terms does not constitute a contractual commitment of the Company or the Investors or an obligation of either party to negotiate with the other.

Expenses:

The Company and the Investors will each bear their own legal and other expenses with respect to the transaction (except that, assuming a successful completion of the transaction, the Company will pay the legal fees and expenses of Testa, Hurwitz & Thibeault, counsel to the Investors).

Finders:

The Company and the Investors will each indemnify the other for any finder's fees for which either is responsible.

Due Diligence:

All terms subject upon successful completion of due diligence within twenty (20) days after successful completion of this term sheet.

Source: Corporate documents.

EXITING PRIVATE EQUITY INVESTMENTS

The third module of *Venture Capital and Private Equity* examines the process through which private equity investors exit their investments. Successful exits are critical to ensuring attractive returns for investors and, in turn, to raising additional capital. But the concerns of private equity investors about exiting investments—and their behavior during the exiting process itself—can sometimes lead to severe problems for entrepreneurs.

We will employ an analytic framework very similar to that used in the first module. We will not only seek to understand the institutional features associated with exiting private equity investments in the United States and overseas, but also to analyze them. We will map out which features are designed primarily to increase the overall amount of profits from private equity investments and which actions seem to be intended to shift more of the profits to particular parties.

WHY THIS MODULE?

At first glance, the exiting of private equity investments may appear to be outside the scope of *Venture Capital and Private Equity*. Such issues might seem more appropriate for courses that focus on public markets. But since the need to ultimately exit investments shapes every aspect of the private equity cycle, this issue is very important for both private equity investors and entrepreneurs.

Perhaps the clearest illustration of the relationship between the private and public markets was seen during the 1980s and early 1990s. In the early 1980s, many European nations developed secondary markets. These markets sought to combine a hospitable environment for small firms (e.g., they allowed firms to be listed even if they did not have an extended record of profitability) with tight regulatory safeguards. They enabled the pioneering European private equity funds to exit their investments. A wave of fundraising by these and other private equity organizations followed in the mid-1980s. After the 1987 market crash, initial public offering activity in Europe and the United States dried up. But while the U.S. market recovered in the early 1990s, the European market remained depressed. Consequently, European private equity investors were unable to exit investments by going public. They were required either to continue to hold the firms or to sell them to larger corporations at often-unattractive valuations. While U.S. private equity investors—pointing to their

This note was prepared by Josh Lerner. Copyright © 1996 by the President and Fellows of Harvard College. Harvard Business School case 297-042.

successful exits—were able to raise substantial amounts of new capital, European private equity fundraising during this period remained depressed. The influence of exits on the rest of the private equity cycle suggests that this is a critical issue for funds and their investors.

The exiting of private equity investments also has important implications for entrepreneurs. As discussed in the first module, the typical private equity fund is liquidated after one decade (though extensions of a few years may be possible). Thus, if a private equity investor cannot foresee how a company will be mature enough to take public or to sell at the end of a decade, he is unlikely to invest in the firm. If it was equally easy to exit investments of all types at all times, this might not be a problem. But interest in certain technologies by public investors seems to be subject to wide swings. For instance, in recent years "hot issue markets" have appeared and disappeared for computer hardware, biotechnology, multimedia, and Internet companies. Concerns about the ability to exit investments may have led to too many private equity transactions being undertaken in these "hot" industries. At the same time, insufficient capital may have been devoted to industries not in the public limelight.

Concerns about exiting may also adversely affect firms once they are financed by private equity investors. Less scrupulous investors may occasionally encourage companies in their portfolio to undertake actions that boost the probability of a successful initial public offering, even if they jeopardize the firm's long-run health: for example, increasing earnings by cutting back on vital research spending. In addition, many private equity investors appear to exploit their inside knowledge when dissolving their stakes in investments. Although this may be in the best interests of the limited and general partners of the fund, it may have harmful effects on the firm and the other shareholders.

THE FRAMEWORK OF THE ANALYSIS

The exiting of private equity investments involves a diverse range of actors. Private equity investors exit most successful investments through taking them public.[1] A wide variety of actors are involved in the initial public offering. In addition to the private equity investors, these include the investment bank that underwrites the offering, the institutional and individual investors who are allotted the shares (and frequently sell them immediately after the offering), and the parties who end up holding the shares.

Few private equity investments are liquidated at the time of the initial public offering. Instead, private equity investors typically dissolve their positions by distributing the shares to the investors in their funds. These distributions usually take place one to two years after the offering. A variety of other intermediaries are involved in these transactions, such as distribution managers who evaluate and liquidate distributed securities for institutional investors.

This module will examine each of these players. Rather than just describing their roles, however, we will highlight the rationales for and impacts of their behavior. We

---

[1] A Venture Economics study finds that a $1 investment in a firm that goes public provides an average cash return of $1.95 in excess of the initial investment, with an average holding period of 4.2 years. The next best alternative, an investment in an acquired firm, yields a cash return of only 40 cents over a 3.7-year mean holding period. See Venture Economics, *Exiting Venture Capital Investments,* Wellesley, Venture Economics, 1988.

will again employ the framework of the first module. We will seek to assess which institutions and features have evolved to improve the efficiency of the private equity investment process, and which have sprung up primarily to shift more of the economic benefits to particular parties.

Many features associated with the exiting of private equity investments can be understood as responses to many uncertainties in this environment. An example is the "lock up" provisions that prohibit corporate insiders and private equity investors from selling at the time of the offering. This helps avoid situations where the officers and directors exploit their inside knowledge that a newly listed company is overvalued by rapidly liquidating their positions.

At the same time, other features of the exiting process can be seen as attempts to transfer wealth between parties. An example may be the instances where private equity funds distribute shares to their investors that drop in price immediately after the distribution. Even if the price at which the investors ultimately sell the shares is far less, the private equity investors use the share price *before* the distribution to calculate their fund's rate of return and to determine when they can begin profit-sharing.

THE STRUCTURE OF THE MODULE

This module begins by exploring the need for avenues to exit private equity investments. To do this, we will examine Europe's private equity markets. As described above, the inability to exit investments has been a major stumbling block to the development of its private equity industry.

We then examine the exiting of private equity investments in the United States. We will examine the differing incentives and actions of venture capitalists and investors during the exiting process. We explore the perspectives of and implications for private equity investors, entrepreneurs, firms, limited partners, and the specialized distribution managers that they hire regarding going public and distributing shares. Once again, we will seek to assess which behavior increases the size of the "pie" and which actions simply change the relative sizes of the slices.

FURTHER READING ON EXITING PRIVATE EQUITY INVESTMENTS

Legal Works

JOSEPH W. BARTLETT, *Equity Finance: Venture Capital, Buyouts, Restructurings, and Reorganization,* New York, Wiley, 1995, chapter 14.

MICHAEL J. HALLORAN, LEE F. BENTON, ROBERT V. GUNDERSON, JR., KEITH L. KEARNEY, AND JORGE DEL CALVO, *Venture Capital and Public Offering Negotiation,* Englewood Cliffs, NJ, Aspen Law and Business, 1995, volume 2.

JACK S. LEVIN, *Structuring Venture Capital, Private Equity, and Entrepreneurial Transactions,* Boston, Little, Brown, 1995, chapter 9.

Practitioner and Journalistic Accounts

JAMES S. ALTSCHUL, "Staging the Small IPO," *CFO* 7 (November 1992): 70–74.

PAUL F. DENNING, AND ROBIN A. PAINTER, *Stock Distributions: A Guide for Venture Capitalists,* Boston, Robertson, Stephens & Co. and Testa, Hurwitz & Thibeault, 1994.

European Venture Capital Association, *Venture Capital Special Paper: Capital Markets for Entrepreneurial Companies,* Zaventum, Belgium, European Venture Capital Association, 1994.

Mark Mehler, "Mangy Mutts Go Public," *Upside,* 4 (October 1992): 48–53, 64.

Ann Monroe, "The High-Tech Crapshot," *Institutional Dealers' Digest* 61 (March 13, 1995): 12–23.

Venture Economics, *Exiting Venture Capital Investments,* Wellesley, MA, Venture Economics, 1988.

Numerous articles in *Buyouts, Private Equity Analyst,* and *Venture Capital Journal.*

Academic Studies

Christopher B. Barry, Chris J. Muscarella, John W. Peavy III, and Michael R. Vetsuypens, "The Role of Venture Capital in the Creation of Public Companies: Evidence from the Going Public Process," *Journal of Financial Economics* 27 (October 1990): 447–471.

Bernard S. Black, and Ronald J. Gilson, "Venture Capital and the Structure of Capital Markets: Banks versus Stock Markets," *Journal of Financial Economics* 47 (March 1998): 243–277.

George W. Fenn, Nellie Liang, and Stephen Prowse, "The Private Equity Market: An Overview," *Financial Markets, Institutions, and Instruments* 6 (#4, 1997): 1–26.

Paul A. Gompers and Josh Lerner, *The Venture Capital Cycle,* Cambridge, MA: MIT Press, 1999, chapters 10–14.

Steven N. Kaplan, "The Staying Power of Leveraged Buyouts," *Journal of Financial Economics,* 29 (October 1991): 287–313.

T. H. Lin and Richard L. Smith, "Insider Reputation and Selling Decisions: The Unwinding of Venture Capital Investments During Equity IPOs," Unpublished Working Paper, Arizona State University, 1995.

Tim Loughran and Jay R. Ritter, "The New Issues Puzzle," *Journal of Finance* 50 (March 1995): 23–51.

John D. Martin and J. William Petty, "An Analysis of the Performance of Publicly Traded Venture Capital Companies," *Journal of Financial and Quantitative Analysis* 18 (September 1983): 401–410.

William C. Megginson and Kathleen A. Weiss, "Venture Capital Certification in Initial Public Offerings," *Journal of Finance* 46 (July 1991): 879–893.

20

The European Association of Security Dealers: November 1994

Dr. Jos. Peeters, chairman of the Capital Markets Task Force of the European Venture Capital Association, felt like a proud father. He had just overseen a one-day meeting that had unveiled a plan to create a pan-European exchange for small-capitalization high-growth firms. This new institution was to be modeled in large part after the United States' NASDAQ exchange, the second largest equity exchange in the United States and the fourth largest in the world.[1] This proposed market, Peeters believed, had the potential to reinvigorate the venture capital industry in Europe. In particular, a large number of venture-backed firms in Europe had been unable to go public, a circumstance that had reduced the ability of venture capitalists to show interesting returns and to raise new funds.

This presentation culminated the work of the task force over the past nine months. At the same time, many concerns remained. These included regulatory hurdles and questions about which design choices would make the market most attractive to issuers, intermediaries, and investors. More fundamentally, there was the challenge of ensuring that the support for the concept remained strong as the effort moved from design to implementation.

THE EUROPEAN VENTURE CAPITAL ASSOCIATION INITIATIVE

The European Venture Capital Association (EVCA) was established in 1983.[2] EVCA had 270 members in November 1994, of which 170 were venture investors; the remainder were law firms, accountants, and the other intermediaries. The members represented more than 50% of the venture capital under management in Europe. The major activities of the EVCA included the publication of an annual statistical yearbook and a number of reports, the organization of working groups, seminars, symposia, and train-

---

This case was prepared by Josh Lerner. Copyright © 1995 by the President and Fellows of Harvard College. Harvard Business School case 295-116.

[1] These are both in terms of market capitalization of listed firms at the end of 1993. If equity exchanges were ranked by the dollar volume of trades in 1993, NASDAQ would be the second largest in the world, after the New York Stock Exchange.

[2] For background information on the European private equity industry, see Chapter 8.

ing courses, and lobbying directed toward the Commission of the European Union. They had a staff of five.

EVCA's initial policy goal had been to address the reluctance to syndicate deals across national boundaries. The different regulatory environments, as well as long-standing cultural barriers, served to dampen the amount of cross-border venture syndication within Europe. Although a Massachusetts-based venture organization was almost as likely to co-invest with a California venture capitalist as with another Massachusetts firm, cross-national syndications were rare in Europe. At the time the task force effort began, the ratio of domestic investments by European venture capitalists to their investments in other European countries was 188:1. This reluctance, the EVCA membership believed, was limiting the expertise and capital that could be brought to deals. Although the effort had met with some success (in 1993, the ratio was 11:1), interregional syndication remained far below U.S. levels.[3]

The formation of the Capital Market Task Force was the EVCA's second major policy initiative. It had been motivated by the recent history of European markets specializing in small-capitalization firms. In the early 1980s, many European nations had pushed to develop secondary markets. These were designed to be more hospitable to smaller firms than the primary exchanges in these countries, which often had rigorous listing requirements (e.g., high levels of capitalization or extended records of profitability were required). At the same time, they sought to retain many of the regulatory safeguards for investors that were found in the major exchanges. (In addition, a number of countries had lightly regulated third-tier markets.) The secondary markets allowed venture capitalists to successfully unwind their positions. Their success, in turn, generated new investments in venture capital. Exhibit 1 shows that in the United Kingdom and France, a wave of initial public offerings (IPOs) by venture-backed firms appeared to trigger fundraising by venture funds.

After the October 1987 decline in world equity prices, IPO activity in Europe dried up, as it did in the United States.[4] But unlike the United States, which recovered with a "hot" IPO market in 1991, in Europe there was no recovery. In 1992–93, there were 432 IPOs on the NASDAQ[5]; on European secondary markets (with 30% of the number of listed firms), there were only 31. In some countries, the decline in IPO activity was even more extreme: only five companies listed in Germany's two secondary stock markets in 1992–93; none listed in Denmark's between 1989 and 1993. Consequently, European private equity investors found that the IPOs of firms in their portfolios were much more difficult to arrange and were more likely to exit firms through the sale of firms to third parties (termed "trade sales"). Exhibit 2 provides a summary of the European small-capitalization markets.

Trading volume in European markets for small-capitalization firms had also lagged. The ratio of total transaction volume to end-of-year market capitalization was 21% in European secondary markets in 1992; for the NASDAQ, the corresponding ratio was 138%. The lack of new issues and diminishing trading in existing shares contributed a

---

[3] These ratios are computed from the various yearbooks of the EVCA. The syndication patterns in the United States are documented in Richard L. Florida and Martin L. Kenney, "Venture Capital, High Technology and Regional Development," *Regional Science* 22 (1988): 33–48.

[4] The following two paragraphs are drawn from Graham Bannock and Partners, *European Second-Tier Markets for NTBFs* (London: Graham Bannock and Partners, 1994).

[5] In the United States virtually all venture-backed IPOs began trading on the NASDAQ: of the 169 U.S. IPOs of venture-backed firms in 1993, 167 went public through a NASDAQ listing, while two were listed on the New York Stock Exchange. (Although these statistics are for venture capital investments only, a similar pattern would appear in exits from buyout investments.)

general decline of interest in these markets. A number of secondary markets, such as the Dutch Parallelmarkt, closed; others suffered precipitous declines.

With the reduction of activity at these secondary exchanges, small firms and their venture backers were left with few options. The most promising firms could list on the NASDAQ in the United States. These firms issued either shares or American Depository Rights (ADRs). These rights were convertible into shares on a one-to-one basis but avoided many of the legal restrictions that nations impose on foreign share-holders.[6] In addition to capital at times when public equity in European markets was unavailable, the firms have found that American offerings had several advantages. For instance, firms believed that American investors understood new businesses better, and consequently assigned more attractive valuations. Second, firms have found that IPOs on the U.S. markets give them greater visibility with potential American customers. Exhibit 3 summarizes recent IPOs on NASDAQ by European venture-backed firms.

But for the vast majority of firms, the only option was staying private. The poor state of the IPO market had led to an inability by venture capitalists to exit these investments other than through acquisitions at often-unattractive valuations. The EVCA estimated that in mid-1994, European venture capitalists held 15,000 private companies in their portfolios.[7] Of these, 90% were mid-sized firms with limited potential for growth.

Most of these firms will ultimately be acquired, but a public offering—if feasible—would be appropriate for some. Even if the bulk of the 90% did not ultimately go public, if they possessed an option to go public, they might receive more attractive valuations when they were acquired by corporations. The remaining 10% were high-growth firms, many of which would be ideally suited to this new market.

A CASE STUDY—THE UNLISTED SECURITIES MARKET

To better understand the problems that European secondary markets encountered, it is worth examining one particular market. The most visible of European secondary markets was probably the Unlisted Securities Market (USM) in the United Kingdom.[8] This exchange had been created in 1980 by the London Stock Exchange (LSE) as a home for small-capitalization stocks that could not meet the strict capitalization and profitability requirements for inclusion on its primary market, the "Official List." At the close of 1989, the USM had 420 listed companies with a market capitalization of $13.5 billion. But by May 1994, the number of companies listed on USM had fallen to 250, with a total capitalization of $9 billion. (During the same time, the NASDAQ composite index had increased by 55%.) The number of IPOs on the USM fell from 103 in 1988 to 12 in 1992 and 1993 combined.

The British venture capital community and other small business advocates attributed the decline of the USM to a number of factors. Some were issues over which Exchange officials had little control, such as the persistent recession in Great Britain which had led to disappointing results for many growth companies. But other factors

---

[6] These institutional considerations are discussed at more length in European Venture Capital Association, *Venture Capital Special Report: An Introductory Guide to U.S. Initial Public Offerings for European Venture-Backed Companies* (Zaventum, Belgium: European Venture Capital Association, 1994).

[7] European Venture Capital Association, *Venture Capital Special Paper: Capital Markets for Entrepreneurial Companies—A European Opportunity for Growth* (Zaventum, Belgium: European Venture Capital Association, 1994).

[8] This description is drawn in large part from Roger Buckland and Edward W. Davis, *The Unlisted Stock Market* (Oxford: Clarendon Press, 1989), and numerous articles in the *Financial Times*.

were direct consequences of actions by LSE officials, such as their willingness to list companies of dubious quality (which had the effect of deterring many institutional investors) and their failure to promote the new Exchange. Furthermore, the LSE had responded to the USM's problems not by heightening efforts to attract new firms to the exchange, but rather by facilitating the inclusion of small firms on the Official List. The number of years of operations required for firms on the Official List was reduced from five to three years, and the profitability and sales requirements for science-based research firms (primarily biotechnology companies) were relaxed.

Many problems could be attributed to the lack of specialized institutions focusing on serving smaller firms. As in other countries, the secondary market was run by the organization responsible as well for the primary market, the LSE. This lack of dedicated institutions also may have explained the speed with which the British investment banks abandoned market making in, and research on, small companies. There was not a well-developed set of investment banks that made the bulk of their money working with smaller firms.[9] In the United States, by contrast, a number of investment banks—for example, Robertson, Stephens & Co., Hambrecht & Quist, and Alex. Brown & Sons—specialized in smaller firms. Consequently, these institutions had powerful incentives to ensure the vitality of the small-capitalization stock market, even during periods when investor interest was not strong.

In December 1992, the LSE announced its intention to phase out the USM by 1997. The decision to close the USM led to protests by the venture capital community exhorting the Exchange to reverse its decision. Ronald Cohen was the first to oppose the Exchange's decision when he raised the issue as a lunch speaker at the Financial Times/Venture Economics Forum very shortly afterward. Ronald Cohen was chairman of Apax Partners & Co. Ltd., the British member of the Apax Partners group, one of the largest international private equity firms managing $2 billion of institutional funds and of which Patricof & Co. is the U.S. member. Prior to founding Apax Partners in 1972, Cohen was a graduate of Oxford University and Harvard Business School and a consultant with McKinsey & Company. He was a past chairman of the British Venture Capital Association (1985–86), a founder–director of the British and European Venture Capital Association, and a pioneer of venture capital in Europe. He was also a member of the Confederation of British Industry's City Advisory Group. Cohen joined the efforts of Andrew Beeson of Beeson Gregory, a new stockbroking firm focusing on smaller companies, in creating a group called the City Group for Smaller Companies (CISCO). CISCO's objective was to bring together all those in the United Kingdom who were involved in financing and advising smaller companies: venture capitalists, brokers, banks, accountants, and lawyers. The response to the Exchange became one of CISCO's major roles. Other members included the stockbrokers Singer & Friedlander and the accountants KPMG Peat Marwick.

LSE officials responded to these protests in April 1994. They argued that the primary barrier to the success of a market geared to smaller firms was the legal and regulatory costs associated with a listing. The LSE suggested that the way to address this problem was to create a new market, dubbed Alternative Investment Market (AIM). This would be a scaled-up version of LSE's third-tier "Section 535.2" market. The

---

[9] This absence of specialized investment banks reflects the more concentrated structure of the European markets. At the end of 1993, the 10 largest listed companies accounted for 74% of the total market capitalization in the Netherlands, 50% in Italy, 40% in Germany, and 23% in London. (These patterns are discussed in the Graham Bannock report cited above.) By way of contrast, in the United States, the 10 largest firms only accounted for 2% of the market capitalization. See Euromoney Publications, *G.T. Guide to World Equity Markets* (London: Euromoney Publications, 1994).

Section 535.2 market, analogous to the "pink sheets" where "penny stocks" were traded in the United States, was an exchange where 236 very small British firms traded in mid-1994. These firms were exempt from most regulatory requirements, and investors' recourse in the case of fraud was very limited.

The proposal to establish an unregulated market for small firms did not satisfy the CISCO advocates. Institutional investors, they believed, would be unlikely to be interested in such an unregulated exchange. Without such investors, it seemed unlikely that the exchange could achieve either the size or liquidity to satisfy the needs of rapidly growing venture-backed concerns. Furthermore, the exchange would not satisfy a recent European Community directive stipulating minimal levels of securities regulations. In response, CISCO began pushing for a new exchange. Initially, they favored a British-based "Enterprise Market" that would not be affiliated with the LSE and would be the first component of a European market. As the proposal to establish a European small-capitalization stock exchange developed momentum on the Continent, CISCO dropped the idea of an independent Enterprise Market in London, and key proponents such as Ronald Cohen began enthusiastically backing the European proposal.

THE CONCEPT OF A PAN-EUROPEAN EXCHANGE

The initial discussions about the need for a European IPO market took place at a conference sponsored by an association of European entrepreneurship academics, the European Foundation for Entrepreneurial Research (EFER). This conference, held in December 1992, highlighted the dwindling number of IPOs in European markets. Most of the papers and informal discussion, however, focused on documenting the problem rather than proposing solutions.

When the EVCA held its business meeting in Venice in April 1993, the same issue surfaced (several EVCA members had attended the December 1992 EFER conference), but no action was taken. At the annual EVCA Symposium in June 1993 in Brussels, the lunch speaker, Ronald Cohen, reviewed the controversy surrounding the demise of the Unlisted Stock Market. He argued for the first time that any new Enterprise Market that was developed should have a European dimension and should be set up along the lines of NASDAQ. At the EVCA annual meeting, which immediately followed, it was decided that a small fraction of EVCA's budget should be made available for a study of the IPO market. They established an informal "Exits Committee" to look at this issue, which held a number of informal conversations over the summer of 1993. In these sessions, the idea of a European small-capitalization stock exchange was first proposed.

In October 1993, the EVCA held its annual strategy meeting with European Community (EC) officials. This was the EVCA's primary lobbying event of the year, although it was more in the nature of an informal discussion with high-ranking officials. Among other issues, the concept of a European exchange for smaller high-growth firms was broached. The EVCA emphasized the potential economic costs to Europe associated with the recent trend of promising European start-ups going public on NASDAQ. If these key sources of economic growth raised their capital in the United States, it was likely that their headquarters and employment would ultimately drift there as well.

These concerns found a receptive audience with the EC officials. Generating entrepreneurial growth as a way to lift Europe from its prolonged recession was a key objective of these officials, who were well aware of the contribution that small and medium-sized enterprises had made to economic growth and competitiveness across the world. The officials had been increasingly troubled by the limited ability of Europe's existing capital markets to accommodate the financial needs of these small firms.

Furthermore, the proposed initiative fit in with the EC's goal of integrating European financial systems. In most of Europe, securities trading had to be routed through a local exchange. Financial institutions based in other European countries that wished to trade on an exchange in countries such as France or Italy were required to set up a separate, well-capitalized subsidiary before they could do so. These requirements for exchange membership were also often very different across nations. For instance, in France, banks had been forbidden from being Bourse members until 1988, while in Germany, only banks could join the exchanges. Many countries also restricted the ability of foreign exchanges to install computer-trading systems in their nations. For instance, until recently, employees in the London office of a German bank could not trade using the IBIS trading system, a screen-based system for trading across Germany's regional exchanges developed by a consortium of banks in that country.

EC officials had tried to encourage greater financial integration in the past, but these efforts had largely failed. For instance, the Euroquote initiative, initiated in 1990, sought to bring together all trading in European securities into a single trading floor or computer system. It encountered resistance from the LSE, which saw it as a challenge to their SEAQ International system, which accounted for about one-third of all trading in French and Italian equities and a smaller but substantial share of German and Spanish trading.[10] It was also opposed by Germany, which was in the midst of a major and costly restructuring of its internal securities markets and did not want to subsidize the system's development.

The EC officials realized that this initiative might have greater chance of success because of recent changes in the regulatory environment. The EC had issued in June 1993, after more than four years of debate and study, its Investment Services Directive (ISD).[11] This legislation required that by January 1996 any firm authorized to trade in one EC member must have a "European passport" that will enable it to trade in every other country. A brokerage based in France wishing to conduct business in Italy, for instance, will simply need to inform the French regulators of its intentions, who will then in turn notify the Italian authorities. The French government will remain the primary regulator of the brokerage, though Italy will be able to impose reasonable restrictions on this and other foreign firms. A directive issued at the same time required nations to adopt at least minimal standards for capital adequacy, insider trading, and financial reporting. Nations were free to set higher standards.

The EC officials invited William Stevens, the secretary general (i.e., administrative head) of the EVCA, to write up a formal proposal for a working group, to be sponsored by the EVCA and funded by the EC. It was not anticipated that the EVCA would be an appropriate organization to run such a market, since they clearly had a set of well-defined interests. But they were seen as an appropriate body to play a catalytic role, initiating discussions with investment bankers, brokers, and others. Furthermore, the EVCA was a truly international body. The European Community officials had a perception that unless a coordinated Europe-wide approach was taken

---

[10] Richard Waters, "Survival Through a Part-Time Exchange," *Financial Times,* April 22, 1993; and London Stock Exchange, *LSE Fact Book 1994* (London: London Stock Exchange, 1994).

[11] This description is based in part on Charles Abrams, *The Investment Services Directive: An Overview* (London: S. J. Berwin & Co., 1994).

early on, there would be numerous initiatives at the national level that would be impossible to coordinate.

THE TASK FORCE DELIBERATIONS

This group was formally begun in February 1994. As noted earlier, Dr. Peeters was recruited as the head of this effort. Peeters was born in Belgium, received a Ph.D. in physics from the University of Louvain, and worked for Bell Telephone Manufacturing Co. as an engineer in its advanced technology department. He then worked for PA Technology, a technology consulting firm, before becoming managing director in 1985 of a new Belgian venture organization, BeneVent Management, N.V. He had recently formed Capricorn Venture Partners, a joint venture between himself and Baring Venture Partners (a U.K.-based private equity advisor). Past chairman of the EVCA, he was a member of the Euromatters Committee. Peeters was chosen as chair of the Task Force for several reasons, including his past service as chairman of the EVCA, his relative abundance of time (he was in the process of raising a new fund, rather than currently overseeing an investment portfolio), and his Belgian nationality (as a representative of a small country, a Belgian was more palatable for an international effort than a British or French venture capitalist). He was assisted in this effort by Jonathan Freeman, who had recently gotten his MBA from the University of Warwick, and the EVCA's secretary–general, William Stevens. The working group's mandate was *(1)* to produce a concrete set of recommendations that promoted the creation of a favorable capital markets environment for entrepreneurial growth companies in Europe, and *(2)* to identify the appropriate bodies to implement these recommendations. Peeters opted for a low-key initial approach, with the hope of building a wave of interest and enthusiasm. Rather than starting off with an ambitious proposal for a European version of NASDAQ, he sought to hold a series of informal discussions of the issues. The first of these was held in Brussels in April 1994. They brought together 28 people from major European exchanges, investment banks, venture capital funds, and institutional investors. Much of the interest in these sessions stemmed from the investment banks, which recognized that their role was much more limited than that of U.S. organizations. In particular, equity issuance, particularly from IPOs, represented a much smaller percentage of their revenues. Among the clearest conclusions to emerge from the meeting was that interest on the part of U.S. and European investors in European small-capitalization stocks was increasing but that many European countries were not able to successfully implement such a specialized market.

After this meeting, the EVCA decided to hold sessions in Paris and London, as the capitals of the two largest nations with a significant involvement in the task force effort. (Germans had played a very minor role in the task force effort.) The Paris meeting was foreseen as two parallel discussions of 20 people each. A week before the Paris session in June, Denis Mortier, a venture capitalist based in Paris and the incoming EVCA chairman, chaired a session in Paris as part of the tenth anniversary of the French venture capital association, AFIC. The panel included Paul Goldschmidt, a director of the EC's eighteenth directorate (and a former Goldman Sachs investment banker), Peeters, Mortier, and Jean-Fran ois Theodore (the president of the Societe des Bourses Francaises, which oversaw the Paris Bourse). Theodore announced that the Paris Stock Exchange was interested in being involved in this effort. This announcement triggered interest in the Paris meeting. Instead of the expected 40 attendees, 70 people turned up (and many others had to be turned away). The success of this meeting stimulated press interest. The Task Force members had been reluctant to talk to the press in the fear of inflating expectations but now undertook some selected interviews. Stories in *Business Week* and the *Financial Times* followed.[12]

Over the summer, following the successful meeting in Paris, Peeters and his team started actions in three distinct areas. First, it was clear from the discussions with the investment banks that creating a specific market for high-growth companies was much more complex than putting a computer system in place. Peeters realized that only limited competence in critical areas such as market-making and research and analysis was available, and that a whole new industry needed to be built very much along the lines of the business that revolves around the NASDAQ trading system in the United States. To achieve this, his working group had to transform itself into a representative body that would be able to foster, stimulate, and direct the development of this new industry. To this end, a Steering Committee was created on which an investment banker from each of five countries, including the United States, were represented. The objectives of this Steering Committee was to put a more permanent association in place, which would continue the activities of the working group after its third meeting.

Second, there was a clear need for a more precise answer to the question of whether enough growth companies existed in Europe that qualified for an IPO on a NASDAQ-type market. The general statement that there were 15,000 venture-backed companies in Europe was not sufficient; there was a need for a closer look. The European Community's thirteenth directorate, which deals with technology transfer and Community research programs, agreed to finance a limited market survey in four countries. Coopers & Lybrand was awarded the contract to undertake this research.

In order to advance the development of the new market proposal, Peeters and Ronald Cohen managed to form an informal consortium between the Paris Stock Exchange, NASDAQ, the EVCA, and a prominent group of 10 people brought together by Cohen to act as the Advisory Board to EASDAQ in the United Kingdom (Andrew Beeson, Beeson Gregory; Ronald Cohen; Sir David Cooksey, Advent; Sir Graham Day; Bill Hambrecht, Hambrecht & Quist; Ron Hollidge, Past Chairman BVCA; Geoffrey Maddrell, Proshare; Sir John Nott; Graham Ross Russell; and Stanislas Yassukovich, SM Yassukovich & Co. Ltd.). Cohen was instrumental in gaining the support of NASDAQ through Alan Patricof's acquaintance with Joe Hardiman, president and chief executive officer of NASDAQ. The group raised the necessary funding to retain the services of Mr. George Hayter, an independent consultant specializing in stock market issues. Over the next three months, this consortium developed a detailed plan for a European equivalent of NASDAQ, called EASDAQ.

The results of these intensive discussions were unveiled at the November 1994 London meeting. Over 200 individuals—drawn from EVCA members, CISCO participants, and British, European, and American investment banks—attended the session. At the meeting, the outline for EASDAQ's proposed structure was unveiled. The structure was similar in large part to NASDAQ's, with a computerized screen-based trading system and no physical trading floor. Four principles would guide the design of the market: an international structure, a strong commitment to regulatory standards, a focus on growing companies, and a reliance on technology already proven in existing markets. Standards for initial listings and the maintenance of listings were similar to those of NASDAQ.[13]

---

[12] Norma Cohen, "Nasdaq Holds Talks on Forming European Exchange," *Financial Times,* June 23, 1994; Richard Evans, "NASDAQ with a European Accent?," *Business Week,* June 27, 1994, 73.

[13] The anticipated entry requirements were $4 million in assets; a net worth of $2 million; a market value of the public float of $1 million; and 300 shareholders. The requirements to maintain a listing were $2 million in assets; a net worth of $1 million; a market value of the public float of $1 million; and 300 shareholders.

EASDAQ, it was proposed, would be organized as a for-profit corporation. An equity interest would be offered to NASDAQ, in exchange for technical assistance, as well as to the major European exchanges. Other shareholders would include major investment banks and brokerages. Although these institutions would be the owners of EASDAQ, the actual exchange would be run by a board of directors, to limit the danger of interference. The task force set an ambitious goal for implementing their vision: to have EASDAQ in operation by January 1996. They hoped to have 50 companies listed by the end of the first year of operations and 500 companies by the end of the sixth. The EASDAQ, it was anticipated, would break even in its fourth year. To finance operations until then, they anticipated that the exchange would need to raise about $11 million.

Before EASDAQ was formally established, however, there were numerous design issues to address. On the day before the London meeting, a not-for-profit companion organization had been established—the European Association of Securities Dealers (EASD). This group would deal with the problems associated with the implementation of EASDAQ. Approximately 20 investment banks and brokerages had signed up as founding members. Its objectives are reproduced in Exhibit 4.

This group faced a series of short- and longer-run challenges. The first was ensuring that the market conformed to the appropriate government standards. Although the EC's ISD had stipulated minimal standards for disclosure, insider trading, and other requirements, each country had the right to set a more stringent standard. For instance, the equity stake that led to an investor being considered an insider (and hence subject to reporting and trading restrictions) varied widely—between 3% in Great Britain to 10% in Germany and Italy. It was unclear whether the legislation of the nation in which the company, the shareholder, or the exchange was located would take priority. A partial solution to this problem was to employ a structure akin to the depository rights that European companies often use to trade on the U.S. exchanges. These are fully convertible into shares on a one-to-one basis but allow the shareholders to avoid some—but not all—of the administrative difficulties associated with actual share ownership. These would be called European Depository Rights (EDRs).

A related problem was posed by differences in tax policies across nations. European governments differed sharply in their tax treatment of securities transactions. For instance, many nations offered reduced capital gains tax rates for certain classes of firms. (In some cases, these preferential rates applied only to private firms; in other cases, to firms quoted on secondary markets; and in yet other cases, to firms that passed certain solvency tests.) Several nations had transactions taxes, and the treatment of dividends varied widely across nations. The taxation of depository rights in some countries was at a higher rate than other securities, whereas in other cases it was at lower rates. It was ambiguous which nation's tax rate would apply in many international transactions.

Another set of problems related to the appropriate design of the exchange. Even if compliance with all governmental regulations could be assured, the EASD faced several choices regarding the appropriate rules and structure. The first related to reporting requirements for companies on the exchange. Europe does not have an accounting standard like the Generally Accepted Accounting Principles (GAAP) in the United States. If companies only complied with its own national accounting requirements, there would be widespread differences in how such items as R&D, depreciation, and inventory were treated across firms. The lack of a common accounting standard could make it easier for substandard firms to be listed. Peeters recalled the experience of the American Stock Exchange, which had set up an Emerging Company Marketplace in 1992 to compete with NASDAQ for new issues. It failed to carefully scrutinize the initial firms that it listed. The questionable background of several of the initial firms listed generated a wealth of unfavorable publicity, and the Market proved unsuccessful in attracting a significant number of listings by growth firms.[14]

Another issue related to the choice of currency. To be a true exchange, the trades must be denominated in a single currency. If pounds, francs, or some other national currency was chosen, it might be perceived as giving too much power to a particular country. But if the EC's currency basket, the European Currency Unit (ECU), was chosen, the liquidity of the market would be affected. For instance, only four dozen banks exchanged ECUs into other currencies. The cost of converting pounds-to-ECU-to-pounds at a British bank was three times the cost of going from pounds-to-francs-to-pounds. Related problems included the choice of a primary language and headquarters location for the EASDAQ.

The settlement process was also problematic. (A trade is settled when the seller has delivered the shares that have been sold and has received the proceeds from the sale.) In the absence of rapid settlement of trades, the liquidity of the market could be impaired. In 1994, many European exchanges took weeks to clear cross-border trades, and there was little coordination of the settlement process between nations. This imposed a substantial cost on foreigners who traded in European markets. From the start the EASDAQ hoped to introduce an efficient international clearing system. At the same time, it acknowledged that "this ambitious goal needs to be tested and refined against the views of member firms and their clients who are used to working in the present setup, and this will be done in the forthcoming consultative period. There will also be consultation with suppliers of the clearing and settlement components."[15] Thus, the precise structure of the settlement process remained to be determined.

A final design issue was the nature of the market itself. NASDAQ assigned several market-makers to each stock, who actively took positions in the firms that they specialized in. This helped ensure liquidity for these stocks. The LSE and many other European systems, as well as the New York and American Stock Exchanges, instead employed specialists, whose primary role was to match orders to buy and sell securities. In many cases, the specialists had inadequate incentives to devote much attention to the smaller firms for which they were responsible, since their primary compensation was a fee based on the volume of transactions that they handled. In contrast, NASDAQ market-makers tended to be the investment banks who had previously underwritten these firms' securities and whose analysts covered these stocks. Ideally, the EASDAQ system would handle trading through both market-makers and order matching in order to maximize the acceptance of the market throughout Europe.

Even if these problems could be overcome and an optimal exchange designed, the problem of implementation remained. There were several powerful institutional barriers to success. For instance, the LSE controlled a large fraction of international European equity trading through its SEAQ International system. Furthermore, many promising British firms currently joining their Official List might instead list on EASDAQ.

Consequently, LSE might possibly view this system as a threat. Furthermore, the committee members, as experienced observers of the European scene, knew that there was a need to maintain cohesion among themselves. In past joint initiatives, as success appeared more probable, there was sometimes a tendency to fragment. Each group

---

[14] See Gary Weiss, "The Amex: A Questionable Seal of Approval," *Business Week,* April 13, 1992, 78–79; and Gary Weiss, "Did the Amex Turn a Blind-Eye to a 'Showcase' Stock?," *Business Week,* September 14, 1994, 80–83.

[15] George Hayter, *EASDAQ: A Concept Paper,* mimeo, November 1994.

might begin neglecting the overall goal of achieving success and instead push for their own ends.

Although these concerns were substantial, Peeters still felt a fundamental pride about the steps that had been accomplished to date and a fundamental optimism about the future. The Coopers & Lybrand survey unveiled at the meeting had identified a considerable demand on the part of entrepreneurial firms for such a market. (Key findings are summarized in Exhibit 5.) Furthermore, the task force effort had succeeded in catalyzing a great deal of interest on the part of venture investors, investment banks, and government officials. Peeters reflected on the progress that had been made to date:

> At the closing of the meeting on November 15, 1994, I was very aware of the enormous challenges ahead, but also conscious of the tremendous impact that the project was making and its significance for the future of Europe's high-growth companies. A significant part of my pride came from the successful establishment of the EASD: the investment banks in Europe and the United States had taken up the challenge and 20 of them had already signed up to carry the effort forward. So the new industry had taken a start.

Exhibit 1   IPO and Venture Capital Fundraising in Great Britain and France

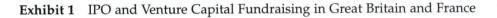

IPOs & VC in the UK

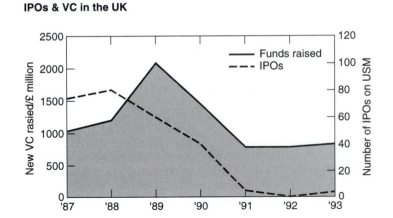

IPOs & VC in France

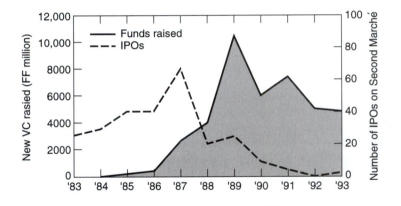

Source: Dr. Jos. Peeters, "Developing Thriving and Efficient European Capital Markets for Entrepreneurial
Companies," mimeo, 1994.

Exhibit 2 Number of Companies, Admissions and Turnover for Second-tier Markets in Europe

Country	Number of Companies	New Companies Admitted (1992 or 1993)	Turnover/ Capitalization Ratio
Belgium	29	0	26.3%
Denmark	9	0	NA
France	276	5	13.9
Total Germany	240	5	39.3
Regulated market	145	3	27.1
Free market	95	2	61.7
Greece	8	0	11.7
Ireland	20	1	5.2
Italy	37	1	4.5
Netherlands	63	1	26.8
Portugal	87	1	59.3
Spain	27	4	6.8
United Kingdom	308	13	14.4
EUR12 Total	1,104	31	21.1%
USA-NASDAQ	3,850	432	138.21%
Japan:	910	100	27.5
Tokyo Stock Exchange-II	433	45	29.7
OTC (JASDAQ)	477	55	25.5

Source: Compiled from Graham Bannock & Partners, *European Second-Tier Markets for NTBFs* (London: Graham Bannock & Partners, 1994).

Exhibit 3   European Community Firms Listing on NASDAQ, January 1991-November 1994 ($ millions)

Issuer	Offer Date	Offer Amount	City	Nation	Industry	Market Capitalization	Pre-offering Assets
Affymax	12/31/91	$ 60.00	Amsterdam	Netherlands	Manufacturing	$289.50	$ 50.30
Cantab Pharmaceuticals	7/01/92	4.00	Cambridge	United Kingdom	Manufacturing	59.50	12.20
British Bio-Technology	7/01/92	15.20	Oxford	United Kingdom	Manufacturing	288.40	102.60
Trinity Biotech	10/21/92	5.30	Galway	Ireland	Healthcare	20.60	12.10
Hibernia Foods	10/22/92	3.00	Dublin	Ireland	Manufacturing	10.70	
Olicom	10/22/92	75.60	Lyngby	Denmark	Pers/Bus/Rep Svc	204.40	27.40
Scandinavian Broadcasting	3/09/93	43.20	Luxembourg	Luxembourg	Radio/TV/Telecom	118.10	49.00
Ethical Holdings	4/01/93	15.00	Ely (Cambridgeshire)	United Kingdom	Manufacturing	56.40	5.50
Stolt Comex Seaway	5/21/93	37.20	Marseille	France	Pers/Bus/Rep Svc	263.50	320.40
Madge	8/04/93	46.00	Hoofddorp	Netherlands	Manufacturing	274.00	44.00
FutureMedia	8/19/93	7.10	West Sussex	United Kingdom	Leisure	32.80	5.80
Coflexip	11/17/93	80.90	Paris	France	Manufacturing	199.00	383.30
Pharma Patch	2/28/94	6.00	Dublin	Ireland	Manufacturing	8.20	6.70
Integrated Micro Products	3/23/94	18.00	Consett Cty. Durham	United Kingdom	Manufacturing	25.70	5.20
Indigo	5/24/94	80.00	Hoofddorp	Netherlands	Manufacturing	1,000.00	38.90
Xenova Group	7/07/94	6.40	Slough (Berkshire)	United Kingdom	Pers/Bus/Rep Svc	105.40	31.60
Bell Cablemedia	7/15/94	167.00	London	United Kingdom	Radio/TV/Telecom	494.30	594.60
Business Objects	9/22/94	26.30	Puteaux	France	Pers/Bus/Rep Svc	238.90	13.70
Phoenix Shannon	10/12/94	6.00	Shannon	Ireland	Wholesale	9.00	4.50
Central European Media	10/13/94	66.50	London	United Kingdom	Radio/TV/Telecom	186.30	43.30
TeleWest Communications	11/22/94	307.80	Surrey	United Kingdom	Telephone Commun		

Source: Securities Data Co.

Exhibit 4   The EASD Objectives

EASD has the mission to develop the securities markets for growing enterprises in Europe. To that end it will pursue the following objectives:

1. To advise on the organization of European stock markets for growth companies and smaller companies alike:

   • To advise on the creation and development of EASDAQ (EASD Automated Quotation), a new prime European market for internationally-oriented growth enterprises, by providing the forum for the consultation process that is now under way, providing members to the Board and the Committees, and to assist in its promotional efforts,

   • To make policy recommendations on the functioning of national and regional markets for smaller company securities by identifying best practice throughout Europe

2. To work towards a more favorable legal, fiscal and regulatory environment, and make policy recommendations at the:

   • national level

   • pan-European level

3. To provide a unique pan-European forum for every participant in the securities business for growing companies by providing information, training, networking and other relevant services. Services could include:

   • Yearbook (Editorial, Market Reports, Directory)

   • Annual conference

   • Seminars on specific topics

   • Training courses

   • A promotional newsletter

   • Briefing notes

   • Special papers on specific topics

Source: European Association of Securities Dealers.

Exhibit 5   Projected Demand for EASDAQ Listing

	France	Netherlands	Spain	United Kingdom
Total number of IPOs, 1993	15	14	6	186
Estimated number of IPOs, 1994	36	29	10	193
Number of EASDAQ candidates expected to go public in:				
1995	26	2	7	47
1996	32	4	11	25
1997	18	4	4	9
1998 or unknown	16	5	6	0

Source: Compiled from Coopers & Lybrand, *Market Survey of IPOs in Europe: A Report for European Commission DGXIII/Sprint Initiative* (London: Coopers & Lybrand, 1994).

Note: The estimated number of EASDAQ candidates are from a survey of venture capitalists and investment bankers in these four countries, conducted in the fall of 1994. The financial intermediaries were asked to identify privately held firms who would be likely to (i) go public in the next four years, (ii) be the anticipated criteria for an EASDAQ listing, and (iii) choose to list on EASDAQ as opposed to their primary or second-tier exchange in their nation or NASDAQ in the United States.

21

ImmuLogic Pharmaceutical Corporation (A): March 1991

In early March 1991, the board of directors of ImmuLogic Pharmaceutical Corporation met to consider an initial public offering (IPO). A series of presentations by investment bankers the preceding week had highlighted the importance of this decision. Like most biotechnology companies, ImmuLogic needed to raise substantially more capital in order to create commercially viable products. The investment bankers had indicated that ImmuLogic might be able to raise as much as $80 million, given the favorable climate for new offerings of biotechnology shares. This capital infusion would assure a strong product development effort and give the firm additional credibility and a competitive edge over a rival firm. At the same time, the directors wondered if going public made sense at such an early stage in the firm's development: ImmuLogic was only four years old and at least four years away from introducing its first product. Would the firm receive a fair price for its shares? What were all the implications of being a public firm? Should the firm instead sign another collaborative agreement with a major pharmaceutical company? Each of the key players saw the issues differently.

THE BIOTECHNOLOGY INDUSTRY IN 1991

The biotechnology industry in 1991 had several features that distinguished it from other high-technology sectors. Foremost among these features were its close links to the scientific community, the large number of active firms, its large capital needs, and the high degree of uncertainty.

The initial scientific breakthrough that sparked the biotechnology revolution was James Watson and Francis Crick's 1953 discovery of the "double helix" structure of DNA, the basic molecule of life. In subsequent decades, biologists explored the chemistry of life intensively. By the 1970s, researchers reached the point of actually being able to "cut and paste" DNA. This ability to rearrange the building blocks of life had revolutionary implications. The possibilities included production of computer-designed drugs to cure age-old diseases; super-productive, disease-resistant animals and plants with superior attributes; and custom-built microorganisms as substitutes for many chemical processes used in industry (e.g., papermaking).

As the technological and financial potential of the biotechnology revolution became clear, scientists began to establish firms dedicated to its commercialization. The first

This case was prepared by Josh Lerner. Copyright © 1992 by the President and Fellows of Harvard College. Harvard Business School case 293-066.

biotechnology firm, Cetus Corporation, was started in 1971 by scientists from the University of California at Berkeley and Stanford University. This pattern was repeated in subsequent years, as new organizations were begun by researchers leaving academic laboratories or research facilities at large pharmaceutical firms, often in conjunction with nontechnical managers from new or established companies. These new firms cultivated close ties to the academic community. They typically employed formal scientific advisory boards, often signed licensing agreements with universities, and in some cases even encouraged researchers to continue to publish in scientific journals.

Most of the activity in these newly formed firms centered around research, product development, and clinical testing. In the first 15 years of the industry, only two products developed by biotechnology firms were approved by the Food and Drug Administration (FDA). Although the pace of approvals by FDA and other federal agencies accelerated in the late 1980s, most firms remained in a development phase. Consequently, major emphases of firms were protecting their discoveries by filing patent applications and raising capital long before revenues or profits appeared. Exhibit 1 summarizes the approval process for a new human pharmaceutical product as well as the probability of success in each stage. Not only was the drug development process lengthy but it was very expensive: a 1991 study by Joseph DiMasi of Tufts University's Center for Drug Development and several other authors had estimated the fully expensed cost of developing a new drug at $231 million.

Many of the early firms had claimed in their promotional material to be "the next Syntex." Founded in 1946, Syntex had been the last firm to join the ranks of the major pharmaceutical manufacturers. (Syntex's history is summarized in Exhibit 2). A major drug for an integrated pharmaceutical company (such as Syntex's Naprosyn, SmithKline Beecham's Tagament, or Glaxo's Zantac) could yield $1 billion or more in annual sales. Not all drugs, however, were that successful. Figure 1 summarizes the discounted value of the after-tax revenues for 100 drugs that received FDA approval during the 1970s.

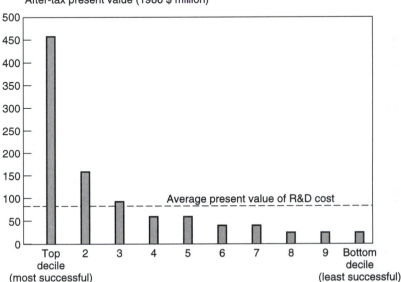

Figure 1　Present Value of After-Tax Revenues from New Drugs Introduced between 1970 and 1980, by Decile.

Source: Compiled from Henry Grabowski and John Vernon, "A New Look at the Returns and Risks to Pharmaceutical R&D," *Management Science* (July 1990). The present value calculation does not include the after-tax R&D cost, which the authors estimate at $81 million (in 1986 dollars).

In the face of setbacks in research and development (R&D) programs and the long path to regulatory approval, however, the early dream that the new biotechnology firms would rapidly evolve into major pharmaceutical companies was gradually understood to be unrealistic. Almost every biotechnology firm that went public was required to raise more capital through seasoned offerings. Start-ups began undertaking alliances with established pharmaceutical firms for marketing, testing, and manufacturing products. In addition to using the extensive marketing network of established pharmaceutical firms, new biotechnology companies entered into strategic alliances to take advantage of the established firms' testing and screening facilities. Another important factor was the pharmaceutical companies' willingness to invest in biotechnology firms at times when the public markets were not receptive to biotechnology offerings and to pay greater prices in recognition of the rights implicit in deal structures.

Although a shakeout of biotechnology firms had often been predicted, Ernst & Young surveys suggested that the number of biotechnology firms remained constant at about 1100 between 1987 and 1991. Of these, approximately 200 were publicly held in March 1991. Although many firms had been acquired or merged, a steady stream of new firms had been formed. These patterns are summarized in Figure 2.

Since few biotechnology firms had been profitable to date, this continued industry activity would have been impossible without outside investors. Biotechnology firms employed several forms of capital from private sources and the public marketplace. The most significant source for early stage companies was venture capital funds, which specialized in financing and overseeing privately held firms. Increasingly important were private placements from established pharmaceutical companies (typically in conjunction with a collaborative arrangement) and institutional investors such as pension funds and insurance companies.

The largest source of funds was public stock offerings. Unlike in most industries, biotechnology companies typically went public long before their products were generating any revenues, much less profits. Biotechnology stocks were characterized by "hot" and "cold" periods. The first of these followed the IPO of Genentech in October 1980,

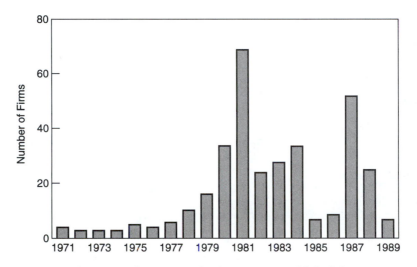

Figure 2 Number of U.S.-Based New Biotechnology Firms Established, by Year, 1980 to 1989

Source: Compiled from U.S. Office of Technology Assessment, various documents; and North Carolina Biotechnology Center, various databases.

which soared from its offering price of $35 per share to $89 per share in the first hour of trading. During subsequent hot periods, such as 1982 to 1983 and 1986 to 1987, valuations were relatively high and equity issues common. These periods were triggered by highly publicized events such as acquisitions (e.g., Eli Lilly's 1986 acquisition of Hybritech), successful public offerings (i.e., Genentech's 1980 offering), and regulatory approvals. These periods had been followed, however, by a sharp decline in market valuations and in offering activity. (These patterns are shown in Figure 3. Similar, though less extreme, patterns were observed in the stock market as a whole.)

IMMULOGIC PHARMACEUTICAL CORPORATION

ImmuLogic was formed in early 1987 by Dr. Malcolm Gefter. A professor at the Massachusetts Institute of Technology (MIT) since 1977, Gefter was one of the leading researchers in the field of immunology. Gefter had been involved in the business world through outside consulting, service on the MIT industrial liaison committee, and as a director of the biotechnology start-up firm Angenics.

The Products

The science on which ImmuLogic was based emerged from Gefter's laboratory at MIT. Beginning in 1980, Gefter's group had been exploring the complex workings of the human immune system. In particular, he explored the question of how T-cells—the white blood cells that identified and directed attacks on infections—recognized invading molecules while avoiding attacks on the body's own products. Along with researchers at other schools, he showed that the body had a fail-safe mechanism to prevent mistakes. No matter how provoked by invaders, the T-cells did not attack foreign molecules unless they

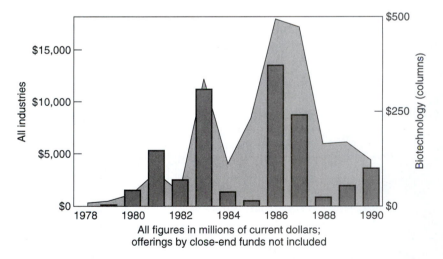

Figure 3 Amount Raised in Initial Public Offerings by All Firms and Biotechnology Firms, 1978 to 1990

Source: Compiled from Venture Economics, Recombinant Capital, Securities Data Company, and casewriter's estimates.

received a signal from a second type of cell, an antigen-presenting cell. The presence of this second class of cells limited the possibility of destructive attacks by "rogue" T-cells.

Gefter identified two applications for these insights into the workings of the human immune system. The first was allergies. An allergy was caused when a foreign agent, such as pollen, was mistakenly recognized by the antigen-presenting cells as harmful. This mistake triggered an inappropriate response by the T-cells, leading to a chain reaction that culminated in an allergic reaction. The standard treatment for allergies had been repeated allergy shots, which introduced small amounts of the allergy-causing substance into the body. Each time the antigen-presenting cells responded, but eventually the T-cells learned to ignore their signal. Allergy shots were expensive, time-consuming, and dangerous if too large an injection were made. Gefter proposed to inject instead the compound by which the antigen-presenting cells communicated to the T-cells. This could accomplish the reeducation of the T-cells with many fewer treatments and without the danger of an allergic reaction.

The second opportunity, expected to take longer to come to fruition, was the treatment of autoimmune diseases such as rheumatoid arthritis and diabetes. In these diseases, the antigen-presenting cells mistakenly identified the body's own substances as foreign antigens. To date, therapies had focused on either addressing only the consequences of these attacks or suppressing the body's entire immune system. Gefter's insight was to address these diseases by disabling those antigen-presenting cells that were mistakenly looking for the body's own substances. If compounds could be identified that only disabled those antigen-presenting cells while allowing other cells to continue their work, these diseases would be cured.

The Company

The first steps in forming ImmuLogic were taken in late 1986. As the commercial potential of Gefter's research became apparent, MIT and Gefter applied for a series of patents on his work. Although MIT's licensing office discussed licensing the technology with Jess Belser, president and chief executive officer (CEO) of Rothschild Ventures, Gefter broached the concept of a new firm with James Bochnowski, then a general partner at Technology Venture Investors. Bochnowski brought the deal to the attention of Henry McCance of Greylock Ventures.

The three venture capital firms—Rothschild Ventures, Technology Venture Investors, Greylock Ventures—undertook the first round of funding of ImmuLogic in June 1987. The three investors purchased 1.7 million shares at $2 per share. The firm as a whole was valued at $5.5 million. Belser, Bochnowski, and McCance all joined the board at the time of the investment. Exhibit 3 summarizes the financing of ImmuLogic through March 1991.

The firm addressed several key issues in 1987, including the leasing of office space, the hiring of a chief financial officer, and the building of a scientific advisory board. Signing a licensing agreement with MIT was another necessity. The agreement called for ImmuLogic to provide the university with 185,000 shares, a deferred payment of $750,000, and a 5% royalty on sales. A final accomplishment was signing a contract research agreement with Merck & Co., Inc. to enhance the immunological properties of a vaccine that Merck was developing. These contract research funds represented almost all of ImmuLogic's operating revenues in the firm's first years of operations. In 1988, ImmuLogic joined with Professors Hugh O. McDevitt, C. Garrison Fathman, and Kenneth L. Melmon of Stanford University, who had all realized a similar scientific approach to ImmuLogic's.

By mid-June 1988, the firm's initial financing was largely gone, and ImmuLogic sought a larger capital infusion. In addition to the three original investors, four new venture funds—Institutional Venture Partners, Mayfield, Bessemer, and Sprout—invested in the firm. In light of the firm's accomplishments over the previous 12 months, the price was fixed at $6 per share, a threefold increase over the original price. The valuation of the firm climbed to $31.4 million. (See Exhibit 3 for terms.)

Management next shifted its attention to developing a relationship with a major pharmaceutical company to pursue autoimmune research, the long-run component of the firm's research agenda. Such a relationship would have several advantages: it would enhance the credibility of the start-up firm, bring access to a major research facility, and might include an up-front payment to ImmuLogic. After negotiations with a number of firms, ImmuLogic entered into an agreement with Merck, with which the firm already had a contract research arrangement. As part of the September 1989 agreement, Merck purchased 1 million shares at $10 per share, with the previous investors purchasing 200,000 shares between them. The valuation of the firm climbed from $31 million to $65 million. (See Exhibit 3 for terms. The distribution of shares after this financing is shown in Exhibit 4.)

At the closing of this third financing, ImmuLogic had a cash balance in excess of $20 million. With an expanded staff of 72, nearly one-third of which had Ph.Ds., and a CEO with extensive pharmaceutical industry experience, Richard Bagley, former president of E. R. Squibb and Sons, the firm's allergy research program made rapid progress. The first product, for cat allergies, was expected to be ready for the marketplace in 1995. Products to address allergies to ragweed, dust, and grass were expected to follow. The firm anticipated that it would eventually need a second strategic alliance with a major pharmaceutical company to market its allergy products successfully worldwide. In the interim, payments from Merck as a part of its agreement to pursue long-run pharmaceutical research continued to be the primary source of operating revenue. Reflecting the fact that the firm was still in a development stage, ImmuLogic continued to lose money. Financial statements are reported in Exhibit 5.

THE PROPOSED INITIAL PUBLIC OFFERING

Prices of biotechnology stocks, which had lagged the market ever since the 1987 crash, began recovering in 1990. Their performance was particularly striking in the rally that coincided with and followed the Gulf War in the winter of 1991 (see Figure 4). At the same time, filings for IPOs by biotechnology firms increased, as Exhibit 6 depicts. Other firms were rumored to consider going public, including ImmuLogic's closest competitor, the Cytel Corporation. In light of this activity, Gefter and his investors began seriously to consider taking ImmuLogic public.

In late February 1991, a series of investment bankers made presentations to the ImmuLogic board concerning a public offering. Several conclusions emerged from these discussions. ImmuLogic, it was widely agreed, would be seen as an attractive offering by the public market. The company's scientific specialization, strong research staff, and influential scientific advisers would all be viewed favorably, as would the presence of a strategic relationship with Merck (especially in conjunction with the pharmaceutical giant's large equity investment in the start-up). Although none of the firm's 11 patent applications had as yet been awarded, the firm was confident they would be shortly.

Most important, the potential market for ImmuLogic's products was very large, both in the medium term (allergies) and the long run (autoimmune diseases). Allergies

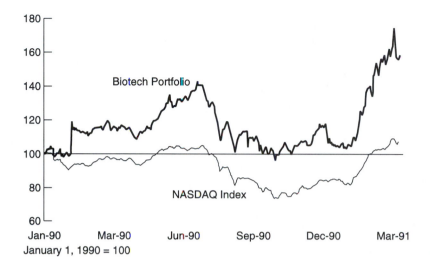

Figure 4   Performance of NASDAQ Value-Weighted Index and Biotechnology Portfolio
January 1, 1990 to March 15, 1991

Source: Compiled from the Center for Research in Security Prices and author's analysis.
Note: The NASDAQ value-weighted index provides a measure of the change in the value of small-capitalization stocks as a whole.

were pervasive among the U.S. population: 5 million people were allergic to cats, 15 million to dust, and 25 million to ragweed and grasses. Some 1 million people were insulin-dependent diabetics, while over 2 million Americans suffered from rheumatoid arthritis. The firm's internal sales projections, which would not be included in any IPO prospectus but might be discussed with the investment bankers, are summarized in Exhibit 7.

A strong case could be made for either going public or delaying the offering. The appearance and disappearance of "windows" for IPOs by biotechnology companies argued for an immediate offering. The market was "hot" now, but there was no guarantee this condition would last. Some firms that tried to go public during "cold" periods found they were unable to sell shares at any price: Verax, MicroGeneSys, and Immune Response Corporation had canceled IPOs in 1989 after being unable to sell shares. (In March 1991, the former two firms remained privately held. Immune Response, on the other hand, went public in May 1990, with a market capitalization of roughly one-half that proposed in its withdrawn IPO filing. An index of biotechnology stocks had appreciated in the interim by over 25%.)

On the other hand, going public at this stage might mean receiving a price for the shares substantially below what an offering in 1992 would garner. In past years, biotechnology firms had typically not gone public until their products were in preliminary (Phase I) human trials, which were anticipated to begin early the next year. Once the firm initiated clinical trials of its allergy vaccines and established a corporate partnership agreement to market these products, its valuation by the market might be substantially higher. An even greater concern was the possibility of a failed public offering. If ImmuLogic were unable to sell its shares, the impact on the firm's reputation and its ability to sell shares in the future might be substantial. Since ImmuLogic had sufficient cash for the immediate future, it could reduce these risks by delaying going public until the firm was more established.

Lending weight to this argument was the prospect of a collaborative agreement involving the allergy product line. The board felt that the allergy drugs would be extremely attractive to pharmaceutical firms, since they comprised an entire product family. Several major pharmaceutical firms were facing the prospect of having very profitable drugs shortly going "off patent," that is, losing their monopoly protection as patents expired. (These are summarized in Exhibit 8.) Although the major pharmaceutical companies had significant product development programs of their own—the Pharmaceutical Manufacturers Association estimated total drug R&D expenditures in 1990 at about $8.1 billion—these firms would be strong candidates for a collaborative agreement to commercialize ImmuLogic's allergy drugs, an agreement that might involve a substantial up-front cash payment to ImmuLogic. Such an agreement could serve as an alternative to an IPO. (Exhibit 9 summarizes the joint ventures and collaborative research agreements that new U.S. biotechnology firms entered into between September 1990 and March 1991.)

Exhibit 1 Milestones in Drug Development and Approval Process

The search for a single commercializable drug in the 1980s typically started with the trial-and-error screening of some 10,000 compounds before testing the most promising of the substances in animals and humans. A significant portion of the total investment—one that consumed tens of millions of dollars and generated thousands of pages of supporting documentation—consisted of taking the drug through the FDA's exacting regulatory process. It was estimated that the average cost of developing a new drug (in current dollars) rose from $1.3 million in 1960 to $50 million in 1979 and topped $230 million by the end of the 1980s. A brief outline of the process appears below.

Initial screening (1 to 2 years) During the initial screening stage, the thousands of compounds regarded as potential candidates for treating a specific medical condition were reduced to approximately 20 through chemical and structural analysis.

Preclinical Testing (2 to 3 years) Preclinical trials involved the testing of compounds in the laboratory and in animals to assess safety and to analyze the biological effects of each of the drug candidates. Approximately five of the compounds would subsequently be accepted as Investigational New Drugs (INDs) by the FDA for clinical testing in humans with respect to a specific indication (disease or other medical condition).

Clinical Testing (6 years) Clinical trials involved the testing of INDs in human volunteers. This stage of the process was divided into three separate phases:

- Phase I Trials (1 year) The Phase I safety trials in humans were designed to determine the safety and pharmacological properties of a chemical compound. Each drug was typically tested in 20 or more healthy volunteers. On average, 70% of all INDs moved on to the Phase II human trials.

- Phase II Trials (2 years) The Phase II efficacy trials were designed to evaluate the effectiveness of the drug and to isolate side effects. Tests were typically conducted with several hundred (volunteer) patients, one-half receiving the IND and one-half receiving a placebo. Only about one-third of all INDs survived both the first and second phases of clinical testing.

- Phase III Trials (3 years) The Phase III efficacy trials measured the effect of the IND on thousands of patients over several years. These trials helped ascertain long-term side effects and provided additional information on the effectiveness of a range of doses administered to a rich mix of patients. Approximately 27% of all INDs moved on to the FDA review stage.

FDA Review (2 to 3 years) Upon the completion of the Phase III clinical trials, firms were required to file a New Drug Application (NDA) with the FDA and submit documentation of all relevant data for review. The FDA created a special advisory committee for each NDA, typically approving the final recommendation of the committee regarding whether or not the drug should be released for commercial sale. Post-marketing safety monitoring continued even after approval. Only 20% of all INDs ultimately made it through the full testing and approval stages.

Exhibit 2 Financial Summary of Syntex Corporation[a] ($ millions)

| | | | | | Fiscal Year Ending | | | | |
	7/31/60	7/31/65	7/31/70	7/31/75	7/31/80	7/31/85	7/31/90	3/15/91
Sales	7	36	90	246	580	949	1521	
Net income	0.3	10	12	42	75	150	342	
Operating margin	3%	26%	14%	17%	19%	23%	30%	
Market capitalization (at fiscal year end)	43[b]	408	256	681	716	1994	6911	8513

Source: Compiled from Moody's Industrial Guide, various years; Daily Stock Price Guide, various years; Value Line Guide, various years.

[a]Syntex went public through a rights offering to the shareholders of the Ogden Corporation in April 1958. Ogden had acquired the assets of Syntex's predecessor firm, which had been a development stage firm throughout most of the 1950s.

[b]Syntex's initial market capitalization in 1958 was approximately $10 million.

Exhibit 3   Financing of ImmuLogic Pharmaceutical Corporation, 1987 to March 1991

Series A Convertible Preferred Stock Agreement

Date: May 21, 1987.

Shares Sold: 1,675,000, at $2.00 per share.

Total Valuation: $5.5 million.

Dividends: Series A shareholders are entitled to receive a dividend of $0.20 per share, beginning on June 1, 1990, if declared by the Board. This dividend is non-cumulative. No dividend can be paid to holders of common stock until the Series A dividend for the fiscal year is paid. Holders of Series A stock must obtain the share of any dividends paid to the common stock equivalent to the amount they would have received had they converted all their shares to common stock.

Liquidation: If the company is liquidated, the company will pay $2.00 for each share of Series A stock, plus any dividends declared but unpaid, before any payments are made to the common stockholders. The remaining amount will be then split equally between the Series A and common shareholders. If the net assets of the company after liquidation are insufficient to pay $2.00 per share of Series A stock, the net assets of the company will be split among the preferred shareholders.

Conversion: Each Series A share is convertible into one share of common stock. If the company goes public at a price exceeding $10.00 per share (adjusted for any stock splits) in an offering which raises at least $10 million, the Series A shares will be automatically converted into common stock.

Voting Rights: Each Series A share is entitled to one vote in any matter submitted to the vote of the shareholders. Holders of three-quarters of the Series A shares must authorize the issue of any shares which are senior or equal to the Series A in dividend or liquidation rights. Holders of three-quarters of the Series A shares must also approve any merger, liquidation or sale of the firm or an increase in the number of the directors of the firm beyond five.

Board Seats: Series A shareholders are entitled to elect four directors of the company. The Board will meet at least six times a year. Each owner of 450,000 shares can send an observer to the meetings.

Redemption: The company must liquidate one-third of the Series A shares outstanding on December 31, 1995, one-half of those outstanding on December 31, 1996, and all remaining shares on December 31, 1997. In each case, the holders of liquidated Series A shares will receive a payment of $2.00. The redemption can only be waived on the vote of two-thirds of the Series A shareholders.

Registration Rights: Series A shareholders can demand that the company include their shares in any registration statement for the public sale of stock that the company files. Series A shareholders can also demand that the company register their securities after December 31, 1992. In the former case, the Series A shareholders will bear their share of the cost of the offering; in the latter case, the company shall bear the full expense of filing the registration statement, legal and accounting fees and other underwriting costs.

Preemptive Rights: Series A shareholders have the right to purchase any class of shares, bonds, options or other securities that the company proposes to sell. This does not includes shares sold to the company's employee benefit plan.

Covenants and Adjustments: The company agrees to pay all taxes and fees, keep accurate accounting records, and other covenants. All restrictions will be adjusted for any stock splits.

Series B Convertible Preferred Stock Agreement [Modifications Only]

Date: July 11, 1988.

Shares Sold: 2,129,167, at $6.00 per share.

Total Valuation: $31.4 million.

Dividends: Series B shareholders are entitled to receive a dividend of $0.45 per share, beginning on June 1, 1993, if declared by the Board as above. [Series A dividends are changed to $0.15 per share, also beginning on June 1, 1993.] Neither Series A nor Series B shareholders can receive dividends without the other.

Liquidation: If the company is liquidated, the company will pay $2.00 for each share of Series A stock and $6.00 for each share of Series B stock as above. The maximum additional payout to Series A and B shareholders is capped at $6.00 per share.

Conversion: Each Series B share is initially convertible into one share of common stock. This conversion ratio may be adjusted upward if the company issues additional shares of common stock. If the company goes public at a price exceeding $15.00 per share in an offering which raises at least $10 million, the Series B shares will be automatically converted into common stock. [The automatic conversion price of Series A shares is similarly adjusted.]

Voting Rights: Each Series B share is entitled to one vote in any matter submitted to the vote of the shareholders. Holders of two-thirds of the Series B shares must authorize the issue of any shares which are senior or equal to the Series B in dividend or liquidation rights. [The required majority for Series A shareholders is similarly changed to two-thirds.] Holders of two-thirds of the Series A and B shares must jointly approve any merger, liquidation or sale of the firm.

Board Seats and Redemption: [Board seat and redemption provisions for Series A shares canceled.]

Registration Rights: Series A and B shareholders can demand that the company include their shares in any registration statement for the public sale of stock that the company files. 30% of all Series A and B shareholders (as converted) can also demand that the company register their securities after December 31, 1992, providing the offering price of their equity will exceed $10 million. [Additional registration rights of Series A shareholders canceled.] Underwriting costs as above.

Series C Convertible Preferred Stock Agreement [Modifications Only]

Date: October 4, 1989.

Shares Sold: 1,200,000, at $10.00 per share.

Total Valuation: $63.3 million.

Dividends: Series C shareholders are entitled to receive a dividend of $0.75 per share, beginning on June 1, 1993, if declared by the Board as above.

Liquidation: If the company is liquidated, the company will pay $2.00 for each share of Series A stock, $6.00 for each share of Series B stock, and $10.00 for each share of Series C stock as above.

Conversion: Each Series C share is initially convertible into one share of common stock. This conversion ratio may be adjusted upward if the company issues additional shares of common stock. If the company goes public at a price exceeding $15.00 per share in an offering which raises at least $10 million dollars, the Series C shares will be automatically converted into common stock.

Voting Rights: Each Series C share is entitled to one vote in any matter submitted to the vote of the shareholders. Holders of two-thirds of the Series C shares must authorize the issue of any shares which are senior or equal to the Series C in dividend or liquidation rights. Holders of two-thirds of the Series A, B and C shares must jointly approve any merger, liquidation or sale of the firm.

Registration Rights: Series A, B and C shareholders can demand registration as above.

Source: Corporate documents.

Exhibit 4 5% Shareholders of ImmuLogic Pharmaceutical Corporation

Name	Shares Beneficially Owned	
	Number	Percent
Merck & Co., Inc.	1,150,000	17.9%
Arrow Partners (Rothschild, Inc.)	941,451	14.6
Greylock Partnerships	705,732	11.0
Technology Venture Investors	628,333	9.8
Institutional Venture Partners	557,663	8.7
Mayfield Funds	371,437	5.8
Malcolm L. Gefter	500,000	7.8
Other officers and directors	314,125	4.6
Other venture funds, consultants and employees	1,267,024	19.8

Source: Corporate documents

Exhibit 5 Financial Statements of ImmuLogic Pharmaceutical Corporation: Balance Sheets, 1988 to 1990 ($ 000s)

	1988	1989	1990
Sponsored research revenues	$ 1,426	$ 3,230	$ 3,265
Operating expenses:			
Research and development	2,721	5,181	7,236
General and administrative	1,982	2,227	3,367
Total expenses	**4,702**	**7,409**	**10,602**
Operating loss	(3,276)	(4,179)	(7,337)
Interest income, net	565	1,034	1,294
Net loss	$(2,711)	$(3,145)	$(6,043)

Exhibit 5 (continued) Consolidated Balance Sheets, December 31, 1989 and 1990 ($000s)

	12/31/89	12/31/90
ASSETS		
Current assets:		
Cash and cash equivalents	$20,084	$14,786
Prepaid expenses and other current assets	199	258
Interest receivable	183	98
Total current assets	**20,466**	**15,142**
Property and equipment, net	3,461	3,266
Other assets	201	195
Total assets	$24,128	$18,604
LIABILITIES		
Current liabilities:		
Accounts payable	$ 271	$ 282
Accrued expenses	239	363
Note payable	150	-
Current portion of capital lease	218	245
Total current liabilities	**877**	**890**
Other noncurrent liabilities	-	750
Capital lease obligation	1,105	859
Total liabilities	**1,982**	**2,499**
STOCKHOLDERS' EQUITY		
Convertible preferred stock:		
Series A, $.01 par value; 1,675,000 shares authorized; 1,675,000 shares issued and outstanding at December 31, 1989 and 1990	17	17
Series B, $.01 par value; 2,129,167 shares authorized, 2,129,167 shares issued and outstanding at December 31, 1989 and 1990	21	21
Series C, $.01 par value; 1,200,000 shares authorized, 1,200,000 shares issued and outstanding at December 31, 1989 and 1990	12	12
Common stock, $.01 par value; 8,100,000 shares authorized; 1,523,288 and 1,324,098 shares issued and outstanding at December 31, 1989 and 1990	15	13
Additional paid-in capital	28,745	28,749
Less note receivable	(81)	(81)
Accumulated deficit	(6,584)	(12,627)
Total stockholder's equity	**22,146**	**16,104**
Total liabilities and stockholders' equity	$24,128	$18,604

Source: Corporate documents.

Exhibit 6   Biotechnology Initial Public Offerings in Registration, March 1991

Company	Filing Date	Shares Filed (millions)	% of Company Represented by These Shares	Filing Range ($s)	Market Capitalization[a] ($ millions)
Applied Immune Sciences, Inc.	3/22/91	2.3	33.8	10-12	75
Cephalon, Inc.	3/15/91	2.3	30.3	17-19	137
Regeneron Pharmaceuticals, Inc.	2/20/91	3.0	21.6	16-19	243

Book Manager	Other Managing Underwriter (1)	Other Managing Underwriter (2)	Issuer's Legal Counsel	Issuer's Auditor
Montgomery Securities	Furman Selz		Latham & Watkins	Ernst & Young
Hambrecht & Quist	Cowen & Co.		Morgan, Lewis & Bockius	Arthur Andersen
Merrill Lynch	Smith Barney	S.G. Warburg	Skadden, Arps	Coopers & Lybrand

Source: Corporate documents.

[a]Market capitalizations calculated using midpoint of filing range.

Exhibit 7 Sales Projections for ImmuLogic Pharmaceutical Corporation, March 1991 ($ millions)

AllerVax sales	1994E	1995E	1996E	1997E	1998E
Cat	0.00	15.00	40.00	60.00	75.00
Ragweed			25.00	65.00	120.00
Mite				40.00	85.00
Grasses					20.00
Allervax royalties		1.50	6.50	16.50	30.00
Allergic rhinitis					20.00
Asthma					20.00
Total	**0.00**	**16.50**	**71.50**	**181.50**	**370.00**

	1989	1990	1991E	1992E	1993E	1994E	1995E	1996E	1997E	1998E
Revenues:										
Product sales & royalties						0.00	16.50	71.50	181.50	370.00
Contract revenue	3.23	3.27	6.10	8.60	11.32	8.48	14.00	12.50	8.50	3.50
Net interest & other	1.03	1.29	1.30	2.20	2.00	3.20	4.00	5.00	6.00	8.00
Total revenue	4.26	4.56	7.40	10.80	13.32	11.68	34.50	89.00	196.00	381.50
Expenses:										
Cost of goods sold							4.13	17.88	50.82	103.60
Research & development	5.18	7.24	11.19	15.13	18.00	22.00	30.00	42.00	60.00	80.00
Selling, general & administrative	2.23	3.37	2.67	3.28	4.50	6.00	14.00	26.00	34.00	50.00
Total expenses	7.41	10.60	13.86	18.41	22.50	28.00	48.13	85.88	144.82	233.60
Income before tax	(3.15)	(6.04)	(6.47)	(7.61)	(9.18)	(16.32)	(13.63)	3.13	51.18	147.90
Taxes									5.12	50.29
Net income	(3.15)	(6.04)	(6.47)	(7.61)	(9.18)	(16.32)	(13.63)	3.13	46.06	97.61

Source: Internal corporate projections.

Note: The average beta of thirteen publicly traded biotechnology companies in 1988-90 was 1.43. The yield on a five-year U.S. Treasury bond in March 1991 was 8.11%. E denotes estimates.

Exhibit 8 Selected List of U.S.-Manufactured Drugs with U.S. Patent Protection Expiring Between April 1991 and December 1995

Drug	Manufacturer	Expiration Date	1990 Rank in Sales of All U.S.-Manufactured Drugs (if in Top Ten)	U.S. Drug Sales ($ mil)	In Year of Patent Expiration (Estimated)			
					Firm's After-Tax Profit as % of Sales	U.S. Sales of Drug as % of Firm's Pharmaceutical Sales	U.S. Sales of Drug as % of Firm's Total Sales	U.S. Earnings From Drug as % of Firm's Total Earnings
Anaprox	Syntex	Dec. 1993		$180	24%	7%	6%	8%
Capoten	Bristol Myers-Squibb	Aug. 1995	2	535	25	6	3	5
Cardizem	Marion Merrill Dow	Nov. 1992	9	425	22	13	13	16
Ceclor	Eli Lilly	Dec. 1992	4	615	23	13	10	10
Dobutrex	Eli Lilly	Oct. 1993		120	24	2	2	2
Dolobid	Merck	Apr. 1992		65	26	1	1	1
Feldene	Pfizer	Apr. 1992		225	14	4	3	5
Halcion	Upjohn	Oct. 1993		95	16	3	2	3
Lopid	Warner-Lambert	Jan. 1993		300	12	11	5	13
Micronase	Upjohn	May 1994		260	16	8	6	8
Naprosyn	Syntex	Dec. 1993		525	24	22	18	22
Tagament	SmithKline Beecham	May 1994	3	440	16	8	4	8
Xanax	Upjohn	Oct. 1993		625	16	19	15	23

Source: Compiled from Cowen and Company, "Industry Strategies: Drug Stocks," (1992); *Medical Marketing and Media* (Aug. 1991); *Pharmaceutical Business News*, 15 Feb. 1991.

Exhibit 9 Joint Ventures and Collaborative Research Arrangements Entered into by U.S.-Based New Biotechnology Companies, September 1990 to March 1991

New Biotechnology Firm	Partner	Partner Nationality	Equity Investment ($ million)	Other Payment ($ million)	Deal Length (years)	Type of Deal	Area of Deal
Bio-Technology General	ABI Biotechnology	Canada	None	$2 - $3	2	Financing for Clinical trials; ongoing joint venture	Human growth hormones
Corvas	Plant Genetic System	Belgium	N/D	None	N/D	Joint product development program	Drugs to treat thrombosis
Curative Technologies	Espace Diversification	France	None	N/D	N/D	Joint venture for product development	Drugs to speed healing of wounds
Enzon, Inc.	Scherling-Plough	United States	None	6	N/D	Joint efforts to enhance existing drug	Polyethylene glycol attachments
Genzyme Corporation	N/D	N/D	None	13	N/D	Joint process development program	Making drugs via transgenic animals
Geritech	Marion Merrill Dow	United States	N/D	N/D	N/D	Equity Investment; licensing agreement	Diabetes medicine
Glycomed	Genentech (Swiss Parent)	United States	7	8	N/D	Joint product development program	Carbohydrate-based drugs for cancer
Immune Response	Rhone-Poulenc Rorer (French parent)	United States	10	36	N/D	Joint venture for product development	HIV vaccine
Isis Pharmaceuticals	Ciba-Geigy	United Kingdom	5	25	5	Joint product development program	Antisense drugs
Isis Pharmaceuticals	Rhone-Poulenc	France	None	N/D	N/D	Cooperative program	Antisense drugs
Isis Pharmaceuticals	Elsai	Japan	None	N/D	N/D	Cooperative program	Antisense drugs
Neurogenetic Corporation	Eli Lilly	United States	N/D	N/D	4	Joint product development program	Neurological pharmaceuticals
Oncogene Science	Pfizer	United States	None	16	5	Joint product development program (renewal)	Cancer treatments
Tanox Biosystems	Ciba Geigy	United States	None	N/D	N/D	Joint product development program	AIDS drugs
Telios Pharmaceutical	Morsk Hydro	Norway	N/D	N/D	N/D	Joint venture for product development, marketing	Matrix peptide technology
Vertex Pharmaceuticals	Chugai	Japan	2	19	5	Joint product development program	Immunosuppressive drugs

Source: Venture Economics, Strategic Alignments database.

22

ImmuLogic Pharmaceutical Corporation (B-1): Malcolm Gefter

Malcolm Gefter was deeply committed to the success of ImmuLogic Pharmaceutical Corporation and had hired a talented group of researchers to commercialize the ideas that originated in his laboratory in the early 1980s. Nonetheless, in his dealings with the firm, he sought to be just as objective as the professional venture capitalists who funded ImmuLogic were. To this end, in July 1998 Gefter sold back to ImmuLogic 250,000 of the 750,000 shares he owned. The $1.5 million he received from this sale and an employment contract with the company were sufficient, he felt, to give up his tenured faculty position at MIT and to ensure that he would approach the company's strategic choices in a dispassionate and professional manner.

Gefter saw two reasons that argued strongly for taking ImmuLogic public in March 1991. The first related to a potential collaborative agreement to commercialize its allergy product line. Gefter felt the product family was a great one, but he also believed that several small biotechnology firms in the past had been forced to accept relatively unattractive terms in arrangements with established pharmaceutical companies because of their financial weaknesses. A public offering would greatly strengthen ImmuLogic's balance sheet and hence its negotiating position.

A second consideration related to ImmuLogic's closest competitor, the Cytel Corporation. Also privately held, this firm was rumored to be considering an initial public offering (IPO) as well. He felt that an offering by Cytel could put ImmuLogic at a competitive disadvantage in a subsequent IPO or even in arranging private financings, since it was often the case that a single leader in a technological subfield attracted the bulk of the institutional money invested in a particular niche.

Gefter realized that the pricing of IPOs involved several arcane features, particularly the deliberate underpricing of the new issues in hopes of creating a "hot issue," which would rise in price during the first few hours and days of trading. Nonetheless, he felt that an appropriate valuation for the company could be gauged by comparing the valuation and development of other biotechnology firms going public as well as by the $10-per-share price paid for ImmuLogic stock by Merck and other investors in the "C" financing round. Exhibit 1 presents some of the information that Gefter considered.

This case was prepared by Josh Lerner. Copyright © 1992 by the President and Fellows of Harvard College. Harvard Business School case 293-067.

Exhibit 1   Biotechnology Initial Public Offerings in Registration: Detailed Comparison

Company	Date of Incorporation	Background of Founders	Number of Employees	Ph.D. Employed
Applied Immune Sciences, Inc.	1982	Assistant professor, Stanford Medical School	71	10
Cephalon, Inc.	1987	3 senior research scientists at Du Pont	49	20
Regeneron Pharmaceuticals, Inc.	1988	Faculty at Stanford, Comell, and University of Texas Medical Schools	91	31

Number of Patents Awarded	Number of Patent Applications Pending	Description of First Product Family
5	6	Devices to capture beneficial cells from blood or bone marrow; these are grown outside the body then returned to the patient.
0	At least 5	Small, biotechnology-based molecules to prevent nerve cell death, which can be introduced into the body nonsurgically.
0	"Several"	Growth factors to treat nerve damage, using recombinant versions of molecules naturally occurring in the body.

Current Status of First Product in U.S. Market	Major Strategic Partner	Largest Non-Management Shareholders
Human clinical trials	Baxter	Montgomery (36%); Nazem and Co. (14%); Aeneas (12%)
Preclinical animal research	Schering-Plough	Burr, Egan, Deleage (23%); Hambrecht & Quist (23%); Oak (13%)
Preclinical animal research	Amgen	Merrill Lynch (24%); Sumitomo (8%); Amgen (7%)

Source: Corporate documents.

23

ImmuLogic Pharmaceutical Corporation (B-2): Henry McCance

Henry McCance, a general partner since 1969 at Greylock, the Boston-based venture capital firm, held that an effective venture capitalist did not need to be an expert at exiting from investments. Rather, it was critical that one made reasonably priced investments in firms with market-leadership potential and great people and then worked with management as an active partner.

Greylock, established in 1965, had raised a series of partnerships with a total equity investment of over $300 million. Like other venture funds, its investments encompassed firms in a broad range of industries and situations. But Greylock had several features that distinguished it from the average venture capital fund. The first such characteristic was the strength of Greylock's ties to its investors (limited partners). Greylock had a relatively small number of investors, individuals, families, and university endowments with which the firm had a long-standing relationship. Second, unlike most funds, Greylock did not charge a fixed-annual management fee based on the assets that it had under management. Rather, the limited and general partners set an annual management fee, below the industry average, based on the partnership's annual operating budget.

Greylock had developed experience in the biotechnology industry by serving as a lead or co-lead investor in two early biotechnology companies, Genetics Institute and XOMA, and as a second-round investor in another biotechnology start-up, Centocor. Through these transactions—particularly the former two, where a Greylock representative had sat on the board of each firm—Greylock's partners had come to understand the unique management challenges posed by the biotechnology industry. In addition to the experience gained through these investments, Greylock acquired a reputation as a savvy investor in biotechnology firms when these three firms proved to be among the most successful companies in the industry during the 1980s.

McCance had been impressed by Malcolm Gefter since their initial introduction by James Bochnowski of Technology Venture Investments, based in Menlo Park, California. Bochnowski had been eager to involve McCance because of Greylock's geographical proximity to ImmuLogic, its biotechnology experience, and its close ties to MIT, which was a Greylock limited partner. McCance was struck by Gefter's combination of business acumen, communication skills, and scientific acuity. McCance, who held

This case was prepared by Josh Lerner. Copyright © 1992 by the President and Fellows of Harvard College. Harvard Business School case 293-068.

a B.A. in economics from Yale University and an MBA from Harvard Business School, could not assess the scientific validity of ImmuLogic's concept himself. As part of his evaluation process, he circulated Gefter's papers for comments to the chief executive officers of biotechnology companies in which he had previously invested. McCance also accompanied Gefter to Colorado for a conference on T-cells, where he was able to assess Gefter's standing with his scientific peers when Gefter delivered a keynote presentation to a packed hall at 10:00 P.M. on the last night of the conference.

McCance realized that the biotechnology industry was very different from others in which he invested. Although he would normally be reluctant to have a company in his portfolio go public that was so far from profitability, this pattern was common in the biotechnology industry and understood by investors. In fact, biotechnology firms' balance sheets were in some senses competitive weapons: without a substantial cash cushion, firms could be hobbled in their dealings with competitors and strategic partners. Finally, ImmuLogic in March 1991, while certainly a high-risk venture, was of high quality relative to other new biotechnology firms.

McCance was also aware of the need to move quickly. The one certainty about the current open window for biotechnology initial public offerings (IPOs) was that sooner or later it would shut again. Furthermore, he had observed that in past periods of intense IPO activity, the best firms tended to go public early in the cycle, while lower-quality firms went public later. Thus, it was desirable for several reasons to get into the queue early. McCance anticipated selling no shares of Greylock in the proposed offering. (Lock-up agreements typically prohibited the sale of shares for three to six months after the IPO, and Greylock typically held their shares for much longer after the IPO.)

To help identify an appropriate price range for the public offering, McCance compared the step-ups between financing rounds for biotechnology offerings. The step-ups for several recent biotechnology IPO filings are reported in Exhibit 1; the distribution from several hundred biotechnology financings are presented in Figure 1.

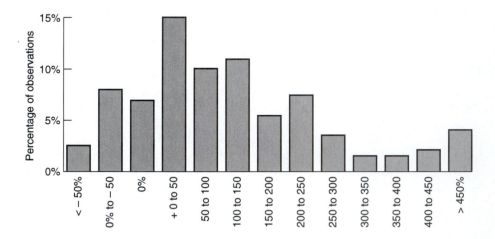

Figure 1 Increases in Per-Share Price between Financing Rounds of New Biotechnology Firms, 1978 to 1989

Exhibit 1 Venture Financings of Biotechnology Initial Public Offerings in Registration

Venture Round	Date	Price per Share of Common Stock	Total Funds Disbursed ($ millions)	Valuation	Investors
		Applied Immune Sciences, Inc.			
C	1984-1986	$1.39 -1.67	$3.1	$6.2	Several venture capitalists
D	1986	2.73	7.1	19.5	Several venture capitalists
E	1987 and 10/89	8.60	8.6	79.8	Several venture capitalists
F	11/89	10.16	7.7	87.1	Several venture capitalists
G	12/90	3.44	15.4	40.5	Several venture capitalists

Rounds F and G also included a total of $9.1 in convertible debt, which was later converted into stock.

Applied Immune Sciences underwent a substantial reorganization between its F and G rounds.

All prices are adjusted for stock splits.

Venture Round	Date	Price per Share of Common Stock	Total Funds Disbursed ($ millions)	Valuation	Investors
		Cephalon, Inc.			
A	10/87	$0.75	$0.5	$0.6	Several venture capitalists
B	5/88-6/88	1.50	4.6	5.9	Several venture capitalists
C	6/89-9/89	2.25	1.8	10.6	Several venture capitalists
D	5/90	8.00	2.0	40.8	Several venture capitalists
E	5/90	20.00	2.0	98.3	Schering-Plough

All prices are adjusted to stock splits.

Venture Round	Date	Price per Share of Common Stock	Total Funds Disbursed ($ millions)	Valuation	Investors
		Regeneron Pharmaceuticals, Inc.			
A	1/88	$0.50	$1.0	$3.6	Merrill Lynch
B	11/88-3/89	3.22	5.9	28.4	Several venture capitalists
C	3/89	4.84	4.4	48.4	Sumitomo
D	8/90	19.02	15.0	205.2	Amgen

All prices are adjusted for stock splits.

Source: Corporate documents

24

ImmuLogic Pharmaceutical Corporation (B-3): Katherine Kirk

Katherine Kirk first became aware of ImmuLogic in 1990, after a *New York Times* story had featured its research into immunological processes. After calling Gefter, she had visited the company. This process of visiting private firms was not unusual for Kirk. Since the competition for underwritings was frequently fierce and because Hambrecht and Quist (H&Q) staked its reputation every time it underwrote a company, the identification of promising private companies was an important facet of Kirk's job.

When the company initially approached H&Q in late 1990 about the possibility of going public, she had indicated it was too early to consider an initial public offering (IPO). Not only would the firm be able to command a considerably higher valuation if it waited until human clinical trials had begun—perhaps $200 million instead of the $100 million valuation it would now command—but the danger of a withdrawn IPO would be considerably reduced. This advisory role was in keeping with another facet of Kirk's job, that of educating chief executive officers (CEOs) about raising capital in the public market. CEOs of privately held firms, she noted, were used to being in total control of their business. As they approached the stock market for the first time, they had to grasp the complex web of supply and demand at the heart of the public offering process.

In early 1991, however, a number of firms still in preclinical trials indicated in preliminary filings with the Securities and Exchange Commission that they intended to go public. To ImmuLogic, the virtues of waiting until clinical trials began to seem less clear-cut.

Kirk found the proposed offering to be attractive for several reasons. Of the current crop of firms considering going public, she felt, ImmuLogic was in the top tier in terms of the quality of its people, its science, and its business strategy. Underwriting an IPO for ImmuLogic might lead to more business if the firm subsequently issued more shares in a secondary public offering. Finally, underwriting IPOs was a substantial source of revenue for H&Q. This was particularly true of high-technology IPOs, which was H&Q's area of specialty. (Exhibit 1 provides overall underwriter rankings for 1990; Exhibit 2 examines biotechnology offerings in the past two years.) While IPOs were typically syndicated among a large number of investment banks, the bulk of the offerings was sold by the managing underwriter or underwriters. Roughly seven cents of every dollar of

This case was prepared by Josh Lerner. Copyright © 1992 by the President and Fellows of Harvard College. Harvard Business School case 293-069.

IPO proceeds went to the investment bankers; of this sum, a little over one-half was the "selling concession," which went to the sales staff's commissions and to the lead underwriters' management fees (20%).

The purchasers of H&Q offerings were typically institutional investors. Unlike retail-oriented underwriters such as Merrill Lynch, H&Q's strength lay in its long-standing relationships with mutual funds, pension managers, and other large purchasers. Mutual funds specializing in individual industries were playing an ever-more-important role. Although some of these institutions might hold on to these offerings as long-run investments, many purchasers only held their shares for a few hours or days after the IPO.

H&Q attempted to ensure that its IPOs would be "hot" deals. Institutional orders—which typically took the form of price-dependent "limit offers"—were compiled by the lead underwriter into a "book" of orders. The underwriter's goal was to set a price at which there were several times more orders than there were shares available. In this way, the underwriter could increase the probability that the share price would surge as trading opened.

Another important customer for H&Q was the venture capitalists who had initially invested in the firm going public. Venture capitalists played an important role in making decisions about when companies in which they invest should go public. Not only did they have formal control rights (the put options and registration rights that were part of many venture capital contracts), but they also served as advisers to many CEOs. (Exhibit 3 summarizes the price behavior of several recent biotechnology IPOs; Exhibit 4 and Figure 1 provide general overviews of both biotechnology offerings and those of venture-backed firms in general.)

Thus, in the ImmuLogic transaction, Kirk needed to balance several concerns. In her decision to recommend proceeding with the deal, she had to balance both the risks and the rewards. Although the deal had many attractive aspects, if ImmuLogic encountered reverses after the offering, H&Q's reputation might be tarnished. Pricing the deal posed another set of conflicts. If the investment bank was perceived as not pricing a particular offering aggressively enough, the venture capitalists—who, reflecting their far greater experience with the initial public offering process, typically advised the entrepreneurs closely—might steer their next deals to other underwriters. On the other hand, if the price of the shares fell immediately after the offering, H&Q's relationship with several major institutional investors could be strained.

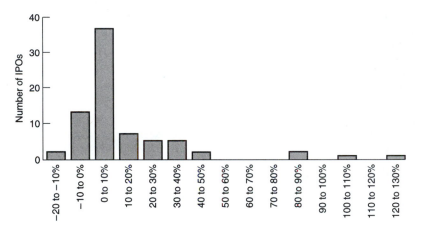

Figure 1   Change between Offer Price and First-Day Closing Price, All Venture-Backed Biotechnology Initial Public Offerings, 1979 to 1990

Source: Casewriter's analysis.

Exhibit 1 Leading IPO Managers, 1990, Excluding Closed-End Funds
(Full Credit to Lead Manager)

Manager	$ Volume (millions)	Rank	%	# Issues
Goldman Sachs	1,246.5	1	27.1	9
Alex. Brown	433.4	2	9.4	16
Salomon Brothers	332.6	3	7.2	5
First Boston	282.7	4	6.1	4
PaineWebber	273.6	5	6.0	10
Morgan Stanley	240.7	6	5.2	7
Smith Barney	239.5	7	5.2	7
Merrill Lynch Capital	221.4	8	4.8	7
Lehman Brothers	202.1	9	4.4	3
Kidder Peabody	141.4	10	3.1	4
Robertson Stephens	135.8	11	3.0	6
Prudential-Bache	98.7	12	2.1	3
Bear Stearns	96.8	13	2.1	2
Dillon Read	81.5	14	1.8	3
D.H. Blair	70.7	15	1.5	13
Hambrecht & Quist	47.2	16	1.0	3

Source: Compiled from *Investment Dealers' Digest* (Feb. 1991 and Feb. 1992).

Exhibit 2 Leading Biotechnology Equity Offering Managers, 1989 to 1990
(Full Credit to Each Manager)

	$ Volume (millions)	# Issues	# IPOs
Hambrecht & Quist	$265.9	9	2
Paine Webber	214.1	6	1
Lehman Brothers	200.3	5	0
Robertson Stephens	144.2	3	0
Merrill Lynch	125.3	4	1
Montgomery	113.2	3	1
Alex. Brown	96.4	4	1
Morgan Stanley	72.2	2	0
First Boston	65.5	2	0
Smith Barney	46.2	2	2

Source: Hambrecht & Quist.

Exhibit 3   Aftermarket Performance of Recent Biotechnology Initial Public Offerings

	Offer Price	Day 1 Close	Day 2 Close	Day 3 Close	Day 4 Close	Day 5 Close	Day 6 Close	Day 7 Close	Day 8 Close	Day 9 Close	Day 10 Close
Cygnus Therapeutic Systems											
Share Price ($)	9	11.75	11	11.5	11.625	11.75	11.125	11.375	11	11.25	11.25
OTC Composite Index	408.5	414.2	417.7	424.8	432.2	439.2	435.0	436.8	444.1	444.0	444.0
Gensia Pharmaceuticals											
Share Price ($)	11	11.125	10.75	10.125	10	9.75	7.75	10.125	10	10.5	10.125
OTC Composite Index	465.6	464.6	465.0	464.1	460.9	462.8	466.6	468.9	467.1	467.6	460.8
Immune Response Corporation											
Share Price ($)	7	6.75	6.875	6.75	6.75	6.875	6.75	7	6.75	6.875	6.625
OTC Composite Index	487.8	491.1	492.1	491.5	491.5	492.5	497.8	493.4	493.9	488.8	478.1

Source: Compiled from *Daily Stock Price Guide*, (1990 and 1991).

Exhibit 4   Characteristics of Biotechnology and All Venture-Backed Initial Public Offerings

	429 Venture-Backed IPOs, All Industries, 1978-1987	72 Venture-Backed IPOs, Biotechnology, 1979-1990
Firm age at time of IPO (years)	5.8	3.9
Earnings/Price Ratio[a]	-0.015	-0.065
IPO Size ($ millions)	$19.1	$15.2
Mean charge from offering price to first day's close	8.4%	12.2%

Sources: Compiled from Chris Barry, et al, "The Role of Venture Captial on the Creation of Public Companies: Evidence from the Going Public Process," *Journal of Financial Economics*, 27 (1990) 447-471; and casewriter's analysis.

[a]Ratio of earnings per share in year before IPO to per-share price of IPO.

25

ImmuLogic Pharmaceutical Corporation (B-4): Phillip Gross

Phillip Gross, a vice president at Harvard Management Company, found the biotechnology investments to present both opportunities and challenges. Although the great bulk of his investments were in large companies included in the Standard and Poor's (S&P) 500, biotechnology was attractive because of its potential for large returns. Because the industry's development was so uncertain, however, the market valuation of firms could swing wildly.

Harvard Management, founded in 1974, managed the $5 billion Harvard University endowment. In the spring of 1991, the largest share of the endowment (almost $2 billion) was allocated to U.S. equities. The remaining funds were allocated to, in order of importance, foreign equities, domestic bonds, venture capital, real estate, commodities (primarily oil and gas), foreign bonds, and high-yield and distressed bonds.

The management of Harvard Management's portfolio of U.S. stocks had undergone a series of shifts over the years. In the mid-1980s, the company had had four portfolios, each with a distinct investment strategy. One of these was a specialized fund targeting emerging growth companies. The firm had extensive biotechnology holdings in the mid-1980s (up until 1986) and then again in the period between August 1987 and January 1988. These holdings had been cut back sharply in the late 1980s as Harvard Management had shifted to "value" investing: instead, large investments were made in firms perceived to be undervalued. In recent years, the domestic equities program had simply attempted to surpass consistently the S&P 500 by a small margin. Its strategy might have been characterized as making many small wagers rather than a few large bets.

The program was divided up among six analysts, each responsible for a set of industries. The amount to be allocated to each industry was proportional to its representation in the S&P 500. Each analyst identified companies in the industries he or she was responsible for that were anticipated to under- or overperform the market in the months and years to come, regardless of the health of the economy and the market. Harvard Management's holdings would be adjusted to reflect these predictions. Less frequently, the domestic equities program would adjust its holdings of entire industries that were expected to do particularly well or poorly. Investments consisted primarily of firms

This case was prepared by Josh Lerner. Copyright © 1992 by the President and Fellows of Harvard College. Harvard Business School case 293-070.

included in the S&P 500, although some smaller over-the-counter stocks were included as well.

Gross was responsible for the retail, transportation, and health care industries. Normally, he did not consider participating in initial public offerings (IPOs). He was aware that the performance of IPOs had been generally poor (see Exhibit 1); in any case, the amount of shares that could be bought in IPOs was too small to be of much interest. He did, however, occasionally consider purchasing offerings as long-run investments when he was able to validate independently the recommendations of investment bankers.

Gross used three criteria to evaluate biotechnology companies. Foremost was an assessment of the quality of the science. He tried to find observers without a financial interest in the industry to solicit for opinions. Second, he considered the relative valuation of the firms. One rough way he used to assess whether biotechnology firms were over- or underpriced was to compare the firms' projected 1997 earnings, the current stage of the companies' development, and their valuations. (These figures for several biotechnology firms publicly traded in the spring of 1991 are provided in Exhibit 2. The first of these firms, Amgen, was the highest valued biotechnology firm. The others represented examples of the mixture of firms in the industry.) In addition, Gross was aware of many other valuation "rules-of-thumb" developed by analysts. One of these is reproduced in Figure 1.

The third and perhaps most important criterion that Gross used was the "karma" of the market. Biotechnology equities had endured an extended slump after the 1987 crash. Although the market had recovered in recent months, Gross was well aware that a single reversal could lead to a sharp downward revision of valuations.

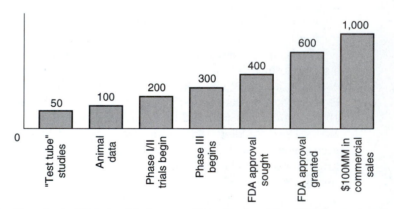

Figure 1 Hypothetical Relationship between Biotechnology Firm Development and Valuation, February 1991. Market capitalization in millions of dollars.

Source: Hambrecht and Quist.

Exhibit 1   Long-Run Performance of Initial Public Offerings, All Industries and Biotechnology

	1526 IPOs, All Industries 1975-1984	68 IPOs, Biotechnology 1979-1987
Average price change from end of first trading day to three years after IPO	+34.4%	+48.9%
Average price change from end of first trading day to three years after IPO, adjusted for performance of over-the-counter stock index.	-15.8%	+21.9%

Source: Jay R. Ritter, "The Long-Run Performance of Initial Public Offerings," *Journal of Finance, 46 (1991) 3-28;* and casewriter's analysis.

Exhibit 2 Biotechnology Companies' Projections and Valuations: Comparison

Company	Projected 1997 Net Income ($ million)	Background	March 1991 Valuation ($ million)
Amgen	348	Marketing heart drug, EPO.	5,541
Applied Biosystems	35	Manufacturing biotechnology instrumentation.	252
Centocor	167	Seeking regulatory approval of septic shock product.	1,112
Chiron	190	Selling hepatitis diagnostic test, ophthalmic products.	1,236
Cytogen	80	Developing biotechnology-based cancer imaging products.	268
Immunex	193	Seeking regulatory approval of colony-stimulating factor.	783
Xoma	154	Seeking regulatory approval of septic shock product.	430

Source: Compiled from Winter and Spring 1991 analyst reports; Compustat; and corporate documents.

26

RogersCasey Alternative Investments: Innovative Responses to the Distribution Challenge

Philip Cooper, president and chief executive officer of RogersCasey Alternative Investments, gazed at the darkening Connecticut landscape pensively. He was considering three alternative strategies relating to distributions by private equity funds in which his clients invested. Each seemed to have considerable promise but also to pose substantial challenges.

Cooper had joined RogersCasey Alternative Investments (RCAI) five months earlier, in August 1993. RogersCasey's founders—Stephen Rogers and John Casey—had given him a broad mandate to expand the firm's role as an adviser to institutions about their private equity investments. After making several crucial hires and undertaking a variety of organizational changes, he felt confident that RCAI was on its way to meeting this objective.

Cooper was intrigued about pursuing an initiative relating to distributions of securities by private equity investors. These investors, particularly venture capitalists, often do not return cash to their investors, but the shares of the firms that they have recently taken public. The proper way to handle these distributions is often unclear.

Like other investment managers, RCAI had been providing distribution–management services for its clients for several years. Upon receiving a distribution, the firm decided whether to sell the shares immediately or to hold them for a considerable period. One possibility might be simply to continue this service.

Alternatively, RCAI could introduce one of two new services. These would serve to differentiate RCAI from other investment managers. They would also build on two of RCAI's strategic strengths: the analytic acumen of its staff and its close ties to its public-market-oriented parent. The first was a co-investment fund. This would invest in the shares of publicly traded firms, either before or at the time of distribution. The second was a distribution–hedging service. This might allow investors to reduce the risk of market swings, lessening the value of their distributed shares. Implementing either of these new initiatives, however, would pose a variety of challenges.

This case was prepared by Josh Lerner. Copyright © 1995 by the President and Fellows of Harvard College. Harvard Business School case 296-024.

STOCK DISTRIBUTIONS IN PRIVATE EQUITY

Venture capitalists[1] typically do not sell shares at the time of an initial public offering (IPO) of a firm that they have financed. In fact, they will typically enter into a "lock-up" agreement with the investment bank underwriting the deal, in which they agree not to sell shares for several months. This makes the sale of shares to the public easier, since investors often fear that if insiders dump large blocks of securities in the months after the IPO, the share price will tumble. Even after they are free to sell shares, many venture capitalists delay liquidating their positions for months or even years.

Once they decide to liquidate investments in publicly traded firms, venture capitalists typically employ one of two approaches. The first alternative is that the venture capitalist sells the shares in the market and distributes the cash to his investors (limited partners).[2] More often, however, the venture capitalist distributes the actual shares to each of the limited partners. Exhibit 1 shows the growing importance of these distributions.

Three reasons explain the frequency of stock distributions. First, SEC rules restrict the size of sales by corporate affiliates (officers, directors, and holders of 10% of the firm's equity). Venture investors often qualify as affiliates because of their role on the board and their equity holdings. (Exhibit 2 summarizes relevant securities law.) The venture capital fund may hold a large fraction of the company's equity. Selling its entire stake may consequently take a long time. By distributing the shares to limited partners (who are not considered affiliates and can consequently sell their shares freely), the venture capitalist can dispose of a large stake quickly.

Second, tax motivations provide an incentive for the venture capitalists to distribute shares. If venture capitalists sell the shares and distribute cash, the limited partners and the venture capitalists are subject to immediate capital gains taxes. The limited partners are likely to include some who are tax-exempt (e.g., pension funds) and others who are not (individuals and corporations). These investors may have different preferences about when the shares should be sold. Furthermore, the venture capitalists themselves may wish to postpone paying personal taxes by selling their shares at a later date.

Third, if selling the shares has a large negative effect on prices, then venture capitalists may want to distribute the shares for two reasons. First, venture capitalists have an incentive to distribute the shares that they think are overvalued because of the way that limited partners and outside fund trackers (e.g., Venture Economics and Cambridge Associates) compute returns. A venture organization's track record is the most important marketing tool when it seeks to raise capital for a new fund. Returns for the venture capital fund are calculated using the closing price of the distributed stock on the day of the distribution.[3] This may not be the actual price received (or even near the actual price received) when the limited partners sell their shares. It may take two or three days, or even longer, before the shares reach the limited partners once a distribu-

---

[1] Distributions are also important in buyout funds. A major university endowment that is a large buyout investor estimates that over 30% of the distributions from buyout funds are in the form of securities. Distributions are also controversial in this setting. For instance, in September 1994 Wasserstein Perella's merchant banking fund distributed its shares of Maybelline, which it had held since 1990. Five days later, Maybelline announced disappointing earnings and its stock price dropped by 36%. In a highly unusual move, Wasserstein Perella bowed to the limited partners' protests and reduced the price at which the distribution was recorded (thereby sharply reducing its profits). See Yvette Kantrow, "Wasserella Fund Investors See Red over Share Payout," *Investment Dealers' Digest* 60 (September 26, 1994): pp. 3–4.

[2] Over 80% of U.S. venture capital funds are organized as limited partnerships. In these limited partnerships, the venture capitalist serves as the general partner and the investors as limited partners.

[3] Many distributions are declared at 5 P.M. after the stock market has closed.

tion has been declared. If the market reacts negatively to the distribution, actual returns to the limited partners could be substantially less than calculated returns. The second reason relates to the venture capitalists' compensation. If the investors in a venture fund have not yet received back the capital that they originally invested, then most funds will distribute nearly all shares to the limited partners. After the capital has been returned, the venture capitalists will collect a substantial share of the profits (usually 20%). Distributing overvalued shares allows venture capitalists to begin receiving profits earlier than they would otherwise.

Many institutional investors can relate stories of shares that fell sharply in value after being distributed by venture capitalists. One example is Media Vision Technology, a company financed by (among others) Brentwood Associates, Nazem and Co., Aspen Venture Partners, and Advanced Technology Ventures. Several venture capitalists distributed their shares in January 1994, when it was trading as high as $46 per share. Within two months, its stock price began falling precipitously, as rumors of manipulated earnings and phantom warehouses began circling the company. By May, its stock price had fallen to $2. It ultimately restated its 1993 financial statements, turning a $20 million profit into a $99 million loss, and declared bankruptcy.[4] More systematic evidence about the relationship between distributions and stock prices is found in a study of nearly 800 such transactions.[5] Exhibit 3 shows the average stock price of firms from three months before to five months after distributions by venture funds. These are net-of-market returns (adjusted for the shift in the relevant stock index). Exhibit 4 displays the returns for various subclasses of firms. The groupings include firms financed by older and younger venture capital organizations, companies taken public by high-, medium-, and low-reputation investment bankers, firms where the venture capitalist did and did not leave the board at the time of the distribution, and cases where the distribution is larger and smaller.

Although the stock prices of venture-backed firms displayed an up-and-down pattern around distributions, the *long-run* returns of venture-backed firms seemed "fair" given their riskiness. A recent study had demonstrated that the average venture-backed IPO at the end of five years performed almost as well (on a risk-adjusted basis) as the NASDAQ market index: a portfolio consisting of recent venture-backed IPOs performed 99% as well as an investment in the NASDAQ index.[6] Returns of IPOs not backed by venture capitalists were much poorer. A portfolio consisting of recent nonventure IPOs performed only 76% as well as an investment in the NASDAQ index. This disparity was due to the very poor performance of the smallest nonventure IPOs.

The distribution process often frustrates limited partners. As Venture Economics notes,

> There are few venture capital fund management issues that evoke so much controversy as the timing and execution of stock distributions. Venture capital managers [and investors] differ in their philosophy as to when stock should be distributed and how those distributions should be handled.[7]

[4] See, for instance, Heather Pemberton, "Media Vision Flounders Amidst Questionable Business Practices," *CD-ROM Professional* 7 (July 1994): 13 *ff.;* "Media Vision Bankruptcy Moves Forward," United Press International Newswire, November 11, 1994.

[5] The results are presented in more detail in Paul Gompers and Josh Lerner, "Venture Capital Distributions: Short- and Long-Run Reactions," *Journal of Finance* 53 (1998): 2161–2183.

[6] Paul Gompers and Alon Brav, "Myth or Reality? The Long-Run Performance of Initial Public Offerings," *Journal of Finance* 52 (1997): pp. 1791–1821.

[7] "Stock Distributions—Fact, Opinion and Comment," *Venture Capital Journal* 27 (August 1987): p. 8.

A Kemper Financial Services survey, for instance, found that only 16% of limited partners preferred stock distributions.[8] First, the distribution of shares poses a substantial administrative burden. Recordkeeping and tax calculations are far more complex when shares are distributed. Second, it is often difficult to decide what to do with the shares. Venture capitalists often distribute shares with little notice. The venture capitalists explain that their behavior is due to the need to avoid providing information to hedge fund managers, who might drive the price down before the distribution by shorting the stock. Finally, distributions of young and obscure firms often come with little supporting information and few recommendations. Venture capitalists respond that under SEC regulations, limited partners are far safer if they are not advised by venture capitalists (see Exhibit 2).

Limited partners have developed three distinct strategies to deal with distributions. The first is an "automatic sell" policy, liquidating distributions immediately upon receipt. An investment banker at Alex. Brown & Sons estimates that as recently as 1990, institutional investors sold one-half of all stock distributions on the day of receipt. In recent years, he suggests, this has fallen to 10%.[9]

A second approach has been to internally analyze each distribution. Often, this is equivalent to an automatic sell policy. In almost all cases, the sell-or-hold decision is made not by the officials responsible for venture investments, but by the analysts handling publicly traded small-capitalization stocks. These analysts have their own lists of favorite stocks, which are unlikely to coincide with the stock distributions. Furthermore, the number of shares received may be small, which may further reduce the analysts' willingness to study the firms carefully.

The third approach has been to rely on a new class of financial intermediaries, known as stock distribution managers. These firms receive distributions from limited partners and make the decision of whether to sell or hold these shares. Profiles of RCAI's five leading competitors in the distribution management area are presented in Exhibit 5.

ROGERSCASEY ALTERNATIVE INVESTMENTS

RCAI's parent organization was established in 1976. Rogers, Casey & Barksdale (later known as RogersCasey) sought to help pension funds understand their liabilities to employees, as well as to plan their investments to meet these needs.

This firm was established at a propitious time. First, the Employee Retirement Income Security Act (ERISA) had been enacted in 1974, which greatly increased the need for corporations to carefully manage their pension obligations. Second, the equity markets about this time reached the trough of a pronounced "bear" market.

Equities lost 49% of their value between the end of 1972 and the beginning of 1975.[10] As pension fund managers grappled with the challenges of funding pension obligations, they increasingly began turning to investment advisers for help. Under the leadership of Stephen Rogers and John Casey, RogersCasey benefited from this growth. By 1979, the firm had 15 clients with $35 billion under management; by 1989, 35 clients

---

[8] Kathleen Devlin, "The Post-Venture Dilemma," *Venture Capital Journal* 33 (May 1993): pp. 32–36.

[9] In between 5% and 10% of the distributions, an institutional investor seeking to sell immediately would be limited by Rule 144 (see Exhibit 2). In these instances, the venture capitalist has distributed shares that have been held between two and three years, and whose rate of sale is restricted by Rule 144.

[10] This is adjusted for inflation. The source is Ibbotson Associates, *Stocks, Bonds, Bills, and Inflation*, Chicago: Ibbotson Associates, 1995.

with $60 billion; and in early 1994, 95 clients with $188 billion. (A profile of RogersCasey in early 1994 is presented in Exhibit 6.)

RogersCasey first began investing in alternative investments, such as venture capital, buyouts, and natural resources, in 1985. This was largely in response to client requests for this service. Pension funds became heavy investors in alternatives in the early 1980s, after a 1979 Department of Labor interpretation of ERISA relaxed their concerns about such investments. In many alternative asset classes, pension funds had become the dominant investors by the mid-1980s.

RogersCasey did not decide to make a formal effort in the alternative investment arena until 1988. At this point, it established RCAI as a wholly owned subsidiary. Many activities performed by RCAI in its first years resembled those of other investment managers (also known as "gatekeepers"): due diligence, portfolio management, reporting, monitoring, and research. Although many of RCAI's activities were similar to those of its rivals, it sought to differentiate itself in two important ways. First, it employed state-of-the-art computer systems, databases, and analytic capabilities. This process was greatly eased by RCAI's close ties to RogersCasey, which had built up a substantial infrastructure for managing its public market investments. The second distinguishing characteristic followed from the first. Rather than focusing on any single-asset class, it sought to employ the full complement of alternatives. These included such diverse investments as timber, mezzanine debt, and oil and gas participating royalties.

Under the leadership of Carla Haugen and Duff Lewis, RCAI gradually grew in size. By mid-1993, RCAI had $600 million under management, which was invested in both partnerships and direct investments. In addition, the firm played an advisory role in the allocation of another $100 million. (Exhibit 7 summarizes RCAI's investment recommendations between 1988 and 1993.)

Philip Cooper joined RCAI in August 1993. A separate board was established for RCAI at the same time to give the organization more autonomy. Serving on this board was Casey, Cooper, Rogers, and Terrence Overholser, a RogersCasey managing director. As an indication of the importance of this effort, Cooper was added to the governing board of RogersCasey. As such, he was the first director other than the firm's founders. Cooper had experience with nearly all aspects of the venture capital business. While working as an account supervisor at the advertising firm BBDO, Cooper—tired of poring over weighty printouts—conceived the notion of a graphics package that would ease the analysis of large data sets. Cooper headed to Boston, seeking to commercialize this idea. He soon met David Friend, an engineer who had developed a software package embodying this concept. Cooper and Friend raised $4 million in 1980 from Greylock, Venrock, and other venture capitalists to finance their new firm, Computer Pictures Corporation. As one analyst noted, Cooper had an extraordinary ability to "incite and excite the mentality of venture capitalists."[11] Two years later, Cullinet Software acquired the firm for $14 million in cash.

After a hiatus as a Sloan fellow at MIT's Sloan School of Management, Cooper formed Palladian Software. This artificial intelligence company developed an expert system to help businesses do financial planning and capital budgeting. Cooper then turned to working on the other side of the venture investment process. In 1987, he and two partners established a small partnership that worked with two large institutional investors—Harvard Management Company and the Vista Group—to identify promising deals. Cooper provided expertise in evaluating potential venture and buy-

---

[11] Michael Ball, "Ring-Around-the-Rosy," *Boston Business Journal* 7 (September 7, 1987): p. 1.

out deals, and then oversaw the firms' managements. On the side, he founded and served as chairman of Business Matters, Inc. (formerly known as Cottage Software), which developed and marketed a Windows-based financial analysis program. Cooper also served as a managing director of Boston International Advisors, a quantitative investment advisory firm with $2.5 billion under management, and chairman of several other firms.

DISTRIBUTION MANAGEMENT AT RCAI

Upon assuming the leadership of RCAI, Cooper sought to boost its analytic capabilities in two major ways. First, he made several critical hires, especially Thomas Philips and John Picone. (Exhibit 8 profiles RCAI's personnel.) He also sought to aggressively expand RCAI's investment management role, rather than primarily selecting other fund managers.

One area to which Cooper assigned a high priority was the management of distributions. This high-growth area appeared to fit well with RCAI's analytic strengths and its close ties to its parent. Cooper considered three alternative strategic approaches in this area. The first was to devote greater resources to RCAI's traditional distribution–management services. Like other investment managers, RCAI had managed distributions for clients for several years.

RCAI had developed a systematic approach to managing distributions. RCAI began compiling information on firms while they were still privately held. Data collection became more intense at the time the firms went public. Thus, once a distribution was received, RCAI's staff had a wealth of quantitative and qualitative information at their fingertips. In evaluating whether to hold or sell the distribution, RCAI employed several criteria:

- The relative valuation of the firm, as measured through ratios such as market-to-book value and price-to-earnings.

- The valuation of the firm relative to the discounted value of the firm's projected cash flows, as estimated in analyst reports issued after the IPO.

- The strength of the firm's management, technology, and business plan, as assessed through conversations with venture capitalists.

- The behavior of the stock price before the distribution. If the shares fell sharply ahead of the distribution, it suggested that the distribution had been anticipated by traders. In this instance, RCAI might be less likely to sell the shares immediately.

- The venture capitalists' apparent reasons for distributing the stock. If the partnership distributing the shares was nearing its end, it might be compelled to distribute the stock, whether or not it was fairly valued. Similarly, venture capitalists might be more inclined to distribute shares prematurely if the partnership agreement governing the fund required them to, or if they held a particularly large position in the firm.

If the firm was sold immediately, RCAI typically executed the trade through the investment bank that took the firm public. If the distribution was to be held for an extended period, however, RCAI would transfer the shares to the custodian (e.g., Boston Safe or State Street Bank) with whom the institutional investor had an established relationship. This deprived the investment banker of the knowledge of whether or not the institution had liquidated its position. Knowledge that large numbers of distributed shares had not yet been sold might encourage short selling, in anticipation of large-block trades that would depress the stock price. Extensive short selling might drive the stock price down before sales by RCAI's clients.[12]

Nonetheless, the extent of RCAI's distribution–management activities was limited until the end of 1992 by the status of its largest client. Due to an early retirement program, this pension fund needed to make payments more rapidly than anticipated. Due to this demand for liquidity, the client asked RCAI to sell most distributions immediately. A detailed justification had to be prepared for each distribution held for an extended period. Another factor that encouraged RCAI to sell distributed shares was the time-consuming responsibility of voting proxies. Clients expected RCAI to vote in all proxy contests. These shares had to be voted following the specific policy guidelines of each institutional investor.

One problem with distribution-management services that RCAI and other investment managers faced was performance assessment. Institutions typically evaluate their money managers against a benchmark such as the S&P 500 or the Russell 2000. It is difficult to find an appropriate benchmark for distribution managers, because they do not choose when to receive the large blocks of thinly traded securities. John Picone, Gary Kominski, and others at RCAI felt that if they were ultimately able to liquidate the shares at the price immediately prior to the distribution, they would be doing a good job.

One possibility, Cooper mused, would be simply expanding RCAI's distribution management services. Two new initiatives, however, also appeared intriguing. The first of these, a public market fund focusing on companies around the time of distribution, had been suggested by John Picone.

Picone had been a public stock manager for many years. While working for Metropolitan Life in 1987, however, he had been asked to help the insurer's venture capital group manage stock distributions. MetLife, like many institutions, had begun investing in venture capital funds in the early 1980s. After venture capitalists took many firms public during the 1986–87 IPO "window," the volume of distributions rapidly increased. Like many institutions, MetLife sold its first few distributions immediately upon receipt. This triggered two concerns. First, in some cases the venture capital group was selling the shares of companies in the open market while the public stock managers were buying shares of the same firm. This was clearly inefficient. More generally, senior management asked whether MetLife was receiving the best price by selling immediately. Picone introduced a variety of initiatives at the venture capital group. One of these was traditional distribution management, along the lines of RCAI's program and those described in Exhibit 5. Picone also developed a second approach. He pioneered a co-investment fund, which bought shares of venture-backed firms that had recently gone public. For instance, he might consider buying shares when a firm had dropped sharply in price around the time of a distribution, or when a venture capitalist that was free to distribute shares in a firm nonetheless delayed the distribution. Picone proposed to create a similar co-investment fund for RCAI's clients.

A second service that Cooper considered offering was distribution hedging. RCAI might mingle distributions from several clients. It could then hedge the risk that this portfolio would decline in value by purchasing derivatives on a small-capitalization stock index, or an industry index such as the CBOE Biotech Index. In this way, changes in mar-

---

[12] At the same time, brokers from the investment bank that took the firm public could be important sources of information. For instance, they would know whether a large number of limit orders had been placed, instructing the bank to sell the shares once the stock reached a certain price.

ket valuations would not wipe out the value of the portfolio. The distributed shares could then be slowly liquidated, and the derivative holdings adjusted accordingly.

Thomas Philips, managing director of Advanced Research, had raised several concerns about this proposal. In particular, he worried about how successfully RCAI could hedge these distributions. Often several venture funds simultaneously distributed the same firm. Thus, a single company might represent as much as 40% of the portfolio. It was unclear how successfully such substantial firm-specific exposures could be hedged using derivatives based on particular indices. Exhibit 9 provides some evidence on this point, reporting the performance of 11 biotechnology firms in the three months after their distribution and the performance of a biotechnology index in the same period.[13]

A second consideration was whether investors would be willing to blend their distributions with those of others. RCAI's proposed hedging strategy would only work if enough distributions could be mixed. Investors, however, might be reluctant to accept the average returns from distributions of their venture capitalists and others'. For instance, they might believe that the venture capitalists in which they invested were likely to distribute a firm like Microsoft, which appreciated sharply after its venture investors distributed it. Why should the superior postdistribution returns of their funds be blended in with the inferior returns of funds selected by other institutional investors?

A third concern was that this product would compete with those offered by some investment banks to hedge individual distributions. The bankers offered derivatives that enabled institutions to "lock in" share prices. One common offering is a "collar," which consists of an equal number of call and put options at slightly different strike (exercise) prices. For instance, if a stock is trading at $15 at the time of distribution, the institution might simultaneously enter into two transactions with an investment bank. First, the institution could sell a call to the bank with a strike price of $17 and then buy a put with a strike price of $12.50. In this way, if the price of the stock falls precipitously, the institution can sell its shares to the investment bank for $12.50. If the share price rises sharply, however, the investment bank is sure to buy the shares for $17. In this way, the institution does not need to sell immediately but can protect the profits from its venture investment.

Finally, however sound the hedging product, it might encounter resistance from potential users. Commenting on derivatives as a tool to manage distribution risks, Russell L. Carson, a partner at Welsh, Carson, Anderson and Stowe, observed:

> I'm kind of skeptical. It seems to me that this is the same kind of thing that has been getting the names of some corporate CFOs into the paper lately. And I can't think of anything that would stop your franchise faster than having to explain to your limited partners that you lost $25 million of their money because you thought you were hedging your position.[14]

An observer of the venture industry, Lisette Keto of Athena Capital Advisors, noted that "the venture capital skill set—working with people, markets and businesses—is very different from the quantitative skills needed to work with derivatives."[15]

---

[13] Biotechnology might be thought to be an industry where hedging of distributions would work particularly well, since the stock prices of many small biotechnology firms are highly correlated with each other and industry indices. Many young, publicly traded firms have no products for sale, but are focusing on developing and getting approval for new drugs. A single event, such as the U.S. Food and Drug Administration's rejection of a drug, often has triggered a reevaluation of the prospects of a large number of firms developing new drugs.

[14] Asset Alternatives, "Are Private Equity Managers Missing the Boat by Ignoring Derivatives?," *Private Equity Analyst* 4 (August 1994): p. 9.

[15] Ibid., p. 12.

Exhibit 1   The Annual Volume of Venture Capital Stock and Cash Distributions

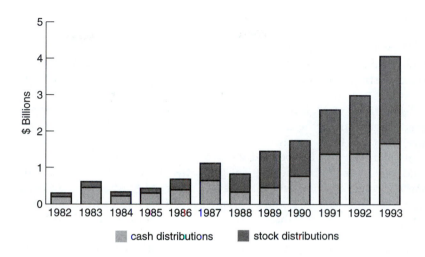

Source: Compiled from information provided by Schott Capital Management.

Exhibit 2   Securities Law Relevant to Venture Distributions[a]

Several SEC regulations are relevant to the distribution of stock by venture capitalists, especially Rules 144, 16(a), and 10(b)-5. The first governs trading in restricted and control stock; the second, reporting of insider transactions; and the third, insider trading around securities issues.

Restricted stock is defined as shares that *(i)* have not been registered with the SEC and *(ii)* are acquired directly from the firm or an affiliate (such as an officer or director). Shares purchased by a venture capitalist from a private company generally meet these two tests. At the time of the case, restricted shares could not be sold for two years, except in the case of death of the owner. Between two and three years after the original issue, the shares could be sold, but only in a limited manner. Among the requirements were that the SEC must be notified of the sale, that the sale must be done through a broker who is a market maker, and that the volume traded in any three-month period cannot be too large.[b] After three years, the shares could be traded freely.[c]

In addition, Rule 144 restricts sales of control stock, even if it is not restricted. Control stock is defined as shares owned by individuals who are affiliates of a firm, such as directors, officers, and holders of 10% of the company's shares. Sales by these parties are only allowed under the same conditions as sales of restricted stock in the two to three years after the original purchase. In a long series of no-action letters, however, the SEC has made clear that distributions from affiliates to non-affiliates (e.g., from a venture capitalist with a board seat to an institutional investor) are not subject to restrictions under Rule 144. Thus, distributions can be as large or small as the affiliate desires, and the recipient of the distribution can sell the shares as quickly as he desires.[d]

Rule 16(a) states that affiliates of a publicly traded company must disclose their ownership of shares annually and any transactions monthly. This information is made available to the public through Forms 3, 4, and 5 (as well as through proxy filings). Provision 16(a)-7, however, explicitly exempts distributions of securities that *(i)* were originally obtained from issuers and *(ii)* are being distributed "in good faith, in the ordinary course of such business." Thus, venture capitalists rarely report distributions to either the SEC or the public.

Rule 10(b)-5 is the general law limiting fraudulent activity "in connection with the purchase or sale of any security." More suits are brought under Rule 10(b)-5 than any other provision of the securities law. If several tests are met, private plaintiffs who have bought or sold shares can recover damages from the defendant. First, damages are only available under Rule 10(b)-5 to purchasers or sellers of the securities in question. Second, the plaintiffs must prove that the defendants had previous knowledge that their statements or actions were misleading. Third, it must be shown that the misrepresentations were not insignificant in nature, but rather "material." Fourth, the plaintiff must prove that he or she was actually misled by the deceptive statement or action on the part of the defendant. Fifth, there must be a casual link between the defendant's actions and the injury to the plaintiff. Finally, it must be shown that the defendant had a fiduciary duty to the shareholders of the firm. Not only are affiliates liable under this final requirement, but so are "tippees": individuals who receive information about publicly traded firms from corporate insiders. In the landmark case *Dirks vs. SEC*,[e] the U.S. Supreme Court ruled that a tippee may be liable if the individual giving the tip *(i)* had a duty not to disclose the information, and *(ii)* stood to benefit in some tangible or intangible way from providing the tip.

While the SEC has not explicitly discussed the applicability of Rule 10(b)-5 to venture capital distributions, venture capital lawyers have applied the same principles that govern the interpretation of Rules 144 and 16(a). An interpretation widely accepted within the industry is that venture capitalists distribute investments in the normal course of the investment process. Consequently, a distribution does not convey information to the limited partners. This presumption does not hold, of course, if the venture capitalist makes an explicit recommendation to either hold or immediately sell the shares. Otherwise, no presumption is typically made that an institutional investor who receives a distribution from a venture capitalist has received any information with those shares. Similarly, an institutional investor who observes that a venture capitalist has failed to distribute shares on which the lock-up period has expired has not received information from the venture capitalist.

Sources: Compiled from Harold S. Bloomenthal, *Going Public and the Public Corporation*, New York: Clark Boardman Callaghan, 1994; James Bohn and Stephen Choi, "Securities Fraud Class Actions in the New Issues Market," Unpublished working paper, Harvard University, 1994; Commerce Clearing House, *Insider Trading and Short-Swing Reporting*, Chicago: Commerce Clearing House, 1992; and assorted other sources.

[a] I thank Katherine Todd, Esq., of Brinson Partners, and Robin Painter, Esq., of Testa, Hurwitz & Thibeault, for helpful discussions of these issues. All remaining legal errors, however, are solely my fault!

[b] The volume sold by any party in a three-month period (including by relatives or any corporation or trust in which the party has a controlling interest) cannot exceed the greater of *(i)* 1% of outstanding shares or *(ii)* the average weekly trading volume in the previous four weeks.

[c] These periods have subsequently been shortened to one and two years respectively.

[d] If, however, the recipient of the distribution held a 10% stake in the company, then Rule 144 would apply. This is unlikely to be the case in distributions from venture funds, since there are usually several limited partners receiving the shares.

[e] 463 U.S. 646, 103 S.Ct. 3255 (1983).

Exhibit 3   The Net-of-Market Returns around Distributions

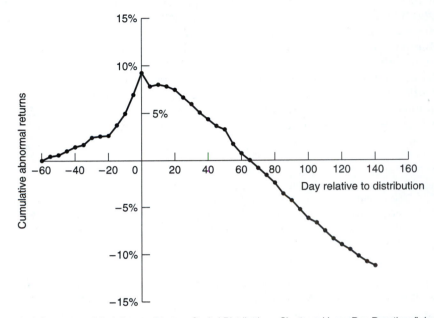

Source: Paul Gompers and Josh Lerner, "Venture Capital Distributions: Short- and Long-Run Reactions," *Journal of Finance* 53 (1998) 2161–83.

Exhibit 4 The Net-of-Market Returns Around Distributions

The pre-distribution return is the return in the period from the sixth month prior to the distribution to the month before the distribution. The distribution window return is from the period from the day of the distribution to three days after. The post-distribution return is from the month after the distribution to twelve months after.

Sample	Pre-distribution Return	Distribution Window Return	Post-distribution Return
1) Full Sample	14.2%	-2.0%	-6.8%
2) Venture Organization Age ≥ Median	15.4	-2.5	-8.3
3) Venture Organization Age < Median	12.7	-1.5	-5.0
4) High Underwriter Rank	10.2	-1.4	-0.1
5) Medium Underwriter Rank	15.8	-1.6	0.6
6) Low Underwriter Rank	14.1	-2.8	-12.9
7) Venture Capitalist Does Not Leave Board	15.8	-2.1	-6.3
8) Venture Capitalist Leaves Board of Directors	15.3	-2.8	-15.9
9) Distributions that are Larger than Median	16.4	-2.2	-6.7
10) Distributions that are Smaller than Median	10.9	-1.6	-4.3

Source: Paul Gompers and Josh Lerner, "Venture Capital Distributions: Short- and Long-Run Reactions,"*Journal of Finance*, 53 (1998) 2161-83.

Exhibit 5   Five Major Competitors to RCAI in Distribution Management

HLM Management

HLM Management, Boston, Mass., processes stock distributions as part of its overall micro-cap stock management services and later-stage venture capital investment program. Formed in 1983 by A.R. Haberkorn, a partner at Harvard Management Company, Judith Lawrie, a senior analyst with Endowment Management & Research Corp., and James Mahoney, general partner of Cowen & Co., the firm "covers the waterfront" of entrepreneurially managed, growth companies, says Ms. Lawrie. Five general partners, assisted by a full-time trader, manage a group of limited partnerships designed to invest in both small-cap public and later-stage private companies. It also invests, as a limited partner, in both venture partnerships and direct venture deals.

The firm's investment approach calls for mandatory in-person meetings with management because "it's important to kick the tires before buying a car," Mr. Haberkorn says. HLM runs two types of stock distribution accounts for its clients, mostly pensions and endowments. The "stand-alone discretionary account," essentially a "hold or sell" account, is funded by distributions received. Ms. Lawrie says this format of stock distribution management is still the most popular with clients. HLM also manages a discretionary stock distribution account that takes in distributions and, with pool of cash set aside by the client, buys pre-distribution stocks during their post-IPO honeymoon period.

QCI Asset Management

QCI Asset Management, Rochester, N.Y., an employee-owned investment advisor, initiated a venture capital stock distribution program in 1988 when it hired Mr. Gavagan, the former director of the investment office at the University of Rochester.

Mr. Gavagan had been with the university endowment for four years and during that time oversaw management of in-kind venture distributions. When he moved across town to join QCI as executive vice president and principal, Mr. Gavagan brought the university's venture distribution business with him.   At that time, the endowment held about $60 million of venture capital partnerships and around $25 million of direct private equity investments.   In addition to the University of Rochester, QCI advises Worcester Polytechnic Institute on its venture capital stock distributions. QCI integrates the management of venture capital distributions with the management of clients' small-cap, emerging growth company holdings. Managing more than $375 million in assets, QCI runs about $40 million of small-cap and newly public, venture-backed stocks.

It offers only end-game distribution management services to investors in venture capital limited partnerships, through both "hold or sell" and "integrated" accounts. QCI neither advises clients on fund investments, nor invests for them.

Shott Capital Management

Founded in 1991 by Mr. Shott, San Francisco-based Shott Capital Management is truly a venture distribution specialist. Administering venture capital stock distributions is its only line of business. Mr. Shott's first venture distribution client was Thomas Ford, general partner of Ford Land Co., developer of 3000 Sand Hill Road. The endowments of Stanford University and the University of Southern California also are clients.

Mr. Shott, Paul Reese, formerly a general partner at TA Associates and founder of First Chicago's first post-venture fund, and three other employees analyze distributions using a "portfolio" approach. The firm has found that evaluating each stock based on how it fits into a client's overall portfolio is the best way to identify big winners. "The key is not to analyze distributions in a vacuum," Mr. Reese says. While it primarily makes hold or sell decisions on behalf of its clients, Shott will buy additional shares of winning stocks in the market for some accounts.

Because the firm is "dedicated to the universe of companies distributed by venture capitalists, [Shott] pledges to know every stock prior to its emergence as an IPO," explains Mr. Reese. To help it keep that promise, Shott last month forged a strategic alliance with Cowen & Co. (Although both groups declined to disclose the details, Stephen Weber, managing director at Cowen, says that his firm, in effect, became a minority shareholder in Shott. In return, Shott gets access to Cowen's research capabilities and other resources.) Like other management distribution specialists, Shott manages distributions on an individual account basis. It also runs two commingled post-venture funds, Technology 2000 and BETA.

T. Rowe Price Associates

The $40 billion fund manager T. Rowe Price Associates, Inc. runs a venture distribution investment service as part of its emerging company investment division. The investment activity of this unit ranges from venture capital to young public companies. Its products include mutual funds, separately managed portfolios, and limited partnerships. T. Rowe Price's venture distribution management service makes only hold or sell decisions and returns all cash proceeds to its clients once stocks are sold, according to Preston Athey, vice president and equity portfolio manager in the emerging company investment division and the head of the venture distribution investment service.

In evaluating the potential of stock distributions received, T. Rowe Price uses the NASDAQ Composite Index as a benchmark. Shares are sold when the advisor determines they can no longer outperform the benchmark.

Clients are managed on an account-by-account basis, Mr. Athey says. "Every account stands on its own and every stock stands on its own." The investment manager's venture distribution client list includes E.I. du Pont de Nemours, the R.K. Mellon Foundation, Sprint Master Trust, the State of Minnesota, and the Meyer Memorial Trust.

From its inception in 1986 through December 1992, the distribution management service has processed distributions of over 177 venture-backed companies and completed 840 sales. Two-thirds of all the venture distributions sold outperformed the over-the-counter market during their holding periods.

Warburg, Pincus

At the request of one of the largest venture capital investors, AT&T, Warburg, Pincus Counsellors' Small Capitalization Equity Management Group began offering post-venture services in 1989. "Having already paid the price of admission to winners as limited partners in venture partnerships," the corporate pension thought it ridiculous to cash out at the venture distribution only to have their small-cap manager buy the same stock in the open market, remembers Richard Klemm, senior vice president.

The firm currently offers three investment programs:

- A hold/sell arrangement in which proceeds from the sale of distributed stock are returned to the client.

- A buy/sell arrangement in which proceeds are used for the open market purchase of securities distributed by other venture capital partnerships.

- A buy/sell arrangement in which the cash proceeds from the sale of distributed stocks are used to purchase other emerging growth stocks not typically found in venture portfolios.

The post-venture/emerging growth services group can seek advice from 13 research analysts with Warburg, Pincus Counsellors and can also leverage the resources of the E.M. Warburg Pincus venture banking subsidiary. The post-venture research team, for instance, meets periodically with Warburg Pincus' technology advisory committee. Warburg, Pincus manages close to $300 million in its post-venture accounts. Its clients participate in over 215 funds managed by over 120 firms.

Source: Excerpted from Kathleen Devlin, "The Post-Venture Dilemma," *Venture Capital Journal*, 33 (May 1993), pp. 33-34.

Exhibit 6   RogersCasey Profile

RogersCasey
One Parklands Drive
Darien, CT 06820

Stephen Rogers, Chairman
John F. Casey, President & Chief Executive Officer
Del Budzinski, Managing Director-Consulting
Robin S. Pellish, Managing Director-Consulting
R. Barry Thomas, Managing Director-Consulting
Steven C. Case, Director-Consulting
Drew W. Demakis, Director-Consulting
Timothy R. Barron, Senior Consultant
Venita L. Bullock, Senior Consultant
Adele Langie Heller, Associate Consultant
Elizabeth L. DeLalla, Research-US Equities
Narayan Ramachandran, Research-US Equities &
    Investment Technology
Carla P. Haugen, Research-Alternative Investments
A.Duff Lewis, Jr., Research-Alternative Investments
Gary J.Kominski, Research-Alternative Investments
Matthew R. Jensen, Research-International
    Investments
Reza Vishkai, Associate Director-International
    Investments
Jeffrey K. Feldman, Research-Fixed Income &
    Derivatives
Gregory T. Rogers, Research-Fixed Income &
    Derivatives
Robert Capaldi, Research-Investment Technology
Ruth Hughes-Guden, Research-Defined Contribution
    Services
Eleanor A. Burns, Research-Defined Contribution
    Services & Master Trustee-Recordkeeping
Philip A. Cooper, Research-Alternative Investments
Peter J. Gavey, Research-Alternative Investments
Dan Lew, Research-NDT
Thomas K. Philips, Director-Advanced Research
John Picone, Portfolio Manager-Alternative
    Investments
Gregg A. Robinson, Research-Defined Contribution
    Services
Gregory T. Rogers, Research-Fixed Income &
    Derivatives

RogersCasey offers a broad scope of investment
services to its clients: full service consulting,
consulting in the area of alternative investments,
special advisory programs (i.e., multi-manager mutual
fund programs) and investment manager diagnostics.
RogersCasey provides its clients with active
investment solutions. Our practice is driven by
applied research techniques, substantial industry
experience, and a commitment to investigation and
evaluation of innovative solutions.

SERVICES

Alternative Investments
Asset Allocation
Asset/Liability Modeling
Client Monitoring/Reporting
Custodian or Master Trustee Search Selection
Due Diligence
Database/Publications
Global Manager Search
International Manager Search
Investment Policy/Objectives
Liability Analysis
Manager Evaluation
Manager Search/Selection
Manager Structure Analysis
Minority/Emerging Managers
Mutual Fund Evaluation/Management
New Theories
Options and Futures
Performance Attribution
Performance Measurement/Analysis
Portfolio Optimization
Quantitative Analysis
Real Estate Manager Evaluation
Reports/Custom Research
Seminars and Lectures
Socially Conscious Investing
Software
Strategic Planning Services

MANAGER DATABASE

Established: 1976
Managers tracked:
    Domestic: 930
    International: 125
    Global: 100
    Equity: 500
    Fixed Income: 250
    Balanced: 210
    Specialty: 180

DATABASE: PIPER

Our database of historical return information is made
available to the institutional community under the
name PIPER (Pension & Investments Evaluation
Report). We produce the PIPER Commingled Funds
report which tracks the performance of bank
commingled funds and insurance company separate
accounts. PIPER Managed Accounts is a similar
database tracking the performance and other
statistical data on independent investment advisors
representative composite accounts. Approximately
ninety percent of all institutional assets are
represented in our PIPER databases. There is no
charge to managers to be included in the PIPER
database.

INVESTMENT ADVISORY SERVICES

Global Developing Markets Fund, a commingled group trust deploying multiple managers to invest in emerging markets around the world. Development funds that contain multiple managers to access new investment strategies or lesser known investment talent. Savings Plan Alternatives that offer an individually tailored selection of mutual funds for retirement, thrift and 401(k) plan assets.

CLIENTS

AlliedSignal, Inc.
American Cyanamid Company
Amphenol Corp.
Appleton Mills
Asea, Brown, Boveri, Inc.
Avon Products, Inc.
BASF Corp.
Bowater, Inc.
Champion International Corp.
Citizens Utilities Co.
Cowles Media Co.
Dexter Corporation
E.I. DuPont de Nemours & Co.
Eastman Kodak Company
Electronic Data Systems Corp.
Fairfax County Retirement Funds
Federated Department Stores, Inc.
FPL Group, Inc.
Gannettt Co., Inc.
GATX Corporation
General Electric Investment Corporation
Group Health, Inc.
GTE Financial Services
Health Insurance Plan of Greater New York, Inc.

Honeywell, Inc.
Insilco Corporation
Axel Johnson, Inc.
Kimberly-Clark Corporation
The Kroger Co.
Lawrence & Memorial Hospitals
Mark IV Industries, Inc.
Mead Corporation
The Mead Corporation Foundation
Michigan Consolidated Gas Co.
New York City Teachers' Variable Fund
New York State Teachers' Retirement System
Northwestern University
Norwich City Employees' Retirement System
Pennsylvania State Employees' Retirement System
Phelps Dodge Corporation
Public Service Electric & Gas Company of New Jersey
RJR Nabisco, Inc.
Rochester Gas & Electric Corp.
Rochester Telephone Corporation
Rush Presbyterian-St. Luke's Medical Center
Saint-Gobain Corporation
Saks Fifth Avenue
Springs Industries, Inc.
Stamford Hospital
The Stanley Works
Texas Instruments, Inc.
Unisys Corp.
University of Colorado at Boulder
University of Missouri System
US WEST, Inc.
Veterans Memorial Medical Center
Virginia Retirement System
Washington Gas Light Company
Witco Corp.
Ziff Communications Co.

Source: Money Market Directories, *Money Market Directory of Pension Funds and their Investment Managers*, Charlottesville: Money Market Directories, 1995.

Exhibit 7 RogersCasey Alternative Investments: Number of Investment Recommendations, 1988-1993

	1988	1989	1990	1991	1992	1993
Funds Evaluated						
Venture capital	91	129	131	96	157	118
Buyouts/mezzanine	48	29	27	9	14	33
Distressed debt	17	19	18	31	19	15
Oil and gas	15	16	15	8	14	11
Timber	0	0	0	0	0	11
Other	0	0	14	9	30	31
Total	171	193	205	153	234	219
Funds Recommended						
Venture capital	6	6	2	5	10	1
Buyouts/mezzanine	6	1	1	1	1	2
Distressed debt	1	0	0	1	0	0
Oil and gas	1	0	1	0	0	0
Timber	0	0	0	0	0	1
Total	14	7	4	7	11	4
Fund Returns						
Recommended funds	18.3%	15.4%	2.4%	1.4%	0.3%	-1.1%
Weighted benchmark index	11.2%	4.8%	0.0%	-2.9%	-10.6%	15.4%

Source: Corporate documents.

Exhibit 8   RogersCasey Alternative Investments: Biographies

Philip A. Cooper
Chairman and Chief Executive Officer

See biography in the text of the case.

Carla P. Haugen
Managing Director

A graduate of the University of Minnesota and the Harvard Business School, Ms. Haugen has managed RogersCasey's alternative investment activities for five years and serves as a member of the firm's operating committee. She has overall responsibility for clients' private equity investments. Prior to joining the firm, Carla had seven years' experience in venture capital and leveraged buyout investing at Oak Investment Partners and Exxon Enterprises.

A. Duff Lewis, Jr.
Managing Director

Mr. Lewis joined RogersCasey's alternative investment group after 26 years with the Eastman Kodak Company. He spent the last nine years there on the Treasurer's staff, working on investments for its $8⬛+ billion pension plans. Prior to working on pension investments, Duff accumulated ten years of experience on the corporate financial planning and analysis staff. Mr. Lewis is a member of the Institute of Chartered Financial Analysts, and holds an M.S. from Purdue's Krannert School of Management.

Thomas K. Philips
Managing Director of Advanced Research

Dr. Philips joined RogersCasey in 1993. He divides his time between RCAI and advanced research projects for RogersCasey. Prior to joining RogersCasey, Dr. Philips spent eight years at the IBM Corporation. The first five were spent at the Thomas J. Watson Research Center, and the last three at the IBM Retirement Fund, where he was responsible for a number of quantitative research projects. Dr. Philips received a Ph.D. in Electrical and Computer Engineering from the University of Massachusetts, Amherest.

John Picone, Jr.
Managing Director

Mr. Picone joined RCAI in 1993, after 14 years with Metropolitan Life Insurance Company and two with Bankers Trust. At MetLife, he was solely responsible for developing and managing its $100 million small-capitalization public investment program, which generated a five-year average return of 25%. During the same period, he also solely managed the Company's venture capital program, which was invested in 42 limited partnerships and 20 direct placements. Prior to that, Mr. Picone managed a large-capitalization equity portfolio and was a securities analyst. He holds an M.B.A. from University of North Carolina at Chapel Hill.

Gary J. Kominski
Director

A graduate of the University of Pennsylvania, Mr. Kominski manages partnership and direct investments and securities distributions. Prior to joining the firm, Gary had six years' experience working with a broad array of alternative investments at Salomon Brothers, Concord Partners (the venture capital arm of Dillon, Read & Co. and Northtown Realty. He also spent four years with the Irving Trust Company, for whom he managed their Grand Cayman facility.

Peter J. Gavey
Senior Analyst

Mr. Gavey joined RCAI from Gabelli & Co., where he worked for nearly four years. During his last two years of employment there, he worked as a securities analyst, trader, and portfolio administrator in the risk arbitrage unit. He holds a B.S. in Management from Fairfield University.

Marsha Tinguely
Senior Analyst

Prior to joining RCAI, Ms. Tinguely had five years' experience in pension consulting, investment research, and private equity due diligence at Principal Financial Securities' Pension Consulting Group, the Renaissance Capital Group (a late-stage venture fund), and Siecor, Inc. She holds a B.S. in Economics and Finance from the University of Texas.

Patrice Bottari
Administrative Assistant

Ms. Bottari is Philip Cooper's Administrative Assistant and supports RCAI's office in Bedford, Massachusetts. Prior to joining RCAI, she spent six years with a start-up biotech company and AT&T American Transtech. She holds an Associate's Degree in Business Administration from Northeastern University.

Donna Rosequist
Administrative Assistant

Ms. Rosequist is the administrative assistant for RCAI's Darien, Connecticut office. Her responsibilities include the coordination and production of periodic client reports and special research reports, and the maintenance of key databases. Prior to joining RCAI, she worked at International Capital Partners and Control Data Corporation in various administrative and financial positions. She holds a B.A. and M.B.A. from the University of Connecticut.

Source: Corporate documents.

Exhibit 9   Biotechnology Firm Stock Price and Biotechnology Stock Index Around Distributions

	On Day Before Distribution		Three Months Later	
Observation	Stock Price	Biotech Index	Stock Price	Biotech Index
Distribution 1	10	1.06	12.75	1.30
Distribution 2	21.25	1.12	11.25	0.77
Distribution 3	35	1.25	27.25	1.48
Distribution 4	24	0.84	24.25	1.01
Distribution 5	21	1.41	22.875	1.12
Distribution 6	18.75	1.52	15.75	1.02
Distribution 7	18.25	1.08	8	0.84
Distribution 8	13.625	0.98	9.75	0.86
Distribution 9	7.375	0.78	8.25	0.93
Distribution 10	20.5	1.21	22.25	1.44
Distribution 11	7.625	0.91	8.125	0.95

Source: Casewriter's analysis. The biotechnology index is computed by the casewriter by examining the returns from a "buy-and-hold" investment in thirteen biotechnology stocks

TRANSPLANTING THE PRIVATE EQUITY MODEL

The final module reviews many of the key ideas developed in *Venture Capital and Private Equity.* Rather than considering traditional private equity organizations, however, the two cases examine organizations with very different goals from the ones we have considered previously. Large corporations, government agencies, and nonprofit organizations are increasingly emulating private equity funds. Their goals, however, are quite different: for example, to more effectively commercialize internal research projects or to revitalize distressed areas. These cases will allow us not only to understand these exciting and challenging initiatives, but to review the elements crucial to the success of traditional private equity organizations.

WHY THIS MODULE?

Since corporate and public venture capital initiatives are so different from traditional private equity funds, one may wonder why these cases are included. There are three main reasons. First, this arena is the focus of intensive activity of late. These funds today are important investors. Second, it is difficult to examine the issues faced in adapting the private equity model without thinking about the rationales for the key features of traditional private equity funds. Thus, this section of the course allows us to review and revisit many of the issues we have considered in the previous three modules. Finally, corporate venture capital programs, in particular, provide an interesting alternative way to break into the private equity field that few students consider.

Interest in adopting the private equity model has exploded in recent years. In an era when many large firms are questioning the productivity of their investments in traditional R&D laboratories, venture organizations represent an intriguing alternative for corporate America. Much of the interest has been stimulated by the recent success of the independent venture sector. While total disbursements from the venture industry over the past two decades have been far less than the R&D spending of either IBM or General Motors, the economic successes of venture-backed firms—such as Intel, Microsoft, Genentech, Thermo Electron, and Cisco Systems—have been profound. The *Private Equity Analyst* estimates that at least two dozen such programs were launched in 1996 alone.[1] Meanwhile, several leading private equity

This case was prepared by Josh Lerner. Copyright © 1996 by the President and Fellows of Harvard College. Harvard Business School case 297-043.

[1] Asset Alternatives, "Corporate Venturing Bounces Back, with Internet Acting as Springboard," *Private Equity Analyst* 6 (August 1996): 1, 18–19.

organizations—including Kleiner, Perkins, Caufield & Byers and Advent International—have begun or expanded funds dedicated to making strategic investments alongside corporations.

The growth of venture funds organized by public and nonprofit bodies has been even more striking. Recent estimates suggest that close to 40% of venture or venture-like disbursements in the United States—and more than half of early-stage investments—came in 1995 from "social" sources: those whose primary goal was not a high economic return. Nor has this activity been confined to the United States. Governments in dozens of countries have established significant public venture programs. In recent years, nonprofit organizations have also become increasingly active in encouraging and overseeing venture funds. Some of America's largest and most prestigious foundations, such as the Ford and McArthur Foundations, have been particularly active backers of community development venture funds. An interesting new trend has been the involvement of successful private equity investors, most notably Henry Kravis, as investors in and advisers to community development funds.

A second reason for the inclusion of this module is that it allows us to review and think about the key features of independent private equity firms. In particular, in adopting the private equity model, features of independent funds have been adjusted or altered. In some cases, these changes have been benign; but in others, the consequences have been disastrous. By reviewing successful and failed modifications of the private equity model to serve the goals of corporate, public, and nonprofit organizations, we will gain a deeper understanding of how traditional funds work. During discussions, we will return repeatedly to the frameworks developed in the earlier modules of the course.

Finally, corporate venture capital programs represent an interesting avenue for entry into the private equity field that relatively few students consider. The intense competition for jobs in traditional private equity organizations allows many funds to demand that new hires already have a demonstrated investment track record. Yet it is difficult to develop such a track record without a job in the industry. Corporations are often much more willing to hire candidates directly out of school. If one can successfully make one's way into a corporate venture group, it can provide valuable experience and serve as a stepping-stone to a position at an independent private equity firm.

CORPORATE VENTURE CAPITAL

The first corporate venture funds were engendered by the successes of the early venture capital funds, which backed such firms as Digital Equipment, Memorex, Raychem, and Scientific Data Systems. Excited by this success, large companies began establishing venture divisions. During the late 1960s and early 1970s, more than 25% of the Fortune 500 firms attempted corporate venture programs.

These generally took two forms, external and internal. At one end of the spectrum, large corporations financed new firms alongside other venture capitalists. In many cases, the corporations simply provided funds for a venture capitalist to invest. Other firms invested directly in start-ups, which gave them a greater ability to tailor their portfolios to their particular needs. At the other extreme, large corporations attempted to tap the entrepreneurial spirit within their organizations. These programs sought to establish a conducive environment for creativity and innovation within the corporate workplace. In an ideal world, internal venture programs allowed entrepreneurs to focus their attention on developing their innovations, while relying on the corporation for financial, legal, and marketing support.

In 1973, the market for new public offerings—the primary avenue through which venture capitalists exit successful investments—abruptly declined. Independent venture partnerships began experiencing much less attractive returns and encountered severe difficulties in raising new funds. At the same time, corporations began scaling back their own initiatives. The typical corporate venture program begun in the late 1960s was dissolved after only four years.

Fueled by eased restrictions on pension investing and a robust market for public offerings, fundraising by independent venture partnerships recovered in the early 1980s. Corporations were once again attracted to the promise of venture investing. These efforts peaked in 1986, when corporate funds managed $2 billion, or nearly 12% of the total pool of venture capital. After the stock market crash of 1987, however, the market for new public offerings again went into a prolonged decline. Returns of and fundraising by independent partnerships declined sharply. Corporations scaled back their commitment to venture investing even more dramatically. By 1992, the number of corporate venture programs had fallen by one-third and their capital under management represented only 5% of the venture pool.

As has been often pointed out in this course, the entire venture capital industry is cyclical. So too has been corporate venturing. At the same time, it appears that the decline of the earlier corporate venture programs was also due to three structural failings. First, these programs suffered from a lack of well-defined missions. Typically, they sought to accomplish a wide array of not necessarily compatible objectives: from providing a window on emerging technologies to generating attractive financial returns. This confusion over program objectives often led to dissatisfaction. For instance, when outside venture capitalists were hired to run a corporate fund under a contract that linked compensation to financial performance, management frequently became frustrated about their failure to invest in the technologies that most interested the firm.

A second cause of failure was insufficient corporate commitment to the venturing initiative. Even if top management embraced the concept, middle management often resisted. R&D personnel preferred that the funds be devoted to internal programs; corporate lawyers disliked the novelty and complexity of these hybrid organizations. New senior management teams in many cases terminated programs, seeing them as expendable "pet projects" of their predecessors. Even if they did not object to the idea of the program, managers often were concerned about its impact on the firm's accounting earnings. During periods of financial pressure, money-losing subsidiaries were frequently terminated in an effort to increase reported operating earnings.

A final cause of failure was inadequate compensation schemes. Corporations have frequently been reluctant to compensate their venture managers through profit-sharing ("carried interest") provisions, fearing that they might need to make huge payments if their investments were successful. Typically, successful risk-taking was inadequately rewarded and failure excessively punished. As a result, corporations were frequently unable to attract top people (i.e., those who combined industry experience with connections to other venture capitalists) to run their venture funds. All too often, corporate venture managers adopted a conservative approach to investing. Nowhere was this behavior more clearly manifested than in the treatment of lagging ventures. Independent venture capitalists ruthlessly terminate funding to failing firms because they want to devote their limited energy to firms with the greatest promise. Corporate venture capitalists have frequently been unwilling to write off unsuccessful ventures, lest they incur the reputational repercussions that a failure would entail.

An illustration of these difficulties is Analog Devices' venture subsidiary, Analog Devices Enterprises (ADE).[2] Analog Devices decided to establish a corporate venture program in 1980. Through these investments, it hoped to gain both attractive financial returns and strategic benefits in the form of licensing agreements and acquisitions. Funds for these investments were provided by Amoco. By 1985, ADE had invested $26 million in 11 firms. The ADE program was suspended in that year, after Amoco ceased contributing capital. Around the time the investment program was terminated, Analog Devices took a $7 million charge against earnings; in 1990, when most of the portfolio was liquidated, it took another $12 million charge. Of the 11 firms in ADE's portfolio, most were terminated, acquired by other companies at unattractive valuations, or joined the "living dead" (ongoing companies whose prospects are so marginal that they cannot be taken public or otherwise harvested). Only one of the firms ultimately went public. In this case, ADE's stake was so diluted by a merger that it was only worth about $2 million at the time of the offering.

The failure of the ADE program can be attributed to several of the concerns outlined above. The program managers were hampered by the lack of a clear objective: they were urged to invest in firms pursuing technologies relevant to the ongoing businesses of Analog and Amoco, to obtain options to acquire firms that interested Analog's management, and to generate high financial returns. Analog Devices' researchers, who saw scarce resources being devoted to ADE, resented the program. Amoco only committed to fund the program for five years, much less time than was needed to grow the early-stage companies. Finally, the incentives of the various parties appear to have been improperly aligned. Not only did the management of ADE believe that they were insufficiently rewarded, but Amoco did not share in the profits generated.

Consequently, concerns linger about attempts to replicate the success of venture capital firms in the corporate setting. The previous two surges in corporate venture capital, like today's activity, were stimulated by well-publicized successes of independent venture investors. When their initial venture investments faltered in the past, corporations rapidly abandoned their programs. Avoiding the mistakes of the past is a major challenge for corporate venture capital programs today. In this module, we will explore how one corporate venture fund is seeking to address these challenges.

PUBLIC AND COMMUNITY DEVELOPMENT VENTURE CAPITAL

The primary motivation in 1946 for the founders of the world's first private equity fund, American Research and Development, was largely not the creation of profits.

---

[2] This account is drawn from David H. Knights, "Analog Devices Enterprises/Bipolar Integrated Technology," Harvard Business School Case No. 9-286-117, 1985; Rosabeth Moss Kanter, Jeffery North, Ann Piaget Bernstein, and Alistair Williamson, "Engines of Progress: Designing and Running Entrepreneurial Vehicles in Established Companies," *Journal of Business Venturing* 5 (1990): 415–30; Bruce G. Posner, "Mutual Benefits," *Inc.* 5 (June 1984): 83–92; and various press accounts and securities filings.

Rather, it was the encouragement of economic growth in the United States and New England. As founder (and former Harvard Business School professor) General Georges Doriot responded, when confronted by some investors who complained about the slow progress of many of his investments:

> You sophisticated stockholders make five points and sell out. But we have our hearts in our companies: we are really doctors of childhood diseases here. When bankers or brokers tell me I should sell an ailing company, I ask them, "Would you sell a child running a temperature of 104?"[3]

Although American Research and Development sought to combine social goals with profits, the Small Business Investment Company (SBIC) program is generally regarded as the first explicit "social venture capital" endeavor. This program was launched by the U.S. government in 1958 in the aftermath of the Soviet Union's launch of the world's first satellite Sputnik. The level of social venture activity remained relatively modest until the late 1970s. During the past 15 years, over 100 state and federal initiatives have been launched. European and Asian nations have also undertaken many similar initiatives. Although these programs' precise structures have differed, the efforts have been predicated on two shared assumptions: (1) that the private sector provides insufficient capital to new firms, at least in certain regions or industries, and (2) that government or nonprofit officials can identify firms in which investments will ultimately yield high social and/or private returns.

Although the sums of money involved are modest relative to public expenditures on defense procurement or retiree benefits, these programs are substantial when compared to contemporaneous private investments in new firms. For instance, the SBIC program led to the provision of more than $3 billion to young firms between 1958 and 1969, more than three times the total private venture capital investment during these years. In 1995, the sum of the financing provided through and guaranteed by social venture capital programs in the United States was at least $2.4 billion. This sum was substantial relative to the $3.9 billion disbursed by traditional venture funds in that year. Perhaps more significantly, the bulk of these funds was for early-stage firms, which in the past decade have only accounted for about 30% of the disbursements by traditional venture funds. Some of America's most dynamic technology companies received support through these programs while still private entities, including Apple Computer, Chiron, Compaq, Federal Express, and Intel. Public venture capital programs have also had a significant impact overseas. Germany, for instance, has created over the past two decades about 800 federal and state government financing programs for new firms, which provide the bulk of the external financing for technology-intensive start-ups.

Many of the same problems that haunt corporate venture programs, however, also bedevil social venture initiatives. Among them are the difficulty of balancing multiple objectives, the investors' frequent failure to appreciate the long-run nature of these investments, and the struggle to design appropriate compensation schemes. In this module, we will examine one community development venture fund's efforts to overcome these barriers.

---

[3] Patrick Liles, *Sustaining the Venture Capital Firm,* Cambridge, Management Analysis Center, 1977, page 70.

FURTHER READING ON CORPORATE AND SOCIAL VENTURE CAPITAL

Practitioner Accounts and Studies about Corporate Venture Capital

ASSET ALTERNATIVES, "Corporate Venturing Bounces Back, with Internet Acting as Springboard," *Private Equity Analyst* 6 (August 1996): 1 and 18–19.

ZENAS BLOCK AND OSCAR A. ORNATI, "Compensating Corporate Venture Managers," *Journal of Business Venturing* 2 (1987): 41–52.

NORMAN D. FAST, *The Rise and Fall of Corporate New Venture Divisions,* Ann Arbor, UMI Research Press, 1978.

ROBERT E. GEE, "Finding and Commercializing New Businesses," *Research/Technology Management* 37 (January/February 1994): 49–56.

PAUL A. GOMPERS AND JOSH LERNER, *The Venture Capital Cycle,* Cambridge, MIT Press, 1999, chapter 5.

G. FELDA HARDYMON, MARK J. DENINO, AND MALCOLM S. SALTER, "When Corporate Venture Capital Doesn't Work," *Harvard Business Review* 61 (May–June 1983): 114–120.

E. LAWLER AND J. DREXEL, *The Corporate Entrepreneur,* Los Angeles, Center for Effective Organizations, Graduate School of Business Administration, University of Southern California, 1980.

KENNETH W. RIND, "The Role of Venture Capital in Corporate Development," *Strategic Management Journal* 2 (April 1981): 169–180.

ROBIN SIEGEL, ERIC SIEGEL, AND IAN C. MACMILLAN, "Corporate Venture Capitalists: Autonomy, Obstacles, and Performance," *Journal of Business Venturing* 3 (1988): 233–247.

Practitioner Accounts and Studies about Social Venture Capital

PETER EISENGER, "The State of State Venture Capitalism," *Economic Development Quarterly* 5 (February 1991): 64–76.

PETER EISENGER, "State Venture Capitalism, State Politics, and the World of High-Risk Investment," *Economic Development Quarterly* 7 (May 1993): 131–139.

JOSH LERNER, "The Government as Venture Capitalist: An Empirical Analysis of the SBIR Program," *Journal of Business* 72 (1999): 285–318.

CHARLES M. NOONE AND STANLEY M. RUBEL, *SBICs: Pioneers in Organized Venture Capital,* Chicago, Capital Publishing, 1970.

STEVEN J. WADDELL, "Emerging Socio-Economic Institutions in the Venture Capital Industry: An Appraisal," *American Journal of Economics and Sociology* 54 (July 1995): 323–338.

27

Xerox Technology Ventures: March 1995

Robert V. Adams, president, CEO and senior principal of Xerox Technology Ventures, contemplated the changes in his organization over its first five years of life. In conjunction with his partners Robert Curtin and Jeffrey Tung, he had designed and implemented a structure for a corporate venturing program and gained acceptance within the Xerox Corporation. This organization had enabled Xerox to commercialize a number of innovations that would have otherwise been developed outside of Xerox, or else been retained by the Corporation only after protracted intellectual property litigation.

While remaining true to his initial vision, the organization's design had evolved over the past five years as unanticipated challenges appeared. Perhaps more significantly, XTV's objectives had also evolved, from a narrow focus in investing in new technologies to the pursuit of a variety of investment opportunities, including acquisitions of divisions that Xerox wished to divest. How would this broadened mission, he wondered, affect the evolution of XTV over the next five years?

XEROX CORPORATION

The Xerox Corporation originated as a photography-paper business called the Haloid Company. The Haloid Company's entrance into what would later become its principal business came in 1947 when it and Battelle Memorial Institute, a research organization, agreed to produce a machine based on the recently developed process named xerography. Invented by a patent lawyer named Chester Carlson, xerography—Greek for "dry" and "writing"—involved a process by which images were transferred from one piece of paper to another by means of static electricity. By 1949, the Haloid company introduced its first copier based on this technology. Although this first machine, the XeroX Copier, was rudimentary and required the majority of its processing to be done manually, the company still managed to sell many of the units and to invest the earnings into research on the second-generation copier.

The Haloid Company in the 1950s was characterized by rapid growth and a redirection of the company's emphasis toward xerography. By 1955, only five years after the first copier contract was signed, Haloid converted its 18 regional offices into showrooms

This case was prepared by Brian Hunt and Josh Lerner. Copyright © 1995 by the President and Fellows of Harvard College. Harvard Business School case 295-127.

for its Xerox machines. By 1958, Haloid would change its name to Haloid-Xerox, indicating the direction of the company away from photography products.

At the turn of the decade, Haloid-Xerox introduced its Xerox 914 copier. The copier had the designation of being both the first automatic Xerox copier and the first plain-paper copier. Although extremely bulky, it was an undoubted success. Haloid-Xerox's sales and rentals of xerographic products doubled in 1961 and continued to grow. In that same year, Haloid-Xerox became the Xerox Corporation.

In light of its success the new Xerox Corporation began to expand. Haloid had already formed the overseas affiliate Rank Xerox with the Rank Organization, a British film company. In addition to taking advantage of the British market, Xerox sought to exploit those in the Far East, forming Fuji Xerox in an alliance with Fuji Photo Film Company of Japan. Xerox maintained this growth throughout the 1960s, opening subsidiaries in Australia, Mexico, and continental Europe, and making various acquisitions, including University Microfilms and Electro-Optical Systems.

In response to IBM's entrance into the copier field in the late 1960s, Xerox experimented with computers and with designing an electronic office of the future. It formed Xerox Computer Services (XCS), acquired Scientific Data Systems (SDS), and opened its Palo Alto Research Center (PARC) in California. XCS, SDS, and PARC were only the beginning of the copier giant's effort to become a force in the computer industry. Throughout the 1970s, Xerox completed several acquisitions in order to further its project for an "architecture of information." Unfortunately, in assembling these noncopier companies and opening PARC, Xerox created a clash of cultures. Differences between its East Coast operations and West Coast computer people would severely impact the company.

The focus for much of this division was PARC. In the 1970s, PARC was remarkably successful in developing ingenious products that would fundamentally alter the nature of computing. The Ethernet, the graphical user interface (the basis of Apple Computer's and Microsoft's Windows software), the "mouse," and the laser printer were all originally developed at PARC. The culmination of much of PARC's innovation was its development of the Alto, a very early bit-mapped computer. The Alto's first prototype was completed in 1973, and later versions were placed in the White House, Congress, and various companies and universities. The key technology in the Alto project was licensed to Apple Computer, after Xerox made $1 million investment in the start-up (which ultimately was worth $50 million). This license included a contract for Xerox to sell the resulting "Lisa" (and subsequent "Macintosh") computer developed by Apple. Xerox, however, terminated the contract, preferring to proceed with its own "Star" computer, which failed in the marketplace after being offered for $25,000.

Inherent in the Star's demise was Xerox's relationship with PARC. Xerox did not have a clear-cut product strategy for its research laboratory, and in turn many of PARC's technologies did not fit into Xerox's strategic objectives. Although it failed to cash in on many of PARC's innovations, Xerox did identify the promise of the laboratory's laser printing technologies. Under the leadership of Robert Adams, Xerox went on to dominate the high-end laser printing business, a sector that generated over $2 billion in revenue for the firm in 1994. Xerox encountered competitive pressures as it attempted to grow during the 1960s. Its main competitor, the Japanese, made great strides in developing copiers. Xerox spent heavily on product development but had trouble introducing new low-cost products and maintaining market share. This drop was compounded during the 1970s, as Japanese companies and later IBM began to make smaller, less expensive, and more efficient copiers that significantly challenged Xerox.

Therefore, in the late 1970s the company began to focus on regaining market share. It reorganized and began to benchmark both American and Japanese companies. This extensive benchmarking was meant to increase business effectiveness in various areas, including quality control and manufacturing costs. Xerox's revamping triggered a comeback for the company. During the 1980s, Xerox introduced a wealth of new products. Xerox's new Memorywriter typewriter had the capability of storing large amounts of data internally and soon outsold IBM's. Xerox unveiled its first new line of copiers since the 1960s, the 10-series copiers. These copiers marked Xerox's entry into the low-end copier market. Meanwhile, PARC was beginning to conduct research that was more integrated with the company's strategic objectives. Other developments spurred by Xerox's commitment to research and development included computer workstations and software, and technological advances in digital copying.

The 1980s also marked Xerox's entrance into the financial services. Xerox began Xerox Credit Corporation, modeled after General Electric's financial subsidiary. It acquired Crum and Forster Inc., a property casualty insurer, and later formed Xerox Financial Services (XFS). This subsidiary would acquire an investment banking firm, other insurance wholesalers, and several other financial services companies. With the Xerox's reputation behind it, XFS was apparently a successful attempt at diversification. By the late 1980s, it was providing the corporation with close to 50% of its income.

As the 1980s came to a close, Xerox was reestablishing its market dominance. After extensive restructuring, which included the creation of a new marketing organization, Xerox was rewarded with Congress's Malcolm Baldrige National Quality Award. This award highlighted the copier giant's regaining the lead in copier quality and was a testament to its ability to adapt. At the turn of the decade, Xerox announced the replacement of its retiring CEO, David Kearns, with Paul Allaire. The company introduced five new types of printers that met various office needs, a digital color copier, and a variety of fax machines and software.

Overcoming its problems of the past, Xerox strengthened the collaboration between its research groups and the parent company. Xerox strove to inform its long-term strategy by its research as much as its research was shaped by its long-term strategy. John Seely Brown, director of PARC, explained: "We expect our researchers to be marinating in the real problems of the corporation. But on the other hand, they should have the absolute freedom ... to step back out of that marination and to think radical thoughts, to reframe the problems."[1] Financial information on the Xerox Corporation is summarized in Exhibit 1.

THE BIRTH OF XEROX TECHNOLOGY VENTURES

Xerox had invested in venture-backed firms since the early 1970s. For instance, it joined a variety of venture capitalists in investing in Rolm, Apple, and a number of other firms. The investments, though successful financially, were made on an ad hoc basis. In the early 1980s, Xerox established two venture funds with an external focus. These did not prove particularly successful, largely due to disputes within the firm about appropriate investments.

The establishment of XTV was driven by two events in 1988. First, several senior Xerox managers were involved in negotiating and approving a spinoff from Xerox, ParcPlace, which sought to commercialize an object-oriented programming language developed at PARC in the 1970s. The negotiation of these agreements proved to be protracted and painful, highlighting the difficulty that the company faced in dealing with these contingencies. More importantly, in this year a book documenting Xerox's failure to develop the personal computer, *Fumbling the Future,* appeared. Stung by the description in the book, Xerox Chairman David Kearns established the task force,

[1] "Interview with John Seely Brown," *Computer World* 26 (August 17, 1992): 80.

with the mandate of preventing the repetition of such a failure to capitalize on Xerox innovations.

The task force, in member Robert Adams's words, rapidly "concluded that we needed a system to prevent technology from leaking out of the company."[2] The committee focused on two options: (1) to begin aggressively litigating those who tried to leave with new technologies, and (2) to invest in people trying to leave Xerox.

The task force reviewed the experience of firms with the two options. Intellectual property litigation was becoming more frequent, as firms increasingly sought to protect discoveries. Not only were firms more aggressively patenting discoveries, but several firms frequently prosecuted employees who left to join rivals or to establish new firms for trade secret theft. These firms felt the high probability of litigation had a deterrent effect, limiting either employees' desire to leave or venture capitalists' willingness to finance these entities. Such a strategy of aggressive litigation, however, might have limited effectiveness.[3] Since cases involving employee noncompetition agreements and claims of trade secret theft were typically heard in the state courts, there was considerable variation in the law across jurisdictions. For instance, California law took a strong position against noncompetition agreements that limited the freedom of employees to change jobs or begin their own firms. (Departing employees in California can still be sued, however, for trade secret theft.) Furthermore, courts in many states had recently been sanctioning firms that they perceived as being too aggressive in enforcing agreements. For instance, a $300,000 judgment had recently been entered against IBM for firing a woman who was dating the employee of a competing firm.[4]

In addition to concerns about the effectiveness of this strategy, a policy of aggressive intellectual property litigation might present other problems. Such a strategy might limit Xerox's ability to recruit the best research personnel, who might not want to limit their future mobility. Similarly, an aggressive legal environment might prevent the establishment of profitable relationships with former employees who were beginning their own firms not in competition with their former employer. Finally, this environment might lead scientists at universities and other research institutions to be reluctant to cooperate with Xerox researchers, lest they embroil their institutions in protracted intellectual property litigation.

Concerning the second option, large companies had experimented extensively with venture capital operations over the 1970s and 1980s, with mixed results. Venture operations generally took two forms, although variations abounded. At one end of the spectrum, large corporations financed new firms alongside other venture capitalists. By entering into venture capital investments, large corporations typically had several objectives. Corporate venture capital investments ideally provided exposure to new technologies and markets, facilitated acquisitions, and generated attractive capital gains.[5] About half of these corporate venture capitalists simply served as limited partners in other venture funds. In many cases, these firms became frustrated because the venture capitalists did not invest in the technologies that most interested the firm.

---

[2] Larry Armstrong, "Nurturing an employee's brainchild," *Business Week* (October 23, 1993), p. 196.

[3] The treatment of these issues at the time of the task force's deliberations are discussed in Wayne E. Green, "Courts Skeptical of 'Non-Compete' Agreements," *Wall Street Journal* (January 11, 1989), p. B1; and Ronald E. Berenbeim, *Safeguarding Intellectual Property*, Conference Board Research Report No. 925 (New York: Conference Board, 1989).

[4] "Privacy," *Business Week* (March 28, 1988), p. 64.

[5] Zenas Block and Ian MacMillan, *Corporate Venturing* (Boston: Harvard Business School Press, 1993), p. 350.

Other firms invested directly in firms, which may have led to closer ties to the companies in their portfolios.[6] In many cases, however, the corporate venture arms did not get offered the best deals by independent venture capitalists, responded too slowly to the potential investments that were offered them, or became embroiled in battles with corporate research officials, who desired that the resources be devoted to internal programs.[7] On the whole, successful corporate venture capitalists have been kept autonomous from corporate activities and have behaved much like normal venture capitalists with the exception of using corporate funds. Thus, the strategic benefits have been limited.

At the other extreme, large corporations attempted to tap the entrepreneurial spirit that emanated from within the company. These programs have sought to establish a setting for creativity and innovation within the often-stifling corporate workplace. The most frequently cited example of such a program, 3M, designates that at least 25% of its business come from products not in existence five years earlier. If 3M's intrapreneurs succeed with their ideas, they can start their own businesses under the umbrella of the parent corporation.[8] Other examples of companies that had successful internal ventures were IBM, which developed the original PC through a special team, and Thermo Electron, which has sold minority interests in a large number of subsidiaries begun by its employees to public investors.[9] In an ideal world, intrapreneuring programs allow entrepreneurs to focus their attention on developing their discovery, while relying on the corporation for financial, legal, and marketing support.

Yet, the intrapreneuring process is not without its disadvantages, as is evident from the number of corporations that have abandoned their programs. Corporate venture programs often attempt to accomplish too many objectives. There needs to be "very clear, defined objectives for a [corporate] venture capital program. It cannot be a mixture of things," as one corporate venture capitalist notes.[10] If a company's program does not have a clear directive, it can cause conflict. In his study of New Venture Divisions within corporations, Fast notes that the short-lived status of many divisions is due to erratic changes in corporate strategy.[11]

Such inconsistency in goals is often manifested in the pay systems for internal ventures. The compensation system is often linked to the achievement of certain sales and profit goals, while the overall corporate strategy dictates investments that may have few direct economic payoffs. In these cases, venture leaders are forced to concentrate on getting their product or technology into the marketplace in order to be paid adequately, and conflict with senior management may result.

Internal venture programs in large corporations have also been characterized by high turnover rates. The frequency of job rotations at many firms has led corporate venture managers to make investment decisions with short-term results in mind. In other

---

[6] Hollister B. Sykes, "Corporate venture capital success," *Journal of Business Venturing* 5 (1990): 37–47.

[7] Robin Siegel, Eric Siegel, and Ian C. MacMillan, "Corporate venture capitalists: Autonomy, obstacles and performance," *Journal of Business Venturing* 3 (1988): 233–47.

[8] Block and MacMillan, op. cit., p. 23.

[9] Gifford Pinchot, *Intrapreneuring* (New York: Harper & Row, 1985), p. 88.

[10] Molly Upton, "Single goal vital to successful corporate venturing," *Corporate Venturing News* 5 (June 1991): 1.

[11] Norman D. Fast, "The future of industrial new venture departments," *Industrial Marketing Management* 8 (1979): 221–25.

cases, the lack of a system of rewards or incentives which matches the risks of innovating or intrapreneuring led disenchanted managers to leave. In a study of employees in six multinational companies, Lawler and Drexel point out that successful risk-taking is inadequately rewarded and failure excessively punished. The majority of the managers studied indicated that their companies' reward systems fostered safe and conservative behavior.[12] A study of compensation practices and venture performance by Block and Omati concludes that incentives used by 207 ventures in 42 *Fortune* 1,000 companies were almost always insufficient.[13]

Differences in the organizational styles of new ventures and their parent corporations also generate conflicts in the internal venture process. Growing, intrapreneurial companies are characterized by a need for high autonomy and rapid decisions. Yet the bureaucracy of their larger parents often moves slowly, delaying access to time-critical resources and in turn stifling the growth of fledgling companies. A new venture manager comments on managing within large corporations: "In the corporate purchasing system, one places an order, and nothing happens. We stay away from most of their systems and build our own."[14] In addition, corporate control systems emphasizing carefully planned improvements and stable growth conflict with the rather unpredictable growth of newly formed ventures. For instance, a venture project at GTE was almost discontinued after it fell behind its corporate plan. After a protracted battle to get corporate approval for extra time and cost, the TeleMessenger unit went on to generate a $70-million-a-year revenue flow for the company.[15]

Finally, corporations often find it difficult to terminate internal ventures. Many managers are unwilling to incur the accounting charges (and the reputational repercussions) associated with writing off an unsuccessful venture. In addition to economic factors, there are social and psychological factors that make it difficult to kill internal ventures in large corporations. Reluctance to disrupt the organization and corporate politics can lead to the continuation of a failing venture.[16] For instance, Time-Life failed to critically examine assumptions about its Cable Week venture (a weekly guide to cable television programs), because the venture was advocated by powerful forces within the organization. As the venture began incurring considerable losses, executives refused to admit that their assumptions were faulty.[17]

Despite these dangers, Chairman Kearns decided to pursue a corporate venture capital program. He agreed to commit $30 million to invest in promising technologies developed at Xerox. As he commented at the time, "XTV is a hedge against repeating missteps of the past."[18] He briefly considered the possibility of asking an established venture capital firm to jointly run the program with Xerox, but decided that the involvement of another party would introduce a formality that might hurt the fledgling venture. Adams was asked to lead the unit, based on his past successes translating laser printing technology into a major business line. As Adams explained his mandate, "the purpose of

[12] E. Lawler and J. Drexel, *The Corporate Entrepreneur* (Los Angeles: Center for Effective Organizations, Graduate School of Business Administration, University of Southern California, 1980).

[13] Zenas Block and Oflar A. Ornati, "Compensating corporate venture managers," *Journal of Business Venturing* 2 (1987): 41–52.

[14] Rosabeth M. Kanter, *When Giants Learn to Dance* (New York: Simon & Schuster, 1989), p. 217.

[15] Ibid., p. 204.

[16] Barry M. Straw and Jerry Ross, "Knowing when to pull the plug," *Harvard Business Review* 65 (March–April 1987): 68–74.

[17] Block and MacMillan, op. cit., p. 246.

[18] Armstrong, op. cit., p. 196.

XTV is to take technical and product development ideas that appear to have a market attraction, but do not fall into the mainline Xerox business strategy."[19]

THE IMPLEMENTATION OF XTV

In planning XTV, Adams—in conjunction with his two fellow principals—emphasized two key design principles. (Biographical information on the XTV principals is contained in Exhibit 2.) These were to model XTV as closely as possible after a venture capital organization and to use the resources of the parent firm to leverage the portfolio firms.

As he looked back over the previous five years, Adams realized he had largely accomplished these goals. The organization had invested in over one dozen companies. These covered a gamut of technologies, mostly involving electronic publishing, document processing, electronic imaging, workstation and computer peripherals, software, and office automation. Although the maturation of these companies had in some cases been slower than expected, they displayed considerable promise. Estimates suggested that the market value of the portfolio was several times the original cost of the portfolio. These firms are summarized in Exhibit 3. XTV had also displayed the willingness to terminate companies when necessary. For instance, Decisus, Inc. had been scuttled because it proved too expensive to enter the market for financial modeling software. XTV had been explored as a model by many other corporations; and AT&T's internal ventures program had been largely modeled after this program.

One successful example of XTV's ability to catalyze the commercialization of technological discoveries was Documentum, which marketed an object-oriented document-management system. Xerox had undertaken a large number of projects in this area for over a decade prior to Documentum's founding but had not shipped a product. After deciding this was a promising area, XTV recruited Howard Shao and John Newton, both former engineering executives at Ingress Corporation (a relationship database manufacturer) to head up the technical effort.

Shao spent the first six months assessing the state of Xerox's knowledge in this area—including reviewing the several 300+-page business plans prepared for earlier proposed (but never shipped) products—and assessing the market. He soon realized that while Xerox understood the nature of the technical problems, it had not grasped how to design a technologically appropriate solution. In particular, the Xerox business plans had proposed building document management systems for mainframe computers rather than for networked personal computers (which were rapidly replacing mainframes at many organizations). With the help of the XTV officials, Shao and Newton led an effort to rapidly convert Xerox's accumulated knowledge in this area into a marketable product. Xerox's accumulated knowledge—as well as XTV's aggressive funding of the firm during the Gulf War period, when the willingness of both independent venture capitalists and the public markets to fund new technology-based firms abruptly declined—gave Documentum an impressive lead over its rivals. (The financing history of Documentum is summarized in Exhibit 4.)

Modeling XTV after venture organizations had several dimensions. The most obvious was the structure of the organization. Although XTV was a corporate division rather than an independent partnership like most venture organizations, Adams crafted an agreement with Xerox that resembled typical agreements between limited and general partners in venture funds. (The "term sheet" from the agreement is reproduced in Exhibit 5.)

---

[19] "Xerox venture unit to invest $10 million a year in projects," *Corporate Financing Week* 15 (July 10, 1989): 7.

The XTV officials insisted on a formal procedure to avoid the ambiguity that had plagued earlier corporate ventures. The agreement made clear that the XTV partners had the flexibility to respond rapidly to investment opportunities, as do independent venture capitalists. They essentially had full autonomy when it came to monitoring, exiting, or liquidating companies. The partners were allowed to spend up to $2 million at any one time without getting permission from the corporation. For larger expenditures, they were required to obtain permission from XTV's governing board, which consisted of Xerox's chief executive officer, chief financial officer, and chief patent counsel.

The spinout process was clearly defined in the partnership agreement, in order to ensure that disputes did not arise later on and to minimize the disruption to the organization. A researcher approaching XTV is asked to prepare a preliminary business plan and to make a list of the resources that he needs, whether laboratory equipment, people, or patents. If the idea seems promising, the XTV personnel will informally contact the researcher's managers for permission. The concept is then reviewed by XTV's board, and then the legal corporation is established by one of Xerox's lawyers. The researchers seeking to commercialize a project are kept inside the laboratory in which they are based until they have developed a full working model. This allows the fledgling entrepreneurs to easily obtain help from other researchers versed in the particular technology being commercialized. Once a working model is developed, the project is rapidly moved out of the laboratory and set up in cheap accommodations.[20] The agreement also specifies that formal transactions between XTV companies and Xerox—whether the procurement of a large amount of technical consulting by a start-up or the repurchase of a company by Xerox—are to be valued on an arm's-length basis. Adams, while acknowledging the importance of his informal ties with Xerox executives, emphasized the necessity of these formal procedures.

Similar to independent venture organizations (but unlike many corporate programs), the program also had a clear goal: to maximize return on investment. Adams felt that the ambiguous goals of many of the 1970s corporate venture programs had been instrumental in their downfall. Adams hoped to achieve a return of investment that exceeded both the average return of the venture capital industry and Xerox's corporate hurdle rate for evaluating new projects. In actuality, the preliminary return of the fund (based on interim valuations) was well above these targets.

Not only was the level of compensation analogous to that of the 20% "carried interest" that independent venture capitalists received, and the degree of autonomy similar, but XTV operated under the same 10-year time frame employed in the typical partnership agreement. As Tung noted, "our job is like any other venture capitalist—we need to generate some return within some finite period of time, usually three to six years, for Xerox, so Xerox can show its shareholders that the money and assets it put in can generate some return."[21] Under certain conditions, however, Xerox could dissolve the partnership after five years.

The analogy to independent venture organizations also extended to the companies in which XTV invested. These were structured as separate legal entities, with their own board and officers. XTV sought to recruit employees from other start-ups that were

---

[20] While the start-up personnel severed their ties to Xerox, in most cases Xerox held onto the patents needed by the start-up. Xerox had broad cross-licensing agreements with IBM and other firms, agreements that might be endangered if the patents were transferred to subsidiary. Instead, Xerox licensed its patents to subsidiaries. These licenses were either exclusive or nonexclusive and for varying lengths of time. Generally, Xerox retained the right to defend the patents and to decide whether to fight or to settle third-party infringements. The cost of litigating these patents, however, was typically borne by the subsidiary.

[21] Mary Eisenhart, "Venture capital: Changing strategies for changing times," *MicroTimes* (September 2, 1991), p. 86.

familiar with managing new enterprises. As Tung noted, "we make sure we have a mixture, not just a culture dominated by a single company."[22] The typical CEO was hired from the outside, on the grounds that entrepreneurial skills, particularly in financial management, were unlikely to be found in a major corporation. XTV also made heavy use of temporary executives who were familiar with a variety of organizations.

The independence of management also extended to technological decision making in these companies. The traditional Xerox product—for instance, a copier—was designed so that it could be operated and serviced in almost any country in the world. This meant not only constraints on how the product was engineered, but also the preparation of copious documentation in many languages. These XTV ventures, however, could produce products for "leading edge" users, who emphasized technological performance over careful documentation.

Like independent venture capitalists, XTV intended to give up control of the companies in which they invested. Transferring shares to management and involving other venture capitalists in XTV companies would reduce Xerox's ownership of the firm. As Tung noted, "our target is that over the long run, after several rounds of financing, Xerox would like to hold from 20% to 50% equity stake."[23] XTV sought to have under a 50% equity stake at the time a spinout firm went public. In this way, it would not need to consolidate the firm in its balance sheet (i.e., it would not need to include the company's equity on its balance sheet, which would reduce Xerox's return on equity). The Xerox lawyers had originally only wanted employees to receive "phantom stock" (typically bonuses based on the growth in the new units performance). Instead, XTV insisted that the employees receive options to buy real shares in the venture-backed companies, in line with traditional Silicon Valley practices. The partners believed that this approach would have a much greater psychological impact, as well as a cleaner capital structure to attract follow-on financings by outside investors.

One difference from venture-backed companies was the timing of when employees received their shares. In a typical venture-backed firm, the entrepreneur started out with the bulk of the shares. His ownership stake was diluted with each venture round, until after the IPO he had approximately a 20% to 30% stake. Here, instead, the initial stake of the management team was small. The shares granted managers increased with time. By the time that firm was approaching an IPO, management's equity stake was intended to be around 20%. Just as the employees stood to make real profits from these ventures, so too did they face real risks. Employees joining XTV companies were required to sign statements acknowledging that they had no guaranteed job to return to at Xerox. This was a sharp difference from most intrapreneuring programs.

The second design principle was to leverage the assets of Xerox Corporation whenever possible. This approach was described by Tom Slechta, marketing vice president of the XTV spinoff ChannelBind: "I've been in other start-ups where you were spun out entirely, and it was sink or swim. You had to create your own entity, but here we were able to walk with a foot in both camps."[24] The XTV partners saw their role as twofold. First, they performed the role of traditional venture capitalists, helping screen proposed transactions, recruiting the management team, attending board meetings, and so forth. Second, they played the role of facilitator to the ventures, ensuring that they received Xerox resources whenever needed. Tung reflected that this hands-on guid-

---

[22] John Rumsey, "Xerox launching new ventures," *Gannett News Service,* July 25, 1991.

[23] Eisenhart, op. cit., pp. 84 and 86.

[24] Ibid., p. 210.

ance and extensive operational involvement differed from that of most traditional venture organizations. All of XTV's principals had stepped into operating roles at portfolio firms as necessary.

This assistance took several forms, depending on the maturity of the firm. The first area of assistance was manufacturing capabilities and procurement. Although Xerox did not supply components to the XTV units, it made sure that the units had access to the corporation's worldwide procurement channels. By purchasing from Xerox-approved suppliers, firms were able to frequently get better prices, as well as the confidence that the suppliers had quality control programs. The units were expected to contract with Xerox to manufacture their products, at least initially, rather than making costly investments in their own facilities.

A second area of assistance is in the area of business services. Firms were expected to initially use Xerox's office space and equipment, as well as to have their accounting and legal services performed by Xerox, which XTV had to reimburse at market rates. As the firms matured, however, they were free to employ the same law and accounting firms that were typically employed by "Silicon Valley" start-ups.

Undoubtedly the most important form of assistance, however, was the certification provided by Xerox. Xerox allowed companies that it owned a majority of to be termed "Xerox companies"; those companies that it owned 33% to 50% of were termed "Xerox-alliance companies." This affiliation allowed XTV start-ups to sell to large companies that they would otherwise not have been able to. For instance, Documentum sold a system to Boeing for use in developing the service and customer documentation of its next-generation aircraft, the 777. Had Documentum been a stand-alone start-up, it would have been very unlikely that Boeing would have made such a critical purchase from them. Xerox implicitly guaranteed that it would back up Documentum if Boeing encountered any problems. As Adams commented, "we operate like a Japanese style *keiretsu* (corporate family) when greasing the skids of our start-ups."[25] This point was also emphasized by Charles Hart, the first CEO of Semaphore Communications, an XTV company that develops security products for computer networks: "[Xerox officials] haven't mucked around much with the management [of Semaphore], but, boy, do they give you credibility when you call up someone and say that you're a Xerox company."[26]

A final, somewhat less important, source of assistance was Xerox's sales force. XTV firms generally hired sales forces of their own. The Xerox sales organization primarily sold items costing $100,000 or more to managers of mainframe computer systems. Most of the XTV firms were making products geared to end users or network administrators that sold for a few hundred or a few thousand dollars. It was anticipated the sales force would not be very interested in selling such small items. Hence, approaches akin to that of ChannelBind, which manufactured units that inexpensively bound xeroxed pages, were typical:

> While the product is complementary to Xerox's, it wouldn't get the same attention alongside a mid-volume copy duplicator that sells for fifty to one hundred times its price. ... So we deliberately have not gone to the Xerox sales organization as a reseller. We've used them as a referral and lead-generating source, and as a way to gain exposure in the marketplace. The sales organization helps us get right to our end-users.[27]

---

[25] "Barefoot into PARC," *The Economist* 328 (July 10, 1993): 68.

[26] Steven W. Quickel, "Venture capital incubators are hatching new companies again," *Electronic Business Buyer* 20 (January 1994): 90–93.

[27] Eisenhart, op. cit., p. 210.

The recent movement in many corporations toward networked personal computers, and the consequent shift in purchasing power to senior management and end users, had somewhat changed this dynamic. Being able to mention the XTV portfolio companies' products had given the salesmen a "foot in the door" with these users. Consequently, the salesmen's interest in the XTV companies' products had been growing. For instance, XTV's portfolio company Document Sciences, which produces software that enables the production of large numbers of customized reports, worked out a relationship with Xerox where both teams of salesmen would get a referral fee for promoting the others' products.

As Adams reviewed the past five years, he realized as well that the implementation of XTV had faced at least three challenges that had not been anticipated at the time the unit was established. One challenge that had not been fully appreciated by XTV management was the amount of time and energy required to establish syndication relationships with other venture organizations. XTV had envisioned syndicating transactions for at least two reasons. First, the involvement of other venture capitalists would leverage XTV's investments, by providing additional funds. More importantly, they would certify the quality of the firm to outsiders, whether today's customers or potential investors at the time of an initial public offering.

XTV initially found venture capitalists reluctant to invest in XTV firms, at least not at valuations acceptable to the partners. This reflected the relative youth of the companies in XTV's portfolio. (During the early 1990s, venture capitalists were investing relatively less money in early-stage investments). In addition, because of the checkered record of earlier corporate venturing programs, the venture community was initially skeptical of whether Xerox was committed to the XTV initiative. Finally, XTV was prohibited by its charter from investing in firms not affiliated with Xerox and not based on Xerox technology. Thus, XTV could not make reciprocal investments in venture capitalists' later-stage deals. This sharing often characterizes the syndication process.

As of March 1995, three transactions had been syndicated with other venture organizations. Syndication partners included Brentwood Associates, Merrill, Pickard, Anderson & Eyre, Sequoia Capital and Norwest Capital. These transactions introduced a variety of legal and organizational changes. Typically, prior to outside investments, 80% of the equity in the firm is held by Xerox, and the remainder is held by (or earmarked for) the management team. Once a transaction is syndicated, Xerox's stake falls below 80%. This means that the subsidiary's losses cannot be consolidated any more for tax purposes. (As long as it owns 50%, Xerox must continue to consolidate the subsidiary for financial reporting reasons.) More generally, when venture capitalists invest, XTV's relationship with the unit becomes more formal. XTV will no longer provide loans for working capital purposes or make formal guarantees of the start-up's debts.

A second surprising outcome had been Xerox's repurchase of one of the firms. At the time, Xerox was marketing (for about $13,000) a desktop publishing workstation, which used a proprietary operating system. Consequently, the software could not run on standard computers that employed DOS or Unix operating systems. The firm, Advanced Workstation Products, sought to shrink the main circuitry and software for the Xerox workstation down to a $400 circuit card that could be added to a $2000 personal computer. The user could then switch between running DOS and running this package. Xerox had rejected this project because it had calculated that the product would cost at least $25 million and take three years to develop.

This start-up was able to complete the project in 18 months and for $4 million. In part, this success reflected the less-constrained design environment that characterized the start-up: they could focus on developing a product that would work for U.S. users.

It also reflected the motivational effect of the powerful financial incentives. The success of this product coincided with the delay of Xerox's next generation graphics workstation, so the corporation decided to repurchase the start-up. The negotiated purchase price was $15 million. Approximately 19% of this price went to the managers, and the capital gains were divided 80%–20% between Xerox and the general partners in XTV.

The XTV principals noted a change in attitude toward XTV on the part of many line managers after this repurchase. Initially, XTV had been approached primarily by frustrated researchers, particularly from the PARC and Webster laboratories, who had been unable to persuade their supervisors to invest in the new products. There had been some concern from operating managers who didn't want to give up control of new technologies, even if they didn't want to spend money commercializing them. (XTV also sought to address this resistance by conducting extensive internal public relations at staff meetings and in publications. These publicity efforts also served to underscore the extent to which the XTV was supported by top management.) Particularly after this repurchase, line management increasingly saw XTV less as a competitor for projects and more as a potential "skunk works" where promising ideas that did not fit within the budget or business plan could be nurtured. XTV began receiving referrals not only from researchers, but also from project managers who terminated researchers' projects because of a lack of strategic fit. Managers assessed proposed products using several criteria. Not only did the technology have to be promising, but the product had to match Xerox's existing delivery system (e.g., Xerox's sales force). Because the cycle between the development of a concept in a research laboratory and its widespread rollout in the market is so protracted—often a decade or longer—these assessments could often differ. XTV offered an opportunity for product champions to obtain a second opinion.

A third surprise had been the evolution of XTV's focus. The firm had originally sought to invest in unappreciated technologies developed at Xerox laboratories. This reflected the broad-based nature of Xerox's research philosophy. As Tung noted,

> Xerox's research philosophy doesn't try to be too specific or narrowly focused. Their philosophy is that in order to attract the best researchers, they need to give them some degree of freedom and latitude to work on various projects in order to come out with innovations. As a result, not all research products or technologies can be readily applicable to their mainline business.[28]

By March 1995, much of XTV's energy was devoted to nurturing these businesses. The venture capitalists actively served on the boards of the portfolio companies, helped arrange key acquisitions or mergers, and occasionally served as interim operating officers. XTV was also considering new investment opportunities, but many of them were of a different type. As Xerox focused during the 1990s, many units were being terminated or outsourced. (Most visible was the $3 billion deal to outsource Xerox's data processing to EDS.) This created many potential opportunities for XTV. As freestanding units, the companies could sell to other firms as well as Xerox. For example, XTV was offered a component facility with $30 million in sales to Xerox (its sole customer). If the firm was spun off, it might be able to identify other business opportunities.

---

[28] Eisenhart, op. cit., p. 84.

Exhibit 1 Xerox Corporation Financial Statements—Consolidated Statements of Income, Year Ended
December 31 (in millions, except per-share data)

	1993	**1992**	**1991**
DOCUMENT PROCESSING			
Revenues:			
Sales	$7,395	$7,485	$7,089
Service and rentals	5,989	5,975	5,645
Finance income	1,053	1,049	898
Equity in income of unconsolidated affiliates and other income	164	172	187
Total Revenues	14,601	14,681	13,819
Costs and expenses:			
Cost of sales	4,227	4,033	3,810
Cost of service and rentals	3,003	3,093	2,851
Research and development expenses	883	922	890
Selling, administrative and general expenses	4,585	4,779	4,497
Interest expense	540	570	536
Special charges, net	1,373	—	175
Other, net	183	80	49
Total Costs and Expenses	14,794	13,477	12,808
Income (loss) before income taxes and minorities' interests:	(193)	1,204	1,011
Income taxes (benefits)	(78)	493	412
Minorities' interests in earnings of subsidiaries	78	149	163
Income (loss) from document processing	(193)	562	436
INSURANCE			
Revenues:			
Insurance premiums earned	2,408	2,326	2,663
Investment and other income	401	552	636
Total revenues	2,809	2,878	3,299
Costs and expenses:			
Insurance losses and loss expenses	1,836	2,725	2,245
Insurance acquisition costs and other insurance operating expenses	785	957	967
Interest expense	215	218	222
Administrative and general expenses	95	106	59
Goodwill write-down	—	400	—
Total Costs and Expenses	2,931	4,406	3,493
Realized capital gains	88	516	122
Income (loss) before income taxes	(34)	(1,012)	(72)
Income taxes (benefits)	(38)	(233)	(74)
Income (loss) from insurance	4	(779)	2
TOTAL COMPANY			
Income (loss) from continuing operations	(189)	(217)	438
Discontinued operations	63	(39)	16
Cumulative effect of changes in accounting principles	—	(764)	—
Net income (loss)	($126)	($1,020)	$454
Primary earnings (loss) per share			
Continuing operations	($2.46)	($2.91)	$3.74
Discontinued operations	62	(.41)	17
Cumulative effect of changes in accounting principles	—	(7.97)	—
Primary earnings per share	($1.84)	($11.20)	$3.91
Fully diluted earnings (loss) per share			
Continuing operations	($2.46)	($2.91)	$3.71
Discontinued operations	.62	(.41)	.15
Cumulative effect of changes in accounting principles	—	(7.97)	—
Fully diluted earnings per share	($1.84)	($11.29)	$3.86

Exhibit 1 (continued)   Consolidated Balance Sheets, December 31 (in $ millions)

	1993	1992
ASSETS		
Document Processing:		
Cash	$ 68	$ 2
Accounts receivable, net	1,613	1,751
Finance receivables, net	3,358	3,162
Inventories	2,162	2,257
Deferred taxes and other current assets	1,167	864
Total Current Assets	$ 8,368	$ 8,036
Finance receivables due after one year, net	5,594	5,337
Land, building and equipment, net	2,219	2,150
Investments in affiliates, at equity	1,094	957
Other assets	883	660
Total Documents, Processing Assets	$18,158	$17,140
Insurance		
Cash	18	41
Investment held for sale	8,344	7,974
Reinsurance receivables	3,835	4,233
Premiums and other receivables	1,443	1,334
Goodwill	291	301
Deferred taxes and other assets	1,487	1,596
Total Insurance Assets	$15,418	$15,479
Investment in discontinued operations	5,174	5,652
TOTAL ASSETS	$38,750	$38,271
LIABILITIES AND EQUITY		
Document Processing:		
Short-term debt and current portion of long-term debt	$ 2,698	$ 2,533
Accounts payable	541	544
Accrued compensation and benefit costs	511	722
Unearned income	335	363
Other current liabilities	1,926	1,296
Total Current Liabilities	$ 6,011	$ 5,458
Allocated long-term debt	5,157	4,950
Liability for post-retirement medical benefits	997	927
Deferred taxes and other liabilities	2,608	1,625
Total Document Processing Liabilities	$14,773	$12,960
Insurance		
Unpaid losses and loss expenses	$ 9,684	$10,657
Unearned income	1,077	1,073
Other liabilities	990	749
Total Insurance Operating Liabilities	$11,751	$12,479
Discontinued operations liabilities—policyholders' deposits and other	4,585	4,958
Other long-term debt and obligations	2,400	2,723
Deferred ESOP Benefits	(641)	(681)
Minorities' interests in equity of subsidiaries	844	885
Preferred stock	1,066	1,072
Common shareholders' equity	3,972	3,875
TOTAL LIABILIIES AND EQUITY	$38,750	$38,271

Shares of common stock issued and outstanding at December 31, 1993 and 1992 (in thousands) were 104,122 and 95,066, respectively.

Exhibit 1 (continued) Consolidated Statements of Cash Flows, Year Ended December 31
(in $ millions)

	1993	1992	1991
CASH AT BEGINNING OF YEAR			
Document processing	$2	$10	$127
Insurance	41	35	20
Total	43	45	147
DOCUMENT PROCESSING			
Cash flows from operating activities	526	(353)	200
Cash flows from investing activities			
Cost of additions to land, building and equipment	(470)	(582)	(467)
Proceeds from sales of land, building and equipment	41	43	25
Net change in payables to insurance	19	395	(58)
Net transactions with insurance	164	(411)	(306)
Net transactions with discontinued operations	(206)	263	256
Total	(452)	(292)	(550
Cash flows from financing activities			
Net change in allocated debt	(151)	1,014	760
Dividends on common and preferred stock	(389)	(373)	(368)
Proceeds on sale of common stock	665	113	26
Redemption of preferred stock	(6)	(6)	(3)
Dividends to minority shareholders	(105)	(121)	(132)
Proceeds received from minority shareholders	12	31	26
Total	26	658	309
Effect of exchange rate changes on cash	(34)	(21)	(76)
Net cash flows from document processing	66	(8)	(117)
INSURANCE			
Cash flows from operating activities	(167)	(595)	(345)
Cash flows from investing activities			
Purchase of portfolio investments	(5,143)	(14,481)	(5,030)
Proceeds from sales of portfolio investments	6,077	14,592	4,792
(Increase) decrease in short-term investments	(1,212)	181	409
Subtotal	(278)	292	171
Other, net	(181)	(201)	(12)
Net transactions with discontinued operations	401	(31)	(46)
Total	(58)	60	113
Cash flows from financing activities			
Net change in allocated debt	366	130	(59)
Net transactions with document processing	(164)	411	306
Total	202	541	247
Net cash flows from insurance	(23)	6	15
DISCONTINUED OPERATIONS			
Income (loss) from discontinued operations	63	(39)	16
Collections and changes in assets, net	418	236	832
Net change in debt	(584)	(378)	(1,239)
Net change in operating liabilities	211	413	601
Settlement of tax benefits with document processing	87	—	—
Net transactions with document processing	206	(263)	(256)
Net transactions with insurance	(401)	31	46
Net cash flows from discontinued operations	—	—	—
CASH AT END OF YEAR			
Document processing	68	2	10
Insurance	18	41	35
Total	$86	$43	$45

Source: Corporate documents.

Exhibit 2   XTV Principals

Robert V. Adams   President, CEO and Senior Principal, is a former executive vice president of Xerox. Since joining Xerox in 1965, Mr. Adams has held a number of marketing, planning and sales management positions. He was named president and general manager of the company's Printing Systems Division in 1979 and elected a corporate vice president in 1981. In 1983, Mr. Adams became a corporate group vice president and president of the Xerox Systems Group, with revenue of $2.6 billion and 9,000 employees. He was then promoted to executive vice president where he was responsible for the Corporate Strategy Office and the Corporate Business Development Office and a newly created Custom Systems Division. He is Chairman of the Board for several of the XTV portfolio companies, as well as outside director of several other non-XTV related companies. In addition to his corporate responsibilities, he serves on several educational and nonprofit boards. Mr. Adams holds an MBA degree from the University of Chicago and a B.S degree in mechanical engineering from Purdue University.

Robert H. Curtin   Vice President and Principal, comes to XTV after 20 years of experience with Xerox Corporation, a majority of it in the financial area. While with Xerox, Mr. Curtin was Director of Corporate Business Development, concentrating on mergers and acquisitions and licensing agreements. In addition, he spent six years abroad with Rank Xerox (the Xerox European subsidiary), three years at the international headquarters in London, where he managed several major PanEuropean financial projects and three years as Financial Director of Rank Xerox Netherlands. Mr. Curtin is a Director of several of the XTV companies. Mr. Curtin received an MBA degree from the University of Rochester and a B.S. degree from the New York State Maritime College.

Jeffrey C. Tung   Vice President and Principal, joined XTV from the venture capital industry. Mr. Tung was an Associate Partner at KBA Partners, L.P., a $100 million technology-oriented venture capital and investment firm. Previously, Mr. Tung was a product manager of a local area network product line for Intel Corporation. Prior to his Intel experience, Mr. Tung was a project leader in a new business unit of Lockheed Missiles and Space Company. Mr. Tung serves as a Director of several of the XTV companies. Mr. Tung received an MBA degree from Harvard Business School and M.S. and B.S. degrees from the Massachusetts Institute of Technology.

Source: Corporate documents.

Exhibit 3   XTV Portfolio Companies

ChannelBind Corporation

ChannelBind Corporation provides professional, highly custom, highly decorative document binding and labeling products to corporate America.

Products:	System 10 is a low cost, nonelectrical binding system designed for lower volume applications (up to 150 sheets).
	System 20 is a high-end, nonelectrical binding system, capable of binding documents up to 300 sheets. It comes with a lifetime warranty. The binding process in both systems is easy to learn and takes less than 15 seconds.
	ChannelBind covers come in 8½" x 11", A4, and other standard sizes. Hard covers come in a variety of popular colors and textures; soft covers are available with or without die-cut windows. Custom covers (including four-color printed and laminated) are available as well in both hard and soft cover format.
	"Titling on Demand" software packages. Titling capabilities include foil imprinting, silk-screening, embossing/debossing, and gold labeling.
	DeBinder comes with both System 10 and 20, and can be used to quickly reopen bound documents. Debound covers can be reused a minimum of three times.
Target Markets:	Office products (NOMDA, NOPA)
	Home office *Fortune* 500 Selected vertical markets
Major Investors:	Xerox Technology Ventures (XTV)
XTV Role:	Incubation, lead investor
Business Phase:	Established products and expanding distribution chain globally; $6 + million in sales and full year profitability in 1993.

Document Sciences Corporation

Document Sciences Corporation provides automated database publishing software and related services on a worldwide basis.

Products:	CompuSet@, the company's flagship product, is the automated database publishing software kernel.
	CompuSeries7 is in a development environment designed to enhance the creation and implementation of CompuSet8 applications.
	CompuPrep7 is the software that automatically tags database information for CompuSet.
	CompuView7 is the PC Windows-based system for viewing the assembled CompuSet document.
Target Markets:	Global Corporate 2000
Major Investors:	Xerox Technology Ventures (XTV)

XTV Role:	Incubation, lead investor
Business Phase:	Company has established product line, was profitable in 1993, and is continuing product development and market expansion.

Documentum, Inc.

Documentum, Inc. develops and markets the Documentum Enterprise Document Management System, a family of open client/server software products that can be tailored to specific business-critical document applications. The Documentum system enables the capture, workflow, assembly and distribution of business critical documents. Documentum delivers the virtual document which allows organizations to create information once and reuse it many times across the enterprise.

Products:	Documentum Server Documentum Workspace (GUI Client) Documentum Toolkit
Target Markets:	Pharmaceutical Build to Order Manufacturing Regulated Industries Government
Major Investors:	Xerox Technology Ventures Brentwood Associates Merrill, Pickard, Anderson and Eyre Norwest Venture Capital Management Sequoia Capital
XTV Role:	Incubation and follow-on rounds investor
Business Phase:	Company has launched its family of products and is moving towards market leadership in multiple segments. Company achieved $10.7 million in revenue in 1994 and reached profitability in the fourth quarter of 1994. Projecting revenue in excess of $25 million in 1995. Closed $7 million of second-round financing in October, 1993, and $5 million third-round financing in September 1994.

FairCopy Services, Inc.

FairCopy Services provides easy-to-use, automated systems for measuring the copying of published and copyrighted material. This sampling data is provided to publishing collectives for their blanket licenses as well as developing and providing support services to collectives, or individuals when prior approval for copyright or reprographic activities is required.

Products:	Page Sampler is used to scan bibliographic and numeric information and store the data on tape cartridges for processing. Volume Sampler counts the number of copyright copies without capturing the bibliographic information.
Target Markets:	Publishing houses Writers Rightsholders' collectives
Major Investors:	Xerox Technology Ventures (XTV)
XTV Role:	Incubation, lead investor

Business Phase:	Continued contract with first major sampling customer Company expects $1 million sales and full year of profitability from copyright business in 1994.
	Development underway for new product line addressing different market.

Opto Generic Devices, Inc.

Opto Generic Devices develops and manufactures miniature precision generic optical encoders, servo motors, and other motion control devices.

Background	Xerox has been working with Opto Generic Devices, Inc. (OGD) since 1987 on the development of a low-cost, high-function, generic optical encoder for its copier/duplicator line of products. The "generic" encoder developed with OGD is designed to replace both shaft and modular encoders. This encoder offers Xerox and other customers an opportunity to "standardize" encoder hardware and software, as well as the supporting documentation and maintenance.
	In the process, Xerox engineers have developed and patented several elements of the new encoder. The Materials Management Group under Steve Tierney was looking for ways to spin out the Xerox technology and, at the same time, support the development of its minority supplier base. They approached XTV for investment support and technology transfer.
	In a separate market, OGD also has co-developed with Xerox new nickel electroformed parts and applications. Specifically, OGD has explored and progressed use of this technology in CVTs (Continually Variable Transmission). This has potential for the automotive industry and beyond.

Pixelcraft, Inc.

PixelCraft is a leading supplier of scanners and computer-based software products that facilitate the integration of images in various open systems environments for printing, publishing and graphic arts services industries. The company enjoys a worldwide reputation and is recognized by numerous industry groups. Its esteemed and patented color software technology is licensed by major imaging and graphics arts vendors, such as Quark and Sharp.

Products:	Pro Imager 4520 RS—imaging system for high-quality transparency images. ColorAcess—color production, image management technology. Pro Imager 8000—high-quality, large-format professional color scanner. Pro Imager 4000—entry-level, letter-sized graphics arts color scanner.
Target Markets:	Printers Publishers Graphic Designers Service Bureaus Trade Shops
Major Investors:	Xerox Technology Ventures (XTV)
XTV Role:	Incubation, lead investor
Business Phase:	Product development and market rollout completed; recent product introductions underway. Revenues have grown at 75% per year. Expecting profitability in 1995.

QuadMark, Ltd.

OuadMark manufactures and markets high-quality portable copiers, printers, fax and multifunctional devices (fax, scanner, printer and copier all-in-one) using full-size, cut-sheet, plain paper at affordable consumer prices.

Products:	Portable copier Portable printer/fax Multi-functional device—copier/printer/scanner/fax
Target Markets:	Consumer Home office Small business Mobile
Major Investors:	Xerox Technology Ventures (XTV) ASCO Technology Leaders
XTV Role:	Incubation, lead investor, participant in follow-on rounds
Business Phase:	Company announcement and first product prototype developed; production ramp-up in 1994. Closed third-round funding with $5 million to be used for manufacturing start-up and market launch. Second product family to be launched in the first half of 1995.

Semaphore Communications, Inc.

Semaphore Communications provides network security products, hardware and software, to corporate America. The company's products protect sensitive data as it travels across enterprisewide global networks.

Products:	Network Security System™ Network Encryption Units and Network Security Center
Target Markets:	Corporate America Global 1000 corporations, universities, government and financial
Major Investors:	Xerox Technology Ventures (XTV)
XTV Role:	Incubation, lead investor
Business Phase:	First product roll out completed. Initial customers include Microsoft McCaw Cellular, Silicon Graphics, Dow, Texas Instruments, Hughes, Hewlett Packard and IBM. Established strategic relationships with AT&T, Novell, IBM, and Infonet.

Terabank Systems, Inc.

Terabank Systems provides proprietary digital tape storage systems with very fast access time, ultrahigh capacity, and high reliability suitable for "near-on-line" applications.

Products:	4MM DAT Tape Drive System 4MM DAT Cartridges
Target Markets:	"Near Line" Data Storage and Retrieval Digital Video
Major Investors:	Xerox Technology Ventures (XTV)
XTV Role:	Incubation, lead investor
Business Phase:	Engineering prototype completed in 1993

Source: Corporate documents.

Exhibit 4   Summary of Documentum's Financial History

The Company was incorporated in January 1990 as a wholly-owned subsidiary of Xerox Corporation ("Xerox"). Between January 1990 and December 1992, Xerox contributed approximately $2.26 million of equity in exchange for one share of Common Stock. In March 1993, the company was recapitalized and 15,999,000 shares of Series A Preferred Stock were issued to Xerox in exchange for the one outstanding share of Common Stock. At the same time, 200 shares of Common Stock were issued to Xerox for $100.

In October 1993, the Company issued 27,395,909 shares of Series B Preferred Stock (the "Series B Stock") for an aggregate consideration of $6.95 million in cash and the cancellation of indebtedness. In connection with such financing, the Company issued (i) 4,730,229 shares of Series B Stock to Xerox in exchange for the cancellation of approximately $1.2 million in indebtedness; (ii) 6,602,611 shares of Series B Stock to Brentwood Associates VI, L.P. ("Brentwood VI") in exchange for cash and the cancellation of approximately $102,000 of indebtedness; (iii) 6,384,725 shares of Series B Stock to Merrill, Pickard, Anderson & Eyre V, L.P. ("MPAE V") in exchange for cash and the cancellation of approximately $102,000 of indebtedness; (iv) 271,886 shares of Series B Stock to MPAE V Affiliates Fund, L.P. ("MPAE Affiliates") for cash, (v) 4,730,229 shares of Series B Stock to Norwest Equity Partners, IV ("Norwest") for cash and the cancellation of approximately $73,000 of indebtedness; (vi) 4,304,509 shares of Series B Stock to Sequoia Capital VI ("Sequoia") for cash and the cancellation of approximately $66,000 of indebtedness; (vii) 236,511 shares of Series B Stock to Sequoia Technology Partners VI ("Sequoia Technology") for cash and the cancellation of approximately $4,000 of indebtedness; and (viii) 189,209 shares of Series B Stock to Sequoia XXIII for cash and the cancellation of approximately $3,000 of indebtedness. In addition to the shares of Series B Stock issued to Xerox, the Company paid Xerox $500,000 of the proceeds from the financing and issued Xerox a convertible subordinated note in the principal amount of $541,309 in full payment of $2,241,320.80 of outstanding indebtedness to Xerox. All of the indebtedness canceled in the financing, other than the Xerox indebtedness, had been issued by the Company in connection with bridge loans made by the Series B investors to the Company on September 30, 1993.

In September 1994, the Company issued 5,625,000 shares of Series C Preferred Stock (the "Series C Stock") for an aggregate consideration of $4.5 million in cash and the cancellation of indebtedness. In connection with such financing, the Company issued (i) 1,431,590 shares of Series C Stock to Xerox in exchange for cash and the cancellation of approximately $573,000 of indebtedness and accrued interest thereon, (ii) 1,039,493 shares of Series C Stock to Brentwood VI for cash, (iii) 1,039,493 shares of Series C Stock to MPAE V for cash, (iv) 744,712 shares of Series C Stock to Norwest for cash, (v) 677,688 shares of Series C Stock to Sequoia for cash, (vi) 37,236 shares of Series C Stock to Sequoia Technology for cash, and (vii) 29,788 shares of Series C Stock to Sequoia XXIII for cash.

John Walecka, a director of the Company, is a general partner of Brentwood Associates, the general partner of Brentwood VI. Kathryn Gould, a director of the Company, is a limited partner of MPAE V Management Company, L.P., the general partner of MPAE V and MPAE Affiliates.

Pursuant to an offer letter of employment, dated July 27, 1993, from the Company to Jeffrey A. Miller, the President and Chief Executive Officer of the Company, Mr. Miller was granted an option to purchase 340,000 shares of the Company's Common Stock at a per share exercise price equal to the fair market value of the Company's Common Stock on the date of grant. The option is subject to vesting over four years from the start of Mr. Miller's employment with the Company. The letter provides that the option be assumed by the acquirer of the Company in the event of a merger or acquisition, or, in the alternative, that vesting be accelerated. Vesting will also be accelerated in the event of a liquidation of the Company.

Pursuant to the terms of the 1993 Equity Incentive Plan, certain officers of the Company exercised options under the Plan and paid the exercise price, either in whole or in part, by issuing promissory notes to the Company. Mr. Miller issued a promissory note in the amount of $99,643, and seven other officers issued promissory notes in the aggregate amount of $139,478. All promissory notes are secured by the shares of Common Stock issued upon exercise. The promissory notes accrue interest at rates ranging from 6.76% to 7.92% per annum and are due five years from the date of issuance. As of March 1995, approximately 3 million options had been granted under the Plan.

Source: Corporate documents.

Exhibit 5 Summary of Principal terms of Xerox Technology Ventures Plan

1. **Entity:** Xerox Technology Ventures, a division of Xerox Corporation.

2. **Purpose:** To manage and nurture start-up ventures consisting of internally generated ideas, products, and technology of Xerox which are not "mainline Xerox products or technologies."

3. **Participants:** Xerox Corporation and the XTV Principals (Adams, Curtin, and Tung).

4. **Term:** 1989 through 1998.

5. **Capital Contributions:**

   A. *Xerox:*

   (1) Ventures and related technology rights, all internally generated by Xerox, at fair market value. Ventures may be offered by Xerox to XTV and may be accepted by XTV.

   (2) A total of $30,000,000 ("committed" cash):

   a. Committed cash draw-downs of less than $2 million made upon the request of the XTV Principals.

   b. Draw-downs of more than $2 million made only with the approval of the Management Board.

   (3) Operating overhead and expenses: all Xerox contributions are reflected in a Memorandum Capital Account ("MCA"). Losses on the disposition or liquidation of a venture are effectively added to the MCA.

   B. *XTV Principals:*

   Contributions will not be required from the XTV Principals.

6. **Management Board:** XTV has a Management Board (including the XTV Principals, Xerox CEO and CFO, and senior staff officer) to which the XTV Principals report.

7. **Management:** The XTV Principals are responsible for management of all ventures, as well as the timing and method of disposition of all ventures.

8. **Distributions:**

   (1) Distributions upon disposition of securities: Upon receipt of proceeds from the disposition of any XTV securities, such proceeds are to be distributed as follows:

   a. To the extent that the value of the proceeds and all of the portfolio assets of XTV exceeds the MCA, 80% to Xerox (with a corresponding reduction to the MCA), and 20% to the XTV Principals (all distributions, as among the XTV Principals, are made in accordance with their interests in XTV Principal Compensation Pool under the XTV Plan); and

   b. The remainder to Xerox (with a corresponding credit to the MCA).

   (2) Any expenses arising from the liquidation of XTV's assets pursuant to an early termination of XTV by Xerox are paid 50% by Xerox, and the remaining 50% is treated as an expense and credit to the MCA.

9. **Rights to reacquire investments:**

    (1) Right of first refusal: Before selling its interest in, shutting down, or otherwise disposing of any portfolio company, the XTV is required to give prior written notice to Xerox which has the right to purchase XTV's interest in such portfolio company at its then fair-market value.

    (2) Right to reacquire: Xerox may at any time require XTV to transfer back to Xerox all of XTV's interest in any portfolio company, at fair market value of such interest as of the date of such transfer plus 5% (the "5% Premium") of the excess of the fair market value of such interest over the XTV's original purchase price of such interest. The 5% premium is distributed to the XTV Principals.

10. **Termination:** In the event of an early termination of the XTV contract by Xerox, and consequent termination of the XTV before December 31, 1998, the XTV Principals have the right to purchase from Xerox some or all of the portfolio securities of XTV distributed to Xerox at value of the asset reflected in the MCA. Any proceeds of such sale will be deemed to be proceeds received upon disposition of such securities.

Source: Corporate documents.

28

Northeast Ventures: January 1996

Nick Smith, chairman and chief executive officer of Northeast Ventures Corporation, a venture capital fund focusing on the development of northeastern Minnesota, gazed over the snowy landscape pensively. Before him lay a well-marked copy of an assessment of his fund, prepared three months earlier by the Chicago-based Shorebank Corporation. The analysis concluded that the fund had been "extremely well-managed" over its first five years, but identified some important issues about the future of community development venture capital.

Smith thought back to five years before, when he had shifted his focus from the day-to-day management of the region's preeminent law firm to the organization of a new $7.7 million venture fund. He had been motivated to take this step by the increased need for equity capital in Duluth and the surrounding region. Since the turn of the century, the area had relied heavily upon the mining and processing of iron ore. The region had lost more than 75% of its mining jobs in the early 1980s, as U.S. steel production declined and imports of ore rose.

Looking back over the past five years, Smith realized that Northeast Ventures had enjoyed many successes. Under the leadership of Smith and President Greg Sandbulte, the fund had invested $4.5 million in 16 firms. Two investments had been successfully exited. The potential profits from a number of firms still in the fund's portfolio seemed substantial, assuming that Northeast could find the right ways in which to exit the investments. In addition, their portfolio firms had created about 200 jobs in the region and had the potential to create many more in upcoming years.

Smith realized, however, that the Shorebank report accurately identified some of the challenges that community development venture capitalists faced. A major issue was how to expand the community of investors who would invest in such funds. Most investors to date had been foundations, economic development organizations, and corporations. In broadening their appeal, community development venture funds would need to revisit the question of how to balance financial and social goals: how to produce attractive returns while making a tangible impact on the local economy. The obstacles to success were many, Smith mused, but the rewards of overcoming them would be even greater.

This case was prepared by Eric K. Jackson and Josh Lerner. Copyright © 1996 by the President and Fellows of Harvard College. Harvard Business School case 296-093.

THE ECONOMIC CRISIS IN NORTHEASTERN MINNESOTA

Northeastern Minnesota was a predominately rural area, with about 325,000 inhabitants in January 1996. The region's largest city, Duluth, had a population of 85,500. (A map of Minnesota is reproduced in Exhibit 1.) The development of the region was spurred by its plentiful natural resources, especially iron ore and wood. When northeastern Minnesota was developing in the first decades of this century, scores of small towns sprang into existence overnight along the region's rich vein of iron ore. Open-pit mines were hastily constructed to extract the mineral. By 1940, high-grade iron ore in the region was mostly depleted. As a result, mining operations shifted to producing and shipping taconite, a lower grade of iron ore. This led to a consolidation of mining activities and an initial economic crisis in the region.[1]

In 1941 Governor Harold Stassen responded by creating the Iron Range Resources and Rehabilitation Board (IRRRB). The IRRRB, a state agency, was funded through a tax that was levied on taconite production. The resulting revenues were channeled to small towns in the region for financial assistance and economic development programs (e.g., marketing campaigns and loans for local businesses). Several other efforts were undertaken to wean the region from its dependence on the mining industry. For instance, the Arrowhead Regional Development Commission, a government planning body, created the Northspan Group, which provided financing to and encouraged procurement with local businesses. These various initiatives, however, did not fully address the region's heavy reliance on the mining industry. In 1980, mining continued to account for 12% of the region's employment and more than 20% of total wages.

The consequences of this failure to diversify were made apparent in the early 1980s. Domestic steel manufacturers encountered heavy competition, both from more efficient foreign producers and domestic "mini-mills." (Rather than making steel from ore, mini-mills melt used automobiles and other scrap.) Among the responses of U.S. steel manufacturers were shuttering obsolete facilities and making increasing use of imported ore from mines in such countries as Brazil.

The result was a substantial decline in the demand for Minnesota ore. Mining industry employment in northeastern Minnesota dropped from 16,450 to 3,800 between August 1979 and December 1984. The effects also damaged mining-related companies and retail and wholesale industries. Overall, the region's unemployment catapulted from 3% in 1979 to almost 16% by 1984. These effects were even more severe in the rural areas of northeastern Minnesota. For instance, the number of jobs (excluding the self-employed) in Lake County fell by 30% between 1980 and 1985, while the average inflation-adjusted salary fell by 25%. In some towns around the mines, unemployment exceeded 90%.[2]

As a result of the bleak job prospects, many of the region's younger and most able workers departed to seek employment opportunities elsewhere. This migration exacerbated the crisis for the economy and placed unanticipated strains on the social welfare system. Despite their declining tax bases, local governments struggled to aid the growing number of residents in need of assistance.

---

[1] This account of the initial crisis in the Minnesota iron mining industry and the public policy response is based partially on James B. McComb, *Iron Mining and Taxes in Minnesota,* Bureau of Business Studies, Macalester College, 1963.

[2] These statistics are drawn from interviews with economic development officials and Bureau of Economic Analysis, Regional Economic Information System, State of Minnesota, "Minnesota Economic Regions and Counties," Unpublished report, January 1995.

THE CONCEPTION OF NORTHEAST VENTURES

In 1985, the Blandin Foundation, based in Grand Rapids, Minnesota, convened a series of meetings of local economic development and business leaders to discuss strategies to counter the devastation. In his presentations at the Blandin conferences, Smith passionately expounded on the potential benefits of a venture fund. Such a fund could encourage long-run economic growth in a way that an expanded small business lending program or a campaign to attract large out-of-state manufacturers could not.

Following these meetings, Smith and a small group of his business colleagues accepted the Blandin Foundation's challenge to further investigate the viability of his vision. They began by conducting an informal survey of business development organizations and local attorneys, accountants, and bankers. The organizations estimated that they received approximately 400 proposals seeking financing annually, of which almost 100 specifically sought equity investments. The businessmen confirmed that they reviewed roughly the same number of new business proposals that needed equity capital infusions. The primary financial instrument used by the existing economic development organizations and local banks and thrift institutions, however, was debt. In many cases, it appeared that the firms could be far better off if they could obtain equity financing.

Initially, the possibility of building upon the pioneering community development venture program of the Kentucky Highlands Investment Corporation (KHIC) was investigated. KHIC was created during the "Great Society" program initiated by President Lyndon Johnson; its venture capital organization officially began operation in 1974. The chronic underemployment and the rural setting of eastern Kentucky posed challenges similar to those faced by northeastern Minnesota. The fund was initially capitalized with a $15 million grant from the federal government. Over the years, the program had had a substantial impact on the employment of the region.

Although Northeast's founders respected KHIC's contribution, they sought to design a venture fund tailored to fit the particular needs of the region. They decided to establish two organizations, operating under a single parent. The for-profit Northeast Venture Development Fund would manage between $5 and $10 million of venture capital investments. A companion organization was the Northeast Entrepreneur Fund (NEF), which was seen as raising $750,000. This organization would provide management assistance and loans to very small businesses and the self-employed. Their services would target the region's low-income and structurally unemployed residents. This would be structured as a nonprofit (501c-3) organization, in order to enable it to accept grants from outside sources. The parent organization, Northeast Ventures Corporation (NVC), would control both entities.[3] (The boards of the organization are summarized in Exhibit 2; biographies of key staff are presented in Exhibit 3.)

The venture fund was designed to operate like a traditional venture organization. The founders set a goal of an annual compounded return of 25% for the portfolio. Potential investments were to be evaluated against a hurdle rate of 33%. The fund sought to balance its portfolio between investments that provided current returns and those that would provide substantial returns later. This would enable them to meet their return objectives, maintain self-sufficiency, and have enough flexibility to pursue additional activities.

Like traditional venture funds, the fund anticipated that it would participate in syndicated investments with other venture capitalists. Initially, this was likely to take the

---

[3] As the fund evolved, NVC's management and board of directors realized that they could achieve savings in overhead costs by restructuring the organization. In a November 1994 restructuring, the Northeast Ventures Development Fund was merged into the parent company. NEF remained a separate organization.

form of investments in other funds' deals. Although the bulk of Northeast's investments would be in northeastern Minnesota, the fund would make a small number of investments in the Minneapolis region. These investments, it was hoped, would generate attractive returns and raise the overall portfolio's performance. Venture capital funds based in the Minneapolis region were gaining increasing recognition: their share of all funds raised had increased from 2.6% in 1979–80 to 5.2% in 1989–90.[4] It was hoped that these co-investments might lead to some of these funds ultimately investing in turn in northeastern Minnesota firms.

The investment review process was also relatively standard. All investments would be authorized by Northeast's board of directors. The management would present their recommendations on pricing and deal structure to this body. The fund would require companies in their portfolio to periodically report on their progress in achieving their financial and social objectives; the fund was expected to hold a voting or advisory position on the firms' boards of directors.

Finally, the fund would also resemble the traditional venture funds in its compensation scheme. Although the base salaries would be below those of typical independent venture funds, the designers attempted to replicate the key incentive structure by retaining 20% of all realized capital gains for a staff bonus pool. As the fund's operating plan explained, "any proceeds from an exited investment will be used first to return 100% of its initial investment to Northeast Ventures, with any remainder divided between Northeast Ventures (80%), and an incentive bonus pool (20%)."[5]

At the same time, Smith realized that the fund would face challenges that traditional venture funds did not. One important concern of potential investors was surely job creation. In its planning documents, Northeast's goal was to create a total of 1400 jobs in its first seven years of operation. It further specified that at least 75% of these jobs would be full-time positions with health insurance in high value-added industries like manufacturing. Northeast also wanted 75% of the businesses it invested in to be majority-owned by residents of the region.

In addition, the venture fund would provide some funding to support NEF. The Entrepreneur Fund was not designed to be self-supporting. The revenues that it would generate from loans were not anticipated to meet the expenses of providing intensive training and consulting to their clients.

Another difference was the proposed structure of the fund. The fund was formed as a corporation rather than a limited partnership. There were at least two motivations for this decision. First, one of the criteria employed by the U.S. Internal Revenue Service to determine whether an organization qualifies for treatment as a limited partnership is the "limited-life test." An organization may fail to pass this test unless its charter defines a set life span or contains provision for dissolution in the event of management turnover. Northeast's founders wanted to build a permanent organization that could play an enduring role in the development of the region. Consequently, structuring the fund as a corporation (which did not need to satisfy this test) was attractive. Second, a corporate structure would facilitate the active involvement of the investors. Most venture capital funds were formed as partnerships because of tax reasons: the structure allows profits to be passed through to investors without being taxed at the entity level. In this way, tax-exempt organizations such as pension funds and founda-

---

[4] This is based on a tabulation of an unpublished database provided by Venture Economics.

[5] Northeast Ventures Corporation, "Northeast Venture Corporation: A Description," May 1988, p. 11. As of December 1995, the fund had a liability on its balance sheet of $146,000 of deferred incentive compensation payable pursuant to this plan.

tions avoid any tax liabilities. Partnership law, however, limits the extent to which the limited partners (the investors) can become involved in the day-to-day operation of the fund. If they play too active a decision-making role, they can lose their limited liability protection.[6]

Because Northeast was structured as a corporation, its investors received less favorable tax treatment. In particular, any capital gains from portfolio firms would be taxed at the fund level, even if the investors were almost entirely tax-exempt organizations. The founders understood the inherent disadvantages of the decision but preferred to have the active involvement of the investors. The fund's outside directors also included financiers and community leaders, who brought to the table a wealth of expertise and personal contacts.

FUNDRAISING

Convinced of NVC's viability, the Blandin Foundation provided the seed capital in early 1989. Smith was asked to continue to lead the effort. As the president of the region's largest law firm, Fryberger, Buchanan, Smith & Frederick, he knew the time and energy needed to grow an enterprise. After careful consideration, however, Smith reaffirmed his commitment to the effort. Despite his other commitments, he could not sit on the sidelines while his community was in need.

Smith began by pursuing funding from major foundations and local corporations with an interest in the development of their region. In addition to the Blandin Foundation, the largest sources of capital were the Ford, MacArthur, and Northwest Area Foundations and Minnesota Power. The Ford Foundation was a natural group to approach. Not only was it one of the largest domestic foundations, but it was particularly interested in experimenting with novel approaches to economic development. Ford was an investor in high-risk economic development projects around the globe, typically participating as a minority investor to ensure the involvement of local sources of support. Thomas F. Miller, the head of program-related investments (PRIs) at the Ford Foundation, had previously headed Kentucky Highlands' venture program. He thus had an intimate understanding of the challenges posed by community development venture capital. Miller was usually very reluctant to support prospective venture capitalists, but he was persuaded by Smith's determination and experience, as well as by the demonstrated needs of the region.

Ford, like many other major foundations, kept its philanthropic investments distinct from the management of its endowment. These PRIs had an explicitly charitable, rather than financial, intent. One potential concern about such investments was that they might be closely scrutinized by the U.S. Internal Revenue Service. If the IRS believed that the foundation's intention was not primarily charitable or that the production of income was a substantial purpose of making the investment, it could designate the PRI as a "jeopardizing investment," which could result in the imposition of an excise tax. As a result, Ford scrutinized Northeast Ventures' charitable purpose carefully and structured its PRI as a loan with a below-market interest rate.[7]

---

[6] These tests are laid out in Treasury Regulations 301.7701-2, also known as the "Kintner regulations."

[7] The Blandin Foundation, on the other hand, decided to structure its PRI into Northeast as an equity investment. Before doing so, it requested (and received) a special ruling from the U.S. Internal Revenue Service authorizing the transaction. Despite this ruling, the IRS could review its Northeast Ventures investment in retrospect.

In September 1990, the Ford Foundation made NVC a loan of $1.5 million at 1% interest, payable annually. It required Northeast to make three principal payments of $500,000, due in September 1997, 1998, and 2000. These funds had to be used primarily for the equity financing of new, restructuring, or expanding businesses located in northeastern Minnesota. The fund was not allowed to invest more than 10% of capital in any one deal or more than 15% of capital outside the region. Ford also insisted that the social return expectations be specified in the covenants to the loan agreement, including specific annual job-creation targets. Not meeting these targets was an event of default in the loan agreement.

The John D. and Catherine T. MacArthur Foundation, sharing Ford's concerns about the inadequacy of debt financing for new firms in disadvantaged regions, had earlier invested in a corporate-sponsored fund to encourage new ventures in the Chicago area. MacArthur structured its PRI in a similar manner to Ford's. In December 1990, the foundation loaned NVC $500,000 at 3.5% interest, payable quarterly, with the principal due in January 2001. Subsequently, in July 1993, MacArthur made another loan to NVC of $1 million, with 5% interest payable quarterly and the principal due in July 2003.

In addition to $3 million of PRI debt from Ford and MacArthur, Northeast raised $4.7 million in equity. Among the first investors was Minnesota Power, a private utility that served northeastern Minnesota. Minnesota Power viewed economic development as an inseparable portion of its business growth strategy. It was actively involved in the Blandin meetings and therefore was very familiar with Smith's efforts to develop Northeast Ventures. In addition to Minnesota Power's $1 million investment, the Blandin Foundation invested $2 million, Northwest Area Foundation, $1 million, Minnesota Technologies, $500,000, and the Northland Foundation, $200,000.[8]

Unlike the limited partners in many traditional venture funds, the equity investors agreed to allow much of the capital gains from their investments to be reinvested by the fund. In particular, they agreed to accept only the amount of distributions sufficient to give them an annual return of no more than 5%, "until such time that a more significant return can be provided (if ever)."[9] All other capital gains accruing to the fund would be reinvested, at least for the foreseeable future.

THE IMPLEMENTATION OF NORTHEAST VENTURES

The implementation of Northeast's strategy, Smith realized, had posed two challenges that he had not fully appreciated when he began the initiative. The first of these was the nature of the investments. The fund managers had hoped to invest in firms in a variety of situations, from start-ups to later-stage deals. Traditional venture capital firms enjoyed the luxury of rejecting 50 to 100 business plans for each one in which they invested. As Smith and Sandbulte soon realized, this was not the case for a fund based in northeastern Minnesota. The limited number of potential investments meant that Northeast had to consider promising-but-poorly articulated business plans that other venture funds might reject out of hand. As a result, many more investments in Northeast's portfolio were early stage than had been originally anticipated. As of January 1996, NVC had invested $4.5 million in 16 firms. A summary of NVC's investments is provided in Exhibit 4; Exhibit 5 presents information regarding the portfolio companies.

---

[8] In addition, the IRRRB had agreed to invest $1 million of equity. This transaction was expected to close in the second quarter of 1996.

[9] Northeast Ventures Corporation, "An Operating Plan for Northeast Venture Development Fund, Inc.," September 1989, p. 4.

A natural consequence of this investment mix was that the Northeast staff was required to spend much of their time working with entrepreneurs. Many of these interactions were similar to those performed by other venture capitalists: attending board meetings, reviewing financial statements, and assisting in key personnel decisions. Similarly, Smith and Sandbulte used their many ties to local leaders to help their firms obtain needed resources. For instance, with the help of Northeast, their portfolio company Larex would be moving into a $6 million manufacturing facility. The plant, which was the first to be located in an industrial park developed by Minnesota Power, was built by the IRRRB and leased to the firm. Minnesota Power acted as general contractor during the construction and agreed to provide utility services at a discounted rate.

The second challenge that Northeast faced was exiting investments. The immaturity and small size of the firms in its portfolio forced Northeast to consider alternatives to initial public offerings. Exiting investments via acquisition raised particularly sensitive issues. The social benefit to the regional economy could be lost when a local company was acquired, if the acquirer relocated or streamlined the firm. Yet acquisitions could also lead to an expansion of social benefits. An example is Kentucky Ventures' exit of American Bag Corporation: the sale of the company to Milliken & Co. resulted in an increase in local economic activity when the acquirer moved production from other facilities to the plant. Other possibilities included the repurchase of shares by managers, the sale of equity to employee stock ownership plans (ESOPs), or the creation of "seasoned pools" of their investments that could be sold to other investors.

As of January 1996, 11 active firms remained in Northeast Ventures' portfolio. Two had been exited profitably, two had been written off, and one was dormant. One firm that had been successfully exited was Diametrics, a medical device company based near Minneapolis. In 1991, Northeast had co-invested with Medical Innovation Partners, one of whose partners, Robert Nickoloff, was a board member of NVC. The company went public in June 1994, and Northeast had liquidated its position by selling shares over the course of 1995. A second exit was that of Partridge River, a manufacturer of quality wood products such as kitchen cabinet parts and artists' easels. Several years after Northeast's original investment, the firm needed significant financing for an upgrade of its equipment. Rather than accepting additional financing from Northeast (which would have entailed the dilution of the entrepreneur's ownership stake to below 50%), the entrepreneur brought in another investor. The investor purchased Northeast's stake at a significant premium to the original investment and contributed additional financing to the firm at a high valuation. This enabled the entrepreneur to maintain a majority stake.

In contrast to these profitable exits, a few of their investments had not been successful. An example was the investment in Minnesota Aquafarms, written off in 1994. Minnesota Aquafarms' strategy was to raise salmon in fresh-water lakes created in local mine pits. The company, however, experienced difficulties in its efforts to comply with the state's environmental regulations. The firm eventually sold off its inventory and closed operations. Exhibits 6 and 7 provide information on the potential exits foreseen by Northeast; Exhibit 8 provides some additional details on the investments.

THE FUTURE OF NORTHEAST VENTURES

On this cold, sunny winter day, Smith was thinking about a variety of key issues that the Shorebank report had raised. The report had been prepared by Shorebank Advisory Services, an affiliate of the Shorebank Corporation. Shorebank was the holding company for the South Shore Bank, the first community development bank in the country and one of the most respected such banks. Exhibit 9 summarizes the evaluation.

One question raised by the report was whether Northeast had found the proper balance between financial and social objectives. The report indicated that the fund had succeeded in generating attractive financial returns.[10] At the same time, Northeast was behind its original target of creating 200 jobs per year. Northeast's calculations suggested that, as of the end of 1995, their portfolio firms had created a total of 418 jobs. A total of 173 of these jobs were in northeastern Minnesota. The report implied that Northeast might be following the traditional venture capital model too closely. If the fund instead made debt investments in more mature firms, more rapid job creation might result.

Smith realized that the relatively limited job growth was due largely to the mixture of investment opportunities. Many early-stage companies grew slowly in their initial years. Employment growth might have been greater had Northeast instead chosen to make loans to established concerns. But Smith believed that employment growth was not the appropriate measure. In particular, the firms that would have received debt financing from Northeast might have financed their projects otherwise through private-sector sources. Much of the employment growth at these firms would have occurred in any case. What was really needed, Smith mused, was a measure of value created by the investments.

A second concern raised by Shorebank was the way in which the fund was structured. Although Northeast's operating expenses (which were paid out of the fund each year) were very close to the amount originally projected, the $82,500 in annual debt service to their program-related investments created a substantial draw against cash flows. Furthermore, the repayment of principal was set to begin in 1997. Shorebank urged Northeast to renegotiate these principal repayments. In January 1996, Northeast and Ford agreed to extend the principal repayments to 2002, 2003, and 2004.

More generally, Shorebank questioned the viability of community development venture capital. Although Smith strongly believed in the need for equity financing for emerging firms, the critique prompted him to wonder about what the future held for the sector. Since the creation of Northeast Ventures, there had been increasing interest in how venture capital could address the needs of underdeveloped regions. In recent years, several organizations had sought to marry social goals with the traditional venture capital model. The Ford and MacArthur Foundations had promoted these efforts by supporting the Community Development Venture Capital Alliance (whose members are summarized in Exhibit 10).

The most significant challenge facing community development funds, Smith believed, was that such investments generally provided lower financial returns than traditional venture capital funds. A study of selected investments by two funds suggested that the returns had been quite low, under 5%.[11] Such returns would limit the ability of these organizations to raise funds from the sources that financed conventional venture capital funds—that is, endowments and pension funds. The managers of these institutions were concerned that investing in funds that promised high risk and modest returns would be counter to their fiduciary responsibilities.

---

[10] The report stated, after calculating the effects of the two successful exits and three write-downs (or potential write-downs), "total net realized return will be $1,009,269, or 24.4% [of the $4.128 million invested through October 1995], closely approximating the 25% portfolio return projected in the plan." Shorebank Advisory Services, "Northeast Ventures Corporation: Interim Strategic Assessment," October 1995.

[11] David L. Jegen, "Community Development Venture Capital: Managing the Tension Between Social and Financial Goals," Unpublished manuscript, Harvard Law School, May 1996, Appendix III. These were gross returns—that is, not adjusted for any management fees or incentive compensation paid to the venture investors.

The limited ability to raise funds to date also had a pronounced effect on expected future returns. Several community development funds recently formed or currently being raised had average management fees of about 4.5% of capital under management. This was more than twice the average of traditional venture funds.[12] These high fees reflected two facts. First, substantial fixed costs were involved in running a venture fund of any size, so the relative share of expenses declined with fund size. Most community development venture funds were very small—as of the end of 1995, only one fund had raised more than $10 million. Second, the young firms typically financed by community development venture funds usually required intensive assistance and monitoring. These high fees would clearly depress the returns to the funds' investors.

Smith believed that if community development funds could consistently produce returns slightly below those of traditional venture funds, they might be more attractive to institutional investors. As of the beginning of 1995, the capital-weighted return for all venture capital funds formed between 1969 and 1990 was 10.5%.[13] If the community development funds could consistently generate returns of 8% or 9%, Smith believed, they might be able to attract pension investments. One complex issue would be how to trade off the social benefits against lower returns. Perhaps a performance index for the traditional venture capital industry could serve as a benchmark, with some adjustment for the added social benefits provided by community development funds.[14]

Another potential source of capital was the public sector. Scores of states established state venture capital programs during the 1980s, allocating about $200 million in public revenues and about $1 billion in public employee pension funds. Although many states had recently abandoned these efforts, several were seeking other ways to encourage entrepreneurship within their boundaries. These might be an important source of capital for community development venture capital funds.[15]

The federal government was also interested in helping community development venture funds raise capital. In July 1995, Congress had authorized $50 million for the Community Development Financial Institutions Fund, to be administered by the U.S. Department of the Treasury. These funds were to be invested in community development venture funds, community development banks, and other organizations. Legislation pending in Congress in January 1996 called for the U.S. Department of Agriculture to establish a pool of federal guarantees for investors in rural community development venture funds. Investors in funds selected for such a program would be assured that they would receive their money back, even if all the portfolio investments went bad. The quasi-government Overseas Private Investment Corporation had

---

[12] Jegen, op cit., p. 16. Data on compensation in traditional venture capital partnerships are presented in Paul A. Gompers and Josh Lerner, "An Analysis of Compensation in the U.S. Venture Capital Partnership," *Journal of Financial Economics* 51 (1999): 3–44.

[13] Venture Economics, *Investment Benchmarks Report: Venture Capital,* Venture Economics, 1995. Had more recent funds been included in this calculation, the average would be lower, because the newer funds held many immature investments.

[14] Although a recent U.S. Department of Labor memo allowed firms to make economically targeted investments, it stated that such "an investment would not be prudent if it would be expected to provide a plan with a lower rate of return than alternative investments with a commensurate degree of risk." See "Interpretative Bulletin Relating to the Employee Retirement Income Security Act of 1974," *Federal Register* 59 (June 23, 1994): 32606–7.

[15] Activity of state venture funds is reviewed in Peter K. Eisinger, "The State of State Venture Capitalism," *Economic Development Quarterly* 5 (February 1991): 64–76, and Peter K. Eisinger, "State Venture Capitalism, State Politics, and the World of High-Risk Investment," *Economic Development Quarterly* 7 (May 1993): 131–139.

employed a similar program since 1990 to encourage investments in venture funds focusing on developing nations.[16]

Although the promise of public money was substantial, it also posed potential concerns. In particular, funds backed by public dollars had in the past encountered political pressures to invest in firms run by politically influential individuals, even if the investments were unlikely to yield attractive financial or social returns. In other cases, public funds had been allocated to venture capitalists with little experience or questionable track records.[17]

Smith wondered what the future held in store. Would he and his peers generate sufficiently attractive returns to lure institutional investors? Would the public sector emerge as an important source of funds? Would the structure of venture funds devoted to community development evolve further? Despite these questions, Smith was convinced that the marriage of community development objectives with the discipline of venture capital had immense potential. As he mused:

> Wealth creation through small business ownership tied to communities has been the backbone of flourishing, empowered communities. The venture capital method, when tied to community development objectives, can be a powerful engine for distressed communities across the nation. We can, and must, make this work.

---

[16] For descriptions of these programs, see Kirsten S. Moy, "Prepared Statement before the Subcommittee on Veterans Affairs, Housing and Urban Development, and Independent Agencies, House Committee on Appropriations," April 1996; and Ray Moncrief, "Testimony Before the Resource Conservation, Research and Forestry Subcommittee, House Committee on Agriculture," May 1995.

[17] To cite the most conspicuous example, the federally guaranteed Small Business Investment Company (SBIC) program was initially plagued with numerous defaults. Although the program was restructured, it continued to experience a high default rate. For background, see Charles M. Noone and Stanley M. Rubel, *SBICs: Pioneers in Organized Venture Capital,* Capital Publishing Company, 1970, and U.S. General Accounting Office (GAO), *Small Business—Information on SBA's Small Business Investment Company Programs,* Report RCED-95-146FS, GAO, 1995.

Exhibit 1   Minnesota Economic Regions and Counties

Source: Corporate documents.

Exhibit 2   Boards of Directors of Northeast Ventures Corporation and Northeast Entrepreneur Fund, January 1996

Northeast Ventures Corporation	Northeast Entrepreneur Fund, Inc.
Nick Smith	Nick Smith
Chairman, CEO, Northeast Ventures Corporation	*Chairman, CEO, Northeast Ventures Corporation*
Chairman	*Chairman*
Fryberger, Buchanan, Smith and Frederick, P.A.	*Fryberger, Buchanan, Smith and Frederick, P.A.*
John Harris	Christopher D. Anderson
Partner	*Attorney*
Faegre & Benson	*Minnesota Power*
Theodore A. Johnson	Mary Ives
President	*General Manager and Co-Owner*
Minnesota Cooperation Office for Small Business & Job Creation	*Mike Ives Realty*
Arthur R. Kydd	Kathryn Jensen
President	*Senior Vice President*
St. Croix Management Group, Ltd.	*Charles K. Blandin Foundation*
Robert S. Nickoloff	Kjell R. Knudson
General Partner	*Director*
Medical Innovation Partners	*University of Minnesota, Duluth Center for Economic Development*
Mark Phillips	Rob Marwick
Director, Corporate Relations	*Vice President—Business Banking*
Minnesota Power	*Norwest Bank Minnesota Mesabi, N.A.*
Kevin Pietrini	Kimberly M. Renner
President	*Owner*
Queen City Federal Savings and Loan Association	*KMR Designs*
Geraldine R. Van Tassel	Kerry Zlebnik
Vice President Corporate Resource Planning	*Instructor*
Minnesota Power	*Imesabi Community College*

Source: Corporate documents.

Exhibit 3   Key Staff of Northeast Ventures Corporation

Nick Smith, Chairman and Chief Executive Officer

Nick Smith founded Northeast Ventures Corporation and Northeast Entrepreneur Fund, its non-profit affiliate, in 1989. He has served as Chairman and Chief Executive Officer of both entities since inception. He is President and a founding director of the Community Development Venture Capital Alliance, a national organization formed in 1993 to provide a network and advocate for community development venture capital in America.

Smith is also Chairman of Fryberger, Buchanan, Smith and Frederick, P.A., a regional law firm based in Duluth, Minnesota. He has over 35 years experience in representing small and medium-sized businesses, assisting clients with financing needs ranging from debt of all kinds to private placements of equity and public offerings, and has earned recognition for his positive influence on the business community. He was named 1990 Business Person of the Year by the School of Business and Economics at the University of Minnesota-Duluth, and was also the recipient of the 1992 Minnesota Financial Services Advocate Award, presented by the United States Small Business Administration.

He is the founding Chairman of Lake Superior Center, an international education center focusing on global issues of fresh water and also serves on the Equity Fund board of Minnesota Technology and the boards of directors of Minnesota Power, North Shore Bank of Commerce, and Advantage Minnesota. Smith attended Amherst College and the University of Minnesota Law School, receiving G.S.L. and J.D. degrees, cum laude, in 1960.

Greg Sandbulte, President and Chief Operating Officer

Sandbulte has been with Northeast Ventures since its inception, and oversees all aspects of its day-to-day operations. Prior to joining Northeast Ventures, Sandbulte served as Executive Director of the Northspan Group, Inc., a private non-profit development consulting group based in Duluth and serving the seven counties of northeastern Minnesota. His work focused primarily on areas of business finance, both debt and equity for clients both private and public, and on issues related to the development and diversification of the northeastern Minnesota economy.

Sandbulte serves on the boards of directors of several portfolio companies, as well as the Northland Foundation, a regional foundation based in Duluth. He attended the University of North Dakota and University of Minnesota, earning B.S.B.A. and M.B.A. degrees respectively.

Tom Van Hale, Vice President

Prior to joining Northeast Ventures in 1990, Van Hale was Director of the Natural Resources Research Institute Business Group in the University of Minnesota-Duluth Center for Economic Development. In that capacity, his efforts focused on assisting businesses seeking to commercialize products based on Minnesota's indigenous resources. Van Hale has managed a variety of small businesses, and sits on the board of directors of several of Northeast Ventures' portfolio companies. He holds a B.S. degree from St. Cloud State University, and an M.B.A from the University of Minnesota-Duluth.

Sandra Miller, Administrative Assistant

Miller provides secretarial support, as well as handling the daily logistics of office management including information storage and retrieval, financial record keeping, and receptionist duties. She has experience and educational background appropriate to her responsibilities.

Source: Corporate documents.

Exhibit 4   Summary of Portfolio Companies

ATAK, Inc., Duluth, Minnesota:[a] ATAK manufactures high-quality bicycle apparel and accessories and markets them directly to independent bike dealers throughout the United States and Canada. The company's strategy of using telemarketers to call on a large number of accounts in a wide geographic area allows it to provide high-quality services and products to an underserviced market at very competitive prices.

Courtland Design, Inc., Duluth, Minnesota:[a] Courtland Design has developed a product referred to as "Suspenders." The product is used to suspend telephones from modular office partitions, thereby creating additional desktop space.

Diametrics Medical, Inc., Roseville, Minnesota: Diametrics developed and is beginning market introduction of a patented bedside blood gas analyzer which rapidly provides highly reliable blood gas information.

Employer Data Communications, Inc., Two Harbors, Minnesota: Employer Data Communications, Inc. (EDC) is a fee-for-service third-party administrator of 125 flexible spending accounts and 401(k) retirement plans. EDC uses specialized computer software to explain the 125 and 401(k) plan concepts to employees, resulting in higher than average enrollment rates.

Husky Manufacturing Company, Tower, Minnesota: Husky manufactures touch-free, automatic rollover carwash equipment. The company supports a wide and growing network of distributors who sell/install/service Husky units.

Integ, Inc., Roseville, Minnesota: Integ is a research and development stage company which has developed, and is pursuing a strategy to ultimately commercialize, a glucose monitoring system which does not require blood samples for its analysis, for use by diabetics. If successful, Integ will not only provide a pain-free and blood-free method for diabetics to monitor their condition, but should also be a significant financial success based on the anticipated demand for such a product.

Larex International, Inc., Cohasset, Minnesota: Larex is a start-up biomaterials company that holds the right to a process patent for refining a type of sugar found in trees of the larch family, particularly western larch and tamarack. The company will identify and develop markets for this product in the biomedical and pharmaceutical industries.

Minnesota Aquafarms, Inc., Chisholm, Minnesota: Minnesota Aquafarms raises trout and Chinook salmon in spring-fed abandoned iron ore mine pits near Chisholm on the Mesabi Iron Range. The net-pen aquaculture operation in this unique water resource provides wholesome fish products to the Upper Midwest market, fresher, faster, and at a lower transportation cost than any competitor.

Northeast Heart, Duluth, Minnesota: Northeast Heart is a research and development project, formed to build a pulsatile blood pump or artificial heart.

Omega Marketing, Inc., Duluth, Minnesota: Omega Marketing is a start-up company manufacturing and distributing odor absorption products. Omega products use granular activated carbon in a receptacle which is applied to the underside of waste container covers to eliminate offensive odors.

Partridge River, Inc., Hoyt Lakes, Minnesota: Partridge River is a specialized manufacturer of precision and wood component parts for furniture and cabinets. Using readily available light-colored woods such as aspen, basswood, birch and maple, the company mills the wood to meet specifications of manufacturing customers throughout the United States.

Ribbon Recyclers, Inc., Rochester and Grand Rapids, Minnesota: Ribbon Recyclers provides new and recycled imaging products to business. Its products consist of a broad range of ribbon-based products which include re-inked products and reused printing cartridges stuffed with new ribbon. The company also sells recharged laser toner cartridges.

Telephone Equipment Supply, Inc., Grand Rapids, Minnesota: Telephone Equipment has developed a message-waiting light for use in conjunction with voice messaging systems. The light is expected to enjoy wide acceptance based on ease of installation and use, low cost, and customer desire for simplifying message notification.

Thomson Berry Farms, Duluth, Minnesota: Thomson Berry Farms is a food processing company which packs and markets a line of fruit jams, syrups, vinegars, and other specialties under its own label, as well as for many private label customers.

Transformer Technology, Northeastern Minnesota: Transformer Technology is a research and development project focusing on acquiring and developing technology relating to electromagnetic devices, primarily electric transformers. The scope of the project includes acquiring the technology from the inventor and working closely with the inventor to complete applications on the technology, to demonstrate the value of the technology for use in manufacturing transformers and to build a prototype of a unique high frequency alternator.

Van Technologies, Inc., Knife River, Minnesota: Van Technologies Inc., (VTI) provides consulting, R&D and custom formulation services for industrial customers wanting to use environmentally compliant coatings to achieve new air emission standards. The environmentally compliant coating technologies used by VTI allow its customers to reduce the level of volatile organic compounds emitted when coating solvents, such as turpentine and lacquer thinner, evaporate. VTI customers include metal castings, plate glass, eyeglass lens, sheet aluminum and adhesive manufacturers.

[a]The Shorebank analyses (**Exhibits 5** through **7** and **9**) do not include ATAK or Courtland Design, in which Northeast made initial investments totaling $71 thousand in December 1995.

Source: Corporate documents.

Exhibit 5   Northeast Ventures Portfolio: Sales, Profitability, Employment, and Ownership, June 1995

Company Investment Purposes Dates	Cumulative Investment	% of NVC Portfolio	NVC Ownership % in the Firm	% of Leverage to NVC Investment	Sales Initial Year	Sales Current Year Estimate	Profitability Initial Year	Profitability Current Year Estimate	Net New NE MN Employees as of 3/31/95	Local Ownership
Partridge River Expansion 11/90; 9/94	225,000	2.92%	42.00%	107.00%	2,500,000	3,800,000	54,000	200,000	17	Y
Diametrics Medical, Inc. Expansion 2/91; 6/91	500,000	6.49%	1.92%	16754.00%	N/A	1,600,000	N/A	-19,776,000	0	N
Employer Data Comm. Turnaround/Start-Up 8/91; 2/92	170,000	2.21%	69.00%	16.00%	106,341	380,000	-54,934	35,000	7	Y
Husky Manufacturing Co. Start-Up 11/91; 12/92; 4/93; 3/94	335,492	4.36%	54.50%	132.00%	0	1,477,000	0	139,000	8	Y
Telephone Equipment R&D/Start-Up 2/92; 11/92; 3/95	540,736	7.02%	73.60%	38.64%	584,000	1,200,000	51,000	100,000	6	Y
Thomson Berry Farms Turnaround 9/92	106,000	1.38%	39.80%	67.38%	437,000	730,000	-38,700	10,000	10	Y
Larex International Inc. Start-Up 5/93; 9/94; 9/95	750,000	9.74%	18.20%	365.00%	N/A	360,000	N/A	-2,540,000	10	Y
Van Technologies Start-Up 4/94; 6/95	160,000	2.08%	42.00%	29.38%	132,889	250,000	-58,389	-40,000	2	Y
Transformer Technology R&D 9/94	75,000	0.97%	100.00%	0.00%	N/A	N/A	N/A	N/A	0	Y
Ribbon Recyclers Expansion 12/94	250,000	3.25%	20.87%	87.50%	1,500,000	same	25,000	same	10	Y
Integ R&D 6/95	250,000	3.25%	0.66%	8867.00%	N/A	N/A	N/A	N/A	0	N
Total*	4,127,959								70	9

488

Exhibit 5 (continued)

*The total invested on the previous page included the following investment amounts written off or projected to be written off:

Company Investment Purpose Dates	Cumulative Investment	% of NVC Portfolio	NVC Ownership % in the Firm	% of Leverage to NVC Investment	Sales Initial Year	Sales Current Year Estimate	Profitability Initial Year	Profitability Current Year Estimate	Net New NE MN Employees as of 3/31/95	Local Ownership
Minnesota Aquafarms (write off 12/94)	380,796	4.95%	Less than 1%	1,817.00%	2,858,000	1,489,000	-1,185,000	-1,782,000	N/A	N/A
Northeast Heart (write off 12/94)	9,935	0.13%	22.12%	171.00%	N/A	N/A	N/A	N/A	N/A	N/A
Omega (projected write off)	375,000	4.87%	42.91%	16.00%	121,000	7,000	-191,500	-16,000	1	N/A
Total Losses	765,731									

Note: Net new jobs for Telephone Equipment and Thomson Berry Farms represent jobs that would have been lost had the firm ceased operations.

Source: Compiled from Shorebank Advisory Services, "NVC Interim Strategic Assessment," October 1995.

Exhibit 6   Northeast Ventures Projected Investment Exits, June 1995

Initial Investment	Investee	Cumulative Investment June 1995 (000's)	Exit Method	Anticipated Timing	Anticipated Value (000's)	
					Low	High
1990	Partridge River	225	Acquisition	95	482	482
1991	Diametrics Medical Co.	500	IPO	95	1,708	1,708
1991	Employer Data Comm.	170	ESOP/Acquisition	97-98	150	250
1991	Minnesota Aquafarms Inc.	381	Write Off	94	0	0
1991	Husky Manufacturing Co.	335	IPO/Acquisition	98-99	1,000	3,000
1992	Telephone Equipment	541	Management Buyback/ESOP	98-99	0	5,500
1992	Thomson Berry Farms	106	Acquisition/ESOP	97-98	600	1,000
1993	Omega Marketing, Inc.	375	Write Off/ Acquisition	95-96	0	375
1993	Larex International, Inc.	750	IPO/Acquisition	97-98	2,250	6,000
1993	Northeast Heart	10	Write Off	94	0	0
1994	Van Technologies Inc.	160	IPO/ESOP	99-00	500	1,000
1994	Transformer Technology	75	IPO/Acquisition	00-01	0	300
1994	Ribbon Recyclers	250	IPO/Acquisition	00-01	500	1,500
1995	Integ	250	IPO/Acquisition	98-99	500	1,250
			TOTAL		7,690	22,365

Note: Exit values for Partridge River and Diametrics are presented according to actual and 12/95 projection.
IPO = Initial Public Offering; ESOP = Employee Stock Ownership Plan.

Source: Compiled from Shorebank Advisory Services, "NVC Interim Strategic Assessment," October 1995.

Exhibit 7   NVC Projected Investment Exits ($000s)

Company	1994	1995	1996	1997	1998	1999	2000	2001
Pessimistic Scenario								
Partridge River (Note 2)		482						
Diametrics (Note 2)		1,708						
EDC					150			
Husky						1,000		
Telephone Equipment					0			
Thomson					600			
Omega		0						
Larex					2,250			
Van Technologies						500		
Transformer Technology							0	
Ribbon Recyclers								500
Integ						500		
Total	0	2,190	0	0	3,000	2,000	0	500
Moderate Scenario								
Partridge River (Note 2)		482						
Diametrics (Note 2)		1,708						
EDC					200			
Husky						2,000		
Telephone Equipment					0			
Thomson					800			
Omega		0						
Larex					4,125			
Van Technologies							750	
Transformer Technology							0	
Ribbon Recyclers								1,000
Integ						875		
Total	0	2,190	0	0	5,125	2,875	750	1,000
Optimistic Scenario								
Partridge River (Note 2)		482						
Diametrics (Note 2)		1,708						
EDC					250			
Husky						3,000		
Telephone Equipment						5,000		
Thomson					1,000			
Omega			375					
Larex					6,000			
Van Technologies							1,000	
Transformer Technology								300
Ribbon Recyclers								1,500
Integ						1,250		
Total	0	2,190	375	0	7,250	9,250	1,000	1,800

Notes: 1.   These projected exits are based upon Exhibit 6.
a.   Pessimistic Scenario: NVC's low anticipated value at the late projected date and possible losses at the early date.
b.   Moderate Scenario: The average of NVC's high and low anticipated values at the late projected date and possible losses at the early date.
c.   Optimistic Scenario: NVC's high anticipated value at the late projected date and no losses.
2.   Exit values for Partridge River and Diametrics are presented according to actual and 12/95 projection.

Source: Compiled from Shorebank Advisory Services, "NVC Interim Strategic Assessment," October 1995.

Exhibit 8   Profile of Northeast Ventures Activities

Excerpts from Income and Cash Flow Statements, 1989-1995 ($ millions)

	1989	1990	1991	1992	1993	1994	1995
Equity raised	4.00	0.70	0.00	0.00	0.00	0.00	0.00
Debt raised	0.00	2.00	0.00	0.00	1.00	0.00	0.00
Revenues from interest	0.17	0.34	0.46	0.36	0.24	0.21	0.24
Operating and interest expenses	0.25	0.34	0.47	0.50	0.55	0.52	0.54
Operating income	(0.08)	(0.00)	(0.01)	(0.13)	(0.31)	(0.31)	(0.30)
Amount invested	0.00	0.22	1.07	0.65	0.70	0.82	1.04
Proceeds from exited investments	0.00	0.00	0.00	0.00	0.00	0.00	2.19

Excerpts from Balance Sheet, December 1995 ($ millions)

	Amount
Current assets (cash + short-term investments)	3.81
Investments[a]	3.48
Current liabilities	0.16

Portfolio Summary, December 1995

Company	Cumulative Investment	Valuation
Current Portfolio Firms:		
1. Larex International	$1,000,000	$1,583,334
2. Omega Marketing, Inc.	375,000	1,000
3. Husky Manufacturing Company	376,932	541,160
4. Telephone Equipment, Inc.	540,736	540,736
5. Thomson Berry Farms	106,000	106,000
6. Employer Data Communications	170,000	170,000
7. Van Technologies, Inc.	160,000	160,000
8. Virginia Magnetics	75,000	75,000
9. Ribbon Recyclers, Inc.	250,000	250,000
10. Integ	250,000	250,000
11. Courtland Design, Inc.[b]	25,000	25,000
12. ATAK, Inc.[b]	45,518	45,518
Exited Firms:		
1. Diametrics	500,000	1,708,105
2. Partridge River	225,000	482,189
Written Off Firms:		
1. Minnesota Aquafarms	337,492	0
2. Northeast Heart	9,935	0
Totals	$4,486,613	$5,938,042

[a]The accountant's methodology for valuing private investments was slightly different than Northeast Ventures'. This accounts for the disparity between the valuation of investments on the balance sheet and the sum of the valuations of the current portfolio firms in the portfolio summary.

[b]The Shorebank analyses (**Exhibits 5** through **7 and 9**) do not include ATAK or Courtland Design, in which Northeast made initial investments in December 1995.

Source: Corporate documents.

Exhibit 9   NVC Social and Financial Performance Benchmarks

Objective	Benchmark in 1989 Plan	Experience-to-Date	Approach in 1995 Plan
Job Creation	*Per NVC:* 200 jobs per year for a total of 1,400 jobs through Year 7; 300 jobs per year thereafter. *Per Ford Foundation Management Letter:* Years 1 and 2 ('91 and '92) 100 Years 3 and 4 ('93 and 94) 180 Years 5 and 6 ('95 and '96) 260 Years 7 and 8 ('97 and '98) 300 Years 9 and 10 ('99 and 2000) 300	NVC management reports 158 full-time jobs created in northeastern Minnesota through June 30, 1995 (middle of Year 6). This represents 14.4% of the NVC benchmark of 1,100 jobs for the same period. 50 of the 158 jobs, or 31.6%, were retained, as opposed to newly created. The job creation numbers reported by NVC do not reflect layoffs nor recalls. There were 54 net new jobs and 16 retained jobs in the region as of June 30, 1995.	Per NVC management, the 1995 Operating Plan formalizes Ford job creation standards. The '95 plan calls for: • 710 jobs to be created over the five-year period from 1995 to 1999 (50.7% of the '89 Plan benchmark). • Not more than 20% of job creation should be in the form of job retention.
Job Targeting	At least 50% of the jobs created will be available to women, low-income and structurally unemployed persons.	NVC management reports that 92 jobs, or 59% of jobs created in northeastern Minnesota, have been filled by JPTA-eligible, low-income employees, *i.e.*, those who are "economically disadvantaged" or "dislocated workers" within northeastern Minnesota. An additional 13 jobs retained have been filled by eligible employees, bringing the total number of eligible employees to 83.9%.	Unchanged.
Job Quality	At least 75% of the jobs created will be full-time.	NVC only monitors full-time job creation and retention. Additional, part-time jobs may have been created as a result of NVC investment but are not tracked.	The 1995 plan appears to ease this requirement by stating that NVC will "*try to* ensure that at least 75% of the jobs created through North-east Ventures' investments will be full-time positions."
Health Insurance Benefits	Compensation for jobs will include health insurance.	Investment closing documents state that portfolio companies must offer employees an opportunity to participate in a healthcare plan in which the employer makes some contribution.	Unchanged.
Targeted Industry	Over 75% of the jobs created will be in manufacturing or value-added industries.	All portfolio companies fall in this category, so this benchmark has been fulfilled.	Unchanged.
Deal Volume	The fund will invest in three to four businesses a year for an average investment amount of $250,000.	1990: $ 225,000 for one firm 1991: 1,070,000; $267,000 average to 4 firms 1992: 647,052; $161,763 average to 4 firms 1993: 695,367; $231,789 average to 3 firms 1994: 815,380; $116,483 average to 7 firms 1995 (6/30): 675,100; $168,775 average to 4 firms The above amounts include both new and follow-on investments. In practice, NVC's cumulative investments in individual portfolio companies range from just under $10,000 to $750,000. An average investment amount is only useful for comparison to the benchmark.	The benchmarks are substantially unchanged. NVC will make at least 15 investments during the five-year period of a total of $5 million, divided between new and follow-on investments.
Leverage	The fund will leverage its investments a minimum of five times on a portfolio.	On a total portfolio basis, the leverage is 2832%, including debt and equity invested in all portfolio companies. If only companies located in northeastern Minnesota are included, leverage drops to 325% (approximately three-and-a-quarter times), including Larex, which was started in the region and will operate a plant there and Minnesota Aquafarms and Northeast Heart, which are now defunct.	Unchanged.

493

Exhibit 9 (continued)

Objective	Benchmark in 1989 Plan	Experience-to-Date	Approach in 1995 Plan
Regional Targeting	The amount of capital invested by NVC in businesses outside the region will be exceeded by the amount of venture capital brought into the region and co-invested with NVC investees. The fund will invest no more than 15% of capital outside northeastern Minnesota.	Over the life of the fund, NVC has invested $750 thousand, or 9.7% of capital, in medical equipment deals which are based in Minneapolis. This counts Larex as a regional firm, based upon NVC's leadership in its organization, and the plan to build a factory employing 60 persons in northeastern Minnesota. When NVC completes the liquidation of its holdings in Diametrics, its percentage of capital invested outside the region will decrease to 3.2%.	The 1995 Plan appears to ease this requirement by stating that the Fund will "try to ensure that the amount of capital invested by Northeast Ventures in businesses located outside northeastern Minnesota is exceeded by the amount of venture development capital brought into the region and co-invested in Northeast Ventures investees." The 15% cap on investment outside the region does not appear in the 1995 Plan.
Local Ownership	Businesses with a majority ownership in northeastern Minnesota will constitute at least 75% of the businesses in which NVC invests.	Nine, or 81.8% of the 11 firms in which NVC has active holdings are majority owned within northeastern Minnesota (these figures do not include the two investments which have been written off, or the one projected to be written off before year-end, all of which were located in northeastern Minnesota).	The 1995 Plan appears to ease this requirement by stating that NVC will "invest in businesses having a majority ownership from within north-eastern Minnesota, with a goal of at least 50% of investees exhibiting such ownership over time."
Portfolio Balance	NVC will balance its investments between seed, start-up, expansion, and buyouts.	One of the most difficult challenges of NVC implementation, per management. Of the 14 companies in which the fund has invested, 10 have been in an R&D or start-up phase, three have been expansions and one was a turnaround.	The '95 Plan does not specifically address this issue, but does articulate 1995 objectives to "make at least one investment with unusually dramatic financial return when compared with the balance" of NVC's portfolio, and "attempt to identify at least one investment in 1995 which can be structured to provide some level of current return."
Exits	ESOPS will be investigated in every NVC deal. The social benefits of NVC investments will be maintained after NVC's exit.	In general, it is too early to assess performance here. For the two exits which have occurred, an ESOP was considered and rejected for Partridge River, and Diametrics was an IPO.	This issue is not specifically addressed.
Self-Sufficiency	NVC will achieve a level of profits from its investments which will fully provide for its annual operating and investment expenses, as well as providing additional revenue which may be used by NVC as it deems appropriate. Generate a return of $1.25 million per year by Year 7 (1996)	Given the early, profitable exits from Partridge River and Diametrics and the slower than planned pace of investment, management reports that it will have sufficient revenue to cover operating expenses in 1995. But financial self-sufficiency beginning in 1996 is less certain.	The benchmark is unchanged, including return targets. The 1995 Plan states that NVC "will achieve exits with a cumulative value of at least $6 million during the period."

494

Source: Compiled from Shorebank Advisory Services, "NVC Interim Strategic Assessment," October 1995.

Exhibit 10   Descriptions of CDVCA Member Organizations

CDVCA members include community development corporations, state-funded venture firms, private venture capital firms, and foundations. Funding sources, organizational structures, and investment strategies vary.

Boston Community Loan Fund   is a ten-year old community development financial institution which has recently expanded from low-income housing lending to a broader range of community investments. It is currently establishing a community development venture capital subsidiary, BCLF Ventures, whose first investment was a highly subordinated loan to help establish a start-up worker-owned home care business.

Cascadia Revolving Fund   is a nonprofit community development financial institution working in Washington and Oregon. Cascadia focuses its lending activities on minority- and women-owned businesses, businesses located in economically distressed communities, and companies whose activities restore or preserve the environment. Cascadia's *Rural Development Investment Fund* is a new initiative to provide investment capital to start-up and existing businesses involved in value-added wood and fish products, manufacturing from recycled materials and other diversified manufacturing industries located in the rural communities of the Pacific Northwest.

CEI Ventures, Inc.   is in development and will be a $5 million for-profit, socially responsible venture capital fund. The fund will create economic opportunities for people with low incomes by investing in businesses that will not only provide competitive returns on investment, but will also provide quality jobs, have a progressive attitude toward employee growth and development, have the potential to grow sufficiently to provide career opportunities for employees, and otherwise advance socially responsible business objectives including producing socially beneficial products and services (including health care and environmental businesses).

Commons Capital, the venture capital program of the Jessie Smith Noyes Foundation,   was established in 1993 as part of a comprehensive strategy to reduce the dissonance between grantmaking and investment management. Commons Capital targets early-stage private companies whose business is consistent with the Noyes Foundation's mission. Commons Capital is particularly interested in shaping affirmatively the culture of young companies with respect to equity, sustainable community development, and environmental impact. The initial capital allocated to this small venture capital investment program is $3,000,000.

Connecticut Innovations, Inc. (CII)   is a quasi-public state agency that provides product development and product marketing capital to small and medium-sized technology-oriented Connecticut Companies. Since 1989, CII has invested approximately $10 million/year and currently has an active portfolio of 100 companies.

Enterprise Corporation of the Delta (ECD)   is a private nonprofit business development organization serving the Delta region of Arkansas, Louisiana and Mississippi. ECD offers assistance in three program areas: Development Finance, Technical Assistance, and Market Development.

Impact Seven, Inc. (I-7)   is a 25-year old community development corporation serving the State of Wisconsin. As a community development financial institution (CDFI), I-7 has five revolving loan funds and a venture capital pool. Recipient of many national and state community development awards, I-7 has, among its many accomplishments, created over 9,400 jobs, constructed 1,156 new units, and rehabilitated 1,141 more.

Kentucky Highlands Investment Corporation   is a community development corporation which has provided funding and assistance to entrepreneurs and companies throughout Southeast Kentucky for the past 26 years. Kentucky Highlands' success lies in a willingness to consider any investment opportunity that has potential for developing into a profitable business while providing economic job opportunities to residents of Southeast Kentucky.

Local Economic Assistance Program, Inc. (LEAP) is a nonprofit formed in 1991 to help create community businesses employing low-income people in New York City. It especially helps in raising equity or seed capital, and is presently creating a venture fund. LEAP (New York) operates from the office of Community Capital Bank, a community development bank. LEAP (California) is a newly formed nonprofit which helps to create community businesses employing low-income people in the Bay Area. It especially helps with locating equity capital and plans to create its own venture fund. LEAP (California) is an affiliate of the Community Bank of the Bay, a community development bank in formation.

Northeast Ventures Corporation is a venture capital firm focusing its investment activity primarily in the seven counties of northeastern Minnesota, a restructured mining region. Northeast Ventures invests in both new and expanding businesses, and will consider investments in a wide range of industries. The amount and terms of its investments are based on the specific needs of the business, though all investments will include some equity component, and "typical" initial investment tend to range from $150,000 to $350,000. For larger financing requirements, Northeast Ventures will assemble both additional investors and appropriate sources of debt, for a complete financial package.

Neighborhood Ventures, Inc., an affiliate of Cleveland Development Bancorporation, is a mezzanine level fund focusing on small growth businesses primarily on the east side of Cleveland. The fund is under development and expects an initial capitalization of about $5 million.

Resources for Human Development, Inc. RHD's Capital To People system, which now includes five for-profit businesses with $1.4 million in product, provides a Mondragon-like system for operating the businesses, and a contract with each business to recycle 30% of profits back to social sector concerns. "We are demonstrating a model while encouraging others to join us in reinventing capitalism."

Source: Compiled from Community Development Venture Capital Alliance documents.

29

A Note on Private Equity Information Sources

Finding information about private equity-backed firms and private equity organizations is often difficult. If the firm is privately held, it is likely to attract little outside scrutiny and to disclose scant public information. Even if the firm is publicly traded, its coverage by the press may be infrequent. These problems are even more severe for private equity organizations. Private equity organizations tend to be extremely reluctant to disclose information about their successes, much less their failures.

Despite these difficulties, there are numerous occasions when it is critical to obtain information. One may be assessing a private firm as a strategic partner or a potential investment, or a private equity organization as a potential employer. This note summarizes the most useful information sources about these organizations. Before beginning, however, it should be stated that the most important information source is not discussed here: word-of-mouth. There is no substitute for informal "due diligence." Private equity organizations will often make 50 or even 75 calls before deciding to invest in a firm. A similar level of scrutiny may be appropriate before one accepts a position or undertakes a strategic alliance with a private firm.

INFORMATION ABOUT PRIVATE FIRMS

Business directories are an important, but rather limited, source of information about private firms. Directories such as Corporate Technology Information Service's *Corporate Technology Directory*, Gale Research's *Ward's Directory of U.S. Public and Private Companies*, and various state and industry directories provide basic information on employment, sales, industry focus, and year of formation. (Since these are based on survey responses, they are not always accurate!) But for more detailed information, one must turn to other sources.

A rich source of information is the press. Almost every firm, no matter how publicity-shy, generates some press attention. The easiest approach is to search well-cataloged databases such as ABI/Inform. Business Dateline provides full text of regional business publications, while OneSource and PROMT cover many of the smaller trade journals and newswires. The coverage of the trade press is more comprehensive through LEXIS-NEXIS, which also includes the *New York Times,* several newswire services, and many

This note was prepared by Josh Lerner. Copyright © 1998 by the President and Fellows of Harvard College. Harvard Business School case 299-018.

smaller papers. It also may make sense to check the *Wall Street Journal* Index. This is available in hard copy, on CD-ROM, or online (which also includes newswire stories not printed in the *Journal*). It also pays to check with industry contacts as to the key trade journals they read.

Three databases are the best sources for detailed financial information on private firms. First, Venture Economics, a unit of Securities Data Corporation (SDC), provides profiles of firms backed by venture capital and (less comprehensively) buyout funds in its VentureXpert (formerly known as the Venture Intelligence) Database. It also provides information about the amount of and the investors in each financing round. A typical entry is reproduced in Exhibit 1. Its Joint Venture and Strategic Alliances Database summarizes corporate transactions.

A second company, VentureOne, provides more detailed profiles, including information on directors and detailed business profiles. Although its coverage does not extend as far back in time as that of Venture Economics and only includes venture-backed firms, the accuracy and detail of its information is generally superior. A sample report is shown in Exhibit 2. Like the Venture Economics database, VentureOne permits extensive screening—for example, it is possible to identify all Internet firms that received seed financing in 1997 and were based in Massachusetts. VentureOne is a professional database, with subscriptions restricted to limited partners in private equity funds and corporations making direct investments.

Finally, information on debt financing is available through Dun and Bradstreet. This includes information on both bank loans and trade credit. It is far better to discover that a firm has defaulted on previous contractual obligations before entering into a business relationship with them rather than afterward!

Private firms sometimes make information available about themselves. It is certainly worth checking to see whether the firm has a site on the World Wide Web. This is easy to determine using the Yahoo index, as well as the various search engines such as Alta Vista. It may also be worthwhile to contact the firm: frequently, one can get the standard kit of information sent out to the press and/or potential customers without being asked too many questions. Although it may be easy to get this information, it may not always be accurate. In addition, a lot of helpful information may be available through a Web site specializing in that particular industry. For instance, Recombinant Capital—which markets a high-priced database on biotechnology–pharmaceutical alliances—has put much ancillary information on biotechnology firms on its Web site (*www.recap.com*).

A final source of information on private firms is the most specialized (and expensive). On occasion, one may be interested in establishing a relationship with a firm that has previously engaged in litigation. For instance, one may wish to enter into a collaborative venture with a firm that has previously litigated a key patent. Obtaining an understanding of the dispute may be important in evaluating the firm. These court records are readily available through a company called Federal Document Retrieval, which will photocopy some or all of the records.

INFORMATION ABOUT PUBLIC FIRMS

Public firms must file extensive information with the U.S. Securities and Exchange Commission. This makes finding out about these firms much easier. To track a company, the basic information is in the firm's initial public offering prospectus (description of the business, five years of financial results, directors and officers, principal shareholders, and financing history), and the annual 10-K filings (description of business and financial results) and proxy statements (officers and directors and principal shareholders). The most recent financial information is available in the quarterly 10-Q statements.

All these documents are available from Disclosure in hard-copy, microfiche, and (for the past decade) on CD-ROM. Much of this information (as well as news stories) are also available in summary form on the Bloomberg machines. Since mid-1996, most companies have also made filings in electronic form, which are available (text only; pictures not included) on the Internet at the EDGAR site *(www.sec.gov)*.

Firms must also file "material" documents. Firms differ in how they define what is material, but generally a firm going public will file copies of its financing agreements with private equity organizations and strategic alliances with larger firms. These will often have a wealth of information not disclosed elsewhere. In many cases, a press release will describe a strategic alliance in glowing terms, but the agreement itself will reveal that the alliance is much more limited in scope. It is interesting to note how often Wall Street analysts repeat what is in the press release, without bothering to check the agreement! When a firm goes public, it will typically file all material documents in a registration statement that accompanies the IPO prospectus (more technically known as an S-1 or an S-18). The index of a typical registration statement is reproduced in Exhibit 3. If the firm signs an important strategic document after it is already public, it will typically be filed in a statement known as an 8-K. These are also available from Disclosure and (since mid-1996 for most firms) at the EDGAR Web site. Firms often will file repeated amendments to their registration statements, scattering key documents across their statements. This makes it very frustrating to find documents. Making life a little easier is the fact that subsequent 10-Ks will often list earlier documents filed by the firm and indicate when they were filed. LEXIS's FEDSEC/REGIS and FEDSEC/EVENTS databases provide a searchable directory of all such filings (and any exhibits contained therein) over the past five years. In general, firms make it difficult to find the most interesting items!

Analyst reports are a somewhat useful source of information. A number of analysts seem to do little more than rephrase corporate press releases, but others do careful and insightful studies. Analyst reports are one of the few public sources of financial projections for firms. Perhaps the easiest way to obtain analyst reports is to contact the head of investor relations at the firm or else the analysts directly. (Analysts covering each firm are listed in *Nelson's Directory of Investment Research,* and the dates of recent analyst reports are indicated in the Bloomberg news file.) Alternatively, many reports are available through the Investext database. Financial projections are available in the FirstCall and Bloomberg databases.

Several databases provide information about the financing activities of public firms. SDC publishes an annual index known as *Corporate Finance: The IDD Review of Investment Banking.* This also includes some large private placements. It is, however, rather awkward to search through. Disclosure's Compact D, which provides summary reports on offerings during the past five years (screened by many criteria) is easier to use. Much more comprehensive, however, is Security Data Company's Corporate New Issues database. This not only contains more detailed information, but it can be downloaded onto a Lotus or Excel spreadsheet for easy analysis. The usage fees, however, are quite high. At least temporarily, a database very similar to SDC's is being provided by a new vendor for free on the World Wide Web *(www.netresource.com/wsn)*.

Many publications cover the public marketplace and highlight financial innovations of all sorts. Among the best are *The Red Herring* (which focuses on high-tech firms),

Going Public: The IPO Reporter, Investment Dealer's Digest, and *CFO.* The periodicals are well worth scanning on a regular basis.

INFORMATION ABOUT PRIVATE EQUITY ORGANIZATIONS

Among the most difficult to track are the private equity organizations themselves. Most actively avoid the press. Although they disclose considerable information to their limited partners in annual reports and offering memorandums, these documents are generally confidential.

To obtain information about private equity organizations, one must thus use other means. It is worth searching LEXIS-NEXIS and other databases for the occasional mention of these firms. Both VentureOne and Venture Economics databases can be used to construct detailed profiles of various funds, but these are difficult to access or are very costly.

Thus, one is often forced to rely on industry directories. *Galante's Venture Capital and Private Equity Directory* profiles venture capital and private equity organizations alike; venture capital organizations only are profiled in *Pratt's Guide to Venture Capital Sources.* The *Pratt's* guide is quite useful, however, as it has been published for several decades. This allows one to answer questions such as which partners of the firm have left and how capital under management has changed. Several other directories list U.S. private equity firms, including the National Venture Capital Association's *Membership Directory,* but these are substantially less informative. A CD-ROM directory has been developed by Infon, from which data can be rapidly downloaded into a spreadsheet or a mail merge program.

Many venture capital organizations make some information available through the World Wide Web. The easiest way to find these organizations is through Yahoo: the list is located at Business and Economy/Companies/Financial Services/Financing/Venture Capital. The quality, informativeness, and accuracy of these Web pages vary widely. Most buyout organizations have been more cautious about embracing this technology. A few of the many more general sites about the venture capital *industry* more generally are informative, though most are pretty dreary. Among the best are PricewaterhouseCooper's *(www.pwcglobal.com/vc)* and Accel Partners' *(www.accel.com).* Additional sites are listed at the author's home page *(www.people.hbs.edu/jlerner).*

Although the above sources include some buyout firms, many more are listed in the National Register Publishing Company's *America's Corporate Finance Directory,* McGraw-Hill's *Corporate Finance Sourcebook,* SDC's *Directory of Buyout Financing Sources,* and the winter issue of *Financial World's Corporate Finance.* Small Business Investment Companies (a specialized type of private equity organization with government sponsorship) are listed in *Directory of Operating Small Business Investment Companies* and the National Association of Small Business Investment Companies' *Membership Directory.*

The names and nature of a fund's investors are potentially very valuable information. (They are also very useful for fundraising.) Two directories provide this information. Venture Economics' *Directory of Private Equity Investors* has better coverage; but considerably greater detail is available in Asset Alternatives' *Directory of Alternative Investment Programs.*

Occasionally, information may be needed about the private equity industry in general. This information falls into three broad classes: statistical analyses, legal guides, and general overviews. In addition to the publications cited below (especially the *Private Equity Analyst* and the *Venture Capital Journal*), there are several sources of statistical data. Particularly useful is VentureOne's *Annual Review* and *IPO Report*. The annual reviews of Venture Economics and the National Venture Capital Association are also helpful. VentureOne also does a variety of other special reports: they are summarized at *www.ventureone.com* (and may also be ordered there). For data on LBOs, it is useful to check the November/December issue of *Mergers and Acquisitions* and the Security Industry Association's (less useful) *Securities Industry Fact Book*. The primary sources for returns data are Venture Economics' *Investment Benchmarks Reports,* which are prepared for venture capital, other private equity (primarily buyouts), and international funds.

A second source of information relates to the legal status of private equity activities. The most useful reference guides are Joseph Bartlett's *Equity Finance*, the Practicing Law Institute's annual volume *Venture Capital,* Michael Halloran's *Venture Capital and Public Offering Negotiation,* and Jack Levin's *Structuring Venture Capital, Private Equity and Entrepreneurial Transactions.* (The first is the best general overview, and the second is the most useful in-depth analysis.)

Finally, there are more general overviews. Many collections of "war stories" by venture capitalists exist, which may make for enjoyable reading. Less entertaining but probably more helpful are the academic overviews of the industry: especially Fenn, Liang, and Prowse's "The Private Equity Market: An Overview." (An earlier version, *The Economics of the Private Equity Market,* is available on the Web at *www.imdr.com/venture/preqmkt.htm*) and (if you are interested in venture capital) Gompers and Lerner's *The Venture Capital Cycle.*

Information is available about European private equity firms in the European Venture Capital Association's *Yearbook* (formerly known as *Venture Capital in Europe,* this also has extensive statistical information), the *Venture Capital Report Guide to Venture Capital in the U.K. and Europe,* Galante's *Venture Capital and Private Equity Directory,* the *Fitzroy Dearborn International Directory of Venture Capital Funds,* and Initiative Europe's *European Buyout Review, European Buyout Monitor,* and *Who's Who in Risk Capital.* Many national venture capital associations in Europe publish (in their native languages) detailed annual reviews and directories. For instance, the British Venture Capital Association prepares a *Membership Directory* and *Report on Financing Activity.* The European Venture Capital Association has done a series of monographs on legal aspects of private equity investing across Europe that are very helpful.

Information on Asian private equity organizations and general trends is available in the Asian Venture Capital Journal's *Guide to Venture Capital in Asia. Galante's Venture Capital and Private Equity Directory* and the *Fitzroy Dearborn International Directory of Venture Capital Funds* have much useful information.

The final source of information—publications devoted to the private equity industry—include not only news stories, but also detailed profiles of organizations and the firms in which they invest. The most useful periodicals about the U.S. market are the *Venture Capital Journal, Buyouts,* and the *Private Equity Analyst.* A general-interest magazine focusing on venture capital is *Upside.* Detailed accounts of transactions are contained in *Private Equity Week* and the quarterly *Venture Edge.* The specialized world of Small Business Investment Companies is covered in the *NASBIC NEWS.* Asian private equity is covered in two publications, the *Asian Venture Capital Journal* and the less satisfactory *Venture Japan.* The European private equity scene is covered by the *European Venture Capital Journal* and the much less satisfactory *Start-Up.* Latin American funds are covered by the *Latin American Private Equity Analyst* and EuroMoney's *LatinFinance.*

WHERE TO FIND NON-INTERNET ITEMS

Asian Venture Capital Journal
80 Maiden Lane
New York, NY 10038
(212) 344-4411 (ph)
(212) 344-8074 (fax)
www.asiaventure.com
Asian Venture Capital Journal
The Guide to Venture Capital in Asia

Aspen Law and Business
A Division of Aspen Publishers Inc.
7201 McKinney Circle
Frederic, MD 21701
(800) 447-1717 (ph)
(212) 597-0335 (fax)
www.aspenpub.com
Structuring Venture Capital, Private Equity and Entrepreneurial Transactions [Levin]
Venture Capital and Public Offering Negotiation [Halloran]

Asset Alternatives
180 Linden Street, Suite 3
Wellesley, MA 02181
(617) 431-7353 (ph)
(617) 431-7451 (fax)
www.assetalt.com
Directory of Alternative Investment Programs
Galante's Venture Capital and Private Equity Directory
Latin American Private Equity Analyst
Private Equity Analyst

Blackwell Publishers
350 Main Street
Malden, MA 02148
(800) 835-6670 (ph)
(617) 388-8232 (fax)
www.blackwellpub.com
"The Private Equity Industry: An Overview" [Fenn, Liang, and Prowse, *Financial Markets, Institutions and Instruments*, Vol. 6, No. 4]

Bloomberg, L.P.
499 Park Avenue
New York, NY 10022
(212) 318-2000 (ph)
(212) 980-4585 (fax)
www.bloomberg.com
Bloomberg Database

British Venture Capital Association
Essex House
12-13 Essex Street
London WC2R 3AA

United Kingdom
44-171-2403846 (ph)
44-171-2403849 (fax)
www.brainstorm.co.uk/BVCA
British Venture Capital Association Membership Directory
British Venture Capital Association Report on Investment Activity

CFO Publishing Group
253 Summer St.
Boston, MA 02210
(617) 345-9700 (ph)
(617) 951-4090 (fax)
www.infonet.com
CFO Magazine

Corporate Technology Information Services
12 Alfred St.
Woburn, MA 01801
(800) 333-8036 (ph)
(781) 932-6335 (fax)
www.corptech.com
Corporate Technology Directory

Disclosure Inc.
5161 River Road
Bethesda, MD 20816
(800) 754-9690 (ph)
(301) 951-1753 (fax)
www.disclosure.com
Compact D Database
U.S. Securities and Exchange Commission Filings

European Venture Capital Association
Keibergpark
Minervastraat 6
B-1930 Zaventem
Belgium
32-27-150020 (ph)
32-27-250740 (fax)
www.evca.com
European Venture Capital Association Yearbook
Startup

Federal Document Retrieval
810 First Street, N.E., #600
Washington, DC 20002
(202) 789-2233 (ph)
(202) 371-5469 (fax)
Litigation file services

Fitzroy Dearborn Publishers
70 East Walton Street
Chicago, IL 60611
(312) 587-0131 (ph)
(312) 587-1049 (fax)
www.fitzroydearborn.com
Fitzroy Dearborn International Directory of Venture Capital Funds

Financial World Partners
1328 Broadway
New York, NY 10001
(212) 594-5030 (ph)
(212) 629-0021 (fax)
Financial World's Corporate Finance

Gale Research
27500 Drake Road
Farmington Hills, MI 48331-3535
(800) 877-GALE (ph)
(248) 699-8061 (fax)
www.gale.com
Ward's Business Directory of U.S. Private and Public Companies

Infon
15600 N.E. 8th B1-161
Bellevue, WA 98008
(800) 654-6366 (ph/fax)
www.infon.com
The Infon Venture Capital CD-ROM

Information Access Co.
362 Lakeside Drive
Foster City, CA 94404
(650) 378-5000 (ph)
www.informationaccess.com
PROMT database

Initiative Europe
Kingsgate House
High Street
Redhill RH1 1SL
United Kingdom
44-173-7769080 (ph)
44-173-7760750 (fax)
European Buyout Monitor
European Buyout Review
Who's Who in Risk Capital

John Wiley & Sons, Inc.
605 Third Avenue
New York, NY 10158
(212) 850-6000 (ph)
(212) 850-6088 (fax)
www.wiley.com
Equity Finance [Bartlett]

Latin Finance
2121 Ponce de Leon Blvd., Ste. 1020
Coral Gables, FL 33134
(305) 448-6593 (ph)
LatinFinance

Lexis-Nexis
P.O. Box 933
Dayton, OH 45401
(937) 865-6800 (ph)
(937) 865-1211 (fax)
www.lexis-nexis.com
Lexis-Nexis Database

McGraw-Hill Companies
1221 Avenue of the Americas
New York, NY 10020
(212) 512-4100 (ph)
(212) 512-4105 (fax)
www.bookstore.mcgraw-hill.com
Corporate Finance Sourcebook

MIT Press
Five Cambridge Center
Cambridge, MA 02142
617-253-5646 (ph)
617-258-6779 (fax)
www.mitpress.mit.edu
The Venture Capital Cycle [Gompers and Lerner]

National Association of Small Business Investment Companies
666 11th Street, N.W.
Suite 750
Washington, DC 20001
(202) 628-5055 (ph)
(202) 628-5080 (fax)
www.nasbic.org
NASBIC News
National Association of Small Business Investment Companies Membership Directory

National Register Publishing
121 Chanlon Rd.
New Providence, NJ 07974
America's Corporate Finance Directory

National Venture Capital Association
1655 North Fort Myer Drive, Ste. 850
Arlington, VA 22209
(703) 524-2549 (ph)
(703) 524-3940 (fax)
www.nvca.org
National Venture Capital Association Annual Report
National Venture Capital Association Membership Directory

Nelson Information, Inc.
1 Gateway Plaza
Port Chester
New York, NY 10573
(914) 937-8400 (ph)
(914) 937-8908 (fax)
Nelson's Directory of Investment Research

One Source Information Services
150 Cambridge Park Drive
Cambridge, MA 02140
(617) 441-7000 (ph)
(617) 441-7058 (fax)
www.onesource.com
OneSource Business Browser Database

Practising Law Institute
810 Seventh Ave.
New York, NY 10019
(212) 824-5710 (ph)
www.pli.edu
Venture Capital

The Red Herring
1550 Bryant St., Ste. 450
San Francisco, CA 94103
(415) 865-2277 (ph)
(415) 865-2280 (fax)
www.herring.com
The Red Herring

Securities Data Publishing
40 W. 57th Street, Ste. 1000
New York, NY 10019
(212) 484-4701 (ph)
(212) 732-4740 (fax)
www.securitiesdata.com
Buyouts
Corporate Finance: The IDD Review of Investment Banking
Corporate New Issues Database
Directory of Buyout Financing Sources
European Venture Capital Journal
Going Public: The IPO Reporter
Investment Dealer's Digest
Joint Venture and Strategic Alliance Database
Merger and Acquisitions
Pratt's Guide to Venture Capital Sources
Private Equity Week
Venture Capital Journal
Venture Capital Yearbook
Venture Japan

Securities Industry Association
120 Broadway
New York, NY 10271
(212) 608-1500 (ph)
(212) 608-1604 (fax)
www.sia.com
Securities Industry Fact Book

Thomson Financial Services
22 Pittsburgh Street
Boston, MA 02210
(617) 856-2704 (ph)
(617) 330-1986 (fax)
www.tfp.com
FirstCall Database
Investext Database

UMI
300 North Zeeb Road
P.O. Box 136
Ann Arbor, MI 48106
(800) 521-0600 (ph)
(734) 761-1032 (fax)
www.umi.com
ABI/Inform Database
Business Dateline Database
Wall Street Journal Index
Wall Street Journal CD-ROM

United States Small Business Administration
409 Third St., S.W.
Washington, DC 20416
(202) 205-6510 (ph)
(202) 205-6959 (fax)
www.sba.gov
Directory of Operating Small Business Investment Companies

Upside Media, Inc.
2015 Pioneer Ct.
San Mateo, CA 94403
(415) 377-0950 (ph)
(415) 377-1961 (fax)
www.upside.com
Upside

Venture Capital Report
The Magdalen Centre
Oxford Science Park
Oxford OX4 4GA
United Kingdom
44-186-5784411 (ph)
44-186-5784412 (fax)
www.demon.co.uk/vcr1978/index.html
Venture Capital Report Guide to Venture Capital in the UK and Europe

Venture Economics Investor Services
Two Gateway Center, 11ᵗʰ Floor
Newark, NJ 07102
(973) 622-3100 (ph)
(973) 622-1421 (fax)
www.ventureeconomics.com
Annual Review
Directory of Private Equity Investors
Investment Benchmark Reports
VentureXpert (Venture Intelligence Database)

VentureOne Corporation
590 Folsom Street
San Francisco, California 94105
(415) 357-2100 (ph)
(415) 357-2101 (fax)
www.ventureone.com
IPO Report
Venture Edge
VentureOne Annual Report
VentureOne Database

Exhibit 1   Sample Venture Economics Report

COMPANY: Network Peripherals, Inc.

This information last updated: 07/26/94

1371 McCarthy Blvd.
Milpitas, California 95035
Tel. 408-321-7300

Business: Designs, manufactures and markets parts for network computing, including products based upon the fiber distributed data Interface (FDDI) standard. The Company's integrated solutions include high performance network adapters, network operating system software drivers, concentrators, and network management software.

Founded: 03/01/89
Status: Public (IPO on 06/28/94)

Audited by
Price Waterhouse

Management: (Name) Pauline Lo Alker   (Title) Chief Executive Officer   (Phone) 408-321-7300

Competition: Cisco Systems/Crescendo, Interphase, SysKonnect, 3Com, Artel, Alantec,

Customers: Ungermann-Bass, Network General, AT&T, Cabletron, National Semiconductor, NetFRAME, Optical Data Systems, Sun Microsystems

Market for Products: 33 million Ethernet connections were installed in 1993 and were expected to increase to 85 million by 1997

Financials ($000s) as of:	Yr Ended 12/31/93	Yr Ended 12/31/92	Yr Ended 12/31/91	Yr Ended 12/31/90	3 Mos End 03/31/94
Sales	10687	7214	1796	246	5945
Pre-Tax Income	377	-795	-2015	-774	1085
Net Income	358	-795	-2015	-774	868
Earnings Per Share	-	-	-	-	-
Total Assets	8728	5338	2060	1436	10191
Shareholders' Equity	-3181	-3559	-2779	-784	6777
Employees:	-	-	-	-	14

Source: Securities Data Company (201) 622-3100

Exhibit 1 (continued)

FINANCING HISTORY:

Round #	Date	Financing Stage	Amount of Round($000)	Post-Round Value of Company($000)
1	**02/01/90**	**Seed**	**3000**	(Unavail.)
	Participants: (Fund)		(Fund Manager)	
	Other Investors		Other Investors	
	Associated Venture Investors		Associated Venture Investors	
	Associated Venture Investors		Associated Venture Investors	
	Alpha Venture Partners III		Alpha Capital Venture Partners, L.P.	
	Batterson, Johnson & Wang L.P.		Batterson, Johnson & Wang Venture Partner	
	Trinity Ventures I, L.P.		Trinity Ventures, Ltd.	
2	**10/01/90**	**Seed**	**1250**	(Unavail.)
	Participants: (Fund)		(Fund Manager)	
	Alpha Venture Partners III		Alpha Capital Venture Partners, L.P.	
	Associated Venture Investors		Associated Venture Investors	
3	**04/01/91**	**First Stage**	**2000**	(Unavail.)
	Participants: (Fund)		(Fund Manager)	
	Alpha Venture Partners III		Alpha Capital Venture Partners, L.P.	
	AVI Partners		Associated Venture Investors	
	National Semiconductor		National Semiconductor	
4	**01/01/92**	**Third Stage**	**3500**	21600
	Participants: (Fund)		(Fund Manager)	
	other Investors		Other Investors	
	Associated Venture Investors II		Associated Venture Investors	
	Alpha Venture Partners III		Alpha Capital Venture Partners, L.P.	
	AVI Partners		Associated Venture Investors	
	International Venture Capital Group of A		Venture Capital Fund of America, Inc.	
	Other Investors		Other Investors	
5	**07/01/93**	**Third Stage**	**1800**	39600
	Participants: (Fund)		(Fund Manager)	
	AVI Partners		Associated Venture Investors	
	C.V. Sofinnova (Burr Egan Deleage)		Burr, Egan, Deleage & Co.	
	Other Investors		Other Investors	
	Alpha Venture Partners III		Alpha Capital Venture Partners, L.P.	

Source: Securities Data Company (201) 622-3100

(*) Asterisked round amounts are for part of the round only. (They are not indicative of any given investor's investment.)

EXHIBIT 2   Sample VentureOne Report

Magnifi

www.magnifi.com

Last Update: October 1998
Last Update Type: General Update

CONTACT INFORMATION:

1601 South De Anza Boulevard
Suite 155
Cupertino, CA 95014

Phone: (408) 863-3800
Fax: (408) 863-7210

Financing Contact: Ranjan Sinha, President & CEO

COMPANY OVERVIEW:

Business Brief: Developer of automated marketing, supply-chain management software
Financing Status: As of 09/98 the company is seeking to raise a $10M round of venture financing that will start on 11/1/98 and is anticipated to close in the later first quarter of 1999. This round is open to new investors.

Founded:	02/96	**Industry:**	Software Development Tools
Employees:	45	**Status:**	Private & Independent
		Stage:	Shipping Product

INVESTORS:

Investment Firm	Participating Round #(s)
Gideon Hixon Fund	1, 2
Draper Fisher Jurvetson	1, 2
Convergence Partners	2°
IDG Ventures	1°, 2
Crystal Internet Venture Fund	1, 2

° = *Lead Investor*

FINANCINGS TO DATE:

Round #	Round Type	Date	Amount Raised ($MM)	Post $ Valuation ($MM)	Company Stage
1	1st	06/97	3.0	6.0	Shipping Product
2	2nd	11/97	5.1	N/A	Shipping Product

FINANCIALS:
(A = Actual E = Estimated P = Projected)

($MM)	**1998A**
Revenue	0.0
Net Income	0.0
Burnrate ($K/Month):	0.41

EXECUTIVES AND BOARD MEMBERS:

Name	Title	Background	Telephone
Ranjan Sinha	President & CEO	Date joined: 02/96 Cofounder, WhoWhere	(408) 863-3807
Eric Hoffert	Chairman & CTO	Date joined: 02/96 Senior Technologist, Apple Computer	
Chris Crafford	VP, Engineering	VP, Rightworks	
Pat Greer	VP, Professional Services	VP, Wallop Software	
Phillip Ivanier	VP, Business Development	Executive, MIT Media Lab; Executive, Apple Computer	
Jim Ogara	VP, Sales & Support	VP, DEC	
David Dubbs	Director, Marketing	VP, Marketing, LookSmart; Principal, Consulting Firm, Intellectual Capital Partners; Executive, AT&T	
Stewart Alsop	Advisory Board	Partner, New Enterprise Associates	(650) 854-9499
Gordon Bell	Advisory Board	Executive, Microsoft	
Dave Davison	Advisory Board	Cofounder, New Media Magazine; Partner, Knowledge Venture Partners	
Shane Robinson	Advisory Board	VP, Engineering, Cadence	
Skip Stritter	Advisory Board	CTO, NeTpower	(408) 522-9999
Susan Cheng	Board Member, Venture Investor	Partner, IDG Ventures	(415) 439-4420
Eric DiBeneditto	Board Member, Venture Investor	Partner, Convergence Partners	(650) 854-3010
Dan Kellogg	Board Member, Venture Investor	Partner, Crystal Internet Venture Fund	(440) 349-6025
Randy Komisar	Former Officer	CEO, Lucas Arts; WebTV	(650) 233-9683
Robert Pariseau	Former Officer	Date joined: 11/97	

BUSINESS INFORMATION:

Overview: Developer of automated marketing, supply-chain management software. The company develops Web-based marketing solutions to automate the marketing supply chain and its core activities and workflow, including encyclopedias, channel management, customer acquisition/retention, business intelligence, and campaign management. The company's patent-pending core technology supports unstructured marketing files such as video images, PDFs, and business documents, and integrates with the RDBMS to allow ROI assessment on marketing investment and establish a marketing process history. The production solution, MarketBase, links the internal and external collaborators of product or campaign development into a common, Web-based platform for managing the marketing process.

Product: Marketing automation software for managing product and advertising development, establishing marketing encyclopedia, acquiring/retaining customers, and supporting channels and customers.

Customers: Customers include CNN, ABC, PBS, Boeing, Time, Citibank, the U.S. Navy, GM, and Microsoft.

Market: The company estimates a $2 billion market for its products by the year 2000.

OUTSIDE PROFESSIONALS:

General Business Banking: Cupertino National Bank
Auditor: Coopers & Lybrand
General Counsel: Venture Law Group

Exhibit 3   Sample Registration Statement Index

INDEX TO EXHIBITS

(1) To be supplied by amendment.
(2) Confidential treatment requested.

A Private Equity Glossary

Adjusted present value (APV)   A variant of the net present value approach that is particularly appropriate when a company's level of indebtedness is changing or it has past operating losses that can be used to offset tax obligations.

Advisory board   A set of limited partners or outsiders who advise a private equity organization. The board may, for instance, provide guidance on overall fund strategy or ways to value privately held firms at the end of each fiscal year.

Agency problem   A conflict between managers and investors or, more generally, an instance where an agent does not intrinsically desire to follow the wishes of the principal that hired him.

Agreement of limited partnership   *See* Partnership agreement.

Angel   A wealthy individual who invests in entrepreneurial firms. Although angels perform many of the same functions as venture capitalists, they invest their own capital rather than that of institutional and other individual investors.

Asset allocation   The process through which institutional or individual investors set targets for how their investment portfolios should be divided across the different asset classes.

Asset class   One of a number of investment categories—such as bonds, real estate, and private equity—that institutional and individual investors consider when making asset allocations.

Associate   A professional employee of a private equity firm who is not yet a partner.

Asymmetric information problem   A problem that arises when, because of his day-to-day involvement with the firm, an entrepreneur knows more about his company's prospects than investors, suppliers, or strategic partners.

Beta   A measure of the extent to which a firm's market value varies with that of an index of overall market value. For instance, a stock with a beta of zero displays no correlation with the market, that with a beta of one generally mirrors the market's movements, and that with a beta greater than one experiences more dramatic shifts when the index moves.

Bogey   *See* Hurdle rate.

Book-to-market ratio   The ratio of a firm's accounting (book) value of its equity to the value of the equity assigned by the market (i.e., the product of the number of shares outstanding and the share price).

Call option   The right, but not the obligation, to buy a security at a set price (or range of prices) in a given period.

Callable   A security on which the security issuer has an option to repurchase from the security holder.

Capital structure   The mixture of equity and debt that a firm has raised.

Capital under management *See* Committed capital.

Carried interest The substantial share, often around 20%, of profits that are allocated to the general partners of a private equity partnership.

Closed-end fund A publicly traded mutual fund whose shares must be sold to other investors (rather than redeemed from the issuing firm, as is the case with open-end mutual funds). Many early venture capital funds were structured in this manner.

Closing The signing of the contract by an investor or group of investors that binds them to supply a set amount of capital to a private equity fund. Often a fraction of that capital is provided at the time of the closing. A single fund may have multiple closings.

Co-investment Either *(a)* the syndication of a private equity financing round (*see* syndication), or *(b)* an investment by an individual general or limited partner alongside a private equity fund in a financing round.

Collar A combination of an equal number of call and put options at slightly different exercise prices.

Committed capital Pledges of capital to a private equity fund. This money is typically not received at once, but rather is taken down over three to five years starting in the year the fund is formed.

Common stock The equity typically held by management and founders. Typically, at the time of an initial public offering, all equity is converted into common stock.

Community development venture capital Venture capital funds organized by nonprofit bodies, often with the twin goals of encouraging economic development and generating financial returns.

Consolidation A private equity investment strategy that involves merging several small firms together and exploiting economies of scale or scope.

Conversion ratio The number of shares for which a convertible debt or equity issue can be exchanged.

Convertible equity or debt A security that under certain conditions can be converted into another security (often into common stock). The convertible shares often have special rights that the common stock does not have.

Cooperative Research and Development Agreement (CRADA) A collaborative arrangement between a federally owned research facility and a private company. These were first authorized by Congress in the early 1980s.

Corporate venture capital An initiative by a corporation to invest either in young firms outside the corporation or in business concepts originating within the corporation. These are often organized as corporate subsidiaries, not as limited partnerships.

Credit crunch A period when, due to the regulatory actions or shifts in the economic conditions, a sharp reduction accurs in the availability of bank loans or other debt financing, particularly for small businesses. The early 1990s were one such period in the United States.

Deposit-oriented lease In venture leasing, a lease that requires the lessee to put up a cash deposit, usually ranging from 30% to 50% of the total lease line.

Dilution The reduction in the fraction of a firm's equity owned by the founders and existing shareholders associated with a new financing round.

Disbursement An investment by a private equity fund into a company.

Distressed debt A private equity investment strategy that involves purchasing discounted bonds of a financially distressed firm. Distressed debt investors frequently convert their holdings into equity and become actively involved with the management of the distressed firm.

Distribution   The transfer of shares in a (typically publicly traded) portfolio firm or cash from a private equity fund to each limited partner and (frequently) each general partner.

Draw down.   *See* Take down.

Due diligence   The review of a business plan and assessment of a management team prior to a private equity investment.

Earnings before interest and taxes (EBIT)   A measure of the firm's profitability before any adjustment for interest expenses or tax obligations. This measure is often used to compare firms with different levels of indebtedness.

Employee Retirement Income Security Act (ERISA)   The 1974 legislation that codified the regulation of corporate pension plans. *See* Prudent man rule.

Endowment   The long-term pool of financial assets held by many universities, hospitals, foundations, and other nonprofit institutions.

Equipment takedown schedule   In a venture leasing contract, the time when the lessee can draw down funds to purchase preapproved equipment.

Equity kicker   A transaction in which a small number of shares or warrants are added to what is primarily a debt financing.

Exercise price   The price at which an option or a warrant can be exercised.

Financing round   The provision of capital by a private equity group to a firm. Since venture capital organizations generally provide capital in stages, a typical venture-backed firm will receive several financing rounds over a series of years.

First closing   The initial closing of a fund.

First fund   An initial fund raised by a private equity organization; also known as a first-time fund.

Float   In a public market context, the percentage of the company's shares that is in the hands of outside investors, as opposed to being held by corporate insiders.

Follow-on fund   A fund that is subsequent to a private equity organization's first fund.

Follow-on offering   *See* Seasoned equity offering.

Form 10-K   An annual filing required by the U.S. Securities and Exchange Commission of each publicly traded firm, as well as certain private firms. The statement provides a wide variety of summary data about the firm.

Free cash-flow problem   The temptation to undertake wasteful expenditures which cash not needed for operations or investments often poses.

Fund   A pool of capital raised periodically by a private equity organization. Usually in the form of limited partnerships, private equity funds typically have a 10-year life, though extensions of several years are often possible.

Fund of funds   A fund that invests primarily in other private equity funds rather than operating firms, often organized by an investment adviser or investment bank.

Gatekeeper   *See* Investment adviser.

General partner   A partner in a limited partnership is responsible for the day-to-day operations of the fund. In the case of a private equity fund, the venture capitalists either are general partners or own the corporation that serves as the general partner. The general partners assume all liability for the fund's debts.

Glass-Steagall Act   The 1933 legislation that limited the equity holdings and underwriting activities of commercial banks in the United States.

Grandstanding problem   The strategy, sometimes employed by young private equity organizations, of rushing young firms to the public marketplace in order to demonstrate a successful track record, even if the companies are not ready to go public.

Hedging   A securities transaction that allows an investor to limit the losses that may result from the shifts in value of an existing asset or financial obligation. For instance, a farmer may hedge his exposure to fluctuating crop prices by agreeing before the harvest on a sale price for part of his crop.

Herding problem   A situation in which investors, particularly institutions, make investments that are more similar to one another than is desirable.

Hot issue market   A market with high demand for new securities offerings, particularly for initial public offerings.

Hurdle rate   Either (i) the set rate of return that the limited partners must receive before the general partners can begin sharing in any distributions, or (ii) the level that the fund's net asset value must reach before the general partners can begin sharing in any distributions.

Implicit rate   Also known as the implicit yield, the implicit rate in venture leasing is the annual percentage rate of return before considering the impact of the warrants included as part of the transaction.

In the money   An option or a warrant that would have a positive value if it was immediately exercised.

Initial public offering (IPO)   The sale of shares to public investors of a firm that has not hitherto been traded on a public stock exchange. An investment bank typically underwrites these offerings.

Insider   A director, an officer, or a shareholder with at least a certain percentage (often 10%) of a company's equity.

Intangible asset   A patent, trade secret, informal know-how, brand capital, or other nonphysical asset.

Intrapreneuring   A corporate venture capital program that invests in business concepts originating inside the corporation. The term often is applied specifically to efforts in which the corporation intends to reacquire its new ventures.

Investment adviser   A financial intermediary who assists investors, particularly institutions, with investments in private equity and other financial assets. Advisers assess potential new venture funds for their clients and monitor the progress of existing investments. In some cases, they pool their investors' capital in funds of funds.

Investment bank   A financial intermediary that, among other services, may underwrite securities offerings, facilitate mergers and acquisitions, and trade for its own account.

Investment committee   A group, typically consisting of general partners of a private equity fund, that reviews potential and/or existing investments.

Investor buyout (IBO)   *See* Management buy-in.

Lease line   Similar to a bank line of credit, a credit that allows a venture lessee a certain amount of money to add equipment as needed, according to a preapproved takedown schedule.

Lemons problem   *See* Asymmetric information problem.

Lessee   The party to a lease agreement who is obligated to make monthly rental payments and can use the equipment during the lease term.

Lessor   The party to a lease agreement who has legal title to the equipment, grants the lessee the right to use the equipment for the lease term, and is entitled to the rental payments.

Leveraged buyout (LBO)   The acquisition of a firm or business unit, typically in a mature industry, with a considerable amount of debt. The debt is then repaid according to a strict schedule that absorbs most of the firm's cash flow.

Leveraged buyout fund   A fund, typically organized in a similar manner to a venture capital fund, specializing in leveraged buyout investments. Some of these funds also make venture capital investments.

Leveraged recapitalization   A transaction in which the management team (rather than new investors as in the case of an LBO) borrows money to buy out the interests of other investors. As in an LBO, the debt is then repaid.

Licensee   In a licensing agreement, the party who receives the right to use a technology, product, or brand name in exchange for payments.

Licensor   In a licensing agreement, the party who receives payments in exchange for providing the right to use a technology, product, or brand name that it owns.

Limit order   In an underwritten IPO, the price-dependent orders made by individual or institutional investors: for example, the agreement by an investor to purchase 10,000 shares, conditional on the price of the offering being under $12 per share.

Limited partner   An investor in a limited partnership. Limited partners can monitor the partnership's progress but cannot become involved in its day-to-day management if they are to retain limited liability.

Limited partnership   An organizational form that entails a finitely lived contractual arrangement between limited and general partners, governed by a partnership agreement.

Lock up   A provision in the underwriting agreement between an investment bank and existing shareholders that prohibits corporate insiders and private equity investors from selling at the time of the offering.

Management buy-in (MBI)   A European term for an LBO initiated by a private equity group with no previous connection to the firm.

Management buyout (MBO)   A European term for an LBO initiated by an existing management team, which then solicits the involvement of a private equity group.

Management fee   The fee, typically a percentage of committed capital or net asset value, that is paid by a private equity fund to the general partners to cover salaries and expenses.

Market-to-book ratio   The inverse of the book-to-market ratio.

Mega-fund   One of the largest venture capital or private equity funds, measured by the amount of committed capital.

Mezzanine   Either *(a)* a private equity financing round shortly before an initial public offering, or *(b)* an investment that employs subordinated debt that has fewer privileges than bank debt but more than equity and often has attached warrants.

Milestone payments   In a licensing agreement, the payments made by the licensee to the licensor at specified times in the future or else when certain technological or business objectives have been achieved.

NASDAQ   The U.S. stock exchange where most IPOs are listed and most firms that were formerly backed by private equity investors trade.

Net asset value (NAV)   The value of a fund's holdings, which may be calculated using a variety of valuation rules. The value does not include funds that have been committed but not drawn down.

Net income   A firm's profits after taxes.

Net operating losses (NOLs)   Tax credits that are compiled by firms that have financial losses. These credits generally cannot be used until the firm becomes profitable (or returns to profitability).

Net present value (NPV)   A valuation method that computes the expected value of one or more future cash flows and discounts them at a rate that reflects the cost of capital (which will vary with the cash flows' riskiness).

Operating lease   In venture leasing, a short-term lease in which the customer uses equipment for a fraction of its useful life. Obligations of ownership may remain with the lessor, including maintenance, insurance, and taxes.

Option   The right, but not the obligation, to buy or sell a security at a set price (or range of prices) in a given period.

Out of the money   An option or a warrant that would have a negative value if it was immediately exercised.

Participating preferred stock   Convertible stock where, under certain conditions, the holder receives both the return of his original investment and a share of the company's equity.

Partnership agreement   The contract that explicitly specifies the compensation and conditions that govern the relationship between the investors (limited partners) and the venture capitalists (general partners) during a private equity fund's life. Occasionally used to refer to the separate agreement between the general partners regarding the internal operations of the fund (e.g., the division of the carried interest).

Patent   A government grant of rights to one or more discoveries for a set period, based on a set of criteria.

Placement agent   A financial intermediary hired by private equity organizations to facilitate the raising of new funds.

Point   One percent of a private equity fund's profits. The general partners of a private equity fund are often allocated 20 points, or 20% of the capital gains, which are divided among the individual partners.

Post-money valuation   The product of the price paid per share in a financing round and the shares outstanding after the financing round.

Preferred stock   Stock that has preference over common stock with respect to any dividends or payments in association with the liquidation of the firm. Preferred stockholders may also have additional rights, such as the ability to block mergers or displace management.

Pre-money valuation   The product of the price paid per share in a financing round and the shares outstanding before the financing round.

Price-earnings ratio (P-E ratio)   The ratio of the firm's share price to the firm's earnings per share (net income divided by shares outstanding).

Private equity   Organizations devoted to venture capital, leveraged buyouts, consolidation, mezzanine, and distressed debt investments, as well as a variety of hybrids such as venture leasing and venture factoring.

Private placement   The sale of securities not registered with the U.S. Securities and Exchange Commission to institutional investors or wealthy individuals. These transactions are frequently facilitated by an investment bank.

Pro forma   Financial statements that project future changes in a firm's income statement or balance sheet. These often form the basis for valuation analyses of various types.

Prospectus   A condensed, widely disseminated version of the registration statement that is also filed with the U.S. Securities and Exchange Commission. The prospectus provides a wide variety of summary data about the firm.

Proxy statement   A filing with the U.S. Securities and Exchange Commission that, among other information, provides information on the holdings and names of corporate insiders.

Prudent man rule   Prior to 1979, a provision in the Employee Retirement Income Security Act (ERISA) that essentially prohibited pension funds from investing substantial amounts of money in private equity or other high-risk asset classes. The Department of Labor's clarification of the rule in that year allowed pension managers to invest in high-risk assets, including private equity.

Public venture capital   Venture capital funds organized by government bodies, or else programs to make venture-like financings with public funds. Examples include the Small Business Investment Company and Small Business Innovation Research programs.

Put option   The right, but not the obligation, to sell a security at a set price (or range of prices) in a given period.

Putable   A security which the security holder has an option to sell back to the issuer.

Red herring   A preliminary version of the prospectus that is distributed to potential investors before a security offering. The name derives from the disclaimers typically printed in red on the front cover.

Registration statement   A filing with the U.S. Securities and Exchange Commission (e.g., an S-1 or S-18 form) that must be reviewed by the Commission before a firm can sell shares to the public. The statement provides a wide variety of summary data about the firm, as well as copies of key legal documents.

Residual value   In venture leasing, the fair-market value of the leased equipment at the end of the lease term.

Restricted stock   Shares that cannot be sold under U.S. Securities and Exchange Commission regulations or that can only be sold in limited amounts.

Right of first refusal   A contractual provision that gives a corporation or private equity fund the right to purchase, license, or invest in all opportunities associated with another organization before other companies or funds can do so. A weaker form of this provision is termed the right of first look.

Road show   The marketing of a private equity fund or public offering to potential investors.

Roll-up   *See* Consolidation.

Round   *See* Financing round.

Royalties   In a licensing agreement, the percentage of sales or profits that the licensee pays to the licensor.

Rule 10(b)-5   The U.S. Securities and Exchange Commission regulation that most generally prohibits fraudulent activity in the purchase or sale of any security.

Rule 16(a)   The U.S. Securities and Exchange Commission regulation that requires insiders to disclose any transactions in the firm's stock on a monthly basis.

Rule 144   The U.S. Securities and Exchange Commission regulation that prohibits sales for one year (originally, two years) after the purchase of restricted stock and limits the pace of sales between the first and second (originally, second and third) year after the purchase.

Running rate   *See* Implicit rate.

Seasoned equity offering   An offering by a firm that has already competed an initial public offering and whose shares are already publicly traded.

Secondary offering   An offering of shares that are not being issued by the firm but rather are sold by existing shareholders. Consequently, the firm does not receive the proceeds from the sales of these shares.

Shares outstanding   The number of shares that the company has issued.

Small Business Innovation Research (SBIR) program   A federal program, established in 1982, that provides a set percentage of the federal R&D budget to small, high-technology companies.

Small Business Investment Company (SBIC) program   A federally guaranteed risk capital pool. These funds were first authorized by the U.S. Congress in 1958, proliferated during the 1960s, and then dwindled after many organizations encountered management and incentive problems.

Social venture capital Either community development venture capital or public venture capital (see definitions).

Staging The provision of capital to entrepreneurs in multiple installments, with each financing conditional on meeting particular business targets. This provision helps ensure that the money is not squandered on unprofitable projects.

Syndication The joint purchase of shares by two or more private equity organizations or the joint underwriting of an offering by two or more investment banks.

Take down The transfer of some or all of the committed capital from the limited partners to a private equity fund.

Takedown schedule The contractual language that describes how and when a private equity fund can (or must) receive the committed capital from its limited partners. In venture leasing, the period after the lease begins when the lessee can draw down funds for the preapproval equipment to be purchased.

Tangible asset A machine, building, land, inventory, or another physical asset.

Term of lease In venture leasing, the duration of the lease, usually in months, which is fixed at its inception.

Term sheet A preliminary outline of the structure of a private equity partnership or stock purchase agreement, frequently agreed to by the key parties before the formal contractual language is negotiated.

Tombstone An advertisement, typically in a major business publication, by an underwriter to publicize an offering that it has underwritten.

Trade sale A European term for the exiting of an investment by a private equity group by selling it to a corporation.

Triple-net full-payout lease In venture leasing, a long-term lease in which the lessee's lease payments cover the entire cost of the leased equipment and the lessee assumes all responsibilities of ownership, including maintenance, insurance, and taxes.

Uncertainty problem The array of potential outcomes for a company or project. The wider the dispersion of potential outcomes, the greater the uncertainty.

Underpricing The discount to the projected trading price at which the investment banker sells shares in an initial public offering. A substantial positive return on the first trading day is often interpreted by financial economists as evidence of underpricing.

Underwriting The purchase of a securities issue from a company by an investment bank and its (typically almost immediate) resale to investors.

Unrelated business taxable income (UBTI) The gross income from any unrelated business that a tax-exempt institution regularly carries out. If a private equity partnership is generating significant income from debt-financed property, tax-exempt limited partners may face tax liabilities due to UBTI provisions.

Unseasoned equity offering *See* Initial public offering.

Up-front fees In a licensing agreement, nonrefundable payments made by the licensee to the licensor at the time that agreement is signed.

Valuation rule The algorithm by which a private equity fund assigns values to the public and private firms in its portfolio.

Venture capital Independently managed, dedicated pools of capital that focus on equity or equity-linked investments in privately held, high-growth companies. Many venture capital funds, however, occasionally make other types of private equity investments. Outside of the United States, this phrase is often used as a synonym for private equity.

Venture capital method A valuation approach that values the company at some point in the future, assuming that the firm has been successful, and then discounts this projected value at some high discount rate.

Venture capitalist   A general partner or associate at a private equity organization.

Venture factoring   A private equity investment strategy that involves purchasing the receivables of high-risk young firms. As part of the transaction, the venture factoring fund typically also receives warrants in the young firm.

Venture leasing   A private equity investment strategy that involves leasing equipment or other assets to high-risk young firms. As part of the transaction, the venture leasing fund typically also receives warrants in the young firm.

Vintage year   The group of funds whose first closing was in a certain year.

Warrant-based lease   In venture leasing, a lease that requires the lessee to grant equity participation to the lessor, usually in the form of warrants.

Warrants   An option to buy shares of stock issued directly by a company.

Window dressing problem   The behavior of money managers of adjusting their portfolios at the end of the quarter by buying firms whose shares have appreciated and selling "mistakes." This is driven by the fact that institutional investors may examine not only quarterly returns, but also end-of-period holdings.

Withdrawn offering   A transaction in which a registration statement is made with the U.S. Securities and Exchange Commission but either the firm writes to the Commission withdrawing the proposed offering before it is effective or the offering is not completed within nine months.

Index

Italicized page numbers reflect pages on which Exhibits, Appendices, Tables, or Figures appear. Page numbers followed by "n." or "nn." and numbers indicate pages which contain footnotes.